# SHAKESPEARE IN PARTS

# SHAKESPEARE IN PARTS

SIMON PALFREY

AND

TIFFANY STERN

OXFORD

UNIVERSITY PRESS

# OXFORD
UNIVERSITY PRESS

Great Clarendon Street, Oxford OX2 6DP

Oxford University Press is a department of the University of Oxford.
It furthers the University's objective of excellence in research, scholarship,
and education by publishing worldwide in

Oxford New York

Auckland Cape Town Dar es Salaam Hong Kong Karachi
Kuala Lumpur Madrid Melbourne Mexico City Nairobi
New Delhi Shanghai Taipei Toronto

With offices in

Argentina Austria Brazil Chile Czech Republic France Greece
Guatemala Hungary Italy Japan Poland Portugal Singapore
South Korea Switzerland Thailand Turkey Ukraine Vietnam

Oxford is a registered trade mark of Oxford University Press
in the UK and in certain other countries

Published in the United States
by Oxford University Press Inc., New York

British Library Cataloguing in Publication Data

Data available

Library of Congress Cataloging in Publication Data

Data available

Typeset by Laserwords Private Limited, Chennai, India
Printed in Great Britain
on acid-free paper by
Biddles Ltd., King's Lynn, Norfolk

ISBN 978–0–19–927205–1

1 3 5 7 9 10 8 6 4 2

To the memory of Eileen Palfrey (1930–1999)
and Geoffrey Stern (1935–2005)

# Preface and Acknowledgements

This book emerged out of a friendship. We each knew the other's first book, one on early modern rehearsal, the other on Shakespeare's late plays. Stern was particularly engaged with the practices of the theatre and with the fragmentary nature of its texts, Palfrey with the peculiar ways in which minds and moments are animated in and by dramatic language. We wondered whether two such different approaches might gel in interesting and even unprecedented ways. So we met and laid out our wares. 'I'm thinking about actors' parts, but I don't know where to start,' said Stern; 'I'm thinking about the vertiginous dramatic moment, and I don't know where to stop,' said Palfrey. This book is the result.

Readers may be curious as to who did what. We thought of saying that Stern gave the cues and Palfrey the speeches, but the fact is that it has been a dialogue throughout. Both of us have read, edited, and reread even those parts that we did not initially write. Whether we have produced something larger than the sum of our respective parts is for others to judge. What we know for sure is the debt each of us owes the other. Neither of us could have written it, or even thought of it, alone.

But obviously we owe thanks to many others. We would like to acknowledge the generosity of the AHRB, which awarded us an 'Innovations' grant, without which this work would never have taken shape. We are grateful, too, to both our then institutions—Oxford Brookes (Tiffany) and Liverpool University (Simon)—for letting us take up the opportunity that the grant gave us, and to our new institution, Oxford University, for providing us with jobs so near to each other and to the Bodleian Library.

We have given papers based on sections of this book at the Shakespeare Association of America and the World Shakespeare Congress: we thank the British Academy for funding travel, and our fellow seminarians for their trenchant comments. Papers based on this book have also been given by each of us at Oxford, Cambridge, and Yale: again, we are grateful to listeners for their suggestions and advice. An earlier version of one of our chapters has appeared as 'What Does the Cued Part Cue? Parts and Cues in Romeo and Juliet', in the *Companion to Shakespeare and Performance*, edited by Barbara Hodgdon and W. B. Worthen (Oxford: Blackwell Publishing, 2005), and we wish to acknowledge Blackwell Publishing which gave us permission to reprint this piece.

Librarians at the Beinecke Library, the Bodleian Library, the British Library, Cambridge University Library, Harvard Theatre Library, the Houghton Library, and the Huntington Library have all been unfailingly generous of their time; librarians at the Folger Shakespeare Library deserve special mention. The several illustrations in this book are reprinted by kind permission from the Governors of Dulwich College, the Folger Shakespeare Library, and the Houghton Library. Thanks also to MOMA (New York), La Scala, and the Giorgio de Chirico estate for permission to use his picture, 'Le Duo (Les Mannequins de la tour rose)', as our cover image.

The artful words of David Scott Kastan and Gordon McMullan were instrumental in helping us get the funds to begin this piece. At OUP Sophie Goldsworthy and Andrew McNeillie have been supportive commissioning editors, and Tom Perridge a patient and understanding editor. Latterly Jacqueline Baker and Jean van Altena have helped see the book through to completion. We also very much benefited from the learning and expertise of three anonymous OUP readers. Our thanks to all of them: their suggestions helped make this a better book.

During the writing of *Shakespeare in Parts* we have both had numerous stimulating conversations with friends, colleagues, and passing acquaintances. Together we had a list of more than a hundred such creditors, so many as to make mention of them fairly meaningless and (accidental) omission doubly insulting. So a blanket thanks to all. Nonetheless, Simon would like to give particular praise to Jo, who is delighted the project is over, and to Georgia, Ella, and Louis, who barely knew it had begun; and Tiffany would like to praise her equally forgiving family, Jonty Stern, Elisabeth Stern, Joy Moore, and—the inspiration for so much that is here—Patrick Tucker.

# Contents

*List of Illustrations*     xiii
*Textual Notes*     xiv

**Introduction**     I

## I. HISTORY

1. **The Actor's Part**     15
   Early Modern Professional Parts     15
   The University Parts     24
   The Restoration Part     29
   Later Parts     31
   Twentieth-Century Parts     38

2. **The Actors**     40
   Casting     40
   Typecasting     43
   'Becoming' the Part     45
   Doubling and Vizards     50

3. **Rehearsing and Performing**     57
   The Reading     57
   The Distribution of Parts     60
   Learning Parts     62
   Instruction     66
   Rehearsal     70
   Performance and the Prompter     73
   Performances and Repeated Performances     75

## II. INTERPRETING CUES

4. **History of the Cue**                                       83
    The Cue                                                 83
    Length of Cue                                           88

5. **Interpreting Shakespeare's Cues: Introduction**            91

6. **Cues and Characterization**                                96
    Early and Inaugurating Cues                             97
    Transitional Cues                                       110
    Recurring Cues                                          113
    Conclusion                                              118

7. **Waiting and Suddenness: The Part in Time**                 120
    Ellipses and Plotting a Part                            121
    Set-Piece: Macduff                                      125
    Cued Action                                             134
    Set-Piece: Bertram                                      136
    Short-Line Cues                                         142
    Conclusion                                              152

## III. REPEATED CUES

8. **Introduction**                                             157

9. **From Crowds to Clowns**                                    165
    Crowds                                                  165
    Clowns                                                  171
    Set-Piece: Malvolio                                     177

10. **Comi-tragic/Tragi-comic Pathos**                          184
     Mercutio                                               186

11. **The Battle for the Cue-Space: *The Merchant of Venice***  192
     Shylock's Repetitions                                  193
     Cues and Power                                         196
     Cues and Comic Uncertainty                             200
     The Trial Scene                                        206
     Conclusion                                             212

12. **Tragedy**                                                 214
     Tragic Bathos: *Romeo and Juliet*                      214

Tragic Pathos                                            218
*Julius Caesar*                                          219
*Hamlet*                                                 219
*Troilus and Cressida*                                   224
*Othello*                                                227
Lady Macbeth                                             237

13. **The Cue-Space in *King Lear***                     **240**
Gloucester                                               240
Poor Tom                                                 247
Edgar and Gloucester                                     250
The 'Mad' Lear                                           255
Cordelia                                                 258
The Final Scene                                          261

14. **Post-Tragic Effects**                              **266**
Antony and Cleopatra                                     266
Imogen in *Cymbeline*                                    271

15. **The Cue-Space in *The Tempest***                   **275**
Cueing the Scene                                         275
Miranda                                                  279
Ariel                                                    284
Caliban (1)                                              288
Ferdinand                                                290
Antonio and Sebastian                                    294
Caliban (2)                                              296
Conclusion                                               305

## IV. THE ACTOR WITH HIS PART

16. **History**                                          **311**
Interpreting Parts: Emotions                             311
Playwrights and Emotions                                 315
Parts and Emphasis                                       317
Parts and Action                                         324

17. **Dramatic Prosody**                                 **328**
Introduction                                             328
Verse/Prose                                              332

Rhyme 340
Short Speech Units (Short Lines, Midline Switches) 346

18. **Prosodic Switches: Pauses, Prompts, and Soliloquies** 353
*Romeo and Juliet* 353
Gloucester/Richard III 358
Richard II 371

19. **Midline Shifts in 'Mature' Shakespeare: From Actorly Instruction to 'Virtual' Presence** 380

20. **Case Studies: Five Romantic Heroines and Three Lonely Men** 390
Portia 392
Rosalind 408
Olivia 415
Helena (*All's Well That Ends Well*) 422
Isabella 434
Mercutio 453
Shylock 456
Macbeth 463

*Notes* 495
*Bibliography* 519
*Index* 533

# List of Illustrations

1. The part of Orlando from Robert Greene's *Orlando Furioso* (1590s). By permission of the Governors of Dulwich College.      14

2. The part of Trico from Ferdinando Parkhurst's *Ignoramus* (1662–4). By permission of the Houghton Library, Harvard University.      82

3. The part of Sir Archy from Charles Macklin's *Love à la Mode* (*c.* 1760). By permission of the Houghton Library, Harvard Theatre Collection, Harvard University.      156

4. The part of Shylock from William Shakespeare's *Merchant of Venice* (1772). By permission of the Folger Shakespeare Library.      310

# Textual Notes

First Folio quotations are taken throughout from the facsimile prepared by Charlton Hinman, *Mr. William Shakespeares Comedies, Histories, and Tragedies* [*The Norton Facsimile*] (New York: Norton, 1968), using the through-line-numbers (TLN) of that edition. Folio speech-prefixes, however, have been expanded and, where necessary, modernized or regularized for ease of reference. Quotations from Quarto texts are from the facsimiles prepared by Michael J. B. Allen and Kenneth Muir, *Shakespeare's Plays in Quarto: A Facsimile Edition of Copies Primarily from the Henry E. Huntington Library* (Berkeley: University of California Press, 1981); pages from that edition are referred to by signature. Quarto speech-prefixes are, similarly, modernized or regularized when necessary. The *STC—A Short-Title Catalogue of Books Printed in England, Scotland, & Ireland and of English Books Printed Abroad 1475–1640*, first compiled by A. W. Pollard and G. R. Redgrave, 2nd edn., revised and enlarged by W. A. Jackson, F. S. Ferguson, and Katharine F. Pantzer, 3 vols. (London: Bibliographical Society, 1986–91)—has been a constant reference throughout, and we have used it to supply the full names of authors when not provided on title-pages. We have silently modernized u, v, i, j, and long s, and have expanded scribal contractions.

# Introduction

'Players action, doeth answere to their partes,' wrote Stephen Gosson in 1579.[1] The sentence seems straightforward enough: players always use action appropriate to the character they are to perform. But 'part' had a wider and more specific meaning in the early modern theatre than it does now. 'Part' signified not just the character in a play. It stood for the written paper, often made into a roll, on which that part was transcribed, and the nature of the way in which the text was presented on that roll. It was the text an actor received, learned from, and in a very real sense *owned*. And that text contained on it all the words the actor was going to speak, but nothing that would be said to or about him. Each of his speeches was preceded simply by a short cue. This cue was usually the last one to three words of the speech immediately preceding his own. The actor was to memorize the cue just as he did his own speeches; the cue was, then, as much a constituent of his part as anything he said. Once the cue was heard, he spoke. So when Gosson writes that the part will dictate the action, he means that that particular fragment of text—the actor's own words and his cues—will be enough to determine his performance.

For actors in the early modern theatre never received the complete text of the play in which they were to perform. No company wanted more copies of the full play to be in existence than were strictly necessary. To a certain extent this was for the mundane reason that paper was scarce, and that producing endless handwritten copies would be laborious, expensive, and—to the thinking of the time—unnecessary. Nor was it in anyone's interest for more copies of a full text to exist than were essential: the more copies of a play, the more likely it was that one would fall into the hands of either a rival company or a printer. But even when such local imperatives ceased to be so pressing—as printing became faster and cheaper, as laws of copyright evolved to protect intellectual property more securely—this same system of transcribing and disseminating parts remained. Extant parts of the eighteenth century, of which there are well over forty, show that even when full printed texts of plays existed, actors continued to be given parts. The conclusion is irresistible, and a basic premiss of our project: there was some kind of virtue, some kind of serendipitous potential, in this rather primitive technology. For both the actor and, we believe, the playwright, the handwritten part offered possibilities—a practical facility, a concentration of effect, a communicative economy—that the full text simply did not.

However, the entire issue of parts has never been addressed interpretatively. Indeed, it has rarely even been alluded to. Perhaps this is unsurprising. The jagged, reduced, apparently lacunal 'part' might be assumed to be a sorry and primitive creature when compared to the complex 'three-dimensionality' of an entire Shakespearean play-text. Indeed, the very idea of parts militates against most thinking about English literature, which is still shaped to Romantic-cum-Victorian notions of either a presiding authorial genius (like 'Shakespeare') or an organically whole text. Yet the very word 'part' (later in history to yield to 'length', then 'side', then 'cue-script') highlights the fact that what an actor was given was a segment only of the play: a part is, of course, not the whole. But as a fragment, it should not be dismissed as some severed or atrophied limb of an erstwhile holistic unity. After all, as at once a physical artefact and an actor's vocation, the part bears both text and context in its own right. Nor is it fatally detached from authorial 'intention' (certainly no more than any other dramatic text). Indeed, in drawing us closer to the processes of theatrical production—logistical, material, and phenomenological—thinking about parts can cast intimate and even secret light upon writerly design.

Shakespeare, an actor as well as an author, undoubtedly wrote his plays with the 'part' always prominent in his mind. When Viola cannot immediately answer a question because it is 'out of [her] part' (TLN 473), when Flute speaks 'all [his] part at once, cues and all' (TLN 912–13), parts are being casually referred to as the unit of performance. It is an open question whether or not Shakespeare cared about printing his plays: certainly he intended to 'publish' (in the sense of broadcast) them in part form. So, though never considered interpretatively until now, the part was actually the first (and perhaps only) unit of text designed by Shakespeare to be examined, thought about, learned, and 'interpreted'. Our book sets out, then, to examine Shakespeare's writing from the perspective he anticipated: of actor's parts that *were* in many ways 'the text', not only as possessed and used by the practitioners, but as worked upon and revised by the playwright or company. Our proposition is that the actor's part is a basic building-block of Shakespeare's craft, and that by 'recovering' it we will be able to capture anew the processes of Shakespeare's theatre. What can parts tell us about early modern theatrical practice? How did they contribute to such practice? What light can they shed upon the processes of constructing and performing a play? How much did they contribute to the astonishing sophistications that the period witnessed in dramatic 'personation'? Did writing in and for parts shape the way in which plays were composed?

Of course, lip-service is routinely paid to Shakespeare as a 'man of the theatre'. So, it is regularly acknowledged that play-texts display an immanent working knowledge of what is theatrically practicable. But the functions tend to be seen as effectively separate ones: there is a play-text, there are actors to give it life; someone, it is often anachronistically suggested, 'directed' the performance. What our book identifies, by contrast, is an actor's part that in a sense concentrates all three, even the non-existent director. And indeed this seems almost inevitable as soon as we recall that this astonishing writer was—already and always—an actor. Before he ever got close to getting one of his own plays on the main stage, he was working on other people's plays. As an actor, there was effectively no such thing as 'the play-text': or rather, his part *was* the play-text in so far as he ever got hold of it. Here is where the young Shakespeare learnt his trade; here is where his imagination, verbal and technical, learnt to roam. The part supplied the whole; or if it didn't, the young Shakespeare must have imaginatively filled out the gaps so as to make it do exactly that. Like any actor, he might have wished his parts better, fuller, funnier; like any fertile young mind, he must have considered ways of secreting infinite riches in his *own* little room. Shakespeare's most impressionable years were probably spent as an actor, finding out what he thought and what he could do as he learnt how to own and communicate a part. And such formative experiences permeate the forms of his mature work. Shakespeare's subsequent achievement as a playwright wasn't inevitable; nor was it easily earned; nor was it the free gift of a transcendent imagination or of some demonic facility for seeing into other people's minds. It could not have happened quite as it did if the actor's part had not been what Shakespeare identified as the vital thing to be opened up and expanded. It should be no surprise, then, that Shakespeare filled the parts he gave to his actors with all kinds of 'directions' for their performance.[2] But more than this, the written part never ceases to be a creative catalyst for Shakespeare;

he seems never to lose the basic trust that these fractured little texts can be as surprising and as self-generating as any living organism. Shakespeare makes his parts, but equally they 'make' whatever Shakespeare becomes.

If we are really to contextualize Shakespeare's parts, it will be necessary to disabuse ourselves of certain very common assumptions about his work and its milieu. One of these is that 'the play', as a finished and masterful organism, ineffably precedes and determines all else. Of course the part will also suggest the larger play; it will distil preoccupations dilated elsewhere in the work, contribute to the unfolding story, to the to-and-fro between characters, the drawing out of ideas and conflicts, and so on. But our project requires that we suspend, or at times even reverse, the common presupposition that, performance or no performance, it is the playwright and/or the finished play that remains the primal fount of meaning and direction. Instead, our project will identify the actor and his part as crucial contributors, both as catalyst and vehicle, to whatever Shakespeare's theatre became.

For this system of transmitting parts highlights the centrality of individual actors, owning the parts they played. The part, exactly because it is at once so severed and so concentrated, becomes inherently magnified the moment we place it back in something like its original context. For the actor, it is *everything*, truly a microcosm. It is learned and memorized in private away from other parts, in the actor's home, in the bedroom, late at night or early in the morning. In Shakespeare's period and beyond, chief actors, having fully learned or 'conned' their own parts, seem often to take a pride in disdaining all else; there are many stories of their refusal to attend group rehearsals, condemning them to know nothing of the plays they are in beyond their own parts.

Consider the situation of Shakespeare, so intimately a member of the same team of men for his entire play-writing career. Even as he was meditating upon some brand new work, deep within the fabled smithy of his imagination, part of the metal must have been his mates, their jokes or aura or expectations, the voices from the previous day's playing or the night's carousing. So he shaped each written part to a particular actor. This helps to explain so much about Shakespeare's work, both the broad brush and the detail. He knew these actors; he knew what they had said about the last play, their last part, how they spoke the words, responded to cues, what they enjoyed, and what they did not. Shakespeare may or may not have been pleased with their performances; they may or may not have been pleased with his scripts. But if an actor were sensitive to verbal nuance, picking up each emotional transition, expressing gradations of emotion with finesse and clarity, then Shakespeare may well have been encouraged to write still more subtly for him: instead of laying one passion after another in the part, for example, Shakespeare may have decided to layer one on top of another, to be felt and communicated simultaneously. In such a case actorly competence helps to elicit rhetorical and psychological complexity. Alternatively, Shakespeare might have noticed an actor *not* picking up all that he wanted. In that case he may have had a quiet word with the performer, he may have let it go, or he may have tried, through his next play, to force the actor to refresh his routine. So he might give the actor a simpler role, a character 'type'; or jolt the actor back into alertness by sewing some unforeseen surprise into his next part, hopeful that a small embarrassment, or sudden shock, or new emotion, would remind the performer that in this company's play-world nothing stays entirely still.

As we shall see again and again, the fact that Shakespeare knew his actors so well meant that, as much as he wrote 'to' their identifiable skills or characteristics, he also wrote 'around' them: he could always add, alter, or deny what the actor was expecting and be confident of the response the change would receive. The very centrality of particular, individuated actors became—perhaps ironically—a primary force for originality; it was also of course a way of keeping things fresh. Mutual knowledge, trust, and confidence—Shakespeare's of and in his actors, his actors' of and in him—allowed for, and perhaps created, the boundary-bending energy of his plays. Shakespeare knew that the actors would pick up the tiniest verbal fidget; they knew how to 'pick' him, however clever or abstruse his constructions. Each could stretch the other.

So, once a trick or a trope was learned, it wouldn't easily be forgotten. At the same time, it must have been clear to Shakespeare's actors that their chief writer was constitutionally restless; Shakespeare's willingness to continue to take risks showed that he would not be sated or calmed by popular success. At every level, micro- and macro-, expressive and technical, Shakespeare continued to experiment. Just as generic locations were daringly conjoined, so too were rhetorical instructions and character 'types'. Consequently, if Shakespeare's actors learnt a technique—say for reading cues, or using rhyming couplets—they had to be ready for the technique both to be repeated *and* to be altered. An initially minor facet of the actors' craft (for instance, repeated cues or short lines), was, through Shakespeare's use of the part-text, turned into something centrally directing. Or Shakespeare might, through the part, ask an actor to employ (or suffer) a known practice in a new or unexpected way (we find this with various cueing and prosodic effects). Or again, Shakespeare's writing might bury some clearly defined, lustily performable, audience-pleasing tropes in locations that the actor could 'see' but would struggle to articulate (we find this with his increasingly latent puns and metaphors). But that too can be newly explicable if we think in terms of parts: for whatever reason, the 'old' ways of acting jokes or making puns were no longer wanted; what was wanted (we might surmise) was that the actors would pick up on puns in their parts, and then visibly struggle on-stage because they could *not* embody them as once they had. The mixture in the actor's mind of insight, hindsight, and frustration corresponds to layered, accumulative experience; his ensuing acting would generate and communicate the same.

In such things the direction of influence between writer and actors doesn't matter. Perhaps the players complained to Shakespeare about his extended similes or his tiresome puns, and persuaded him to try new ways of writing; perhaps it was he who made them give up their favourite party-pieces. What matter are the years and years of experience, of working in each others' pockets, that ensures both repetition and difference; what matters is the individual actor working with the part by himself, picking up everything, identifying with everything, remembering and anticipating everything. This is a system that ensures tremendously intense collaboration. To the extent that the actors tried to influence the scripting, they almost certainly came at the writer from numerous angles at once, as one after another expressed his particular suggestion, fear, or grievance. And perhaps the experience of one part produced suggestions about that actor's *next* part: power and expectation then return to the company playwright, who can work with any suggestions in the 'larger' but unfinished context of a new play. The main point is irrefutable: the knowledge and practice that accrue from working in a single company ensure both continuity and innovation.

All of this suggests new ways of understanding the early modern theatre. For we can see that a play in performance was in many ways an accumulation, or a meeting, of numerous separate parts. Add to that the fact that theatrical companies performed different plays every day, while the various parts for the plays seem to have been written and circulated in the same hand, and it will be clear how a 'part' in one play will have easily been comparable with—even conflatable with—a part in another play. The part has a *physical* economy that facilitates not only intra-play but also inter-play references. If all these fragments had a unity of appearance, then we might need to reconsider the notion of the separateness of one play-text from another. Just as parts jostled and nestled with one another, like cards shuffled in a deck, so too might plays have formed a mutable corpus of work, by Shakespeare and indeed others, in which the distinctions between each were nothing like as hard and fast as the bibliographical certitude of modern books can suggest. Once more, we see how if the play bestows the part, so too the part bestows the play. The physicality of this circulating, multiplying part, then, might modify our very picture of a 'play-text'.

Rather than thinking of plays as finished books, we might better conceive of them as loose-leaf sheets, commissioned or swapped or shuffled with facile aplomb. This was a milieu, after all, in which collaborations between playwrights were hardly less common than single-author plays (Shakespeare, Jonson, Middleton, Marston, Fletcher, Beaumont, Dekker, Massinger, *et al.* all wrote collaboratively); in which dialogue or dances could move almost seamlessly from play to masque, and back (*Two Noble Kinsmen*, a collaboration between Shakespeare and Fletcher, reproduces the second antimasque of Beaumont's *Inner Temple Masque*, for instance), in which 'Hey ho the wind and the rain' can be sung in two radically different plays, a comedy (*Twelfth Night*) and a tragedy (*King Lear*); in which big set-piece soliloquies were both a popular staple, almost like an operatic aria, and at times dispensable (Hamlet's famous 'How all occasions doe informe against me', is in the 1604 Quarto (K3a—b) but not the Folio). Above all, this was an age in which many plays were in the repertoire at once, as old favourites were brought back to play alongside new plays, as actors learned and performed multiple roles in a single week, as both old and new plays were cut or augmented to adapt to fashion or respond to necessity. This kind of theatrical world is much easier to countenance once we recognize that the prime material of circulation was the part: easily handled, swapped, scribbled over; easily inserted into or extracted from an existing piece; conveniently rolled or folded by the actor all together; facilely rewritten or conceived brand new, perhaps by the jobbing hack happy to respond to commission, perhaps by the established artist anxious that a flight of fancy or sharp new joke should find its way into his work. It is a theatrical milieu buzzing with cross-reference and allusion, stock conceits and sensational variations, out of which new plays were born. There is a sense in which the magpie John Webster, whose plays can seem to consist of one set-piece 'quotation' after another, and whom one can imagine haunting the upper-class playhouses, scribbling down the best bits to rehash them in his own constructions, was less the plagiarist than paradigmatic of a theatre whose circulation of conceits and clichés was channelled and symbolized by this busy traffic in sheets.

For the fact is that many plays were composed not only of, but also at times *in*, part 'blocs'. Sustained evidence of this comes from play revisions. Often, as in *Hamlet*, revisions occur within a speech so that the cues can be left intact and will not have to be relearned: the nature of the part defines the kind of revision likely to take place.[3] Where revisions are thorough and extend through the length of a play, as in *Lear*, they nevertheless retain the cue-effect even as they alter the cue, with 'repeated' cue matched by different repeated cue. Either way, revisions suggest a habitual attention to the part's primacy as mediator of performance. The additions to the 1602 Quarto of the *Spanish Tragedy* are a striking example of composing in parts, the title-page broadcasting the 'new Additions of the Painters part' in the text.[4] Most telling are the fascinating alterations appended to the end of William Percy's manuscript plays *The Cuck-Queanes and Cuckolds Errants* and *The Faery Pastoral*. The tiny reworkings and alternative lines he suggests are not placed *in situ* as part of the plays themselves. Instead, they are tacked on at the end of the manuscript, to be inserted or not into the actors' parts ('Whither's the whither you may chuse the Better'). In each case the revision is given specifically by cue (headed 'Quu' or 'Qu'):

Act V Scen 4

Christ. Quu——Now beginneth the charme to work, see.
Dau. A whist, Gentlemen, a whist, And God and St Sepulcher to boote.

Act V scen 5

Or. Qu——Is this a Tyme to Squirill-hunt with Harlots and with Pages etcaet.
Vide locum.[5]

In other words, authors with any knowledge of the theatre wrote with parts and their cues at the forefront of their mind, and revised and restructured along 'part' lines. We see this again with *The Spanish Tragedy*: Hieronimo distributes parts for his play-within-the-play, insisting that each be written in a different language. The projected play will have to be an accumulation of separate roles, each following its own rules, and utterly isolated from all other parts by dint of its incommunicable language. Other plays, too, show a careful distinction between part and part. In Beaumont's *The Knight of the Burning Pestle*, Master Humphrey always speaks in rhyming couplets, but his lover, Luce, always speaks in blank verse. Each actor is likely to be taken aback by the other's verbal metrics: it is as though they belong to two different play 'worlds', which, in many senses of course, they do.

Generally it is thought that not enough information survives either about parts or about acting to understand clearly the way in which the early modern theatre operated. That is based on the (false) assumption that most available information about the early modern theatre has already been gathered and processed. In this book we will draw upon several hundred 'new' sources for our material; our readings of the individual parts will build a still more detailed and intimate picture of a working theatre company. We will frequently identify material that is occluded or invisible when looking at a full play-text, and is suddenly brought to light by reading in part-form. Necessarily, much that is salient to actors' parts will not be our subject. As a rule, if something can be seen or understood as easily in full text as in part-text, then we will pass it by. This includes matters that are fundamental to the writing and performing of parts, such as rhetorical tropes and figures of speech, and the generic 'types' that underlie particular characters (e.g. the Vice in Iago or Richard III). We will concentrate upon phenomena that cannot be seen unless we take the cued part as our text, or which are transformed in so doing.

In order to achieve this, we often try to place the 'whole' play under erasure: that is, we endeavour to presuppose neither the full play-text nor the subsequent history of part and play in performance, criticism, or popular reputation.[6] A basic method of ours involves reproducing the parts, much as the prompter might have in Shakespeare's theatre, and very simply studying them (much as an actor might have). By thus 'bracketing' them, we hope to see more than would be seen by reading these parts within their familiar textual space. It is these imaginatively reconstructed part-scripts, then, that have been our working texts; as far as possible we have tried to pretend that no one has ever seen them before; that we are as the first actors were, searching for entrance-points into parts made up of a formidable array of materially specific signs and techniques. From this we move back 'out' to Shakespeare's larger development as a writer: but any such judgements or generalizations proceed from the information suggested by the discretely analysed part. Of course, we cannot grasp the part without first sensing the whole; but equally, we will not know the whole without first rethinking the part.

Before summarizing what we do in this book, we should briefly explain what the book is not. It is not a comprehensive history of actors' parts in the early modern theatre; it does not explore the uses that playwrights other than Shakespeare make of the part-based techniques which we identify. We do not ascertain whether different practices were common to different playhouses, or theatrical companies, or collaborations; nor whether certain techniques were more in vogue at one time than another. We do not explore the question of influence, either of other writers upon Shakespeare or of him upon them. The first large section of the book establishes the public theatre's regular practice, over a long period of time, in terms of the writing, circulating, rehearsing, playing, and watching of parts. However, the only way to get close to the specific use or adaptation of these practices by other writers or companies is to study closely the parts written by or for them. We have done this only with the parts written by Shakespeare. So after this 'historical' section, we pretty much leave other writers and companies alone. As a consequence, we do not make any judgements about how unique or otherwise Shakespeare's practices were; nor do we offer any generalizations about other writers. Inevitably, many of the techniques we analyse were common to many writers, or became common once they were established. But this is material for another book (perhaps by us, perhaps by others). We hope that our work will inspire further questions and research, whether challenging our methods and conclusions, or pursuing them further in other subject areas.

We should confess that we began with the ambition of looking at the whole of early modern theatre. That we did not in the end do this is partly because we might never have finished, but more profoundly because Shakespeare's use of parts seemed immediately so interesting and so various as to warrant treatment on its own. We were encouraged in this decision by the newness of our subject. The subject of parts is, we think, in many ways revelatory of the early modern theatre; so too, we hope, are the methods we are pioneering in its study. If these things are to become more widely known, then by far the best means is a clearly defined book about Shakespeare's use of parts.

But having made this decision, we found as we researched and wrote the book that there was a rationale for our choice other than expedience and marketability. Partly the rationale is simply that Shakespeare, more than any other writer of the time, turns every technique, however apparently mechanical, into an expressive language: if we want to seek out the possibilities in any given technical or material form, then his work will reveal them. Partly the rationale turns and returns to simple biographical facts, unique to Shakespeare amongst all of his peers. First, he was an actor; second, he wrote always and only for the same group of players for most of his career. It is, we think, these facts that, in the end, vindicate our choice of subject.

This book has four major sections. First, using printed and manuscript sources, many of which have not been brought to light before, we will provide the most complete history of the part to date: what parts looked like, how they worked, what they did and did not contain, who used them and how. Then, using this historical information as our premiss, we will explore the creative, expressive, and interpretative possibilities that ensue.

In Part II we place cues under the microscope, identifying each part's cues as a second narrative running along the right-hand side of an actor's text. We examine the links between cuer and cued, and between cue and cued speech; we explore their length, the narratives they tell or foretell, the information they give to actors, and the ways in which various cue-effects help to direct or orchestrate action; we discuss cues as indicators of character or comments upon the dramatic moment. In Part III we examine Shakespeare's increasingly ambitious use of premature or repeated cues. Equally, we explore the cue-space itself—the space in between and encompassing 'cuer' and 'cued'—as peculiarly promise-crammed or meta-dramatically suggestive.

In Part IV we study the specific directions for acting contained within the cued actor's speeches: how such speeches direct shifts of mind, focus, emphasis, or body. In particular, we study techniques such as midline switches, movements between verse and prose, full line and short line, blank verse and couplets. This means looking at the ways in which parts communicate to the actor transitions from self-address to dialogue, or from one emotion or passion to another. What did these actors search for, what did they concentrate upon, knowing that their choices alone must pace and measure their character's relationship to the on-stage world and to the audience?

Throughout, then, we consider not only how Shakespeare's actors read and embodied their parts, but also how working from parts produced particular effects in performance. We see how parts influenced the kinds of characters Shakespeare wrote and the techniques he used to produce them. And we ask how we might interpret parts and plays differently if, like Shakespeare's actors, we were to limit ourselves to the cued part as our working text. At the same time our book is also a 'how to' guide: it not only asks how actors responded to parts in Shakespeare's day; it offers suggestions as to how *we* might do so today. As we see it, the cued part is a unique keyhole on to hitherto forgotten practices and techniques, and into the theatrical shorthand, or sleights of hand, that were once, perhaps, taken for granted. These actors were trained, through practice and daily intimacy, to become Shakespeare's 'understanders' as probably no one has been since. But by looking at parts we not only discover a newly active, choice-ridden actor; we discover a new Shakespeare, whose part-based understanding and experimentation lead to remarkable innovations in creating subjectivity and engineering dramatic affect, producing on-stage drama of unprecedented immediacy.

# PART I

## History

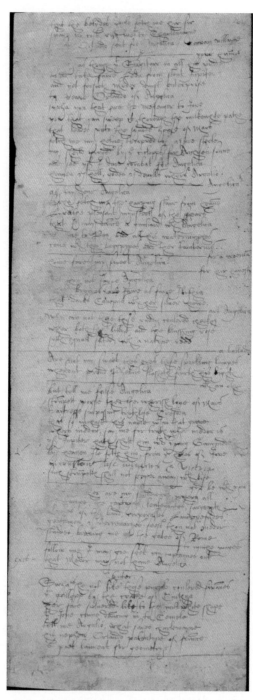

The part of Orlando from Robert Greene's *Orlando Furioso* (1590s).

# I
# The Actor's Part

## Early Modern Professional Parts

Much uncertainty has arisen from the erroneous assumption that there is only one surviving early modern written 'part' from which all knowledge of actors' texts must be gleaned. But in fact there are a handful of extant parts in English both from the Renaissance period and earlier; and from later—the Restoration and the eighteenth century—there are large quantities of surviving professional theatre parts. Examining a wealth of parts reveals their consistencies with each other and over time. On record there are more than forty British professional theatrical parts surviving from the eighteenth century, one dramatic and one musical part from the Restoration, four university parts (bound together) from the early seventeenth century, an amateur and a professional part from the sixteenth century, three parts (bound together) from the fifteenth century and one that is separate, and three from the fourteenth—and fragments of parts are attached to plays in manuscript. In addition, the tendency of writers of the early modern period, both in and out of the playhouse, to use the theatre as a metaphor results in a large number of detailed references to the nature and use of parts. From the Continent there are parts in abundance; Switzerland provides at least twenty sixteenth-century examples, France ten, Germany upwards of twelve in German and Latin, Holland at least one, Italy at least four—and these are only the ones recorded in articles. Even a classical Greek part—for Admetus in Euripides' *Alcestis*, dating from between 100 BC and AD 50—has lately been identified.[1] Each country's scholars puzzle over the information given as well as denied an actor in a part; few countries are conscious either of similar holdings in other countries, or of the similar questions they provoke.

We begin with a description of early sixteenth-century parts from England, France, and Germany; perversely, more parts survive from then than from later that century. Having established the characteristics of these parts, that information will then be compared with the information offered by the early modern professional part of 'Orlando'. As the question that is important to our project is whether 'Orlando' is typical, further contexts will be explored: we will consider what professional theatre parts look like over the two centuries following the performance of *Orlando*, asking where 'Orlando' fits into the history of actors' parts.

The earliest English parts, like the early German and Italian ones, give the actors only their lines to speak; no cues of any kind are provided.[2] This must relate to the way early medieval parts were learned for performance. Without having any cues at all, the actor cannot himself identify the moment when he is to speak: he needs to be given this information by another. Famously, Continental illustrations of early medieval performance, like Jean Fouquet's 'Sainte Apolline', show a prompter standing mid-stage with a book in one hand and a baton (originally the *baculus* of the clerical Master of Ceremonies) in the other. Indeed, the book-and-baton is something of a prompter's motif in this period; other surviving pictures also show the two.[3] In France and Germany at this time—and, we are conjecturing, also in England—actors were literally 'conducted' as to when to speak. But, from the early sixteenth century, parts with cues—the final words of the preceding speech—become increasingly frequent over Europe. Again, we must use conjecture here. We are guessing that the cue relates to a shift in acting style; in particular, that parts started to be cued when prompters lost their batons and moved off the stage into the tyring-house.[4]

The earliest parts with cues seem to be 'The Ashmole Fragment', an English part from the fifteenth century in the Bodleian Library, the thirty French and French-Swiss parts, all of which date from between the 1510s and the 1530s, and two medieval German parts in Latin. The Bodleian's 'Ashmole Fragment' is for 'Secundus Miles', the second soldier, in an unknown play.[5] Two cues are provided for the actor; neither of the speakers of the cues is named. This, as we shall see, is entirely normal, but ignorance about not naming cue-speakers led to the text's misidentification in the 1950s (the cues were thought to be odd stage-directions); thus the earliest cued part in England was not identified until the 1970s. The cues, 'ρουρ ye were' and 'To the hye trenite', are separated from the text by being centred on the page and 'boxed' with oblique lines on either side and a line beneath. So the cue is made to relate to the spoken text whilst being differentiated from it (another point to which we will return). 'The

Ashmole Fragment' is a detachable document from a miscellany, so its provenance is unclear; it is also unknown how long the whole part was, and whether it was given to the actor on a roll or in a book. The French and German parts of the same period, however, seem to provide some answers about length and appearance of parts—or at least refine the questions.

The largest single cache of parts is from Vevey in Switzerland, and is now in the Fribourg archive.[6] It dates from just before 1520 and consists of some twenty-three parts—possibly more: each part is fragmentary, and it has not always been possible to identify which pieces belong together. The story of the Fribourg fragments gives a sense of how actors' manuscripts were valued—or, rather, not valued. These parts ended up in the hands of a sixteenth-century bookbinder as waste paper. He took them with other, similar waste—accounts, sonnets, posies, letters, and medicinal recipes—and glued them together to make a thick cardboard. This he trimmed and shaped and made into the hard cover of a book. Four hundred years later, in the 1920s, the scholar Paul Aebischer, intrigued by the cardboard, had it unglued; it resolved into a jigsaw puzzle of fragments.[7] Out of the debris Aebischer identified twelve actors' parts; Graham Runnalls later found a further eleven amongst the pieces. The parts are particularly useful because of their quantity; any concerns that they might be relevant only to Swiss performance are negated by their similarity to other European parts.

Each of the Fribourg parts seems, originally, to have been about 10 cm in width; the width one would get by halving a folio-size page vertically. These strips were then attached to one another top to tail and fastened. Though few of the joins survive—the bumpy edges seem to have been purposefully cut away by the bookbinder—just enough evidence remains to show that a variety of pinning, gluing, and sewing was used to attach the separate strips into a long continuous paper. The actor's words were written on one side of this paper; the other was left blank. Four of the Fribourg fragments contain the end of a roll, and in each case the last, blank 6 cm of paper contain holes made by pins or nails, seemingly so that the strip could be fastened to a wooden baton and then rolled around it. This suggestion is bolstered by the French words used for parts at the time—they were called *roole*, *rollet*, *roullet* (from which we get our term 'role');[8] German parts, similarly, were known as *Rolle*; Italian parts, *rotuli*. Indeed, though the word 'part' (and sometimes 'parcell') were the usual terms used in England at the time, William Percy the playwright enjoins actors—probably Paul's boy players—to make no mistakes and to observe 'your rouled Parts'.[9]

At the top of each sheet, the name of the character in the play for whom the part was intended—'Baltasar', 'Jesus'—is inscribed; at the bottom is written the word *Explicit*. Cues are indented and appear in the middle of the line, as with 'The Ashmole Fragment'; again as in 'The Ashmole Fragment', the speaker of the cue is not named. As for cue-length, which varies from one to three words, there seems to be no clear set of rules to determine the number of cue-words provided. Cues are not, for instance, chosen in order to help with versification: indeed, intricate rhyme patterns are sometimes hard to spot, as they are shared between characters, not all of whose parts have survived. Tellingly, then, actors frequently lacked the advantage of having a mnemonic rhyme on their own individual parts.[10] What did they have instead? Stage-directions are placed, boxed, to the right of the text, and there are manuscript markings to the left, generally of horizontal lines, which seem to relate to action and may be guides as to blocking, indicating specific movements across the stage.[11]

One extract, from 'The Priest's Role' in a play similar to *Prêtre Crucifié*, will suffice to give a general idea of the appearance of a Fribourg role. It shows one to three cue-words—with no indication of the cue-speaker—and it also contains a stage-direction relating to the movement of other actors in performance. One thing that cannot be replicated here is the state of the roll: it is, like all of them, described as being (surprisingly) 'carelessly written and full of error'.[12]

> *blan*
> J'ay le cherubin ja tout blan!
> De la bulure ja je suis mort!
> *veisez.*
> Helas, m'amie, je ne say!
> Il m'a tout brulé le vellant.
> *a vue vot.*
> Ma bel'amie, fermé bien tout,
> Devant que vous entrés dedans!
> *t'ouvre!*
> Qu'esse, m'amie?                    *Il va en la le crucefis.*
> *ne quan.*
> Helas, helas!
> *ne bien.*
> Helas, helas![13]

Other parts are scattered around the archives of France: 'The Rôle of Tripet', 'The Rôle of the "Minister" in the *Mystère de Saint André*', 'The Rôle of Saint Simon', 'The Rôle of "Péché" "Sin" in a morality play', 'A Comic Rôle from Sion', 'The Rôle of Saint Barbara (Barbe)' in a morality play, 'The Farce of Thévol'.[14] There are also Victorian accounts of French rolls found and now lost again: 'The Rôle for Moréna' in a Nativity play', 'The Rôle of God' and 'Rôles for the Passion Play performed in Paris in 1539 by the Confrérie de la Passion'.[15] Of particular interest amongst these is the part for Saint Barbara; unlike the other French parts listed above, all of which are short in nature (being from farces, morality plays, or for secondary characters), the 'Sainte Barbe' part is for a substantial character—and it occurs in a different format. As ever, it consists of unattributed cues and speeches, but it is written into a stitched book instead of on to a roll. One suggestion that has been made on the strength of this is that shorter parts were disseminated as rolls, and longer parts as books; evidence from other European parts does not entirely back up that conjecture, however.[16]

From sixteenth-century Britain we have the part of God in a miracle play. It, too, is in a roll, and is the first English part to survive with cues, generally of three or four words. Yet it differs in one significant aspect from the other rolls: in this part the speaker of the cue is named.[17] In fact, from the middle of the sixteenth century onwards, various parts across Europe name the speaker of the cue. In the German 'Strassburg Salvator-Rolle' (roll of Our Saviour) for the Lucerne Passion, 1616, the speakers of the 'Stichwörter' are indicated. Linke, who draws attention to this cued part, mentions its similarity to other German parts (without describing them in much detail): a Latin role from Berlin of a high priest—probably Annas—in a Passion play of the fifteenth century, and a Latin 'Merchant's roll', described as medieval and not dated.[18] So performers readying a miracle play seem to have regularly been told to whom their speeches were addressed. This is symptomatic of intimate staging—on pageant wagons, for instance—in which eye contact with the relevant person is a possibility. Still more importantly, knowing the name of the speaker gave vital additional 'help' to the uncertain performer. We need to recall here that the performers of miracle and morality plays were also always employed in other jobs: as actors they were strictly amateur. Whether the speaker of the cue was named or not in the early modern British *professional* theatre is another question, and obviously one of consequence for our book; we will now look in detail at the surviving evidence for the answer.

The most obvious and first place to turn is the one known English professional theatre part of the 1590s: the part of 'Orlando' in Robert Greene's play *Orlando Furioso*. This is the nearest survivor to Shakespeare's parts—it was penned at a time when Shakespeare was alive and writing for the theatre; it was intended to be used by Burbage's rival Edward Alleyn.

The remaining strips of 'Orlando', now separate, were clearly originally stuck together in a roll of about 18 feet in length, as worm-hole evidence shows. So here is a very long part—a part for a major protagonist—disseminated as a scroll; this suggests that the choice of roll or book is not necessarily connected to the length of the part.[19] Rather, the choice of roll may have been made because the formula preserves paper: unlike a book, in which blank pages are simply wasted, the end of a roll can be trimmed, and left-over paper can be used to make another part. That said, there is also an essential difference between a roll and a book: a roll will be for one play only—otherwise it will become thick and unwieldy—whereas, as we will show, a book can contain several parts for several plays.

This particular part, headed 'Orlando' at the top of each strip (just as French-Swiss parts are headed)—presumably to ensure that separate strips are attached to the correct roll—is amongst the papers which Alleyn left to Dulwich College. The part includes on it manuscript corrections in the hand of a 'corrector'. This is quite possibly Alleyn himself, the actor 'inserting' himself into the part as he attempts to make it render sense; for the part, though neat, has blanks and gaps for words that its scribe could not read in the text he was copying. It has been conjectured that the part—improved by correction, but still not perfect—is itself a rejected text.[20] For our purposes the question is immaterial: used or unused, the part is written to the formula adopted at a public theatre. But what is interesting to us is that a certain sloppiness seems to be endemic (see above and below). This reflects the hasty production of parts in a busy playhouse, and the very local and private circulation they were intended to have; but it also allows the actor the intimacy with the text that 'correction' offers. (The evidence of 'Orlando', and many later parts, is that they were always very 'busy' documents, alive with scribbles and emendations.) Another confusion surrounding 'Orlando' is that it bears an odd relationship with the full Quarto of Robert Greene's *Orlando Furioso* published in 1594. The problem is that the version of the play reflected in the part seems to be the one given a performance at the Rose in 1591/2, while the Quarto records a different version of the play, perhaps the result of the fact that Greene sold *Orlando* twice, to two different companies, the Admiral's Men and the Queen's Players.[21] As a result, direct comparison between the two texts is less revealing than might otherwise have been the case.

Here is a section of that part, just to show how much Alleyn was and was not given in his script. As this section makes clear, Alleyn's part, like all other parts, consisted of what he was going to say—but did not include what was to be said about or to him (cue apart). Unlike the French cues, the cues in 'Orlando' are heralded not by centring on the page, but by a long preceding line (called the 'tail'; see Part II). The cue-words themselves are aligned to the right of the manuscript, and the cue-line visibly cuts across the actor's speeches. In this the part resembles what was seen in the earlier parts. Alleyn's cue was, of one to three words: length of cue is thus broadly flexible, but that seems to be because its content is *not* random. If the addition of a word helps to give the cue a tangible presence or memorability, then a word will often be added; conversely, if one or two words give a sufficiently pithy picture, then a third word will often be deemed redundant. Consecutive cues in 'Orlando' read:

> —————————————————— the world
> —————————————————— no answerr
> —————————————————— doth lye
> —————————————————— penylesse
> —————————————————— by force
> —————————————————— I give
> —————————————————— souldioures

Small variations, however, are often employed to distinguish between similar-sounding cues. In 'Orlando' 'lord' and 'my lord' are interchanged, no doubt as a mnemonic aid for the actor:

> —————————————————— my lord
> I pray the tell me one thing, dost thou not
> knowe, wherfore I cald the
> —————————————————— neither
> why knowest thou not, nay nothing thou
> mayst be gonne, stay, stay villayne I tell
> the Angelica is dead, nay she is in deed
> —————————————————— lord

                                      but my Angelica is dead.
                           _____ my lord
he beat*es*. A.            and canst thou not weepe
                           _____ Lord[22]

Thus the part of 'Orlando', in its length and use of cue is broadly representative of the conventions of its time. Like the Swiss actors, Alleyn is
given additional stage-directions in the left margin that tell him important
material relevant to his performance, including not only his own actions
but, occasionally, those of other players (as this damaged section of the
manuscript indicates):

he beat*es*. A.       and canst thou not weepe
                      _____ Lord
                      why then begin, but first lett me geve you
A. begins to          you$^r$ watchword· Argalio, Ang <el
weepe                 stay <          > begin to so <

But unlike the Swiss actors, Alleyn here is given no hint about 'blocking'
more generally on the stage—where or at whom he is to look, how far
forward he is to walk, and so on. Such very basic matters are simply not indicated. If the 'Orlando' part is indeed representative—and in this it almost
certainly is—then we have to conclude that, while certain specific actions
may be dealt with in a part's stage-directions, many more general movements are either so 'stock' as not to deserve mention, or are simply left to
the actor to determine as he cons the part and, of course, when he performs.

   Amongst the information that Alleyn is *not* given is how long he will
have to wait to hear his cues, guidance that all actors seem to have done
without. He is also ignorant as to who speaks the cues. And he is given
very little punctuation as a speaking guide, though lineation indicates verse
lines to him. The following passage from the part is a fight scene in which
Orlando attacks a French peer. On stage at this moment, according to the
equivalent scene in the Quarto, are Marsillus, Mandrecard, twelve peers of
France, and Angelica. What Alleyn gets in the manuscript part is this:

                  Twelve peres of frau*n*ce, twelve divylles, whats y$^t$
                  what I have spoke, ther I pawne my sword
                  to seale it, on the helme, of him that dare
                  Malgrado of his hono$^r$ combatt me
                                                        of
                  _____ Lord*es* Jndi<a

|  | You that so proudly bid him fight |
|  | out w<sup>th</sup> your blade, fo<sup>r</sup> why your turne is next |
|  | tis not this champio*n*, can discorage me· |
| *pugnant* | ——————————————————————— |
| *N. victus* | You sir that braved your < c > hevaldry |
|  | wher is the honor of the howse of frau*n*ce |
|  | ———————————————— to doe |
|  | ffaire princesse what I may belong*es* to the |
|  | wittnes I well have hanseled yet my sword |
|  | now sir you that will chastyce when you meet |
|  | bestirr you french man fo<sup>r</sup> Ile taske yo*u* hard |
| *Oliver victus* | ——————————————————————— |
|  | Provide you lordes, determyne who is next |
|  | pick out the stoutest champio*n* of you all |
|  | they wer but striplin*ges*, call you these y<sup>e</sup> pe<sup>r</sup>s |
|  | hold madam, and yf my life but last it out |
|  | Ile gard your *person* w<sup>th</sup> the peires of frau*n*ce |

Let us first compare this with the equivalent scene in the (revised) Quarto text of the same play. The scene is run slightly differently, but many of Orlando's speeches can still be recognized, and the passage gives a sense of how the plot and staging were managed altogether. We should note here not only the difference in content, but also the difference in presentation, of the stage-directions. As is clear from this section of the full text of *Orlando*, the stage-directions in a complete printed version of a play may record a past performance, or prescribe a future one; directions in part-text have to tell a specific actor what to do or what is happening at a specific moment. Consequently—and hardly surprisingly—stage-directions in full text will very often not have been quite the same as stage-directions in part-text (a point confirmed by extant Restoration parts—see below).

| *Orlando* | How Madam, the twelve Peeres of France? |
|  | Why let them be twelve divels of hell: |
|  | What I have said Ile pawne my sword |
|  | To seale it on the shield of him that dares |
|  | Malgrado of his honor combat me. |
| *Oliver* | Marrie sir, that dare I. |
| *Orlando* | Yar a welcome man sir. |
| *Turpin* | Chastise the groome (Oliver) & learne him know, |
|  | We are not like the boyes of Africa. |
| *Orlando* | Heare you sir: You that so peremptorily bad him fight, |
|  | Prepare your weapons for your turne is next, |

Tis not one Champion that can discourage me,
Come are yee ready.

*He fighteth first with one, and then with another, and overcomes them both.*

So stand aside, and Maddam if my fortune last it out,
Ile gard your person with twelve Pieres of France.

Extraordinarily, then, as the comparison between the two varieties of text shows, the part of 'Orlando' gives the actor a complex fight scene in which he knows who to fight and who will win (in the Quarto text he consistently wins, in the part he does not): but he is not actually told to whom he is speaking. But is 'Orlando', with its absences and lacunae, representative of professional theatre parts of its time? Comparison with earlier French and English parts has suggested that 'Orlando' fits comfortably with late medieval and early modern parts, but has raised the possibility that some varieties of part might name the speaker of the cue-words. Contemporary and later evidence will now be examined in order to determine how normal 'Orlando' is in this and in other respects.

## The University Parts

There are four surviving early modern British university parts, all bound together in a part-book, which are in several significant ways different from 'Orlando'. These parts, for single performances at Christ Church (Oxford) in the 1620s, have cue-lines considerably longer than those discussed so far. Each cue-line, moreover, is fronted with the name of its speaker. The parts are also not in a roll but are preserved in a book, in which they are written consecutively: thus the four parts are visually similar, breaking down the boundaries between play and play.

The university parts are 'Poore' (in English, from a lost play), 'Polypragmaticus' (in Latin, from Robert Burton's *Philosophaster*), 'Amurath' (in English, from Thomas Goffe's *The Courageous Turk or Amurath the First*), and 'Antoninus' (in Latin, from the anonymous *Antoninus Bassianus Caracalla*).[23] The second and fourth of these are written in the hand of Thomas Goffe—who probably also played from them.[24] These parts tell us a great deal about the carefully prepared single performances that were put on by students in universities. But do they tell us anything about professional performance? The question is vexed. Long(er) cues are, sometimes, found in later professional theatre parts: Kemble's many surviving eighteenth-century parts tend to have cues of five words or so. But the naming of the cue-speaker has no parallel in professional theatre parts of any period. It relates, as illustrated, to earlier and amateur performance—performances, that is to say, by people who were not accustomed to acting on a daily basis and who put on plays only irregularly, and after careful rehearsal. 'All four university parts', observes Carnegie, comparing them to 'Orlando', 'consistently make life easier for the amateur actor.'[25] In other respects the four university parts are like professional theatre parts: the actor receives only his own speeches; additional information, when necessary, is supplied to the right of the text. For instance, 'Poore' has the additions 'Badg: gives him y$^e$ lre' and 'To Med:', though, as Carnegie comments, 'the explicit directions appear an arbitrary choice; they do not fall into identifiable or important groupings distinct from the implied directions'.[26] It may be, of course, that implied directions do not need the bolstering of an additional stage-direction and are directions in their own right. That said, there are also present on the parts of 'Poore' and 'Polypragmaticus' vertical marks to the left of the writing and crosses, both in pencil and of unclear date. The marks may, like the similar marks in French-Swiss parts, indicate movement across the stage.

Two more features of these parts deserve special mention because central to our project in this book. One is that the university parts do not draw attention to cue-words that are to be given out more than once. For instance, in the full, published play of Goffe's *The Courageous Turk or Amurath the First* (which relates closely to the part of Amurath) there is a moment at which the cue 'and mine' is given out twice, once by Eurenoses, once by Chase-Illibeg:

|  |  |
|---|---|
|  | Our Tutor, *Eurenoses*, Captaines, welcome! |
|  | Gallants, I call you to a spectacle: |
|  | My breast too narrow to hoard up any joy: |
|  | Nay, gaze here (Gentlemen!) give Nature thanks, |
|  | For framing such an excellent sence as (Sight) |
|  | Whereby such objects are injoy'd as this! |
|  | Which of you now imprison not your thought |
|  | In envious and silent policy. |
| *Schahin* | My Lord to whatsoever you shall propose, |
|  | My sentence shall be free. |
| *Eurenoses* | **And mine.** |
| *Chase-Illibeg* | **And mine.** |

| | |
|---|---|
| *Amurath* | Which of you then dare chalenge to himself, |
| | Such a pathetique a Prærogative ...[27] |

The manuscript part for Amurath, however, does not indicate that the cue
will be heard twice:

> Our Tutor, Euren: Captaynes, welcome
> Gallants I call you to a spectacle
> My breaste to narrow, to hoard up my ioy
> Nay gaze here Gentle~, give nature thancks
> For framinge such an excellent sense as sight
> Whearby such obiects are enjoyd as this
> Which of you all, imprison not yr thougth
> In envious, and silent pollicie
> Chas: _____ And mine:
> Which of yu then dares challenge to himselfe
> So a pathetique a praerogative

Because he is told who is speaking the cue-line, the actor of 'Amurath'
is not bound to start his reply at the 'wrong' time—but nevertheless the repeated cue presents a 'danger' to which the actor is not
alerted. Perhaps ensemble rehearsal, such as there was, would sort out
such problems. But the fact of the textually unacknowledged repetition
raises interesting questions. Was there any way of indicating on the part
that the cued actor must wait for the cue's second articulation? If not,
does it matter if Amurath starts speaking at the first 'and mine'? After all, the two 'and mines' illustrate the slavishness of Eurenoses and
Chase-Illibeg alike; were Amurath indeed to speak over their shared
submissiveness, that itself would reinforce their insignificance relative to
Amurath's power.

When it is very important that no 'over-speaking' happens, in fact, the
university parts have a way of dealing with the problem. For example,
Amurath has to speak after a marriage ceremony that includes a wedding-
song. The song has a repeated chorus, which Amurath must not interrupt.
Here is the song and its preceding stage-direction as it is presented in the
full, printed text:

*Enter Amurath at one doore with Nobles Bajazet, Enter at th'other, Hatam,*
*richly attended, they meet, salute in dumbe shew; Amurath ioynes the hands of the*
*Prince, and Princesse; whilst this is solemnizing, is sung to soft Musicke, this Song*
*following.*

*Song.*
*Thine O Hymen, thine: O shee,*
*Whose Beauties verse Calliope,*
*Sing to Marriage rites an Io,*
    *Io to Hymen.*
*Chorus.*

*To thee Apollo is my sute,*
*Lend me a while thy silver Lute,*
*O what a woe it is to bring,*
*A Bride to Bed and never sing.*
    *Io to Hymen.*

*When she's old, still seemes she young,*
*When she's weake, to her be strong!*
*Be Cyprus, both, and Paphos here,*
*Love, sing with merry cheere.*
    *Io to Hymen.*

*Amurath*     You Gods of Marriage: sacred Protectoresse
Of lawfull propagations, and blest Love
Be most propitious to these grafted stemmes![28]

Amurath's part at the same stage looks like this:

Am: gives Baiazet in marriage

Son:    3 Io to Hymen
Am:    you Gods of Marriage, sacred protectoress
      Of lawfull propagation, and blest love
      Bee most pertious, to thease grafted stemms

The '3 Io to Hymen' clearly tells the actor not to speak his lines until he has heard 'Io' three times, an instruction that will prevent premature speaking, and this appears to be another careful amateur 'help': nothing of its kind is found on the contemporary or later professional theatre parts. That said, we need to bear in mind the options that it raises for preventing unnecessary or uncalled for over-speaking: and of course the reverse—the opportunities created for deliberate over-speaking when repeated cues are *not* indicated by the cued part (explored in detail in Part II).

Comparing the full printed play and the manuscript part reveals other differences between the two varieties of text: stage-directions in full play and in part-script serve distinct purposes. Amurath's stage-directions, hardly surprisingly, directly concern the actor, and ignore other players except in so far as they affect *him*; by contrast, the stage-directions in the printed play, which seems to have been prepared for reading, are full and explanatory, and concern the story as a whole. Again, this alerts us to the possibility that the stage-directions we receive on printed texts are not necessarily what the actors were given on their parts; we can be conscious of this problem but cannot conclusively resolve it. We cannot know what stage-directions may have been added to—or indeed omitted from—Shakespeare's actors' lost parts, particularly given that university parts relate uncertainly to public theatre parts.

Verse is also indicated by lineation in the parts—as it is in 'Orlando'. But three of the four university parts are in complex verse in which one actor is obliged to complete a verse-line started by another; in this they manifestly imitate what had long been common metrical practice in Jacobean plays (unlike the much earlier 'Orlando', in which speeches regularly finish with a full verse-line). What is intriguing in the university parts is that incomplete verse-lines are indicated with long dashes that, unlike cue-lines, can follow as well as precede a speech to show the speaker where he is within a line of verse. So 'Poore' contains the following verse exchange:

> Snaile:   I nere wrongd you _____
> Poore:    _____ nor ere mistrusted him?
> Snaile:   No on my life. _____
> Poore:    _____ nor wife, I knowe it well
> Sir hye you home; if now you meet not w^th him ...

(ll. 615–19)

Again, this is not a method found in professional theatre parts either of this time or later. There may, however, have been a known playhouse method of 'handing on' verse in some way (an issue we explore further in Part IV).

Though the university parts of the 1620s raise many interesting questions, they are frustratingly unlike either earlier or later parts. They illustrate that methods existed for showing when verse-lines were shared, for indicating (and not indicating) repeated cues, and for establishing the speaker of the cue-lines. However, no contemporary professional or foreign actors' part so far examined exploits any of these. The university parts seem uniquely different from other parts, no doubt because university acting was differ-ent—more studied, more careful, more in need of safety nets—than public theatre acting. Carnegie, considering these parts and 'Orlando' concludes:

> The more extended cues in the university parts would have allowed the actor studying his part in private a fuller knowledge of the plot, character, and

dynamics of those parts of the play in which he was involved. The academic actor may therefore have been able to prepare a more consistent character-ization or a more coherent reaction to plot action than minimal parts and negligible rehearsal time would have allowed his professional counterpart facing a first production ... We have, unfortunately, no evidence of which I am aware that might clarify whether the production of the college plays, in entirely different circumstances, in any way signals that professional prac-tices were changing twenty years on, or whether the greater possibility for dramatic interaction that I infer from the university manuscript is simply a by-product of the amateur student actors' simplifying memorization of both lines and action.[29]

The later history of professional theatre parts suggests the answer.

## The Restoration Part

There is, on record, a part that belonged to the Earl of Portland, and that W. J. Lawrence saw in private hands in the 1930s.[30] That has proved impossible to trace—meaning that the single cued part known from the Restoration comes from Ferdinando Parkhurst's play of *Ignoramus* which belonged to the Duke's Company and was put on in the Cockpit and at Whitehall in 1662.[31] The part itself was owned by Matthew Medbourne, who played 'Trico'; it is written in the hand of the actor. 'Trico' is thus a professional theatre part, and as such we should look at it against 'Orlando' for similarities and differences.

First, the cues. 'Trico' has cues mostly of one to three words; nevertheless, in some instances just a syllable is thought sufficient: cues vary in length from 'horne', 'Play', and 'Court' to 'contracted now to Ignoramo' (at four words—and nine syllables—the longest cue). Here we have a professional theatre part, then, in which cues are usually short and pithy. Langhans, writing of the part in 1975, noted:

> One might expect to find longer cues at the ends of lengthy speeches, or after Trico has had no lines for some time, but such is not the case, and there appears to be no logic behind the selection of cue length. At the beginning of II, v, Parkhurst inadvertently wrote out the whole speech of Antonius as a cue: 'Trico I like this plot'—but then he went back and crossed out the first three words to make it a shorter cue.[32]

Another feature of the part to which Langhans drew attention is the way that no differentiation is made between a cue that is part of a speech and a cue that is the speech in its entirety. One such example is when the full manuscript play contains a passage reading:

> Tric:   approach not neere her sir, take my advice,
>         see you not that old woman?
> Ant:   what of her?

The part of Trico for this moment reads:

> Approach not neer her Sir, take my advice,
> See you not that old woman?
> _____ what of her?

The cue-tail here 'misleads' the actor: it suggests the potential for other words that precede this question: but there are none, and Trico must respond at once to this rapid-fire cue.

As with 'Orlando', the name of the speaker of the cue-line is not provided. Occasionally, though, entrances of named speakers are supplied (perhaps also helping an actor identify his likely addressee). Another similarity to the 'Orlando' part is that an elongated cue-like line heralds the stage-directions—which, again, are sometimes about other actors—on the right. Here is a passage from Trico, showing cue-length, unnamed cue-speaker, and some clarifying stage-directions:

> _____ engaged for me
> mine lyes at stake too, therefore have a care
> _____ sparkleth truly?
> ha, ha, ha, how it sparkleth truly!
> and now Pyrupus thou art a true Sparke
> (thank Trico for it)
> here prethy let thy boy convey these clothes
> to the Ancor for my Master.—
> _____ yea
> farewell, truly-simple: ha, ha, ha—
> Now sir go dress your selfe with expedition
> _____ how then
> Ile teach you a trick to cosen him:
> If any thing chance to crosse your expectation,
> Be patient still, for ffortune has her end
> _____ our friend    (Exit Ant)
> (Ent Cupes) Now Cupes how dost find thy wife?
> _____ upon her.
> that's well; then take these Robes & carry 'em to her;

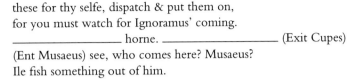

these for thy selfe, dispatch & put them on,
for you must watch for Ignoramus' coming.
_____ horne. _____ (Exit Cupes)
(Ent Musaeus) see, who comes here? Musaeus?
Ile fish something out of him.

Comparisons between the part and the full manuscript play show that, as with the university parts and 'Orlando', stage-directions differ between the two. In the passage above, for instance, Musaeus's entrance is placed before Trico's speech, but in the full text it occurs after Trico's speech and is positioned at the start of the next scene.[33] There are further differences concerning stage-directions: when, in v. vii, the part tells Trico first to exit and later to re-enter, the full text is not clear about the exit; when, in IV. v, the part tells Trico to hide after saying 'to your work with celerity', the full text omits the stage-direction altogether.[34] Here follows Trico's part for IV. vi and IV. x, which in the part are consecutive:

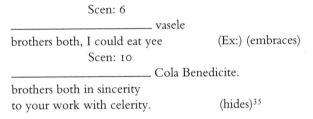

Scen: 6
_____ vasele
brothers both, I could eat yee          (Ex:) (embraces)
Scen: 10
_____ Cola Benedicite.
brothers both in sincerity
to your work with celerity.          (hides)[35]

Parts serve a different purpose from the full text. While they might verbally follow the complete play, they are likely to be more accurate locally, at least as far as stage-directions are concerned. In such incidental features the parts of Trico and Orlando are very similar. What does this mean for editors who struggle to find the 'right' place for a stage-direction? We simply have to acknowledge that surviving plays do not provide all the additional staging information that parts *may* have done—though we should be alert to the stage-directions that parts do not offer as well as those they do.

## Later Parts

Eighteenth-century professional parts were always in books—the roll no longer seems to have been used. These books might contain one or several parts: in handing on a book of parts, then, an actor would give a series of parts—perhaps his 'acting line'—to another player. (Conversely,

in handing on a roll, he would have given neither more nor less than
that specific part.) Shakespeare's practice here is difficult to discern. In *A
Midsummer Night's Dream* the actors are simply given 'parts', though their
names are written on a 'scroll'; as both existed and both were used at the
time, it is hard to be sure.

Part-books of the eighteenth century are usually personalized: the name
of the actor for whom the part is intended is written in the book, making
the actor himself an element of the part. Indeed, if a new actor takes over
an old part-book, he tends to assert his ownership by himself becoming
inscribed on his part. Thus texts survive that relate a mini-history of their
own, like the part for Falstaff that was handed on from famous actor to
famous actor for more than fifty years, as its cover relates: 'Mr Quins Part
of Falstaff [1792]—given by Mr Garrick to Mr T King by Mr King to
w Dowton in 1798'.[36] Parts were evidently still treated as fiercely owned
personal possessions in which one's fictional and real character were united
on the title-page, analogous to the widespread merging of role and reality
that is such a feature of actors in Shakespeare's time.

Parts were called 'lengths' in the eighteenth century, the word referring
both to a sheet of writing and to a number of lines—'each length should
be forty-four lines including the cues', explains Tate Wilkinson; 'Take half
a sheet of foolscap paper and divide it, the two sides are called a length
by the players; and in this form their parts are always written out by the
Prompter or his clerk', adds Boaden.[37] And 'length' as a word is, of course,
resonant—for it was the 'length', the bulk of the part, that defined the
actor's self-image: the more lengths, the more important he could think his
character. It came to be habitual to note, at the bottom of a part, the total
number of lengths it contained ('Shylock/in the/Merchant of Venice/For
Mr: Wm: Ward/Doncaster October 25th: 1772/Lengths 10'); whole books
were published informing actors of *the Number of Lengths Noted that Each Part
Contains* in popular plays.[38] Clearly actors prided themselves on the number
of lengths they could learn in a certain space of time; there seemed to be
little notion that one variety of part or one type of character might require
more time than another. And indeed, this effectively had to be the case:
preparation time before the performance of a play was not varied for depth
of character; hence the workaday claims made by performers like Thomas
Holcroft: 'I can repeat any part under four lengths at six hours' study.'[39]
The 'length' was, then, the unit in which a role was learned—suggesting,
as we will consider later, the sequential learning of a part from start to end.

In this period, parts continue to look much as they had done before. They give cues of generally no more than four words, and still do not indicate who speaks the cue-line except, occasionally, at the beginning of scenes: as ever, entrance cues are no longer than other cues, though they are sometimes differentiated by being prefixed with the word 'at'.[40] Here, for instance, is the second act of Macklin's 1734? part of Scrub in George Farquhar's *The Beaux Stratagem* (the part itself is one of several parts in separate plays, all to be performed by Macklin, that are united in one part-book):

Act 2<sup>d</sup>

Enter L.D.P.S. [Left Door Prompt Side]

at _____ Scrub

Sir!

_____ Week is this

Sunday, an't pleasure your Worship.

_____ Scrub.

Sir!

_____ of your Razor          {Exit[41]

Cues clearly continue to be of short but unequal length, though again we see how any such fluctuation is basically attributable to the content. It is easier to remember something meaningful than something floating and arbitrary, not least because it genuinely does 'cue' something. Macklin's cues often appear to be discrete clauses, or proper nouns, or questions that glance back to what has been said whilst setting up a response. His part for Lovegold in Fielding's *The Miser* in the same part-book, for instance, has on one page consecutive cues of:

_____ on the ear

_____ No really sir

_____ curmudgeon

_____ The matter, sir!

_____ what, Sir?'[42]

Where the words are bland and instrumental ('The matter, sir', etc.), they offer a clear invitation to speak; in other instances, the cue is animated and memorable ('curmudgeon', 'on the ear'), conveying a colourful mood or passionate attitude that can similarly set up an appropriate tone of response. Another sheet from the same part shows something similar: 'Terms you please', 'old Rascal', 'these eight months [*Pick up a Pin here*]', 'by these

scandalous Extortions?', 'at such Interest?' Merely to list the cues is to
pick up much about the exchange; complete ignorance of any context
is no bar to organizing genuinely coherent playing. For the evidence
here suggests that cues are cut and shaped to convey as much as possible
in as little as possible; if an extra word transforms nullity into content,
then the extra word can be included in the cue. On the odd occasion
when cues are not telling enough, Macklin himself writes in some further
cue-words—whether adding them from the prompt-book or as a result
of ensemble rehearsal is unclear (this was a period in which ensemble
rehearsal was prized for the first time). But Macklin's actions also show
how important it was to get the cue-length 'right'.

Revision in Macklin's parts also usefully tells us something about parts as
units in which plays were not just conceived but altered. The ways in which
parts can be individually revised to avoid complete rewriting is illustrated in
different ways in Macklin's part-book. It contains several revisions which
are made by pinning a thin piece of paper over a section of the part (the
surviving pin or, in some cases, a pin-rust trace of it, illustrates this); alternatively, there are sections in which a new piece of text is stuck on top of the
old one with glue or a plug of wax (both forms of revision can be found in
Macklin's part of Scrub). These methods show different textual possibilities.
The first does not destroy the passages underneath (the revision is a 'flap'
on top of the part), meaning that the original passages can, if necessary,
be resurrected; the second renders access to the passages underneath almost
impossible—the revision is permanent. The existence of either shows, of
course, that play revision had a knock-on effect (it enforced part revision)
and that part revision certainly took place: it is worth wondering whether
plays were often revised along part lines rather than over the full text.[43]

Parts continue to look similar over time. They also continue to be
distributed even when players have barely a line to speak—or when a full,
printed text is available. Below is a tiny complete part for Peaseblossom
in a 1763 Garrick production of *A Midsummer Night's Dream*; it includes a
cross-reference to a printed book:

Peaseblossom,            In, A Midsummer-night's dream

    Act.3: page 26                                                    {Enter
at _____ Peaseblossom, cobweb, moth mustard seed ^
Ready.

_____ your name, honest Gentleman.

Peaseblossom.
at _____ bring him silently {Exit w<sup>th</sup> Others
      Begin 4. Act with ye Queen & Others.
_____ where's peaseblossom.
Ready.
at _____ and be always away {Exit}[44]

Cues do seem to become slightly longer—up to five words or so—towards
the end of the eighteenth century: Kemble's parts, of which thirty-four
survive in the Folger Shakespeare Library, regularly have cues of five
words, but still do not name the speaker of the cue line.[45] We might
wonder why, at this stage, parts even exist, given that not just Peaseblossom
but all the eighteenth-century Shakespeare parts discussed in this section
include on them handwritten page references to a full book containing the
complete play—usually a printed edition—accessible to the part-learning
actor. Clearly actors got something from parts that the full printed text
did not give them. For our purposes, it is very telling that the actors
chose to continue to receive parts—though these had to be separately
handwritten—simply in order to receive their lines in a form in which
they are extracted and isolated from the busy full text. Again, why this
might have been so is one of the basic questions we explore.

Professional eighteenth-century parts in their other features continue to
differ from the university parts, and resemble 'Orlando'. They do not name
cue-speakers, and, perhaps more strikingly, they do not seem to employ
the method used to indicate verse that the university parts employed. In
these professional parts, actors are not told when they are involved in a
verse exchange—or what is often thought to be a verse exchange. This
raises two questions: were there other ways of 'handing on' verse? And are
all exchanges said to be verse actually so?

Garrick's 1745 part for 'King John' contains a section that is generally
lineated as follows by editors:

    KING JOHN. Thou art his keeper.
    HUBERT.                   And I'll keep him so
        That he shall not offend your majesty.
    KING JOHN. Death.
    HUBERT.          My lord?
    KING JOHN.         A grave.
    HUBERT.                        He shall not live.
    KING JOHN. Enough.

In Garrick's part this exchange is rendered:

_____ yr Majesty

Death.

_____ my Lord?

A Grave

_____ not live.

Enough.[46]

Similarly, there is a section of *Macbeth* that is conventionally presented:

LADY MACBETH.  I heard the owl scream and the crickets cry.
                        Did not you speak?
MACBETH.                                When?
LADY MACBETH.                                Now.
MACBETH.                                          As I descended?
LADY MACBETH.  Ay.

But in Kemble's 1785 part for Macbeth, in which cues are centred, the section the actor is given reads:

10 re-enter O.P.[opposite prompt] at,
          As he slept, I had done't.—


          My Husband!
I've done the Deed.—Did'st thou not hear a noise?
          Did not you speak?
When?
          Now.
As I descended?
          Ay.
Hark!—[47]

As we will discuss in detail in Part IV, it is almost impossible to sustain pentameter rhythm over a large number of split lines—nor, it seems, is there a way to indicate this on parts. Such examples, we believe, show a Shakespeare text that has been over-corrected over time: we doubt that these are in fact shared pentameter lines.

But there are also exchanges that are much simpler, in which one character clearly takes on another's pentameter—or gives out a partial pentameter to someone else. We are interested in the fact that these, too, are not indicated in eighteenth-century parts. For instance, take the passage in *Merchant of Venice* that is conventionally rendered:

| ANTONIO. | If thou wilt lend this money, lend it not |
| | As to thy friends—for when did friendship take |
| | A breed for barren metal of his friend?— |
| | But lend it rather to thine enemy |
| | Who, if he break, thou mayst with better face |
| | Exact the penalty. |
| SHYLOCK. | Why, look you, how you storm! |
| | I would be friends with you and have your love, |
| | Forget the shames that you have stain'd me with, |
| | Supply your present wants and take no doit |
| | Of usance for my moneys, and you'll not hear me: |
| | This is kind I offer. |
| BASSANIO. | This were kindness. |
| SHYLOCK. | This kindness will I show. |
| | Go with me to a notary, seal me there |
| | Your single bond; ... |

True, the iambics here are slightly awkward: Shylock's 'Why, look you' continues a line started by Antonio, but makes it hexameter; in enunciating his 'Of usance' line, he must violently contract the word, 'moneys', or else break rhythm; Bassanio's 'This were kindness' completes Shylock's pentameter, but then Shylock's next line has only three feet—and a two-foot gap. These issues, however, are to do with Shakespeare's experiments with the possibilities and parameters of iambic verse; the broad iambic structure of the exchanges is clear. Yet now let us look at that same passage as it is rendered in the part for Shylock performed by Mr Ward in 1772:

> ———————————————————— Exact the Penalty.
> Why, how you storm!
> I would be friends with you, and have your Love;
> Forget the shames that you have stain'd me with;
> Supply your present wants, and take no Doit
> Of Usance for my Monies, and you'll not hear me;
> This is kind offer.
> ———————————————————— this were kindness.
> This kindness will I show;
> Go with me to a Notary, seal me there
> Your single Bond ...[48]

Shylock's 'Why, look you, how you storm!' has been 'improved' to 'Why, how you storm!', seemingly so as to make the complete line a more regular

pentameter. And yet the part-script does not, in layout, make clear the giving or taking of iambic lines—though the general verse-form is indicated by
the capitals at the beginning of each line. Clearly the actor is in a verse exchange—but how can he know the difference between 'This is kind [I] offer' which starts an iambic exchange, and 'This kindness will I show' which
is free-standing. Will he think 'This kindness' completes a pentameter, and
only find in performance that it does not? Again, we will consider just how
actors may have 'handed on' verse-lines, and what the implications might
have been if they realized they were not in fact giving or taking a verse-line
when in a verse exchange. For the moment suffice it to say that there was a
way of indicating verse-lines extant by the 1620s and used in university parts;
and that professional theatre parts do not seem to have used that convention.

## Twentieth-Century Parts

Parts continued to be used, at least in repertory companies, into the
twentieth century, with similar attention given to script rather than full text:
American actor William B. Wood relates how 'many pieces (manuscripts
chiefly) were acted which the performers who played in them never
had a chance of even hearing read...It was by no means an uncommon
thing when I left the theatre [1846] to hear an actor inquire of another
during the performance, "What is this play about?" '[49] Parts, in the
twentieth century, came to be called 'sides', as they were now thought
of as single, typed, sides of paper. So Philip Godfrey records, in an
offhand fashion, that 'An experienced actor, being offered a part, is
unimpressed by the number of "sides" it contains, a "side" being a half-
quarto sheet of typescript.'[50] That he feels the need to say this would
seem to indicate the reverse: that twentieth-century actors, like their
predecessors, noticed the length of their parts against other people's. Other
twentieth-century accounts confirm the modern part's similarity to earlier
parts—and its supposedly continuing disadvantages. Dolman writes in the
1940s:

> Because plays are usually produced before they are published, professional
> actors, from the earliest times, have been accustomed to learning their parts,
> not from printed books, but from what are often called 'sides'. These are
> simply pages of manuscript containing the lines of one part, with a short cue
> for each speech consisting of the last two or three words of the preceding

line—usually with no indication of which character speaks it. Only the prompt copy contains the whole play, and the actor does not know what it is about until he has attended enough rehearsals to enable him to remember the continuity.[51]

Without the number of rehearsals that a modern theatre imposes, an actor without a printed text—like the early modern actor—did not have easy access to 'which character speaks' and 'what it is about'. What kind of access he *did* have will occupy much of our subsequent analyses.

# 2

# The Actors

## Casting

As we outlined in the Introduction, Shakespeare's unique situation, writing solely for and working with the same actors for many years, gave him unrivalled opportunities for stretching both his actors and his writing. But still his innovations drew and depended upon a system common to all playwrights in the community. We are accustomed to thinking of actors being 'made' for parts; in the early modern theatre it was more common for parts to be made for actors. There is a poem that concerns a minor playwright attached to the Globe theatre. It is never quoted, perhaps because it was not published until 1661. Nevertheless, the text, which must date from much earlier (by 1661 the Globe had already been pulled down), gives a tiny glimpse into a moment in the running of the Globe theatre during vacation. It portrays an overwrought poet anxious about an uncompleted work:

> Now Poet small to Globe doth run
> And vows to Heaven four acts are done,
> *Finis* to bring he doth protest:
> Tells each aside, his part is best.[1]

The author is hardly transcendent here, scurrying from actor to actor as though from one creditor to the next; the unwritten fifth act, one can imagine, might be determined by the kinds of promises he makes as he seeks to mollify impatient players. At the same time the poem contains a wry reference to artistic aspirations: 'Heaven' is patron of the playwright's masterpiece (the heaven of the skies doubling with the stage's internal roof, the 'heavens'), but the grand old theatre itself dwarfs the poor poet ('Poet small to Globe doth run', playing on the ever available global pun). The relationship that the Globe poet has with both the players and the theatre is a telling one. He 'owes' them a play, and because he is late with the script, he woos each actor individually with the promise that he has the 'best' part. But what is significant from the above text is that the playwright who, like Shakespeare, is a 'Globe' author, has written not all-purpose parts, but rather parts *for* the particular actors who will perform his play. There is, it seems, some kind of house style, and it is the *players* who are its safe-keepers. Consequently, if this poet is 'small'—at least when compared to Shakespeare, a shareholder in the company as well as its pre-eminent writer—he may not lack talent so much as privilege: Shakespeare really knew these actors; he worked with some of them for thirty years. In all kinds of ways the parts Shakespeare wrote must have been contiguous to the lives enacting them: imitating them, commenting upon them, teaching them, laughing at them, compensating for them, even predicting them.

On the surface it is no more than common sense to say that any early modern playwright who knew the company for whom he was designing a play wrote for those actors. Nevertheless, the very suggestion can today cause tension in the critic (who resists the idea that the playwright's creativity is determined by an unknowable and foreclosed selection of individuals) and in the actor (who prefers all parts to be equally 'available' to everyone). But the fact is that an early modern playwright with an attachment to a company had no choice: he wrote a play with actors already in mind, shaping each written part to a specific player, creating lines that explicitly matched an actor's size, vocal range, and mannerisms. Modern practices of audition and subsequent casting were irrelevant. Even an unattached author hoping to appeal to a particular company would write clearly designated parts fitted to the company. If he did not, his play would lack both appeal and practical facility. Character type, then, was important to both player and playwright: it described the playing range of the actor, and so prescribed the writing range to the author. Accordingly, it is repeatedly obvious that playwrights (often known as 'poets' at the time) specifically created and designated parts suited to the particular range and talents of individual actors:

> [W]e oft have seene,
> Him act a Beggar, who a King hath beene:
> For no default, but that the Poets art
> Thought at that time he best would fit that part.[2]

That word 'fit' crops up repeatedly in writing of the time to describe what a playwright does. Nathaniel Richards, a minor playwright of the 1630s, refers to the mixture of pains and art that poets use in order 'to advance and fit' an actor with a part, and William Cartwright specifically praises Fletcher because in his plays 'Parts are so fitted unto parts'.[3] Indeed, it is Richard Baker's contention that reading a play is less good, less clear, than seeing it, as only on-stage can one appreciate how carefully the speech is 'fitted to the Person'.[4] It was for this reason that Heywood, a playwright for the popular Red Bull theatre, claimed that actors should always be 'men pick'd out personable, according to the parts they present'.[5] Similarly, Gainsford, writing of child players, was comfortable with Epictetes' doctrine that the master of a comedy should 'adapt the dispositions of his boyes to such severall parts, as shall well befit their natures and inclinations'.[6]

At a time when 'directors' were yet to come into being, and when a playwright would often have very little right to attend what minimal full rehearsal there was (unless he were already attached to the theatre), 'casting' through or while writing was, for the playwright, a welcome source of control; indeed, casting was effectively a kind of patronage. Pen power could promote or demote players; responses to recent performances could dictate future ones. To the actors of the Red Bull, playing secretly in the autumn of 1648, one irritated writer issued a reminder of this ever latent capability: it was playwrights who could

> advance you to the Dignity of Kings, Dukes, Earles, and Knights; and sometimes least you should [inspired with ignorance] imagine your selves to be those whom you personate, we abate your overweening thoughts, putting on you the habit, and prescribing unto you the language of Beggars ... [7]

The fact that the actor's part was a product of the playwright's intentions was so commonplace that it was one of the staples of the over-used Renaissance analogy between man's life and the theatre. Accordingly, 'God' writes (or perhaps wrote) a play in which he formed certain specific parts for each one of us. 'God which is on high ... appoints every man his part and apparell on the worlds stage.'[8] When it is Fortune who writes the play, the comparison remains the same: 'On him whom [Fortune] most favors, she bestowes | A Kingly vesture: ... | The habit of a servant poore and bare | She puts upon another.'[9] Even when 'we' are in the hands of the Devil, the essential comparison is unaltered, though the threat behind it is darker: 'Doth Satan play the Poet, and fit every Player with a part that hee is best able to act?'[10] But though the casting may have been chosen by the author, the people who made up the playing company were a given; a shareholder like Shakespeare probably had no more say in employing new members of the troupe than anyone else with a stake in the company. In all sorts of specifics the author had free choice. But still the players were 'there' from the beginning: indeed often *before* the incipience of a particular part.

# Typecasting

That Shakespeare wrote to a variety of types that his actors could play is suggested by the fact that only late in the creative process would he actually flesh out his characters with fictional names. This is clear from looking at Quarto and Folio speech-prefixes where the fictional name of a character—Gertrude, Don Adriano di Armado, Peter—jostles against the name of that character's 'type'—Queen, Braggart, Clown. *Hamlet*'s Osric is called in Quarto 1 (1603) '*a Bragart Gentleman*' (I2a). The same character designation of 'braggart' is also given to Don Adriano di Armado in the Quarto (1598) of *Love's Labour's Lost*, III. i, where '*Braggart* and his *Boy*' (C3b) signifies Don Adriano and Moth. Evidently, then, 'braggart' was one regular character-type that Shakespeare sometimes wrote to—because this was a role that someone in his company could play. Some 'types' keep their generic speech-prefixes and are never given 'names' at all, like 'Fool' in *King Lear* or 'Nurse' in *Romeo and Juliet* or 'Queen' in *Cymbeline*. Even Lady Macbeth, for all the subsequent infamy of that appellation, is never once called that either on page or on-stage: she is '*Macbeths Wife*' (TLN 348) on her first entrance and, apart from one entrance as '*Macbeths Lady*' (TLN 1151), she is for every speech and entrance simply '*Lady*', nothing more.

Other characters unaccountably change names (though retain characteristics) inside their plays. 'Balthazar', 'Boy', 'Peter', and 'Will Kemp' (the name of the company clown) are all used for Romeo's man in *Romeo and Juliet*; Pistol's wife in *Henry V* slips from 'Nell' (TLN 353) to 'Doll' (TLN 2976); even Polonius in *Hamlet* may be a second thought for the 'Corambis' of the First Quarto. Hamlet in *Hamlet* thinks of the players he meets not in terms of the wide range of fictional characters they have played, but rather in terms of a limited selection of 'types' that will (indubitably) crop up in every play the company has in its repertoire. He welcomes 'He that plays the King', adding that 'the adventurous Knight shal use his Foyle and Target: the Lover shall not sigh *gratis*, the humorous man shall end his part in peace' (TLN 1365–70). Hamlet's conception of the company and their plays in terms of typecasting has often been queried, but only because of a misunderstanding surrounding the term 'typecasting' itself, a modern word that does not quite describe how it was that actors were given their parts.[11]

When we use the word 'typecast' in this book, we do not mean to imply that a single actor could play only one variety of character. Early modern actors often played various parts; indeed, this is another staple of the theatre–world analogy: 'This day one playes a Monarch, the next a private person. Heere one Acts a Tyrant, on the morrow an Exile: A Parasite this man too night, to morrow a Precisian … '[12] Yet typecasting was a primary feature of the early modern theatre, in that actors were cast along the lines of personality 'type'. Thus the fat and exuberant had fat exuberant parts given them, while the lean and melancholy had lean melancholic types to perform. This is not quite the same as modern typecasting, where an actor has a *character* he is to play all the time: in the early modern theatre a lean melancholy player might be good or bad, villain or hero; his parts were not the same, but his type—his body and his mood—always shaped them. From what we can gather about Shakespeare's group of actors, for instance, John Sincler (Sincklo or Sinklo), who was notably emaciated, played 'thin' parts: but this might embrace equally Andrew Aguecheek or Cassius.[13] Then again, a quality like thinness was thought to spread beyond body weight: being thin was an aspect that fed into—and that helped create—your dominant 'humour'. Which of the four humours you most exhibited made up your actual character, and thus determined the parts you played. Of the four humours, for instance, the thin Sincler appears to have been melancholy. His parts, then, will be thin/melancholy ones: Slender and Starveling are obvious roles, but his range might have extended to Antonio, Shallow, or Jaques, for example, all very different 'characters', but all potentially concordant with a certain actor's nature. So, though there was not one-character typecasting, there were particular characters written for certain body and humour types; an actor might show a skill at one type of behaviour, for instance, like the player who was talented at performing 'weeping parts'.[14]

Nor was typecasting limited to minor characters (or what today we might call 'character actors'). It extended to the sharers in companies; even 'masters' or 'chief players', who were famed for the ability to play all parts, were to some extent typecast, despite the fact that lead characters appear to be many different kinds of men. Randolph said of his university friend Thomas Riley, who performed lead roles in Randolph's own plays, that he was

> [A] Proteus, that [could] take
> What shape he please, and in an instant make
> Himself to anything; be that, or this,
> By voluntary metamorphosis.[15]

The word 'Proteus'—the god of shape-shifting—gives the clue. The term is used here not to imply an ability to change character so much as an ability to 'become' whatever character one was playing. Riley can make himself *be* whoever he has been given to perform (and he is, in fact, generally given 'the lead'). The same praise is bestowed upon Richard Burbage, Shakespeare's chief actor: Burbage was 'a delightful *Proteus*, ... wholly transforming himself into his Part, and putting off himself with his Cloathes'.[16] Though the passage may not reveal much about Burbage, it certainly shows the qualities prized in a 'master' player: the ability to internalize a part fully, and to elide the barrier between performance and identity.[17] Good early modern actors were said to turn into the part they were given: easier to do, perhaps, if a part was written for you. Moreover, important actors were, however loosely, typecast by the very nature of their principal positions in the company: their 'type' was the hero, usually 'tragic' or 'romantic'. In a sense an actor like Burbage 'is' a Proteus: this is his type. That is, the great actor is awesome precisely because of his radical emptiness and mutability; he owns a magical capacity for self-erasure in the interests of becoming another. The heroic 'type' is thus no plaster-cast archetype. It is an invitation to command the stage, and more often than not the audience's sympathies—a privilege that can then be adapted by and to the particularities of the lead actor. So Edward Alleyn was praised for his pre-eminent skill in one mode above all: 'he made any part (especially a Majest[i]ck one) to become him ... '[18]

## 'Becoming' the Part

It will come as no surprise that early modern actors invariably identified closely with parts that had been written for them. Parts were self-revealing, self-describing, and, perhaps most pertinent of all, self-fulfilling. Often there developed a need, beyond mere ambition, to 'Act Great Parts'.[19] Self-worth and part became intertwined. Relying on parts as a means of self-definition was so common that there was a set phrase to describe the process: to 'stand by' or 'stand on' one's parts. Thus at the accession of James I it was said that even the 'worst players Boy stood upon his good parts'.[20] Or again, here is Dekker on a pair of highly competitive players engaged in a kind of job challenge:

> [They] refused to put themselves to a day of hearing (as any Players would have done) but stood onely upon their good parts. Why saies the one, since thou wouldst faine be taken for so rare a peece, report... what excellent parts thou hast discharged?... I (quoth he) have playd the Sophy: the Sophy, replyed the second: what a murren was he? What was he saies the other: why he was a Turke: right quoth his adversarie, get to play as many Turkes partes as thou canst, for ile bee hangd if ever thou playst a good Christian.[21]

The punchline to the argument depends upon puncturing the distinction between merely playing and 'being'. Of course any kind of relationship—ribbing, rivalrous, collusive, even genuinely 'Christian'—might underlie the joke: it is enough here to notice how easily the membrane between part and player can snap, or prove suddenly and pointedly transparent.

Accordingly, actors were easily tempted into transporting facets of their stage-character—sometimes physical, sometimes attitudinal—out into the world. At its most trivial, this might mean simply that the actors were given to wearing their stage clothes in the streets. But even that was fiercely (and regularly) criticized at the time; anti-theatricalists picked up any stick with which to beat the playhouses, and the example of actors so 'living' their parts seemed a literal translation of the theatre's inverting and insolent simulations. At the very least, such behaviour gave out 'confusing' social signals. The magnitude of the offence is illustrated by Henslowe, financier of the Rose Theatre, who levied a fine of 'ffortie pounds' not just on players who left his premises in play clothes, but on those who consented that anyone else should do so—larger than the fine for anything else.[22] An actor who 'do's not only personate on the Stage', but also walks the streets 'maskd still in the habite of a Gentleman', might be in danger not only of persuading others that he was a gentleman, but of convincing himself as well.[23] (Hence, too, the slight regard offered to an actor like Shakespeare when he went so far as to purchase himself the status of gentleman.) Divines relished reminding players that by statute they were nothing more than 'rogues, vagabonds and sturdy beggars'.[24]

But it is not simply that actors took their playing clothes into the world with them and carried on performing. It was a question of mental familiarity, indeed identification: 'no *Actor* well can play the *King*, | That is not one in his imagination'.[25] The usual salutary tales attend on this too. Like the player who continued to be a 'king' in his daily life:

> I ...
> Did him approach; but loe, he casts his Eye,
> As if therein I had presumption showne:
> I, like a Subject (with submisse regard)
> Did him salute, yet he regreeted mee
> But with a Nod, because his speech he spar'd
> For Lords and Knights that came his Grace to see.

Clearly this poem mocks the player's absurdity—all the time 'I well knew him (though he knew not me) | To be a player'—but we can see why 'parts' were often said to corrupt, magnifying an actor's pretensions, pride, or susceptibility to suggestion.[26] Thus an actor chosen to play a tyrant would already be presumed to cherish a small 'corner' of the tyrant within; correspondingly, he would 'whet his minde unto tyranny that he may give life to the picture hee presenteth'.[27] Anti-theatricalists gathered much grist for their mills from the part-system: quite simply, actors learned how to sin through playing (or, more likely, how to sin better). The part or role, then, was not just a written text. It was an adjunct to the actor's being, a tangible experimentation in imaginative 'becoming'.

Unsurprisingly, a number of stories circulated about actors who were permanently taken over by the characters they portrayed. There were tales of players left 'stuck' with the mannerisms of the characters they had played, as though overwhelmed by an inward truth suddenly given such public head. Examples include the player who performed Antonio in *The Changeling*, and who 'so lively and corporally personated a Changeling, that he could never compose his Face to the figure it had, before he undertook that part'.[28] An old Interregnum story told how Hugh Peters had once been an actor before becoming a preacher and revolutionary. It was said that he was tainted, not just by his earlier profession, but by the fact that he used to play women. Effeminized by the experience, his social and subjective bearings lost, it is little wonder (said the tale-tellers) that he wobbled into revolution. 'Sam Rowley, and he were a Pylades,

and Orestes, when he played a womans part at the Curtaine Play-house,'
goes the taunt, and, reading the part back into the person, concludes that
this 'is the reason his garbe is so emphaticald [*sic*] in the Pulpit'.[29] Warning
stories were circulated to prevent innocent young men thoughtlessly acting
at university and having their natures permanently altered as a result.
There was the scholar who played Richard III in college in such a lively
manner that 'ever after he was transported with a royall humour in his
large expences, which brought him to beggary'.[30] Or again there was
the nobleman's son who played a beggar, and then 'ever after perswaded
himself to be in his whole life, what he had personated on the Stage for
one hour'.[31] Shakespeare, too, is forever conscious of how perilous and
exciting it can be to 'fit' a characterization so snugly.

   An actor who did not perform to his type was treated warily. Had he
actually 'acted' at all? Harvey claims to feel bemused and cheated when
he finds that Tarlton, player in and author of *The Seven Deadly Sins*, is
not in fact performing the sin he most practises, lechery: 'Oh but that,
M. Tarleton, is not your part upon the stage, you are too-blame, that
dissemble with the world & have one part for your frends pleasure, an
other for your owne.'[32] Because of the powerful personal association
between actor and part, there was a notion, keenly felt, that a play would
itself languish when the main actor concerned in it could not perform his
role. When a worthy actor dies, says a writer of additions to *Overburies Wife*
(probably the playwright Webster, perhaps the playwright Dekker), 'wee
cannot be perswaded any man can doe his parts like him'; when Burbage
died, at least one elegy lamented not just his passing, but the end of all
performances of Shakespeare's plays:

> Hees gone and wth him what a world is dead
> wch he revived, to bee revived so
> no more: young Hamlet, ould Hieronimo,
> kind Leir, the greived Moor, and more beside,
> that livd in him have now for ever died.[33]

In other words, plays were not secure without their actors; once bereft
of the specific performances designed for them, they appeared perishable,
and possibly worthless. Attempts to keep famous plays going in the face of
the deaths of the most relevant players often frame themselves hesitantly,
even apologetically. The belief that only one actor could 'really' play a
part—others being second-rate imitations of that first actor—remained

very much alive. It was to worry many subsequent performers over the next two centuries. Heywood's prologue to Marlowe's *Jew of Malta*, written for Perkins who was to perform the Jew, is an elongated apology for taking over the part after the death of its originator, Alleyn. Whilst Alleyn was 'Roscius for a tongue', Perkins has no

> ambition
> To exceed, or equall, being of condition
> More modest; this is all that he intends,
> (And that too, at the urgence of some friends)
> To prove his best, and if none here gaine-say it,
> The part he hath studied, and intends to play it.[34]

Writers with some historical perspective might point out that the comedies of Plautus and Terence continued to be read and performed without seeming to be compromised by the fact that their performers were dead; indeed, they seemed to be 'at this day the very same Comedies, which they were a thousand yeares agoe, albeit the persons, that then acted them be chaunged'.[35] But for many, the fact remained that 'Jew' belonged to Alleyn, and that Hamlet, Lear, and Othello were Burbage's—indeed, in a sense *were* Burbage.[36] These were not parts written for Everyman or every actor: they were parts written for specific people. In the next century, similarly, Cibber was to write his play *A Woman's Wit* for Lincoln's Inn company, and to rewrite the characters when it was to be played by the Theatre Royal company instead; while Dennis was to declare that it was 'absolutely impossible … that any Actor can become an admirable Original, by playing a Part which was writ and design'd for another Man's particular Talent'.[37]

What may seem strange, given the obsession with parts, is that dramatis personae in printed texts of the time scarcely ever name the actor. But then plays were written for performance, in which it would be entirely clear who played what, while published plays either relied on audience memory, or perhaps were regarded as being a different species from a play performed. Throughout the period there is confusion as to whether to offer for publication the play that was acted on the stage or the play in a longer, more 'ideal' form: playwrights often opted for the latter, casting out their less famous co-writers—as happened with Jonson or Marlowe—or simply providing the long text that did not make it to performance.[38] Nevertheless, the play as first written, provided it was written with a company in mind (as all of Shakespeare's plays were), was clearly thought of in terms of parts for specific actors, and we must bear this in mind: when dividing plays back down into actors' parts, we are also in some sense recovering Shakespeare's separate players with their separate bodies, mannerisms, and verbal abilities.

## Doubling and Vizards

Shakespeare's actors, then, might expect their parts from one play to another to have shared some characteristics. Occasionally, like the university actor who owned four 1620s parts in one pamphlet, or like Macklin, who similarly received a collection of parts in a single book (see Chapter 1), the actor might have received several parts from different plays stitched together to create one entity. If that were the case, the distinctiveness of one play and part from another may have been annulled: the actor may have seen a collection of fool roles or heroine roles—or, at any rate, 'his' roles—as one semi-continuous piece of work. But what if the actor doubled roles in a single play?

Doubling was of course a common recourse of any acting company, faced with enormous cast lists and necessary limitations upon budget and personnel. As 'Albert' in *Antonio and Mellida* explains to his fellow actors, 'The necessitie of the play forceth me to act two parts…'[39] Particularly amongst lesser parts, doubling was routine. This was so whether the performers concerned were permanent members of the company ('sharers') or temporary 'hirelings'. Quarles, who wrote religious and non-religious books, explains that his own work differs as a courtier differs from a churchman, 'But if any thinke it unfit, for one to play both parts, I have *presidents* for it'.[40] A system that allowed for doubling was particularly necessary, because there were no understudies at the time: the word, and the concept, of understudying dates from the late nineteenth century. In earlier theatre, where actors specifically owned the scroll or book in which their parts were inscribed, there was no way one player could learn another's text, and no payment system set up for him to do so. Thus, if a player were ill, and a performance could not be cancelled, another member of the company—a person with a smaller or more disposable part—had to stand in, learning the new lines hastily, or perhaps taking the written part with him on to the stage as happened in later times.[41] So Henslowe is concerned to hear of the illness of Edward Alleyn, his lead actor and friend. Rumour has told Henslowe that another actor, whose name he does not know, is to take on Alleyn's roles—or at least is prepared to do so: 'we hard that you weare very sycke at bathe & that one of your felowes weare fayne to play your parte for you wch wasse not lytel greafe unto us'.[42] The problem was that the player who had taken on a new part could often not jettison his own role, and would have to manufacture a way of performing both. Hence the anecdote about Tarlton, who played his own role of Clown in a play about Henry V, and also took on a fellow player's part of Judge:

> At the Bull at Bishops-gate was a play of *Henry* the fift, wherein the Judge was to take a boxe on the eare, and because he was absent that should take the blow: *Tarlton* himselfe ... tooke upon him to play the same Judge, besides his owne part of the Clowne: and *Knell* then playing *Henry* the fift, hit *Tarlton* a sound boxe indeed, which made the people laugh the more, because it was he: but anone the Judge goes in, and immediately *Tarlton* (in his Clownes cloathes) comes out, and askes the Actors what newes? O saith one ... Prince *Henry* hit the Judge a terribl[e] box on the eare: What man, said *Tarlton* ... it could not be but terrible to the Judge, when the report so terrifies me, that me thinkes the blow remaines still on my cheeke, that it burnes againe.[43]

Of course, there was usually nothing improvised about doubled roles. But we do not really know the form in which a doubling actor would have received his parts. Some idea, though, is suggested by an odd part that survives from the Restoration period: a musical manuscript containing a series of bass parts for the singer Richard Leveridge in Purcell's *The Indian Queen*; it is the earliest surviving operatic part.[44] The designation of the part is confusing: it is titled 'Mr Leveridge: Indian Queen', yet it does not contain the role that Leveridge is known to have sung in that opera, Ismeron. It seems to represent an earlier version of the opera in which Leveridge had various lesser roles; thus the part contains the complete chorus bass line, interspersed (in play order) with the solo sections for the High Priest in Act v and followed, under the heading 'Last Act', by the part of Hymen in Daniel Purcell's masque, and then by 'Grand Chorus'. In placing in one manuscript these various roles, the part may provide a fascinating insight into the nature of doubling: here, at any rate, different characters for a single player are all placed together in one stitched booklet, each melding into one another.

This musical part thus raises one of the great questions about the distribution of parts for doubling in the theatre. If multiple parts were regularly transcribed on to one roll or book, were they presented as 'discrete' entities, with one complete part being followed by another? Or were they, as in Leveridge's booklet, transcribed in 'play order', so that lines spoken by one character were interspersed with lines spoken by a different character? Other, later information sheds little light on this question. It is true that all the surviving theatrical parts are for single, discretely packaged characters; but this may be because parts were invariably handed out separately, or because most surviving parts are long, written for major characters who are unlikely to have doubled. Leveridge's example makes learning sense for an actor memorizing a script in the order in which he is to speak (or, in this case, sing) it. And it raises the possibility that doubling actors received a text in which one character and his words were interspersed with another's, the whole unified by the body and character of the actor performing the roles. If so, this would make for a considerably more continuous, even organic connection between the process of learning and the experience of playing multiple parts—and, indeed, between the internalizing of one part and another. Perhaps the actor would have identified his doubled characters as specifically indebted to *his* well-attested aura and skills, beholden to the fact that he and no one else is given the words to speak. Equally, he might have felt encouraged to seek out distinctive points of difference or comparison: anticipating that the audience would recognize 'him' as the actor of, say, two parts, he might be alive to the possibility either of exploiting this recognition (if the two parts enjoy a counterpointing or continuous relationship with one another) or of effectively burying it (if there were little to be gained from it). Alternatively, if the doubling actor received his parts in separate physical rolls, he would still have carried with him expectations consonant with the type he habitually played: but he might have been more likely to infer from each roll a unique character as the part's material self-sufficiency confers or implies an identity 'anterior' to his own possession of it.

If we know little about how doubled roles were recorded on the paper part, we know more about how the doubling was signified in performance. The above anecdote about Tarlton shows how the doubling was effected—with a change of clothing to indicate the 'new' character. However, it also suggests that the singleness of the one actor-performer shone through the doubling of both roles. Tarlton seems to have internalized Judge and Clown and made them both adjuncts of himself. Or, rather, whichever fictional character is represented, the cohering personality of the performer, Tarlton the clown, is an equally significant presence.

A change of apparel, as in this instance, was the most common way of effecting and representing a 'doubled' part. However, as with Tarlton, different clothes could not change the appearance of a character too greatly; sometimes they scarcely altered it at all. Thus 'type' was frequently maintained across a clothes change, and important physical links between disparate characters could be exploited. Presumably Brabantio, Desdemona's father, and Brabantio's brother Gratiano, who announces Brabantio's death, were performed by the same player in *Othello*; for the same reason, the Ghost of Old Hamlet and Claudio, again brothers of roughly the same age, were probably doubled in *Hamlet*. Doubling may also have extended to join characters who are strikingly cognate in role and function, such as Posthumus and Cloten in *Cymbeline*, or Mamillius and Perdita in *The Winter's Tale*. No doubt doubling was also used to exploit theatrical ironies: for instance, the actor murdered as Duncan returns as Macduff to 'discover' his own murdered body.[45] We are wary about drawing conclusions concerning conceptual doubling when so little evidence survives on the subject. What *is* clear is that so standard was doubling by changing clothes that there was a need for actors who changed clothes *without* actually changing character to explain (often repeatedly) what was happening, like Kent or Edgar in *Lear*, or Rosalind in *As You Like It*. At the same time, the audience's sense that personality was linked with clothes would undoubtedly have shaped the way it understood those altered characters. There would have been something alien or cross-fertilizing, an engagement with new possibilities, about characters whose clothes were transformed—as again we find with Kent, Edgar, and Rosalind once their clothes are transformed. Indeed, the system of doubling on the stage at the time made it easier—perhaps, expected—that personalities should subtly change with altered clothes.

One half-way point between changed apparel and changed appearance was the beard. Adding a phoney beard to the face or taking one away was another very usual way of effecting doubling. In this case the actor's face was semi-'deleted', though body type remained the same. 'There's no disguise in't', crows Nabbes of his play *The Unfortunate Mother*, 'no false beard, that can | Discover severall persons in one man'; but Cleveland talks of there being 'False beard enough, to fit a stages plot' in his *Character of a London Diurnall*, and the internal play within *Thomas More* cannot take place until a false beard is found for Wit.[46] As other visual aspects of the actor remained fixed—age, height, mannerisms, and, most significantly, face—it is hardly surprising to find that extant records of doubling that do not involve a 'grotesque' part happen, as they must do, along physical and character lines (that is, again, by 'type'). In Massinger's *The Roman Actor* (Q 1629) Thomas Pollard plays both Aelius Lamia and Stephanos, and Curtis Greville plays Latinus and a Tribune; similarly, in Thomas Nabbes's *Hannibal and Scipio* (1637) Hugh Clark plays Syphax and Nuntius, William Sherlock doubles as Maharball and Prusias, and Robert Axen plays both Bomilcar and Giscon.[47]

As important as the clothes was the exit: a character would generally leave the stage as one person and enter as another, even when doubling within a scene.[48] Indeed, long act-breaks, such as those in private theatres, could be specifically necessary for careful reclothing. Inflammatory love-songs, sung in theatrical act-breaks, were said to hold the double purpose of delighting the audience whilst also filling 'that … vacant Interim which the Tyring-house takes up, in changing the Actors robes, to fit them for some other part in the ensuing Scene'.[49] Even when a single actor took on every part in a display of protean talent, he would still separate one from the other by exiting and re-entering. Robert Armin, the 'wise fool' player of Shakespeare's company, writes of the time he spent as clown for the Lord Chandos's players, when he would perform plays in gentleman's houses: '[D]oing all himselfe, King, Clowne, Gentleman and all having spoke for one, he would sodainly goe in, and againe returne for the other, and stambring, so beastly as he did, made mighty mirth.'[50] We might see here how doubling could itself *be* the entertainment. Once again, habitual theatrical practice offered the playwright and player all sorts of opportunities for exploitation. So when looking at the plays of Shakespeare we rarely *know* which characters doubled with which others, but we do have information with which to speculate: that actors changed clothes to double, that actors left the scene as one character and re-entered as another, and that the doubled parts they played would both resonate in some way with their actual characters.

The alternative method through which the actor could present more than one part was by wearing a mask or 'vizard'. Hence an alternative version of the popular analogy of the world as a stage: it is a place 'where net-maskt men do play their personage'.[51] Indeed, 'vizard' was a slang way of referring to the actor himself. So, in *Rythmes against Martin Marre-Prelate*, it is related that 'A Vizard late skipt out upon our Stage'.[52] And the connection between vizards and stage-playing remained a staple, even as the new theatre of the Restoration came into being. Whether or not the Restoration stage still turned to masking as a device—and it almost certainly did not—Bishop Fuller, whose mind was forever straying towards the theatre of the Caroline period, linked the two in his criticisms, opining that there were 'Never more st[r]ange Stage-Players then now, who weare the vizards of Piety and holiness'.[53]

Puttenham traces the popularity of masks back to ancient Rome ('one *Roscius*... brought up these vizards, which we see at this day used'), and puts forward a number of reasons why actors continue to find them useful. Vizards, he concludes, could

> supply the want of players, when there were moe parts then there were persons, or that it was not thought meet to trouble & pester princes chambers with too many folks. Now by the chaunge of a vizard one man might play the king and the carter, the old nurse & the yong damsel, the marchant & the souldier or any other part he listed very conveniently.[54]

The passage illustrates that plays could be specifically written for more people than there were in a company, but also, interestingly, that performers at court were under some obligation not to fill the palace with too many people. Both should be borne in mind with respect to the companies for whom Shakespeare wrote, all of which performed regularly at court.

Puttenham also makes clear that a vizard, unlike a mere change of clothes, allows one character to play quite radically different parts. A brief look at the regular references to acting with vizards, however, suggests that they were not generally used for all varieties of role. Instead, vizarded characters had a type all their own: they were usually 'grotesques', as were their masks. Hence Jonson's joke about the player 'Mumming' who, as Carol reports in *Christmas, his Masque*, 'has not his vizard': 'No matter', responds Christmas, 'his owne face shall serve for a punishment, and 'tis bad enough.'[55]

Masks were usually confined to parts that required exaggerated features: ghosts, fools, devils, animals. So the Ghost in the ur-*Hamlet* had a special 'pale' vizard; the fool in general was vizarded ('some [mountebanks in Italy] weare visards being disguised like fooles in a play'); the Devil had a characteristic vizard face that was imitated when 'Popish imposters' feigned bedevilled people whom they could miraculously cure (the 'she-devil' became angry, and 'in choler had like to have pulled off her devils vizard, and shewed her owne face').[56] A telling reference to the appearance of the Jew of Malta in the play of that name shows both how Semitic features were exaggeratedly reproduced on the stage, and also how the Jew was played—and perceived—as a grotesque with fool or demonic qualities: Rowley the playwright compares a supremely ugly face to a 'visage (or vizard) like the artificiall Jewe of *Maltaes* nose'.[57]

Special animal vizards were similarly stock features of the playhouse—Willis looks back with an old man's fondness at a play he saw when little, in which a sleeping prince had 'a vizard like a swines snout' put on his face; Henslowe's list of playhouse properties include 'owld Mahemetes head', 'Argosse heade', 'Jermosses head', 'i bores heade & Serberosse iii heades', 'i bulles head', 'ii lyn heades'.[58] The vizard in such instances would signify an often violently different body and temperament, and the underlying actor was, if not invisible, then under a kind of agreed erasure. But occasionally vizards might be used to create eerie similarities, as when parallel characters were made to look exactly alike—possibly one way that identical twins were portrayed: William Percy in one of his zany play-scripts asks that 'The two coupples of young men' be 'counter-vizarded a lyke'.[59]

As it is, limitations of space—and a care not to heap conjecture upon conjecture—means that our book will not be overly concerned with Shakespearean doubles, despite the practice's centrality to both the composing and the playing of parts. Occasionally, however, we will identify characteristics from one part's language and mannerisms that are reflected in, and help to mould, another's.

# 3
# Rehearsing and Performing

## The Reading

The one time when a play as a whole was presented to the actors, or at least to some of them, was the 'reading'. But as plays actually went through more than one kind of reading before performance—though all are called 'readings'—it is worth defining what happened in each, and how the playhouse reading differed from others.

One variety of 'reading' has little to do with actors. This was the reading that an author might give to a friend or—equally often—to a potential backer. Such private readings were couched as requests for advice, though generally their purpose was to flatter, deflect future criticism, and win present support. So a jest-book tells a story of how playwright George Peele 'read a Play booke to a Gentleman'. In the story, Peele's 'gentleman' was a fool of whom Peele had grown tired. Knowing that the man relished the privilege of critiquing plays, Peele lured him with the promise of 'halfe a score sheetes of paper'; then 'betweene every sceane [Peele] would make pauses, and demaund his opinion how hee liked the cariage of it … '.[1] The end of the story is that Peele prolonged the reading until it was too late for the gentleman to go home. Peele invited him to stay, put him to bed, saw him to sleep, then robbed him of money, clothes—and reputation—and ran away. The rancour that underlies the jest shows the real attitude of playwrights who had to submit to the indignity of amateur judgement as one way of securing their play's success. Thomas Dekker is infused with the same rage. He bitterly advises gallants to 'put your selfe into such true *scaenical* authority, that some Poet shall not dare to present his Muse rudely upon your eyes, without having first unmaskt her, rifled her, and discovered all her bare and most mysticall parts before you at a taverne'.[2] But such references have no direct connection to playhouse readings—they are concerned with the construction of the play, not its presentation to the players.

The playhouse did, however, witness a similar variety of occasion. It involved one or more 'sharers' in the company—sharers who were often actors, but who were hearing the 'reading' in their capacity as financial backers. Would this play be good or not? Would it 'take'? Most importantly, should the company commission the play and pay for it? 'Mr Henshlowe', writes the actor/sharer Robert Shaa to the financier, 'we have heard their booke and lyke yt their pryce is eight poundes, wch I pray pay now'; similarly, Rowley the sharer, actor, and playwright has 'harde five sheets of a playe of the Conqueste of the Indes & I dow not doute but It wyll be a verye good playe therefore I praye ye delyver them fortye shyllynges In earneste of It'.[3] The text might at this stage be a largely unwritten scenario (called, confusingly, a 'plot'), or a semi-written play. This was, then, a professionalized extension of the reading to a 'friend' described above—and most references to playhouse 'readings' are to this kind of occasion. That the play would be accepted at this reading was, inevitably, of tremendous concern to the author; thus the habitually impecunious Daborne regularly begs for readings—in the hope that he will get a financial advance on the strength of them ('if yu please to appoint any howr to read to mr Allin I will not fayle'[4]). Naturally, he always fears their outcome: 'Sr if yu doe not like this play when it is read yu shall hav the other which shall be finished wth all expedition for before god this is a good one & will giv yu content.'[5] But none of these readings is related to rehearsals as such.

Quite different, and considerably less often referred to, was the reading at which the main actors were invited to be present to hear a completed play. Daborne again makes clear that such a reading did take place. He draws a distinction between a judgemental reading and the reading to 'the general company': 'one Tuesday night if yu will appoint I will meet yu & mr Allin & read some for I am unwilling to read to ye generall company till all be finisht'.[6] Such a company reading seems to be recorded by Henslowe when he noted, with typical tight-fistedness, that he lent (rather than gave) money 'unto the company for to spend at the Readynge of that boocke [*Henry I*] at the sonne in new fyshstrete'.[7] Later, in a more generous mood, there was money 'Layd owt for the companye when they Read the playe of Jeffa for wine at the tavern'.[8] These tavern readings (the place determined, perhaps, on account of the free evening use of candles) were no doubt a mixed blessing for the anxious playwright. There would have been good humour, geniality, conversation—and doubtless increasingly drunk actors and raucous auditors. Nevertheless, playwrights needed such occasions: they were sometimes the only opportunity to illustrate, through recital, what they wanted the actors to do with their part-texts. Posthaste, the playwright of Marston's *Histrio-mastix*, is depicted in a tavern reading his play. This seems to resemble more closely a reading to interested gentlemen than to actors, but it nevertheless gives something of the sense of what such an occasion might have been like. Here the playwright intersperses his reading with drinking, which, together with the enthusiasm of his reading, sends him into a passion of tears leading to the recitation being given over altogether:

> *Hee reades the Prologue, they sit to heare it.*
>
> POSTHASTE. *When Aucthours quill, in quivering hand,*
> *His tyred arme did take:*
> *His wearied Muse, bad him devise,*
> *Some fine play for to make.*
> And now my Maisters in this bravadoe,
> I can read no more without Canadoe.
>
> OMNES. What hoe? some Canadoe quickly,
>
> Enter *Vintner* with a quart of Wine.
>
> POSTHASTE. Enter the Progidall Child; fill the pot I would say,
> *Huffa, huffa, who callis for mee?*
> *I play the Prodigall child in jollytie.*
>
> CLOUT. O detestable good.
>
> POSTHASTE. Enter to him Dame Vertue:
> *My Sonne thou art a lost childe,*
> (This is a passion, note you the passion?)
> *And hath many poore men of their goods beguil'd:*
> *O prodigall childe, and childe prodigall.*
> Read the rest sirs, I cannot read for teares,
> Fill mee the pot I prethe fellow *Gulch*.[9]

Readings of this kind continued to be held over the next 200 years, remaining the only place at which the full play was introduced before the distribution of the parts.[10] In later times parts were distributed sometimes immediately after the reading—if the playwright was a trusted one—and sometimes a few days later (if changes to the text had been demanded). The same may have been the case in the early modern period, though other possibilities are suggested below. Either way, it was with whatever information and pointers a reading had given them that the major actors learned their texts—unless they hated the play so much that at this late stage they rejected it (for if this reading took place in front of the major shareholders of the company, it would retain elements of an audition).[11] Hirelings, however, who played small roles and were paid piecemeal by the week, would not have been provided for in the tavern. Mostly they would not even have been acquired by the company at this early stage in the play's life. Never part of the judgemental process, they would not have been expected to attend any kind of play-reading before performance and would probably have learned their parts without having had the benefit of hearing the full play.

## The Distribution of Parts

Adrian Kiernander has suggested that the playwright's reading to the actors might also have been a dictation, so that the writers of actors' parts 'might have been, or might at least have included, some of the more literate actors in the company who could have used this transcription process as the start of their memorisation of the lines'.[12] His suggestion demands that casting be made before the reading—as we have argued, most plays were cast by playwrights during the writing process—but that distribution happens in the light of it. This makes a certain sense. Were actors to have the opportunity of copying their own texts, then their ownership of parts would extend beyond identification with the character or ownership of the paper on which the character was inscribed: they would meet 'their' characters, learn them, internalize them, through the medium of their own handwriting. The process would have the further advantage of familiarizing the actors with the rest of the play and introducing them to some of the speakers of their cue-lines. And at least one early modern author suggests this might sometimes have been the case. William Prynne in his hysterical anti-theatrical tract *Histrio-mastix*, reckons university and professional theatrical activity in terms of the time they waste that could otherwise be spent in church: 'how many houres, evenings, halfe-dayes, dayes, and sometimes *weekes*', he demands, '*are spent by all the Actors* (especially in solemne academicall Enterludes) *in coppying, in conning, in practising their parts*, before they are ripe for publike action?'[13] It is feasible that university actors, and possibly other performers, sometimes copied out their parts: the four university parts, bound together, are in two different hands, and at least one of those is the hand of the author (and perhaps actor) Thomas Goffe; the Restoration part of Trico is also in its actor's hand (for more on both, see above). Nevertheless, this is to presuppose writing literacy, and may be more likely with university players than with professional players. And even then, the manuscript university play that most clearly anticipates the division into parts—Richard Legge's *Richardus Tertius* in the Bodleian manuscript—is marked up with a series of written signals, seemingly for a scribe rather than a set of listeners: each different character's speeches have a unique pattern of dots and slashed lines after them, presumably so that the part-writer can easily see on whose roll or part-book the words should be inscribed.[14]

John Downes the Restoration prompter says that 'writing out all the Parts in each Play' is one of his daily jobs, and from thenceforward it is prompters or their scribes who are described as regular part-writers.[15] And there is a suggestion that early modern prompters (or 'book-holders' as they were occasionally known) often had a similar job.[16] For when Henry Herbert, Master of the Revels, chooses to write a grumpy note about the distribution of actors' parts amongst the King's Men, he sends it to Edward Knight, their prompter. The play he's been looking at, writes Herbert, is unacceptable, and he has been obliged to alter some of its words. Yet the players already have it in parts. Now the prompter must 'purge their parts, as I have the booke', admonishes Herbert; in future 'the players ought not to study their parts till I have allowed of the booke'.[17]

Herbert's irritation also tells us something about the playhouse: the urgency with which a play might be divided into parts sometimes when it had barely been written, so that the actors could start the learning process at once, between and around other performances of other plays. On this occasion, parts have clearly been distributed before the formal process of accepting the play has been completed: here no sooner was the play received in its final written version than it was resolved into parts. On another occasion the parts were created before the play was even fully written. Daborne the playwright writes to ask that changes be made to parts already distributed and semi-learned: 'I have took extraordinary payns wth the end & altered one other scean in the third act which they have now in parts.'[18] In this case at least, a full text of the play does not yet exist; there can have been no public 'reading' to anyone beyond that of the plot.

One more point: if parts in different plays were generally in one hand—whether that of the prompter, or the actor, or a scribe—then a 'part' in one play will have been easily comparable with a part in another, not just in appearance but also in feel. If so, this can only have strengthened the identification of the actor—particularly a typecast actor—with a series of similar roles. The consistent 'character' of the handwriting may have encouraged presumptions of a consistent 'character' in the actor's personae: one that varies in details and emphases, but remains in identifiable ways continuous.

## Learning Parts

What an actor would do having received a part is illustrated in most plays-within-plays: he would take it away in order to learn it in solitude. So Quince in *A Midsummer Night's Dream* tells the actors 'here are your parts', and asks them to 'con them by too morrow night' (TLN 361), when the group rehearsal will take place. In fact, when the mechanics' collective rehearsal does begin, it becomes clear that one of the players, not understanding the way in which his fragment of text is meant to work, has done more than simply learn his part off by heart: he has committed to memory every word on his roll, and he goes on to repeat it, 'cues and all' (TLN 913). This is the danger of solitude: he learned his part where no one more knowledgeable than he could correct his error. Here is another essential difference between early modern actors and actors of the present day. A modern actor often learns his role when the period of group rehearsal starts: much of his part is internalized during the shared rehearsal process itself. This is because the modern actor needs to learn not just his part, but his interactions with other characters on the stage: the ensemble qualities of modern performance are established during and by the rehearsal process. For the early modern actor, the emphasis of playing was quite different. The part was more important to the production than the group interaction. It was learned in full *before* any group rehearsal; consequently, collective rehearsals were far less important, and indeed occasionally dispensed with altogether, as we will show. This was the same whether a country actor, a university actor, a boy actor, or a professional were preparing. Romney locals putting on a play have 'receyvyd players Speachys or pαrtes in the seyd playe'; they must now 'learne ... theire pαrtes ... & be redye then to playe the same'.[19] It is not that group rehearsal did not take place; just that it was not essential to the performance in the way that learning parts was.

The private learning process took up most time before performance. It is frequently referred to in all kinds of contemporary discourses, though vocabulary had not yet fixed on a single term for it: 'conning', 'studying', 'practise', and 'rehearsal' can all refer to that same private, solitary event. Where did it occur? Not, it seems, in the place of performance, but at home. So Dekker draws an analogy in which a chief actor goes 'into his bed-chamber, where he [is] fast enough lockt all night, to rehearse his parts by himselfe': the bedroom and the locked door illustrate the private investment in the whole process; alone in his room, the actor might literally dream himself into his roles.[20] Alternatively, the fact that learning happened away from the playhouse released the player, allowing him to nurture his passions and hone his intensity in ways that would, later, give urgency to his performance: 'the Player so beateth his parte too him selfe at home, that hee gives it right gesture when he comes to the scaffolde'.[21] It was not only the words of the part that were learned at home. The whole tone and manner of the character were likewise determined in isolation: despite the fragmentary nature of the part, its contents were expected to provide everything the actor needed to furnish *his* particular persona on the stage. Thus Mackenzie explains how 'skilfull Comedians, ... act still at home those personages which they are to represent publickly upon the stage'.[22]

This 'conning' process might happen at any time in the day, squeezed in between and around performances, meals, and sleep. It was not regularized or organized entirely, precisely because it was private. The actor could pick his own moment for learning. So while Breton suggests that seven o'clock in the morning—before breakfast—is the time for 'the Player, to conne his part', Fletcher, in *Maid in the Mill*, has it happening mid-morning, when it is, of course, far more in danger of interruption.[23] Bustofa, the mill owner's son in *Maid*, has been asked to appear in a country performance that will occur later that day, and wanders round his house intoning the ridiculous lines he is to speak: 'The thundring Seas, whose watry fire washes | The whiting mops: | The gentle Whale whose feet so fell | Flies ore the Mountains tops.' His father, Franio, meanwhile, has a question for him—but Bustofa is furious that anyone should interrupt what is meant to be a private and solitary period of memorization:

> FRANIO.   [*within*] Boy.
> BUSTOFA.  The thundering—
> FRANIO.   Why boy *Bustofa.*
> BUSTOFA.  Here I am—the gentle whale—
>
> > *Enter* Franio.
>
> FRANIO.   Oh, are you here Sir? where's your sister?
> BUSTOFA.  The gentle whale flies ore the mountain tops.
> FRANIO.   Where's your sister (man)?
> BUSTOFA.  Washes the whiting-Mops.
> FRANIO.   Thou ly'st, she has none to wash! mops?
>          The Boy is half way out of his wits, sure:
>          Sirrha, who am I?
> BUSTOFA.  The thundring Seas—
> FRANIO.   Mad, stark mad.
> BUSTOFA.  Will you not give a man leave to con?[24]

Note, too, that Bustofa learns through reciting, practising the sounds and the pauses, and that, for him at any rate, rhyme is both helpful and dangerous: he seems to find it more memorable than meaningful.

Unlike Bustofa, 'Boy' in *Return from Parnassus* has been less keen on his practice. He, too, has had a role to learn, but he has given over his evenings 'when you should be conning your part' to playing cards and socializing; as a result he forgets his words when he comes to the stage. This instance also provides further useful information, at least about academic rehearsal: the 'Boy' in *Return* believes he should have been allowed to take his part home sooner for private learning, and turns on the stage-keeper accordingly—'Its all long of you, I could not get my part a night or two before that I might sleep on it.'[25]

When not called 'conning', the process of learning a part was known as 'study', with all the educational connotations that this implies. William Kemp, for a while the main clown in Shakespeare's company, is depicted in John Day's *Travails of Three English Brothers* describing himself as good at extemporization, but 'somewhat hard of study'; Snug in *A Midsummer Night's Dream* similarly calls himself 'slow of studie' (TLN 330), and, like the Boy, desires to have a written part as early as possible.[26] In a theatre in which different plays were performed every day, and in which parts might not be repeated on a regular basis, the ability to learn quickly, to be 'quick of study', was imperative.

The aim of study was to learn off by heart not just the words, but the gestures and pronunciation required by the part—all of which would be worked out and committed to memory at the same time. Words and motions so went together that Middleton, comparing spiders to actors preparing, writes of their 'stalking' around the ceiling of a bed-chamber 'as if they had been conning of *Tamburlaine*'.[27] So it was only when he had committed mental and physical choice to memory—as well as the actual words—that an actor could claim to be 'perfect' in his part. Thus the actors who, in the induction to *Antonio and Mellida,* ask one another 'are you ready? Are you perfect?', are testing whether the other performers have not just learned but internalized their roles.[28] Is the play in a 'perfect' state such that each actor is 'ready' to perform properly? Tellingly, they ask this question as the play itself is about to begin; equally, they do not know what each other's performance will be like. Consequently, whatever the answer, there will simply be no time to correct any 'imperfections' before the start of the production. Playwrights—and plays—depended on actors prepared to choose to put the time into learning their parts properly: a badly prepared player could get a play 'damned' and pulled from performances. Hence the poet Nathaniel Richards, drawing an analogy in which the ideal person is a well-prepared actor and God is the playwright, writes of the paragon who 'makes … pretious use | Of his faire Part' so that he never wrongs his holy writer: he

> Ponders with sweet celestiall affectation
> On his soule-pleasing Part, dares not venter
> To tread Times *Stage*; nor unadvis'd to enter
> Till perfect in that part … [29]

A good actor, then, brings time and meditation to his part, and does not go out on to the stage until perfect. This conning, studying, or rehearsal, reliant as it was on the part rather than the full text, resulted in the actor committing the words of his speeches to memory invariably before having too much sense of the play as a whole. As slight as a part might look, it had to provide enough information to determine an actor's entire performance: for it was the only knowledge that was absolutely assured.

# Instruction

Though the actor in the 'study' period was away from the full play-text and many of the other performers, an 'instructor' offered occasional help with preparing to perform the part; instructors might similarly work with subgroups of actors. Such instructors, who generally came from the company, might on occasion include the playwright himself. Thus when Quarles, like Richards, compares God to a playwright, he imagines a writer/God who not only provides an excellent text but who also carefully instructs the player what to do with it—if the player is prepared to listen. God's wisdom, writes Quarles, 'will direct | Thy painfull hand, his mercies will correct ... and teach thee to proclaim'.[30] But, as instruction was unpaid, it is unlikely that jobbing playwrights routinely helped out with this kind of rehearsal. The instructor was only the playwright if that playwright had some kind of personal or financial relationship with the rest of the company—like Shakespeare. Thus in writing a Hamlet who 'instructs' a player how to perform the section he has added to *The Murder of Gonzago*, Shakespeare shows his own familiarity as a playwright with instruction. Ben Jonson, similarly, took a personal interest in productions of his plays, and, indeed, seems to have prided himself on the teaching he gave the actors. Perhaps he liked the power and control over the text that instructing gave him; perhaps he was proud to have been allowed the level of involvement that instruction involves; certainly he makes a point of regularly mentioning instruction in his texts. At the start of *Cynthia's Revels* it becomes clear that three boys have all been trained by the playwright to speak a single prologue, seemingly a sign of unnecessary or over-concerned preparation. 'I studied it first,' says boy number 2; 'That's all one', replies boy number 3, 'if the Authour thinke I can speake it better.'[31]

But instruction was by no means confined to playwrights. Every actor needed instruction of some kind, and a system had to be in place to ensure that they received it. So all sorts of people were dragooned into instructing. Plays of the time frequently refer to actors who have been or will be instructed, as when Domitela in *The Roman Actor* says that she has been 'instructing | The Players', or when Butler in Wilkins's *Miseries of an Inforst Marriage* makes sure that all the plotters are ready, telling them to 'play but your part': 'you knowe your kues, and have instructions howe to beare your selves'.[32] The ridiculous Sarpego in Chapman's *The Gentleman Usher* claims that his schooling has taught him to be an excellent instructor: he can 'teach | To any words' because in Padua he once had a four-line part from which he projected 'Forty faire actions'.[33]

Actors, however, were the main instructors. So in a play that features fictionalized versions of Burbage and Kemp, both the famous actors are made to promise to 'instruct' new actors' performances.[34] Actual records survive of the actor Heminges being paid to teach a boy a speech to be said to the king: actors clearly could acquire a name for offering good instruction.[35] Richard James writes, comparing himself to an actor, 'I must | before [I] to tiring roome of dust | return, instruct some scene'; indeed, when the theatres closed at the start of the Interregnum, one actor, pleading his cause, argued that theatres were no longer full of obscenities. On the contrary, he claimed, brawling and railing had been repressed, and 'we have endeavoured, as much as in us lies, to instruct one another in the true and genuine Art of acting'.[36] This made sense: junior actors could learn from senior actors during instruction, but senior actors too had something to learn or relearn. Instruction meant that a company style could be collectively maintained, actors overseeing other actors, even though there were few ensemble rehearsals. It was that confusion of individual performances and shared collective end that made its way into anti-theatrical texts, where instruction was turned back not just on actors but on whatever religion they could make 'acting' represent. So even when only one phoney Catholic takes to the 'Stage', writes Gee, 'there are diverse others within the tyring-house, that take a great deale of paines to … instruct the Actor'.[37]

Boy performers were taught by adults, of course. In the masque in Middleton's *Your Five Gallants*, Fitsgrave has privately instructed the boy to play Mercury (and pickpocket): 'Is the boy perfect?', asks Taylbeer; 'That's my credit sir, I warrant you', replies Fitsgrave.[38] It seems obvious that apprentice actors were instructed by their 'masters'; Scott McMillin suggests that in certain plays, 'women' respond to cues from—or give cues to—one particular man: Desdemona, in the second half of *Othello*, for instance, has more than half her lines exclusively 'cued' by Othello, and more than half her lines exclusively answered by Othello, perhaps because the boy player of 'Desdemona' was apprenticed to 'Othello', who 'instructed' her/him in reality as much as in the play. It might be that 'new' boy players were more likely to be given parts containing substantial sections in which they could be carefully instructed by a single person, while plays written for more practised boys were not similarly confined to dialogue with only a few people. Again, theatrical contingency helped to mould the construction of plays.[39]

Thus, despite the fact that actors did not get much in the way of full rehearsal, they were nevertheless rehearsed carefully in private. But what does this mean, exactly? What was it that an actor needed to 'study' or be taught? The teaching of boy players gives a clue. Munday, in the brief period in which he rejected the stage, fulminated against schoolmasters who took 'yong boies' who they then 'trained up in filthie speeches [and] unnatural and unseemelie gestures'.[40] They were trained, then, by their schoolteachers, in two distinct arts, speech ('pronunciation') and gestures ('action'). Indeed, the nature of the instructors goes some way towards explaining where the training came from. The boys were being taught what all schoolchildren and university students were taught by their teachers—the public side of the art of rhetoric, *pronuntio* and *actio*. Putting on plays—not necessarily in public—was regularly encouraged in schools and universities precisely because it provided excellent training in just these public aspects of rhetoric, and thus 'embolden[ed] ... *Junior* schollers' in the public-speaking jobs they were likely to hold in later life as clerics, lawyers, or teachers.[41]

But instruction did not always mean mutual work on a part, or coming to a shared understanding about what that part was offering. When instructing a more minor actor, 'instruction' might have meant simply showing the actor what to do by example: instruction could be largely based on imitation. But that, again, is to do with *actio* and *pronuntio*. There were rules about how to deal with text verbally and physically, and an instructor was someone who knew, or thought he knew, those rules particularly well.

Time and again references to 'instruction' present an instructor reciting the part to another actor. Hamlet has clearly pronounced his way through the text when showing the actor how to perform the lines he has written, for he reminds the player to 'Speake the Speech ... as I pronounc'd it to you' (TLN 1849–50). In Thomas Tomkis's *Lingua* (IV. ii), Phantastes instructs Comedus how to play his lines 'quid igitur faciam' by saying 'doe it thus. *Quid igitur, &c.*'[42] This imitative method extended into the way a new actor of any standard would receive an old part. For a part was not simply physically handed to the new actor. It was simultaneously given over and taught, so that all the gestures and emphases established by the original actor would be conveyed with it—as though the gestures and emphases themselves were attached to the part. So when Burbage in *3 Parnassus* wants to teach one of his most famed parts, Hieronymo in the *The Spanish Tragedy,* he says, 'observe how I act it, and then imitate me'.[43]

As the discovery and replication of the 'ideal' gestures and pronunciation were so linked to the words of the part, when an actor who had possessed a part died or retired, if his roles were handed on at all, it was page by page and gesture by gesture. Moreover, an actor's full collection of parts in different plays was generally inherited *en masse* by another actor when the time came—confirming the idea that there was a variety of typecasting in operation in the theatres—and the new actor would have to learn from the old actor (if alive and able) or from someone familiar with the old actor's performance (if not). A jest-book story about Gamaliel Ratsey has him robbing an actor who he also advises to go to London and prepare to take over Burbage's parts. Says Ratsey:

> Get thee to London, for if one man were dead, they will have much neede of such a one as thou art. There would be none in my opinion, fitter then thy selfe to play his parts: my conceipt is such of thee, that I durst venture all the mony in my purse on thy head, to play Hamlet with him for a wager.[44]

In a sense, then, a new actor had to 'act' in a way that the part's originator had not had to: whereas the first actor had established the character's distinctive template, the best the new actor could hope for was to recover a respectful simulacrum of the 'true original'. Predictably, with a theatre of this kind, the Interregnum terrified performers and audience alike: the great fear was that if theatres were closed too long, 'inheritance' would be lost, and the correct way of performing the parts would be forgotten. In fact, the inheritance made it over the divide—through memory and make-believe— and performances of the 1660s were said to be traceable back to the originals; famously, Betterton was said to have 'inherited' Hamlet and Henry VIII as taught by Shakespeare.[45] And inheritance remained the way of handing on parts for the next 200 years and more. Only when David Garrick took to the stage was early modern inheritance done away with, and he did so only in order to establish a new line of inheritance stemming from him.[46]

This means that new parts in new plays were particularly prized, and that actors receiving new parts for the first time had an enormous responsibility. Their combination of interpretation and imitation would 'create' the way the part was *meant* to be; their decisions would become aspects of the part itself.


# Rehearsal

Just before performance, there would be (if there was the time for it) a 'private practise of [the] publick Play': at least one full rehearsal, whatever that might mean.[47] As a different play was performed every day (London was too small to sustain a play 'run' at any theatre), it is extraordinary to discover that full rehearsals were generally held during term time (there were four legal terms a year), thus coinciding with the acting period. A contract for the actor Robert Dawes that survives amongst the Alleyn documents is suggestive:

> Robert Dawes shall and will at all tymes during the said terme duly attend all suche rehearsal which shall the night before the rehearsal be given publickly out; and if that he ... shall at any tyme faile to come at the hower appointed, then he shall and will pay to the said Phillipp Henslowe and Jacob Meade their executors or assignes Twelve pence.[48]

Group rehearsal, then, happened in the morning of a term in which (at least in Henslowe's company) up to forty different daily plays might be put on, all of which the actor will also have had to 'con' or at least relearn. And, as this document also makes clear, group rehearsal did not take place daily: rather, when a rehearsal was to happen, the actors would be warned the night before. No wonder, then, that full rehearsals were kept to the absolute minimum, and that playwrights had cause to complain of

> Th'unworthy *Actors*, dull, imperfect skill
> Bred by distemper, grosse neglect in studdy,
> Carelesse Rehearsalls, and a skull so muddy,
> As never minds th'infinite paines and Art,
> Penn'd, to advance and fit him with a part
> That might immortalize ... [49]

It is not really possible to establish an average number for the full rehearsals generally held before performance, but country accounts suggest that non-professional players varied their number of group rehearsals (known, usually, as the 'general rehearse') from one to three according to region;

one was usual.[50] One seems, too, to be the number most often referred to in plays: there is one in Shakespeare's *A Midsummer Night's Dream*, in Marston's *Histrio-mastix*, in Munday's *Downfall of Robert, Earl of Huntington*, and Middleton's *Your Five Gallants*; there is none in Kyd's *Spanish Tragedy*, Jonson's *Cynthia's Revels*, Beaumont and Fletcher's *Maid in the Mill*, Chapman's *The Gentleman Usher*, Carlell's *The Fool would be a Favourite*, Shakespeare's *Hamlet* (though in each of these there is a suggestion of intensive studying and learning of parts). Gayton refers to a single 'trial' before performance of a university play, and Blount to a single 'essay': 'Among Comoedians the tryal or proof of their action, which they make before they come forth publiquely upon the Stage, is their *Essay*.'[51] Group rehearsals, then, seem to have been anything from zero to about three in number, with an emphasis on one as normative. Lack of consistency, however, always meant that more were possible if necessary: should, for instance, rehearsal reveal a play to be grossly under-prepared, the performance could be called off, and another play substituted while further learning took place.

In truth, however, more than one rehearsal was rarely desirable: the event was unpaid, and actors who were anyway concentrating on solo performance simply did not have the same concern to practise together. Rather, having been reminded of the basic plot in which they were performing, they were expected to be able to act: Gee writes an analogy in which Jesuitical plotters are like the people in a tyring-room who 'take...paines to project the plot' to the actor.[52] Many plays of the time contrast careful learning with the little attention given to group rehearsal: the boy actors of Marston's *Antonio and Mellida* enter on to the stage for performance 'with parts in their hands' and do not yet know which of their fellow actors have been cast in which role; Bassiolo in Chapman's *Gentleman Usher* precedes performance asking, 'Are all parts perfect?', to which Sarpego answers, 'One I know there is' (that is, he knows that he has learned his own part); Bustofa performing his play in *Maid in the Mill* does not know whether Gerasto is meant to snatch Venus away, as 'he never rehears'd his part with me before'.[53] Concomitantly, over the next couple of centuries, during which 'parts' continued to be the unit in which plays were learned, chief actors consistently refused to attend such group rehearsals as there were; famous stories are told about lead players who knew nothing of the plays they were in beyond their parts, like Hannah Pritchard, who Samuel Johnson said 'had never read the tragedy of *Macbeth* all through. She no more thought of the play out of which her part was taken, than a shoemaker thinks of the skin, out of which … he is making a pair of shoes.'[54] The part remained the indispensable unit of learning, practising, and performing; in Shakespeare's *A Midsummer Night's Dream*, just before performance, the last check that Bottom asks each actor to make is to 'look oer [your] part' (TLN 1782–3).

It is no surprise that the playhouse documents that seem to have flanked professional performance are all aids for actors who are individually knowledgeable but have not had much time to work on ensemble techniques. So a 'plot' containing essential dramatic information was hung backstage. This was a clearly written sheet of paper mounted on cardboard and attached to the tyring-house wall (surviving plots contain square holes in their centre for the purpose). Divided into two columns, each of which is subdivided into scenes, the plot provides not the story of the play, but the sequence of dramatic events in the play. Specifically, it contains actors' entrances—and some additional details about properties and who else would be on-stage; exits are not necessarily given: 'Enter aspida & validore disguisd like rose wth a flasket of clothes to them rose wth a nother flasket of clothes to them the panteloun to them pescodde.'[55] Plots thus inform the individually prepared player (or a call-boy for the individually prepared player) what is happening more generally to him and to others in the scene, mapping his progress through the play in a series of entrances and properties; simply put, they make collective performance from separate parts easier.

With such helps provided by the playhouse, the extent to which a full rehearsal even involved all of the words in a play is open to question. If actors had already been instructed, there would have been little need to check that they knew how to say what they had learned (as there was for the uninstructed actors of *A Midsummer Night's Dream*). By contrast, particular *group* elements of the play—jigs, songs, dances, sword fights, perhaps crowd or climactic scenes—will have benefited from ensemble rehearsal. The few surviving hints about rehearsals suggest that moments, rather than the full text, were what the occasions were often about. So Ben Jonson in *Every Man Out of his Humour* (1599) has Carlo refer to 'a thing studied, and rehearst as ordinarily … as a jigge after a Play', while the boys in Chapman's *Gentleman Usher* are heard 'practising' their song in the play (the other performers are not with them).[56] Even blocking notes, when they survive, are for similar such specific moments in plays.

Thus Percy's manuscript plays, which include detailed pictures to describe the blocking of songs and dances—as when North, South, East, and West meet together in *Arabis Sitiens or A Dreame of a Drye Yeare*—are so vague as to other stage-directions that they cannot be directly attributed either to an adult company (and their brand of performances) or to a boy one (and their brand of performances).[57]

## Performance and the Prompter

Performance itself, of course, had to find ways to unite the actors with their separate parts, gestures, and actions. This was done with a variety of helps, one being the plot, and another the person who may well have written the plot and who certainly 'ran' the performance: the man usually called the prompter and occasionally the 'book-holder'. So Thomas Rogers, conceiving of political events as though they were happening in a theatre, writes that 'lame brooke should hould the booke, and sit him still | to prompte, if any mist or acted ill'.[58] Leaving the analogy aside, Rogers indicates what the book-holder did in the theatre: he prompted not simply 'mist' words, but also ill action; he had a responsibility for what happened verbally *and* physically on-stage.

Medieval prompters had been responsible for words and action visibly: they had stood on-stage throughout performances, Prospero-like (*Tempest* may be making the analogy), holding the book, the source of the words, whilst, with their batons, 'conducting' some of the blocking. But in the early modern theatre, the prompter's role was no longer so visually explicit. The functionary now resided in the tyring-room, though his duties—prompting missing words and directing blocking—remained similar. He was there to set the players going again when they had missed or not observed their cue: Mistress Caroll in *Hide Park* suggests no one try to be 'prompter' and 'insinuate the first word of your studied Oration'.[59] Hardly surprisingly, the early modern variety of terms for referring to the title and concept of the functionary's job —ranging from 'prompter' to book-keeper—all emphasize a fundamental association with 'the [play] book' ('the prompter', as Higgins calls him, 'or booke-holder' is one that 'telleth the players their part when they are out and have forgotten'; 'a prompter', as Florio defines it, is 'one that keepes the book for plaiers, and teacheth them ... their kue').[60]

Against this book, the actors had something fragmentary: only 'part' of the text.

Despite being out of the sight-line of the audience, the prompter still oversaw what was happening on-stage and—sometimes audibly—'directed' it. From his position in the tyring-house he was able, when necessary, to observe what was happening on-stage through grilles in the doors or openings—and perhaps loopholes in the curtains; he could shout commands both to the actors backstage awaiting their entrance, and to those on-stage.[61] So one Prologue knows the play is about to start as he hears, from behind the *frons scenae* (the wall that divided stage from tyring-house) 'the players prest, in presence foorth to come'.[62] But the prompter's voice also directs those already on-stage: a Prologue in *Staple of News* hears the book-holder calling out, 'Mend your lights, Gentlemen. *Master Prologue*, beginne', while Will Summers in *Summers Last Will* hears the book-holder ordering the players to 'Begin, begin'.[63] Indeed, the prompter's cry from 'within' of 'Dismisse the Court' becomes part of Brome's *Antipodes*: the actor Letoy takes this up with 'Dismisse the Court, cannot you heare the prompter?'.[64] Thus when Othello suggests that he needs no one to tell him when to start fighting, he too is making a theatrical analogy: 'Were it my Cue to fight, I should have knowne it | Without a Prompter' (TLN 301). The suggestion here is that Othello's action, like the timing of entrances and opening speeches, might also be prompter-controlled; and indeed, it is material of this kind, advance notices for actors' entrances, necessary properties, and important events—like music, dances, and songs—that are marked up in surviving playhouse books. Years later Aaron Hill was to describe a prompter as one who so strictly controlled the performance that 'I have seen the merriest of mortals not dare to crack a joke till [he] gave them their cue, and the most despairing of lovers refrain from sighs and tears till they had permission to be miserable'.[65]

For our purposes, what is important here is that the prompter offered ways in which separately prepared actors could be successfully brought together on the stage: certain ensemble elements of the drama—the kind of things that might not be gathered from a part in advance—could be controlled or 'conducted' from backstage by the prompter. Use of prompter together with backstage 'plot' were two ways to bring the separate constituents together to make a full play. There simply was no need for over-much ensemble preparation before performance.

# Performances and Repeated Performances

Performances themselves were shaped by and to 'parts': as we have shown, 'parts' defined the way the audience watched plays, just as they had defined the way actors prepared them. Performers who had played 'good parts, and play'd them Bravely-well' were rewarded with applause; others would 'goe hissed off the Stage. And that is for want of being perfect in those good parts, which are put into them.'[66] Thus separate actors in the same play would be separately judged on pronunciation and on gesture. While the play itself might be applauded or hissed at its conclusion, the actors were acclaimed or booed for their abilities throughout. They were also judged on their interactions with one another—this being likely to be the worst pitfall of a separately studied text.

Accounts suggest that a 'bad' actor was someone so intent on his part—and his part alone—that he adopted his character only for the moments at which he himself was to 'act'. Such a player was *too* part-focused, and so would lose interest as soon as his words stopped: 'when you have spoke, at end of every speech, | Not minding the reply, you turne you round', says Letoy of bad players in Brome's *Antipodes*.[67] Trained in a system that encouraged actors to play for themselves rather than for the ensemble, the second-rate performer might go hunting for audience approval, neglecting the dialogue and situation that he serves, so that 'when he doth hold conference upon the stage; and should looke directly in his fellows face; hee turnes about his voice into the assembly for applause-sake'.[68] That said, crowd-conscious performing of this kind might occasionally be a part-based necessity: not being told who would speak the next cue on the part, it might be easier to address the audience than risk speaking to the wrong person on a busy stage.

Over the next couple of centuries, the same criticisms continued to be made: that some actors performed only when speaking, and lost possession of their character when not. The great Restoration actor Thomas Betterton complained that 'the Actors…who are on the Stage, and not in the very principle Parts, shall be whispering to one another, or bowing to their Friends in the Pit, or gazing about'.[69] Years later, exactly the same complaint still had currency; there were actors who would 'relax themselves as soon as any speech in their own part is over, into an absent unattentiveness to whatever is replied by another…only watchful of the cue, at which, like soldiers upon the word of command, they start suddenly back to their postures'. The result could be 'a Speech calculated *to excite a latent Passion* ... received with perfect *Apathy* and *Indifference*; and the Answer all at once, preposterously returned in the *Rage* of *Passion*, or *Theatrical Throws* of *Distress*'.[70]

We are assuming that in Shakespeare's time, as during the Restoration, part-based problems of this kind were confined to minor or unprofessional actors. The regulars who made up a company—financially as well as in acting terms—no doubt developed a keen sense of how to perform with one another.

But here we should consider a fundamental question about working in parts: that is, the question of subsequent performances of a single part. We need here to remember one basic but perhaps under-regarded fact: there was no guarantee that a play would ever receive a second performance. This was a time in which there were no play 'runs', and different plays were put on every day. A 'new' play might be repeated regularly if it were making money, or never be performed again if it were not. Actors were expected to have upwards of forty roles in their heads or to hand, and might regularly be asked to learn new plays while performing an endless series of old ones. In Henslowe's 'diary', for instance, accounts show that the Admiral's Company performed six days a week in season, and added a new play to their repertory roughly once a fortnight. So in their 1594–5 season, for instance, they offered thirty-eight plays altogether, of which twenty-one were new.[71] The actors' parts, then, were always written *for* the first performance. Everything in them presupposes that the actors are coming at the part for the first time. This first performance simply had to be the most important one—because it could easily be the only one. Equally, if the actors did indeed play the part again, it was this inaugurating experience that established the template for so doing. True to so many Renaissance phenomena, it was recapturing the 'original' that conferred validity and legitimacy; the players had to convince themselves and their audiences that this first 'cauldron' was still burning within; for in a culture so entranced by supposedly inceptive truths, only a method that claimed to 'sustain' inception would allow the cultural and subjective force needed for a long-running, successful public theatre company.

There is no doubt that audiences often went more than once to see the same play. Taylor writes of the man who 'scornes to see a Play past twice'; but sophisticated plays were positively recommended as needing repeated viewing: Jonson's plays are described as being so far above 'Vulger' understanding that they 'took not so well at the *first stroke* as at the *rebound*, when beheld the second time'.[72] Plays of the time abound with references to audiences who are familiar with the jokes in the production, having been at many performances—like the man in Webster's induction to Marston's *Malcontent* who has 'seene this play often' and who, as a result, has 'most of the jeasts heere in my table-booke'.[73] So, though no two performances are ever the same, we also do not think that two performances would have been allowed by the watchers to be markedly different. We suspect that both actors and audience were grounded by the fact that the actor played his part as learned—as it had worked in performance by him or by his predecessors. Consequently, practised members of the audience could recite, in anticipation, the speeches they were hoping to hear in just the manner they were hoping to hear them—like the 'Neophyte' described by Crites in *Cynthia's Revels*, who mutters 'part of speeches, and confederate jests, | In passion to himselfe' as he waits.[74] Of course, certain players—particularly improvising jesters such as Tarlton—may have been famed (or decried) for wandering from the script: but even this accords with popular anticipation.

Obviously, when discussing the ways in which actors respond to parts during performance on the stage, we need to consider the 'gap' between one performance of a play and the next performance of the same play. What effect did this have on repeated performances? Would performers 'solidify' knowledge over the interim, or forget it, or revise their parts to embrace it? If a misapprehension or oddity were found in a part on first performance, would subsequent performance straighten it out? After all, what was shocking or horrifying or confusing on the first day would no longer be unexpected on the second or third.

Our conclusion, having looked at many plays in part-form, is that if a moment were simply 'wrong', then it would, of course, be corrected. But we think that surprising moments are often *not* 'wrong'—more often than not, they are the very heartbeat of the part. To take just one example: if Shakespeare, himself a performer from parts on a daily basis for years, chooses to write a cue that is given out repeatedly during a speech, we are sure that he does this deliberately. He cannot have done so through ignorance, and the sheer ubiquity of the technique argues against sloppiness (the decisive argument, of course, is powerful expressive effect, which we will come to in Part II). The repeated cue is not a minor annoyance, one that might bedevil a first performance but is open to be 'corrected' in the second. For confirmation, we might note how often time-worn plays, plays regularly revised and changed, or plays that seem to be printed from prompters' 'books', still contain such repeated cues. But this is merely one of the many 'surprises' that a cue-script can hold. We will identify numerous ways in which apparent confusion or ellipses—endemic to the part-technology, but also easily avoided or overcome by careful scripting—are in fact meticulously orchestrated and gradually refined by Shakespeare: first to produce specific, foreseen responses in his actors; and from this to produce very particular expressive or thematic results. Shakespeare was far less suspicious of actors than, say, Jonson seems to have been; he gave his players crucial freedoms, moments of actorly choice, often no doubt terrifying moments, that invariably coincide with moments of decision for the character. And it is these moments that will be inscribed—as defining of the part, as literally self-constituting—in the mind of the actor; the more exposed the uncertainty or sudden the recognition, the more imperative it is that this experience should be remembered, revered, and in future performances recovered.

However—and this point is fundamental to our method and argument—we do not base our conclusion upon any preconceptions concerning what an actor's relationship should or must be to his parts; still less do we base our argument (as it were pre-emptively) upon expectations of actorly neuroses, or motivational techniques, or empathy exercises, or anything of the kind. Rather, as with everything in the book, we proceed 'inductively' from the particular instances—the evidence about contemporary practice of rehearsal/conning, and the evidence of Shakespeare's play-texts—generating conclusions from the accumulation of discrete phenomena.

In one sense, the actor learning a part and bringing it to the production is something like a trumpeter learning his part in an orchestral piece. He brings a separately learned piece—one in which he will have decided phrasing and mood—to an ensemble performance. There he is 'directed' in his performance by a prompter who, like the orchestra conductor, is responsible for basic timing, and for melding the individual pieces together. In another sense, the actor working from a part is nothing like so secure: the 'classical' score is subjected to the jazz-like peril and contingency of performance. As we shall see, neither rehearsal nor performance is ever finally definitive; each subserves the other. This is not true of all drama.

However, it is powerfully true of plays that are patched together from, or cut up into, individual actors' parts. But to reiterate: these actors must *never* go off script; if there is a god in this machine, it is moving and whispering throughout the part-text. In this particular theatrical economy—one in which the part-script, the rehearsal, and the performance are never quite complete, never quite finished with—we find one of aesthetic history's great creative tensions.

# PART II

## Interpreting Cues

——————— value not.

but 'tis not well to bring such men oth' stage.

——————— philosopher.

'tis true Musæus;

but Trico has another part to act,

prethy tell me, where's thy Master Ignoramus?

——————— Rosabella.

is he going for her then?

——————— think

as thou lou'st me hasten with all speed to Cupes

and bid him remember the horne,

——————— whats that?

he know's my meaning, it concernes the Lawyer.

therefore away, I prethy away.

——————— Master!                                    (Exit Musæ

run Musæus run,

if Cupes come not quickly, wa're undone.

## Scen: 7.

(Ent. Ignor.) ——————— sweet Rose

how finely these men watch

——————— to night

not yet?

——————— persona.

oh how they linger, I must not let him pass

nor know I how to keep him while the come;

'saue you sir

——————— mittimus

a poore man sir, spent my whole estate in law,

——————— away.

I beseech your councell.

——————— legem pone.

this greedy Cerberus must haue a morsell,

and I haue nothing left, but one poore soul.

perhaps he may fasten on't —

indeed sir I am a very poore man.

——————— nihil dicit.

a slender fæ sir, I beseech your councell.

——————— the case

Issue — peseeds out, what shall I say now?

yes sir, issue

——————— the action

The part of Trico from Ferdinando Parkhurst's *Ignoramus* (1662–4).

# 4
## History of the Cue

### The Cue

The word 'cue', variously written 'cue', 'Q', 'kew', 'qu', and 'queue', was glossed in early modern dictionaries in a variety of ways. Each gloss shows a different facet of the cue itself. The etymological root of 'cue' is unclear, but in the Renaissance the word was generally traced to the letter 'q', which starts both the Latin *qualis* (what) and the Latin *quando* (when). 'What' or 'when' together propose the cue as a precise indicator of occasion: the particular moment when the next actor must begin: a verbal version of being pointed at by the conductor's baton. The 'q' was usually defined as being of one word in length—that is, the final word of the preceding speech (the 'Qu', wrote Minsheu in 1625, shows 'at what manner of word the *Actors* are to beginne to speake one after another hath done his speech'[1]). Edmond Malone, the eighteenth-century theatre historian, hand-wrote a 'correction' of the etymology of 'Q' in his copy of Butler's 1633 *English Grammar*, perhaps because he had been reading Samuel Johnson's *Dictionary*. 'Queue', as Johnson and Malone preferred it, comes from the French, and signifies 'the tail or last word of a speech, which is the hint to the next speaker'.[2] This is unlikely—cue in French is not 'queue' but 'réplique', and, as we have seen, surviving French roles have cue-words but not cue-tails. What is interesting, however, is how important the 'tail' is to English writers: for Malone and Johnson, the line before the cue-words is part of the cue itself.

So the tail, which both flows into and remains distinct from the 'last word' of the speech, is important: it gestures towards anything and everything that might be said by other actors in between one's own speeches. The tail is a visual representation of absence, signifying all the bits of preceding speech(es) that have not been given. But for the actor, the tail more pertinently represents *his* approaching moment: it is a call to present arms. In this sense, the cue-plus-tail shrinks the actor's known world into nothing but what serves the part's world. We can see this graphically illustrated by the very long cue-'tail'—almost the entire width of the page—in the 'Orlando' part. The effect is very explicitly to parcel the blocs of speeches off one from another, almost like self-sufficient entities; 'boxed' by the cue-line in this way, each speech appears to generate or belong to its own context; this graphic style may well recommend learning speeches one at a time, like distinctive 'gobbets'.

In a joke description of an echo it was said that 'She were good to make a Player of the Stage, for she would take her cues excellently well.'[3] The purpose of the cue was to let the actor know when he should speak: not having a full text of the scene in which he was performing, he would need to listen carefully on-stage for the cue and then say the passage he had learned following it. This is a staple of metatheatrical references: 'your speech being ended, now comes in my cue' (Heywood); 'Your qu. | ... 'twill be spoken quickly | Therefore watch it' (Middleton and Rowley); 'Speak count, tis your Qu' (Shakespeare).[4] The important fact to realize here is that actors must know their cue as thoroughly as they do their subsequent speech: they had to learn a cue-to-speech 'sandwich', the one entirely linked to the other. Only in this way can a play performed from cues work.

References repeatedly return to the fact that early modern actors are reliant on their cues. In a theatrical analogy in *The So[l]dered Citizen* the Doctor says that everything is ready for the play to go smoothly ahead: 'all's fitted, | If you be perfect, in yor. Cues, and action'.[5] Actors who do not know their cues as well as their speeches are in serious trouble, for no other person on-stage can help them if they are 'out' (a term meaning 'not "in" one's part')—other actors, of course, knowing only *their* own lines, not the full text. Dialogue frequently harps upon the terrifying idea of being 'out', or the absolute necessity of *not* being out: 'Act but thine owne part, and be not out *Sam*, | and feare nothing,' says Gilbert in Brome's *Sparagus Garden*; Baltazar in Dekker's *Noble Spanish Soldier* speculates what would happen 'if you being the King, should be out of your part'.[6] Jokes similarly hinge upon the isolation of being 'out': since no one else knows what the actor is meant to be saying, no one on-stage can do more than cajole or curse until the prompter brings relief. There was, for instance, the story of the boy who was performing in a university play in front of Queen Elizabeth. He, like the actor in Shakespeare's Sonnet 23, 'with his feare [was] put besides his part'; the only thing his embarrassed tutor could do to set him back on track was pinch him—which did not have quite the desired affect:

> In a Play presented in the Universitie, before Queene Elizabeth: It happened a young lad, something daunted with her presence, had forgot himselfe, and was quite out of his part (being at a stand) which a Master of Art, at that time, one of the prime Actors perceiving, gave him a pinch by the arme, which made the teares stand in his eyes: which the Queene perceiving, call'd to the young Scholler, and commanded him to tell her, why his countenance was so suddenly changed; To whom hee answered, with that verse out of Virgill:

> In fandum Regina iubes renovare dolorem.[7]

Plays also nervously depict what would happen if an actor waited for his cue—and did not hear it. What would he do? Carlell's *The Fool would be a Favourit* features a terrible amateur performer, Young Gudgeon, who lies 'dead' on-stage waiting for his cue. Meanwhile, the play in which he is performing has been called to a halt...

| MAN. | Master, Master, rise, rise. |
|---|---|
| YOUNG GUDGEON. | That's not my cue, he's out. |
| MAN. | The Princesse is gone. |
| YOUNG GUDGEON. | Gone is not my cue neither. |
| MAN. | The play is done. |
| YOUNG GUDGEON. | Thou lyest, I must be kis'd first; I wil not open mine eyes till I be kis'd.[8] |

Hardly surprisingly, when likening man's life to a stage-play, Thomas Howell warns us to 'Take heede...and kepe eche Cue so right, | That Heaven for hyre unto thy lotte may light.'[9]

Actors who did not *give* their cues well would also bring a performance to a standstill: lacking the right cue, the next actor would not know that it was his turn to speak (until the prompter alerted him). Will Summers threatens to use this in Nashe's *Summer's Last Will*: he declares an intention to 'play the knave in cue' in order to 'put you besides all your parts'.[10] There is something of the house of cards about this method: one cue falls and the whole show collapses:

| BOYET. | Why that contempt will kill the keepers heart, |
|---|---|
|  | And quite divorce his memory from his part. |
| QUEEN. | Therefore I doe it, and I make no doubt, |

The rest will [n]ere come in, if he be out.

*(Love's Labour's Lost,* TLN 2041–4)

Actors were tied to their cues, and judged by their ability to respond quickly and accurately to them.[11] So much did this continue to be the case that when, years later, the actor John Palmer failed to learn his role of Lord Russel on time, he simply spoke words from a different character, homing in on the Lord Russel cues so as not to muddle his fellow actors:

> he dexterously introduced some passages from the Earl of Essex, which he contrived to fit into the cues received by Lord Russel ... It will be remembered that to his audience this play was completely new; while the dialogue was in progress, and not seemingly irrelevant, there were no means of detection.[12]

Cues might, occasionally, have been non-verbal. This is perhaps particularly true of entrance cues. Dekker suggests waiting to take one's stool on-stage until 'the quaking prologue ... is ready to give the trumpets their Cue, that hees upon point to enter': here the backstage actor communicates with the trumpeters in the music room that it is time they 'announced' his entrance with the customary two blasts.[13] This suggests some kind of backstage access between the tyring-house and the music room, so that the actor can wave—or possibly shout—his cue at the musicians. And at moments in 'Orlando' when the character is to enter an empty stage (at the start of an act when there are no words for him to listen for), the text simply says 'enter'. Presumably the entrance of Orlando, too, is cued in some non-verbal way, either by the prompter or by a fellow actor. Thomas Adams draws an analogy in which 'the more men act, the more they affect; and the exit of one sin is another's hint of entrance, that the stage of his heart is never empty till the tragedy of his soul be done': the exit of the previous actor could itself, perhaps, also be an entrance cue.[14] It is worth observing here that it is a feature of actors' parts for entrances only sometimes to be cued, whereas exits are almost universally indicated; furthermore, as with miscellaneous stage-directions, exits on parts frequently do not correspond to exits in the play-text.[15] The reverse is the case on surviving backstage 'plots' or 'plats', which state all entrances, but often do not contain exits at all. 'Plots', the documents that seem to have hung backstage, provided a scene-by-scene list of when actors should enter and, sometimes, further information concerning whom actors were to 'enter to', what they were to carry (and so forth); exits, however, are recorded only erratically. The implication, then, is that the actor using the plot needs to be apprised of entrances, whereas the actor using the part needs to know when to exit. As the plot is backstage, and the part refers to on-stage activity, it stands to reason that the two are opposite as well as complementary.[16]

Whatever the cue was, it was the thing that often defined the actor in popular parlance. Samuel Harsnett, the man whose writings against 'egregious popish impostors' influenced Shakespeare in writing the part of Edgar in *King Lear*, uses a suggestive term to express his contempt for players. Accusing his popish *bêtes noires* of play-acting rather than really ridding themselves or anyone else of devils, Harsnett shuns the words 'player' and 'actor' in favour of 'cue-fellows'.[17] The coinage is derogatory: a 'cue-fellow' is someone entirely determined by the cues of another, a puppet of the insidious master (Pope or playwright). 'Cue-fellows' act from moment to moment, dangerously unbeholden to any visibly unifying script. But the term also shows how the cued part, not the full text, described the world of the actor. Indeed, the inevitable association of effective part-playing with effectively taken cues was such that even a (probably apocryphal) performing dog was said to have taken his cues 'well':

> [The dog] eate the pyson, and presently (drunkard-like) stackered up and downe, ... as his Part was; and at last fell downe, stretcht himselfe upon the stage, and lay for dead. Soone after, when his Cue was spoken, first by little and little he began to move himselfe, ... then he arose, and came to him to whom his part was he should come: which thing ... moved wonderfull admiration in olde Vespasian.[18]

This dog, who has simply been taught what to do, is nevertheless described as having a part with cues: parts were physical, but they were also so much the language of the theatre that to perform a part and to have a part-text were considered almost indissoluble; cues too are so integral to the idiom of play-acting that the very notion of them becomes synonymous with performing a part.

This fact informs perhaps the shortest epitaph of the seventeenth century: one written for Richard Burbage, Shakespeare's master actor. Often reproduced as merely its verbal content, the full epitaph as printed in Sir John Mennes's *Facetiae* in fact reads like this:

_____ Exit Burbage.[19]

This of course is an exit cue, identified as such by the 'tail' before the instruction. Here, the epitaph announces, is the parting cue in Burbage's long roll of parts: it is said to have been inscribed on Burbage's grave. But the choice of this particular form represents more than a conceit. It crystallizes the importance of the cue, and its specific textual form. It declares absolute confidence in the fame of England's great actor, but also the fame of the standard format for cueing all actors. Indeed, some of the pathos of this format derives from a recognition that Burbage's dignity came from his profession: so, though he and his parts have gone, the form that allowed him still survives. In a sense, then, this succinct epitaph is a testament as much to the iconic status of the written part—and most particularly its tailed cue—as to the actor who receives and delivers it. 'Burbage' here stands for much more than a sick old actor; the name calls forth and reanimates all those other parts that the actor was in his lifetime 'cued' to perform—hence the gravity and portent in the exit cue's long walk into silence.

The fact that an actor's text is scored along its length by the lost bits has continually frustrated European commentators: rolls are 'barely comprehensible—or incomprehensible—to the reader', writes Linke, 'because the speeches transcribed always lack textual context, and … the context of the action as well'.[20] In this book, however, we dispute this verdict: just as Burbage's career is powerfully inscribed in his epitaph's tail, so the actor's text, however fragmentary, is anything but incomprehensible. All kinds of contexts breathe in its ellipses.

## Length of Cue

The proposition that the professional actors' cues could have been so lacking in content and context can seem alarming: was the information given to an actor *really* as limited as this? The answer is not only that it was thus limited, but that it was limited for powerfully creative reasons: far from being the accidental sacrifice of a theatre rushed off its feet, the cue's spareness is a strategic astringency. Gabriel Harvey's marginal notes to *Oikonoma* describe 'The lest qu, or hit' as 'ye lest overture, ye smallist or dimmist Light, sufficient to A nimble, & pregnant conceite': as the link between smallness and pregnancy suggests, the very terseness of the cue is an invitation to extrapolate; it beckons imaginative filling out, depending upon the actor's 'nimble', 'conceit'-driven imaginative possession.[21] So when Lyly creates a 'cue' for himself and takes it—a sign of just how familiar he expected general readers to be with the theatrical notion of cueing—he gives himself a single-word cue, 'hangd': 'it runnes still in my minde that they must be hangd. Hangde is the Que, and it comes just to my purpose.'[22] The dictionary quotations above show the expectation of one-word cues, and professional plays confirm that one to three words was entirely acceptable. In James Shirley's *Humorous Courtier* the fool Deppazi has learned a set speech to say to the countess: he loses track, however, when she does not end her own speech with the anticipated one-word cue 'oblivion': 'I beseech your grace, speake your part right, | "Oblivion" is my qu. I doe remember.'[23] As so often, the overt reference to cueing signals a joke that also shows the weight and importance of the cue-word. Here the clown pedantically draws attention to the fact that the cue 'oblivion', meaning to be forgotten, has indeed been forgotten. He in turn is mocked by his boastful 'I doe remember': he purports to counter the countess's oblivious 'oblivion' with his own remembrance of oblivion; the irony, of course, is that it is he who has missed his original cue. If we try to use this to identify the conventional length of cues, it is ambiguous: 'oblivion' is one word, but four syllables, and, more than that, strikingly memorable. Even so, it shows that one-word cues are quite normative.

Entrance cues, which one might expect to be slightly longer, seem in practice to have similarly been of one to three words. So in the rehearsal scene of *A Midsummer Night's Dream*, Bottom/Pyramus is chastised by Peter Quince for missing his two-word entrance cue ('never tyre'): '*Piramus* enter, your cue is past; it is never tyre' (TLN 913–14). Bottom/Pyramus is throughout the rehearsal unclear how to use his 'part' appropriately; later, in the performance itself, he glosses his new-found understanding of entrance cues: 'Curst be thy stones for thus deceiving mee,' he exclaims, followed by a helpful aside to the audience—'*Deceiving me* | is Thisbies cue; she is to enter...' (TLN 1983–6, our italics, another two-word cue). In each case we might again notice how the cue has a choric or characterizing function: 'never tire' 'cues' a joke about the exhaustion of 'Pyramus', an exhaustion indicated by his failure to appear. 'Deceiving me' is a similar gift to the audience, joking benignly upon Bottom's basic condition: he spends the play in the happiest state of self-deception and ignorance. We see here, then, how the apparent flexibility of cue-length feeds a certain flexibility of usage.

Another example comes from George Wilkins, who in his prose narrative of *Pericles* gives Lysimachus a one-word cue of entrance—the word 'come':

'hastily into the Chamber came the Pandar unto them, who ... told them, that the Lorde *Lysimachus* was come, and as if the word Come had beene his kew, he entred the Chamber with the master bawde'.[24] Here we have a terse, one-word cue that is anything but empty: 'Come' is the governor's 'kew', as the eager Bawd and Pandar know to their regular profit. Wilkins may well have co-written the stage-play *Pericles* with Shakespeare; but whether he did or not, it is likely that his prose version is a report of a recently witnessed Globe performance. The mangled Quarto text of the play has 'Here comes the Lord *Lysimachus* disguised' (G3b), a comment echoing Wilkins's 'come[s]'. Indeed, the play's phrasing sounds suspiciously like an observation of the action that has simply been transferred to a convenient speaker. What is interesting here is that play and novel alike take up the mundane tropes of theatrical exchange at the same point in the narrative. Thus, in the play, both the fact of entrance *and* the fact of disguise are referred to; the 'joke' about the Duke's see-through disguise then reinforces the likelihood that the same moment on-stage makes a joke about him 'coming'. Either way, Wilkins's commentary suggests that parts were written and heard with ears highly tuned to the contextually allusive, punning possibilities of cues.

# 5
# Interpreting Shakespeare's Cues: Introduction

In this section we examine various ways in which Shakespeare exploits the limitations and possibilities of the cue, and in particular we see how cues are used to orchestrate performance and contribute to characterization.

Upon receiving his part, an actor's attention would be drawn to its two connected but separate elements. On the left he would see the 'body' of the text: all the speeches he had to learn. Examining that slab of text in part-form, he would be under no illusions as to the length or character of 'his' bit. Flanking his speeches above and below but situated to the right of his text were the cue-words, their long 'tails' extending back into the space occupied by his speeches. That list of cues would attract as much attention as the text to be learned: for, as we shall see, cues can stand for considerably more than 'themselves'. His own speeches apart, cues amount to much of the knowledge that the actor will have of the play he is in, and pretty much all of the knowledge he will have been 'given' to take home. The right-hand text thus possessed its own visual and functional unity. For the actor, this 'cue column' is far more than an accidental and disparate collection of words. Huddling slightly aside from the actor's speaking text, a chain of cues can contain its own mini-narratives, bearing potentially telling relationships to the larger narrative of full scene or play. Parts were regularly written—and played—with ears highly tuned to the contextually allusive—indeed, punning—possibilities of cues. Because the cue is slightly beyond the immediate motives of its speaker, it is also a place where the playwright can annotate or otherwise 'block' the part of its receiver. It thus offers numerous clues to the rest of the play-world, as well as numerous specific prompts for the actor's own performance.

Of course, many cues do nothing, as it were, but their basic job. But Shakespeare's actors had to be prepared for their cues to own the same range of addressing options as any other scripted unit of speech; like many other instances of compacted word use, the cue can play off adjacent words, comment upon a situation, project into future possibilities; it can point toward consequences, judgements, or alterations that are otherwise not yet in play. But the cue also exists on its own terms, independent of any full-play context to which it contributes. Above all, it belongs to an actor with *that* cue on *his* part. This means that the cue is twice remote from any 'larger' contexts: marooned in a part that is already marooned from the larger play. Given this distinctive placing, cue-words must in some sense always be taken at face value, whatever the larger dramatic context that ostensibly produces them. The elisions in the part demand that this be the case; the actor may guess at what comes before each cue, but however conscientiously or otherwise he does this, at some level he has to take the cue-words as they are, and infer their most likely meaning. As we shall see, there is much room here for the writer to play upon discrepancies between part-text and play-text, or between the inferences of private rehearsal and the 'proof' of public performance.

And cues too were learned—had to be learned—with the fervency with which a speech was learned, and listened to and for by actors as they listened to no other bit. If a cue were missed, the action would stop, the illusion break, the play grind to a halt. So, given the way in which parts were memorized, it might be expected that the speaker of the cues would be 'named', so that an actor would always know who he was talking to. But as we have seen, cues were generally not attributed in the professional theatre. Again, this looks like making trouble, complicating the play unnecessarily by withholding essential information. But there was no intention specifically to deny the actor what might be useful: it was simply that what was designated as useful then was not what we might think useful now. The fact is that knowing the speaker of the cue-line was not thought to be generally necessary; it was the kind of incidental information only 'careful' university actors and other 'non-professional' players might need. Indeed, we might go further here, and suggest that detailing the cue-speaker was thought positively undesirable.

In a text in which the speaker of the cue-line is *not* named, all cues are 'equalized': they all look roughly the same, and all share equally the burden of giving the actor information about his part. Designate every last cue to a specific interlocutor, and the actor's part is immediately fragmented, its specific integrity ineffably weakened. We may think that naming the cuer allows the cued actor useful knowledge of his changing context. But in fact this strictly limited information is more likely to raise than answer questions. The actor will be prone to have half a mind casting about for the motives or contexts of his interlocutor; he may feel pressure to fit in to this still inadequately given context, or obscurely to defer to it. But if the part does not name the speaker of the cue, then the cues are his cues, for and about *him* and his part. To the actor initially learning from such a part-text, he cannot know whether he is addressed by one person or many, or across a short or a long period of time. The part cannot tell him; he doesn't (for the moment) need to know. Without such answers or the right to ask such questions, all parts seem to be shored up, complete in themselves; without knowing who else you are talking to, you yourself seem always to be at the core of the play.

This is emphatically not to say that the rest of the play becomes a thing of no interest to the actor. But he *begins* with his own part, and always moves out into the world with that as his founding prepossession. Each actor's identification with his part ensures that, as in life, every subject assumes his own existence as the predicate of all else. In turn, two or more actors engaging with each other—each emerging from his own 'solipsistic' process of possessing his part—will help to produce the electric reactivity of living drama. So this particular technology—not naming the cuer—ensures that the event of performance will retain its own urgent immediacy. The things that are happening are happening *now*, in the present; the actor has to stay on edge; he simply cannot afford to doze off in the blithe knowledge that the player currently speaking is not the one who is to give him his cue. Because the cue just *might* come from anyone, the actor must always remain 'on cue'.

The cue is in some senses the most 'fixed' bit of a part. An actor can change the middle of a speech, and only the prompter who follows from a copy of the full text will even notice that he has done so. The cue, by contrast, is inviolable. So we have to consider a system in which not just contextual information for the actor but also anything of permanent importance to the play is put towards the bottom of speeches and into the cue, the playwright all the time acutely aware of the cue's pivotal position in his 'score'. Shakespeare accepts this, and exploits it. Time and again he makes the cue-sign and cue-space resonate with information, instructions, and power.

So for all of its apparent brevity and functionality, the cue inherits an immense burden of mediation. It is the main conduit between one part and another, as it is between one part and the rest of the play. In being co-owned by two actors (the one who speaks the cue and the one who hears it), the cue is the hinge between addressor and addressee. In one sense it belongs to both of them, and is a locus of sharing and co-dependence. In another sense, however, it lays extraordinary focus upon the separation of one mind from another: after all, the cue-phrase may well mean one thing to its speaker and something completely different to its recipient. As we shall see, Shakespeare repeatedly exploits the potential opened up by the 'shared' cue for pressing upon that tender and sometimes explosive point where two minds meet—or fail to meet. Furthermore, we will see how the cue does not necessarily retain a fixed meaning for the cued actor: the cue can suggest one thing in private rehearsal, but reveal something quite different in public performance. In all of these ways the cue is a fundamental tool of Shakespearean characterization, as well as a vehicle and epitome of the dynamic 'dramatic moment'.

To create cued parts, we have had to rely on the 'earliest' Shakespeare texts we could get hold of: the problem being that each text has a different heritage—and none is that early. We use quartos and folios (both when there are two that are considerably different textually), whilst being aware that some of the texts behind the printed ones are nearer and some further from the 'theatrical' text. Naturally, in 'creating' the actor's cued parts we would like, ideally, to be using the text from which the playhouse made its parts. But not only are we obliged to work with texts in the form in which history has handed them to us, we also feel that this is not dissimilar to what happened in the playhouse. As has been detailed in Part I, we know of times when scenes from the playwright's rough copy were made into actors' parts (Daborne's text was divided into parts piecemeal as it was written); we know of times when parts were created before the full play had been approved by the Master of the Revels, and of parts being recalled for alteration even while still being learned by the actors. We know, too, of a full play-text that may have been re-created *out* of actors' parts when the official 'book' was lost (*The Winter's Tale*, some think, was re-formed this way). And we know that 'parts' might reflect revisions that the full text did not: we have detailed the playwright William Percy's manuscript for *The Faery Pastoral*, where the revisions added to the end of the fully scripted play are made not scene by scene, but cue by cue, ready for insertion into the actors' parts.

All of this gives us enough information to know that we will never be able to find which text a playhouse used for parts—because the question 'which text' is basically misconceived. Nor will we ever know which text parts best reflect. So we are content to use both texts near authorial draft (because they are closer to what the playhouse was given) and texts that reflect performance scripts (because they resemble what cued parts became). When there is a choice as to which text to use, we use both, or whichever seems to us most suggestive about likely company practice. Texts that may be cleaned-up scribal copies for presentation and reading are inevitably a problem (though perhaps less so with Shakespeare than with, say, Ben Jonson)—but we can only use the text that we have.

We have also had to make some assumptions about cues. First, we have followed the rough idea, too casual to be quite a rule, that the length of a cue was determined by its sense. We have assumed generally one-, two-, or three-word cues, but allow for the possibility of four-word cues when it is important for the actor to understand a little bit more about what is said to him. This assumption is based on the surviving parts with their one- to three-word cues (discussed in our historical introduction). But it is an assumption, and at appropriate moments we discuss the variant consequences of being given reduced or enlarged cues.

We have also made an assumption about the way in which cued parts were learned. It is clear that actors had to learn their cues with the same assiduity with which they learned their text; they also had to learn cue and subsequent text together as a unit: hear the cue, say the speech that follows it. But one question we have continually come up against is the extent to which the actor learned his text in linear fashion: did he learn the 'order' of the cues, or did he learn the cue–text sandwiches as isolated fragments? Specifically, did he have a sense of sequence, knowing precisely where he was in his text so that he would not respond wrongly if he heard a phrase that was one of his cues elsewhere? We have assumed that, broadly, actors did learn their text linearly—particularly as they often received those texts on 'rolls' that forced linearity on them (it is hard to compare Act I and Act V when they are on a single rolled-up strip of paper). So we think that an actor would usually not respond mistakenly across scenes.

Finally, this is a Section not about facts but about possibilities. Some suggestions seem inevitable, many seem likely, but all strike us as at the very least worth seriously considering.

# 6

# Cues and Characterization

Shakespeare's cues are more than 'empty bells' prompting entrance or speech. This is eloquently suggested by the terms in which Hamlet (in the Folio text), having witnessed the visiting player's passionate performance, castigates his own inactivity:

> What's *Hecuba* to him, or he to *Hecuba*,
> That he should weepe for her? What would he doe,
> Had he the Motive and the Cue for passion [and that for passion Q2]
> That I have?
>
> (TLN 1599–1602)

Hamlet uses 'Cue' here partly in its metaphorical sense, to indicate 'occasion' or 'prompt'. But in a speech that is throughout powerfully about the decorum of acting, the hendiadys of 'the Motive and the Cue' suggests something rather more specific: a motive is a cue, a cue is a motive. The first of these is simple enough. If we have a motive, then we will act on it. It is in the second, however, that Shakespeare plays most explicitly with the materials of actors' parts. That is, the written 'Cue' can itself be a motive. For not only does a cue prompt action (in the form of speech): it can also house the reasons for such action. In the terse address of a cue, then, the actor might locate the forces—internal or external—that compel his character. A similar meta-dramatic suggestiveness distinguishes the following moment in *King Lear*, when Edmund contemptuously notes his brother Edgar's entrance; here it is in Folio (Q places Edgar's entrance in the margin, parallel to Edmund's speech):

> *Enter Edgar*
>
> Pat: he comes like the Catastrophe of the old Comedie:/my Cue is villainous Melancholy, with a sighe like *Tom/o'Bedlam.*——O these Eclipses do portend these divi-/sions. Fa, Sol, La, Me.          (TLN 462–5; lineation ours)

The principal effect of this passage is to predict what will soon occur. Edgar's entrance is the 'cue' for Edmund to change his passion and make a transition into 'villainous Melancholy'; in turn Edgar, 'cued' by the villainy of Edmund, will make his next entrance on to the stage disguised as '*Tom o'Bedlam*'. Shakespeare's use of the word 'cue' is thus radically metamorphic: not merely a prompt to speak or to enter, but the source of a sequence of dramatic mutations or 'divisions' to come: within a single character; between one character and another, from one character to another; between the mere inscription of a phrase ('my Cue is … ') and its acoustic/emotional performance ('with a sighe … '). Edmund's 'Cue' is a site of detonating potential; all sorts of sounds and bodies can be born from it. Shakespeare's actors, we want to suggest, would have known exactly what he meant.

## Early and Inaugurating Cues

Although looking in general at characters' first lines has always been thought to be important, looking at their early or 'inaugurating' cues is never really considered. But it can be profoundly revealing. Of course, the part's first or early cues will usually provide information about the immediate locality of any dialogue and the particular stimulus into speech. But more than that, inaugurating cues are consistently used to instruct the actor in his own basic character, the range of passions his part will entail, and his relationship to the plot. When an actor is anxiously trying to pick up his character from particulars of nuance and address, the cue will give directions for just such matters; the acting direction held in the cue thus often doubles as a pithy characterization, or an implicit commentary upon the scene into which this character has entered. It can work very simply. The Hamlet-part begins like this:

-------------------------------------------- [and] [my] Sonne?
A little more then kin, and less then kinde.

(TLN 244–5)

The cue's questioning of filiality feeds into the first line's quibbling with the semantics of kinship: the actor will thus straightaway draw on the part's emotional taproot of perverted, abrogated, or coerced familial relations. Macbeth starts like this:

—————————————————— [Charme's] [wound] up. *Enter* ...
So foule and faire a day I have not seene.

(TLN 135–6)

The actor will immediately wonder what the relation is between the
wound-up 'charm' and his own entrance. Has his character been conjured
up by black magic? Is he in a spell? Does he possess volition? Furthermore,
the fact that Macbeth clearly does not respond directly to the cue tells the
actor that his character is oblivious to whatever occult forces are at work.
The part is premissed upon discrepant lines of knowledge, and probably of
sight: the audience sees it all; the actor knows something (but not enough);
the character knows still less. This 'objective' condition of bewilderment
is reinforced by the part's first line, with its air of confused fairy-tale,
collapsing opposites, and sensory dysfunction ('I have *not* seene'). The actor
will identify a character entering *in medias res*—mid-conversation, well into
a 'day' that already befuddles his categories of understanding—but into a
situation that he can do nothing about and that will instead act upon him.
    Martius/Coriolanus begins like this:

—————————————————— [hayle,] [Noble] *Martius.*
Thanks. What's the matter you dissentious rogues
That rubbing the poore Itch of your Opinion,
Make your selves Scabs.

(TLN 173–6)

The taciturn 'Thanks', in response to the greeting-cue, will tell the actor
that speech for this character is a burden rather than a pleasure; whether
from pride, obtuseness, or embarrassment, social proprieties in this part
will be assumed rather than observed. In turn—and as the rest of his
opening line attests—fulsome words will be like a disgusted expectoration,
channelled into 'proper' form (here the exactly observed pentameter), but
all the more violent for it. It is the apposition between respectful cue
and contemptuous response—a response not asked for by the cue—that
establishes the part's founding schism.
    So here we have three 'heroes', three first cues and first lines, and all
of them as distinct from each other as they are descriptive of character,
prescriptive of speaking register, and distilling of present and future tensions.
Of course, preliminary cues do not work equally on all parts. If a part's
early speeches are sufficiently coloured and individuating, then its cues
might be relatively empty, or simply there to 'feed' and frame the dialogue.

This is particularly likely for clearly defined types, especially those with idiosyncratic idioms. For example, the actor playing Justice Shallow in *2 Henry IV* hardly needs cues to help him 'place' the role when his first speech (cued by the previous scene's 'Exeunt' of king and company) begins 'Come-on, come-on, come-on: give mee your hand, Sir; give mee your Hand, Sir' (TLN 1534–5). The actor will read through the roll and see speech after speech marked by the same senescent reiterations; when a part is so unchangeable, so awash with its own predetermined discursive manner, the influence of cues upon it is inevitably diminished.

As a rule, the more a character is susceptible to change or to circumstances—the more unfinished or unpredictable that character's reach or remit—the more likely it is that his cues will have a dramatic function beyond that of 'timing' his moments to enter or speak. This is particularly the case with big parts. The principal actors in the company would *always* have expected their cues to be packed full of information, and to work in dialectically suggestive relation to their speeches. A good example of this is the part of Hotspur. His first speech is a forty-line *tour de force*, narrating his recent experience on the battlefield and memorable for its disdainful portrait of the fastidious 'Popingay' (*1 Henry IV*, TLN 351–91). The actor might be tempted to think that his own speeches are all he needs to fill out the role. But—despite initial appearances—this is *not* a part without shades or subtleties. For all the part's rumbustious immediacy, for all the direction and confidence effortlessly given by speeches such as Hotspur's first, it remains a part that must express more than vaulting and careless self-estimation. It is one function of the part's cues to suggest Hotspur's difficult, perhaps shifting relationship to others. And the actor will find this exemplified in the enigmatic conjunction of Hotspur's opening cue with his opening line:

> _____ [not] [my] Sonne.
> My Liege, I did deny no Prisoners.
>
> (TLN 350–1)

We cannot know what was in the original part: perhaps 'Sonne', perhaps 'my Sonne', perhaps 'not my Sonne'. Which ever, when learning the part the actor is very likely to assume that '[not my] Sonne' will be spoken of and by the same man that he now addresses: 'My Liege'—that is, the king. He of course knows that his character is not the king's son; he knows that the king's son is Hal. But the cue—whether it is of two or three

words—will tell the actor that questions of filial and paternal identity are
at the very genesis of his role. If the cue-words speak of Hal, then the
premiss of the Hotspur-role will be competition with this rival 'sonne'; if
they speak of Hotspur, the actor may assume the role will be one in which
the fact that Hotspur is 'not' the king's son will be a live issue, an occasion
for wistful regret or whimsical agitation on the part of either father *or* son.

However, this is not the end of the matter. For even though the cued
part will tell the actor much that he needs to know, Shakespeare often
scripts his parts so as to orchestrate disjunctions or surprises when that
part comes to be played. Learning the part suggests one thing; playing
the part reveals another. So it is here: the cue is *not* in fact given by
the king, but rather by Northumberland, Hotspur's real father. The actor
may well not know this before performance. It is unlikely that a scene
like this received a detailed group rehearsal, or certainly not one that
meticulously placed and directed each actor in the smallest things; it is
similarly unlikely that the Hotspur-actor's part-text would have 'blocked'
such basic things as who to look at or when to turn from one fellow
actor to another. He had to glean what he could from his script, and
for the rest stay alert in performance. And the fact is that the part here
*does* give the Hotspur-actor enough dramaturgical guidance to let him get
going with confidence. His first words are 'My Liege', quite sufficient for
him to know precisely where to look and whom to address: the king. In
performance he will quickly identify how his speech works in context: so,
he is picking up the baton of argument from his father, whose preceding
speech is defending his son's honour against the suspicions of the king.
In this sense, father and son present a united front. At the same time,
and as the actor will see and relish, Hotspur's first speech leaves all others
languishing in its wake: he speaks from vaulting independence far more
than he does from filial obedience. So, as much as the basic acting lines
are clear and powerful—the Percies as one against the king—the actor
of Hotspur should at the same time recognize how the ambiguity of his
inaugurating cue-space (who is speaking/what is it speaking of) is not
so much resolved as fleshed out and dilated: he is cued by an actor, but
addressed by no one; in turn, he addresses the 'highest' character without
being asked to do so; he is 'with' his father but also beyond him; his
opening narrative suggests more an interruption or a trumping of his father
than a continuation of the family theme (certainly it ignores conventional
decorums of deference and precedence); his speech 'drops' his father, or

forgets him—just as the cue-space does. But if Hotspur's speech forsakes his father, it does not follow that the actor does as well. Acting is about much more than position of the body or perspective of the eyes. It is about the actor's mind-in-process, always an embodied thing but very often an invisible one. And crucial to this are suspicions, apprehensions, or apperceptions that the actor intuits well enough, but that he cannot easily manifest or act towards. So it is here with Hotspur's very first exchange. The part's initiating cue, then, encapsulates the character's distinctive function in the play: as the barely governable son of Northumberland, the shadow son of the king, and the rival son to the prince. The very first cue is thus a reminder of the actor's responsibilities to the play, and to the character. It is a part-starting beacon: it should point the actor in the direction, first, of the role's structural and thematic homologies, and second, of the competitiveness, pathos, and disappointment that frame both Hotspur and his relationship to others.

Of course, it is not only the very first cues that are informative. The actor will always check for meaningful sequences of cues. Consider the opening cues of the role of Proteus in *The Two Gentlemen of Verona*:

———————————————————— [to] [love] begin.
———————————————————— [for] [my] successe?
———————————————————— [crost] [the] *Hellespont.*
———————————————————— [swom] [the] *Hellespont.*
———————————————————— [boots] [thee] not.
———————————————————— [by] [folly] vanquished.
———————————————————— [feare] [you'll] prove.

(TLN 13–41)

The cues alone are eloquent: he is engaged to love ('to love begin'); he is being measured against mythic romantic heroes ('crost the *Hellespont*'); he is being mocked for his passion ('by folly vanquished'); and his interlocutor has his own ego and may perhaps prove a rival ('for my successe?'). The train of cues encapsulates the story in which the actor is to engage. The early cues given to Romeo are similarly informative; here is his 'right-hand' cue-text in sequence, shorn of Romeo's speeches, and again assuming up to three words (where possible) as cues:

———————————————————— [Good] [morrow] Cousin
———————————————————— [New] [stroke] nine

————————————————————— [lengthens] [*Romeo's*] houres?
————————————————————— [In] love.
————————————————————— [Of] love.
————————————————————— [rough] [in] proofe.
————————————————————— [I] [rather] weepe.
————————————————————— [good] [hearts] oppression.
————————————————————— [do] [me] wrong.
————————————————————— [that] [you] love?
————————————————————— [tell] [me] who.
————————————————————— [suppos'd] [you] lov'd.
————————————————————— [is] [soonest] hit.
————————————————————— [still] [live] chast?
————————————————————— [thinke] [of] her.
————————————————————— [Examine] [other] beauties.

(TLN 170–236)

These 'inceptive' cues move from acknowledging that Romeo is 'in love' to a brisk, even cynical, narration of the possibilities 'of love'. If you love—and, assuming a three-word cue, the sceptical 'if' is a real presence in cues such as 'suppos'd you lov'd'—then make it count. That is, make her have sex with you. Failing this, move on: 'thinke of her'—who exactly?—and 'Examine other beauties'. The effect of the cues is double. First, they succinctly express the prevailing sexual ethos of Verona's young men. Of course in full text this is already apparent: but the cues here make sure that the Romeo-actor knows the world he is entering. Second, they hint at what the Romeo-actor may *not* know: that the love he will not name is indeed a love he can learn to 'forget'. The cues look ahead to 'her' usurpation by some other beauty—as, indeed, Rosaline will be usurped by Juliet. This introduction to the Romeo-part is typical: in a part's first scene the cues are always working to place, furnish, and frame the character.

Inevitably, trains of cues work in often piquant dialogue with the lines that answer them; here is the opening of the part of Parolles in *All's Well That Ends Well*:

————————————————————— [Who] [comes] heere?

*Enter Parrolles*

————————————————————— [on] [superfluous] follie.

Save you faire Queene.

————————————————————— [And] [you] Monarch.

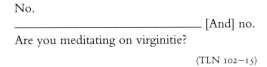

No.
_____ [And] no.
Are you meditating on virginitie?

(TLN 102–15)

The first cue that sets Parolles on to speak—probably 'superfluous follie'—sums up both his qualities and his situation: a born fool, of no use,
suspended between entrance and speech. Here the scripting may again
be playing upon discrepancies between rehearsal and performance. The
Parolles-actor may not learn until performance that after his entrance cue
('Who comes heere?'), he must hover in silent limbo as Helena speaks
seven more lines, in which she fleshes out for audience and player alike
the character of Parolles: 'notorious Liar' (TLN 105), 'a great way foole'
(TLN 106), 'solie a coward' (TLN 106). Parolles is on-stage, dumbly
listening, with his part allowing him no response to these insults. So he
stands inert or impotent, awaiting his ever more appropriate speaking cue,
'superfluous follie'. His next two cues, '[And] [you], Monarch' and '[And]
no', work against each other, like glancing, insulting repartee. Together
they flank Parolles' 'no', playing off one another by predicting and annotating the range of the part (a monarch of his moment? *No*). They thus
complete a brisk sketch of null self-arrogation and absurd pretence—one
that the part will duly flesh out. The part-script, memorized by the actor, tells him most of what he needs to know; the act of performing
reveals unexpected marginality and small but wounding humiliations. The
artfully delayed flow of information to the actor—combined with the
character's already evident 'type' as overweening windbag—is likely to
manufacture precisely the attention-hungry, garrulous pretension that the
part demands.

Similar orchestrations mark Lady Capulet's early cues and speeches; she
has a single line in her first scene, but it is her second scene that really
establishes the part:

_____ [of] [mine] owne.
*Enter Capulets Wife and Nurse.*
Nurse wher's my daughter? call her forth to me.
_____ [is] [your] will?
This is the matter: Nurse give me leave awhile, we/must talke in
secret. Nurse come back againe, I have re-/membred me, thou'se
heare our councell. Thou knowest/my daughter's of a pretty age.

——————————————————————— [unto] [an] houre.
Shee's not fourteene.
——————————————————————— [to] [*Lammas*] tide?
A fortnight and odde dayes.
——————————————————————— [and] [said] I.
Inough of this, I pray thee hold thy peace.
——————————————————————— [have] [my] wish.
Marry that marry is the very theame
I came to talke of, tell me daughter *Juliet,*
How stands your disposition to be Married?
——————————————————————— [from] [thy] teat.
Well thinke of marriage now, yonger then you
Heere in *Verona*, Ladies of esteeme,
Are made already Mothers. By my count
I was your Mother, much upon these yeares
That you are now a Maide, thus then in briefe:
The valiant *Paris* seekes you for his love.
——————————————————————— [man] [of] waxe.
*Veronas* Summer hath not such a flower.
——————————————————————— [a] [very] flower.
What say you, can you love the Gentleman?

(TLN 350–425; prose lineation ours)

The way the lines and cues interrelate changes half-way through. For the
first half, it is clear enough that Lady Capulet addresses the Nurse; for
the second half (from 'tell me daughter…'), it is similarly clear that she is
addressing her daughter. The actor learning the part may not know what
intervenes to mark this transition from one addressee to the other (it is
in fact the long reminiscence of the Nurse about feeding and weaning
the baby Juliet). Once again, the cued part suggests one story-line—a
hesitant mother asserting authority over her daughter—whilst the full play
suggests quite another—the baleful absence of any such authority. The
actor will have identified certain distinctive character traits from the lady's
own speeches: something brusque and peremptory, at once impatient
and strangely whimsical; a mixture of impatient command and sudden
apology; the interlacing of declaratory statement and something close to
malapropism, as she has to correct herself, or stumbles unintentionally
upon word-play. But it is only when we identify the 'cue-joke' that
we can make the connection between Lady Capulet's nervy manner
and her domestic situation. Read in part-terms, it looks as though the
daughter responds to the mother's cues. But she does not: again and

again it is the Nurse who says the things that the actor of Lady Capulet must at first have assumed were to come from her child. The comedy, exasperation, and fear of sabotage are all mutually stoked: felt by the actor, and so all the more present to the audience. Shakespeare here exploits the cue's ability to control the emotional flow and orchestrate the chain of command. If the cue is not taken up, then her power is in abeyance.

The first scene in the part of Mercutio is a good example of how cues can be about the cued character as much as about the context in which he acts:

                                             [beare] [the] light.
Nay gentle *Romeo* we must have you dance.
                                             [I] [cannot] move.
You are a Lover, borrow *Cupids* wings,
And soare with them above a common bound.
                                             [pricks] [like] thorne.
If love be rough with you, be rough with love,
Pricke love for pricking, and you beat love downe,
Give me a Case to put my visage in,
A Visor for a Visor, what care I
What curious eye doth quote deformities:
Here are the Beetle-browes shall blush for me.
                                             [I] [am] done.
Tut, duns the Mouse, the Constables owne word,
If thou art dun, weele draw thee from the mire.
Or save your reverence love, wherein thou stickest
Up to the eares, come we burne day-light ho.
                                             [that's] [not] so.
I meane sir I delay,
We wast our lights in vaine, lights, lights, by day;
Take our good meaning, for our Judgement sits
Five times in that, ere once in our fine [five?] wits.
                                             [wit] [to] go.
Why may one aske?
                                             [dreame] [to] night.
And so did I.
                                             [what] [was] yours?
That dreamers often lye.
                                             [dreame] [things] true.
O then I see Queene Mab hath beene with you.
... This is she

——————————————————————— [talk'st] [of] nothing.
      True, I talke of dreames…

(TLN 465–547)

The cue-phrases give the information 'Mercutio' needs to place his part. The cues which the actor receives divide broadly into three types: comments from Mercutio's addressor about himself ('I cannot move' and 'I am done'); direct questions or responses to Mercutio ('that's not so', 'what was yours?', 'talk'st of nothing'); and statements that offer a more general picture or proposition whose provenance and trajectory are unclear ('beare the light', 'pricks like thorne', 'wit to go', 'dreame to night', 'dreame things true'). All three work very precisely toward focusing the Mercutio-part. This is true even of those cues that are self-evidently about his addressor (who in both cases is Romeo). For these two early cues set up Mercutio to be their counter and opposite: if the interlocutor (Romeo) is 'done', Mercutio has barely begun; if he 'cannot move', Mercutio will be all animation. This is the context for Mercutio's impatient responses to Romeo's abject cues: both times he refuses Romeo's sense, transforming the lover's somnolence into category-defying activity (a flying body, a burning day-light) in which sexual abandon (flying Cupid, love sticking up to the ears/arse) is overwhelmed by imaginative intensity.

But we should also see how the cues themselves establish Mercutio's peculiarly antagonistic relationship to others. It will be clear from Mercutio's responses to the cues that a principal aspect of his role will be its provoking, oppositional, ribbing quality. His first five speeches are all to some degree rebuking his addressee: teasing him, correcting him, bullying him with fanciful or whimsical imperatives. In each case, the cue explicitly draws the response, suggesting that this is a part akin to that of a clown. But Mercutio's sights are elsewhere. It quickly becomes apparent that brisk repartee does not begin to satisfy or define the role. His conversation is far less *social* than this, and far more obliquely internalized. This is clear enough from the sudden transition he makes from hectoring advice to the lovesick Romeo ('Pricke love for pricking…') to unprompted dwelling upon his own ugliness ('what care I | What curious eye doth quote deformities'). But what we need to see is how the early cues will already have helped to make apparent this disjunction between public aggression and private insecurity. The tension between the subject of the cue-words in full-play-form and the subject of the cue-words in part-form illustrates the performative value of having supposedly neutral, context-free cues. All the cues as received describe or comment upon Mercutio, even when their function within the full scene or speech has nothing to do with him: bear the light, prick like thorn, wit to go, dream tonight. None of these cues is in fact talking 'about' Mercutio; in the full play-text they are all about Romeo, as the hero bemoans the pain of love. Nonetheless, they almost meticulously place Mercutio, like the four sides of the frame in which he works: he brings to the group light, prickliness, wit, and dream, and not so much one followed by the other as one *in* the other. As briskly accumulating 'cues' for a part, they couldn't in a sense be clearer.

As the examples of Lady Capulet and Mercutio suggest, the 'surprises' that can lurk in cues are not limited to producing merely comic mistakes, resentment, or exasperation. The discrepant perspectives that can crop up between between cued part and full play, and between the inferences of rehearsal and the experience of performance, are strikingly explored in all of Shakespeare's tragedies. The Othello-part, for example, begins with a carefully worked asymmetry of part-information to play context, seeding the dissociation of character from his social world. Whereas the full text dwells remorselessly upon the scandal of Othello and Desdemona's elopement and love-making, the Othello-part's first scene is studiously vague about anything other than Othello's conviction of self-merit and the fact that he loves Desdemona. He boasts a few times of his indispensable virtues, and he breaks up a fight. But, as to the substance of any threat, Othello's lines offer precious little information: 'Is it they?' (TLN 238), 'What is the Newes?' (TLN 243), 'What is the matter, thinke you?' (TLN 247), 'Tis well I am found by you: | I will but spend a word in the house, | And goe with you' (TLN 257–9), 'Have with you' (TLN 267), 'Holla, stand there' (TLN 272), 'Whether will you that I goe | To answere this your charge?' (TLN 303–4). A similar deferring of content characterizes the cues that the Othello-actor gets. For an opening scene, the cues are unusually *devoid* of usable information concerning Othello's character or function:

| | |
|---|---|
| _____ | [under] [the] Ribbes. |
| _____ | [give] [him] Cable. |
| _____ | [best] [go] in. |
| _____ | [I] [thinke] no. |
| _____ | [on] [the] instant. |
| _____ | [search] [you] out. |

——————————————————————— [will] [you] go?
——————————————————————— [to] [bad] intent.
——————————————————————— [am] [for] you.
——————————————————————— [at] [his] perill.
——————————————————————— [thee] [to] answer.

(TLN 208–307)

These cues vividly communicate a sense of imminent threat, but its source or content is as yet unspecified. Othello is somehow under siege, or being called to account, but why or for what is left curiously hanging. Once again, cued part and full text are telling different stories; as always, these differences exist *only* for the actor, and are only recognized by the actor in those initial, self-inaugurating, role-distilling moments when the actor first morphs into the character.

What will the Othello-actor experience? First, he will see that he speaks a rhetoric of unassailable security; indeed, Othello may seem like an actor, confident that his role is thoroughly conned and possessed and that his part-script is not about to surprise him ('Were it my Cue to fight, I should have knowne it without a Prompter' (TLN 302–3)). But the actor may well equally identify in his part an objective ignorance of the facts. For all of his physical and oratorical authority—and the part's first scene is written in such a way that the actor can hardly *not* assume an air of easy invincibility—the Othello-actor must also feel something more chill and worrying. Perhaps he will recognize the predictive menace of the cues (early cues, like dramatic prophecies, pretty much always come true) and the troublingly unanswered questions of his part-script; perhaps he will learn—and then perform—his next scene emboldened by the character's assurance that he is beyond untoward surprise; perhaps he will genuinely not understand quite what awaits, and so go more or less sleep-walking into battle. In either of these last two situations, the actor shares the character's fatal obliviousness—and so prepares to share the horrible surprises that lie ahead. The opening cue–speech relationship is always crucial in determining the fit between actor and character: and part of this fit can be in *not* fully preparing the actor for what will unfold.

The opening of the Lear-part shows a different manipulation of the same techniques. Lear enters to some part of 'The King is comming' (TLN 36), and his first cue to speak is Gloucester's '[shall,] [my] lord' (TLN 40). The attitude required of the actor appears clear and defined: Lear is confident in his kingship; his behaviour is not in question. However, this very quickly changes—but the change is one for which the actor learning the part will be prepared. So he should immediately notice a worrying equivocation in the cues he has been given for this opening scene.

> ————————————————— [and] [be] silent
> Of all these bounds even from this Line, to this,
> With shadowie Forrests, and with Champains rich'd
> With plenteous Rivers, and wide-skirted Meades
> We make thee Lady. To thine and *Albanies* issues
> Be this perpetuall. What sayes our second Daughter?
> Our deerest *Regan,* wife of *Cornwall?*
> ————————————————— [then] [my] tongue.
> To thee, and thine hereditarie ever,
> Remaine this ample third of our faire Kingdome ...
>
> (TLN 67–86)

Whereas in full script, as it were in the ears of the world, Lear hears Goneril's 'I love you' (TLN 66) and Regan's 'deere Highnesse love' (TLN 81), in part-terms the actor will see 'be silent' and 'my tongue': Cordelia's very differently tuned words. Even though Cordelia's passages are spoken as 'asides' on-stage, they directly cue Lear in his part, as the full text for this passage shows:

> GONERIL.   Sir, I love you more then word can weild y matter,
>               Deerer then eye-sight, space, and libertie, ...
>               A love that makes breath poore, and speech unable,
>               Beyond all manner of so much I love you.
> CORDELIA.  What shall *Cordelia* speake? Love, and be silent.
> LEAR.        Of all these bounds even from this Line, to this, ...
>               We make thee Lady. To thine and *Albanies* issues
>               Be this perpetuall. What sayes our second Daughter?
>               Our deerest *Regan,* wife of *Cornwall?*
> REGAN.      I am made of that selfe-mettle as my Sister,
>               ... I professe
>               My selfe an enemy to all other joyes,
>               Which the most precious square of sense professes,
>               And finde I am alone felicitate
>               In your deere Highnesse love.
> CORDELIA.  Then poore *Cordelia,*
>               And yet not so, since I am sure my love's
>               More ponderous then my tongue.

LEAR.        To thee, and thine hereditarie ever,
             Remaine this ample third of our faire Kingdome ...

(TLN 60–86)

There is thus a split between the courtly to-and-fro of the scene and the internalized to-and-fro of the part. But the apparent contradiction is in fact absolutely faithful to the scene's emotional and political truth. The 'public' cues (from the bad daughters) are indeed dangerously equivocal: the doubts and hesitancies of the part's 'private' cues thus interpret for the Lear-actor what the Lear-character is oblivious to. An attentive actor, then, will try to convey incipient doubt or fear 'inside' whatever arrogance or bluster his titular authority (as registered in the flattering 'public' cues) requires. As it happens, the cues given to Lear will very swiftly declare his abrupt loss of security—'[Nothing] [my] Lord' (TLN 93), '[Nothing]' (TLN 95), '[more] [nor] less' (TLN 99), 'thou dost evill' (TLN 180). But the stark distinctions between the 'private' and 'public' cues have already told the actor that within this 'performed' authority lurks falsehood, embarrassment, and fatal misjudgement.

These examples of parts' early cues show just how attentive to per-formance, and how cross-textually layered, are Shakespeare's strategies of characterization. Writing in and for parts is here integral. Shakespeare clearly wants his actors to share in the surprise and tentativeness of the experiences he unfolds for his characters. This is, indeed, the surest way of achieving the requisite immediacy of successful theatre. And a fundamental method Shakespeare uses for doing so is to make the information offered by the cued part tell a slightly differently-angled story from the simultaneously unfolding 'whole' scene. We see here how cues can help achieve the 'psycholog-ical' sophistication, and that almost tangible reality of feeling, for which Shakespeare has been so often celebrated. Cues become almost the glands of the part, small nodal points that structure and serve the larger organism, synthesizing, secreting, distributing whatever chemistry is here at work.

## Transitional Cues

Entrance cues are often—and understandably—portentous. But so are many cues that mark important shifts in the definition or development of a character—moments when something new 'enters' the purlieu of the particular role, when the character's presence or orientation is up for grabs, or when sudden alterations are in the air. Above all, parts had to cue 'transitions' between one passion and another. Such transitions are almost always marked by rhetorical and prosodic shifts (see Part IV). But cues were another vital way of indicating—and commenting upon—abrupt changes in temperament. For an actor learning a part's twists and turns and, more than that, developing a sufficiently sensitive critical attitude to them, such interpretive aids were indispensable.

So, even apparently straightforward types do not always stay on the same tracks throughout: and if a comic type does indeed alter, then so too will the use that the part makes of cues. This is true, for instance, of Malvolio in *Twelfth Night*. The part's first two cues—'[he] [not] mend?' (TLN 365–6), '[to] [that] *Malvolio*?' (TLN 374)—set up two speeches of scornful contempt for his rival household underlings. The cues are not so much independently meaningful as situationally functional. But Malvolio will go on to endure experiences that go beyond his original remit as a comic butt. In the 'torture scene', the character's definition changes, as measured by his relationship both to other characters and to the audience. And this alteration is pointed up by the cues, which cease to be merely comic tee-ups, and instead render the external situation which Malvolio resists:

Who cals there?
_____ [*Malvolio*] [the] Lunaticke.
Sir Topas, sir Topas, good sir Topas goe to my Ladie.
_____ [said] [M.] Parson.
Sir Topas, never was man thus wronged, good sir Topas do not thinke I am mad: they have layde mee heere in hideous darknesse.
_____ [house] [is] darke?
As hell sir Topas.
_____ [thou] [of] obstruction?
I am not mad sir Topas, I say to you this house is darke.
_____ [in] [their] fogge.
I say this house is as darke as Ignorance, thogh Ignorance were as darke as hell; and I say there was never man thus abus'd, I am no more madde then you are, make the triall of it in any constant question.
_____ [concerning] [Wilde-]fowle?
That the soule of our grandam, might happily inhabite a bird.
_____ [of] [his] opinion?
I thinke nobly of the soule, and no way aprove his opinion.

(TLN 2006–41)

Malvolio knows immediately how he is being treated: his first cue is 'Lunaticke'. And the actor learning this part will quickly pick up on the basic situation: his early speeches reiterate that he is in 'hideous darknesse', enforced by cues of 'darke', 'obstruction', and 'fogge'. This is evidently a mental as well as a physical darkness. Meanwhile the actor's lines repeatedly tell him that Malvolio is 'not mad'. So he knows that he is accused, and, as his part illustrates, that he is not actually insane. Much as the actor will pick up straightaway upon a context of humiliation, Malvolio's own take upon the situation, as portrayed in the part, is resistant, and more indignant than afraid. The actor receiving such a part has his defiance 'cued' at the start of the scene. This newly appositional, dialogical relationship between cue and speech marks the movement of the part out of straitened 'type' into an unpredicted manner of being.

We see similarly how cues can be used to signal transitions in a character's disposition or destiny in Romeo's fourth scene in *Romeo and Juliet*. He enters with Benvolio, Mercutio, and five or six other maskers. His cues are these:

———————————————— [to] [happy] daies.

*Enter Romeo, Mercutio, Benvolio, with five or sixe other Maskers, Torch-bearers.*

———————————————— [and] [be] gone.
———————————————— [have] [you] dance.
———————————————— [a] [common] bound.
———————————————— [a] [tender] thing.
———————————————— [to] [his] legs.

(TLN 452–87)

The cues give us the basic picture: they are broadly choric, building up the sense that the masked ball will propel Romeo into some unforeseen 'bound' or 'dance'. Romeo is being egged into action by his friends. This focus shifts when Romeo refuses to dance, saying 'Ile be a Candle-holder and looke on, | The game was nere so faire, and I am done' (I. iv. 37–8; TLN 491–2). From this point onwards the cues Romeo receives cease to have *him* as their clear focus:

———————————————— [burne] [day-light] ho.
———————————————— [our] [fine] wits.
———————————————— [may] [one] aske?
———————————————— [so] [did] I.
———————————————— [dreamers] [often] lye.

[This] [is] she.

[come] [too] late.

(TLN 496–556)

The Romeo-actor receives a series of instrumental cues, which do little more than oil the brisk conversation. But, on a deeper level, the phrases also signify that Romeo will no longer be 'cued' by his friends. This is signalled, in particular, by a cue that is, again, more striking out of its immediate dialogical context than it is in it: 'This is she.' For whereas the previous five cues have been traded line-by-line, the Romeo-actor will have to wait for about *forty* lines before hearing this cue. Yet the actor does not have in his script either the long wait or the reason for it—that Mercutio is delivering his Queen Mab *tour de force*. Mercutio possesses the stage during his 'Mab' fantasy, but, as the cue shows, he has emphatically not possessed the hero. Whereas everyone else may be watching Mercutio in astonished awe, the Romeo-actor has to retreat into a lengthy, suspended, and uncertain silence waiting for the words 'This is she'.

Furthermore, although 'This is she' actually refers to Mab, for the Romeo-actor the 'she' may well set up an expectation that some woman— probably the long-awaited Juliet—is going to enter the scene. But Juliet does not appear. The 'she' turns out to be his friend's grandstanding flight of fancy. Consequently, Romeo's irritation at Mercutio's endless speech—'Peace, peace, *Mercutio*, peace', and, tellingly, 'Thou talk'st of nothing' (TLN 545–6)—can be all the more pressingly felt by the actor. The part encourages the actor to respond with appropriately urgent exasperation, though not necessarily for the appropriate reason. In turn, because the 'she' of Romeo's returning cue is not present on-stage, it allows the very next cue he receives, 'come too late', similarly to invoke his absent other half. It is precisely because the cues are *not* satisfied entirely by immediate circumstances that they gather this predictive capability. The cue-text and full text are working in a subtly distinctive contrapuntal fashion. The effect is to point—for both the actor and the audience—Romeo's decisive entrance into destiny: one that 'is she' will also, fatally, come 'too late'.

## Recurring Cues

We have seen how the cues that come early in a part often help the actor to 'characterize' the part he is playing. A variation upon this is the cue that crops up time after time: what we will call a 'recurring cue'. The simple fact of intensive repetition argues for importance: whatever the cue 'says', the actor will assume that it carries essential information concerning his character's station, circumstances, or preoccupations. It might draw attention to a specific context, in particular one that presses or harasses (for example, the recurring cue of 'S/sir Topas' given to the Malvolio-actor): in such cases the relentlessness of the recurring cue indicates a world pressing in upon the cued character, and so the world against or towards which the actor must direct his acting.

A distinctive example of a recurring cue is the cue which is a simple term of address, such as a proper name or a title. Shakespeare is in fact sparing with these, probably so as to ensure against confusion (the danger being that the responding actor, hearing the 'same' cue, will come in with the wrong—earlier or later—speech). But a remarkable exception to this is the part of Hamlet. Not only is this the longest role in Shakespeare, but it has by far the greatest occurrence of any single cue-phrase. Perhaps suggesting a recoil against the insolence or presumption of the part's first two cues, 'my sonne', and 'on you', the part is saturated with the cue 'my Lord'. In different scenes with Ophelia (III. ii) and Polonius (II. ii) the actor gets this cue no less than nine times in a row;[1] with Horatio, with the Players, with Rosencrantz and Guildenstern, 'my lord' crops up as almost every second cue. Obviously the cue defers to Hamlet's princely status, just as the absence of the cue will defer to the status of Hamlet's addressees. So, the socially 'superior' King and Queen do not cue Hamlet with 'my Lord'; the simple absence of the ubiquitous cue is itself a character note for the actor, perhaps encouraging a clipped and bitter tone, a less forthcoming façade (unless instructed differently, as he palpably is in the 'closet' scene with Gertrude). Elsewhere, the 'my Lord' cue necessarily defers to the Hamlet-actor's *performance*, and to something like the Hamlet-character's self-sufficiency. It cannot be that this effectively 'meaningless' cue is truly prompting him into action; instead, the springs of thought and action are to be found within. This in turn links the 'my Lord' cue to Hamlet's intensely self-centring, even solipsistic qualities. The cue is particular prevalent when Hamlet is teasing others, and thus playing 'to' himself: the cue works as effective permission, almost an imprimatur, of an actorly *tour de force*. But even 'To be or not to be' is thus cued: on the one hand, suggesting the 'my Lord' cue as a portal into self-dialogue; on the other hand, provoking the hoary old question whether the actor will know for sure if he is alone or not. It is noticeable that the 'my Lord' cues abate only when Hamlet is temporarily taken 'outside' himself by thrilling or terrifying action: with the Ghost, when he hears of the players, when he confronts his mother, or in the fencing match, during which events the cues become much more immediately descriptive.

There is a fascinating variation upon Hamlet's 'calling-card' cue in the part of Polonius. For this part's recurring cue is also 'my Lord'—but not only as a cue he receives, but as a cue he many times gives. First, here are the lines spoken to him when he is on stage with Reynaldo, whose part would have looked like this:

| | |
|---|---|
| ——————————————————— [these] [notes] *Reynoldo.* | |
| I will **my Lord.** | |
| ——————————————————— [Of] [his] behaviour. | |
| **My Lord**, I did intend it. | |
| ——————————————————— [marke] [this] *Reynoldo?* | |
| I, very well **my Lord.** | |
| ——————————————————— [youth] [and] liberty. | |
| As gaming **my Lord.** | |
| ——————————————————— [goe] [so] farre. | |
| **My Lord** that would dishonour him. | |
| ——————————————————— [of] [generall] assault. | |
| But **my** good **Lord.** | |
| ——————————————————— [you] [doe] this? | |
| I **my Lord**, I would know that. | |
| ——————————————————— [man] [and] Country. | |
| Very good **my Lord.** | |
| ——————————————————— [did] [I] leave? | |
| At closes in the consequence: | |
| At friend, or so, and Gentleman. | |
| ——————————————————— [have] [you] not? | |
| **My Lord** I have. | |
| ——————————————————— [fare] [you] well. | |
| Good **my Lord.** | |
| ——————————————————— [in] [your] selfe. | |
| I shall **my Lord.** | |
| ——————————————————— [plye] [his] Musicke. | |
| Well, **my Lord.**          *Exit.* | |

(TLN 860–969)

The Polonius-actor, on-stage with Reynaldo, will have repeatedly heard 'my Lord'; he will already have seen that the cue-words 'my Lord' occur

eight times in quick succession. Obviously this tells the actor that his
addressee is of a lower rank; it places the character in a world sensitive to
such matters; and it readies the actor to play command, ascendance, and
irresistible self-interest. Repeatedly cued by 'my Lord', the actor is bound
to feel that *his* character is the one being deferred to, and more than that,
that his character must be, in some sense, the subject. By teeing him up so
overtly, the recurring cue recommends that Polonius's speeches become a
*performance* of his eminence, his wisdom, and his basic command of address.
The Polonius-actor will then notice a sudden change with the simultaneous
exit of Reynaldo and entrance of Ophelia; his cues are now these:

———————————————— [beene] [so] affrighted.
———————————————— [comes] [before] me.
———————————————— [do] [feare] it.
———————————————— [light] [on] me.
———————————————— [accesse] [to] me.

(TLN 971–1007)

Instead of obsequiously deferring to Polonius, the cues now speak immediately of his daughter's experience: 'beene so affrighted', 'comes before
me', 'do feare it', 'light on me', 'accesse to me'. This alone demands a
complete shift in the Polonius-actor's manner: a quickening switch into
busy urgency. The previous scene's recurring cues of 'my Lord', then, can
be seen to work as an allegory and agent of Polonius's complacency: they
encourage an inert preening and inflation of self, feeding into the decadence
and redundancy of his intended surveillance of Laertes abroad; this is swiftly
punctured by the sudden transition, heralded by the cues, into the genuine
stuff of love and lives. But the transition is not a simple wake-up call,
out of vicarious meddling and into direct paternal concern. For whilst the
subject of this second phase of cues is emphatically Ophelia, the subject of
Polonius's *speeches* is the prince Hamlet: 'Mad for thy Love?' (TLN 981),
'What said he?' (TLN 983), 'This is the very extasie of Love' (TLN 999),
'That hath made him mad' (TLN 1008). In other words, Shakespeare is
writing the part so as to embed one narrative in the cues—proposing a
radical shift from oneself to another—and a subtly different narrative in
the speeches—a much less radical shift from prying into his son's affairs to
prying into Hamlet's.

   This, then, is the context for the Polonius-part's next two quick transitions: first a scene with the king and queen when all he says is puffed up

with self-regard ('My Liege, and Madam, to expostulate | What Majestie should be ... ' (TLN 1113–14), 'What do you thinke of me?' (TLN 1158), 'Hath there bene such a time, I'de fain know that, | That I have possitively said, 'tis so, | When it prov'd otherwise?' (TLN 1183–5)), and then to a scene with Hamlet in which—as the actor will clearly see—this obsessive conceit ricochets back as now servile mockery:

Do you know me, **my Lord?**

_____ [y'are] [a] Fishmonger.

Not I **my Lord.**

_____ [honest] [a] man.

Honest, **my Lord?**

_____ [of] [two] thousand.

That's very true, **my Lord.**

_____ [you] [a] daughter?

I have **my Lord.**

_____ [Friend] [looke] too't.

How say you by that? Still harping on my daugh-/ter: yet he knew me not at first; he said I was a Fishmon-/ger: he is farre gone, farre gone: and truly in my youth,/I suffred much extreamity for love: very neere this. Ile/speake to him againe. What do you read **my Lord?**

_____ [Words,] [words,] words.

What is the matter, **my Lord?**

_____ [Betweene] who?

I meane the matter you meane, **my Lord.**

_____ [could] [go] backward.

Though this be madnesse, yet there is Method in't: will you walke out of the ayre **my Lord?**

_____ [Into] [my] Grave?

Indeed that is out o'th' Ayre:/How pregnant (sometimes) his Replies are?/A happinesse,/That often Madnesse hits on,/Which Reason and Sanitie could not/So prosperously be deliver'd of./I will leave him,/And sodainely contrive the meanes of meeting/Betweene him, and my daughter./**My Honourable Lord,** I will most humbly/Take my leave of you.

_____ [life,] [my] life.

Fare you well **my Lord.**

_____ [tedious] [old] fooles.

You goe to seeke **my Lord** _Hamlet_; there hee is.

(TLN 1210–63; lineation ours)

The actor will identify the recurring cue of 'my Lord' as a simple joke 'against' his character. In one scene the cues impose servility upon another;

now they impose it upon himself. In between the two, the character is seen to miss the chance to leave busy obsequiousness behind and genuinely to engage with another's pain. Polonius never escapes the 'quotation marks' of these cues, whether given or received (and nor in a sense do Ophelia and Hamlet: his daughter remains his sacrifice for a greater service; the prince remains his reactive, reflexive, and ultimately deadly nemesis).

# Conclusion

Through carefully distributed, sequentially unfolding cues, Shakespeare can be seen to be purposively scripting cross-purposes, lateral recognitions, and meta-performative surprises. In turn, his actors' experience of these things helps to produce on-stage something that closely resembles self-sufficient existential identity. In the disjunctions and discrepancies between play-text and part-text, in the false starts and mistaken attributions that ensue, Shakespeare is often scripting a battle for understanding, definition, and recognition that carefully reconstitutes the most elemental challenges of achieving sustainable selfhood.

This is not to propose a straightforward contiguity between the actor's ego and emotions and the character's. It is all to do with the different forms in which the to-be-acted text circulates. The play in performance has no less constitutive authenticity than the cued parts or the full [prompt] book. The playwright wrote all of them—wrote for all of them—and a crucial element of this is the recognition that play and part allowed for simultaneous but differing narrative lines. The play-text is telling one story; the part-text is telling another. If we add to this the likelihood that different part-texts are telling different stories at the same time, then we might be getting closer to the ways in which this apparently primitive technology helped to facilitate plays that have for so long been celebrated for their sustaining of multiple perspectives, and for their presentation of characters whose presence seems so real as to exist beyond the performance that frames them. If the actor in some sense has to fight for his presence, for integrity, coherence, or acknowledgement, then it is likely that the 'character' thereby embodied will give off the sparks of this authentic struggle. The fact of each role's isolation—that the part is written, transcribed, learned, and acted as a separate unit—helps to ensure the character's claims to independence. But more than that, it helps to ensure the free-standing status of character itself: in other words, the part makes a claim to its own ontological integrity. This apparently primitive manner of textual circulation becomes a crucial motor of the affective power, integrity, and sophistication of Shakespeare's plays.

# 7
# Waiting and Suddenness: The Part in Time

As we have foreshadowed in the discussion of early cues, a simple but important fact about cues is that the actor would often not know how long the gap in time or action is between one cue and the next. When the cueing actor is not named, such ellipses become all the more embedded, and all the more influential to the way parts are both written and performed.

For perhaps the starkest thing about parts remains the gaps and truncations that inevitably scar the text. One result is that the part can function in simultaneously distinct time schemes. The scenes of a play unfold at a certain pace; the scenes of a part unfold coterminously, but with a much more accordion-like rhythm, as the speeches and action intervening between the player's particular speeches are squeezed out of the picture. There is nothing metaphysically remote about the different time schemes of part and play. It is a present and working fact for the actor whether he is learning, rehearsing, or performing his role. Shakespeare was an actor. He earned his stripes by acting parts that, of necessity, usually exclude the reasons why a particular mood, attitude, or action is arrived at. He knew the real force of suddenly experienced emotion that parts could give to changes that might otherwise seem fickle or improvised: sudden shifts in passion, sudden recognitions, sudden alterations of state, place, or mentality. It hardly matters how long the interim is between one manner and another; it does not matter how long the scene is: for the actor any such change is *learned* as abrupt and even violent, quite possibly under-motivated, quite possibly inexplicable—but all the same inevitable, predestined, implacably one's own.

Shakespeare's sense of what a role might be is conditioned by his experience of playing parts, and so by a repeated confrontation with just such suddenness. Through learning parts he must often have felt that strange nervousness that comes from knowing that 'something' is coming but not quite knowing what or when it will arrive. He must often have experienced the intense projecting into hypothetical possibilities, as the actor imagines reasons or motives or provocations for a given action. Equally, he will have known the anxiety that his speculations might simply be wrong and, as the line between actor and character grows ever thinner, that he may end up fatally marooned in a context where everyone else seems safely at home. The actor's exclusion from much of the play's working machinery will always prompt an alert and eager gathering of any clue that might fill out his place and purpose. Like Autolycus at the fair, the actor must be a 'snapper-up of unconsidered trifles' (*The Winter's Tale*, TLN 1693–4); like Hamlet at the play, he must 'eate the Ayre, promise-cramm'd' (*Hamlet*, TLN 1949–50). For in a sense, working in parts is always about 'making minds up'. Of course this means the inventing of dramatic personae by author and actor. But it also means the actor's progression—or occasionally his leap—from ignorance to awareness, from doubt to commission, or from mental prevarication to physical singularity. In time, the part-technology, and the powerfully expressive effects it allows, begins to provide the nuts and bolts of a whole range of Shakespeare's characters, from the thinnest 'type' to the most layered and lifelike persona.

## Ellipses and Plotting a Part

If an actor wants to construct a coherent emotional journey, then he needs to find his signposts and pathways from the pock-marked script he is given. Shakespeare of course knows this, just as he knows that the actor, especially of principal parts, will expect a journeying passage of this kind. Of course we cannot glibly assume that the part offers a pre-novelistic, naturalizing notion of grounded and rounded individuality. But it may well be that learning from parts—requiring a frequently isolated and in many ways solipsistic process of unfolding, unrolling, and accumulating information—makes it more rather than less likely that the actor will want to search out a meaningful self-pilgrimage.

Here we can propose two basic ways in which a part's ellipses and abbreviations might be used by the actor. The first is when things happen abruptly within a contracted or concertinaed span of space or time: this is the experience of learning from the part and plotting the character's journey from the written role. In this case the part-script possesses its own pithy coherence, designed by the playwright to accentuate what is wanted, exclude what is not, and so allow the actor to furnish in performance the required manner and attitude for the part. The actor may well gain a basic security from the fact of his relative ignorance; indeed, there are many parts that, in terms of self-motivation or self-definition, work in blissful exclusion of the rest of the play. This is particularly true of any role whose function is to remain throughout in a broadly similar key or humour (that is, basically a 'type'). The actor of a type will know at once the sort of part he is being asked to play; all of his speeches will be written in an identifiable mode, to be delivered in a consistent register. This is obviously true of a clown-role such as Dogberry in *Much Ado*, in which every single speech is in malapropizing prose; but no less true, for example, of any number of soldiers, noblemen, or prelates in the history plays, including quite distinctive parts such as the Lord Chief Justice in *Henry IV* or Canterbury in *Henry V*. It is crucial to the plays that such personae remain (for better or worse) unchanging; there is enough mutation and metamorphosis going on amongst the more 'central' figures. So, even if such character-types are occasionally bested or teased or become the victims of irony, the humour of the role depends upon its unalterable sameness, self-possession, and institutional rectitude. The actor's job, therefore, is to keep 'in' his allotted humour. To this end, the elliptical part is heaven-sent: the less he knows beyond his own cued speeches, the better.

The second effect of the part's elliptical constitution is when things—expected and unexpected—happen very abruptly on the stage. This is the experience of having to wait for one's cue, and therefore being left open to various surprises: perhaps from the source or nature of the cue; perhaps from the length of time it takes to come; or perhaps from the statements or actions of other characters that are not evident from the cued part, but that bear directly upon the character, and demand of the actor in performance some kind of un- or barely rehearsed response. In this scenario, the actor's ignorance of what happens outside his part is a *false* protection, and can be exploited by the playwright for some edgy purpose that only performance can put to the proof.

We might assume that an actor's ignorance of what comes between his speeches presents, in practice, little problem, and that most actors will remain firmly 'in character' throughout the periods when not speaking.

But we know that this is not the case, and that actors who are not being addressed can drift from secure possession of their parts. So we have to be careful here not to superimpose too many modern assumptions upon the very different textual and theatrical economy of the early modern theatre. The elliptical part-text, privacy of rehearsal, and relative ignorance of 'outside' parts and contexts all made it more difficult for the actor to be sure that his adopted persona and associated manners would inevitably bridge any gaps or surprises that the full play performance unveiled. An actor would no doubt want to possess, and may very often assume, a confident prepossession of his role. But to do so had to be a risk. These actors must always have been open to anxiety, even if only at the fringes of their minds. And, in particular, they must have been wary of the knock-on effects that the unforeseen dialogue or movements of other players might have upon their own acting.

There can be no single rule about how this might have worked. Many actors may have prided themselves upon their brisk adaptability to non-cued provocations or invitations, responding with easeful immediacy to 'action-prompts' arising in the middle of other actors' speeches (many of which they may not have known about until the first performance). Others may have prided themselves upon the opposite—an implacable faithfulness to the cued part, certain that if unambiguous movement or response is required, then his part will tell him—and that if another part seeks to 'move' him in some unauthorized way, his job is precisely to act the resistance he feels. This doesn't mean that he refuses to budge, or assumes sulky high dudgeon: his resistance might be thoroughly dramatic and contextually appropriate, redolent of subjective possession, and of the fact that something important is at stake not just for him but for the person speaking to him. We might recall the many occasions when Richard III's menace is suddenly switched to a particular person. Very often the one so menaced is not alerted to the fact by the part; the prompt for it is found only in the Richard-part's heavy midline 'turns' (see Chapter 18). There are far worse ways of acting the response to such assault than basically doing nothing, or doing nothing for as long as it is possible to do so: massive tension will fill the motionlessness, rather as it does a harangued silence. And indeed Shakespeare may well have anticipated the responses of the actors—all of course familiar to him—to certain varieties of part, and may have used that knowledge to create his midline movements and silences.

The crucial gift, as so often with parts, is the tension founded in the moment when an actor has to make a decision. Whatever choice is made will have a definite pay-off. Consider the climactic scene of *1 Henry IV*: Falstaff fights with Douglas and *'fals down as if he were dead'* (TLN 3040–1); Hal and Hotspur immediately enter and have their fight to the death; first Hotspur speaks his own dying epitaph; then Hal speaks one for the dead Hotspur; finally Hal notices the prostrate Falstaff and, assuming he is dead too, speaks various mordant jokes about his old friend's girth whilst pointedly refusing him the solemn epitaph just conferred upon his adversary, Hotspur. Now, the actor playing Falstaff knows that his character is not dead; he knows that he has to play dead until he hears his cue to rise (probably Hal's exit). But how precisely will he do so? If the choice is the actor's, then it is a simple but profound one. He can choose to stay stock still, deferring to the protagonists' climactic duel, whilst sowing in the audience some small doubt as to whether Falstaff is injured, faking, or just maybe dead. This is a decision that connotes historical and thematic seriousness, or at least uneasy ambivalence. Or he can at one or another moment (most likely Hal's epitaph) choose not to stay still—an animated face, or an eye opening to the audience, is all he needs—and act his responses to the words or action around him. This is a decision to emphasize festive comedy, with Falstaff the irreverent jack-in-the-box in the midst of nation-making events. Alternatively, the Falstaff-actor might sustain both possibilities: he might remain frozen until the moment when *he* at last is spoken of; now that the battle has been won, relief can suddenly be manifested in the actor's opening eye or raised head, as he registers his indignation at Hal's punning dispassion.

The question to consider is precisely how the dialogue bears upon the actor even though he is 'out' of the action and unable to respond. This is such a big moment in *1 Henry IV* that there may of course have been a very firm company direction or agreement as to how it should best be played. Stage-directions may indeed have been added to the parts to make that movement clear. But equally they may not. This example can stand for any number of occasions, big and small, when the part-script leaves it to the actor to block his own movements as he deems appropriate. In this particular instance, the Falstaff-actor knows that he will be cued back into action at any moment, and knows that his ignominious situation almost invites the dry slander of others: he will be prepared to hear himself alluded to, and thus be prepared to make visible—or not—the most apt response. He will read 'ahead' in his part to get clues as to what happens when he is silent and prostrate; this will help him to organize his on-stage freeze. But above all, he will have to attend to what happens whilst he is thus frozen; he will have to be prepared for the unexpected, that he may suddenly become the 'target' of another player, and hence that *his* target, even in silence, will mutate from one thing to another.[1] Once again this means that the silently cogitating mind of the actor—his self-conscious processes of response and interpretation—is enabling, and substantively furnishing, both the acted moment's force-field and (a crucial part of this) the character's sensibility. The uncued 'action prompt', then, helps elicit and define the most basic kind of actorly craft: taking everything into account, what is apposite and 'natural'?

## Set-Piece: Macduff

Sometimes the actor's ignorance of most things outside his own part will give him a securing protection; sometimes it will threaten a more uncertain exposing; and sometimes it will be a mixture of both. This last is what we find with the part of Macduff in *Macbeth*.

When first read by the actor, Macduff probably appealed as a fairly transparent part. He arrives in relaxed humour and speaks engagingly to an underling; he embodies good sense and unoppressed candour; eventually he gets to kill the tyrant and proclaim the restoration of order. The actor will assume a fairly normative part—the secondary 'hero' with a reliable moral compass. In line with this, he will expect that a basically open and honest manner will sustain his acting throughout. And in many ways he will be correct: the part is written so as never to allow the slightest ambiguity of manner. But, as we shall see, the implications of such singularity are not quite so straightforward.

So, if there is one thing that characterizes the part of Macduff, it is a curious belatedness. He is from the start threatened with being late, or asked to catch up with events that have already happened. This is a textbook instance of how a part can be temporally discontinuous, even asymmetrical, to the enveloping play. For instance, the play is almost half over by the time Macduff speaks his first words; he arrives after the most dilated 'entrance cue' in all of Shakespeare, with his 'knocking' first interrupting the Macbeths' guilty terror, and then sustained throughout the Porter's long soliloquy; Macduff's purpose upon arriving is to waken Duncan, but of course Duncan is already dead. That this belatedness is far more than an accident of structure is evident from the part's first words:

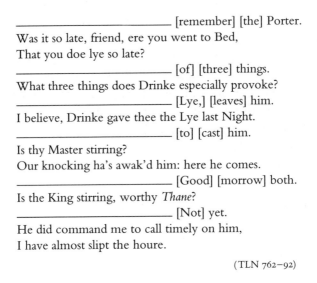

_____ [remember] [the] Porter.
Was it so late, friend, ere you went to Bed,
That you doe lye so late?
_____ [of] [three] things.
What three things does Drinke especially provoke?
_____ [Lye,] [leaves] him.
I believe, Drinke gave thee the Lye last Night.
_____ [to] [cast] him.
Is thy Master stirring?
Our knocking ha's awak'd him: here he comes.
_____ [Good] [morrow] both.
Is the King stirring, worthy _Thane_?
_____ [Not] yet.
He did command me to call timely on him,
I have almost slipt the houre.

(TLN 762–92)

In performance Macduff's opening dialogue can seem like meaningless pleasantries; certainly the actor can only play the exchange with unsuspecting _bonhomie_. But Shakespeare is seeding much more than this into the scene: he is giving the actor his character's 'theme'. So, almost everything that Macduff says here harps upon either sleeping or lateness, or both; the cues, similarly, touch enigmatically upon neglecting others ('leaves him', 'cast him') or deferring time ('morrow both', 'Not yet'). In due course, we will see that 'I have almost slipt the houre' might be the calling card of the part. Furthermore, this first exchange is less the unknowing lull before the storm as the oblivious lull _after_ it—or in the interim between the event and its actable recognition by Macduff. For even though the actor would know how inappropriate his character's banter is (because the King lies dead), he is given no room to 'act' his anxiety. We thus come upon the second of the Macduff-part's founding rules: the actor must play a single passion at a time, one doled out after another in duly permitted order. However out of time or out of turn it may secretly seem, his job is unambiguously to embody a singular 'attitude'.[2]

His next appearance licenses his next 'incarnation', this time as the spokesman of passionate horror ('O horror, horror, horror…Confusion now hath made his Master-peece' (TLN 816–19). He announces the murder; he relays the information that the King's sons have fled and that Macbeth is now King: and then he is gone from the stage for no fewer than eight scenes (more than 800 lines of a very short play). When he returns, he continues speaking in the same vein as before, now bemoaning Scotland's ills. So, he leaves one scene hoping that things don't get worse for his country and enters his next scene bemoaning the fact that they have. The Macduff who reappears in England—the actor will assume—is the same man who left Scotland many scenes earlier. The chronology of the part-text is decisively swift, and its logic apparently simple. Thematic continuity suggests narrative continuity: together they argue strongly for a seamless style of acting.

However, in the interim between the Macduff-actor's two appearances, we have witnessed Macduff's whole family put to the sword. Now, the actor will learn of the atrocity as soon as he has read his part through—but even so, he can really do nothing with this knowledge. The speeches given to the 'ignorant' Macduff when he re-enters express nothing but concerned civic compassion. In other words, the limitations of the part-text help to reinforce the savage ironies of the full play: Macduff speaks passionately for the howling orphans and wives of Scotland, oblivious that the howling of his own wife and son has immediately preceded his reappearance. The temporal disparity between part and play is used to cocoon the actor, or his acting, from the alarming suddenness all around. In this case, the actor simply need not know what has been said about his character whilst he has been absent from the stage (for instance, by his wife, his son, and Macbeth). Indeed, we might think that, for clarity's sake, it is best that he not know. But uncomplicated obliviousness does not seem to be quite what Shakespeare had in mind either.

So Shakespeare now proceeds almost to canonize the ignorance of both his actor and his character: to insist upon it, even to rub their noses in it, by *partially* ameliorating it. We see this exemplified in Macduff's strange exchange with Malcolm in England. Malcolm is supposedly testing Macduff's 'truth and honour'. Initially he does so by insinuating that Macduff is doubly treacherous—first as a spy in the service of the tyrant Macbeth, then as a deserter of his wife and children. Malcolm then goes on to accuse himself of every sin under the sun ('Your Wives, your Daughters, | Your Matrons, and your Maides, could not fill up | The Cesterne of my Lust', etc. (TLN 1884–6)). In other words, the speeches could hardly be more insulting or provocative. But what kind of 'acting' do they allow the Macduff-actor?

The start of the scene seems to present no problems; having been off-stage for 800 lines, the part begins again with four appropriately passionate lamentations:

> _____ [sad] [bosomes] empty.
> Let us rather
> Hold fast the mortall Sword: and like good men
> Bestride our downfall Birthdome ...
> _____ [an] [angry] God.
> I am not treacherous.
> _____ [still] [looke] so.
> I have lost my Hopes.
> _____ [I] [shall] thinke.
> Bleed, bleed poore Country,
> Great Tyrrany, lay thou thy basis sure,
> For goodnesse dare not check thee ...

(TLN 1813–52)

But as clearly directing as these speeches seem to be to the actor, in performance he might find a nasty surprise hiding in the speech Malcolm gives him, and that cues Macduff's fourth speech ('Bleed, bleed...'):

> Why in that rawnesse left you Wife, and Childe?
> Those precious Motives, those strong knots of Love,
> Without leave-taking. I pray you,
> Let not my Jealousies, be your Dishonors,
> But mine owne Safeties: you may be rightly just,
> What ever I shall thinke.

(TLN 1844–9)

The killing question, of course, is the one about Macduff abandoning his wife and child: it is the question that _everyone_ has on their mind, including (perhaps) the Macduff-actor, who has read ahead in the part and knows that a big occasion for acting grief waits just around the corner. But what can he do at this particular moment? This reminder of his family is 'inside' a speech rather than in a cue-line: hence it is _not_ on his part. He has no cued response. Malcolm does not say that wife and children are dead, so does not invite any precipitous 'playing' of shock, tears, or desolation. Instead, the moment almost necessarily produces a stunned recognition of paralysis and impotence. Placed thus strategically, Malcolm's words are a taunt whose humiliations the Macduff-actor must in some murky or half-admitted way share. That is, he is goaded to respond, but as yet cannot; the furtiveness of the taunt (in part-terms) is thus in league with the larger play's cruel ironies. 'Macduff' knows nothing, his actor knows it all: but neither of them can *do* anything. The result is a sequence of singular, delineated attitudes, that must be sustained whatever the motives or mania all around, and obeyed whatever the actor's furtive doubt or—such doubt's corollary—the character's furtive guilt.

This shows how the part-script can embed in the actor a continuity of attitude (Macduff is throughout the passionate patriot) *and* make this continuity itself a form of accusation (here of blameworthy evasiveness or belatedness). The actor is not so much inured to experiencing surprises, as prevented from exhibiting any response to the surprises other than acting in the manner already determined upon. Clearly Shakespeare is here pushing at the comfort zone of his actor. For he does *nothing* to protect the actor from the scene's puzzling indirections or its confusions as to narrative purpose and ethical centre: indeed, rather the opposite.

So, thereafter the actor will see that the cues he receives (with perhaps the ambiguous exception of 'confinelesse harmes') are benign, orthodox, and seemingly consistent with rectitude and hope—and thus with what he will still assume to be his part's dominant register:

————————————————————— [still] [looke] so.
————————————————————— [I] [shall] thinke.
————————————————————— [that] [shall] succeede.
————————————————————— [my] [confinelesse] harmes.
————————————————————— [one] [to] reigne.
————————————————————— [them] [for] wealth.
————————————————————— [unity] [on] earth.
————————————————————— [I] [have] spoken.
————————————————————— [Why] [are] [you] silent?

(TLN 1840–1965)

In puzzling contrast, however, he will find that his own speeches have become enigmatically and abruptly inconsistent: though he has a sequence in Macduff's familiar vein of patriotic compassion and indignation ('Bleed, bleed poore Country' (TLN 1850), 'Not in the Legions | Of horrid Hell can come a Divell more damn'd | In evils, to top *Macbeth*' (TLN 1877–9), 'O Scotland, Scotland' (TLN 1927) ), it is interspersed with two lengthy rationalizations of vice, one admitting 'Boundlesse' intemperance (TLN 1890), the other barnstorming 'Avarice' (TLN 1903). The problem for the actor is the unexplained, contextless thematic shifts, and thus the peculiar weightlessness of the exchanges. It is as though Shakespeare is exploiting the lacunae of the part-script so as to keep the Macduff-actor somehow inert, responding each time from a standing start, forced to generate momentum from nothing but the abstract portent of his rhetoric. What adrenalin can possibly be mustered from these lulling, gentlemanly cues? To the Macduff-actor, grappling with his speech's de-contextualized intensities, the cues may well seem like missives from some inhumanly anaesthetized dimension, one where horses are shod in felt and every scream is silent (as his family's screams were to him). Perhaps the actor will assume that he is in some moral maze, where intellectual hypotheses assume the place of action. But if so, what to make of the abruptly unexplained transitions he is supposed to enact, one after another: moving from ameliorating kingly crime, to praising the 'sainted' Duncan and his queen, to banishing himself despairingly from Scotland? Suddenly it seems that Macduff and Scotland, far from bearing autocracy with permissive sophistication, must be forever ruined.

The difficulty for the actor is that the writing frustrates not simply an intellectual understanding of the context, but also the confident embodying of whatever passions are required. For the scene appears to be written so as to tease the Macduff-actor into, out of, back into, and then back out of, precisely such physical confidence. He starts off passionate, retreats into specious rationalizing, returns to passionate indignation—before another equally sudden return to uncertain silence. Here is the close of this scene's first movement, as the Macduff-actor would have learned it:

> Fare thee well,
> These Evils thou repeat'st upon thy selfe,
> Hath banish'd me from Scotland. O my Brest,
> Thy hope ends heere.
> _____ [are] [you] silent?
> Such welcome, and unwelcom things at once,
> 'Tis hard to reconcile.

(TLN 1938–67)

The silence with which he is upbraided by the cue is, typically, *not* of the Macduff-actor's choosing. It is produced, instead, by the midline pause in

Malcolm's speech—a speech that has already 'silenced' the Macduff-actor for the previous twenty-four lines:

> Now wee'l together, and the chance of goodnesse
> Be like our warranted Quarrell. [SHIFT] Why are you silent?

(TLN 1964–5)

The pause creates a silence that the *audience* will construe as Macduff's: he does not immediately take up Malcolm's strident offer of arms and confederacy, perhaps wondering whether this latest apparent truth is yet another labyrinthine ruse. But the Macduff-*actor* cannot do a thing, just as he could not when taunted about leaving his family in the lurch.

We are seeing a very distinctive manipulation of the part-script's abbreviations: here the Macduff-actor has absolutely no improvisatory liberty; instead, he is forced to weigh his every move against a very part-specific sense of permission and indecorum. Both the actor and the character have been placed at the very edge of embarrassment in this scene—they have been asked to perform things, before an audience, for which they are made to feel increasingly ill prepared. The actor will work hard to keep any embarrassment checked and hidden, but it is almost certain to produce in him two connected resolves. One, he will want to be sure that any subsequent shift in emotion or manner has the vouch of external circumstances; and two, he will be desperate to speak and to move with unfettered, fully embodied physical passion.

This is precisely what now happens, as the part-script (eventually) tells him that his family has been killed; it does so gradually, indeed tortuously, leading the actor into a slowly dawning new manner:

> _____ [yet] [they] heard.
> Humh: I guesse at it.
> _____ [bids] [it] breake.
> My Children too?
> _____ [could] [be] found.
> And I must be from thence? My wife kil'd too?
> _____ [this] [deadly] greefe.
> He ha's no Children. All my pretty ones?
> Did you say All? Oh Hell-Kite! All?
> What, All my pretty Chickens, and their Damme
> At one fell swoope?
> _____ [like] [a] man.
> I shall do so:

But I must also feele it as a man;
I cannot but remember such things were
That were most precious to me: Did heaven looke on,
And would not take their part? Sinfull *Macduff*,
They were all strooke for thee ... Heaven rest them now.

(TLN 2049–77)

Once again, the distinctive time frame in which the part doles out the facts recommends a studied, sequential form of acting. 'Macduff' is asked to display an almost statuesque procession of single-note passions: first, stolid but vicarious concern; second, barely credulous, barely articulate grief (as the statue threatens to crumble); and third, a resolve to revenge:

O I could play the woman with mine eyes,
And Braggart with my tongue. But gentle Heavens,
Cut short all intermission: Front to Front,
Bring thou this Fiend of Scotland, and my selfe
Within my Swords length set him, if he scape
Heaven forgive him too.

(TLN 2080–5)

The meta-dramatic reference ('O I could play...') is a simple instruction for the actor to renounce all ambiguity, whether of attitude, movement, or intonation. Once again we see how Macduff's role (at times, it seems, almost parodically) is to embody *one* thing at a time, each an increment in slowly concretizing history; his often tortuously delayed recognitions correspond to gradually awakening public opinion and belatedly returning agency. So, another seven scenes pass between Macduff's vow to fight and his chance to do so; much happens in the interim; but none of this bears upon the Macduff-actor, or his part-script during this period:

Let our just Censures
Attend the true event, and put we on
Industrious Souldiership.
_____ [advance] [the] warre. *Exeunt marching.*
_____ [on] [our] backe.
                                 *Drumme and Colours.*
                                 *Enter Malcolme, Seyward, Macduffe, and*
                                 *their Army, with Boughes.*
_____ [we] [cannot] fight.
Make all our Trumpets speak, give them all breath

Those clamorous Harbingers of Blood, & Death. *Exeunt*
——————————————— [a] [Woman] borne.          *Exit.*
*Alarums. Enter Macduffe.*
That way the noise is: Tyrant shew thy face,
If thou beest slaine, and with no stroake of mine,
My Wife and Childrens Ghosts will haunt me still:
I cannot strike at wretched Kernes, whose armes
Are hyr'd to beare their Staves; either thou *Macbeth,*
Or else my Sword with an unbattered edge
I sheath againe undeeded. There thou should'st be,
By this great clatter, one of greatest note
Seemes bruited. Let me finde him Fortune,
And more I begge not. *Exit.*          *Alarums.*
——————————————— [better] [upon] them.
*Enter Macduffe.*
Turne Hell-hound, turne.
——————————————— [of] [thine] already.
I have no words,
My voice is in my Sword, thou bloodier Villaine
Then tearmes can give thee out.          *Fight: Alarum*

(TLN 2309–2446)

His part-script truly has 'cut short all intermission': the actor can establish
an attitude, exit for as long as required, and then re-enter with exactly the
same mind, manners, and adrenalized motivation.

The complications in which the Macduff-character partakes are never
fully given to the actor (they are mainly worked in by way of textual
echo or adumbration with other parts).[3] The actor is left working 'outside'
most of the contexts that frame the character, as the gaps in the part
exploit a decidedly appositional relation to the larger play-world and its
calamities. Always, however, the actor's partial exclusion from knowledge
serves the performed play. So, the image of his family running for their
lives is all the more atrocious in the light of Macduff's unwavering stolidity
(however much the Macduff-actor is tacitly cursing his impotence). The
same is true of the 'temptation' scene with Malcolm, in which, as we
have seen, the Macduff-actor is forced, very consciously, to 'perform' a
sequence of dead-end, impotent, self-echoing attitudes. Reduced thus to
stagey ineffectuality, *both* actor and character may well sense a loss, even
a mockery, of efficient libido. But there is a vital dramatic pay-off: the
actor's sense of alienation can itself suggest—and produce on-stage—the
fear and ego loss entailed in accommodating tyranny. Or again, Macduff's

directness in enacting revenge puts the radically contrasting manners of Macbeth—with his despairing ironies and nostalgic indirections, his mind darting in multiple directions even as his actions contract into ferocious singleness—into poignant and perhaps puzzling relief. We can thus see how writing in parts contributes powerfully to Shakespeare's hoped-for effects: first, through the distinctive temporal situating of the part compared to the play; second, through drip-feeding to the actor strictly limited amounts of contextual information.

It is perhaps no mystery that so many of Shakespeare's deep-seeming characters—Macduff no less than Macbeth—should be in their most basic motives opaque or elusive. This opacity—made up of best guesses bridged only by lacunae—is built into the very structure of the part-technology that allows them.

## Cued Action

Fully cued actions will inevitably possess the most thoroughly grounded and directing status for the actor. But at the same time the erratic and elliptical appearance of the cue typifies the part-text's floating elusiveness. The cue brings an actor home, no question: but exactly when and why it does so is always open to question.

The cue can uniquely provoke—indeed, it can distil—fundamental questions about the relationship between thought and action. Am I being acted upon, or am I choosing an action? Does the cue give me something to respond to in the way of a choice or a challenge? Is it accessible to reason, sympathy, or contextual awareness? Or is it an empty signifier, offering nothing but a pre-articulate command to act—*now*—in some definitively undefined new way? In this way we can posit a model of cognition and volition grounded in the actor's cue: one that will focus with unusual sensitivity upon the very possibility of acting with a fully attentive and accountable mind. The actor can be forced genuinely to experience the vulnerability of not knowing what lies around the corner. And what is true of the actor is symbiotically true of the character he plays.

As he learns the part, the actor will study the cues for clues as to why such changes happen; and when he acts the part, he must wait keenly for the cue to come. The wait may at times be unconscionably long. In

*As You Like It*, IV. i, a scene of more than 200 lines, the Celia-actor enters at the start but does not receive his first cue ('marrie us' (TLN 2036)) until the scene is two-thirds gone; she/he gets to say two brief lines, then must wait another eighty lines for the next cue. This period during which the actor is left waiting in silence for his cue accompanies a character who is left similarly lingering, impotently and perhaps angrily at odds with the surrounding acceleration into hasty marriage. Similarly, in the opening scene of the Macbeth-part, the part-text gives the actor necessary contextual information—but it also frustrates him by leaving him hanging for what is in fact more than twenty lines between his seemingly twinned statements to the witches of desperate curiosity, 'what are you?' and 'tell me more'.

> Speake if you can: what are you?
> ——————————————————— [*Macbeth*,] [all] haile.
> Stay you imperfect Speakers, tell me more ...
>
> (TLN 147–70)

It was reported that the famed nineteenth-century actor William Charles Macready 'could scarcely repress his impatience' during Banquo's 'lines of interrogatory':[4] a shared feeling of frustration here unites actor and character, as each helps to produce the other.

Occasions such as these can be multiplied. But what they always show is a subtle exploiting and conjoining of the various lacunae that shape actors' parts. First, there is the simple swiftness with which events are arrived at in the scripted part: Celia is suddenly to be 'sundred' from her inseparable companion. Things happen quickly to these dramatic beings; existence is unpredictable, and choices few or compelled. Second, there is the lengthy gap between entrance on-stage and invitation to speak. What is to be done in the interim? How to 'act' without script or instruction? Yet how to switch off or relax in the knowledge that the cued response is surely due any moment? Here we are not assuming the incompetent or inexperienced actor who might 'leave' character as he leaves speaking. We are instead assuming an actor intimately known to Shakespeare and knowledgeable about his techniques: one whom Shakespeare could tease, and exploit, delight or terrify, and from whom the smallest shifts in the written part could reliably produce unexpected but thoroughly scripted performative decisions.[5]

## Set-Piece: Bertram

A part constructed around such surprises is Bertram in *All's Well That Ends Well*. His first scene establishes the context:

> ————————————————— [a] [second] husband.
> And I in going Madam, weep ore my/fathers death anew; but I must attend his maje-/sties command, to whom I am now in Ward, evermore/in subjection.
> ————————————————— [up] [against] mortallitie.
> What is it (my good Lord) the King languishes of?
> ————————————————— [Fistula] [my] Lord.
> I heard not of it before
> ————————————————— [it] [soone] mortall.
> Maddam I desire your holie wishes
> ————————————————— [him:] [Farwell] *Bertram.*
> The best wishes that can be forg'd in your thoghts/be servants to you: be comfortable to my mother, your/Mistris, and make much of her.

(TLN 8–80; lineation ours)

These cues are obviously not 'about' Bertram as a character; similarly, his own speeches reveal next to nothing about his nature. Bertram is introduced as a cipher, framed only by death ('mortallitie') and disappointment ('soone mortall... Farwell'). He gathers his own negative picture from this framing negativity. Lacking all personal information other than this situating within somebody else's bleak and languishing world, the actor can only act the scene with neutrality, or diffidence, or some enigmatic lack of colour. In his next scene of any substance (II. iii), he enters with the king and various other courtiers, knowing that his first cue to speak will herald a decisive and, for the character, outrageous transition: 'shee's thy wife'. But the actor is left hanging for more than 100 lines before the cue comes. In other words, Shakespeare writes the part so as to engineer a tacit collision between the attitude so far assumed—diffident, offhand, remote, almost anonymous—and the manner now suddenly expected of him: thrust centre-stage and told to embrace his 'romantic' fate.

The crucial disjunction is between the abrupt story told by the written part, and the suspended one enacted in performance. The actor sees what is coming, but doesn't see it come; he feels the clash between a necessarily internalized acting manner and an unpractised and unprepared openness, imposed from 'above' by playwright and king. In other words, the part is written to make this suddenly transfixing cue seem, to the actor as well as to the character, like an outrage: a provocation for which he cannot be prepared, one that allows him no real *bodily* response at all. And this is precisely because the part has put the actor on the back foot, either colourless in the courtly throng or engaging in dialogue to which his own presence is only ever incidental. A likely consequence is that the actor—originally almost certainly Burbage, accustomed to playing stage-centre parts timed by hugely satisfying shifts in passion—will himself begin to feel edgily protective of his character's rights; we might imagine his almost truculent progress through boredom, impatience, complacency, irritation, into thinly aggressive defensiveness. Taken together we get the moods so elemental to the querulous Bertram.

But the part-script does not give the actor merely one moment of alarm; here is how the scene proceeds for 'Bertram':

———————————————————— [shee's] [thy] wife.
My wife my Leige? I shal beseech your highnes
In such a busines, give me leave to use
The helpe of mine owne eies.
———————————————————— [done] [for] mee?
Yes my good Lord, but never hope to know why I should marrie her.
———————————————————— [my] [sickly] bed.
But followes it my Lord, to bring me downe
Must answer for your raising? I knowe her well:
Shee had her breeding at my fathers charge:
A poore Physicians daughter my wife? Disdaine
Rather corrupt me ever.
———————————————————— [wealth,] [from] mee.
I cannot love her, nor will strive to doo't.
———————————————————— [Speake,] [thine] answer.
Pardon my gracious Lord: for I submit
My fancie to your eies, when I consider
What great creation, and what dole of honour
Flies where you bid it: I finde that she which late
Was in my Nobler thoughts, most base: is now
The praised of the King, who so ennobled,
Is as 'twere borne so.
———————————————————— [ballance] [more] repleat.
I take her hand.

(TLN 1003–81)

The cues briskly 'tell' Bertram's moment. If he had received two-word cues, he would have been given 'thy wife', 'for mee?', 'sickly bed', 'from mee', a succinct capsule of his recoiling emotions; if he had received one-word cues, he would have had 'wife', 'mee', 'bed', 'mee', vacillating equally appropriately between Bertram's trademark selfishness and his situation's nightmarish inescapability. But the part reveals much more. First, there is Bertram's gaucheness, so much clearer here than in the full text. Given a cue of 'bed' or 'sickly bed', Bertram's sexualized response (punning on 'raising') is, intentionally or not, grossly insolent. Bertram's part, of course, does not tell the actor what is signified by this 'raising': he may assume that he is commenting on an old man's illicit sexual appetite rather than on his magical resuscitation from infirmity. Bertram is thus almost 'set up' here by his lacunal part, tricked into an automatic but inappropriate wink or leer or other pseudo-collusive *faux pas*. Secondly, the part-text's ellipses accentuate the suddenness of Bertram's shifts in situation: here, from defiance ('I cannot love her') to submission ('I submit | My fancie to your eies') with only the most glozing explanation as to why. Thirdly, this rhythmic and emotional disjunctiveness is accentuated by the prosody: in full text Bertram's capitulation is capped by two thoroughly abrupt shared pentameters (with the King):

> BERTRAM.   …I finde that she which late
> Was in my Nobler thoughts, most base: is now
> The praised of the King, who so ennobled,
> Is as 'twere borne so.
> KING.                          Take her by the hand,
> And tell her she is thine: to whom I promise
> A counterpoize: If not to thy estate,
> A ballance more repleat.
> BERTRAM.                          I take her hand.

> (TLN 1073–81; layout ours)

Bertram's irresolute 'Is as 'twere borne so' is forcibly welded into iambic and social order by the King's 'Take her by the hand'; this is then the instruction—the *order*—that Bertram must now take up to complete the King's half-line: 'A ballance more repleat. | I take her hand.' This metrical fit represents still further coercion: it is ugly and atonal, with Bertram's presence in the shared line little more than that of a programmed zombie.[6] We might almost say the same of the actor, who has almost *no* control over the scene's pace or the character's purposes. It might well be as great a relief to the player as to his character to take the first opportunity he can to run off into the callous prose of the military scenes.

The role of Bertram is one whose relation to supposed 'truth' is always strained—even when it is not directly coerced. The actor often needs to double-check or guess whether his character is telling outright lies, making shrewd evasions, or simply airing his own obtuse sincerities. During the military scenes this is less of a problem. There he speaks mainly in clearly directed prose, thinly consonant with his smug officer type, thinly responsive to passing occasion. Of course, the actor will know that the military scenes are a leave-taking from the darker promises (of death and marriage) that his character has fled. He will thus anticipate a final change of scene to produce some resolving comeuppance, recognition, or restoration, in which his character can decisively 'come home' in terms both of plot and of full comic-romantic type. But he will not quite find what he expects.

So, having been off-stage for some 300 or so lines, and with the end of both part and play nearing, Bertram makes a final re-entrance to the court of his upbringing:

————————————————————— [high] [in] fame.
*Enter Count Bertram*

————————————————————— [is] [faire] againe.
My high repented blames
Deere Soveraigne pardon to me.

————————————————————— [of] [this] Lord?
Admiringly my Liege, at first
I stucke my choice upon her, ere my heart
Durst make too bold a herauld of my tongue:
Where the impression of mine eye enfixing,
Contempt his scornfull Perspective did lend me,
Which warpt the line, of everie other favour,
Scorn'd a faire colour, or exprest it stolne,
Extended or contracted all proportions
To a most hideous object. Thence it came,
That she whom all men prais'd, and whom my selfe,
Since I have lost, have lov'd; was in mine eye
The dust that did offend it.

————————————————————— [upon] [her] finger.
Hers it was not.

————————————————————— [stead] [her] most.

My gracious Soveraigne,
How ere it pleases you to take it so,
The ring was never hers.

(TLN 2733–98)

He enters seemingly contrite: prepared to be rebuked by the king and to make a repentant acknowledgment of his error. This will take the specific form of recognizing how perverted his judgement of one particular woman has been, and how his scorn, contempt, and irritation have been a form of warped self-torture. He is ready at last to love what he had lost. When learning his part, the actor would surely assume that 'she whom all men prais'd' is Helena, whom Bertram dismissed like so much offensive 'dust'. He would likewise have assumed that his next two speeches, insisting that 'The ring was never hers', must then refer to some other woman: he would presume Diana. The Bertram character, he would think, is reforming according to type; he is repairing mistakes; the ring was truly his wife's. But all of these assumptions would be proved wrong in performance. In full text, the woman he now acknowledges that he unworthily disdained is someone we have never met, a character never seen on-stage and never before mentioned: a daughter of Lord Lafeu, who in the wake of Helena's 'death' is being touted as a possible wife for Bertram. Moments later Lafeu disappears again: Bertram's continuing lies persuade Lafeu to call off all thoughts of a match. But such details are by the way. This entirely hypothetical 'character' has no function other than as a screen for the perversities and pathologies of Bertram's erotic judgement. One effect is to give psychological layering to the character of Bertram; the accumulating instances evoke Bertram's compulsively 'real' bent of mind. But it seems more profoundly to work upon the *actor*, by seeding uncertainty as to which of the (now three) women he is talking about at any one time. For it seems highly likely that the actor will be left stranded, assuming with blithe confidence that he has accepted Helena, before learning that he continues to reject Helena. Neither his cues nor his speeches have proved a safe guide to context; the actor's part-text has simply elided crucial information concerning who or what he is addressing.

And so it continues to the end. Here are the Bertram-part's final few lines:

_____ [Ring] [of] yours.
I thinke she has; certain it is I lyk'd her,
And boorded her i'th wanton way of youth…

She ...
Subdu'd me to her rate, she got the Ring,
And I had that which any inferiour might
At Market price have bought.
———————————————— [me] [mine] againe.
I have it not.
———————————————— [spoke] [the] truth.
My Lord, I do confesse the ring was hers.
———————————————— [not] [the] thing.
Both, both, O pardon.
———————————————— [are] [doubly] wonne?
If she my Liege can make me know this clearly,
Ile love her dearely, ever, ever dearely.

(TLN 2936–3054)

Would the actor know which woman he is left accepting, or which rejection he is ambiguously ('dearely, ever, ever dearely') undertaking to undo? After all, he has viciously scorned and traduced three women; his part gives no clue as to why or whether any of them particularly deserve or demand more considered attention. If the actor seeks direction from the chain of cues that his part gives him at this moment, he will only find reinforced this riddling, elusive context:

———————————————— [Ring] [of] yours.
———————————————— [me] [mine] againe.
———————————————— [spoke] [the] truth.
———————————————— [not] [the] thing.
———————————————— [are] [doubly] wonne?

All the cues harp upon possession and identity, but in the way of a contract that keeps on breaking, or an exchange that never satisfies: 'yours' then 'mine again', 'truth' then 'not the thing'. Just as any repeated positive appears set to turn recursively into a negative ('dearely, ever, ever dearely'), so the cue-promise of 'doubly wonne?' threatens to unravel into its own lurking puns—doubly *one*, meaning doubly alone? or doubly *won*, meaning won by one and then by the other, so that the initial victor becomes the loser, or the whole thing ends up in a mutually negating 'tie'? The keyword is 'If': it begins the final speeches of both Helena and Bertram, while the King's closing encomium twice hinges on the word's treacherous contingencies.

So, how *can* the Bertram-actor fully commit to this moment? And what would such commitment entail? The equivocations of the last lines inhibit any unabashed leap into traditional comic forgetfulness: the fulsome smile, the surge of relaxation that comes when the body arrives home. But the withholdings of the part-text leave the Bertram-actor still more estranged from the context, more aware of its coercions and of the trammelled obedience they command. For the actor is not really allowed even the pretence of serendipity. He knows that *someone* returns to him, but he may be unsure quite which one: the only thing he can be sure of is that it *might* be his character's wife. Any 'surprise' is pre-empted by a tacit shuffling of options, all of them manageable, none of them blissfully releasing. In this context, even satisfaction is a kind of disappointment. The actor may well feel relief at the end of the performance, but in the moment of reaching his destination his thoughts are likely to remain equivocal and even wistful: perhaps silently casting after missed alternatives, perhaps wondering whether what seems to have happened really has, perhaps thinking that the shadow of some more pleasing solution may still be discovered inside or alongside the putatively closing contract. In all of this, it seems by design, the actor shadows his character. Will subsequent performance reveal more? Probably not, for the ambiguities remain even when *known*: day after performance day the actor of Bertram must revisit his surprise and irritation, still unable to alter or even productively rethink his options.[7]

It is hard to imagine a part-script that less prepares its subject for libidinous self-forgetfulness; hard to imagine one that more encourages a frigid separation from the pleasures of others, or indeed from the pleasures of theatre. Even inwardness here lies unexpressed, and somehow unrecognized. If Bertram is 'dismissed to happiness' (as Dr Johnson had it), then the Bertram-*actor* remains exactly where he is: energies unreleased, preparations subtly embarrassed, and tricked into petrified submission.[8]

## Short-Line Cues

We need here to consider some basic questions about the practice of giving and taking cues. First, would the actor being cued 'hear' any aural indication from the cueing actor that the cue is about to come? Second, would he be able to tell from either the evidence in the written part or the experience of performing whether he is sharing a pentameter line with the other actor (either because he is giving a 'short' cue-line, or starting his speech with a shortened verse-line), and therefore whether the writing expects, or presupposes, a tight rhythmic connection between the performers, and thus (invariably) a tight emotional connection between the characters? And third, what happens if no such foreknowledge can be relied upon?

From fairly early in Shakespeare's career, cueing lines are often short lines. By the late 1590s it became as normal for a speech to end with a short as with a full line; in later Shakespeare it became unusual *not* to end a speech with a short line. One of the major tasks confronting a Shakespeare editor from the eighteenth century onwards has been to decide whether two half-lines, spoken in succession by different parts, are really supposed to complete one another or not. Often there is not a consensus. Our problem in making and analysing actors' parts is the same as the editor's: when confronted with iambic lines that may complete one another, we do not absolutely know which really are free-standing and 'incomplete' and which are not.[9] Parts may or may not have conveyed the answer to the actors; in early Shakespeare shared lines in full text are usually clear; in the plays from roughly 1600 on, it is often effectively impossible to distinguish between shared pentameters, 'squinting' lines (where the exchange is in verse but there are more half-lines that can be fitted into complete pentameters), and prose. But whatever we deduce from a full play-text, the problems with part-texts are distinctive. As we saw from extant university parts, there did exist a way of indicating 'handing on a verse line'; we looked at parts in which an actor spoke an incomplete verse-line that ended with a long dash—a sign that another speaker would be expected to take on the rhythm of the line. We also saw that an actor might, in a similar way, know when he is to complete a verse: he might be given a long cue consisting of the incomplete verse-line in its entirety ending with a dash under which his own words (the completion of the line) are given. But public theatre parts do not seem habitually to have used this convention.

The question of shared pentameters, particularly in sections of less regular verse, highlights one of the difficulties we have faced in constructing parts. It seems to us impossible to write a script in such a way that the actors would know they were speaking a pentameter line when it is divided into separate exchanges. Indeed, it was only in the eighteenth century that Shakespeare texts were published in which shared lines were indicated by layout—a practice introduced by Edward Capell. It is a leftover of the eighteenth-century editorial habit of turning any line that *might* be a pentameter into one that *is* that has created some exchanges that would, we think, never work in 'part' terms. When several speakers are involved in a single pentameter line, the whole status of the iambic pentameter formula is put under threat.

Whilst thinking in terms of parts often confirms decisions made by modern editors, there are also moments where it challenges common editorial practice. So, for instance, we doubt that actors would have been able to spot a pentameter rhythm—or even know that they were speaking a pentameter—in the exchange in *Macbeth* that is commonly rendered:

| | |
|---|---|
| MACBETH. | … though the treasure |
| | Of nature's germens tumble all together, |
| | Even till destruction sicken: answer me |
| | To what I ask you. |
| FIRST WITCH. | Speak |
| SECOND WITCH. | Demand. |
| THIRD WITCH. | We'll answer. |

(IV. i. 72–5)

Here the fact of parts provides information for all editors. It would be difficult indeed to indicate on the part of the Third Witch that she speaks the fifth iamb (and a feminine extra stress) of a pentameter line. The actor of Macbeth may, through recognizable shifts in rhythm and accentuation, have indicated when passing on the words 'To what I ask you' that he is speaking an incomplete pentameter. However, the First Witch, whose part reads simply 'Speak', would probably not have been able to sustain the requisite rhythm (nor is she likely to have known to do so). The result of her hesitation before or after her word may have resulted, of course, in the emergence of a slow, elongated pentameter line: 'To what I ask you.' '… Speak …' '… Demand …' 'We'll answer …'. Or the result may have been an exchange that was rendered like prose. Indeed, a prose exchange allows each pause to have a weight of its own: Macbeth has asked for answers that he also fears to hear. So 'Speak' might be followed by a pause during which the Macbeth-actor can do nothing (this is not his cue); 'Demand', too, is followed by a brief hiatus, during which Macbeth and the audience alike wait to see what will fill Macbeth's rooted pause. Finally, 'We'll answer' is spoken: but this is not Macbeth's cue either. The character remains silent; the actor performs the frustrated, cueless dread that the character feels. Indeed, the First Witch, as the full text makes clear, has to prompt Macbeth into words: 'Say, if th'hadst rather heare it from our mouthes, | Or from our Masters' (TLN 1595–6). Only then does Macbeth reply: 'Call 'em: let me see 'em.' This half-line reply completes a 'shared' pentameter with the cueing line ('Or from our Masters'); and perhaps the Macbeth-actor identifies the completion as his prompt to abandon all delay and to rush immediately into fatal union with the witches.

Perhaps: but the dread-heavy silences and temporal disjunctions of the surrounding context might just as easily render defunct such coercive metrical allegories. The actor may well 'see' the sign hinting at a shared pentameter; but looking at the context of his words, he might equally feel one instruction pushing him this way, another that. Of course, flouting a convention does not mean ignoring it, still less that it is lost from view. The struggle for a shared line between hero and witch—Macbeth coerced into it, resisting it, needing it, getting it but still deferring it—also encapsulates the dramatic moment. In that case, the actor's consciousness of being tugged in contrary directions informs the character's similar sensibility. An auditor may or may not 'hear' the metrical struggle—but, knowingly or not, he will always experience its effects in the staged action.

Could the performing actor know, or confidently guess, that his cue was about to come? We can only hypothesize. The actors may have habitually paced and stressed a cueing line differently from a non-cueing line, and a cueing half-line differently from a cueing full line. It is impossible to discern any general rule about this merely from the prosody of the texts that we have inherited. But, just as a musical score, or simply the custom of musical performance, very often gives the closing bars of a tune a rhythm that is both slower and more emphatic, so too might the closing line of a speech have received a more emphatic, 'teeing-up' delivery. The 'receiving' actor would hear the rhythmic shift, and thus ready himself for his re-entrance into speech (although this would be of limited use in a scene when a number of actors are each simultaneously waiting for their next cue). Clearly this could protect against unwanted silences: but equally it might allow for very loaded, intentional moments of silence. That is, if the actor senses that his cue is about to come, then he can be prepared *not* to reply instantaneously if he so wishes, allow a brief suspension in which the cued action—as distinct from the cued speech—has its necessary moment. The delay becomes a choice, and therein loaded.

The choices for the actor, and the emotional possibilities for the characters, are intensified in the case of a short-line cue. It might come as a surprise to the cued actor, because it signals an abrupt end to a speech otherwise in full pentameters. He is momentarily taken aback; he feels the suddenness as a challenge, a provocation. But again, any subsequent delay before the cue is taken—it need be no more than a second—will be tacitly animated by whatever is at stake between the cuer and the cued. Either way—the actor forewarned of the cue or the cue coming as a surprise—the fact of the short line can intensify the transaction's immediacy (to actor *and* audience). Furthermore, in such cases the actor will always have to keep in mind the possibility that his 'short' cue-line serves as the first half of a pentameter, to be completed by his addressee. There may have been practised ways in which an experienced group of professional actors shared such lines with one another. Perhaps an actor starting what looked to him like a foreshortened pentameter would 'hand it on' rhythmically: it then might or might not be taken up by the next actor. For if an actor had a sense that he was giving—or receiving—an incomplete verse-line, that would have changed not just his performance but also his perception of the lines themselves (usually suggesting a closer tie with the interlocutor).

In its basic form, the importance of the short cue-line can be adduced from the parts of Juliet and Romeo. In both parts most speeches end with a full line. Consider these examples from the Romeo-part:

> O she is rich in beautie, onely poore,
> That when she dies, with beautie dies her store.
>
> (TLN 223–4)

> I cannot bound a pitch above dull woe,
> Under loves heavy burthen doe I sinke.
>
> (TLN 475–6)

> Because it is an Enemy to thee,
> Had I it written, I would teare the word.
>
> (TLN 852–3)

> My life were better ended by their hate,
> Then death proroged wanting of thy Love.
>
> (TLN 876–7)

Thou cut'st my head off with a golden Axe,
And smilest upon the stroke that murders me.

(TLN 1825–6)

More fierce and more inexorable farre,
Then emptie Tygers, or the roaring Sea.

(TLN 2891–2)

Read in isolation, none of these really declare themselves as invitations to another actor. Though their content may gesture towards someone else on-stage, their structure does not *require* anyone else—they are complete in themselves. But now compare these speech-closing *half*-lines, also from Romeo's part:

This love feele I, that feele no love in this.
Doest thou not laugh?

(TLN 187–8)

What is it else? a madnesse, most discreet,
A choking gall, and a preserving sweet:
Farewell my Coze.

(TLN 200–2)

Sin from my lips? O trespasse sweetly urg'd:
Give me my sin againe.

(TLN 688–9)

O that I were a Glove upon that hand,
That I might touch that cheeke.

(TLN 816–17)

*Tibalt*, *Mercutio*, the Prince expresly hath
Forbidden bandying in *Verona* streetes.
Hold *Tybalt*, good *Mercutio*.

(TLN 1519–21)

In what vile part of this Anatomie
Doth my name lodge? Tell me, that I may sacke
The hatefull Mansion.

(TLN 1922–4)

Without exception the speech-closing half-line very explicitly reaches out to another actor or actors: the metrical incompletion indicates and facilitates

dramatic 'want'. Whether the short line is a discrete unit of speech or part
of a sentence carried over from the previous line makes no difference: the
very fact of the incomplete pentameter signals to the part-conning actor
that there are other actors to bring into play, and a wider physical context
to be produced.

   The Juliet-part similarly has largely full-length cueing lines, but sometimes includes what then comes to seem suggestive: a speech-closing
half-line. However, Juliet's uses are often more daring and pioneering than
Romeo's:

> Without that title *Romeo*, doffe thy name,
> And for thy name which is no part of thee,
> Take all my selfe.
>
>                    (TLN 841–3)

> What man art thou, that thus bescreen'd in night
> So stumblest on my counsell?
>
>                    (TLN 847–8)

'Take all my selfe', the actor says: the half-line here completes what
is in effect an overheard soliloquy (Juliet addresses herself throughout),
encapsulating an existential risk that the actor too must partly share in.
The actor is fully aware of Romeo's presence on-stage; he might suspect
that the speech with his half-line cues, then, will come from Romeo, but
he cannot know whether it will be addressed to 'Juliet' or not. So the
suspended line, at once closing one speech, resigning all other thoughts
to silence, and beckoning someone else to come and 'take' the cue, is to
this extent a leap into the dark: she/he may well be left alone with her
pleading half-line. Thus, when the response from Romeo does come—'I
take thee at thy word'—completing her pentameter *and* picking up the
verb in her cue-line ('Take'), it may well provoke a *frisson* in the actor of
delayed surprise and suddenly satisfied expectation.

   The second speech—in fact, the Juliet-part's very next speech—is
different. Here it is in full text:

> ROMEO.  Call me but Love, and Ile be new baptiz'd;
>          Hence foorth I never will be *Romeo*.
> JULIET.  What man art thou, that thus bescreen'd in night
>          So stumblest on my counsell?
>
>                    (TLN 845–8)

'What man art thou' is specifically asking for an answer from another. More than that, the whole speech is one single sentence, ending with the short line, 'So stumblest on my counsell?' Again, the actor will not know quite what is coming. The Juliet-actor's cue might be 'will be *Romeo*', in which case the responding speech could be spoken with expectant hope or even conspiratorial confidence ('What man art thou ... ', she asks, while already knowing). Alternatively, the cue might be 'never will be *Romeo*', proposing a much more nervous, alarmed, menaced—and even ashamed—emotional register. In full text there is no mystery at all. We see Romeo on-stage, just as we see that he completes Juliet's short lines with his own: the second time also furnishing a perfect pentameter with 'By a name ... ' (TLN 849). Depending on the cues *he* is given, the Romeo-actor may similarly always know, or have guessed, about the shared line (and the emotional reciprocity it allegorizes). Alternatively, he too may have had to wait for performance: in which case the speech-closing half-line is again orchestrating communicable pleasure through a mixture of ignorant separateness (what will come?) and serendipitous union (she/he has come!).

The Juliet-part is always much more intimate to such processes than the Romeo-part. It consistently gives the actor choices to make—is this self-address or confession, or (as perhaps here) is the character simply left in the dark? The actor is often forced to commit absolutely to the emotion, and to the passion and physicality of its expression ('Take all my selfe' (TLN 843) ), without quite knowing whether satisfaction will come immediately, soon, or not at all. Romeo's cueing half-lines never work in this way. They are always much more assured, the statement definitively pre-empting any possibility of opposition or equivocation. For if the Romeo-actor's relation to the world beyond him is a given, the Juliet-actor—like his character—is more open to the peril of boundary-less passion. Both actor and character are frequently only a mistake—or a mistaken cue—away from being utterly abandoned in their respective commitments to a *single* decision.

We can see here that a speech ending with a 'pleading' or hanging half-line does not necessarily imply dialogue. The end of a speech might instead declare a mental movement away from further discussion. That is, the actor will automatically identify mental closure—perhaps local and temporary, but always impelled and possessed by the self. The short cue-line speaks of *his* powers of release and retention; the 'missing' half-line stands for both unspoken secrets and opened-out opportunity. The actor is holding things in reserve: as we shall see, this reservoir can powerfully suggest the character's inferable 'privacy' or inwardness.[10] For there is always a *want* suspended in the missing iambs: for obedience, for privacy, for love, or simply for an answer. The actor may or may not know from his part the rhythm with which he will be answered; he certainly will not know what (if any) words will come back at him. The moment's possibilities will be all the more intense because the answers are not quite at hand. Again and again working in parts produces this inestimable benefit: the actor is in his moment—which in fact means never quite in complete possession of it.

Here is an example from *Lear*, as it is printed in the Folio:

> GLOUCESTER.  There is a Cliffe, whose high and bending head
> Lookes fearfully in the confined Deepe:
> Bring me but to the very brimme of it,
> And Ile repayre the misery thou do'st beare
> With something rich about me: from that place,
> I shall no leading neede.
> EDGAR.  Give me thy arme;
> Poore Tom shall leade thee. *Exeunt.*
>
> (TLN 2258–65)

Editors generally assume that Edgar completes Gloucester's verse-line, and so set the passage like this:

> GLOUCESTER.  ... Ile repayre the misery thou do'st beare
> With something rich about me: from that place,
> I shall no leading neede.
> EDGAR.                                        Give me thy arme;
> Poore Tom shall leade thee. *Exeunt.*

This setting seems appropriate. The Folio sets the first four of Edgar's words on a separate line, distinguishing them from the following words—and so encourages the reading above. We, like editors of this scene, conjecture that the above reading is correct. But now let us consider how the respective parts might look *if* the actors playing Gloucester and Edgar were alerted therein to the shared verse. Here is a part for Edgar in which the cue-line indicates to the actor that he is being handed a half-line of incomplete verse:

> ———— I shall no leading neede ————
> Give me thy arme;
> Poore Tom shall leade thee. *Exeunt.*

The Edgar-actor would see that he must immediately respond to Gloucester's suggestion that he shall need no leading—with the offer to give him
just that: Edgar asks for the old man's arm and declares that he 'shall
leade thee'. The Edgar-actor would probably speak his cued half-line
immediately, while simultaneously grabbing Gloucester's arm (which the
Gloucester-actor may already have given to Edgar even as he hands on
his half-line). Furthermore, the actor would know to stress both 'shall'
and 'lead', as they clearly pick up on the cue given him: the two words
thus 'stolen' from Gloucester's cue-line together manifest Edgar's defiance of instruction and his effective power. Indeed, this second short
speech ('Poore Tom shall leade thee') may well be acted as an aside,
as Edgar's powerfully determined vow to himself. Whatever choice the
actor makes, the twin imperatives (*shall* and *lead*) are now in his character's possession.

   The actor playing Gloucester, meanwhile, may have seen the exchange
like this:

> ———————————————————— [I] Master.
> There is a Cliffe, whose high and bending head
> Lookes fearfully in the confined Deepe:
> Bring me but to the very brimme of it,
> And Ile repayre the misery thou do'st beare
> With something rich about me: from that place,
> I shall no leading neede ————————————

If the part was transcribed in this way, with a cue-like 'tail' following
his speech-ending half-line, then the Gloucester-actor would probably
have expected his final line to be completed by another. Of course he
does not know what that other will say: something affirming, rebuking,
consoling…? Either way, an actor keeping pentameter rhythm while
'handing on' a verse-line, would be wise to stress his iambs carefully to
help out his interlocutor. As a result, 'shall', 'lead', and 'need' would stand
out in his cueing line, ready, though Gloucester does not know it, for the
response which (as we have seen) plays on those same words: '… Poore
Tom shall leade thee'.

   Of course there is much more in the speech that the actor may pick
up: the wry pun upon 'the *misery* thou do'st beare' (meaning both Poor
Tom's thankless task and Gloucester himself), and the internal rhymes of 're-
payre/beare' and 'leading/neede'. Both the puns and the rhymes inscribe
a rival voice or manner 'inside' the dominant blank verse: their private

candour suggests an alternative perspective upon Gloucester's headlong despair, with all three 'jokes' complicating the framing speech's apparent purposes (is Gloucester needing or leading, repairing or bearing, the thing being
borne or the thing doing the bearing?). We need not explore these effects
here. Suffice it to say that Shakespeare always expects of his actors close attentiveness to such content, and that the answers the actor comes up with
will always directly inform the way he plays the more obviously 'actable'
information such as (in this instance) the short cueing line and consequent
shared half-lines. Here this comes down to simple but profoundly salient
questions: all encapsulated in the 'cue-space'. How certain is Gloucester of
his path? How much might the actor see, by way of anticipated options or
alternatively sketched fates, that his character does not? How much are *we*
asked to judge Gloucester differently from the way he judges himself? How
comic—how hedged in by expectations of protection or 'repayre'—is this
suicide bid *before* it happens? All of these questions are compacted into the
speech's complex rhetorical patterns. But equally, they are all centred in the
particular moment when Gloucester hands his line and his arm to Poor Tom:
or in other words, in a cue-space that is given renewed tension and expectancy
in being 'framed' by two half-lines.

The speech-closing half-line—whether the text indicates that it is to be
completed or not—thus typifies how parts can concentrate a sense of life
at a cusp. The technique requires activity of mind in both speakers, and so
the filling out that comes with subjective commitment (fear, desire, hope,
memory, and so on). This spatial contingency thus also implies temporal
fluidity, as the gap between cue and response speaks equally of what has
been, what is, and what *might* be to come. It is a classic example of how
working in parts pre-empts what might be construed as the metaphysical
presumptuousness of the complete play: the sense that everything has been
pre-written, masterminded to the last detail. The various lonely spaces in
parts—epitomized in the speech-closing half-line—show that more than
one mind, and more than one choice, goes to make a moment.


# Conclusion

It might be objected here and elsewhere that a 'surprise' can never
work the same way twice; that if an actor is kept waiting for his cue
unconscionably long, or if it comes suddenly in the middle of his script,

then the second time he plays the scene he will know exactly what is coming: expecting it, he assimilates and neuters the *frisson* of surprise or recognition. We suggest, however, that this shows a fundamental misunderstanding of the kind of acting required by Shakespeare. A crucial part of our argument is that 'surprise' will not simply be overtaken or overcome in rehearsal, or in second or subsequent performances. As we outlined in the 'history' Part, there was no promise of a second go at any of these parts; furthermore, performances of the 'same' play years apart were routine. The first performance is the thing, the event for which the part is written, and the touchpaper that must be relit if the actor is ever asked to play that part again. Recovering the 'original' is the key to early modern notions of truth and authenticity: so it is here, and with bells on. But this has nothing to do with a dry antiquarianism; the kind of theatre here expected could not be further from a museum piece, in which interested spectators cast an expert eye over some much-praised old classic. Renaissance humanism was all about making things new, burnishing them for *now*: a bow should be drawn between first things and present things, but that bow must quiver with expectation, compulsion, necessity. Correspondingly, everything about Shakespeare's drama is premissed upon immediacy: presence in Shakespeare is all about imminence, a continuing condition of 'about to be'. We have described Shakespeare working for a core group of actors who worked inside Shakespeare's language in part after part, year after year. They and he knew what was expected, and how to orchestrate it. Almost above all, the actors learned to trust and respect such possibility of surprise. They would have learned through practice to cherish any such happening, as crucially constitutive of that specific part or scene; they knew that what was needed was the power to recover such feeling (in the event of a second or subsequent performance) as the mark of an authentic or compelling possession of the part.

Certainly the players knew that the one thing they must at all costs avoid is the appearance of 'reciting' the words as though a chronicle of times past (a doleful practice occasionally mocked by Shakespeare, as in the interminable pedantry of Canterbury in *Henry V*, I. ii). If they did not, then Shakespeare repeatedly forces them to remember: again and again he makes actorly surprise unavoidable. Of course, many of the sources of such surprises would themselves have become conventions, to be consciously searched for by the actors. But all that this means is that the actor, if he sees before performance that a particular technique has been scripted—as he often would with repeated cues, for instance—will have more time to consider and practise the immediate range of options. Indeed, it might be things such as this that the instructor helped him isolate and work on. If the actor feels the dramatic rightness of a 'surprise', feels how this rightness originated in his own experience (of uncertainty, anger, shock, etc.), then his job in a subsequent performance will be to recover such feeling with as much freshness and gusto as he can muster. We might liken it to a small wound or trauma that *needs* to be repeated; it may even be that 'surprise' was itself an aid to memory, or at least to the memorable etching of *that* particular persona 'in' the actor's sense memory. Almost everything written about early modern actors attests to an aesthetic of seeming spontaneity, howsoever calmly or even coldly arrived at. Hence the mother-lode of Shakespearean characterization: parts wherein the osmosis of actor and character is respected, and exploited, as never before.

# PART III

# Repeated Cues

Hm! he is well enough for a Squire ha, ha
—————— Back of the others.
Ha, ha, ha!
—————— the odds my dear.
Ha, ha, ha!
—————— done first — damn me.
Ha, ha, ha!
—————— Are you not a Squire?
Ha, ha, ha!
—————— he'll make Love in Irish!
Something very like it, I dare say, Squire.
Let us retire, here they come. [Retires.]
—————— I come to Action.
~~Ha, ha, ha!~~
—————— side of my Voice.
Ha, ha, ha!
—————— let us Steal off. Exit.
Enter with Sr Archy at —

The part of Sir Archy from Charles Macklin's *Love à la Mode* (c. 1760).

# 8

# Introduction

B y 'repeated cues' we mean a cue-phrase that is said more than once within a short space of time: usually within a single speech, but not necessarily so. If we take the function of cues very literally, as an actor might who speaks his part absolutely on cue, oblivious to anything else, then the repeated cue means that one speaker will interrupt or talk over another speaker. If there were little more than a single full group rehearsal before taking a new play on-stage, then this interruption and over-speaking might happen in the full glare of the public. What then? The play becomes a shambles, its players at incoherent cross-purposes, unsure who goes first or what comes next? This is exactly what happens in the mechanicals' rehearsal scene in *A Midsummer Night's Dream*, in which not only does 'Thisby' speak 'all [his] part at once, cues and all', but in trying to repair the mistake he repeats the cue-phrase—'never tyre'—that Peter Quince has already once repeated (TLN 909–17). It is somewhere in this multiply cued confusion that Bottom enters wearing the ass's head—an apt symbol, we might think, of the hapless ineptitude of any actor who misses his cue, or any playwright who repeats one. Surely, then, a playwright—particularly one who was also an actor, would repeat cues at his peril. But this is not the case. Shakespeare does not repeat cues carelessly, but he does repeat them often enough to demand some answering hypothesis. This is what we offer, test, and expand upon in the discussions that follow. We shall see that when Shakespeare repeats a cue, the repetition is meticulously pointed and plotted. Unavoidable to the actor in the process of learning his part, the repeated or premature cue becomes an instruction—an invitation—all of its own.

We have compared the system of cues to a conductor's baton; the repeated cue might accordingly be seen as indicating two—or more—instruments or voices at once. It seems likely that the simple fact of repetition within speech and at the end of a unit of speech is an indication of some kind of cross-dialogue, or of different characters speaking independently of each other, perhaps ignorant of each other, in orchestrated counterpoint. This is a technique that makes drama audibly and indeed visibly a thing of dialectical instantaneity. Read in a book, a play looks linear, one speech following on from another in duly sequential order. Performed from cued parts, a play can become something much more lifelike.

To illustrate by example, let us take a simple passage of text that contains repeated cues. We will look at it, first in full, then broken down into the relevant parts. It starts at the midpoint of one of the lengthy speeches of the garrulous Nurse in *Romeo and Juliet*. Presented on the printed page from the Folio it looks like this, save for the fact that we have boldfaced one (or perhaps two) moments when the Nurse sends out her cue early:

NURSE. ... the day before she broke her brow, and then my Husband,/ God be with his soule, a was a merrie man, tooke up the/Child, yea quoth hee, doest thou fall upon thy face? thou/wilt fall backward when thou hast more wit, wilt thou not/*Jule*? And by my holy-dam, the pretie wretch lefte/crying, **& said I**: to see now how a Jest shall come about./I warrant, & I shall live a thousand yeares, I never should/forget it: wilt thou not *Julet* quoth he? and pretty foole it/stinted, **and said I**.

OLD LADY. Inough of this, I pray thee hold thy peace.

NURSE. Yes Madam, yet I can not chuse but laugh, to/thinke it should leave crying, **& say I**: and yet I warrant/ it had upon it brow, a bumpe as big as a young Cockrels/stone? A perilous knock, and it cryed bitterly. Yea quoth/my husband, fall'st upon thy face, thou wilt fall back-/ward when thou commest to age: wilt thou not *Jule*? It stinted: **and said I**.

JULIET. And stint thou too, I pray thee *Nurse*, say I.

(lineation ours)

But when we consider the parts of the Old Lady (Juliet's mother) and Juliet we find something rather interesting. The Old Lady's part will have looked like this:

_____ [and] [said] I.
Inough of this, I pray thee hold thy peace.

Juliet's part like this:

_____ [and] [said] I.
And stint thou too, I pray thee *Nurse*, say I.

Both Juliet and her mother have a cue that will lead them to interrupt the Nurse not separately as the text suggests, but in unison, and more than once. The only way to prevent this happening would be to give the two women longer cues. Elongating the cues to 'stinted, and said I' could prevent mid-speech interruption (where the words are 'crying, and said I') but will not prevent the two women from responding at the same time: both share the longer cue, 'I/it stinted and said I'. Indeed, stretch the cues to longer still, creating a six-word cue (and this far exceeds any on record in a professional part), and even that is not much help: the Old Lady has 'foole it stinted…', Juliet has 'Jule? It stinted…' The rhyme is almost guaranteed to confuse the two actors. It seems near impossible to prevent Juliet and her mother speaking together. Indeed, given the normality of cues of three or fewer words, the mid-speech interruptions seem similarly plotted. The only other alternative would be to provide the Old Lady and Juliet with indications that they must hear the cue more than once and remain silent before the 'actual' cue. That would necessitate adding to their parts something along these lines:

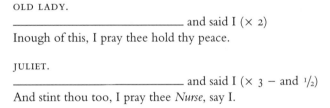

OLD LADY.

_____ and said I ($\times$ 2)
Inough of this, I pray thee hold thy peace.

JULIET.

_____ and said I ($\times$ 3 − and $^1/_2$)
And stint thou too, I pray thee *Nurse*, say I.

Any such device requires the writer of the actors' parts (the prompter?) first to notice that the cue is repeated on the Nurse's part, then to count how many times, and finally to mark up the two parts 'Old Lady' and 'Juliet' with the extra information: all very troublesome in the hectic theatre of the time. It requires, too, Shakespeare the writer-actor repeating a cue thoughtlessly, oblivious to the difficulties to which it will give rise. This is yet more unlikely. But the strongest argument in favour of the intended repeated cue is that the sense of the play at this point can only be enhanced by interruption. This is so in two basic ways. First, if it is the Nurse who is interrupted, then the humour of the scene is emphasized. She is recalling a story that she has told many times before; indeed, she repeats a familiar cycle of retelling the story even within her two consecutive speeches. She is thus seen comically to tire one or both of her addressees. No one hears her gleeful reminiscence without escalating exasperation—'Inough of this', 'stint thou!' Everyone wants the Nurse to shut up. Second, it might be that the two instantaneously 'cued' respondents interrupt not only the Nurse, but also each other. Alongside the garrulous humour are terse disagreement, familial tension, and a divisive past and future in miniature.

Let us consider the first option, and assume that the interruption is scripted. We now have actors with very different kinds of information about the scene. The actor of the Nurse will see at once that she (or he) gives out repeated cues. The actor can thus play with his fellow actors. Perhaps he pauses as the first 'cue-like' speech is given, letting the other actors begin their interruption before riding over their speeches with the continued text—'to see now how a Jest shall come about', 'and yet I warrant…'. Perhaps he lets the actors speak their entire lines before going on to give them the cue again—forcing the entire text once more—and once more still. Both comedy and bathos are enhanced by repetition. In turn, once the Old Lady and Juliet recognize what is happening, they too can 'play' the moment. When the Old Lady, for instance, hears her cue, 'she' begins to speak her cued line. What happens when she then hears her cue once more? She has three options. She can stop speaking, wait until the cue is finished, or start her own cued line again from the beginning. She can simply keep on speaking so that the cueing and cued voices speak over one another. Or she can continue from where she left off, 'drip-feeding' her lines every time she hears the cue until the cueing actor indicates to her that she can see her line through. She can vary one against the other on different days of performance.

Depending on how the actors play one another, the text might go something like:

| NURSE. | **and said I** [*pause*]— |
| OLD LADY. | Inough of this,— |  [JULIET *and* OLD LADY *exchange glances*]
| JULIET. | And stint thou— |

—to see now how a Jest shall come about. I warrant, & I shall live a thousand yeares, I never should forget it: wilt thou not *Julet* quoth he? and pretty foole it stinted, **and said I.** [*long pause*]

| OLD LADY. | [*pause*] Inough of this, I pray thee hold thy peace. |
| JULIET. | [*pause*] And stint thou too, I pray thee *Nurse*, say I. |

NURSE.   Madam, yet I can not chuse but laugh, to thinke it should
         leave crying, & **say I** [*raises warning finger*]—and yet I warrant/it
         had upon it brow, a bumpe as big as a young Cockrels stone?
         A perilous knock, and it cryed bitterly. Yea quoth my husband,
         fall'st upon thy face, thou wilt fall backward when thou commest
         to age: wilt thou not *Jule*? It stinted: **and said I.**
OLD LADY.   [*shouts*] Inough of this, I pray thee hold thy peace.
JULIET.   [*wearily*] And stint thou too, I pray thee *Nurse*, say I.

Or something like this:

NURSE.   **and said I** [*pause*]—
OLD LADY.   Inough of this,— [JULIET *and* OLD LADY *exchange glances*]
JULIET.   And stint thou—
         —to see now how a Jest shall come about. I warrant, & I shall live a
         thousand yeares, I never should forget it: wilt thou not *Julet* quoth
         he? and pretty foole it stinted, **and said I.** [*long pause*]
OLD LADY.   [*hesitant*]—I pray thee … [JULIET *and* OLD LADY *exchange glances*]
JULIET.   [*hesitant*]—I pray thee …
NURSE.   Yes Madam, yet I can not chuse but laugh, to thinke it should
         leave crying, & **say I**—[*mischievous slight pause*]
OLD LADY.   —hold …
JULIET.   —*Nurse* …
         —and yet I warrant it had upon it brow, a bumpe as big as a young
         Cockrels stone? A perilous knock, and it cryed bitterly. Yea quoth
         my husband, fall'st upon thy face, thou wilt fall backward when thou
         commest to age: wilt thou not *Jule*? It stinted: **and said I.** [*pause*]
OLD LADY.   [*long pause*] thy peace! Inough of this, I pray thee hold thy peace.
JULIET.   [*long pause*] say I! And stint thou too, I pray thee *Nurse*, say I.

The second possibility—that the scene might be setting-up Juliet and her
mother to be talking to each other as much as to the Nurse—becomes all
the more likely once we grant to the players a certain performance-attentive
liberty. The moment might even go like this:

NURSE.   … said I—
OLD LADY.   [*to Nurse*] Inough of this.
JULIET.   [*to her mother*] And stint thou too.
OLD LADY.   [*to Juliet*] I pray thee hold thy peace.
JULIET.   [*to Nurse*] I pray thee *Nurse*, say I.

In this scenario, the Nurse's double cue—cueing mother and daughter simultaneously—becomes a cue for their simmering tensions suddenly to boil over. After all, the context of the scene is the mother preparing to tell her unwilling 13-year-old child to 'thinke of marriage now'. And there is a subdued but uncertain rivalry between the mother and her surrogate, the Nurse ('Nurse give leave awhile...Nurse come backe againe'), who has such an easy and affectionate relationship with Juliet. Indeed, the Nurse's reminiscence might have been designed to irritate and rebuke a semi-absent parent. Many theatre productions of *Romeo and Juliet* for this reason choose to play the mother as a nervous and fidgety matriarch, herself abandoned to the altar when a child, at odds with her adolescent daughter and obscurely jealous both of her and of her Nurse.

The opportunities for the Juliet-actor in this scene are still more acute. The cue-effect can give to the player a certain tense alertness to context: she (or he) knows that the role is premissed upon filial rebellion as much as love at first sight, and here is her mother, in her very first scene, interrupting a joyous recounting of Juliet's past. Looked at in this way, the cue-effect is a comic foreshadowing of much greater 'extemporizing'—Juliet's disobedience to the 'cues' of her parents—to come. So, Juliet's '*Nurse*, say I' can be understood as a defiant *return* of the cue to the Nurse: as though to say, 'ignore my resentful mother; tell me more of me, but remember that I am no longer the child you speak of'. Juliet's interruption of her mother, as she gives the stage back to her Nurse, becomes a preparation to do and be without either of them. For as we have seen, Juliet could be interrupting the Nurse just as much as her mother is. The Nurse's words are hardly less provoking to the adolescent than to the mother. She repeats the same joke twice, quoting her merry husband to the effect that Juliet will 'fall backward' when she has more wit and comes of age; this when the toddler Juliet has a bump on her brow 'as big as a young Cockrels stone'. The tone is genially bawdy, but there is at the same time something mercilessly predetermining about the whole anecdote. For Juliet, her sex is her own to withhold or to give; for the Nurse, it is always somehow public. Whichever way we see the Juliet-actor using this gift of a free-floating cued response—as a rebuke to her mother, or to her Nurse, or to both—it is Juliet who in every sense possesses the cue-space.

This first example, then, can suggest some of the many possibilities of the repeated cue: it is indeed a highly fertile technique. However, there is an inevitable objection to such readings. If Shakespeare had wanted interweaving voices, why didn't he simply script them in that way? There are many answers to this objection, as we hope the examples that follow in succeeding chapters will show. Briefly, however, the answer is simple. If every last phrase that an actor is asked to speak is independently cued on his part, then the resulting performance will be different than if the occasional statement is spoken in the kind of 'gap' created by an early or repeated cue. When a speech is clearly scripted, each actor must wait for his cue, pause until the other ceases speaking, and then say his piece: the play performed is as linear as the play written. But what if Shakespeare does not want linear performance? Played from cues, each actor speaks not after but around, or inside, the other. When Shakespeare wants to create parallel or mutually oblivious lines of thinking, with one character in one 'mental space' and the rest somewhere quite different, repeated cues can obviate the need for what can be produced typographically only by parallel columns.

To summarize: there are a number of possible ways of acting, or responding to, a repeated cue. There are always at least two players to take into account: the one giving the repeated cue, and the one (or ones) being cued to speak by the cue. Their respective relations to the repeated cue are quite different from one another. Important here is the fact that the cue is always co-owned. The actor throwing out the repeated cue will know that he is scripted to do so. He can therefore choose to do so in various ways. He can 'play' the moment; he can equally 'play' the actor whom he is cueing: the repeating cues may be fired out like shots, sudden and stunning; they may be delayed, floating, teasing. It is crucial to any reading of cued parts, and repeated cues within them, that this 'foreknowledge' of the actor giving the cues be factored in to possible reconstructions of the dramatic moment.

Linked to this is the fact that the same actor may at one point be the speaker of a repeated cue, and at another point its receiver (perhaps not in the same play, but indubitably in, say, a season of plays). This reinforces the likelihood that, once he hears a cue being repeated, or senses that the other actor has not 'closed' his speech and may be about to repeat his cue, the actor receiving the now 'premature' cue will instinctively or intuitively draw upon the stock of options that experience has given him. Actors famously, or notoriously, need to be 'in' their moments, as though surprised by them, to give the play a compelling charge: repeated cues, representing at once a practised array of techniques *and* an abrupt, serendipitous, or mischievous interruption to expectations, are a perfect vehicle for this imperative.

We need to remain alive to the full context of this theatre at this juncture. When an actor received a part, he might receive it in effective isolation from the other parts in that play, but he did not receive it in isolation from other parts that he had played. Above all, as we have argued earlier, each actor was accustomed to playing (perhaps a variety of) certain 'types'. If a clown or jester, then certain communicative techniques would be almost reflexively in his personal repertoire; if a counsellor, or a king, or a pastoral virgin, quite different ones. Furthermore, we need to recognize here that the repeated cue could have acquired a peculiar status as a performance 'instruction' in its own right that alerted the actor reading *or* hearing such a cue to a range of possibilities. For an interesting fact is that in the majority of cases where Shakespeare repeats the same word or phrase in brisk succession, the repetition is also a cue. In other words, merely to read or hear such repetition becomes a prompt to recall techniques associated with the repeated cue. It is not that the repeated cue is ubiquitous: if it were, it would probably lack any significance—as a particular type of cue—whatsoever. Rather, the repeated cue is arresting, and therefore, when it does occur, pointed. Almost always its appearance signifies one of a few things: the early delineation of a garrulous, embarrassed or isolated character (usually of a certain fusty or superannuated type); the pointing of intense conflict between one figure and another; as a variation upon the first of these, the creation of a 'self-speaking' moment, where the actor exists in his own spatial or existential bubble, and the repeated cue is effectively a self-cue; and as an operatic technique of ascending, usually tragic, climax. In other words, the repeated cue was distinctive enough to alert the actor to a fairly specific set of options.

But how to approach repeated cues given the sparseness of specific information about them? We have been obliged to adopt a number of different models, privileging no single one above another, as we cannot know absolutely how repeated cues were handled—and whether they were always handled in uniform fashion (we suspect that they were not). But each model acknowledges the fact that repeated cues were meant to encourage some variety of early response.

# 9

# From Crowds to Clowns

I n the sections that follow we will explore how Shakespeare develops the simple device of the repeated or premature cue so that it becomes a highly sophisticated technical instrument, used to point and orchestrate moments of rare emotional intensity. But, as with most of the theatrical 'languages' honed to unprecedented resourcefulness by Shakespeare, the depth and daring do not come overnight. Much of Shakespeare's audacity in using the technique—and indeed, the performative centrality that ensues—depends upon the actors' familiarity with it. And it seems likely that an important contributor to such company-wide awareness were scenes which, of their nature, included all or many of the company at one time, performing simultaneously on-stage in an intricate tug of war: by this we mean, of course, the crowd scene.

## Crowds

Crowd scenes are an obvious instance in which the repeated cue can be a useful means of creating the required polyphony, or, more particularly, 'cue' a scene where voices intercut and compete, shouting across one another and interrupting 'extemporally'.

Throughout his career, Shakespeare makes repeated cues pivotal to his crowd scenes. *Coriolanus* uses the technique on numerous occasions, beginning with four successive such cues from '*All*': '**Speake, speake**' (TLN 6), '**Resolv'd, resolv'd**' (TLN 9), '**We know't, we know't**' (TLN 12), '**away, away**' (TLN 15); similarly, in the climactic scene of Coriolanus's banishment, the speeches of '*All*' are, consecutively, 'To'th'Rocke, to'th'Rocke with him' (TLN 2356), '**It shall be so, it shall be so**: let him away: Hee's banish'd, and **it shall be so**' (TLN 2391–2), and '**It shall be so, it shall be so**' (TLN 2407). *The Tempest* begins similarly, with the confusion of the storm and the crew orchestrated by a series of repeated cues ('bestirre, bestirre', 'all lost…all lost', 'we split, we split, we split' (TLN 7–9, 60–1, 70–3) see pp. 275–9). Shakespeare is doing something similar at the start of his career. So, in *2 Henry VI*, '*All*' are given three speech-acts in a scene of rival demagoguery between Buckingham, Old Clifford, and the rebel Cade: these speeches are '**God save the King, God save the King**' (TLN 2795), '**Wee'l follow Cade, Wee'l follow Cade**' (TLN 2810), and '**A Clifford, a Clifford,** | Wee'l follow the King, and **Clifford**' (TLN 2830–1).

There is more in this than an economical gesture toward the mindless multi-headed monster. The crowd's repetitions seem to be clearly designed to echo through, cut across, or comment upon the speeches that the speakers are assembled to hear. This is as near a proof as any that Shakespeare scripted interruptions—from cuer or from cued—in exactly the way we are suggesting. He does not detail the precise moment of intervention because he does not need to: he trusts his company, and he knows that dramatic exigencies and the imperative of immediacy are improved by a certain flexibility. And more than that, the crowd's repeated cues suggest that the technique itself gathered—perhaps from the kind of poetically symmetrical uses of it we see in *2 Henry VI*—an almost comical *cachet*, and an identifiable resonance both as a performative prompt and as a characteristic of a particular 'type': that type here is the 'orchestrated' crowd, but there are many different but recurring situations that similarly call forth such repetitions. Everyone in the company must have played a 'part' in the crowd at some point; for an actor merely to see on his roll a repeated cue was to spot an invitation to and opportunity for interruptive counterpointing.

*Julius Caesar* has perhaps the most crafted examples of such crowd effects. So, the plebeians say this at the close of Brutus's speech to them after Caesar's assassination:

| | |
|---|---|
| ALL. | Live *Brutus*, live, live. |
| 1ST GENTLEMAN. | Bring him with Triumph home unto his house. |
| 2ND GENTLEMAN. | Give him a Statue with his Ancestors. |
| 3RD GENTLEMAN. | Let him be *Caesar*. |
| 4TH GENTLEMAN. | *Caesars* better parts, |
| | Shall be Crown'd in *Brutus*. |

(TLN 1578–83)

It is likely that the thrice-repeated 'live' here echoes throughout the acclamations. The first gentleman's shout, if cued by 'live', might set him on immediately to 'Bring him with Triumph...house', itself setting on 'Give him a Statue' and so forth, while, perhaps, the body of the crowd continues its shouts of 'live, live' (perhaps indeed this is a standard format for 'crowd-speak' that indicates rebounding for as long as is appropriate). The effect will be like an oratorio in which each 'singer's' phrase prompts an answering phrase from the chorus. The successive communal 'live's might work like exclamation marks, punctuating and celebrating the individual offerings. The effect would be to change an unrealistically static and staccato crowd scene into something sweeping and echoing; at the same time it would be less an example of 'realism' than of orchestrated expressionism.

Another example is Mark Antony's famous oratorical 'winding-up' of the crowd. Here the plebeians are scripted to speak not at indiscriminate angles, but rather at exact moments of maximum incendiary impact (and indeed comedy). The best example is when Antony teases the crowd with reading Caesar's will. It is necessary to quote it at length:

ANTONY.  ...heere's a Parchment, with the seale of *Caesar*,
I found it in his Closset, 'tis his Will:
Let but the Commons heare this Testament:
(Which pardon me) I do not meane to reade,
And they would go and kisse dead *Caesars* wounds,
And dip their napkins in his sacred Blood;
Yea, begge a haire of him for Memory,
And dying, mention it within their Willes,
Bequeathing it as a rich Legacie
Unto their issue.

4TH CITIZEN.  Wee'l heare the Will, reade it *Marke Antony*.

ALL.  The Will, the Will; we will heare *Caesars* Will.

ANTONY.  Have patience gentle Friends, I must not read it. ...
...being men, hearing the Will of *Caesar*,
It will inflame you, it will make you mad;
'Tis good you know not that you are his Heires,
For if you should, O what would come of it?

4TH CITIZEN.  Reade the Will, wee'l heare it *Antony*:
You shall reade us the Will, *Caesars* Will.

ANTONY.  Will you be Patient? Will you stay a-while?
I have o're-shot my selfe to tell you of it,
I feare I wrong the Honourable men,
Whose daggers have stabb'd *Caesar*: I do feare it.

4TH CITIZEN.  They were Traitors: Honourable men?

ALL.                 The Will, the Testament.
2ND CITIZEN.   They were Villaines, Murderers: the Will, read the Will.
ANTONY.           You will compel me then to read the Will:
                          Then make a Ring about the Corpes of *Caesar*,
                          And let me shew you him that made the Will:
                          Shall I descend? And will you give me leave?

(TLN 1665–98)

Thinking about how the parts were written will highlight what is happening in this passage. The word 'will' here occurs twenty times, as well as being punned upon at least twice more (as a verb—'we will hear Caesars Will', 'Will you be Patient?' 'Will you stay a-while?'—and as a homophone—'Wee'l heare the Will'). Though the word 'will' is *spoken* continually by Antony and by his crowd, it is specifically—and only—Antony's cue (of the crowd in this passage it will be seen that '4' has cues of '[Unto] [their] issue', '[come] [of] it?', '[do] [feare] it', '[give] [me] leave?'; 2's cue is '[Will,] [the] Testament'). Throughout the larger scene, the whole of which resonates with the word 'will', Antony continues to be the only person with 'Will' as a cue. So, while the players of the crowd will see straightforwardly enough their own desire to hear 'the Will' framed with a bustle of varying cues, the player of Antony will see his three successive speeches here cued by 'Will': the cues are '*Caesars* Will', '*Caesars* Will', and 'read the Will'. And, during the rest of the scene, he will see that he continues to be repeatedly cued by 'Will': his part is, in the most literal sense, 'will-full', with text and cue playing off one another. But these repetitions work in quite a different way from the other cued repetitions we have been looking at. These are not 'premature' cues—Antony sees quite clearly that 'Caesar's Will' occurs twice in consecutive cues—so there is no 'early' passage that they provoke (though the actor of Antony might well 'jump' a speech, the '*Caesars* Will' cue sending him past 'Will you be Patient?' and straight to 'You will compel me': in writing similar cues next to one another, Shakespeare perhaps indicated passages that could, if necessary, be cut). But if these are not premature cues, what are they for? Cues such as these, we suggest, are performance notes to the player of Antony, but performance notes that may also have shaped the way in which Shakespeare wrote this scene in the first place.

So what does the obsessive recurrence of 'Will' as a cue tell the Antony-actor as he learns his speech? For one thing he will see that his cues repeatedly ask him for the will (testament) of Caesar, and that he delays handing that testament over. For another he will see that he starts playing with the demand: the more he is asked for the 'Will', the more he teases the waiting crowd, toying with the obvious dual referents of the word with his mocking rejoinders '*Will* you be patient?' and, still more provokingly, '*Will* you stay a-*while*?' (our italics). So he will notice that, by a simple verbal trick, he continually reminds the crowd that Caesar's last will and testament are in danger of not being effected because of the new regime; *and* that, in general, the great man's 'will' (wish) has been stopped following his death ('will', then, becomes a dynamic metonym of the larger scandal). That the crowd's common 'will' is being denied is made to seem just another element of the all-purpose prevention of 'will' in all its senses brought about by Brutus. Whether Antony in his word-play is understood to be spotting a chance and then seizing it, or following a conception through to its end, he divides the word 'will' into and against itself, multiplying its implacability. By ensuring that the simple noun becomes a kind of doubtful verb, he draws out all of the combined frustration and violence that inhere in the basic noun: and therein the word's latent mixture of expectancy and explosiveness.

But Shakespeare makes still more of his recurring cue; after all, as various sonnets suggest, 'will' is one of his most favourite and promiscuously divisible words. So, looking at the flurry of word-games and repetition around the word 'will', the Antony-actor may also see something suggestive, sexually charged, in his character's conquest: an escalating frenzy, as the 'will' at issue is endlessly magnified into enormity. In turn, this teasing quality traces the distribution of the cue-word. For, rather than growing more and more bloated, in moving from '*Caesars* Will' to '*Will . . . a-while*', the word itself is progressively *deflated* throughout Antony's part. Just as the 'Will' at issue is both a shared public longing and a secret scroll, so too does Antony's 'will' hover between an imperative and an uncertainty. The cue-word is turned into a kind of challenge, and thereby an invitation: 'will' you be cued into 'will' or not? The crux of the scene is then the way in which the cue-word collects into itself all of the energies of the dramatic moment. These energies are surely enough political, psychic, and sexual, and correspond exactly to the semantic folds within the word 'Will'.

But Shakespeare is attempting still more in giving the actor a part with so much emphasis—and in the most eye-catching bits of text on the scroll—on 'will'. He appears to be taking the potential of the cue *per se*, its latent or inhering generative power, and turning *it* into the object of the moment. Here we need to think in more indicative terms about how cues work. For the kinds of political and dramatic energies at a crescendo in this scene are also energies peculiar to the simple facts of a cue-word, particularly a reiterated, echoing cue-word. All cues bridge *and* overcome a gap between two statements (indeed, two actions). Rather than any kind of hiatus, then, the cue is much more profoundly a sort (and source) of energy. The technique is astonishingly simple and absolutely 'of' the early modern theatre. This particular scene is, politically, all about lighting a fuse; and dramatically, about a cue-word being man-handled to the very edge of permission, being bounced and shared and split about so much that the single word begins to take into itself the entire momentum of this 'world-historical' moment. The civil wars are about to start, and the movement from one 'Will' to the next is like the fissioning of an atom into explosion. So, Caesar's last 'Will' becomes Antony's delayed will; the crowd's imploring will becomes Antony's granted will; all of these together becomes the unstoppable will of 'mutiny': or, as Antony says at scene's end, 'Mischeefe thou art a-foot, | Take thou what shape thou *wilt*' (TLN 1799–1800, our italics). In due course, 'will' as a decision—'we will!'—is the result. 'Will' becomes a metaphor of the fully taken cue: the civil wars a detonation of the same thing.

The audience too is being played with here; it is very overtly being 'cued', just as the plebeians are. Shakespeare intuits this absolutely; or rather, he intuits the theatrical force of such metatheatrical confederacies, and so meticulously scripts them. We can watch with the eyes of Brutus, his gullible trust so mocked; with the eyes of Antony, watching himself turn the screw; or the eyes of the plebeians, exultant at witnessing mastery and at the prospect of bloodletting. The political direction of the moment is up in the air; the direction of audience sympathy is concomitantly up for grabs. Nothing here is preordained; even Antony can respond only to extraordinary and fickle occasion, and as much as he manipulates his audience, he is also taking his cues from it and duly running.

Nonetheless, this is Antony's moment, and one in which his possession of the cue-space—the way he can speed it up or slow it down, make it supercharged with portent or as slow as a bell—means that he really is given here much of drama's basic potency. This is of course a scene that is *about* the power of theatre to move great assemblies. Antony's techniques are there for all to see. He is knowingly playing the part of demagogue, knowing that it is known. But at the same time, Antony is given that demonic Shakespearean charm: he can lay his cards on the table, require our knowledge of their duplicity, yet still expect that we will fall for the trick. Theatrical enthralment is here specifically rhetorical, and therein open to lead either to action or to horror at such action. To fall under the spell of theatre might be to commit to bloody 'mutiny': equally, the rhetorical tricks, as typified by Antony's use of 'will', are so blatant that we can simultaneously see in the 'persuasion' egregious mendacity and gullibility. We watch the shamelessness of theatre ratcheted up into both sublimity and menace. And we watch it in a basic sense from *inside* the cue-space, sensitive to every fidget, aware of just how un-taken *and* explosive the cue at this moment is.

## Clowns

In Shakespeare's earliest comedies there are very few repeated cues. No doubt this is partly because Shakespeare well knew the importance of clear and orderly cues. But it was also because he had not yet been scripting parts long enough; no doubt it took a few seasons to develop an intimate, intuitively trustful relationship with a core of actors who, knowing what had been written for them, would be all the more sensitive to what was about to come. What we see of repeated cues in the earliest plays, then, is almost entirely limited to brief comic moments, and in particular moments in which an actor of clown parts is invited to indulge in a little *sotto voce* repartee—and perhaps *apparent* improvisation—with the audience. We know that clowns on the Elizabethan stage were famous, or notorious, for their extemporizing, whether this was in the form of jokes, asides, jigs, or cartwheels. We know that sometimes these fools were the most loved characters in a play, and that some plays were set up principally as frameworks, or prompts, for a particularly gifted clown's improvisations. Conversely, we might also suspect that Shakespeare wanted clowns, like the rest of his players, to subserve the larger fiction; not only are his fools regularly vilified for their tired puns or otiose practice, but Hamlet specifically curses stage clowns for veering from the scripted part: 'And let those that play your Clownes, speake no more then is set downe for them. For there be of them, that will themselves laugh, to set on some quantitie of barren Spectators to laugh too, though in the meane time, some necessary Question of the Play be then to be considered: that's Villainous, & shewes a most pittifull Ambition in the Foole that uses it' (TLN 887–93).[1] Nevertheless, the very early comedies (*Two Gentlemen of Verona*, *The Taming of the Shrew*, and *The Comedy of Errors*) show evidence of a strategic *rapprochement* between impatience and permission: evidence rooted in how repeated or premature cues allow the meshing of clownish improvisation with obedience to the script. That is, Shakespeare seems to have scripted specific exchanges in clown parts so as to make improvisation a potential, an opportunity to be grasped or not depending upon the mood of the moment. In this way, the technique at once respects and renovates a looser style of folk entertainment—indeed, a looser style of acting, wherein relatively wooden or inert scripts were the backdrop or the counterpoint to a clown's extemporizing innovations.[2]

In *Two Gentlemen*, for instance, we find this exchange, here in full text:

VALENTINE.  Ha? Let me see: I, give it me, it's mine:
                 Sweet Ornament, that deckes a thing divine,
                 Ah *Silvia, Silvia.*
SPEED.         Madam *Silvia*: Madam *Silvia.*
VALENTINE.  How now Sirha?
SPEED.         Shee is not within hearing Sir.
VALENTINE.  Why sir, who bad you call her?
SPEED.         Your worship sir, or else I mistooke.
VALENTINE.  Well: you'll still be too forward.

                                        (TLN 400–8)

The crucial cues are on the part of the servant/clown, Speed:

_____ [Ah] [*Silvia,*] *Silvia.*
            Madam *Silvia*: Madam *Silvia.*

The actor will see that he is to give out a repeated cue-phrase; it is likely that his part would also have told him that this repeated cue was itself cued by the repeated cue of 'Silvia'. If it did not, then he would come in early with his 'Madam Silvia'; if it did, then he may still have interpreted the repeating cue-word as an instruction to come in early, and so to take his ensuing lines as very much his own, to be acted in the time and space that he thinks immediately appropriate. For he will of course anticipate that the repeated cue-phrase that *he* has to speak ('Madam Silvia') will itself be interrupted. In other words, the cues are scripted to allow a classic moment of foolish licence and servant disobedience. Here this will take the form of Speed's mischievous insolence, as he patrols the stage, shouting out 'Madam Silvia' as though genuinely owning some claim upon her movements. As he does so, Valentine tries vainly to keep to decorum, with his (perhaps repeated) 'How now Sirha?' turning between indignation and amazement. The subsequent exchange seems to vindicate this reading. So, Speed's 'She is not within hearing Sir' is spoken as though returning and reporting from duty, oblivious to his master's intervening 'How now...' Similarly, Valentine's next two speeches both appear to comment, as though meta-dramatically, upon the impudent liberty displayed by the servant in so exceeding his script: 'who bad you call her?', and 'you'll still be too forward'. The repeated cue invites the clown precisely to go 'forward', all the way to the edge of the stage, creating a shared channel in which the fool and the audience can indulge in the pleasures of knowing irreverence.

Something similar might be scripted a little further on in the same part; here again is the full script:

> VALENTINE. No (Madam) so it steed you, I will write
> (Please you command) a thousand times as much:
> And yet ———
> SILVIA. A pretty period: well: I ghesse the sequell;
> And yet I will not name it: and yet I care not.
> And yet, take this againe: and yet I thanke you:
> Meaning henceforth to trouble you no more.
> SPEED. And yet you will: and yet, another yet.
> VALENTINE. What meanes your Ladiship?
> Doe you not like it?
> SILVIA. Yes, yes: the lines are very queintly writ,
> But (since unwillingly) take them againe.
> Nay, take them.
>
> (TLN 503–15)

There are two exchanges going on here: one between Valentine and Silvia, another between Speed and the audience. He is our intermediary, commenting upon the nervous equivocations between the two would-be lovers. Neither of them pays any attention to what Speed says, a fact made clear to the actors by making the line cued by Speed (to Valentine) explicitly addressed to 'your Ladiship'. The Speed-actor, meanwhile, has one line to play with, a line that repeats the cue-word 'yet' twice. Now we cannot know whether the cue that Speed gives to Valentine was 'yet', or 'another yet', or even 'and yet, another yet'. Only the second of these will prevent the Valentine-actor coming in early, perhaps as early as Speed's very first 'And yet'. But even if the cue was 'another yet', and the Valentine-actor does *not* jump in precipitately, the Speed-actor may well identify in his line an invitation to extemporize: to dole out further 'and yets' and 'another yets' as the negotiations between the other two continue. This becomes still more likely when we consider the context of the full script: 'And yet' is Valentine's heavily weighted cue to Silvia, a qualification which she in turn speaks another *four* times. One thing is certain: that Shakespeare is here building the exchange around an echoing cue-phrase, a fact which suggests still more precise invitations to the actors. So, even if the Speed-actor was unsure what to do with his 'repeated' cue-word 'yet', the occasion of performance might well have provided his answer: the clown will seize the word 'yet' just as Silvia has, though for slightly different purposes. So, he will listen to their ensuing conversation, hear Silvia continue with nervous evasions and polite equivocations—'Yes, yes', 'But', 'Nay', 'I, I'—and confide unto us the requisite mocking comment, 'and yet', 'another yet', 'and yet...': one which points both to the immediate occasion (of crossed motives) and to the future qualification (they part at odds now, 'and yet' will not be at odds for ever).

The Speed-actor may well find an extension of the same liberties at the end of this scene. His parting words, which also close the scene, are 'oh bee not like your Mistresse, be moved, be moved' (TLN 564–5); this cues the exit of himself and Valentine and the entrance of Protheus and Julia, heralding this passionate leave-taking:

> PROTHEUS. Have patience, gentle *Julia*:
> JULIA.    I must where there is no remedy.
> PROTHEUS. When possibly I can, I will returne.
> JULIA.    If you turne not: you will return the sooner:
>           Keepe this remembrance for thy *Julia's* sake ...
>
> (TLN 568–72)

The question here is how the Speed-actor would have interpreted his closing repetition, 'be moved, be moved', which might have been part of the entrance cue for the succeeding scene (perhaps alongside 'exeunt', or 'exit Valentine and Speed'). In line with his role in the preceding scene as the audience's 'conductor', and the confident privilege this confers, it is possible that the actor would have taken the doubled-up 'be moved' as a scene-straddling joke. So, the words are already a pun: Speed wants his master to 'be moved' to pity him for his hunger, and more pertinently to 'move' his body (off the stage and to the 'victuals'); there is thus intentional bathos in comparing Silvia's resistance to Valentine's love-letter with Valentine's resistance to Speed's need for a meal. With the meaning of the verb already so shifting and mobile, and Speed's current role likewise one of meta-dramatic impishness, the actor might assume that a single 'be moved' is sufficient as an exit/entrance cue, thus keeping the second in reserve to speak directly to the audience as soon as Protheus and Julia enter: 'be moved', he implores, by the lachrymose parting you are all about to witness. The clown thus darts across and between scenes, orchestrating the audience's ironic remove from the half-blind follies of the lovers.

A related use of repeated cues in the early comedies is to prompt and frame moments of physical comedy or confrontation, and in particular for farcically normative violence. Usually this means the violence suffered by a servant from his master; the repeated cue can be the cause of the violence (because he annoys the master by speaking out of turn or speaking too much); it can perpetuate the violence (because the servant/clown does not quickly escape the moment of culpability/vulnerability); or it can be an escape from the violence (giving the servant/clown a little space in which to appeal against the injustice to the audience).[3] A typical example of this comes at the start of the role of the servant/clown Grumio in *Shrew*:

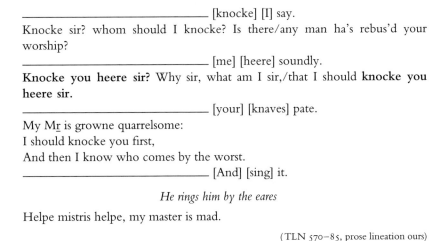

_____ [knocke] [I] say.
Knocke sir? whom should I knocke? Is there/any man ha's rebus'd your worship?
_____ [me] [heere] soundly.
**Knocke you heere sir?** Why sir, what am I sir,/that I should **knocke you heere sir.**
_____ [your] [knaves] pate.
My Mr is growne quarrelsome:
I should knocke you first,
And then I know who comes by the worst.
_____ [And] [sing] it.

*He rings him by the eares*

Helpe mistris helpe, my master is mad.

(TLN 570–85, prose lineation ours)

Both context and character conform to a clear type: the actor will know that his part is one of the naughty servant, taking delight in foiling his master, seeking applause for so doing, but of course getting beaten for his pains. The actor will recognize the repeated cue he gives out, 'knocke you heere, sir', as a perfect occasion for this archetype to be set in motion. So the fact of the repetition suggests, first, the intentional misconstruing of his master's orders (*'heere sir'* working like a fake malapropism), and second, his acting upon this miscontrual (by either ignoring or 'knocking' his interlocutor); this insult asks for an immediate rebuke, in the form of the early return of the cued response ('Villaine I say...'), which in turn 'frees' the rest of Grumio's line to be enacted as the player wishes, perhaps facilitating slapstick violence, perhaps sudden intimacy with the audience, perhaps simply mischievous pretence. The technique is reprised a few lines later; here Grumio gives out the potential repeated cue of 'at the gate', while recalling the earlier freedoms of his last repeated cue of 'Knocke me heere':

| PETRUCHIO. | I bad the rascall knocke upon your gate, |
| | And could not get him for my heart to do it. |
| GRUMIO. | Knocke **at the gate**? O heavens: spake you not/ |
| | these words plaine? Sirra, Knocke me heere: rappe me/ |
| | heere: knocke me well, and knocke me soundly? And/ |
| | come you now with knocking **at the gate**?/ |
| PETRUCHIO. | Sirra be gone, or talke not I advise you. |
| HORTENSIO. | *Petruchio* patience. |

(TLN 604–11, prose lineation ours)

Of course the clown-actor remains tied to his script: but the effect of the repeated cue is to lengthen his leash considerably, albeit with the end result of yoking him violently back into place. This is not a meaningless piece of ribbing or ribaldry: Petruchio's struggle to 'tame' his 'ancient trusty pleasant servant' works dramatically as a precursor to his similar struggle to tame the heroine. That Shakespeare might be intimating, or lightly enabling, a genuine power struggle is reinforced by the metatheatrical context. As we have intimated, the 'old' extra-textual liberties of the clown were in the process of being pegged back by the professional theatre; there is little doubt that many in the company wanted it that way. And here Shakespeare seems to be at once exploiting and disciplining these liberties. In cases like these, it is not at all unlikely that the principal actor—here playing

Petruchio—will join with his character in wishing that the servant/clown would 'talke not' (TLN 610). At the very least, the effect might be to get the Petruchio-actor off and running with the necessary impatient velocity. After all, this episode with Grumio takes place in his very first scene: to have his imperatives doubted, his will frustrated, his playing space cramped; to have him forced into violence where assumptions of authority fall down—some such combination might have been just the 'cue' that Shakespeare planted.

## Set-Piece: Malvolio

The comic potential of repeated cues is exemplified, and interestingly stretched, by the part of Malvolio in *Twelfth Night*. For instance, in the episode in which Malvolio is watched and overheard by Sir Toby and friends, the script offers these 'witnessing' actors five repeated cues, all in lines that cue the actor playing Malvolio: Andrew's 'Pistoll him, pistoll him' (TLN 1052), Toby's 'Peace, peace' (TLN 1053), Fabian's 'peace, peace' (TLN 1066) and 'now, now' (TLN 1073), Toby's 'what, what?' (TLN 1086). The effect of these is simple enough; assuming that at least some of the doubled-up cues are in the Malvolio part-text, all of the actors will know that the scene is one in which Malvolio's central line of speech is overheard and commented upon; the repeated cues establish the freedom of the actors other than Malvolio to speak around and 'inside' his egotistical meditation, a freedom already presaged by the fact that all of their dialogue is palpably 'aside' from the central figure on the stage. But now, coinciding with Malvolio's discovery of Maria's planted letter, the ownership of repeated cues suddenly shifts to Malvolio alone:

MALVOLIO.　　*M.O.A.I.* doth sway my life. Nay but first/let me see, let me see, let me see.
FABIAN.　　What dish a poyson has she drest him?
SIR TOBY.　　And with what wing the stallion [*sic.* staniel?] checkes at it?

(TLN 1123)

The actor playing Malvolio will see that he throws out the same cue-phrase, 'let me see', three times. Here this clearly presages the fact that he is speaking to himself: the repeating cues capture a mind engrossed in its

own miraculously opened sense of possibility; meanwhile another channel
of dialogue proceeds elsewhere on the stage. The scene might proceed
as follows:

> MALVOLIO. Nay but first let me see—
> FABIAN.   What dish—
> MALVOLIO. Let me see—
> TOBY.     What dish … [—a poyson—]
> MALVOLIO. Let me see.
> FABIAN.   [What dish a poyson—] has she drest him?
> TOBY.     And with what wing the stallion checkes at it?
> MALVOLIO. *I may command, where I adore …*

The repeated cue does not so much interrupt the oblivious Malvolio, as
frame his absurdity: it isolates and magnifies his portentous self-absorption.
If the player wants to exploit the cue-effect, he can leave a considerable gap in between each 'let me see'—the longer the better for
comic effect. Each moment spent in rapt silence is a cause for glee in
an audience, who can enjoy his pseudo-pedantry, his ponderous narcis-
sism, and the ever so slow maturing into delighted [mis-]recognition.
Here then is a variation upon the potential already identified in the
technique—to accentuate victimhood by isolating a character from all
others (also the reason, of course, why it can facilitate unusual intimacy with the audience). The character is marooned in his privacies,
oblivious to the fact that the world is looking on and laughing. If
used as a purely comic technique, then, the premature cue has affinities with scapegoat mechanisms: it is a means of isolating a single figure,
in the full gaze of the crowd, for the purposes of gloating, invasion,
or dismissal.

   Shakespeare continues to play with the technique as the role proceeds.
Malvolio's next scene gives him two repeated cues to say, both in the
service of his overweening self-conceit. The first is when he meets Olivia,
convinced of her love:

> ————————————————————— [How] [now] *Malvolio?*
> Sweet Lady, ho, ho.

> (TLN 1538–9)

Malvolio chuckles, while Olivia is half-unmoved, half-amazed ('**Smil'st
thou?**', goes her deadpan observation): the repeated cue strands Malvolio

in his over-scripted affect. A little later the technique returns, this time to
frame Malvolio's disdain for his courtly rivals:

> ———————————————————— [with] [you] man?
> Go off, I discard you: let me enjoy my private: go off.

(TLN 611–13)

As we quite often see—particularly in comedy—the content of the line
apostrophizes the performative instruction. For the two units of speech
after his first 'Go off'—'I discard you', 'let me enjoy my private'—are the
perfect commentary on the comic freedoms released, or assumed, by the
premature cue.

The part of Malvolio attests to Shakespeare's easy mastery of the repeated
cue as a comic instrument. But the part's final uses of the cue-effect
also suggest something considerably deeper: that the repeated cue can
harness complex or troubling emotional effects; and that in itself the cue
technique can help mark for the actor decisive moments of emotional and
performative transition. We see this in Malvolio's next scene, when he is
locked in darkness and tormented by Feste/Sir Topas. We noted earlier
how the consistency and clarity of the part's cues here tells the actor that
he has entered into new terrain; for all of the sensory confusions heaped
upon Malvolio, he knows where he is, and he knows who he is. But this
self-possession does nothing to alleviate his isolation; nor does it prevent
Shakespeare from intensifying his status as the scapegoat: separated from
the crowd, punished for his difference, jeered at for fun, and exiled from
community. All of this is part of the effect of the scene's repeating and
ricocheting cues; but by no means the only effect:

CLOWN.  Fare thee well: remaine thou still in darkenesse,/thou shalt hold
th'opinion of *Pythagoras*, ere I will allow/of thy wits, and feare
to kill a Woodcocke, lest thou dis-(oblique) possesse the soule
of thy grandam. Fare thee well.

MALVOLIO.  Sir *Topas*, sir *Topas*.

(TLN 2042–6, prose lineation ours)

CLOWN.  Hey Robin, jolly Robin, tell me how thy Lady does.

MALVOLIO.  Foole.

CLOWN.  My lady is unkind, *perdie*.

MALVOLIO.  Foole.

CLOWN.  Alas, why is she so?

MALVOLIO.  Foole, I say.

(TLN 2058–63)

CLOWN.     Maintaine no words with him good fellow.
           Who I sir, not I sir. God buy you good sir Topas: Ma-/rry Amen.
           I will sir, I will.
MALVOLIO.  Foole, foole, foole I say.

(TLN 2084–7)

Whether through 'straight' linear scripting (as in the second example above), or through repeated cues (as in the other two), Malvolio is left yelling into emptiness as the Clown parades his tricks. Once again the effect is starkly to highlight the two lines of action: Malvolio stuck in one place, his tormentor[s] in another. But there is a difference here from the earlier uses of the technique. In the earlier scenes, only one opinion of Malvolio is really possible, and it accords with the opinion of his on-stage witnesses; the repeated cues freeze Malvolio in his absurd self-love and snobbery, whilst 'framing' the indignation that this causes in others. In this torture scene, Feste is to all intents closed to and from the audience; we do not share in his perspective; the cues in no sense bring him any closer to us. The effect is simply to make his performance invincible, impenetrable to our intervention or sympathy: it is a force of will that we can only observe. Conversely, the repeating and ricocheting cues (there are many of these in this scene) force us at once to witness and feel with *Malvolio*'s exasperation: if he is on the outside, desperate for entrance or recognition, then so in a basic sense are we. And we should recognize here how carefully Shakespeare is seeding these uncertain or disquieted responses. For it is not 'modern' sensibilities alone that prevent any easy sharing with the tormentors: this is scripted in the cues' mix of obtuseness and exclusion.

Malvolio's final scene reveals still another variation upon the actor's possession of repeated cues—and therein the character's possession of self:

_____ [How] [now] *Malvolio?*
           Madam, you have done me wrong,
           Notorious wrong.

(TLN 2496–8)

It is of course quite likely that 'Notorious wrong' is the cue here, and that the cued actor (Olivia) does not come in early (after Malvolio's initial 'wrong'). But even if this is the case, we still have to factor in the likely response of the Malvolio-actor to this repetition of his final cue-word. He is coming to the end of a part in which, as we have seen, repeated cues figure prominently; he will probably not know what cue has been transcribed on to the part of Olivia; he must thus ask whether, once again, the 'early' cue is helping to point some vital emotional or political switch. Consequently, he might at the very least pause after the first, heavily emphasized 'done me *wrong*'; Olivia may well not come in; if she does not, the silence will ring with just accusation. If Olivia does come in early—if the cue on the part is simply 'wrong'—then Shakespeare scripts it so that her line too is appropriately split by a pause: 'Have I *Malvolio*?' she says, before asserting 'No'. In this case, the lines may interpenetrate as follows:

MALVOLIO. Madam, you have done me wrong—
OLIVIA.    Have I *Malvolio*?
MALVOLIO. Notorious wrong.
OLIVIA.    No.

Olivia is not permitted to stay breezily ascendant; she is forced to account, precisely by the implacability of Malvolio's repetition.

This in turn prepares for Malvolio's penultimate speech (before his closing 'Ile be reveng'd on the whole packe of you' (TLN 2548)): fifteen lines of careful accusation, as he hands Olivia the letter and recapitulates the abuses he has suffered. Once more, the speech seems to be written so as to give the actor a subtle but centring prepossession of his character's right: of something very close to subjective integrity. And once again this prepossession is founded in the trace of premature cues, or of cue-words that hold a private portent for the actor who speaks them:

> Lady you have, pray you peruse that Letter.
> You must not now denie it is your hand,
> Write from it if you can, in hand, or phrase,
> Or say, tis not your seale, not your invention:
> You can say none of this. Well, grant it then,
> And tell me in the modestie of honor,
> Why you have given me such cleare lights of favour,
> Bad me come smiling, and crosse-garter'd to you,
> To put on yellow stockings, and to frowne
> Upon sir *Toby*, and the lighter people:
> And acting this in an obedient hope,
> Why have you suffer'd me to be imprison'd,
> Kept in a dark house, visited by the Priest,
> And made the most notorious gecke and gull,
> That ere invention plaid on? Tell me why?

(TLN 2500–14)

Of course there remains much that is comic here, as he rehashes the
funniest moments in the play (yellow stockings, etc.), all the time plainly
mistaken in his accusation of Olivia. Still, both the actor and the character
are given powerful measures of dramatic control. Most pregnant here is
the simple muscular clarity of the blank verse. But within this, once again,
is the fact—or the intimation—of false or early cues. So, it is possible
that the cue given to the addressee here (Olivia) is a single 'why'. If this
is the case, then Olivia may twice try to intervene with her more or less
sorrowful denial ('Alas *Malvolio*', 'this is not my writing' (TLN 2525)). But
Malvolio will brook no interruption: the prosody barely allows it, with the
positioning of both 'Why's at the start of a flowing pentameter arguing
strongly for continuing rather than pausing in the line. Consequently
Malvolio ploughs on with his indictment, as Olivia struggles to get a
word in edgeways. If there are indeed 'actable' premature cues here, the
result will be to intensify the moment's taut comedy: Malvolio tilting
between pride, vindication, and humiliation; Olivia under challenge but
with invincible reserves of knowledge. Of course, because he is given such
a potentially striking three-word cue-phrase—'Tell me why?'—it is likely
that the actor playing Malvolio will anticipate *not* being interrupted at
these two earlier 'Why's. This reinforces the likelihood that, if Olivia does
indeed come in early, she will immediately be forced to desist, and to defer
to Malvolio's complaint. Equally, however, the Malvolio-actor will see
the three anticipations of his cue-phrase—'tell me', 'Why', 'Why'—just
as he will see the pregnant gap immediately before he gets to speak his
cue: 'That ere invention plaid on?——*Tell me why*?' The combination
of these things might then work exactly as his previous speech has done
(with its potentially repeated cue-word and potentially indignant pause).
That is, the actor will identify all of these 'anticipations' of the cue as
moments of latent potency; all give to him a power of foreknowledge,
and thus of tremulous withholding. For there is tremendous force in the
way the climactic challenge—'Tell me why?'—gathers into itself, and
suddenly detonates, the questing, accumulating, bitten-down indignation
of the earlier 'tell me', 'Why', 'Why'. A similar technique was used in the
torture scene, when Malvolio's line 'Foole, foole, foole I say' compacts
three consecutive cueing speeches into one, 'Foole', Foole', 'Foole, I say'.
There is no question that the actor will be alive to these constructions:
they harness a force that the Malvolio-actor, and no one else, can identify,
possess, and discharge. It is thus highly likely that he will *use* the break

before his 'actual' cue, in the way of a giant suspended swell before the final crash; use it to force Olivia, and everyone else, into a more or less baited waiting. It may well make the perpetrators feel cowed or ashamed, as it often does in (modern) performances. At the very least, it gives Malvolio an authentically centred possession of his unswayable and unassuageable emotions. And it is the actor's intimacy with his cues—built up throughout the part—and the private knowledge that they instil, which both grounds and releases this resolute, unfinished, strangely self-measuring character.

# 10
## Comi-tragic/Tragi-comic Pathos

The movement in the part of Malvolio (a character produced around half-way through Shakespeare's writing life) from contemptible butt, to pathetic victim, to implacable accuser, is a triumph of affective and technical sophistication—and an achievement to which repeated cues make an important contribution. But how did Shakespeare arrive at such effects? In particular, where or when did Shakespeare recognize that the repeated cue could be used to facilitate much more than comic ascendancy or chaotic cross-purposes? Certainly Shakespeare must have long identified in the technique the thrilling, perhaps dangerous licence it gives to the actors; he will have seen how it takes the fiction to the edge, and often blurs the boundaries between one mode or mind and another; how it can bring both actor and character unusually close to the audience; how it allows for all kinds of spatial rearrangements and doubled-up perspectives. Above all, perhaps, he must have recognized a dramatic instrument of rare mobility and instantaneity, in which the experience of the actor, and the decisions he makes in the moment, can suddenly be exposed, and thereby mobilized, as never before. Seen in this way, the repeated cue offers almost an epitome of living theatre. So let us now return to early in his writing life, and see whether we can identify the evolution of this promise-crammed technique.

An early experiment in its possibilities is the memorable climax to *Richard III*. For the immortal line, 'A horse, a horse, my kingdom for a horse', is in fact a twice-spoken cue:

> Enter Richard
> RICHARD. **A Horse, a Horse, my Kingdome for a Horse.**
> CATESBY. Withdraw my Lord, Ile helpe you to a Horse
> RICHARD. Slave, I have set my life upon a cast,

> And I will stand the hazard of the Dye:
> I thinke there be six Richmonds in the field,
> Fiue have I slaine to day, in stead of him.
> A Horse, a Horse, my Kingdome for a Horse.
>
> (TLN 3834–40)

This is the cue both for Catesby's response ('Withdraw my Lord...') and for the alarum that marks the entrance of Richmond for his final fight with Richard. The effect is to open up the possibility for interruption and cross-purposes. As he does quite often, Shakespeare uses the repeated cue in part to orchestrate the chaos of battle. More than one party is on-stage at once, there is more than one centre of action, thus allowing a more vital and compelling enacting of war. Equally importantly, the repeated cue encourages improvisation, for because of it the actor might be surprised by sudden entrances, or mugged by untoward and unexpected appearances. Richard thus has to get his lines spoken while all the time fending off enemies. What we have to imagine, therefore, is that the first 'Kingdome for a Horse' stages a visual collision between the various agents here in opposition. So, we can no longer be certain to whom Richard speaks his scornfully punning riposte:

> Slave, I have set my life upon a cast,
> And I will stand the hazard of the Dye:
>
> (TLN 3836–7)

Perhaps he rebukes Catesby's offer to help him, in which case the line expresses Richard's almost comical petulance. He calls desperately for a horse, but then spits at such escape when it is offered. This is in line with his customary maltreatment of those who serve him. Or again, he might speak the lines to the approaching 'Richmond'—or, rather, to the enemy that he supposes to be Richmond. This can help explain his third and fourth lines, 'I thinke there be six Richmonds in the field, | Fiue have I slaine to day, in stead of him': he is commenting upon what he is *doing* rather than upon what he has done. The premature cue, in that case, draws action and commentary together. And the redundancy of the second cue points to a further alternative: the second time the cue is spoken explicitly marks the fact that Richard is speaking to absolutely no one. He is cueing thin air; his power is past; the wan repetition is a last collusion with the audience that he is about to leave. The fact that the cue-phrase '[Kingdome] [for a] Horse' is not only on the part of the Richard-actor, but also on the scripts of Catesby, Richmond, and perhaps sundry others on the Tudor side, is a telling symbol of the king's loss of control over both script and action.

We might therefore recognize here an early example of what becomes Shakespeare's favourite device for orchestrating tragic climax and the surge of emotions that attends it: the early cue that leaves the principal on his own, occupying his own space-time. The repeated cue, then, is a device that simultaneously maroons *both* character and actor. This wasted or redundant second cue freezes Richard in his tragedy.

Shakespeare here makes the repeated cue a highly effective trigger simultaneously for a crowd scene, for comic scapegoating, and for tragic isolation: the tried and trusted uses here combine to produce something deep and new. But it will be some time before Shakespeare really explores the potential for inward pathos in the technique. When he does so, it will not be with anything like a conventional tragic protagonist, but with two of his most unique and generically elusive figures: Shylock in *The Merchant of Venice* and Mercutio in *Romeo and Juliet*.

## Mercutio

Repeating cues herald a series of decisive transitions in Mercutio's character. Consider the cue for Romeo's entrance in II. iv:

MERCUTIO.　　… these fashion Mongers, these par/don-mee's, who stand so much on the new form, that they/cannot sit at ease on the old bench. O **their bones, their/bones.**

　　　　　　*Enter Romeo.*

BENVOLIO.　　**Here comes *Romeo*, here comes *Romeo*.**

MERCUTIO.　　Without his Roe, like a dryed Herring. O flesh,/flesh, how art thou fishified? Now is he for the numbers/that *Petrarch* flowed in: *Laura* to his Lady, was a kitchen/wench, … Signior *Romeo*, *Bon jour*, there's a French salutation to your/French slop …

　　　　　　　　　　　　　　　　　(TLN 1136–49, prose lineation ours)

In both F and Q2 Romeo's entrance is surrounded by two repeated cue-phrases, for Benvolio also repeats his cue (in the corrupt Q1 there is just the one, Mercutio's 'their bones, their bones'). The moment might work something like this:

| MERCUTIO. | [To Benvolio] O their bones. |
| *Enter Romeo.* | }*Mercutio*   [to audience/himself] their bones |
| BENVOLIO. | [to Mercutio] Here comes *Romeo.*   } |
| MERCUTIO. | [to audience/himself] Without his Roe, like a dryed Herring. O flesh, flesh, how art thou fishified. |
| BENVOLIO. | [to Mercutio again] Here comes *Romeo.* |
| MERCUTIO. | [to Benvolio/audience] Now is he for the numbers that *Petrarch* flowed in … |

The repeating cues give to the Mercutio-actor a rare improvisatory power. The actor will see that the cue-phrase he is to give—'their bones'—is spoken twice. He may not know exactly what he is cueing, but he will know that he can keep one of the cue-phrases 'in reserve'. He can let the next actor start speaking, then break in with his line once more. Doing this allows the repetition to split rather than reiterate its reference; it gives to this particular cue the charge of a tart, semi-private pun. So, the first 'bones' enacts the soreness of sitting on the 'old bench'; having spoken it once, Mercutio has cued the entrance of Romeo and/or Benvolio's herald of this entrance. This now frees up the compulsive punner to adapt his cue-phrase into a reference to the entering lover: 'their bones' now means either penises or the bone-ache (the pox), leading irresistibly into Mercutio's further dilations upon the spent sperm and the fishified flesh ('dryed Herring', etc.) In so far as the second 'their bones' is a pun, it is delivered 'to' no one. The extra cue-phrase, that is, functions like an aside, and allows a similar privacy. In this sense, the repeated cue works to substantiate Mercutio's habit of flying beyond the awareness of his addressees, off into his lonely obsession with sex and mortification.[1]

Another occasion in which Mercutio paces much of his discourse by giving repeating cues is in his penultimate scene, which is mainly taken up with bawdy teasing of the Nurse. Q1 again differs slightly from Q2 and F here, this time offering still more examples of the technique. Assuming that the Q1 text approximates in some way to an acted version, then we see how central floating cue-words are to the Mercutio-part. Here are Mercutio's ends of lines, illustrating the cues that he will give out from the entrance of the Nurse on:

| Q1 | Q2/F |
|---|---|
| ——————————— [A saile,] [a | ——————————— [and] |
| saile,] a saile | [a] Smocke |

| | |
|---|---|
| ——————— [of] [the] | ——————— [the] |
| two. | [fairer] face? |
| ——————— [den] [faire] | ——————— [gooden] |
| Gentlewoman. | [faire] Gentlewoman. |
| ——————— [pricke] [of] | ——————— [pricke] |
| noone. | [of] Noone. |
| ——————— [noted,] | ——————— [ifaith,] |
| [wisely,] wisely. | [wisely,] wisely. |
| ——————— [A baud,] [a | ——————— [A baud, a |
| baud,] a baud. | baud, a baud.] So ho. |
| ——————— [fathers] [to] | ——————— [to] |
| supper? | [dinner] thither. |
| ——————— [farewell] | ——————— [Farewell] |
| [sweete] Ladie. | [Lady,] [Lady,] Lady. |

The details differ ('A sayle, a sayle' (TLN 1202) is given to Romeo in Q2/F, perhaps mistakenly), but in both versions the Mercutio-part is structured by cue-words that he will speak two or three times. What is striking is how aimless these repeating words seem. Both this semantic emptiness and the fact of repetition indicate Mercutio's superfluousness to the action. As the full text shows, the cues that Mercutio gives are respectively for Benvolio, the Nurse (four times), Romeo (twice), and the Nurse once more, but only Benvolio pays any sort of attention to Mercutio. It is he who speaks an aside to Mercutio; other than that, the Nurse does no more than dismiss him with one brief 'out upon you'. Mercutio's improvisations thus largely occupy his own space, and each single word—one 'saile', one 'baud', one 'wisely', one 'Ladie'—may be enough to cue the succeeding speaker. So, having spoken the cue once, the remaining one or two enunciations of the cue-words simply 'float' over an unnoticing stage, to sting, punch, or drift away as the actor desires. Perhaps he chooses to hover around the scene's principals (the Nurse and Romeo), buzzing in like an unwelcome wasp to deliver his mocking choric judgements. Or perhaps he leaves these unlikely confederates alone, and offers his excess solely to us, the audience—his only remaining confidantes. Perhaps he flits between the two, hoping for comic victims one moment, exiled in abject isolation the next.

Either way, what seems clear is that repeated cues are once again a crucial orchestrator of Mercutio's pathology, helping channel his passage through—and eventually beyond—the tragedy. This is apparent enough from the cue-words' non-content. What is Mercutio on about, reduced to these unfunny echoes, desperate for a laugh while everyone just wishes him away? Shakespeare seems to be orchestrating the cue-effect so as to generate Mercutio's exile and exit from the centre.

So, to recapitulate: a repeating cue, when used in basically comic scenes, is mainly there to give the cuer freedom to improvise. The actor can choose his moment, surprise his addressee with interruptions or echoes, or seek thrilling intimacy or complicity with the audience. In such instances, cues are all about seizing the conductor's baton: pacing the scene's rhythms, scoring its moods, dictating its dilations and closures. Yet there is something in Mercutio's performance beyond the comic. The decisive problem is not so much that his jokes here are not funny, or even that his 'addressees' are by turns disgusted ('Out upon you: what a man are you?' (TLN 1214)), impatient ('What hast found?' (TLN 1230)), and dismissive ('A Gentleman... that loves to heare himselfe talke, | and will speake more in a minute, | then he will stand to in a Moneth' (TLN 1245–7)). It is that we too are leaving him: Mercutio's wit is meta-dramatically (as well as situationally) marooned. Principally this is because he is intruding upon the play's primary interest: the thrilling and still secret love of Romeo and Juliet. It isn't until Mercutio leaves this scene that the Nurse can get on and tell Romeo how to pursue his affair. This is what we want to hear too, and for this to happen Mercutio must be dismissed.

This, therefore, is the final purpose of Mercutio's parting cues: 'Lady, Lady, Lady', he says in Q2/F, and it may well be that he keeps on returning, haunting the others' private conference like some jealous imp, reluctant to let matters take their course, or like a jack-in-the-box who cannot put a lid on himself. What we thus see is a reversal of Mercutio's usual scenic presence. Normally he enters slightly off-centre, and proceeds to suck all energies into himself and his tunnel vision. But in this scene—where the Nurse is squarely the agent of Juliet—he starts off at the centre, turns into a margin-haunting echo, and then floats reluctantly away. It is the repeated cues—or more than that, it is Mercutio's devolving into virtually nothing but an emptied-out self-cue—that is the harbinger of his disappearance from the play.

Mercutio's part ends half-way through *Romeo and Juliet*—but not without one final prod at what has hitherto been thought appropriate for a 'tragedy'.

It comes at his moment of death and, if it *is* a repeated cue, it must have been thoroughly unexpected. In F/Q2 it is this:

MERCUTIO.   ... I was hurt under your arme.
ROMEO.      I thought all for the best.
MERCUTIO.   Helpe me into some house *Benvolio*,
            Or I shall faint: a plague a both **your houses**.
            They have made wormesmeat of me,
            I have it, and soundly to **your houses**.          *Exit.*
ROMEO.      This Gentleman the Princes neere Alie,
            My very Friend hath got his mortall hurt
            In my behalfe ...

                                         (TLN 1537–45)

If the first 'your houses' cues Romeo's anguished self-castigation, then Romeo's response may be spoken not after Mercutio has been carried off-stage, but rather whilst he is still visibly dying: 'This Gentleman the Princes neere Alie | My very Friend hath got his mortall hurt | In my behalfe ... '. We can thus immediately see a cold dramatic logic in the Mercutio-part's sudden switch from direct to general address: '*They* have made wormesmeat of me'. He no longer belongs to either side; he no longer really belongs to the action at all. Instead he enters a liminal zone all his own, from where he addresses a single chilling line to the audience. And he speaks as though *after* life but *before* death: the repeated cue facilitates the character's entrance into pathetic metaphysical limbo. This helps turn his final repetition into a memorably cursing prophecy: *and soundly to your houses*. Whereas the earlier repeated cues used comic redundancy to ameliorate existential abandonment, here we have the real thing.

And it is not only Mercutio who is liberated by the cueing technique into 'tragedy'. Romeo is too. Just as Mercutio is stranded in the midst of surrounding action, so too is Romeo. If we read the scene in full text, we might assume that the events happen one after another, in doleful but logical order: Mercutio leaves the stage to die, and only then does Romeo speak his 'This Gentleman the Princes neere Alie ... ' soliloquy. We get one event—the mortal fight—and then another event—the speech summarizing the implications of this event. However, if we reconceive the scene as the part-text seems to suggest, we are forced to witness the simultaneous anguish of Mercutio and Romeo, played out on slightly different parts of the stage. The fact of visible simultaneity *stages* the accumulated portent of what is happening: actions have consequences; no one's experience is truly free to roam; each part exists in the margins or interstices of the other. Mercutio's part is *in* the part of Romeo, who cannot and will not escape from the consequences. And nor does Shakespeare: he will not turn back from the opportunities here opened up.[2]

# II

# The Battle for the Cue-Space:
## *The Merchant of Venice*

Cues can be an integral constituent of characterization, and of no one is this truer than Shylock. But our interest in this chapter is to explore not only how cue-effects contribute to the Shylock-part, but how cues can be the 'plumbing' of a play, at once visible and subterranean, directing the flow and determining the temperature. *The Merchant of Venice* is always uneasily a comedy. Likewise, the role of Shylock is one of the great provocations in dramatic history: how to play him, where does he fit in, what is he doing in a 'romantic comedy'? Might Shakespeare have indeed produced a Jew-baiting pot-boiler? One way or another, the play presents a problem. Can cues help us?

A playwright who wanted 'directorial control', in an age years before a director was thought of, had only the medium of parts through which to guide the players: premature cues could be an important means of such determinative scripting. Now, a cue always means both an arrest (for one speaker) and a beginning (for another). The audience's attention shifts correspondingly. But in the case of a repeated or premature cue, we have a false arrest and a frustrated beginning: not only might voices interrupt or interweave in unpredictable and unwelcome ways, but the audience's security, its unquestioning identification with or attention upon a particular speaker, can itself be questioned. Who to look at? Whose confidence to trust? Cues provide the most basic technique by which to channel, block, or confuse audience sympathies. If so, might they be similarly pivotal in structuring the play's relationship, as it were, to itself? Can they help clarify just what sort of entertainment Shakespeare was producing? Might the analysis of cues help us recover something like the 'original' conditions of performance of this notoriously problematic work?

# Shylock's Repetitions

There is no part in Shakespeare so awash with repetition, 'internal' and otherwise, as Shylock. It is, for instance, a Shylock habit to make puns to himself, both within specific speeches and across consecutive speeches. So, talking of the different kinds of thieves who may plunder Antonio's goods, he observes 'there be land **rats**, and water **rats**, water theeves, and land theeves, I meane Py**rats** ... ' (I. iii). Shylock's pun, first and foremost to himself, is (as always) finely chosen: he is cherishing his dexterity with the word 'rat', despised by others but here his own particular plaything. This example takes place within a single speech, but later Shylock comments on the exchange itself, punning across speeches with himself, this time on the homonym 'rate':

> Three thousand ducats, 'tis a good round sum.
> Three months from twelve, then let me see the **rate**.
> _____ [beholding] [to] you?
> Signior *Anthonio*, many a time and oft
> In the Ryalto you have **rated** me
> About my monies and my usances ...
>
> (TLN 431–6)

This second instance, in particular, tells the player that whatever the interlocutor (in this case Antonio) says to Shylock is of little import: Shylock speaks along his own trajectory, his point of reference generally being what he has just said rather than what other people say to him. The player will quickly identify how Shylock is unable—or reluctant—to take in the speeches of others. Indeed, he is an insultingly bad listener to anyone except himself. 'Cursed be my Trybe,' he mutters, 'If I forgive him', while Bassanio tries to bring him back to their business deal: '*Shylock*, doe you heare?' But Shylock perseveres—out loud—with his own obsessive musing: 'I am debating of my present store ... ' (TLN 375–7). Likewise, other people's jokes seem entirely to pass him by (although always with Shylock there is a choice for the actor of whether he misses the joke or simply ignores it). Of course, Shylock's isolation works both ways: he is obsessed by the fear that no one is listening to *him*. In his first conversation he claims, 'I would be friends ... and youle not heare me' (TLN 465–9); at home, Jessica will not or does not hear him until the clown also joins in, prompting a sequence of anxious imprecations ('What Jessica ... what Jessica ... Why Jessica I say', 'heare you me Jessica...' (TLN 838–41, 864)); later still, when Solario and Salarino purposefully misunderstand him for the sake of a few cheap laughs, he takes it into his head that they have not attended:

> My owne flesh and blood to rebell.
> ———————————————————— [at] [these] yeeres.
> I say my daughter is my flesh and bloud.
>
> (TLN 1249–51)

Perhaps it is the case that Shylock—the outsider, the misfit—is not taken seriously, not heard through in the same way that the other characters are. If so, the part helps the actor to act that. Equally, however, the part advertises a self-contained completeness that will of itself work to isolate Shylock and antagonize all others: and it is his verbal repetitions that epitomize and ensure this effect.

The actor receiving the part of Shylock would have been immediately aware not just of repetitions, but specifically of cue repetitions. So, the part begins with three lines in which the apparently throwaway 'well' is the cue:

> Three thousand ducats, **well**.
> ———————————————————— [for] [three] months.
> For three months, **well**.
> ———————————————————— [shall] [be] bound.
> *Anthonio* shall become bound, **well**.
> ———————————————————— [know] [your] answere.
> Three thousand ducats for three months, and *Anthonio* bound.
> ———————————————————— [answere] [to] that.
> *Anthonio* is a good man.
>
> (TLN 326–37)

We find here a precise snapshot of how this part will unwind. The actor will already see how Shylock's rhetorical system revolves around his own consecutive phrases—the passages spoken in between do not affect this internal pattern. Shylock builds networks around a single word or phrase, as if cueing himself, or setting up solipsistic puns or conceits for his own grim amusement. So, here we catch Shylock in the middle of a typical cogitation, adding up costs, deducing losses and gains. (The trope he uses is epistrophe, meaning the repetition of the final word in a clause rather than this clause's putatively most 'important' word.) This repeatedly stressed 'well', preceded by a repetition of what it is that has just been said *to* Shylock, might seem a somewhat empty or perfunctory mumble: but it is nothing of the kind. Instead, the repetition of the apparently marginal thing *is* the point: Shylock treasures a different measure of centrality, discursive and ideological, from the rule-makers. His circularity suggests a single process of meditation, as Shylock shores up his strength by warding off interruption. It very precisely suggests privacy and suspension: a space for deferred or suspended decision making that no 'addressee' can ever penetrate. But if this miser's incantation is a shield, it is also a barb: each 'well' forestalls *and* interrupts his interlocutor's anxious desire for closure.

The actor will see that Shylock keeps returning to his own obsessive private calculations. However, it is vital to recognize that Shylock does so only after factoring in everything offered by the Christians: 'for three months', 'Anthonio shall become bound'. Of course the two men are deadly enemies: but they are also feeding off one another. Shylock thus takes the cues of his adversary ('for three months') and immediately turns them to his own use ('for three months, well'). It is indeed a kind of discursive 'interest', borrowing for the purposes of quickly hoarded increase. But in doing this he also shows just how much he needs what the Christians, in turn, give him. The claustrophobic menace, the sense of trouble brewing, in these twofold repetitions—Shylock's repetition of both 'his' word ('well') *and* their words ('three months', 'bound')—comes from a cohabitation that is and will continue to be mutually and treacherously exploitative. So, while Shylock appears ascendant in his vengefulness, we should notice how the cue technique is at the same time setting up the terms for their revenge upon him.

The repetitions are here very finely tuned to suggest the play's icy political balance. Looking at Bassanio's part reinforces this point. The Bassanio-actor will probably see (depending on length of cue) that Shylock will simply 'return' whatever he has just said, supplemented by 'well'.

———————————— [thousand] [ducats] well
I sir, for three months.
———————————— [three] [months,] well.
For the which, as I told you, *Anthonio* shall be bound.
———————————— [become] [bound,] well.
May you sted me? Will you pleasure me? Shall I know your answer?
———————————— [and] [*Anthonio*] bound.
Your answere to that.

(TLN 326–36)

Here the echoing cue gives the actor of Bassanio a certain interpretive liberty. As so often in early Shakespeare, the lines have a rhythmic and almost mathematical symmetry; the structure works rather like an unfolded joke. So, Shylock's thrice-repeated 'well'—implicitly a refusal to answer Bassanio's 'cue-questions'—is concluded by (or rather, provokes) Bassanio's three consecutive questions: 'May you sted me? Will you pleasure me? Shall I know your answere?'. If the actors simply follow the script, then the audience will expect the pattern already established to happen again: Shylock will continually repeat each element of Bassanio's final sentences, adding to each a suspending 'well'. But he ceases to do so: the absent 'well' therefore invokes the secrecy (indeed, almost the torture) that Shylock's repeated 'well' has already presaged. In play terms, Bassanio's exasperation will be centred in the silence of Shylock in between the ensuing and repeated questions he asks. Indeed, the effect may be that *Bassanio* is forced mentally to supply the 'well' that Shylock tantalizingly denies: 'May you sted me? [*Well!?*] Will you pleasure me? [*Well!?*] ... ' Shylock's refusal either to take *or* to offer a cue, with its relish in another's pain, offers a foretaste of the sadism that is likewise hinted at in Bassanio's angry questions.

It is Bassanio here who is in all likelihood scripted to possess the audience: for Shylock's refusals become Bassanio's opportunity to comment upon these refusals. Rather than a desperate pleading for mercy, then, 'Shall I know your answere?' and 'Your answere to that' might be offered to the audience as disgusted reflections upon Shylock: 'look at this malignant dog ... '. The Jew is exposed as cruel, but also as a comic butt. The uneasy fact is that the repetitions enveloping Shylock, and which help to create his aura of separateness, can also be orchestrated simply to isolate him as the laughing-stock. They allow the Christian to seize a moment, somewhere inside or in the gaps of Shylock's obsessive repetitions, in which to turn to the audience, assume a confessional intimacy, and ensure their complicity in hatred. The cue-effect distils the terms of the tribal warfare between Jew and Christian, exemplifying the knotted antagonisms that make up the Venetian (and perhaps the comic) world.

## Cues and Power

In this play repeated cues always evoke a battle for possession of the cue-space. But rarely is any actor or character given unalloyed ascendance. All use it; all are used by it. Let us consider the following instance:

> *Enter Anthonio*
> BASSANIO. This is signior *Anthonio.*
> SHYLOCK. How like a fawning publican he lookes.
> I hate **him** for he is a Christian:
> But more, for that in low simplicitie
> He lends out money gratis, and brings downe
> The rate of usance here with us in *Venice.*
> If I can catch **him** once upon the hip,
> I will feede fat the ancient grudge I beare **him.**
> He hates our sacred Nation, and he railes
> Even there where Merchants most doe congregate
> On me, my bargaines, and my well-worne thrift,
> Which he calls interest: Cursed be my Trybe
> If I forgive **him.**
> BASSANIO. *Shylock* doe you heare.
>
> (TLN 363–77)

Now, the most likely interpretation here is that Shylock is speaking a soliloquy—the cue 'doe you heare' suggesting both a comment on his obliviousness to others and an instruction to the Shylock-actor to return to the fold after his monologue. However, if the cue on the Bassanio-part is a single 'him', then he might three times be prompted to speak his line, '*Shylock* doe you heare', over the top of his preoccupied addressee. Of course, he may well have a longer cue—indeed, one might expect this, were it not that his cued line seems to helplessly comment upon the circumstances, and in particular upon the likely consequences of the repeated cue (Shylock appearing not to hear or listen). So let us suppose that Bassanio greets each 'him' with 'Shylock doe you heare'. Clearly, there is room here for comedy: Bassanio might speak the first attempted interruption to Shylock and, having failed, the second or third or even fourth to the audience. Again, the repetition is an invitation to deride: 'deaf old fool', 'self-obsessed villain', and so forth. But it can also work in directly the opposite fashion: Bassanio tries and fails to interrupt what he assumes is Shylock's reverie. However, not only does he fail to interrupt the Jew, but he flatly fails to understand what Shylock is doing. Shylock here is at once ignoring *and* commenting upon Antonio's entrance; the words make clear he has noticed it. Bassanio, however, seeing Shylock talking to himself, assumes that Antonio has not been seen. In the meantime Shylock is forging his own confederacy with the audience. Bassanio's chorus of 'doe you heare's is multiply mocked: first because Shylock absolutely hears; second, because he refuses to answer; third, because he uses the attempted interruption for further self-articulation; and fourth, in doing so he overtly goads the Christian in the eyes of the audience. This is a bravura performance made out of fake impenetrability: in fact, Shylock absolutely takes in and absorbs the way he is treated; as so often, his particular delight is in 'better[ing] the instruction' (TLN 1283).

The premature cue, if this is indeed an example of one, proffers two characters simultaneously seeking the chuckling confidence of the audience, by simultaneously attempting to turn the other into a derisive object. And the battle being staged is not only between the two speakers but also in the minds and hearts of the witnesses. To see how plotted this is, we have to recognize how Shakespeare gives to the cue-effect a sort of narrative arc. So, Shylock begins as though speaking exactly so as to be hissed: 'I hate **him**', he confides, and if there is an interruption, then it mainly sets up Shylock's shameless explanation: 'for he is a Christian' (TLN 366). As a speaker before a 'Christian' audience, he will seem more the ingrate than ingratiating. The next cue moves from generalized hatred to specific brutality: 'If I can catch him'—'*Shylock, do you heare?*'—'once upon the hip, I will feede fat…' (TLN 370). Here Bassanio's line is a chorus to Shylock's vengeful barbarity, and might itself begin to turn: perhaps the question 'do you heare' is no longer for Shylock, but for the audience, asked to take stock of this reprobate's extremity ('*do you heare?*'). But having done so, what do we hear? Again, the shift in tone and point is marked by the premature cue: 'the ancient grudge I beare **him**'—'*Shylock, doe you heare*'—'He hates our sacred Nation…'. Suddenly, Shylock is no longer the stage Jew, Christian-baiter, and usurer. He is the persecuted refugee, speaking for a beleaguered nation. We might notice, then, how the string of 'him's suddenly stops: Shylock is left alone to complete his statement of mitigation. The sudden silence of Bassanio, the arresting of interruptive subversions, *presents* the stage to Shylock.

There is a kind of victory here, however uneasily borne by an Elizabethan audience. If we allow the effect, it is one of curiously Brechtian alienation, forcing the audience to look at itself. After all, much of this play is about being the subject of perception; following from this, it is also about the power to turn others into an object. But we might see here how the audience is similarly turned into the object open to criticism: 'we' are always the perceiving subject at a play, but in this one, particularly and notoriously, we are alienated from our stock sympathies and prejudices.

Crucial here is another fact that repeated cues both hail and ensure: that the Venetian world can never quite allow soliloquy. There are *almost* some soliloquies in *The Merchant of Venice*: there are various nervous or vicious 'asides', but no straightforward soliloquies.[1] This absence is starkly surprising in the part of Shylock. Certainly the actor first given the Shylock-role might *think* that many of his speeches were indeed soliloquies: they are so long, so involved, and so self-absorbed. But they are never once spoken *solus*, and, as we are seeing, are almost always interrupted. This is another fundamental point about the part. Shylock is never free from his context; everything, his every last curse, wish, and fable, is in hock to either his tribe or his trade. On the other hand, just about everything that Shylock says is indeed a kind of soliloquy: he is the man who in every sense *talks to himself*. Hence the cue-effect, and its direction to an actor: where it looks like a soliloquy, it will be interrupted; where it looks like dialogue, it is more pertinently monologue. This, then, might be almost a working crib for the actor playing the Shylock-part, or rather a 'meta-cue' for its execution: Shylock is the frustrated or aspirant soliloquizer.

A similar technique interweaves Shylock's next-but-one speech:

> SHYLOCK. Signior *Anthonio*, many a time and oft
> In the Ryalto you have rated me
> About my **monies** and my usances:
> Still have I borne it with a patient shrug,
> (For suffrance is the badge of our Tribe)
> You call me misbeleever, cut-throate dog,
> And spet upon my Iewish gaberdine,
> And all for use of that which is mine owne.
> Well then, it now appears you need my helpe:
> Goe to then, you come to me, and you say,
> *Shylocke*, we would have **moneyes**, you say so:
> You that did voide your rume upon my beard,
> And foote me as you spurne a stranger curre
> Over your threshold, **moneyes** is your suite.
> What should I say to you? Should I not say,
> Hath a dog money? Is it possible
> A curre should lend three thousand ducats? Or
> Shall I bend low, and in a bond-mans key

> With bated breath, and whispring humbleness,
> Say this: Faire sir, you spet on me on Wednesday last;
> You spurn'd me such a day; another time
> You cald me dog: and for these curtesies
> Ile lend you thus much **moneyes**.
> ANTONIO. I am as like to call thee so againe,
> To spet on thee againe, to spurne thee too ...
>
> (TLN 434–58)

This time, let us consider the possibility that Antonio is cued by 'moneyes' to say 'I am as like to call thee so againe ... ' Shylock throws out this cue-word three other times (plus one 'money'), each time in a context where he is quoting and ridiculing Antonio's hypocrisy: 'rated me about my monies', 'you say, *Shylocke*, we would have moneyes', 'You that did voide your rume upon my beard, | And foote me as you spurne a stranger curre | Over your threshold, moneyes is your suite'. Each time, Antonio's cued line, or a part of it, makes immediately spiteful sense: 'I am as like to call thee so againe, To spet on thee againe, to spurne thee too'. The repeated cue and response reinforces the implacability of the Shylock–Antonio hatred, and gives their history in a brief splenetic snapshot. But again the effect of the repeated cues is poised between two incompatible political and affective keys: perhaps Antonio, calm and ascendant, speaks his contempt to the audience as Shylock repetitively rages; or perhaps Shylock, calm and ascendant, speaks *his* contempt to the audience as Antonio repetitively rages. The cues are pointers in a game of murderous *quid pro quo*; but it is up to the actors how to 'play' them.

## Cues and Comic Uncertainty

Perhaps the play's paradigmatic case of repeated cues is in III. iii. Solanio, Shylock, and Antonio are on-stage. Read in full text, Shylock rants, Antonio then interjects to demand that Shylock hear him speak, Shylock refuses, and finally Solanio chimes in to call Shylock an impenetrable cur. But, in part-form, the scene takes on a different momentum. Here is the part for Antonio in this scene:

> _____ [looke] [to] him
> Heare me yet good *Shylok*
> _____ [at][his] request

I pray thee heare me speake

(TLN 1688–97)

While Solanio's part will look like this:

_____ [have] [my] bond.
It is the most impenetrable curre
That ever kept with men.

(TLN 1703–5)

Now here is Shylock's part:

Jaylor, **looke to him**, tell not me of mercy,
This is the foole that lends out money *gratis*.
Jaylor, **looke to him**.
_____ [yet] [good] *Shylok*.
Ile **have my bond**, speake not against **my bond**,
I have sworne an oath that I will **have my bond**:
Thou call'st me dog before thou hadst a cause
But since I am a dog, beware my phangs,
The Duke shall grant me justice, I do wonder
Thou naughty Jaylor, that thou art so fond
To come abroad with him at his request.
_____ [heare] [me] speake.
Ile **have my bond**, I will not heare thee speake,
Ile **have my bond**, and therefore speake no more.
Ile not be made a soft and dull-ey'd foole,
To shake the head, relent, and sigh, and yeeld
To Christian intercessors: follow not,
Ile have no speaking, I will **have my bond**. *Exit Jew*.

(TLN 1684–1703)1703)

It is a classic case of Shylock's refusal to listen. So, after Shylock says 'looke to him' once, Antonio may enter with his cued line, 'Heare me yet good *Shylok*'. But Shylock has not finished, and proceeds to repeat his cue with insolent menace. Perhaps Antonio is forced to repeat his plea for a hearing; perhaps he is shouted down by Shylock's repetitions and gives up, exasperated. Either way, the effect of the repeated cues is intensified antagonism. Antonio now has to wait for his next cue ('at his request'), before reiterating his baleful request ('I pray thee heare me speake'). Antonio has been battered into submission. However, this is not the end of the exchange's cue-orchestrated complications—or provocations. So, the next actor to be cued is Solanio, by Shylock's '[have] [my] bond'. But Shylock says this not once, but *six* times, both before and after the second cue given to Antonio ('at his request'). In part-form it might work, then, like this:

SHYLOCK.       Ile **have my bond**, [Solanio: It is the most
                     impenetrable *curre*...] speake not against my
                     bond,
                     I have sworne an oath that I will **have my
                     bond**: [It is the most impenetrable *curre*...]
                     Thou call'st me *dog* before thou hadst a cause,
                     But since I am a *dog*, beware my phangs...
                     Ile **have my bond**, [It is the most impenetrable
                     *curre*...] I will not heare thee speake,
                     Ile **have my bond**, [It is the most impenetrable
                     *curre*...] and therefore speake no more.
                     Ile not be made a soft and dull-ey'd foole,
                     To shake the head, relent, and sigh, and yeeld
                     To Christian intercessors: follow not,
                     Ile have no speaking, I will **have my bond**.
SOLANIO.        It is the most impenetrable curre
                     That ever kept with men.

                                                                    (italics ours)

Does Solanio's 'impenetrable curre' speech, which looks on paper to happen only once, begin six other times? If so, then the reference to curs might also be important: enraging Shylock anew with the recollection that Antonio has been ready enough to label him 'dog'; hence, perhaps, his sudden change of direction: '*Thou* call'st me dog *before* thou hadst a cause, | But since I am a dog, beware my phangs' (our italics). The premature cue gives new force to the simple ubiquity of racial insult: how often has Shylock been called 'curre' or 'dog' by these Christians? It is the specific insult he perhaps harps on more than any other, and here it is again: no wonder he refuses to shut up, instead taking the 'cue' given him—Solanio's 'impenetrable curre'—and biting back. That this statement occurs immediately after 'my bond' reinforces the likelihood that the cues are here teeing-up a vicious to-and-fro of insulting repartee. And, of course, the scripting makes it inevitable that Shylock will be ready and waiting for *whatever* the Christians throw at him: the actor sees the sixfold spoken cue-phrase; he knows that an interruption is coming; and he knows that this interruption will have to be shouted down. Whatever is said to him, it will provoke still more vitriolic indignation. The Shylock-actor will therefore comb his speech, searching for the tastiest insult, for the right phrase to stick his enemies with. In a part context like this, *nothing* is innocent: even violent surprises are expected, getting turned instantaneously into equally violent ricochets.

If Solanio's interjection is shouted down over and again, then this itself might provoke situationally appropriate rage and indignation in both actors. Still more, the phrase repeatedly cued carries a powerful meta-dramatic charge. First, it invokes a 'cur', meaning grumbling or braying, suggesting the grating voice of the unpalatable foreigner (again doubling as an acting direction); second, 'impenetrable' is the perfect word for a speech that simply will not accede to the cues it seems to offer. Solanio appeals to a fairer auditor than Shylock: this 'impenetrable cur' rides roughshod over the cues of others; he will not play the game; so please share my contempt, feel my rage, and laugh at him for me.

In other words, the cue-scripting suggests that Solanio's repeating accusation is not in fact spoken again and again *to* Shylock. Instead, having spat it out to Shylock and got nothing but (from the Christian perspective) proof of its justice, Solanio turns to the audience and, in a different voice, perhaps amazed, perhaps wry, sarcastic, confiding, repeats the now sadly inevitable conclusion: 'It is the most impenetrable curre | That ever kept with men.' The repetition—that of *both* parties—here creates the space for divergent lines of address. Certainly this is what the stage-directions suggest: 'follow not, | Ile have no speaking' snarls Shylock, implying considerable stage distance between them and thereby distinct lines of communication with the audience. And indeed, in the full script Shylock is marked to exit *before* Solanio manages to speak his cued line (of course, the part may have prescribed a different exit cue):

> SHYLOCK. ... Ile have no speaking, I will have my bond. *Exit Jew.*
> SOLANIO.  It is the most impenetrable curre ...

If this is the case, then abandoned to nothing but his indignation, Solanio can only now speak his line to the (apparently defeated) Antonio or, as anxious compensation, to the audience.

Whatever the particular choices made by the actors, there seems little doubt that the premature cue here is designed to allow the Solanio-actor a range of ways of speaking his judgement, a gradation that might encompass anything from fury to astonishment, irony to abjection. Concomitantly, the repeating cue sets up the line potentially to be *addressed* to a full range of hearers: to Shylock, to Antonio, to himself, and to the audience. Possible audience sympathies ricochet as swiftly as the exchange. The cue-effect thus pitches and encapsulates the play's taut political and emotional affects.

This ambiguous, or rather ambivalent, deployment of repeated cues connects with the play's violent, almost self-sabotaging approach to comic certainties. Crucial here is the way in which Shylock is positioned in relation to normative ethics and aesthetics. In many ways he deserves the fear and loathing he attracts; he is as vicious and gruesome a character as Shakespeare ever composed. His cruelties move him utterly beyond the pale, beyond even customary sorts of marginality or exclusion. But even as we judge him, we see how badly he is treated. Every single character reviles or mocks him. Even supposed cohorts like Tubal or Gobbo take every opportunity to mimic him into confusion or dizzy him into rage. And again, repeated cues do much of the work. Consider the way in which, as though by osmosis, they are taken up by other characters as a means of ridiculing or tormenting the Jew. An example is Solanio and Salarino's report of Shylock's grief over his lost daughter and ducats:

> SOLANIO.  I never heard a passion so confused,
> So strange, outrageous, and so variable,
> As the dogge *Jew* did utter in the streets;
> My daughter, O my **ducats**, O my daughter,
> Fled with a Christian, O my Christian **ducats**!
> Justice, the law, my **ducats**, and my daughter;
> A sealed bag, two sealed bags of **ducats**,
> Of double **ducats**, stolne from me by my daughter…
> She hath the stones upon her, and the **ducats**.
> SALARINO.  Why all the boyes in Venice follow him,
> Crying his stones, his daughter, and his ducats.

(TLN 1067–77)

Again, the cue might be 'ducats' *solus*, in which case Salarino can be cued into a chorus of affirmation at any point; or it might be the distinct '[and the] ducats', spoken only once. The former possibility makes this little scene more of a set-piece to the audience than a conversation between two people. Both speakers have, after all, witnessed what they are recalling, and the exchange is therefore strictly pointless except as an amplification of established attitudes. But suppose the point is that the two Christians offer a shared 'aria' filled with repetition and affirmation, that parodically recalls Shylock's echoing cues. Then the whole town is shown joining in to mock Shylock with their own Shylockian discord. This report, then, might be a cacophonous and (putatively) hilarious consummation of Shylock's habitual repetition: a deeply satisfying communal goading of the scapegoat into the captive and paranoid replaying of his persecution.

The same 'joke' recurs in Shylock's next scene (III. ii), when Tubal flips with rhythmic symmetry from 'cruel' words about Jessica's betrayal to 'kind' words about Antonio's calamity at sea. At this stage Shylock is almost overwrought with repetitions—in particular, diacope and conduplicatio, both rhetorical devices said to indicate deep feeling. The actor cannot but have recognized such emotional pointers: that is, identified the prompt and worked hard on it to make it effective. And the effect is, as ever, that Shylock is throwing out premature cues: the actor will be either continually talking over or continually interrupted by his interlocutor. His text we have rendered as:

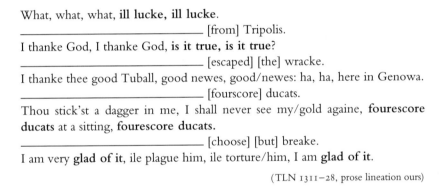

What, what, what, **ill lucke, ill lucke**.
————————————————— [from] Tripolis.
I thanke God, I thanke God, **is it true, is it true?**
————————————————— [escaped] [the] wracke.
I thanke thee good Tuball, good newes, good/newes: ha, ha, here in Genowa.
————————————————— [fourscore] ducats.
Thou stick'st a dagger in me, I shall never see my/gold againe, **fourescore ducats** at a sitting, **fourescore ducats.**
————————————————— [choose] [but] breake.
I am very **glad of it**, ile plague him, ile torture/him, I am **glad of it.**

(TLN 1311–28, prose lineation ours)

It seems that Tubal, Shylock's interlocutor, will spend most of this scene talking half over the 'friend' whom he is enraging with his mischievous 'comfort'. But at the same time Shylock is never simply the butt of the joke. His repeating cue-phrases—'glad of it', 'is it true', even 'ill lucke'—are all expressions of glee, connoting his private visions of plenteous revenge and joyous come-uppance. An actor can cherish them, fully aware that the 'second' articulation of the cue can be for him alone. The repeated cues thus work in two interweaving ways. First, they liberate Shylock into rapt visions of consummate revenge (because Antonio is 'undone'); he veers off from merely exchanging information, locates a dimension of discourse and cogitation entirely his own, and indulges in the freedom of imagining a dream come true. Second, they allow Tubal to reinterrupt Shylock with killing tales of his daughter's fecklessness in betrayal: Shylock *cannot* escape.

The cue-effect at once pins Shylock down when he seeks to fly and embarrasses him when he wants to triumph. As Shylock over-speaks in one direction, and Tubal over-speaks back, it has the inescapable symmetry of classic farce. But it is also an epitome of this particular claustrophobic play-world. Again, then, we witness repeated cues helping to set up the *Merchant*'s keynote mood: triumph in torture, victimization in isolation, experienced coequally by both parties upon each other simultaneously (Tubal here the comic surrogate for Shylock's enemies).

## The Trial Scene

Everything in *The Merchant of Venice* builds up to the climactic trial scene in which power of all kinds is finally put to the proof. Correspondingly, it is the scene in which comic 'Law' puts its foot down: there are to be no more ambiguous affects or ambivalent sympathies. If this is indeed a comedy, then here is where suffering must be forgotten, subversion exiled, and laughter become untarnished by shame. Accordingly, this is the scene in which ultimate possession of the cue-space finds its exclusive and violent resolution.

The scene begins with Shylock as arrogant in his premature cues as he ever manages. Here is his first speech, a reply to the Duke's request for a 'gentle answer' (IV. i):

> SHYLOCK.  You'l aske me why I rather choose to have
> A weight of carrion flesh, then to receive
> Three thousand Ducats? Ile not answer that:
> But say it is my humor; Is it **answered**?
> What if my house be troubled with a Rat,
> And I be pleas'd to give ten thousand Ducates
> To have it bain'd? What, **are you answer'd** yet? ...
> [I can] give no reason, nor I will not,
> More then a lodg'd hate, and a certaine loathing
> I beare *Anthonio*, that I follow thus
> A loosing suite against him? **Are you answered**?
> BASSANIO.  This is no answer thou unfeeling man ...

(TLN 1945–68)

Shylock characteristically turns the request for an answer into an intentionally taunting fake question: the repeated cue-phrase, 'are you answer'd?'

This is indeed more rhetoric than 'answer', as Bassanio is cued three times (or perhaps twice, depending on the length of the cue) to point out: 'This is no answer' and '*This* is no answer'. In throwing out his cue-phrase two or three times, Shylock plays his interlocutors, teasing them with gratuitous reasons. The actor playing Shylock will identify that his cue-phrase is given early, and therefore that his part is inviting interruption; again this is seized as a rhetorical weapon. Hence the—entirely plotted—pseudo-rationality of Shylock's 'answer'. For as so often, Shylock's discourse is a confluence of quotation, parody, scandal, and rage: he is the play's most appropriative speaker, and the premature cues here serve perfectly his vicious ventriloquism.

So, on one level Shylock is playing the part, or pretending to play the part, of the alien abroad, having nothing at his disposal but folk parables of pigs and cats; on another level he is the Jewish scholar, apeing a show of pedantic casuistry, and mocking the Christian 'justice' which he knows as arbitrary and capricious. Hence his oratory's spurious staging of proof and its carefully whimsical outrages: 'say it is my humor'. Bassanio takes the bait, leaping in with his prematurely cued 'This is no answer thou unfeeling man'. The injustice, for Shylock in this moment, is exquisite: so he moves on to his next, still more outrageous and insulting justification: 'What if my house be troubled with a Rat, | And I be pleas'd... To have it bain'd? What, are you answer'd yet?' Again Bassanio's button has been pushed, and he leaps in once more with either the whole line, '*This* is no answer!', or 'thou unfeeling man!': each dramatically appropriate, each entirely satisfying to Shylock. For he is thereby cued to begin all over again, constructing yet another baroque or absurd or sophistic fable of motive: 'Some men there are love not a gaping Pigge...' There is hardly a more insolent, profane, knowingly indecorous speech in all of Shakespeare than Shylock's here, responding to the Duke's hope of a 'gentle answer', amid all of the assembled Magnificoes, with taunts about 'others' who, when 'the bag-pipe sings i'th'nose, | Cannot contain their Urine for affection'.

Here then is Shylock's triumph of subversion, and it is set up and emblematized by his premature cues: they both make his interruption likely and draw the Christians in, transforming their experience of offence into his experience of impenetrable triumph. Hence the way the first two premature cues, inviting indignant or amazed interruption, give way to what is *not* a cue—but sounds alluringly like one: '*now* for your answere' (our italics). This can indeed cue only expectant silence. And Shylock's answer? There is no answer, or nothing but a 'lodg'd hate, and a certaine loathing': '*Are you answer'd?*'

Without the games that Shylock here plays with cues, the sheer goading insult of the speech is diminished. We might also miss how the speech's to-and-fro structure is a terminal example of the city's Jew–Christian relations: one inside the other, compulsively cued by the other, so that even the Jew's inveterate isolation, and the 'self-cueing' that might seem to attend it, is in truth a response to the cue of the enemy. Shylock can take revenge, as here, and possess the 'cueing' power: but the revenge can only take the form of a ricochet. There is no escaping, as it were, the constitutive cue-space.

Effects like these encapsulate the *Merchant*'s strangely Janus-minded style of comedy. For as much as Shylock here 'plays' the moment, he does not entirely possess it. His taunts are a foretaste of the cruelty he would like to impose, evoking the 'Christian' animals he would so love to 'bain' or torture: but he cannot and will not. Hence the way in which the repetition also works like a refrain, almost like a ballad: vicious melodrama is overlaid with something more akin to comic operetta. The result is both to thicken the claustrophobia and menace, and to promise release from it. For the refrain—'Are you answer'd' | 'This is no answer'—always works partly above the intentions and intensities of the principals; it is to and for the audience, both a puzzle or mystery *and* the implicit future solution to that puzzle. That is, *yes* he will insist on his bond; *no* he will not get away with it.

For of course any triumph experienced by Shylock is short-lived. He may get nothing of the money he lent Antonio, but in every other sense he is utterly paid back. The process whereby Portia as the young lawyer teases Shylock with victory only to make his loss all the more humiliating and absolute is well known; so too is how troubling the scene can be to readers or audiences uncomfortable with the scene's tit-for-tat atavism. The resolution of the scene is remorselessly 'anti-Semitic': the Jew is stripped of his possessions, his faith, all rights over heredity. As so often, politics attends the generic machinery; the comic machinery is also Christian machinery. But what is less often recognized is how Shakespeare sustains the cue-effect—and the battle for the cue-space—right through until its final killing inversion.

The scene turns after a brief interlude of spousal jokes. Shylock is cued back into voice with 'unquiet house' (a reminder perhaps of his own once 'sober house' whose 'eares' were fatally invaded by the 'vile squealing' of fifes played by 'Christian fooles' (TLN 864–9)). His part then proceeds thus:

> These be the Christian husbands: I have a daughter
> Would any of the stocke of *Barrabas*
> Had beene her husband, rather then a Christian.
> We trifle time, I pray thee pursue sentence.
> _____ [doth] [give] it.
> Most rightfull Judge.
> _____ [Court] [awards] it.
> Most learned Judge, a sentence, come prepare.
> _____ [o] [learned] Judge.
> Is that the law?
> _____ [a] [learned] Judge.
> I take this offer then, pay the bond thrice,
> And let the Christian goe.
> _____ [take] [thy] forfeiture.
> Give me my principall, and let me goe.
> _____ [me] [that] word.
> Shall I not have barely my principall?
> _____ [thy] [peril] Jew.
> Why then the devil give him good of it:
> Ile stay no longer question.

>                          (TLN 2210–63)

The moment of transition is starkly there to see: it is when Shylock's gloating cry of 'learned Judge' is suddenly thrown back as the cue that *he* must respond to. This is also almost the first time that Shylock is left to speak a single, plaintive, unreiterated, and uninterruptible question: 'Is that the law?' We notice, then, that not only is this moment marked by the delirious echoing (by Gratiano) of the Jew's hitherto delirious cue, but it is also marked by the Christian's replication of 'Shylock's' repeating cue-effect. So, whereas the actor playing Shylock sees as his cue only 'Judge' or 'learned Judge', the actor playing Gratiano is in fact *three* times asked to throw out what look like premature cues: 'O upright **Judge**, | Marke Jew, o learned **Judge**' (TLN 2228–9), followed by the still more specific 'O **learned Judge**, mark Jew, a **learned Judge**' (TLN 2234), and then once more 'O Jew, an upright **Judge**, a learned **Judge**' (TLN 2240). Moments later Gratiano twice more reprises what was Shylock's exultant cry, 'A Daniel, a *Daniel* Jew' (TLN 2250), 'A *Daniel* still I say, a second *Daniel*' (TLN 2257), mocking the Jew's earlier 'A *Daniel* come to judgement, yea a *Daniel*' (TLN 2134). Gratiano's jeering 'a second' says it all. Shylock's discursive habits—the repeating cue as taunt or insult, the vengeful quotation of the enemy—are here irrevocably stolen from and turned upon him. As Gratiano says, 'I thanke thee Iew for teaching me that word' (TLN 2257).

The repeating cues here set off a whole sequence of such devices. They work as the play's ultimate enacting of revenge: exactly of the 'eye for an eye' quality that this world so fetishizes. Either we can see here Shylock desperately speaking over Gratiano, trying to bring him to say something to the point—'I take this offer then … ', or we can see Gratiano's repetition 'playing' the Jew: in the sense of both mimicking and ridiculing Shylock's own earlier glee, or reprising Shylock's habit of hording his cues so as to taunt his adversaries, stab them, as it were, semantically in the back. What Shylock did to the Christians a few moments earlier in his 'Are you answer'd' speech, Gratiano here returns with interest.

In other words, cues here meta-dramatically underscore the action: the point to recognize is how pointed, how utterly mathematical and plotted, this 'cue closure' within the Shylock plot is. As we often find in comedy, a certain geometrical symmetry—in language and plot—takes precedence. Consider, then, Portia's speech, hitting Shylock as he falls:

> PORTIA..  … Tarry Jew,
> The Law hath yet another hold on you.
> It is enacted in the Lawes of Venice,
> If it be proved against an Alien,
> That by direct, or indirect attempts
> He seeke the life of any Citizen,
> The party gainst the which he doth contrive,
> Shall seaze one halfe his goods, the other halfe
> Comes to the privie coffer of the State,
> And the offenders life lies in the **mercy**
> **Of the Duke** onely, gainst all other voice.
> In which predicament I say thou standst:
> For it appears by manifest proceeding,
> That indirectly, and directly to,
> Thou hast contriv'd against the very life
> Of the defendant: and thou hast incur'd
> The danger formerly by me rehearst.
> Downe therefore, and beg **mercy of the Duke.**

GRATIANO.  Beg that thou maist have leave to hang thy selfe
            And yet thy welth being forfeit to the state,
            Thou hast not left the value of a cord
            Therefore thou must be hang'd at the states charge.

                                    (TLN 2264–85)

Clearly, Gratiano can here continue the cueing liberties that began moments
earlier with 'o learned Judge'. He gets his cue half-way through Portia's
speech, and is thereby invited to speak his lines whenever appropriate—that
is, whenever they can exact maximum damage upon his now defeated prey.
He speaks only to Shylock—and of course to the audience—and each
single line is like a twist of the knife. The premature cue, then, here works
by slicing the stage into something like 'serious' and 'comic' spaces; as
Portia and the Duke finesse the details of justiciable humiliation, Gratiano
takes over as the candid, choric jester of comic lore and ritual shaming. All
assume the audience's delighted approbation.

There is, then, no escape for Shylock from his epitomic cue-space: it is
the oxygen in which he lives and perishes. Here is his part's end:

    _____ [not] [for] *Anthonio.*
            Nay, take my life and all, pardon not that,
            You take my house, when you do take the prop
            That doth sustaine my house: you take my life
            When you doe take the meanes whereby I live.
    _____ [dost] [thou] say?
            I am content.
    _____ [deed] [of] gift.
            I pray you give me leave to goe from hence,
            I am not well, send the deed after me,
            And I will signe it.

                                    (TLN 2291–2316)

The cues he receives here are all definitively and ironically murderous: could
there possibly be two 'unkinder' cuts for the Jew than '[for] [*Anthonio*]' and
a '[deed] [of] gift', or two placed with more brutal comic relish? But it is
the penultimate cue that really effects meta-dramatic as well as 'mimetic'
closure here. The cue the Shylock-actor receives is simple enough: '[dost]
[thou] say?' But it is in fact preceded by a 'failed' or false cue: 'Art thou
contented Jew?' The actor will not know of it until spoken; he can do
nothing to it, offer absolutely nothing, but a bereft and suspended silence.
The script is fully alive to the performative effect. 'What dost thou say?'

is Portia's follow-up question, at once ensuring Shylock's silence (because asking the Portia-actor to delay this second question), mocking it (as though to say 'did you mumble something I couldn't quite hear ... ') and finally *allowing* him to speak (because only now cueing the Shylock-actor). But this is merely the final occurrence of a technique which, from the moment when the trial scene turns against Shylock, is used with repeated relish. Again and again the Jew is directly addressed, but the actor is not cued: 'Marke Iew' (2229), 'mark Iew' (2234), 'O Iew' (2240), 'a Daniel Iew' (2250)—all from Gratiano; and 'Why doth the Iew pause' (2251) and 'Tarry Iew' (2264), both from Portia, and again seeming meta-dramatically to point and gloat over Shylock's paralysed silence. The technique is plaintive and awful, the play's ultimate come-uppance via inversion. In every other scene, Shylock is unreachable, impenetrable; he may be isolated, but if so, he is isolated in his garrulous over-speaking, and by his fierce sabotaging of the prerogatives of question and answer. In his final scene, he is repeatedly marooned and stupefied by the simple effect of a false cue.

As always in this play, we can resent the effect, invert the affect, even hiss and berate this cruel comic machinery rather than its equally cruel victim. But we can do so only in the gaps, or in our own minds, in defiance of both meta-dramatic and dramatic architecture. As much as Shakespeare appears to have been fully aware that his villain embarrasses and somehow shrinks everything else in his play, he also seems comprehensively to have plotted Shylock's ultimate alienation. The cue-effects in Shylock's final scene are remorselessly vengeful. This might suggest that in its plumbing, its anterior or subterranean design—deciphered here at a level of 'sub-performative' orchestration—this play really is a hate-full piece of work.

# Conclusion

At this stage of Shakespeare's career—the period of *Romeo and Juliet*, *A Midsummer Night's Dream*, and *The Merchant of Venice*— the repeated cue is used when the unstable genre of the play—tragedy, comedy, or something in between—is palpably up for grabs. Shylock and Mercutio embody this struggle; they alike scuff or straddle the supposed boundaries between comedy and tragedy. In the parts of Shylock and Mercutio they are the characters who usually control the repetition. The players of Shylock and Mercutio can thus retain the 'extra' cue-phrase for themselves, stretching the moment to suit them, playing or goading the audience, to ensure that they (and their characters) will never be humbled into scenic or generic obedience. But, by the same token, this elusiveness also foretells the characters' precariousness within their respective play-worlds. The 'anti-generic' premature cue becomes a preparation, curiously enough, for the premature sacrifice of the anti-generic troublemaker.

But if these characters threaten the balance of their respective plays, they also tilt the balance decisively in the direction of Shakespeare's 'tragic' future. We can identify such a future in the unusual gravity of their jokes; in the excessiveness and privacy of their conceits; in their hostility to audience ease or comfort; in their defiance of expectation; and in the sense that the way they speak, so uniquely their own, offers channels into unspoken terrors and fears. The false or floating cue helps them create space in which to ridicule or isolate their addressees; it helps to certify their own elusiveness, or even something demonic in their irresponsibility; it helps to evoke their indifference to normal conversational decorum. Because no one else on-stage is 'with' Shylock or Mercutio, there is nothing to deflect the fact of being watched in one's isolation by thousands: and one is never more alone than when being observed by the many who *cannot* intervene.[2]

# 12
# Tragedy

## Tragic Bathos: *Romeo and Juliet*

Perhaps the most extravagant use of repeated cues in all of Shakespeare occurs in *Romeo and Juliet*. It is also Shakespeare's first extended attempt to use the technique for something approximating full-on tragic affects: the scene of mistaken mourning for the presumed-dead Juliet. Of course, this is tragedy with a twist. The heroine is not dead; everyone watching knows it; and so the extravagant mourning is mercilessly ironized. The repeated cues can therefore retain their association with comedy and even slapstick: in some sense pathos here mingles with bathos. In this case the repeating cues deflate solemnity, levelling private grief into something crowd-like and anonymous. At the same time they are foreshadowing the effects that so distinguish Shakespeare's later tragedies.

In the 'bad' Q1 text of *Romeo and Juliet*, IV. v is written like this, with repeated cues and communal speaking highlighted in bold:[1]

| | |
|---|---|
| NURSE. | … ah me, alack the day, some Aqua vitae hoe. |
| | *Enter Mother* |
| MOTHER. | How now whats the matter? |
| NURSE. | Alack the day, **shees dead, shees dead, shees dead.** |
| MOTHER. | Accurst, unhappy, miserable time. |
| | *Enter Oldeman.* |
| CAPULET. | Come, come, make hast, wheres my daughter? |
| MOTHER. | Ah **shees dead, shees dead.** |
| CAPULET. | Stay, let me see, all pale and wan. |
| | Accursed time, unfortunate olde man … |
| | O heere she lies that was our hope, our joy, |
| | And being dead, dead sorrow nips us all. |
| | *All at once cry out and wring their hands.* |
| *All cry* | **And all our joy, and all our hope is dead,** |

|                          | Dead, lost, undone, absented, wholy fled. |
|--------------------------|-------------------------------------------|
| CAPULET.                 | **Cruel, unjust, impartiall destinies,** |
|                          | Why to this day have you preserv'd my life? |
|                          | To see my hope, my stay, my joy, my life, |
|                          | Deprivde of sence, of life, of all by death, |
|                          | **Cruell, unjust, impartiall destinies.** |
| CAPULET. [sic. Paris?]   | O sad fac'd sorrow map of misery, |
|                          | Why this sad time have I desird to see. |
|                          | This day, this unjust, this impartiall day |
|                          | Wherein I hop'd to see my comfort full, |
|                          | To be deprivde by suddaine destinie. |
| MOTHER.                  | O woe, alacke, distrest, why should I live? |
|                          | To see this day, this miserable day. |
|                          | Alacke the time that ever I was borne, |
|                          | To be partaker of this destinie. |
|                          | **Alacke the day, alacke and welladay.** |
| FRIAR.                   | O peace for shame, if not for charity ... |

(Q1, I1b–I2a)

It is clear from the Q1 transcription that the scene, as remembered or recorded, involved a variety of cross- and communal outcries: '*All at once cry out and wring their hands*'. The text even gives two lines that '*All cry*', perhaps indicating that all of the mourners are to intone the words as one; perhaps indicating that each actor is to choose a word or phrase to make his own. But what is abundantly clear is the connection between criss-crossing voices and repeated cues. If the writer/recorder of Q1 recalls or requires a scene rife with echo and interruption, then he also knows exactly how the parts must be—or must have been—written.

The script of Q2 and F is different in various details, but there the use of repeated cues is even greater:

| MOTHER. | *O me, O me, my Child, my onely life:* |
|---------|------------------------------------------|
|         | Revive, looke up, or I will die with thee: |
|         | **Helpe, helpe, call helpe.** |
|         | |
|         | *Enter Father.* |
| FATHER. | For shame bring *Juliet* forth, her Lord is come. |
| NURSE.  | **Shee's dead: deceast, shee's dead: alacke the day.** |
| MOTHER. | Alacke the day, **shee's dead, shee's dead, shee's dead.** |
| FATHER. | Ha? Let me see her: out alas shee's cold, |
|         | Her blood is setled and joynts are stiffe: |

Life and these lips have long bene seperated:
Death lies on her like an untimely frost
Upon the swetest flower of all the field.

(TLN 2596–2607)

The words differ from Q1, but the effect is identical. So, we see that the cue
for Capulet to speak (Lady Capulet's 'shee's dead') comes early—for the
Nurse also speaks these words as her very first expostulation after Capulet's
entrance. Consequently, Capulet can be cued to begin his five-line speech
the same moment that the Nurse begins her speech, rather than waiting
for Lady Capulet; if that were the case, Lady Capulet's thrice-spoken
'shee's dead' would be not so much Capulet's cue as her own echo of the
Nurse's early cue. The effect could be to free both the Nurse-actor and
the Mother-actor to speak their brief sighs of grief—'shee's dead', 'alacke
the day', 'deceast', 'shee's dead'—at any propitious moment during the
father's expatiation over the corpse:

Shee's dead.
Ha?
—deceast—
Let me see her:
—shee's dead.
—out alas shee's cold,
Her blood is setled and joynts are stiffe:
—alacke the day.
Life and these lips have long bene seperated:
—alacke the day.
Death lies on her—
—shee's dead—
like an untimely frost—
—shee's dead
Upon the swetest flower of all the field.
—shee's dead

Of course, there are all sorts of variations possible; the two women
might time their interventions to 'answer' Capulet's gradually horrified
recognitions; or they might dole them out as though they are suspended
in their own private horror, oblivious to his awakening. Either way, the
effect of the cues is to punctuate and counterpoint the father's potentially
stilted and academic apostrophizing.

Unique to the Q2/F script is the role of the Nurse in escalating the scale of mourning. Very early in her speech she gives out the cue-phrase, thus inviting the subsequent two speakers to join her in a round of woe:

> O wo, O wofull, wofull, **wofull day,**
> Most lamentable day, most **wofull day,**
> That ever, ever, I did yet behold.
> O day, O day, O day, O hatefull day,
> Never was seene so blacke a day as this:
> **O wofull day, O wofull day.**

(TLN 2629–34)

As in Q1, the speech is set up with innumerable potential pauses, ripe for interruption.

The distinctive speaking style used by Shakespeare throughout this scene—monotonous, list-like, heavily repetitive—makes much more sense once we identify the cue technique. And an alternative explanation offers itself as to how the 'all cry at once scene' of Q1 might be intended to be acted or have been acted (depending upon whether the text reports or prescribes a performance). For the first of the three individual speeches of misery, Capulet's, is in fact topped and tailed by the same line: 'Cruell, unjust, impartiall destinies'. In other words, the speech begins with the cue that also marks its end; as soon as Capulet has spoken his first line, the next speaker has been cued. Capulet's five lines might then be interspersed with Paris's answering or echoing five lines. (In turn, the mother's cue, 'suddaine **destinie**', is itself suggested by the final phrase of Capulet's repeated cue, 'impartiall **destinies**'. Perhaps she too is cued to chime in simultaneously with her 'O woe ... ')

Played in this fashion, and with either text, the scene is no less ritualized, no less formulaic and ceremonial than a 'linear' performance in which actors speak one after another. But it is almost certainly more dramatic, allowing for a mixture of communal ritual and, in its gift to the actor of choice, spontaneity, and improvisation, something closer to the recklessness of grief. The effect of the repeated cues is to help the actors achieve a scene that is precariously balanced between sincerity and irony, communality and individuality, tragedy and its subversion. The hysteria in the mourning keeps us partly aloof from it; the palpably bad verse can seem insincere and even blameworthy. But as much as the grief is misplaced and embarrassing, it is also genuine and prophetic: Juliet will very soon be dead. To the extent that the misplaced mourning is a burlesque, then it is the violent carnivalesque precursor to the 'gloomie peace' in store. The mingled messages sent out by the cues are the very emotional affects that Shakespeare is orchestrating.

The mechanics' play in *A Midsummer Night's Dream* (TLN 2099–2131) uses the same technique: depending on our dates, perhaps reinforcing the argument that 'Pyramus and Thisbe' is a parody of *Romeo and Juliet*. Pyramus ends his 'dying' speech with 'Now dye, dye, dye, dye, dye', which cues a sequence of sarcastic judgements from the noble audience ('No Die, but an ace for him', 'For he is dead, he is nothing', 'With the helpe of a Surgeon, he might yet recover, and prove an Asse') which can clearly be performed whilst Pyramus continues to 'die'. The same effect is then used with Thisbe's final speech, when she or he finds the dead Pyramus: 'And farewell friends, thus *Thisbie* ends; | Adieu, adieu, adieu'. The two examples of the mechanics' play and the mistaken mourning for Juliet suggest how indecorous repeated cues seemed in tragedy, at least in 1595. But this would not be the case for very much longer.

## Tragic Pathos

When Shakespeare returned to tragedy, he had in the early or repeated cue a sure-fire technique for evoking what he needed perhaps above all: a taut sense of pathos that is evoked *not* through (potentially bathetic) self-articulation, but through the sectioning, and thereby the intense *individuating*, of stage space and time. In Shakespeare's mature tragedies, repeated cues are used at moments of the gravest, most terrifying, or most exquisite climax: as we shall see, they help measure and pace the clamour surrounding Desdemona's murder; the reconciliation of Lear and Cordelia; the leave-taking of the mad Ophelia; the sleep-walking of Lady Macbeth; the deaths of Lear and Hamlet, and much else besides. The epitaphs for Burbage paid particular compliment to his art in dying truthfully on-stage: clearly the dying moment was central not only to tragic teleology, but to contemporary appraising of an actor's relative mastery of his craft. The playwright knew that an actor's passing required fastidious pacing: a deep actorly knowledge breathes in the report of Cawdor's death, that 'Nothing in his Life became him, | Like the leaving it. Hee dy'de, | As one that had been studied in his death' (*Macbeth*, TLN 287–9). An actor would have homed in upon his final moments with rare avidity: no death or leave-taking can ever have been scripted untidily. In this, as in much else, repeated cues become absolutely fundamental.² Shakespeare so develops the technique that it becomes a crucial means of orchestrating the passions, awe, and memorability of tragedy.

## *Julius Caesar*

*Julius Caesar* uses repeated cues in two distinct but characteristic ways: to evoke popular turbulence, particularly in the scene when Mark Antony inflames the Roman crowd (see pp. 166–71); and to evoke subjective loneliness, when the hero Brutus prepares to die. Here is the full text of this latter moment as it appears in the Folio:

> BRUTUS.  Night hangs upon my eyes, my Bones would rest,
> That have but labour'd, to attaine this houre.
>                  *Alarum.*                  *Cry within, Flye, flye, flye.*
> CLITUS.  Fly my Lord, flye.
> BRUTUS.  Hence: I will follow:
> I prythee *Strato*, stay by thy Lord ...
> Hold then my Sword, and turne away thy face,
> While I do run upon it. Wilt thou *Strato*?
>
> (TLN 2686–95)

We have here a combining of the technique's two most common uses—the crowd or battle scene and the tragic end. So, Brutus's cue for his suicide plea—whether it is Clitus's whole line, or 'my Lord, flye', or merely 'flye', is first anticipated and quickly surrounded aurally by the off-stage cries of 'Flye, flye, flye'. It doesn't really matter whether or not the Brutus-actor takes the off-stage 'flye' for his cue: either way this generalized panic instigates or echoes Clitus's supplication. Brutus's isolation is framed all the more starkly: everyone is being cued to fly; everyone is cuing *him* to fly; he can do nothing but stay on-stage and speak his resignation into death. The simple cueing context envelops and magnifies the hero's effective oblivion.

## *Hamlet*

Here is the exit of the mad Ophelia from *Hamlet*:

> OPHELIA.  Come, my Coach: **Goodnight** ladies: **Goodnight** sweet Ladies:
> **Goodnight, goodnight.** ['Come my Coach, **God night** Ladies, **god**

**night.**/Sweet Ladyes **god night, god night**': Quarto 2 1604/5][3]

KING..    Follow her close,
       Give her good watch I pray you:
       Oh this is the poison of deepe greefe, it springs
       All from her fathers death. Oh *Gertrude, Gertrude*...

                                 (TLN 2804–14)

The King would have had as his cued part something along the lines of:

           _____ Goodnight.
       Follow her close...

Or possibly:

              _____ Goodnight, goodnight.
       Follow her close...

Ophelia's repeated 'god night' or 'goodnight' is the key to way in which the speeches here are effectively self-directing. If the cue was a single 'goodnight', then this would have invited all kinds of possibilities of cross-dialogue and interruption. The very first 'goodnight' could cue Claudius's initial response; Ophelia could remain somewhere on-stage, or depart and quickly return, and Claudius's words, words that are about her but not to her, could continue to 'splice' into hers. Both parts are interrupted, fragmented, with Ophelia's mad speech interspersed within Claudius's 'sane' one. So one possibility is that Ophelia's repeating cue keeps breaking in on the calm authority of the King; that instead of his customarily masterful rhetoric, his speech is rendered edgy and stuttering, almost as haunted as her own. The cue-effect then gives a tangibility to the 'battalions' that the King feels creeping in upon his security. Orchestrated thus, the part might have played like this (with modernized punctuation):

OPHELIA.  Goodnight—
KING.    Follow her...!
OPHELIA.  Ladies! Goodnight—
KING.    Follow...!
OPHELIA.  sweet Ladies! Goodnight!
KING.    Follow...?
OPHELIA.  Goodnight!    *Exit.*
KING.    [*shouts*] Follow her close!
       Give her good watch I pray you!
       [*to Gertrude*] Oh this is the poison of deepe greefe; it springs
       All from her fathers death. Oh *Gertrude, Gertrude*...

The premature cue is often as simple as a direction to be interrupted. But as we have seen, it can also have a special effect that sections the stage, splitting the focus of interest and allowing simultaneous action and commentary: again, like an aside, it speaks *of* but not *to* a present character. This spatial effect is also a temporal one, in that splitting the focus on stage can represent minds in different places, at different moments, operating at distinct velocities. The scene may be happening simultaneously in 'real' time, but at subtly dislocated moments in 'dramatic' time. So another possibility is that Ophelia hovers around and inside the King's speech, as the Ophelia-actor identifies his repeated cues and delays his second or subsequent articulation of the cue-word. It could be orchestrated something like this (a number of variations are possible):

OPHELIA. Goodnight.  
KING.     Follow her close—  
OPHELIA. ladies Goodnight.  
KING.     Give her good watch I pray you  
OPHELIA. sweet Ladies Goodnight—  
KING.     Oh this is the poison of deepe greefe, it springs all from her  
          fathers deathe.  
OPHELIA. Goodnight.    *Exit.*  
KING.     Oh *Gertrude, Gertrude* ...

Claudius speaks of Ophelia whilst Ophelia speaks 'her mind'; his speech is situationally based, and responsive to circumstance; hers is fantastical, obsessive, and entirely cocooned. The mark of her insanity is that she is severed from mutual or reciprocating dialogue. Claudius acts as though each moment and action simply follow one another ('Follow her close, Give her good watch ... ') whilst Ophelia is frozen in repetition. The repetition, then, becomes her 'character note': trapped in a single but eternalized moment in time, the moment of farewell: 'goodnight, goodnight ... '.

In *Hamlet* it is Ophelia who is the chief subject of the climactic echoing cue. Gertrude, however, is scrupulously denied by Shakespeare the technique's distinctively redeeming isolation. Here are her very final words:

———————————————————— [see] [them] bleede.  
No, no, the drinke, the drinke.  
Oh my deere *Hamlet*, the drinke, the drinke  
I am poyson'd.

(TLN 3787–90)

The ingredients for pathetic death are all there: in particular, the fourfold repetition of what Gertrude suddenly identifies as the bearer of tragic mistake and betrayal: 'the drinke, the drinke…'. However—pitilessly, mercilessly—these climactic repetitions cue nobody. They are effectively unheard, so no one else is brought 'inside' Gertrude's death anguish. On-stage and off-stage, everyone else remains basically a passive bystander. Shakespeare must have known what he was doing—hinting at a powerful cue-effect, and simultaneously withholding it. The Gertrude-actor might well have recognized a tantalizing, almost cruelly denied temptation to seize the stage and die like a true queen. And this fastidious refusal of repeated cues is an emphatic sign that we, like the Gertrude-actor's fellow players, are not ultimately to be allowed 'in' to her dying, as we weren't into her life. She dies alone, and remains as impenetrably opaque as ever.

Unsurprisingly, the play's great adversaries, Hamlet and Claudius, are chorused into death by repeated cues—at least in the Folio text. Here is Claudius's last exchange, as it might have appeared in the actor's part:

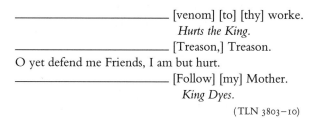

                   [venom] [to] [thy] worke.
                   *Hurts the King.*
                   [Treason,] Treason.
O yet defend me Friends, I am but hurt.
                   [Follow] [my] Mother.
                   *King Dyes.*

                             (TLN 3803–10)

The cue for Claudius's final line—'Treason, Treason'—is spoken by '*All*': once again we see a conjunction of crowd scene and private anguish. Each actor with 'Treason, Treason' on his part would identify this as a single line made up of a repeated cue; so each would have the opportunity to play the second 'Treason' as occasion demands. Each actor receiving this line may or may not realize the further complication that the repeated cue is also to be spoken by any number of other actors at the same time. As we have seen, this simple enough device allows the single line to be distended as far as the situation requires: each 'Treason' can be at once simultaneous and consecutive. Here is the confrontation in full in the Folio text:

LAERTES.        … Thy Mothers poyson'd:
          I can no more, the King, the King's to blame.
HAMLET.   The point envenom'd too,
          Then venome to thy worke.
          *Hurts the King.*

ALL.        Treason, Treason.
KING.       O yet defend me Friends, I am but hurt.
HAMLET.   Heere thou incestuous, murderous,
                Damned Dane,
                Drinke off this Potion: Is thy Union heere?
                Follow my Mother.                    *King Dyes.*
LAERTES..  He is justly serv'd.

(TLN 3800–11)

The cry of 'Treason' seems to be directed chiefly against Hamlet as he wounds the King. But a series of things—Laertes's accusation, the pre-knowledge of Horatio concerning the King's guilt, the sense throughout the play that Hamlet retains considerable sympathy at court and beyond—make it perfectly likely that Claudius as much as Hamlet is here the accused. Accordingly, the withheld second 'Treason' may extend not only into Claudius's final line, but even into Hamlet's enraged response to it. For remember, every actor cued (and it could be virtually the entire ensemble) has at least two opportunities to say the word:

ALL.        Treason, Treason.
KING.       O yet defend me Friends, [Treason!] I am but hurt. [Treason!]
HAMLET.   Heere thou incestuous, [Treason!] murderous, [Treason!]
                Damned Dane, [Treason!]
                Drinke off this Potion: [Treason!] Is thy Union heere? [Treason!]
                Follow my Mother. [Treason!]                    *King Dyes.*
LAERTES.   He is justly serv'd.

At any rate, the echoing cue-phrase produces a ferocious space of confusion and cross-angles, one in which 'Treason' can by turns be spoken in outrage at, or in league with, *both* Hamlet and Claudius. The word can mutate from impotent shock (on the part of Claudius loyalists) to maliciously triumphant revenge (the cry of 'Treason' a justifying exclamation as Hamlet forces the deadly potion home). And unlike his wife, Claudius perhaps retrieves here a certain abandoned pathos: as the words ricochet around him, his calls for help ('defend me Friends', 'I am but hurt') grow ever more faint, mortal, and beleaguered. At the same time, the repeated cues help to achieve simple emotional resolution, founded in the way the action on-stage finally accords with the hopes and expectations of those off-stage. For it is necessary that 'Treason' should thus come home. Revenge belatedly finds its target, and justice is given some vestige—albeit mockingly fleeting—of restored balance.

Hamlet's dying words in F, it may surprise many, repeat the technique—only this time he is the one speaking the echoing cue:

> On *Fortinbras*, he ha's my dying voice,
> So tell him with the occurrents more and lesse,
> Which have solicited. The rest is silence. O, o, o, o. *Dyes.*
>
> (TLN 3845–7)

Of course, it may be that these four closing 'O's' were not in the part-script, and that 'rest is silence' was the cue for Horatio's 'Now cracke[s] a Noble heart: | Goodnight sweet Prince, | And flights of Angels sing thee to thy rest' (TLN 3850–2). The words are, after all, absent from Q2. But it seems certain that the Folio text directs or records some version of the moment as acted under Shakespeare's eye, or at least his fellow actors'. That is, whatever the Horatio-actor's cue, Hamlet continues 'beyond' his final farewell—whether we identify this farewell in his own 'rest is silence' or in Horatio's 'Goodnight'. Suffice to say here that this is a consummate example of a repeating final speech—the 'O, o, o, o' can be conceived of as a single dying moan; equally, each 'o' might represent a quite distinct performative utterance[4]—that forges for actor and character an effectively separate existential dimension: rather like Mercutio's dying curse, it is spoken from a place that is *almost* posthumous, and that gives to 'Hamlet' a privileged position at once inside and beyond his own play.

## *Troilus and Cressida*

This is in stark contrast to the catastrophes in *Troilus and Cressida*. Notoriously, all of the principals are allowed to survive bar one—Hector. But even though Hector is killed on-stage, he is denied both parting words and the repeated cues that so often frame these deaths. Consequently, both he and we lack the channels into inwardness that the repeated cue so often produces at moments of passing. In *Troilus and Cressida* Shakespeare mainly uses repeated cues to orchestrate his actors inside the chaos of battle—but not in the way of crowd scenes familiar from other plays, but rather to indicate isolated selfishness within the confusions of war. A typical

example is the Greeks' tracking of their enemy, Troilus; here is the passage
in the Folio:

> ACHILLES. *Hector*, wher's *Hector*? I will none but *Hector*.
>
> *Enter Ajax.*
>
> AJAX.      *Troylus*, thou coward *Troylus*, shew thy head.
>
> *Enter Diomed.*
>
> DIOMED. *Troylus*, I say, wher's *Troylus*?
> AJAX.      What would'st thou?
> DIOMED. I would correct him.
> AJAX.      Were I the Generall,
>             Thou should'st have my office,
>             Ere that correction: *Troylus* I say, what *Troylus*?
>
> *Enter Troylus.*
>
> TROYLUS. Oh traitour *Diomed*!
>
> (TLN 3424–35)

The names of the prey—Hector and Troilus—are also the two operative
cue-words. As both are repeated more than once, this may allow for
precipitous entrances and competitive interruptions: Ajax might come in
before Achilles has finished, Diomed before Ajax has finished, and Troilus,
perhaps, before any of them have noticed his presence. The Troilus-actor's
cue for the (would-be) ultimate battle with his love rival Diomed is 'what
*Troylus*', or perhaps simply a shouted '*Troylus*'. But his name at any rate is
thus shouted no less than seven times in the fourteen lines that precede his
vengeful self-announcement ('Oh traitour *Diomed*!'). Diomed's line reads:
'*Troylus*, I say, wher's *Troylus*?', followed a second or two later by Ajax's
actual cueing line of '*Troylus* I say, what *Troylus*?': it is difficult to believe
that the script is not orchestrating a gloating comedy, allowing Troilus to
appear on-stage (cued by 'wher's *Troylus*?'), in full view of the relishing
audience, before his adversaries see him. This gives a further ribald, almost
slapstick, context to Diomed's first response to Troilus's appearance, 'Ha,
art thou there?'

    This all makes good enough stage sense, and certainly helps to give
vivid realization to Troilus's separateness. But we are not here witnessing
the separateness of inwardness; there is very little metaphysical distinction
between the 'early' entrances for any of the characters in this scene. The
only distinction concerns which of them the audience identifies with. This
is likely to be Troilus: we alone are privy to his stealing entrance, whereas

the Greeks' emulous attempts at trumping each other are brazenly on view
and clearly ridiculous. Either way, Shakespeare here uses repeated cues in
a strictly limiting way. Troilus later says that he will 'dare all imminence'
(TLN 3549): yet it is precisely 'imminence', the sense that the minds and
bodies on-stage are at the very cusp of decisive happenings, which is here
withheld. As we shall see, it is in this witholding that *Troilus and Cressida*'s
repeated cues particularly differ from those used in unequivocal tragedies
such as *Othello* and *King Lear*.

In *Troilus and Cressida* the repeated cue, as a means of forging individual
experience that is unreachable by anyone else, is given only to the
disreputable jesters, Pandarus and Thersites. We get Thersites's onanistic
frenzy—'frye, lechery, frye', 'Now the pledge, now, now, now' (TLN
3039, 3048)—as he watches Cressida unbuckle with Diomed. This is truly
a man alone in his passion, the premature cues like small gifts to be
obscenely cherished and rubbed. Or we get Pandarus, whose trademark
position—caught between voyeurism and solicitation—is time and again
engineered by repeating cues:

PANDARUS. ...Nay, you shall fight your/hearts out ere I part you. The
Faulcon, as the Tercell, for/all the Ducks ith River: **go too, go
too**.
TROYLUS. You have bereft me of all words Lady.

(TLN 1683–6, prose lineation ours)

HELEN. My Lord *Pandarus*.
PANDARUS. What saies my **sweete Queene**, my very, very **sweet Queene**?
PARIS. What exploit's in hand, where sups he to night?
HELEN. Nay but my Lord?
PANDARUS. What saies my **sweete Queene**? my cozen will/fall out with you.

(TLN 1553–9, prose lineation ours)

HELEN. ...by my troth sweet Lord thou hast a fine fore-head.
PANDARUS. **I you may, you may**.

(TLN 1580–2, prose lineation ours)

All of these examples work similarly: they give the Pandarus-actor room
for play. (Here it actually makes little difference whether Pandarus speaks
or receives the repeated cue. The parts of Cressida, Helen, and Paris all
give out repeated cues to Pandarus; as much as he is in his world, they are
in theirs.) This is appropriate for a role that seizes any opportunity to leer,
wink, cajole, and insinuate his lasciviousness into the audience. The other

characters can go about their love business whilst Pandarus moves in and
around them, half the peeping Tom, half the grotesque choric muse. This
is a mutation out of a clown's licence to improvise. So, the premiss of the
repeated cue in this part seems to be that Pandarus is also *our* pander: his
lewd ingratiations leak beyond any putative fourth wall and challenge us to
feel the heat.

It is faithful to the play's refusal to admit glamour or nostalgia that
Pandarus should be given the climactic echoing cue:

> TROYLUS.      … Strike a free march to Troy, with comfort goe:
>               Hope of revenge, shall hide our inward woe.
>
>               *Enter Pandarus.*
> PANDARUS.     But **heare you? heare you?**
> TROYLUS.      Hence broker, lackie, ignomy, and shame
>               Pursue thy life, and live aye with thy name.
>
>                                               *Exeunt.*
> PANDARUS.     A goodly medicine for mine aking bones: oh world,
>               world, world! thus is the poore agent dispisde …
>                                          (TLN 3566–73)

Pandarus's twice-spoken 'heare you' cues Troilus's departing insult ('Hence
broker, lackie, ignomy, and shame | Pursue thy life, and live aye with thy
name'). Clearly it is possible that Pandarus repeats the phrase because he
cannot get Troilus's attention. Equally, he might say one 'heare you' to
Troilus, and one to us—'heare you' how faithful service is repaid. Either
way, it is left to Pandarus alone to retrieve whatever he can from the
wreckage all around.

## *Othello*

In *Othello* the climactic potential in the technique returns at full throttle.
Before this climax, however, Shakespeare offers a characteristically daring
variation upon the repeated cue's ability to 'conduct' one character's
separateness from others. Here is the conclusion to the part of Bianca, the
courtesan:

> _____ [with] [my] shirt.
>
>               *Exeunt.*
>       What is the matter hoa? Who is't that cry'd?

_____ [is't] [that] cry'd?
Oh my deere *Cassio*,
My sweet *Cassio*: Oh *Cassio, Cassio, Cassio*.
_____ [him] [easily] hence.
Alas he faints. Oh *Cassio, Cassio, Cassio*.
_____ [shake] [at] that?
He supt at my house, but I therefore shake not.
_____ [upon] [thee] Strumpet.
I am no Strumpet, but of life as honest,
As you that thus abuse me.

(TLN 3173–3229)

The repeated cue ('Cassio, Cassio, Cassio') is used to place the character in a disparate mental—and perhaps physical—space from the rest of the cast. No one on-stage much cares about Bianca's fear and terror, any more than they care about her love; perhaps no one off-stage much cares either. So they may interrupt or ignore her with impunity. The part's emotional climax—Bianca's paroxysms of grief over the wounded Cassio—is to be shared by no one else. But the explanation for the cue technique used here is only partly traceable to Bianca's character. It is also a variation upon the play's central themes and looming catastrophe. Like Othello, Bianca is the internal outsider, never more alien, isolated, or indeed contemptible than in her profoundest misery. So, rather like the mistaken mourning over the drugged Juliet, Bianca's excessive grief over redeemable injury is Shakespeare's way of preparing the audience for the absolute losses to come. Her words are sincere enough, of course, and speak directly from the character's passions: but the cue technique does not. It comes from elsewhere—from Shakespeare's larger purposes in the play—and at once precedes, frames, and leaves behind 'Bianca's' particular crisis. Consequently, the isolation produced by the repeated cues works to marginalize rather than accentuate this sincerity. A technique associated by actors either with comic victimization or tragic pathos is used for a purpose that is neither one nor the other, but one that draws from the memory or expectation of each. Bianca and her cues are thus part of a medley of emotional effects that are better ascribed to the author's intentions than to those of either the character or the actor.

For Shakespeare sees in the repeated cue a mode of stage language that is as layered, delicate, and variously interpretable as any other language. Thus, Othello's response to the technique—and the Othello-actor's relationship to it—is utterly different from Bianca's. This is particularly in evidence from the decisive moment when, suddenly certain that Cassio has lain 'with' and 'on' his wife, Othello faints. This moment is already powerfully marked by a transition from verse to prose (see Part IV). And the pretty much simultaneous entrance of early and repeating cues is yet another sign of Othello's sudden severing from self and society. This is most emphatic in the Quarto:

OTHELLO.     Lie with her, lie on her? We say lie on her, when they bely/
             her; lye with her, Zouns, that's fulsome, **handkerchers,**
             Confession,/**hankerchers.** *He fals downe.*
IAGO.        Worke on my medicine, worke: thus credulous fooles are/
             caught, and many worthy and chaste dames, even thus all guilt-
             lesse,/meete reproach...

                                                    (Q1, I3b, prose lineation ours)

Here what looks like an early cue-word may invite Othello to move into his 'epileptic' fit while still having 'Confession, hankerchers' to splutter out; in turn, Iago's vicious words of triumph ('Worke on my medicine, worke...') can accompany, even demonically compel, the general's fall—the super-insidious Iago working like poisonous 'medicine' in Othello's mind. (There is no early cue in the Folio text: the speech closes with 'Confesse? Handkerchiefe? O divell', at which Othello 'Falls in a Traunce'.)

If this first example is only in the Quarto, phrasal repetitions in both Q and F pepper Othello's new prose-cum-verse, many of them doubling up as early cues. Some of them occur when Othello 'withdraw[s]' so as secretly to watch Iago question Cassio (about, as he thinks, Desdemona):

_____ [you] [heare] *Cassio?*
Now he importunes him
To tell it o're: go too, **well said, well said.**
                        (TLN 2499–501; no repetition in Q)

_____ ha, ha, ha.
**Do ye triumph, Romaine? do you triumph?**
                        (TLN 2504–5; same in Q)

We often see the early cue used as a means to separate one character from another, and thus to split both the stage physically and the mind notionally. Here this is explicitly achieved: Othello occupies one 'space', Iago and Cassio another; the repeated early cues ensure the Othello-actor a certain freedom to pace his own movements of mind, voice, and body. So, Othello has five cues to respond to, and three of them are 'ha, ha, ha' (at TLN 2504, 2508, 2525). Almost certainly the Othello-actor will see these as a simple sign of laughter. He doesn't have to wait for the laughter to finish before he begins speaking. On the contrary, the laughter invites the actor to choose his own moments of response. By helping the Othello-actor, in particular, to retain or parcel out his words at unpredictable intervals, *we* can see and hear Othello dividing himself from others, and thus partially separating from his socially endorsed self.

The pathos that the technique can engineer may be further ratcheted up once Iago returns to confer with his general. Perhaps here even single words are repeated cues:

——————————————————— [it] [his] whore.
I would have him nine yeeres a killing.
A fine **woman**, a faire **woman**, a sweete **woman**?

(TLN 2561–3)

——————————————————— [I] [too] gentle.
Nay that's certaine:
But yet **the pitty of it,** *Iago*: oh, *Iago*, **the pitty of it/***Iago*.

(TLN 2579–81, lineation ours; Q has 'but yet **the pitty** of it *Iago*, **the pitty**')

——————————————————— [That's] fouler.
Get me some poyson *Iago*, **this night**. Ile not/expostulate with her: least her body and beautie unpro/vide my mind againe: **This night** *Iago*.

(TLN 2589–92, lineation ours; same in Q)

——————————————————— [she] [hath] contaminated.
**Good, good:**
The Justice of it pleases: very **good.**

(TLN 2594–6; same in Q)

And again when he is next alone with Desdemona:

————————— [am] [I] false?
Ah, *Desdemon*, **away, away, away.**

(TLN 2734–5; same in Q)

Here the repeated 'away' may invite the Othello-actor suddenly to pull 'away' from all others and enter a space of radical separation from everyone and everything but his echoing obsession. Other actors can enter in—but he will not hear them. The technique is immediately repeated:

OTHELLO.    Was this faire Paper? This most goodly Booke
Made to write Whore upon? **What commited,
Commited?** Oh, thou publicke Commoner,
I should make very Forges of my cheekes,
That would to Cynders burne up Modestie,
Did I but speake thy deedes. **What commited?**
Heaven stoppes the Nose at it, and the Moone winks:
The baudy winde that kisses all it meetes,
Is hush'd within the hollow Myne of Earth
And will not hear't. **What commited?**

DESDEMONA. By Heaven you do me wrong.

(TLN 2767–77)

The speech here being cued by 'What commited'—cued apparently three or even four times—is Desdemona's 'By Heaven you do me wrong'. Whereas the Q text seems to preclude any confusion or interruption—'what commited' is spoken twice, but 'impudent Strumpet' is Desdemona's cue—the Folio text appears to invite it. If this is the case, and Desdemona does indeed try vainly and repeatedly to assert the 'wrong' being done to her, then we are presented with a much more roused, more defiant Desdemona. But more than that, we find a scripting that wants to make porous the boundary between character and actor, as 'Desdemona's' frustration escalates in an arhythmic beat to 'Othello's' violent disregard.

    The technique almost certainly returns—here around a single distinctive cue-word—as climax draws ever closer:

OTHELLO.    By Heaven I saw my **Handkerchiefe** in's hand.
O perjur'd woman, thou do'st stone my heart,
And makes me call, what I intend to do,
A Murther, which I thought a Sacrifice.
I saw the **Handkerchiefe**.

DESDEMONA. He found it then:
I never gave it him: Send, for him hither:
Let him confesse a truth.

(TLN 3314–21)

The memorable cue-word, 'Handkerchiefe', is spoken early. It is thus possible that Desdemona leaps in at this first enunciation—an 'interruption' easily anticipated and accommodated by the Othello-actor.

Here we should perhaps pause, and ask what the pay-off is of this seemingly ubiquitous technique. After all, if Shakespeare wanted Desdemona immediately to rebut Othello, why not write it like this:

OTHELLO.      By Heaven I saw my **Handkerchiefe** in's hand.
DESDEMONA.  He found it then: I never gave it him.
OTHELLO.      O perjur'd woman…

This would be to continue the to-and-fro rhythms of earlier in the scene, when Othello's allegations are met by Desdemona's swift rebuttals:

OTHELLO.      That Handkerchiefe
              Which I so lov'd, and gave thee, thou gav'st to *Cassio*.
DESDEMONA.  No by my Life, and Soule: send for the man,
              And aske him.

(TLN 3396–9)

But the early cue proposes a different kind of acting. It suggests escalating desperation and, more profoundly, an unbridgeable chasm between the two lovers. So, Desdemona hears 'Handkerchiefe', and leaps in to deny it: 'He found it then'; Othello barely pauses as he relives what he thinks he has seen, and feels again the terrible bodily intimacy of betrayal:

—in's hand—

Desdemona continues in her frantic denials ('I never gave it him'), denials that Othello damns as a false oath ('O perjur'd woman'). Still she perseveres, struggling for entrance into her husband's foreclosed mind ('Send', 'for him hither')—but he has gone:

… thou do'st stone my heart,
And makes me call, what I intend to do,
A Murther, which I thought a Sacrifice.
I saw the Handkerchiefe.

(TLN 3315–18)

It is the *impossibility* of Desdemona getting a word in that marks the tragedy. Only by not separating the speakers into a 'linear' exchange can their mutual isolation truly be felt; only by not ordaining the particular moment where Desdemona attempts to interrupt—and then attempts again—can the gravity of refusal come home. Once again, it is the actor's responsibility for timing his precise moment of intervention that ensures the presence and urgency of emotion. And this is indeed the fatal moment: Othello's next words, 'he has confest', mark the end of Desdemona's hopes.

Shakespeare knows that in a particular kind of tragic extremity—when passions are exceeding articulation—dialogue must provide openings for the actors to *feel* whether and when to commit. But as much as the script has to anticipate and serve the player's body, the use of early cues here extends beyond any single actor's possession. At its most perilous and delicate, the repeated cue can become the audience's. As we have been stressing, the technique often helps centre and intensify the individual actor's feeling for his character's inwardness. However, because the repeated cue is founded in the interstices between words and between characters, it can also 'breathe' with the larger emotional content of the scene. In *Othello* these emotions are by no means confined to any single character. They involve a shared apprehension, at its most intense where it is least communicable, of tragic mistake spreading like wildfire. It is this anticipation of unrecoverable loss that the 'communal' repeated cue-space invites and elicits, as it opens out to the audience's suddenly accelerated and magnified empathies. The repeating cues in the climax of *Othello* thus help to produce a shared actor/audience space of emotional response, one that is alive with recoil, fear, longing, and anxiety.

This reaches its height in the murder scene. In the full Q text it is presented thus:

| | |
|---|---|
| OTHELLO. | Downe strumpet. |
| DESDEMONA. | Kill me to morrow, let me live to night. |
| OTHELLO. | Nay, an you strive. |
| DESDEMONA. | But halfe an houre, but while I say one prayer. |
| OTHELLO. | Tis too late. *He stifles her.* |
| DESDEMONA. | **O Lord, Lord, Lord.** Emilia *calls within.* |
| EMILIA. | **My Lord, my Lord,** what ho, **my Lord, my Lord.** |
| OTHELLO. | What voyce is this? Not dead? not yet quite dead? |
| | I that am cruell, am yet mercifull, |
| | I would not have thee linger in thy paine,—so, so. |
| EMILIA. | What ho, **my Lord, my Lord.** |
| OTHELLO. | Who's there? |
| EMILIA. | O good my Lord, I'de speake a word with you. |
| OTHELLO. | Yes, tis *Emillia*, by and by: shee's dead... |

(Q, M2a–b)

The Folio has this:

| OTHELLO. | It is too late.          *Smothers her.* |
| | *Aemilia at the doore.* |
| AEMILIA. | **My Lord, my Lord? What hoa?** |
| | **My Lord, my Lord.** |
| OTHELLO. | What noise is this? Not dead? Not yet quite dead? |
| | I that am cruell, am yet mercifull, |
| | I would not have thee linger in thy paine? |
| | So, so. |
| AEMILIA. *within.* | What hoa? **My Lord, my Lord?** |
| OTHELLO. | Who's there. |
| EMILIA. | Oh good my Lord, I would speake a word with you. |
| OTHELLO. | Yes: 'Tis *Aemilia*: by and by. Shee's dead ... |

(TLN 3342–53)

In both versions the part of Othello is cued twice by the repeated phrase, 'My Lord, my Lord'; on the first occasion 'my Lord' is spoken four times. Othello, then, is apparently invited to come in early with his line, 'What voice is this?' The scripted confusion is reinforced in the Quarto: it gives Desdemona an extra line, 'O Lord, Lord, Lord', that offers not only a repeating cue (to the Emilia-actor) but anticipates the cue that Emilia, in turn, is to give Othello. The effect may be to create a maelstrom of fear and panic and, with the deepest possible irony, 'mistaken' cues. It might go along these lines:

> *(from Desdemona?)* Lord!—
> > What noise is this?
> > > (from Emilia *and* Desdemona?) Lord!—Lord!
> > > > Not dead?
> > > > > *(from Desdemona?)* Lord!
> > > > > > Not yet quite dead?
> > > > > > > (from Emilia?) Lord!
> > I that am cruell, am yet mercifull ...

Othello's speech is itself now both capped by a repeated cue—'so, so'—and met by another ('My Lord, my Lord'). The actors are being directed by these cue-effects into a semi-blindness or semi-deafness, where the addressee may be the speaker, or the audience, or simply the dramatic moment. Here all three of the actors are getting the same cueing instructions at one point or another. So even Desdemona's part 'finishes' with what might be an early cue:

_____ [Revenge] [growes] harsh.
O falsely, false murder'd.
_____ [sweet] [Mistris], speake.
A guiltlesse death, I dye.
_____ [done] [this] deed?
No body: I my selfe, **farewell**:
Commend me to my kinde Lord: oh **farewell**.

(TLN 3383–93; same in Q)

The effect has to be one of fatal misdirection. This is similarly true of the
play's second married couple. So, with typical bravura, Shakespeare offers a
pitiless reprise of the central couple's crossed cues in the final confrontation
between Emilia and Iago:

EMILIA.     … She false **with *Cassio*?**
            Did you say **with *Cassio*?**
IAGO.       With *Cassio*, Mistris?
            Go too, charme your tongue …
EMILIA.     **Villany, villany, villany:**            [this speech not in Q]
            I thinke upon't, I thinke: I smel't: O **Villany:**
            I thought so then: Ile kille my selfe for greefe.
            O villany! villany!
IAGO.       What, are you mad?
            I charge you get you home …
EMILIA.     'Twill out, 'twill out. I peace?
            No, **I will speake** as liberall as the North;
            Let Heaven, and Men, and Divels, let them all,
            All, all, crie shame against me, yet **Ile speake.**
IAGO.       Be wise, and get you home.

(TLN 3462–3513)

Emilia's repetitions may here cue Iago's repeated attempts to interrupt and,
more pertinently, silence her. If that is the case, then the early cue becomes
the medium and metaphor of spousal rebellion. The early cue has here a
function that is as symbolic as it is actable. It is used as a working symbol
and agent of *separation*: as lived experience, and as metaphysical condition.

But the beauty of the technique remains in the fact that the movements
it elicits are always both the actor's and the character's. This really is a
technique in which the puzzle of love—of living bewilderedly in a feeling
body, of locating metaphysical essence in flesh and sense, of defining oneself
by connections that may never be sure or secure—can come terribly home.
Ultimately, therefore, repeated cues return emphatically to Othello. First is

the speech that, with a weeping abandonment of rhetorical control, marks
Othello's loss of secure public identity:

> Whip me ye Devils,
> From the possession of this Heavenly sight:
> Blow me about in windes, roast me in Sulphure,
> Wash me in steepe-downe gulfes of Liquid fire.
> **Oh** *Desdemon*! Dead *Desdemon*: dead. **Oh, oh!**
> ———————————————— [most] [unfortunate] man.
> That's he that was *Othello*: heere I am.

(TLN 3577–85)

Second is his response to Cassio's devastating explanation as to where he
found the handkerchief:

> ———————————————— [to] [his] desire.
> **O Foole, foole, foole!**

(TLN 3632–3)

The Othello-actor will see that this line of 'foole[s]' prepares for his final
suicide speech; equally, he will recognize for the last time that he has a
repeated cue-word whose first and last addressee is 'himself'. He is the
'foole' more than ever before, and the second and third cries of this repeated
cue are for the Othello-actor alone. He can ignore whatever clarifications
are spoken (by Cassio and Lodovico) between the part's final echoing curse
('Whip me ye Devils') and its final substantive speech ('O Foole...'). In
fact, Cassio speaks for six lines, Lodovico for eight, both as agents of justice
and the state. But in terms of the tragic denouement, the fourteen lines of
Cassio and Lodovico extend no longer in time than Othello's 'self-cues'
('Foole, foole, foole...'). For the part-dictated actor must always draw an
imaginary bow from cue to cue, speech to speech, and pretend that each in
succession is the predicate and occasion for the next. Often it is not: here
it absolutely is. The space occupied by the repeating cues draws into itself
the fullest weight of Othello's guilt, contrition, and suffering.

We see in the part of Othello a model example of how early or repeating
cues can create an acting 'chamber' that speaks more intimately and
inwardly than many a soliloquy or aside. The player *knows* that any putative
privacy he has between his repetitions is in fact besieged and stolen, and
at every moment might break or be broken back into. It helps to produce
the most lacerating representation of 'interior' suffering. Nevertheless, the
repeated cues in *Othello* reveal a tragedy that is far from being characterized

by a single climactic *anagnorisis*. The play presents a series of calamities that are at once desperately individual and tragically shared: embodied most passionately in waves of sound that, although they collide, are never fully accompanied by a meeting of minds. The catastrophes are doled out with an almost mathematical attention to necessity. Above all, the repeated cue is here the basic means of probing, and suddenly discovering, the *distance* between people who think they know one another, and whose lives are inextricably welded together.

## Lady Macbeth

Perhaps the single most striking instance where the premature cue is used as a sign of existential separation is in Lady Macbeth's final scene. She enters carrying a taper, watched by the doctor and a waiting woman; they talk about her for ten or so lines, during which time the Lady Macbeth-actor will perform her distracted sleep-walking. The premiss of the scene is mental, sensory, and spatial separateness—which is precisely what the repeated cues soon build upon:

_____ [she] [ha's] knowne.
Heere's the smell of the blood still: all the per/fumes of Arabia will not sweeten this little hand.
**Oh, oh, oh.**
_____ [in] [their] beds.
Wash your hands, put on your Night-Gowne,/looke not so pale: I tell you yet againe *Banquo's* buried;/he cannot come out on's grave.
_____ [Even] so?
**To bed, to bed**: there's knocking at the gate:/Come, come, come, come, give me your hand: What's/done, cannot be undone. **To bed, to bed, to bed.**

*Exit Lady*.

(TLN 2141–60, lineation ours)

The actor will inevitably see the repeated cues as an instruction to follow his own emotional line: to listen first and foremost not to the scripted cues but to his character's unravelling truth. Just as Lady Macbeth keeps on rehearsing what should be past and buried, so the early 'to beds' represent the impossibility of escaping the haunted mind: she would 'cue' herself out of the moment (this is, indeed, her 'exit' cue), but cannot; the end is the beginning, and the beginning is the end. That the cue-phrase starts and finishes the part's very last speech symbolizes and enacts inescapable despair; it lends a physical and visible reality to the sheer loneliness of the Lady's eventual exit.

That Shakespeare is scripting precisely this is reinforced by the immediate comments of the watching doctor and waiting woman. In full play-script the dialogue goes like this:

> LADY.                    ... What's done, cannot be undone. To bed, to bed, to bed.
>
> > *Exit Lady.*
>
> DOCTOR.          Will she now go to bed?
> GENTLEWOMAN. Directly.

> (TLN 2158–62)

Doctor and Gentlewoman might whisper this conversation after the first 'To bed, to bed', questioning *when* she will exit—will it be 'now', 'Directly'? For although the Folio marks Lady Macbeth's exit before this exchange, it seems clear that she remains on-stage, and that they both hear her intention ('To bed') and see her wavering. It is certain that Lady Macbeth exits after her final 'to bed'—but hardly less certain that this doesn't come until after the Gentlewoman's 'Directly', which must, then, be spoken in holding fashion, as they continue nervously to watch the Queen's movements and await still further shocking admissions. We cannot know which line the Lady Macbeth-actor was actually given as his exit cue. It may be that he remained on-stage still further into this dialogue: the Doctor's final speech in the scene is nine lines long, and includes at least three moments which might find reinforced theatrical resonance if Lady Macbeth is indeed still in view ('More needs she the Divine, then the Physitian', 'Looke after her', 'still keepe eyes upon her' (TLN 2166–9)). Whatever the precise details, the basic function of the repeated cue is clear: it gives to the Lady Macbeth-actor a determining control over the pace of his character's climactic moments, while giving the other actors a concomitant *lack* of control. It intensifies the Lady Macbeth-actor's possession of her slow steps toward extinction, by effectively erasing all others, or reducing them to barely apprehended whispers in the margins. Actors and characters both defer one last time to their mistress. They cannot quite know what she will say or when she will go; they cannot quite know how much her words or her movements, or the simple menace of such, will continue to shadow their own. Of course the actors will not share their characters' nervous terror, any more than they need share their solicitousness or disapprobation. But the cue-effect reinforces the scene's sickly air of 'infected mindes' (TLN 2164): the Lady's presence seeps beyond the boundaries of her own part into the parts of these other actors, thus frustrating clear demarcations between good and bad. The repeated cues thus help to pace and point the scene's rumbling under-theme: the slow exposing of fastidious health to ethical contamination.

# 13

# The Cue-Space in *King Lear*

*K*ing *Lear* uses repeated cues throughout, forcibly pointing shifts of
mood or power. Repeated cues direct actors toward real ensemble
playing, and to dialogues that are interruptive, staccato, polyphonic, chorused, or harmonically scored. Repeated cues here facilitate and interpret
emotional climaxes and political swings; they are peculiarly intimate to
moments where generic or plot symmetries click satisfyingly into place
or, alternatively, suffer some kind of abrupt and worrying arrest. Rather
like a piano player's left hand, cueing always controls a scene's rhythm:
repeated cues in *Lear* have a tremendous, often barely sensed role in altering
a given moment's pace or order. And repeated cues also at times segue,
inevitably, into entrance cues, drawing figures on to the stage before an
ongoing part has finished. They consequently help manipulate what and
who an audience sees: they can create dual or competitive perspectives;
they can work the thin division between tragedy and comedy (or make
their coexistence unforgettable). In all of this, repeated cues become basic
instruments of Shakespeare's generic momentum.

Let us look at some examples, and see the ways in which Shakespeare's
manipulation of cues accompanies and at times carries the play's vast
emotional range.

## Gloucester

Shakespeare will often plot the development (or derogation) of a character specifically through that character's different uses of repeated cues.
Gloucester is a good example of this, particularly in his early scenes. The
first repeated cue offered by Gloucester is to Edmund: the (apparently)
impatient 'Let's see, let's see', spoken to make the bastard show 'Edgar's'
incriminating letter. Here it is in the Folio:

| | |
|---|---|
| BASTARD. | I shall offend, either to detaine, or give it: |
| | The contents, as in part I understand them, |
| | Are too blame. |
| GLOUCESTER. | **Let's see, let's see.** |
| BASTARD. | I hope for my Brothers justification, hee wrote/this |
| | but as an essay, or taste of my Vertue. |
| GLOUCESTER. | *Reads. This policie, and reverence of Age, makes the/* |
| | *world bitter to the best of our times …* |

(TLN 376–83; prose lineation ours)

The cue on Edmund's part might be a single 'Let's see'; it might be 'Let's see, let's see'. If the former, the Edmund-actor can come in early with his fake 'excuses', provoking the patriarch into furious reiteration ('Let's see … let's *see*!!'). If it is the latter, then the Edmund-actor will not interrupt Gloucester; but even so, the Gloucester-actor is unlikely to know this. The repetition of 'let's see' at the end of his speech will suggest the possibility of an early cue, and therefore invite the actor to retain the second 'let's see' for himself. So, the first 'let's see' might be peremptory and demanding; the second, with letter in hand, more curious or nervous. Alternatively, he might speak the first with patience, the second—the letter still in Edmund's hand—with angry insistence. Either way, the repetition cues through escalation and emphasis the decisive shift from blustering complacency to sudden vulnerability: 'my Sonne *Edgar*, had hee a hand to write this? A heart and braine to breede it in?' (TLN 391–2). The effect of the repeated cue is to separate the actor from the character: whereas the actor is basically in control, the character is opened to unexpected, isolating mortification.

Another characteristic suggested by Gloucester's early use of cues is the comic, buffoonish edge to his role. That this was an element in the conception of the part is suggested by the exit he is given at the end of I. ii. Having been fooled by Edmund into believing in Edgar's villainy, he departs the stage after a lengthy meditation upon how these 'late eclipses in the Sunne and Moone portend no good to us', concluding in the Folio, ' 'Tis strange' (TLN 433–46). In the Quarto his parting words are these: '*Kent* banisht, his offence honest, **strange, strange!**': the 'strange' being a repeated entrance cue for Edmund, who is to come in and say, 'this is the excellent foppery of the world …' (Q, C2a). (The Folio text may lack the repetition for reasons of space: its 'strange' huddles up against the stage direction '*Exit*' without any gap at all.) It is therefore possible that Edmund enters with his scoffing soliloquy, but that Gloucester continues droning on; the old man thus fades away rather than decisively exits, as his 'strange' anxieties are over-ridden by Edmund's sceptical rationalities. Accordingly, the Bastard's insouciant '*This* is the excellent foppery of the world' can point both to the world and to Gloucester: as the old world drifts from focus, the new chillingly arrogates the stage's centre. The cues reinforce Gloucester's early status as the victim of every irony going: marooned with his redundant second 'strange', he is the oblivious buffoon whom no one wants or needs. By making audible and visible his isolation, the cue-effect prepares pitilessly for Gloucester's accelerating superannuation.

Gloucester is being 'placed' for both actor and audience by these sorts of cue. Their effect is often political, as we see in the part's next use of the technique. It occurs at a very particular moment of transition: as the symbols of Gloucester's comfortable world-view go crashing down, and an impatient and unsentimental ruling order rises (II. i). Here is the Folio script (the Quarto barely differs):

> REGAN.         ...how dost my Lord?
> GLOUCESTER.  O Madam, my old heart is **crack'd**, it's **crack'd**.
> REGAN.         What, did my Fathers Godsonne seeke your life?
>                He whom my Father nam'd, your *Edgar*?
> GLOUCESTER.  O Lady, Lady, shame would have it hid.
> REGAN.         Was he not companion with the riotous Knights
>                That tended upon my Father?
> GLOUCESTER.  I know not Madam, 'tis **too bad, too bad**.
> BASTARD.      Yes Madam, he was of that consort.
>
> (TLN 1028–36)

Each one of Gloucester's replies contains a repeated phrase of grief. Two of the repetitions are cues—but only in the sense that they close his speeches. To the audience it would seem that Gloucester is 'cueing' no one: no one else on-stage responds to the old man—instead everyone throws questions at him and then interrupts him when he tries to answer. His immediate fury having abated, he is buried deep here in the circularity of stunned bereavement and the muteness of shame. The repetitions speak disbelief as much as self-pity; a lingering on the fact of ruin, regret for what has gone, perhaps a superstitious idea that to dwell in what is 'crack'd' is somehow to keep a hold upon its relevance. But the more Gloucester turns into a mournfully nostalgic echo of himself, the more he becomes an obstacle, easily ignored but better removed. Hence the repeated cues: a simple but effective marker of accelerating belatedness and marginality:

REGAN.              _____ how dost my Lord?

GLOUCESTER.  O Madam, my old heart is crack'd—

REGAN.       What…

GLOUCESTER.  —it's crack'd.

REGAN.       [What] did my Fathers Godsonne seeke your life?
             He whom my Father nam'd, your *Edgar*?

GLOUCESTER.  O Lady, Lady, shame would have it hid.

REGAN.       Was he not companion with the riotous Knights
             That tended upon my Father?

GLOUCESTER.  I know not Madam, 'tis too bad—

BASTARD.     Yes—

GLOUCESTER.  —too bad.

BASTARD.     —[Yes] Madam, he was of that consort.

(TLN 1028–36)

Edmund answers for Gloucester, and Regan then answers Edmund: the 'old man' is out of the picture. Gloucester's repetitions are both naturalistic markers of an old man's muttering grief and precise conductors of the political moment. These early scenes are all about the sudden acceleration of consequences that have been long gestating. Gloucester suffers entropy *and* explosion; the cues likewise bear both in their wake.

A slightly earlier moment of defused or derailed confrontation between father and son shows this very starkly, while at the same time illustrating one of Shakespeare's important variations upon the repeated cue: that is, the repeated statement that is spoken as though it is a cue to be answered, but which is not in fact responded to at all. We might call this a secreted or refused cue (we saw something similar with the mocking 'false cues' in *Merchant*'s trial scene):

O Villain, villain: his very opinion in the Let/ter. Abhorred Villaine, unnaturall, detested, brutish Villaine; worse then brutish: Go Sirrah [Q: sir], seeke him: Ile/apprehend [Q: I apprehand] him. Abhominable Villaine, where is he?

(TLN 409–12; prose lineation ours)

The part cued here is again Edmund's, which would then look something like this:

_____ [where] [is] he?
             I doe not well know my Lord…

(TLN 412–13)

Edmund's part suggests a very straightforward question and answer, but in the scene he will discover that it is nothing of the kind. The two parts, Gloucester's and Edmund's, seem to be written to accentuate an almost comical disparity between their attitudes. So the player of Edmund will be waiting for his simple cue ('where is he?'). In the meantime the player of Gloucester rages on, shouting 'Villaine' five times, garnished by five furious adjectives and two apparent attempts to cue the 'good son' to appropriately immediate action ('Go sir', 'seeke him'). Whilst Gloucester windily blusters, Edmund is still and silent. The parts are written as though from different plays; the cue on Edmund's part gives no suggestion of the sheer heat and frustration with which it will be spoken. But what it absolutely gives is Edmund's take on the scene: Edmund's simple, processional, instrumental control. Meanwhile Gloucester's is written so as to invite the audience to *expect* the old man to be interrupted. Not only does the simple fact of consecutive repetitions invoke thoughts of interruption, but so too—for Gloucester at least—does the basic filial and sibling context. Surely one brother will defend the other; surely Edgar is being wronged? But the play is pitiless. Edmund ignores Gloucester's 'attempted' cues, whether implicit ('Villaine') or explicit ('Go sir/Sirrah', 'seeke him'). This forces Gloucester into further repetitious invective, followed by a second cue-on-a-plate. So, while Gloucester turns into a mocking self-echo, Edmund is as diffident, as detached, and as brutally hard as a stone. Gloucester can only exhaust his fury and then, silence all around, cue his son through the most simple and helpless question: 'where is he?' The father is now serving the son: the moment absolutely marks the transfer of power.

There is a terrible reprise of the same technique later in Gloucester's story. Fittingly, it occurs when the shift of power presaged in all of Gloucester's repeated cues finds its devastating *coup de grâce*: this moment, of course, is Gloucester's blinding. Gloucester's cued part would be something like this:

_____ [sent] [the] King?

To Dover.

_____ [him] [answer] that.

I am tyed to 'th'Stake,
And I must stand the Course.

_____ [Wherefore] [to] Dover?

Because I would not see thy cruell Nailes
Plucke out his poore old eyes ...

(T LN 2120–9)

But the full dialogue goes like this:

| CORNWALL. | Where hast thou sent the King? |
|---|---|
| GLOUCESTER. | To Dover. |
| REGAN. | **Wherefore to Dover?** |
| | Was't thou not charged at perill. |
| CORNWALL. | **Wherefore to Dover?** Let him answer that. |
| GLOUCESTER. | I am tyed to'th'Stake |
| | And I must stand the Course. |
| REGAN. | **Wherefore to Dover?** [Q: Wherefore to Dover, sir? ] |
| GLOUCESTER. | Because I would not see thy cruell Nailes |
| | Plucke out his poore old eyes ... |

(TLN 2120–9)

The striking difference is that the key cue is spoken not once but three times: 'Wherefore to Dover?' Or this at least is the case with F. In the Quarto the actual cue-phrase is made distinct from the two earlier articulations of the question: the cue is not 'Wherefore to Dover?' but 'Wherefore to Dover, sir?' (Q, H1b). So we have to imagine two scenarios. One involves Gloucester hearing his cue one time only (Q); the other involves him hearing his cue on three quickly consecutive occasions (F). If the part used by the player resembles the Folio script, then this raises the possibility that upon hearing Regan's first demand the Gloucester-actor would have wanted to charge straight in with his defiant 'Because I would not see thy cruell Nailes ... ' The Regan-actor will of course see that he is to speak his cue-phrase twice; rather as we saw earlier with Shylock, this knowledge prepares the actor to be interrupted, and in turn to meet this interruption with contemptuous vehemence, shouting his interlocutor down with the words still to be spoken. It is the perfect technique for emboldening the actor into true malice aforethought. But it also helps orchestrate something of the heady, escalating, improvisatory rage of suddenly unbridled cruelty: the inquisitors, in their rage or eagerness, almost compete with one another to elicit the killing confession; physical torture is matched by verbal torture, as the old man is manhandled, tied to a chair, his speech sabotaged. It might work something like this:

| REGAN. | Wherefore to Dover?— |
|---|---|
| GLOUCESTER. | Because I— |
| REGAN. | —Was't thou not charg'd at perill [?] |
| CORNWALL. | Wherefore to Dover?— |

| | |
|---|---|
| GLOUCESTER. | —[Because I] would not— |
| CORNWALL. | —Let him answer that. |
| GLOUCESTER. | I am tyed to'th'Stake, |
| | And I must stand the Course. |
| REGAN. | Wherefore to Dover? |
| GLOUCESTER. | Because I would not see thy cruell Nailes |
| | Plucke out his poore old eyes ... |

In this scenario, when, finally, the question 'Wherefore to Dover?' is *not* immediately followed with a counter-demand (to him) or a cross-rebuke (to Regan), and Gloucester is at last given breathing space to answer, we might imagine a sudden silence, taut with barely withheld violence. Perhaps Gloucester leaps immediately into his great speech of defiance, accelerating into his destruction; or perhaps, cued in this water-torture fashion, he pauses, before unwinding his speech in a gradual release of all the things that he has so long been denied expression. Either way, the distinctive cue-effect—whether left hanging and unanswered, or proffered and then over-ridden—helps engender a scene of terrifying, visceral fear.

The alternative is the Quarto version. In this version, the Gloucester-actor will hear the question, '[Wherefore] to Dover?', he will be readied with his cued response, but the absence of the cueing 'sir?' will force him into silence. This version, then, is one that ratchets up the tension. The repeated demand 'Wherefore to Dover?' works powerfully as a representation of an interrogation already little short, if at all, of torture. There is a tremendous accumulation of suspense and fear as Gloucester persists in his silence; concomitantly, and perhaps for the first time in the play, we are absolutely 'with' him. His refusal of this 'false' cue, then, is a mark of integrity. When, finally, he is permitted to speak—once Regan adds the ingratiating 'sir?'—it is a powerful moment of self-restitution.

We might thus see how Shakespeare partly sets up this switch of audience feeling—a movement from distrust or perhaps neutrality to unequivocal compassion—through symmetrical but opposed practices of cueing. In the earlier 'Villaine' scene with Edmund, it was Gloucester who was the intemperate interrogator; the silence with which his demands were met dignified the bastard's taciturn but ascendant ironies. In this later scene, Gloucester reverses the role: first, by owning the moment of silence 'before' the illegitimate cue (a silence demonically imitated by Edmund earlier); second, through the cathartic and empathy-generating experience of truthful accusation. Shakespeare is orchestrating almost sub-liminally felt key-changes, corresponding to very basic emotional responses to the action, through the symmetrical reprising and inversion of cue practice.

# Poor Tom

Edgar's 'part within the part' of Poor Tom circulates all kinds of echoing cues: his sudden appearance and apparent madness signify an escalation of cross-talking mayhem within the play in general. But the Tom-persona haunts, echoes, or mirrors considerably more characters than merely its creator Edgar. Poor Tom works as a fantastic allegory of the moment of the play that he appears in; he is also an allegory of the moment's meta-dramatic techniques.

In the Folio, Tom's first words are 'Fathom, and halfe, Fathom and halfe; poore Tom' (TLN 1819), met by the Fool's repeated cue, 'helpe me, | helpe me' (TLN 1820–1); in the Quarto, Tom has not yet spoken, but the fact of his presence has prompted the Fool's repeated demand for help. The hovel is now occupied by a fool, a 'madman', and a mad/foolish king: unsurprisingly, overlapping speech is common. Tom's first long speech in the Folio ends as follows, cueing the Lear-part: '**There** could I have him now, **and there**, and **there** againe, **and there**' (TLN 1842). The cue-word, 'there' (possibly 'and there') is spoken up to four times, inviting Lear's fascinated or horrified interruption; but more than an interruption, the repetition is a cue for cross-purpose interplay between fracturing minds:

> EDGAR. There could I have him now, and there—
> LEAR. Ha's his Daughters ...
> EDGAR. —and there—
> LEAR. [Ha's his Daughters] brought him ...
> EDGAR. —againe, and there.
> LEAR. [Ha's his Daughters brought him] to this passe?
> Could'st thou save nothing? Would'st thou give 'em all?
> FOOL. Nay, he reserv'd a Blanket, else we had bin all sham'd.
>
> (TLN 1842–6)

The repeating word, 'there' or 'and there', accompanied no doubt by pointing or other gesture, is the perfect word for the lunatic moment:

empty enough to conjure up any scene of loss, violation, or larceny that
Lear might wish; and both empty and pointed enough to suggest how
Edgar-Tom's aim here is at once scatter-shot and deadly purposeful. (In Q
the line is 'There could I have him now, and there, and there againe'(Q,
G2a) with no 'scripted' repeated cue: the 'there againe' might possibly be
an instruction to say 'there' again (and again ... ), or a performance memory
of such on the part of the scribe.) For if Lear is starting to play out fantasies
of revenge or compensation, then so too is Edgar. But his role here is
not limited to what 'Edgar' (as the disguised noble son) might wish. Poor
Tom both serves and exceeds 'Edgar': Edgar's cues generate a momentum
beyond Edgar's, or indeed Tom's, control. Anyone and everyone might be
drawn into his 'there', just as anyone might be engrossed or shadowed by
his cascading figurations: his 'there' can cue the lot of them.

This might suggest how Tom's repeating cues are also a metaphor for the
role. Poor Tom causes others to make 'transitions', and as such is himself a
kind of scrambled cue: coming from who knows where, directed to who
knows what. The figure of Tom is almost literally cued by Lear's famous
prayer for the 'poore naked wretches'; in turn, Poor Tom's appearance
appears instantaneously to cue Lear's decisive entrance into insanity ('Did'st
thou give all to thy daughters?' (TLN 1830)). And whether others try to
shun him (Gloucester) or shout him down (the Fool), Poor Tom ends up
in some devastating way prompting each character into his consummation.
Accordingly, when later in the night the eyeless Gloucester has to try to
restructure his life in the light of his new knowledge, he does so not only
through the material help of his unknown son, but also from his vision
'i'th'last nights storme, I such a fellow saw; | Which made me thinke a Man,
a Worme. My Sonne | Came then into my minde ... ' (TLN 2216–18).
As though himself an impelling cue, Poor Tom sets in train strangely
irresistible mutations, mental and otherwise.

His next repeated cue in Folio and Quarto alike is a striking instance of
this magnetic capability:

LEAR.    Those Pelicane Daughters.
EDGAR.   Pillicock sat on Pillicock hill, alow: a**low, loo, loo**. (Q: a lo lo lo)
FOOL.    This cold night will turne us all to Fooles, and/Madmen.
                                        (TLN 1856–9; lineation ours))

There are two cued processes going on here. First, Tom plays upon the
phrase underlying Lear's cue (the proverb was 'Pelicane Daughters spawn

the Pillicock'); second, the Fool comments disdainfully or fearfully upon Tom's cue. Clearly the cue–cued comments work against and within each other, rather like puns; but they are puns with a rare and troubling reach. If we are to understand exactly how the cross-cueing here works, we need quickly to survey the dense, multiple agencies within the exchange.

First, then, what does Edgar see, and seize, in Lear's cue? Lear's cue, 'Pelicane Daughters', is a reference to the fable that the pelican feeds its children with its own blood. But mad Tom takes it up for its sound, mutating Pelicane into 'Pillicock', a penis. Matching Lear's perception of himself as a victim of his daughters is Edgar's perception, equally lucid, of himself as a victim of the world of sexual ethics. Tom thus rehearses the primal crime that so haunts Edgar throughout the play: had Gloucester not been so fecklessly led on by *his* 'Pillicock', there would have been no conception, and so none of the murderous familial world that ensued. Furthermore, 'Pillicock hill' invokes the 'mound of Venus', upon which this little lost member sits, doleful and deflated. 'Pillicock sat on Pillicock hill', then, suggests the disinherited son, cast out—indeed, castrated—from family and generation and his own body. The words thus suggest Edgar's self-perception as the unhappy survivor—exiled, deracinated, abandoned. Consequently, the 'alow, loo, loo' cue he gives out—perhaps drawing upon the melody of the lost nursery rhyme that the 'Pillicock hill' evokes; perhaps a bird sound, and so part of the Darwinian range of animal life at Tom's disposal—can be understood as almost the plaintive signature tune of this wounded and lonely heart. It becomes specifically Edgar-Tom's recitative. The echoing cue becomes a mourning song, a complaint to the air that necessarily overleaps its scripted functionality. In appealing to everyone and no one, in expecting no kind of answer, all addressees are at once bound up and erased in the cue's song of self-pity. This particular reverberating cue-sound thus works rather as the Edgar-role itself does: as a repetition, and a cue for recognition, of a compounded and accumulating suffering.

But this cue also possesses an overriding violence. It evokes hunting, and more particularly the cry used to incite dogs to the chase. Of course, in this context everyone and anyone might be the hunted hare, not least Edgar himself. It fits well enough with the masochism of Edgar's role-play that he should be calling the chasing dogs on to himself; for the apparently arbitrary pretence is in fact a paranoid replaying of his own experience (as the 'proclaim'd' man who 'escap'd the hunt' (TLN 1253)). Tom is victim and agent; he is menacing, but also menaced.

We need a very subtle sense of how exactly Edgar's cue 'cues'. By not stopping with one 'loo', or even with two, Tom ensures that his cue is in one sense a trick cue, an invitation that will immediately get swallowed up or drowned out by his ululation. Others will 'speak into' his part; he will sing into theirs. And this echoing quality also means that at some level it overrides its supposed addressee (the Fool). We might here recall how the Fool disappears in the next scene, as though chattered by Tom into redundancy (perhaps his first response to the vision—'helpe me, helpe me' (TLN 1820)—was indeed a recognition of mortal danger). This fact might give an oddly tangible reality to the way in which the cue works: directed *to* one who is being prepared to pass into all or nothing; directed *by* one who takes into his own role the functions that his cue at once cues and seems to eradicate.

It is thus possible to identify in this echoing cue some kind of taunt, or challenge. So, either the Fool interrupts the beggar, or the beggar overrides the Fool: or of course both:

> EDGAR.  Pillicock sat on Pillicock hill, alow—
> FOOL.   This cold—
> EDGAR.  —alow—
> FOOL.   This cold [–night will]—
> EDGAR.  —loo
> FOOL.   This cold [–turn us all]—
> EDGAR.  —loo.
> FOOL.   [This cold night will turn us all] to Fooles and Madmen.

The Fool is manifestly clearer in his speech than the 'madman': and precisely in this decorum lies insecurity. When the Fool talks about the 'Madmen', then, he is only partly self-referential; the movement from 'Fooles' to 'Madmen', surrounded by the lunatic cries of 'loo, loo', is egged on by what it attempts to disdain. Edgar's echoing, returning cue provokes the Fool's annihilation: the abandonment of hierarchy is facilitated and symbolized by this inescapable cue-sound. 'Loo, loo, loo, loo' howls the Fool out of commission, into one of the 'Madmen', and finally into 'nothing'.

## Edgar and Gloucester

The entrance of Edgar's father, Gloucester, into this febrile scene seems to prompt another of Edgar-Tom's terrible repeated cues, in which his father is linked with devils and demons and filial wounding: 'This is the foule Flibbertigibbet...[who] hurts the poore Creature of earth'. Appropriately, the cues close a song about a meeting between saintliness and possession:

| | |
|---|---|
| EDGAR. | *Swithold* footed thrice the old, |
| | He met the Night-Mare, and her nine-fold; |
| | Bid her a-light, and her troth-plight, |
| | And **aroynt thee** Witch, **aroynt thee.** |
| KENT. | How fares your Grace? |
| LEAR. | What's he? |
| KENT. | Who's there? What is't you seeke? |
| GLOUCESTER. | What are you there? Your Names? |

(TLN 1900–7)

As always, all sorts of possible stories and magnetic connections tumble out of Poor Tom's inventions, here capped by the repeated cue-phrase: 'aroynt thee Witch, aroynt thee'. So, as the song cues a series of uncertain questions—'How fares your Grace?', 'What's he?', 'Who's there?', 'What is't you seeke?', 'What are you there?', 'Your Names?'—Poor Tom can be envisaged singing in between and around the befuddled questioners, perhaps darting or dancing from one to the other with his injunction to disappear: 'aroynt thee!', 'aroynt thee!' The cry is at once protective and accusatory; no one can escape the accusation of witchery. Once more, Tom's echoing cue hovers as the moment's choric key. In over-leaping the decorum of cue-giver and cue-taker, in *not* resting in his own part, the Edgar-part challenges the distinction of one character from another; indeed, he challenges the very notion *of* distinction. Hence this particular moment's final joke: the beggar-man's repeated 'aroynt thee's, we might surmise, have forced the noble characters into their helpless merry-go-round of questions. His jabbering is like a verbal fog, preventing clear sensory apprehension. But then, when a question is finally answered—Gloucester's desperate 'Your Names?'—it is the Edgar-part that in fact seizes the cue: 'Poore Tom, that eates the swimming Frog...' (TLN 1908). Everyone, once again, is submerged in Tom's parables.

Perhaps the most famous and striking 'echoing' cue in this scene is not in fact a repeated cue, but a 'recurring' one: Edgar's cry of 'Tom's a cold'. Occurring at disparate moments in the scene, the expression is never placed so as to interrupt or be interrupted. But this plaintive cry is given as a cue three times, and it epitomizes Edgar-Tom's role. The phrase 'Tom's a cold' has become famous because of its wistful repetition, and because the repetition declares that the statement goes unheeded. Tom may be 'a cold', but no one is listening.

However, the cue-effects of Poor Tom are always equally for or about him and for or about others, who take their transitions from him: anyone might find in the vagrant an unexpected cue back into their *own* destinies. So it is with 'Tom's a cold'. It first cues Lear's question, 'What hast thou bin' (TLN 864), and thereby the King's recognition in this 'Philosopher' of an experience somehow universal and secret-solving. But in part terms it is Tom's oblivious father, Gloucester, who is put in focus, or suddenly revealed, by the recurring cue. Here, then, is the Gloucester part from this first 'Tom's a cold' to the scene's end:

> _____ [Tom's] [a] cold.
> Go in with me; my duty cannot suffer
> T'obey in all your daughters hard commands ...
> _____ [wits] [begin] t'unsettle.
> Canst thou blame him?
> His daughters seek his death: Ah, that good Kent,
> He said it would be thus: poore banish'd man:
> Thou sayest the King growes mad, Ile tell thee Friend
> I am almost mad my selfe. I had a Sonne,
> Now out-law'd from my blood: he sought my life
> But lately: very late: I lov'd him (Friend)
> No Father his Sonne dearer: true to tell thee,
> The greefe hath craz'd my wits. What a night's this?
> I do bessech your grace.
> _____ [Tom's] [a] cold.
> In fellow there, into th'Hovel; keep thee warm.
> _____ [take] [the] Fellow.
> Take him you on.
> _____ [Come,] [good] Athenian.
> No words, no words, hush.

(TLN 1925–65)

Let us imagine the Gloucester-actor working through his part for the first time. He notices the same cue twice in quick succession; he will probably assume that the same character, 'Tom', speaks both. He will also notice that his own responses to the repeated cue-phrase are themselves synonyms: 'Go in with me' and 'In fellow there'. Apparently, however, they are not spoken to the same character: the first seems to be to the King ('... my duty ... your daughters'), the second ('in fellow ... keep thee warm') cannot be. This second cued response, he may assume, will be to the cue-speaker: he is told that 'Tom's a cold', and therefore acquiesces, 'In fellow... keep thee warm'. But the succeeding cues given to the Gloucester-actor continue to harp upon the unresolved issue of the beggar-man: he is the 'Fellow' and the 'good Athenian' that is the parting subject of controversy. Consequently, either Gloucester's response to the second cue of 'Tom's a cold' was *not* to Tom, but rather to the Fool or to Kent; or some sort of battle is going on over possession of Tom, or over the right to keep *him* company. So, Gloucester either tells him to get in, partly out of pity and partly to stop him haunting the King's person, or he ignores him completely. Meanwhile the King insists that he will go in only 'With him... my Philosopher' (TLN 1958–9). Gloucester therefore either relinquishes the beggar to the King ('Take him you on') or reluctantly permits—as the nominal patriarch of the hovel—the beggar to join them as the fractured King desires.

The function of cues as 'narrative capsules' is here very tightly pitched: they are pointers to the part's formative and, in this case, tragic ironies. For the point about Tom's repeated cue-line is that it puts into sharp relief *Gloucester's* state of mind: his continuing ignorance, his emerging compassion, and his recognition of the wrong he has done his (now twice unknown) son. Gloucester is of course not allowed fully to open to his disguised son; the actor on-stage will be well aware of this simply from having read his part through, and of course from the immediate performance context. Nevertheless, the elisions of the part-text will force the player to act 'feelingly': to wonder who exactly he is talking to; to wonder whether his obliquely present son ('Tom's a cold') is in fact 'recognized', if not as his son, then by the simple but plaintive fact of being directly addressed.

Hence the beautiful mystery, the delicacy of choice, contained in Gloucester's closing line: 'No words, no words, hush.' Who, again, is he addressing? Is it the same addressee three times, or does he switch midline from one (King/Tom) to another (Tom/King)? He will know that this is his last line in the scene, but he may not know whether he cues anyone else to respond (he may suspect that he does if his line is not immediately succeeded on the written part by 'exit' or 'exeunt'). And if it does cue a response, he will see that it might be played as a repeated or echoing cue: perhaps because the line seems to enact the same thing three times; perhaps because he suspects that the cued actor will have 'no words' rather than 'hush' (or variations) transcribed on his part; perhaps because the onomatopoeic 'hush' resembles the oft-seen cue of 'O', figuring a potentially long-dilated, unpredictably reverberating sound, rather than a brief bite of diction. Consequently, the actor might anticipate some other voice 'entering' into his own speech. This in turn raises the possibility that Gloucester switches address from the one who cues him (Lear, who is in fact addressing Tom) to the one who interrupts him: and this, of course, is Poor Tom with his scene-closing recitation. Here is the exchange in full context:

> LEAR.            Come, good Athenian.
> GLOUCESTER.  No words, no words, hush.
> EDGAR.         Childe *Rowland* to the darke Tower came,
>                      His word was still, fie, foh, and fumme,
>                      I smell the blood of a Brittish man.

One possibility is that Gloucester takes the suddenly childlike Lear under his wing with a soothing caress of 'no words' and 'hush'. There may be problems here with decorum: as a general rule, Gloucester, like Kent, sticks to the forms of deference as though the imprimatur of sanity. And it is equally likely that Gloucester, so sensitive to the moment's awful indignities, is throughout talking to Tom: first trying to pre-empt any words from him; then, once disobediently 'interrupted' (with the 'early' cue of 'no words') telling him again to be quiet.

Of course, Edgar-Tom must complete his song: the child disobeys the father, first by interrupting him, second by refusing to be silent, and third by singing of a 'childe' smelling his way to some kind of displaced parricide. In other words, the Edgar-actor too must 'feel' his way here, somehow balancing his character's high-wire combination of pretence, 'Oedipal' transgression, insolence, and the deepest, most oblique, most unspeakable love. Simultaneously, the Gloucester-actor must negotiate his own swirling and eddying emotional currents, as he moves between apparently incommensurable but strangely coalescing acts of care, or of fraternal-cum-paternal sympathy: for the vulnerable King, and for the hardly less vulnerable 'fellow'. So, as the boy interrupts with his rhyme, perhaps the man is pitched back into a lost familial scene: his boy kept awake by doom-laden nursery tales, and Gloucester again—or is it for the very first time?—the good father, wishing his child peace and sleep. Of course, there is another option—worried solicitation for the King ('no words ... '), and a sudden rebuke for the beggar ('hush'). Whichever interpretation is chosen, the actor has to *experience* the presence of options, and decide upon just what stage in his pilgrimage Gloucester has here reached.

To reiterate what is here at stake: the Gloucester-actor will suspect, if not know, that the recurring cue, 'Tom's a cold', comes from his character's lost son; his character will suspect, if not know, that his character is as yet *not* allowed to act on this fact. Throughout this exchange, so delicate in its balance of sympathies and extension of care, the Gloucester-actor will wonder whether, and if so *how*, he can speak to the one who, he knows, must in the end 'save' him. Hence the strategic way in which the two cues of 'Tom's a cold' bracket Gloucester's speech of love: 'I had a Sonne…I lov'd him (Friend) | No father his Sonne dearer.' 'Tom's a cold' is more than the scribal frame for this speech: it is its emotional spur *and* factual consequence. The actor will intuit all of this. He will expect the scene to make the presence of 'Edgar' to Gloucester less oblique; but he will equally know that his character's primary care *has* to be for the King. It is in finessing this balance, and the 'sentimental' movements it requires—movements in the focus of sympathy and sensibility; movements in the relative visibility of objects of pity—that the scene-closing repeated cue locates its purpose. The choices left to the actors here are crucial; Tom's song could interrupt and then intimately interweave with Gloucester's line; or it could be intoned at a quite separate part of the stage, as Gloucester has thoughts only for the King. Either way, the actor should see the options, and see in them his character's future in the instant. The scripting ensures the presence of the lost son in the margins or interstices of Gloucester's purview. As we often find, it is the actor's *apperception* which attends, or foreshadows, the character's perception.

## The 'Mad' Lear

Shakespeare uses the repeated cue to help represent Lear's madness in one particular way, both distinctive and appropriate. That is, he gives the King a single word which he then repeats three or four or five times, and the line cues someone else's speech or entrance. The actual cue, then, might equally be the single or the repeated word. An obvious but effective consequence is that other figures can apostrophize upon or enter the scene while the King continues to repeat the cue-word. As stagecraft, this is economical;

more importantly, it can symbolize the King's severance from custom and sanity. Babbling away in his own discursive bubble, the King (if not his actor) is oblivious even to the fact that he is repeatedly giving out his own cues.

A striking example is when Lear comes to the close of his 'preaching' to the blind man. Here is what the Gentleman-part might have recorded:

––––––––––––––––––––––––––––––––––– [kill] [kill] kill.

*Enter.*

Oh here he is: lay hand upon him, Sir.

(TLN 2629–31)

Here is the larger context:

| | |
|---|---|
| LEAR. | And when I have stolne upon these Son in Lawes, |
| | Then kill, kill, kill, kill, kill, kill. |
| | |
| | *Enter a Gentleman [F]; Enter three gentlemen [Q]* |
| GENTLEMAN. | Oh here he is: lay hand upon him, Sir. [Q: sirs] |
| | Your most deere Daughter—— [Q: your most deere] |
| LEAR. | No rescue? What, a Prisoner? I am even |
| | The Naturall Foole of Fortune. |

(TLN 2628–34; [in Q this whole passage is in prose])

Lear says the cue-word 'kill' six times. (A line such as Lear's ('kill, kill, kill … ') makes the whole issue of timing of entrances and exits problematic—the actor sees that his speech ends with a repeatedly spoken cue-word, and so will know that he can delay the later speaking of the word as he sees fit; the 'line' or phrase is not indentured to any specific rhythm, and thus not to any predictable time span.[1]) Clearly there is scope here for the gentlemen to enter after he has said 'kill' one or two or three times—or indeed any number of times up to six; similarly, there is equal scope for the Gentleman to start his speech 'O here he is' at any point during Lear's 'kill'-ing frenzy. One effect will be to point both pathos and ironies. So, the King is caught *in flagrante*; his loyal servants, mortified as much by their own as by the King's violence, seek to apprehend their master, but are forced embarrassingly to chase him, all the time speaking over his words. The Gentleman's attenuated second line, left incomplete verbally and rhythmically ('Your most deere [Daughter]—— ') suggests struggle; iambic measures give way under the disjunctive exigencies of the moment. Further ironies emerge once we see that the Gentleman's lines might *provoke* as much as respond to or follow the King's 'kill[s]'. So, he is attempting to turn the King's mind away from killing towards love, towards his 'deere Daughter', unaware that in Lear's mind none of his daughters is 'deere', and invoking them will only drive the King out of rage into despair. Of course, the effect is uncomfortably comic; the improvisations thereby allowed reinforce how the Dover scene is structured around surprise, interruption, and brutal humour. So, the six 'kills' can be turned *on* any one, and are *about* any one. Equally, the repeated injunction gathers together various of the roles played by Lear in this fantastic scene: judge and executioner, vengeance-taker, exiled monarch—or child in the sandpit. Once more the repeated cue-word is at once pointed and open-ended, allowing for all kinds of contexts:

LEAR.          Then kill,—


                         *Enter Gentlemen*
GENTLEMAN.     Oh—
LEAR.          —kill!—
GENTLEMAN.     —here he is—
LEAR.          —kill!—
GENTLEMAN.     —lay hand upon him
LEAR.          —kill!—
GENTLEMAN.     —Sir!
LEAR.          —kill!—
GENTLEMAN.     Your most deere Daughter ——
LEAR.          —kill!

Seconds later, Lear is off again, and once again his mind's fracturing anarchy—'I am cut to'th'Braines' (TLN 2636)—is given stark contextual pointing in the Folio by repeating cues:

LEAR.          ...I am a King, Masters, know you that?
GENTLEMAN.     You are a Royall one, and we obey you.
LEAR.          Then there's life in't. Come, [Q: nay] and you get it,
               You shall get it by running: **Sa, sa, sa, sa**. [Q omits
               'sa, sa, sa, sa']                              *Exit.*
GENTLEMAN.     A sight most pitifull in the meanest wretch,
               Past speaking of in a King.
                                                    (TLN 2642–7)

Lear's Folio 'sa, sa, sa, sa' is his exit cue and the Gentleman's speaking cue. It is likely, however, to be strictly neither. The repetition is once more an invitation to auditory polyphony—choosing when and where to speak—and physical liberty—choosing when and where to move. Lear, whose part tells him to exit running, might start to dash off stage with his first 'sa', and then return with his next; he might reprise what he did moments earlier with 'kill', only this time devolving from murderousness to a kind of play or farce ('sa' is probably a hunting cry), even a knockabout comedy. (This staccato exit is absent in Q, and we have to wonder, as often with Folio and Quarto distinctions, whether the difference is a revision or an addition, and why it is there.) Equally, the repeating 'sa' creates a space for others' apostrophizing: the Gentleman's 'a sight most pitifull' can be spoken not so much after the King has departed, but as he performs:

> Sa—
> A sight most pitifull in the meanest wretch—
> Sa, sa—
> Past speaking of in a King.

These apparently meaningless repetitions, then, do much more than represent galloping senility or delusional lunacy. They are stage-directions of simplicity and sensitivity. The generic daring of the scene is released and ensured by cues that place the lunacy within mundane sanity.


# Cordelia


*Lear*'s pilgrimage through experience can be tracked through its use of repeated cues. Even the play's most delicate moment uses the technique:

| | |
|---|---|
| LEAR. | …Do not laugh at me, |
| | For (as I am a man) I thinke this Lady |
| | To be my childe *Cordelia*. |
| CORDELIA. | And so **I am: I am.** [Q: And so I am] |
| LEAR. | Be your teares wet? |
| | Yes faith: I pray weepe not, |
| | If you have poyson for me, I will drinke it: |
| | I know you do not love me, for your Sisters |
| | Have (as I do remember) done me wrong. |
| | You have some cause, they have not. |
| CORDELIA. | **No cause, no cause.** |

| LEAR. | Am I in France? |
|---|---|
| KENT. | In your owne kingdome Sir. |
| LEAR. | Do not abuse me. [Q: Doe not abuse me?] |
| GENTLEMAN. | Be comforted good madam ... |

(TLN 2823–37)

Both of Cordelia's responses in the Folio are in the form of repeated cues: 'And so I am: I am' and 'No cause, no cause'; in the Quarto only Cordelia's second response is repeated. Cordelia's emotions are at first glance utterly different from Lear's 'mad' repetitions in the previous scene. There is, however, a similarity in the way in which the repeating cue creates around the speaker a kind of cocoon. If the player throws out his full cue-line, then the rest of the scene can progress in due order. But if he throws out only his first cue-phrase, keeping the second, identical one in reserve, then he remains bound within the gravity of the moment. This might be used to signify obliviousness, as in the mad scenes when the King comi-tragically mirrors his imploding nation. Or it might, as here with Cordelia, signify an emotional fullness, and a concomitant feeling of the brittleness of both words and voice.

The Cordelia-actor will notice that the part gives him two successive repeated cues. Consequently, the gap between 'And so I am' and 'I am' can have any temporal length the Cordelia-player likes. The actor can speak the first 'I am' and—presuming the cue on the Lear-part is a single 'I am'—wait for Lear to enter with his cued response. This leaves the Cordelia-actor free to complete his line in his own time: the silence that exists between the two cue-phrases ('I am ... I am'), becomes specifically that of Cordelia's concentrated 'interiority'. (This need not, of course, mean literal silence on the stage; other characters can keep on speaking their lines. But it might easily enough be played to create such general silence, as for instance Cordelia says her second cues 'to the air' and the other characters stop momentarily to observe her.) In this way, an intense attention 'outwards' on the actor's part will represent an intense contemplation inwards on the character's part. So each first cue-phrase responds to what Lear says; each second cue-phrase is for herself alone.

Shakespeare's repeated cues at climactic tragic moments have one overriding purpose: to focus with sudden and rare intensity upon the extremities of private feeling within a public context. And the device can bring us all the closer to the feeling at issue, making the feeling much less easily mollified.

This is because in the suspended moment between the two cues—inside the cued actor's very own cue-space—the suffering seems to be so locked up and incommunicable. Here, the intense beauty of the scene is premissed upon the terrifying fragility of any achieved meeting of minds, as much as upon how hard it has been earned. Shakespeare's use of the repeated or floating cue both carries and seems to intuit this combined sense of achievement and hazard.

Here the other characters join the audience in noticing, and thereby re-inforcing, the irreducible integrity of this privacy: 'Be your teares wet?' and, some moments later, 'Be comforted, good madam'. Equally profoundly, therefore, the repeated cue here marks *connection*: specifically the connec-tion between father and child, but equally the audience's connection with the emotions that have for so long been occluded or interrupted. Cordelia is overcome, in a kind of daze, but also at the edge of childlike unfurling, into a bawl or a hug, after so much lonely rectitude. Whereas the repeating cues throughout the storm and mad scenes reinforce discontinuity and severance, here they establish a community before or beyond words. If Cordelia is silent, then hers is the silence often associated in psychoanalytic discourse with the return to a primal source: the end of striving, severance, and, in some fundamental sense, words. For there is neither fear nor mystery in Cordelia's repetitions; they rather reinforce basic primal facts: that *I am*; that there is *no cause* for no love.

The first repeated cue here in the Folio is absent in the Quarto. Ironically, however, the Quarto text may well give evidence supporting this reading of the Folio cues (in turn suggesting something more general about the relation between the two texts). For the repeated cues in the Folio seem to be an economical translation of what in the Quarto text is a wordy and euphuistic eulogy; in other words, the specific scene about Cordelia that is in the Quarto but *not* in the Folio is an attempt 'poetically' to report exactly what the Folio cues dramatize. (This says nothing about the priority of Q and F: the Quarto could articulate an effect seen in a Folio-based performance; or the Folio could cut a scene thought redundant and reproduce the effect in the pauses and mimes produced by repeated cues.)

> KENT.          O then it moved her.
> GENTLEMAN. Not to a rage, patience and sorrow streme
>                     Who should express her goodliest you have seene,
>                     Sun shine and raine at once, her smiles and teares,

> Were like a better way those happy smilets,
> That played on her ripe lip seeme not to know,
> What guests were in her eyes ...

(Q, H4b)

The Gentleman here is trying to articulate an expression or emotion that does not quite fall into established categories: hence the vagueness of 'like a better way' and the qualification of a normative verb by an unusual noun in 'happy smilets'. That is, neither the witness nor the witnessed quite possesses a language for their experience: 'her ripe lip seeme not to know ... '. As lachrymose or even bathetic as the speech can seem, it is scrupulous in its precision. For this description anticipates the silence of Cordelia in the reconciliation scene, while the Quarto's next description anticipates the repetitions that, in the Folio, cue this silence:

> Faith **once or twice** she heav'd the name of father,
> Pantingly forth as it prest her heart,
> Cried **sisters, sisters**, shame of Ladies **sisters**:
> *Kent*, **father, sisters**, what ith storme ith night,
> Let pitie not be beleevt there she shooke,
> The holy water from her heavenly eyes,
> And clamour moistened her, then away she started,
> To deale with grief alone.

(Q, I1a)

So, we can see that what the Folio gives compacted dramatic expression to in its two repeated cues, the Quarto here dutifully reports: first, the passionate reiterations of 'father', 'father', 'sisters', 'sisters', all of which evoke a repeated or echoing cue; and second, Cordelia's passing through these reiterations into isolation, into a silent space corresponding to her emotional intensity: 'away she started, | To deale with grief alone'.

## The Final Scene

Many of the techniques we have been identifying return one last time in the scene of Lear's death. The end of *Lear* is filled with either repeated cues or repeated 'refused' cues. Each cue seems to have the same aim—to frame and focus the King—thus consolidating many similar effects earlier in the play. The cues forge co-habiting but distinct sensory perspectives; the stage is divided in two; Lear is projected into his own unique space-time, producing an experiential separateness that is at once the centre of everything and detached from everything:

> ALBANY. ... All Friends shall
> Taste the wager of their vertue, and all Foes
> The cup of their deservings. O **see, see**.
> LEAR. And my poore Foole is hang'd: no, no, no life?
> Why should a Dog, a Horse, a Rat have life,
> And thou no breath at all? Thou'lt come no more,
> Never, never, never, never, never.
> Pray you undo this Button. Thanke you Sir,
> Do you see this? Looke on her? Looke her lips,
> **Looke there, looke there.**                    *He dies*.
> EDGAR. He faints, **my Lord, my Lord**.
> KENT. **Breake** heart, I prythee **breake**.
> EDGAR. Looke up **my Lord**.
> KENT. Vex not his ghost ...
>
>                                   (TLN 3274–87)

> DUKE. all friends shall tast the wages of their vertue, and al foes the cup of their deservings, O **see, see**.
> LEAR. And my poore foole is hangd, no no life, why should a/dog, a horse, a rat of life and thou no breath at all, O thou/wilt come no more, never, never, never, pray you undo this button,/thanke you sir, O, o, o, o.
> EDGAR. He faints **my Lord, my Lord**.
> LEAR. **Breake** hart, I prethe **breake**.
> EDGAR. Look up **my Lord**.
> KENT. Vex not his ghost ...
>
>                                   (Q, L4a; lineation ours)

The part of Albany sets things up with the repeated cue, 'see, see'. On one level this demand to 'see' is Albany's prediction about the future—foes will be punished, friends rewarded, just wait and see. On another level it is a direction to the others on-stage to observe the King, a direction spoken twice: the second 'see' might be delivered after a pause to heighten the pathos and draw all eyes to the terrible grief being enacted on the floor. If the actor playing Lear is cued with only one 'see', he may start in with his 'And', as though continuing Albany's sentence ('see ... , my poore Foole is hang'd'). Yet in what way is the hanging of Cordelia (or even the Fool) a proof—as Albany has just been suggesting—of just reward and punishment? It is of course the reverse. Lear not only cuts into Albany's speech; he cuts down its bland claims of poetic justice—as the assembled others can well 'see'.

The separateness of Lear is of course mainly achieved by the plangent force of his grief: no one and nothing can reach him. But it is precisely this state of grief that the echoing repetitions are designed to enable, protect, and reinforce. This is emphatically achieved through the Quarto's repeated cue of 'O, o, o, o' (the same technique used, for example, to script Hamlet's death in F). The repeated 'O' expects or invites the cued actor (Edgar) to talk over the King's death rattle. But what of the single line in F, 'Never, never, never, never, never' (the word is said three times in Q)? It is, of course, a powerfully resonant word in this play; Lear here takes the ubiquitous trope of 'nothing' and seems to multiply it as the sum of present suffering. However, in neither text is it a cue-word. But perhaps Shakespeare is here invoking the *expectation* that the multiply repeated single word will indeed be a cue for someone. In this case, the other actors—and there are a lot of them surrounding the King here—will hear the repetition and perhaps expect one of them to interrupt and placate the King. But no one speaks. They might look from one to another, back down to the King, guiltily hoping that one of them will relieve the horror: but no one has a word to say; their parts forbid it. This line, then, might be characterized—like Gloucester's 'villainous' and the torturers' 'Wherefore to Dover?' (TLN 2122, 2127)—as a 'refused' cue. It cues the expectation of a response, the fear of a response, the desperate need for a response: but most profoundly, it cues no response whatsoever.

And this is the point: there is no answer. Earlier, Lear's accumulative repetitions had cued some kind of intervention: a measure of sanity or ethical propriety had entered to contain the lunacy. In those instances the repeating cue isolated the insanity and brought forth a cure; the 'premature' intervention offered hope. Here, things are closer to posthumous than premature. Intervention will come too late. Like Albany's belated 'great thing of us forgot' (TLN 3192), the most important cues are increasingly lost. So it is with Lear's chain of 'never's. The sheer weight of experience simply overwhelms any possible answer. For Lear, dying on his dead child, there are no cues left to give or to receive. This is the ultimate meta-dramatic conclusion.

The Lear-actor, of course, has one cue left to give: or so it may seem. In F the final cue-phrase is 'looke there'; in Q it is 'breake' (or 'O' if we think that Q1 and Q2 mistakenly transpose the line 'Breake heart, I prythee breake' from Kent to Lear). But in both texts the cue-phrase is repeated: the actor does not have one cue left to give, but two (or perhaps three or four if his last words are 'O, o, o, o ...'). This repetition first ensures the tragic hero's necessary cocooning: Lear remains entirely in his own dimension. But the repetition is also a way for Shakespeare to open out the death scene with a great charge of contrapuntal voices. So, as Lear is reduced to a single perception, thought, and expression, the repetitions that he speaks invite interpolation from those who watch. But this is still not the end. For Shakespeare makes each of the witnesses to Lear's death throw out still further repeating cues of their own. The effect in F might be something like this:

| | |
|---|---|
| LEAR. | **Looke there**— |
| EDGAR. | He faints, **my Lord**— |
| LEAR. | —**looke there**.     *He dies.* |
| EDGAR. | —**my Lord**. |
| KENT. | **Breake**— |
| EDGAR. | Look up— |
| KENT. | —heart, I prythee **breake**. |
| EDGAR. | —**my Lord**.     [Folio] |

Or this:

| | |
|---|---|
| LEAR. | Do you see this? Looke on her? Looke her lips, **Looke there**— |
| EDGAR. | He faints, **my Lord**— |
| KENT. | **Breake** heart— |
| LEAR. | **Looke there**—     [and/or, *Edgar.* Looke up—] |
| EDGAR. | **My Lord**—   [and/or, *Kent.* Vex not his ghost] |
| KENT. | I prythee **breake**— |
| EDGAR. | Looke up **my Lord**. |
| KENT. | Vex not his ghost ... [or, O let him passe ... ] |

Or this in the Quarto:

| | |
|---|---|
| LEAR. | **O, o**— |
| EDGAR. | He faints— |
| LEAR. | —**O, O** |
| EDGAR. | —**my Lord**— |
| LEAR. | **Breake**— |

EDGAR.   —my Lord.
LEAR.    —hart, I prethe **breake**.
EDGAR.   Look up my Lord.

Apparently consecutive statements become interchangeable, and indeed themselves repeatable. Even Kent's 'Vex not his ghost', which in the full text follows Edgar's 'Look up my Lord', may find itself cued in performance by Edgar's earlier 'He faints my Lord, my Lord'. So as Lear begs his own heart to break—his last words in the Quarto—Edgar and Kent speak over him, one insisting that he is alive, the other acknowledging that he is dying. One voice abuts another, each voice interweaves with the next. Whatever words Lear dies on, the death draws in the dissentious harmonies of the living. As the King looks incredulously upon the death of his child, and in the process does his own dying, the attendant world is magnetized into the moment.

The repeating cues thus absolutely serve the play's climactic event. This is the event of all events, the double death that might end or redeem the lot. But Lear's repeated cue is here the prompt for no answer except yet another self-returning cue. Everything spoken is a cue, repeated and interrupted over and over. Rather than any surceasing or even future-harking response, the echoing cues elicit only a kind of polyphonic tautology, corresponding to an eternalized and universalized question-mark: 'looke there', 'my Lord', 'breake', 'Looke up', 'prythee breake', 'my Lord'. There are no final answers here; there is no escape from the 'wheel'. This is a bracing achievement of dramatic polyphony; indeed, it is almost operatic, as Lear, like Don Giovanni, sings down as he is sung down to his predetermined end. Equally, this presents the cue—the theatre's basic linking tool, its instrument of pledge and trust in others—at the edge of its *own* exhaustion. The end of the play is, then, also a kind of ceasing of communicative possibility: this is explicitly felt by the survivors, but a certain kind of 'naturalistic' theatrical capability is itself here broaching its own limits. The fate of the cue is here a metaphor as well as an instrument of Shakespeare's end-game.

# 14

## Post-Tragic Effects

### Antony and Cleopatra

The roles of Antony and Cleopatra can seem removed from raw tragic emotion; by and large, this is not a play that utilizes repeated cues to help embody tragic effects. Briefly it does so in the scene after Antony's humiliation at sea. Here is Antony's part:

> Leave me, I pray a little: pray you now,
> Nay do so: for indeede I have lost command,
> Therefore I pray you, Ile see you **by and by.** *Sits downe.*
> ———————————————— [Oh] *Juno.*
> **No, no, no, no, no.**
> ———————————————— [you] [heere,] Sir?
> **Oh fie, fie, fie.**
> ———————————————— [Sir,] sir.
> Yes my Lord yes…

(TLN 2046–60)

The repeated cue-words signal the familiar tragic self-absorption, as Antony's apprehension of mutiny not in others, but in himself, tempts him to curl up into ashamed hibernation. His oblivious repetitions ride over all attempts to solicit his attention or raise his spirits (whilst ensuring that other actors do not hear him through). Antony's example seems then to inspire Cleopatra, for she immediately follows suit, simulating a swoon—a process marked by repeating or dilated cues, both by her and by others: one from Eros, 'The Queene, my Lord, the Queene' (TLN 2067), and two from Cleopatra, 'Well then, sustaine me: Oh' (TLN 2070), 'Pardon, pardon' (TLN 2099, preceded by a single 'O my pardon'). But this is in a different register from that which we have witnessed in the earlier tragedies. The manifestly performed, craftily simulated nature of the trick of repetition (like the trick of swooning) suggests something close to parody. The implication is that repeated cues *per se* have a reputation as being appropriate for high tragic pathos—hence the feeling that these two protagonists are rehearsing or remembering a tried and trusted theatrical technique, rather than discovering it as though for the first time in the moment of acting.

It is thus not accidental that, unlike the deaths of so many of Shakespeare's tragic heroes, neither Antony's nor Cleopatra's death is framed by repeated cues. The technique would simply be inappropriate: it is premissed upon feelings of waste, impotence, and desolation, and of death as the greatest loss into the still greater unknown. In *Antony and Cleopatra*, the approach to death is quite different. According to the 'high Roman fashion' of suicide, death is celebrated as a passage to greater consummations. Integral to this is the control that the character has over the moment of passing. So, whereas the main point of Shakespeare's 'tragic' repeated cues has been to give the *actor* possession of his character's ultimate dispossession, here the *character* controls script and performance.

The play does, however, provide one example of early cues being used for genuine theatrical innovation. Unsurprisingly, it shows Shakespeare experimenting with the scenic possibilities of stage space. *Antony and Cleopatra* has more quick shifts of scene, more individual and group exits and entrances, and presumably more stage clearings, than any other play. This is due particularly to three things: the vast geographical spaces which the play travels (especially its movement back and forth between Rome and Egypt); the years of battle it has to condense into stageable narrative compass; and the fact that the play needs to keep equal focus upon two different central figures—Antony and Cleopatra—who for all their intimacy are often not playing in the same scene. The risk, obviously, is that emotional concentration will be diffused. It may be in response to this danger that, at a crucial point in the story, Shakespeare places two strikingly early cues. Here is the full play-text:

ANTONY.     Vanish, or I shall give thee thy deserving,
              And blemish *Caesars* Triumph. Let him take thee ...
              Patient *Octavia*, plough thy visage up
              With her prepared nailes.        *Exit Cleopatra.*
              'Tis well th'art gone,
              If it be well to live. But better 'twere

> Thou fell'st into my furie, for one death
> Might have prevented many. *Eros*, **hoa?**
> The shirt of *Nessus* is upon me, teach me
> *Alcides*, thou mine Ancestor, thy rage.
> Let me lodge *Licus* on the hornes o'th'Moone,
> And with those hands that graspt the heaviest Club,
> Subdue my worthiest selfe: The Witch shall die,
> To the young Roman Boy she hath sold me, and I fall
> Under this plot: She dyes for't. *Eros*, **hoa?**    *Exit.*

*Enter Cleopatra, Charmian, Iras, Mardian.*

CLEOPATRA. Helpe me my women: Oh hee's more mad
> Then *Telamon* for his Shield, the Boare of Thessaly
> Was never so imbost.

CHARMIAN. **To'th'Monument**, there locke your selfe,
> And send him word you are dead:
> The Soule and Body rive not more in parting,
> Then greatnesse going off.

CLEOPATRA. **To'th'Monument:**
> *Mardian*, go tell him I have slaine my selfe:
> Say, that the last I spoke was *Antony*,
> And word it (prythee) pitteously. Hence *Mardian*,
> And bring me how he takes my death **to th' Monument**.

*Exeunt.*

*Enter Antony, and Eros.*

ANTHONY.    *Eros*, thou yet behold'st me?
EROS.        I Noble Lord.
ANTHONY.    Sometime we see a clowd that's Dragonish,
> A vapour sometime, like a Beare, or Lyon,
> A toward Cittadell, a pendant Rocke,
> A forked Mountaine, or blew Promontorie
> With Trees upon't, that nodde unto the world,
> And mocke our eyes with Ayre.
> Thou hast seene these Signes,
> They are blacke Vespers Pageants.
EROS.        I my Lord.
ANTHONY.    That which is now a Horse, even with a thoght
> the Racke dislimes, and makes it indistinct
> As water is in water.
EROS.        It does my Lord.
ANTONY.     My good Knave *Eros*, now thy Captaine is
> Even such a body: Heere I am *Antony*,

Yet cannot hold this visible shape (my Knave)
I made these warres for Egypt, and the Queene,
Whose heart I thought I had, for she had mine:
Which whil'st it was mine, had annext untoo't
A Million moe, (now lost:) shee *Eros* has
Packt Cards with *Caesars*, and false plaid my Glory
Unto an Enemies triumph.
Nay, weepe not gentle *Eros*, there is left us
Our selves to end our selves.

(TLN 2790–2849)

We have here what look like two successive instances of a repeated cue.
First, Antony's 'Eros, hoa?' is the cue for Cleopatra and her ladies to enter,
*and* his cue to exit—but he says it seven lines early. Clearly, he won't
exit early; but the others may well enter. Second, Antony's cue to re-enter
(with Eros)—'To'th'Monument'—is itself twice spoken early: once by
Charmian and again by Cleopatra. This time Antony may well come on
stage 'early'—which is to say, at any of the repetitions. The likelihood is
that Shakespeare is using the criss-crossing entrance cues to set up not just
two sets of characters, but two separate spaces or 'rooms' in different parts
of the stage. So, Cleopatra exits as required (before Antony's ''Tis well
th'art gone'), but re-enters whilst Antony is still speaking, or is still engaged
in his long and furious speech. Cleopatra's lines—also cued by Antony's
'Eros, hoa?'—then proceed to comment ironically upon Antony's. So, his
allusion to the great but betrayed Hercules ('Alcides')—which is also an
allusion to his god, and hence to himself—is matched and perhaps mocked
by Cleopatra's to the loser Ajax ('Telamon'). In turn, with Antony already
on-stage, the first 'To'th'Monument' (spoken by Charmian) can cue *Eros*'s
entrance. That the same cue-phrase is put twice on Cleopatra's part might
be intended to ensure that the actor will expect *someone* to enter (if not
speak) early; if Antony has now exited (perhaps during or immediately
before Charmian's speech), it might cue his re-entrance, as he searches for
his elusive servant. Equally, any of the three 'To'th'Monument'[s] may cue
Antony's now 'early' speech to Eros ('Eros, thou yet behold'st me?'), in
which case Cleopatra may now witness his 'dislimes' meditation ('They are
blacke Vespers Pageants'), and his continuing bitterness toward her ('shee
Eros has | Packt Cards with *Caesars*, and false plaid my Glory'): hence she
repeats the urgent command to tell Antony that she is dead. Mardian might
then merely cross the stage, rather than re-enter, when Cleopatra tells him

to go ('Hence *Mardian* ...') and Antony greets him with surrogate abuse ('Oh thy vilde Lady ...'). According to this reconstruction, lines 2820 and 2850 could become immediately successive.

Of course, much of this is speculation. It is not necessary for Cleopatra to 'hear' Antony's speeches (it is clear that neither Antony nor Eros 'hears' Cleopatra's plan), or even for the two camps' dialogue to be interwoven or cross-cut in ways not represented by the Folio text. Very powerful effects can still be achieved by the simple expedient of stage sectioning, and therefore visual juxtaposition. Above all, both parties are 'frozen' in space—as though for a moment or two given a furtive claim upon, or presence at, the despair of the other. The two camps are on-stage throughout; we keep both in view, and can witness their effects upon one another. For the stake on both sides is unavoidable—death—as are the terms in which it will be played: Antony's would-be monumentalizing epitaphs to himself, Cleopatra's monumental performance. We can see how they share a stage but are presently lost to each other; physical adjacency reinforces the barrier between them. The split-screen effect allows the audience to register both at once, to be at one with each of them simultaneously.

We are perhaps slightly more 'with' Cleopatra than with Antony, especially if she is given the privilege of ironic overhearing and he is not. But either way, the effect of seeing both at once must be to require reunion as the only emotionally satisfying resolution. The technique of 'invisible' contiguity embodies the pathos and peril of true emotional dependency: the fiercer the intimacy, the more absolute the separation. Equally, the technique can represent a near-parody of the 'public' privacy that has characterized their relationship, in which the most sonorous resolves are always an inch away from the mockery of gossipy hearsay.

Of course, we might ask what is gained by any of this that could not be achieved by the simple textual device of parallel columns, or brackets, to indicate simultaneous stage actions: and the answer might be nothing. It may well be a scribal accident or limitation that stops Shakespeare's text from looking as Jonson's occasionally do (e.g. *Bartholomew Fair, Sejanus*), when he choreographs distinct groupings on the stage, acting at once independently and contrapuntally, often with one group commenting candidly upon the other. Equally, it may be that Shakespeare here wants to intensify what the cue can always give him: that crucial edge of experiential surprise, and thus the imperative to make decisions *in the moment*, or 'suddenly' to overhear what you know (or think you know) you have no warrant to hear at all.

# Imogen in *Cymbeline*

A very peculiar use of what might be a premature entrance cue is found, perhaps unsurprisingly, in one of Shakespeare's most peculiar scenes: when Imogen wakes up next to the headless body of the man who was hoping to rape her, meticulously identifies it as the body of her husband, and is then discovered lying on top of the mistaken trunk, her face smeared with its blood, apparently sleeping, by some very stolid Roman soldiers (IV. ii).

IMOGEN.                                                *... Pisanio.*
       All Curses madded *Hecuba* gave the Greekes,
       And mine to boot, be darted on thee: thou
       Conspir'd with that Irregulous divell *Cloten*,
       Hath heere cut off **my Lord**. To write, and read,
       Be henceforth treacherous. Damn'd *Pisanio*,
       Hath with his forged Letters (damn'd *Pisanio*)
       From this most bravest vessell of the world
       Strooke the maine top! Oh *Posthumus*, alas,
       Where is thy head? where's that? Aye me! where's that?
       *Pisanio* might have kill'd thee at the heart,
       And left this head on. How should this be, *Pisanio*?
       'Tis he, and *Cloten*: Malice, and Lucre in them
       Have laid this Woe heere. Oh 'tis pregnant, pregnant!
       The Drugge he gave me, which hee said was precious
       And Cordiall to me, have I not found it
       Murd'rous to'th'Senses? That confirmes it home:
       This is *Pisanio*'s deede, and *Cloten*: Oh!
       Giue colour to my pale cheeke with thy blood,
       That we the horrider may seeme to those
       Which chance to finde us. Oh, **my Lord! my Lord!**

   *Enter Lucius, Captaines, and a Soothsayer.*

CAPTAIN.  To them, the Legions garrison'd in Gallia
          After your will, have crost the Sea, attending
          You heere at Milford-Haven, with your Shippes:
          They are heere in readinesse.

                              (TLN 2634–59)

The scene offers a severe assault to notions of the decorous pastoral heroine, and is tonally ambiguous throughout. For we, the audience, are 'in on' the joke played at Imogen's expense. We know full well that the dead body is that of the loathsome Cloten, not Posthumus. The heroine is the victim of an apparently callous (even gloating) irony. She makes a mistaken identification, and is forced almost literally to swim in it, gore and all. More than this, she is witnessed in her absurdity and error. But how exactly is she witnessed? In what terms, within what kinds of frame, is her extravagant grief mediated? The problem for actors is well known: can the speech be played straight? or is it, in its excruciatingly detailed mistakenness, simply broad and even slapstick bathos? How much do we let Imogen off the hook? And how much do we let Shakespeare off the hook for so embarrassing our favourite character?

There is no way of determining such issues definitively by reference to parts and cues. But we can perhaps get closer to the particular way in which the scene was played, its order of on-stage entrance and observation, by noticing the speech's single premature cue.

The Roman soldiers' entrance is cued by Imogen's expostulation: 'my Lord! my Lord!' Having entered, the soldiers talk about the war for a considerable time—twenty-four lines—before Lucius sees something prostrate and headless: 'Soft hoa, what truncke is here? | Without his top?' (TLN 2680–1). The formality itself has a certain gruesome and inopportune comedy, magnified by the fact of its risible belatedness (they have missed everything and understand nothing). The Romans enter and gibber on about military conscription and dreams about birds; this is in the wake of the play's most alarming scene, and with the heroine still in full sight, centre-stage, hugging the body of her enemy. Clearly, no one is getting off lightly here. If Imogen is embarrassed by misdirected passion, then these portentous Roman narcissists are hardly less so. (It is just about possible from the text that the Romans are cued actually to hear her speak: 'The ruine speakes', says Lucius, although this is more likely to be the start of an observation that the body of Cloten is impressive: 'The ruine speakes, that sometime it was a worthy building' (TLN 2681–2).) We might then ask whether the repeated 'my Lord! my Lord!' is a signal for anything: particularly as two of the words of the cue-phrase 'my lord' do indeed occur earlier in Imogen's speech as well ('Hath heere cut off my Lord'). It is just possible, then, that this first within-speech 'my Lord' cues the entrance of the Romans, and that they are visible witnesses as Imogen proceeds in the second half of her speech: in which she shifts from meticulously tracing each limb to deducing, hysterically, that Pisanio and Cloten are to blame. As Imogen is doing this, do the Roman army enter? Were that to be so, then we, the audience, would be half-aware both of the renewed danger of capture and, more powerfully, of multiplied humiliations. As much as we are privy to Imogen's mistake, we might wish to protect her from further prying eyes. In a curious way, then, if this is indeed a premature cue of entrance, it might ameliorate rather than intensify the scene's exploitation of its heroine. The familiar technique of splitting the stage, by means of the 'early' cue, fleshes out the context and poses a very *consciously* felt challenge to our own responses.

Imogen is the 'victim' of one other repeated cue, again at a moment in which the pathos of recognition is threatened by alarming slapstick. Posthumus has just realized that he has been duped into believing Imogen unfaithful, and delivers a speech of overwrought guilt and grief:

> POSTHUMUS. I am *Posthumus*,
> That kill'd thy Daughter: Villain-like, I lye,
> That caus'd a lesser villaine then my selfe,
> A sacrilegious Theefe to doo't. The Temple
> Of Vertue was she; yea, and she her selfe.
> … Oh *Imogen*!
> My Queene, my life, my wife: oh *Imogen*,
> *Imogen, Imogen.*
> IMOGEN. Peace my Lord, **heare, heare**.
> POSTHUMUS. Shall's have a play of this?
> Thou scornfull Page, there lye thy part.

> (TLN 3499–3512)

This is reminiscent of the climactic exchanges between Desdemona and Othello. Like Desdemona, Imogen comes in before Posthumus has finished; initially oblivious with rage, he turns his violence upon her as soon as he notices the interruption; this coincides with *his* interruption of her. Shakespeare may here be effectively scripting simultaneous lines. It is likely that both actors will have had each of the two repeated cues fully transcribed on their parts: one as speaking text, one as cue to speak. If this were the case, then they would surely have picked up the 'instruction' to repeat a cue. Here, they will assume, must be a moment of heightened tension and potential revelation: this is almost always the case with repeated cues, and never more so than when they top or tail speeches of heightened emotion. Shakespeare's conviction seems to have been that such climactic moments are always better played if the actors are given that little bit of extra rope that repeated cues allow, and thus invited to risk or wager just that little bit more.

There is one other interesting thing here, characteristic of this most reflexive, backward-casting of plays. That is, Shakespeare expounds the situation through a succession of meta-dramatic puns that seem to dwell specifically upon the technology and consequent opportunities of working in parts. First is Imogen's repetition, 'heare, heare', meaning both 'listen' and 'in this place'. The cue-words thus point to Posthumus's present failure either to see or to hear her: both of which can only be happening if he is still wrapped up in his own hysterical speech (in other words, if the early cue is orchestrating cross-voices). Posthumus's reply continues the theme: first he calls Imogen's interruption 'a play', then a 'part'; in calling her a 'Page' he alludes to her appearance as a young male attendant, whilst punning upon the single 'page' that would constitute a minor 'part'—one that in his view here 'lye[s]', meaning both tells untruths (because in his eyes Imogen is not 'heare') and lies flat on the floor (because he has just thrown the interrupting 'Page' to the ground). Of course, the moment is partly comic, because Posthumus is simply mistaken. This is where the meta-dramatic note ricochets back upon Posthumus. So the crux of his insult is that this 'Page' has dared to interrupt his big set-piece speech. Here is the moment of tragic recognition (*anagnorisis*), of mythic self-objectification ('every villaine | Be call'd *Posthumus Leonatus*'), to be followed in the necessary course of things by violent self-sacrifice. On this construction, Posthumus's fury at being interrupted—'Shall's have a play of this?'—becomes a petulant actor's jealousy. 'Posthumus' was all set to play his apportioned role to the hilt, and then this little Jack jumps up and spoils it. *Cymbeline* is often arch in just this way, seeming to lay bare and laugh at its own artifice. So it is here: a technique that in other contexts helps engineer the rawest pathos is here on the verge of being little more than a metatheatrical joke.

# 15

# The Cue-Space in *The Tempest*

I t may be that the repeated cue began merely as a useful instrument for orchestrating the actors. But by surveying its use in all sorts of different plays, we see that such cues crop up at a specific moments. Whatever they help to embody—emotional crisis, metaphysical desolation, comic cross-purposes, the splitting of the stage, meta-dramatic ironies—they are always somehow defining a play's specific focus and orientation. This suggests that the repeated cue becomes a divining stick, or lightning rod, for whatever experiments Shakespeare is engaged with. We have seen time and again how the repeated cue has a uniquely dramatic capability. It takes the multi-form suggestiveness of the cue *per se*—and then intensifies it. Shakespeare continually explores its gift of moving at once forwards and backwards in time and space, and so of placing action and mind, or speech and body, in more than one location simultaneously. This is the great virtue of the technique: it always renders dramatic moments nervously kinetic, rather than inert. Again and again, repeated cues help reveal how dramatic *presence* is always flushed back and forth between future and past, mind and body, self and others, this self and that self. Furthermore, in using repeated cues, Shakespeare insists upon the active decision making of the actor, who is placed in dynamic but unspeaking dialogue both with other actors and with his part-script. This rare mix of technical practicality and metaphysical suggestibility offered by the repeating cue makes it far more than simply an aid to performance. This is supremely in evidence in *The Tempest*.

## Cueing the Scene

That repeated cues are part of the propelling design of *The Tempest* is attested by their frequent appearance in the opening scene:

MASTER.          Good: Speake to th'Mariners: fall/too't, yarely, or we
                 run our selves a ground,/**bestirre, bestirre**.        *Exit.*

     *Enter Mariners.*

                                          (TLN 7–9; lineation ours)

          *Enter Mariners wet.*

MARINERS.         **All lost**, to prayers, to prayers, **all lost.**
BOATSWAIN.   What must our mouths be cold?

                             (TLN 60–1)

               *... A confused noyse within.*

GONZALO.      Mercy on us.
              **We split, we split**, Farewell my wife, and children,
              Farewell brother: **we split, we split, we split.**
ANTONIO.      Let's all sinke with' King.

                                    (TLN 70–3)

All of these take the form that we have often seen in Shakespeare's 'crowd'
scenes, helping to suggest multiple combatants and chaotic comings and
goings. The effect of the repetitions is reinforced by two scripted instances
of off-stage yelling: '*A cry within*' at TLN 45 and '*A confused noyse within*' at
TLN 70. So we get a storm, and inside the storm we get on-stage shouts,
and inside the shouts we get off-stage cries and noise. The noise seems to
echo in a chain of consequence from outside to inside, macro to micro,
cosmic indifference to individual suffering. But it is not in fact so simple.
The 'inside' howling cues 'outside' curses; inside curses cue outside cries.
The same applies to the foul weather and wild seas: the tempest itself is
'cued' by Prospero's art, which is in turn 'cued' by the play's pre-story.
The storm itself can thus be imagined as an echoing, floating, ricocheting
cue—and, as we shall soon see, so too can the island that is its magnet.

     Only a few of Shakespeare's play-texts start in anything like this fash-
ion—with a scripted, sonic cue. *2 Henry VI* begins with a '*Flourish of
Trumpets*', *3 Henry VI* with an alarum—decisive entrance cues, both.
*Twelfth Night* perhaps begins with music, but the text does not prescribe
this, and it is possible that Orsino's 'play on' in the first line is the mu-
sician's cue. *Macbeth* begins with '*Thunder and Lightning*', presaging the
entrance of the three Witches, and suggesting the demonic bowel from
which the weird sisters first spill forth and into which they quickly return. Equally, it is an aural mark of their separation: the thunder cracks,
the witches chant, and almost as suddenly they vanish; immediately an

'Alarum' marks the radically contrasting entrance of the King and his attendants. It may well be that thunder should punctuate this first scene of *Macbeth* throughout, or close it with a single reprising clap. But neither text nor performance demands this. *The Tempest* is quite different. It begins with a similar aural cue—'*A tempestuous noise of Thunder and Lightning heard*'—but in this case it is clear that the 'noise' has *not* been swept away with the subsequent entrances. Whether or not the actual sounds of thunder continue throughout the scene, the idea of them remains inescapably in the air: 'Blow till thou burst thy winde', 'you do assist the storme', 'be patient. | When the Sea is...', 'what cares these roarers for the name of King?', 'if you can command these Elements to silence, and worke the peace of the present, wee will not hand a rope more...', 'A plague——upon this howling: they are lowder then the weather' (TLN 13, 21, 23–4, 24, 29–31, 44–6). In other words, *The Tempest* begins with a multiply *repeating* sound-cue. As we shall see, the whole action of the play is premissed upon just this kind of repetition. In this play-world the big things—life, identity, desire, authority, love, death—must be borne, and often born, inside a repeated, echoing cue.

Of course, even if the 'tempestuous noise of thunder and lightning' recurs throughout the scene, it is not working in the same way as more conventional repeated cues. For the cue is in a sense 'taken' as soon as the shipmaster and boatswain enter, or at least as soon as the Master speaks the play's first word. No other actor's part, we can assume, has the 'tempestuous noise' written down on it as a cue either to enter or to speak. But the noise doesn't pass as a more conventional cue is supposed to; it echoes beyond its nominal function. It may be that this is neither here nor there for the actors. After all, we might think, what do they care if the prompter or backstage boy is bashing away on a drum or rattling some tin? But in this case, it is not only the actors who are at issue.

For Shakespeare sets it up so that the entire *scene*, embodied both in the stage-as-ship and the troupe-as-crew, is captured and animated 'in' a repeating cue. He thoroughly subsumes the cue-effect's usual dilemmas for the actor (concerning choice, timing, and spatial discipline) and its usual character-defining capabilities (concerning internal or inter-subjective conflict), and he transfers them into the thematic substance of the scene. To see more precisely what is at stake here, we need to identify what the 'tempestuous noise' actually cues. It is less a simple give-and-take than a sequence of possibilities, of provocations and responses. So, it cues frenzied attempts to ward off death and, in the struggles that ensue, collateral conflicts and attempts at consolation; ultimately, or so it seems to all those 'inside' it, the noise cues annihilation. In other words, it reprises the most usual context of Shakespeare's repeated cues: varieties of bewilderment, desolation, and loss. Shakespeare is here beginning where he has customarily ended, presenting in miniature compass a proto-tragic panorama.

But the crucial fact is that this sound cue—which continues beyond each particular act of speaking—is never ultimately 'taken'. Final deliverance of the cue is deferred; the cue is still sounding as the scene ends. In other words, Shakespeare uses this unprecedented, scene-long repeated/repeating cue as a means of suspending 'in the air' the basic tragic end. This heralds a transformation in the significance of repeated cues. In Shakespeare's dark comedies and tragedies, repeated cues invariably herald endings. In the great tragedies of love and desire, with their twin central furies of the family and the mind—*Macbeth*, *Othello*, *Lear*, *Hamlet*—this end is of love or self. In *Coriolanus*, by contrast, there is a switch from private to public: the civic body is constantly at the edge of fatal detonation; so repeated cues are continually used to orchestrate its angry crowds, furious battles, and other explosive public conflicts. In *The Tempest*, however, the teleology has been reversed, in line with the new genre in which it is functioning. It has become a space of secretion, resistance, and in due course inception: whereas in the tragedies the repeated cue attends things that are dissolving or dying, in *The Tempest* it helps to produce the opposite.

And what is true of the hunkered-down nobles on the ship will in due course be true of a sequence of characters on the island. For each of the play's most 'promise-crammed' parts—all of those young characters who must possess any future—are subjected to the same spacious and reverberating entrances or re-entrances. It will then be their job to take as they can the subsequent 'mutations' or translations of this inaugural sonic cue.

But if we want to move closer to these individual characters, we have to move closer to the actors who embody them. As we have seen, conventional early cues always involve presenting actors with some kind of choice, often involving a climactic 'possession' of their very own zone of the stage. For the *characters*, however, things are usually quite different. Their identities are dissolving, or they are moving into death; the repeated cues accentuate such desolation, but sometimes allow for some consoling mental self-sculpting before the fall. *The Tempest* works differently. Here, the options or movements offered to the actor, mental or physical, also establish the *character*'s choices. As we shall show, player and persona both lack full possession of self or context; both feel incomplete in, or insufficient to, the unfolding moment. They consequently draw—or are drawn—unusually close to one another. Each is enthralled *and* animated in the cue-space; each is asked to 'see' the options, to watch them tick by, as though in a dreamlike mental pageant—and then to make a choice. Sometimes this choice will result in perceivable action or performance, sometimes only in mental movements of the self-observant actor/character. Either way, the repeated cue-space produces a sketch of possibilities, one that future occasions, if not present incarnations, might flesh out.

To see how this works, we will look at four individual parts—those of Miranda, Ariel, Ferdinand, and Caliban—before considering how each role's discrete use of repeating cues contributes to a cumulative (and again unfinished) text of civic, erotic, and subjective potential.

# Miranda

We have seen how a part's inaugurating cues, or those that mark an important transition in its orientation, are often very specifically for the actor, who can shore up his own role 'against' that of the larger play. Repeated cues, meanwhile, involve the creation of space in which the actor can make his *own* mind up, whilst dealing with (or ignoring) the surprising irruption of others into this space. Where *The Tempest* is unusual is in joining the self-possessing intensities of entrance/transitional cues with those of repeated cues. By joining together these two types of cue, Shakespeare gives to the characters' inceptive moments—entering upon stage for the first time, or for the first time alone; emerging out of consciousness into sleep, or sleep into consciousness; discovering some radically promising novelty—a truly seed-like, even foetal suggestibility.

We find a fascinating example of this with the first major transition in the part of Miranda—here 'cued' by Prospero from waking into sleep:

> ... my fortunes
> Will ever after droope: Heare cease more questions,
> Thou art inclinde to sleepe: 'tis a good dulnesse,
> And give it way: I know thou canst not chuse.
>
> (TLN 294–7)

We cannot know precisely how the Miranda-actor is cued into sleep on his own part. It may well be that the part transcribes 'music' as the prompt for sleep, as happens later for Alonso and his courtiers—if so, this reinforces the effect of the speaking text (as recorded in the Folio). This is because the potential cue-phrases work just as music would, at once prompting the actor to act asleep *and* continuing to be spoken after this action. In the passage above, the successive phrases, 'ever after droope' (even though these words in fact refer to Prospero's 'fortunes'), 'cease more questions', 'inclinde to sleepe', and 'a good dulnesse' are all suitable enough cues for sleep. Depending upon which is the sleep cue, the script might offer as many as five successive addresses to Miranda that happen after the actor has, as it were, stopped acting. They may be addressed 'hypnotically' to the Miranda-character, but they are not addressed to the Miranda-actor. Instead, they circulate in a peculiarly suspended place. Even if the sleep cue is, say, 'inclinde to sleepe', there still remain three 'commands' that float out to a space beyond the Miranda-actor's part, and then float back as a strangely superfluous instruction. This is typical of the play's to-and-fro temporalities: but here the actor too is drawn inside just such a spatio-temporal pendulum.

We might think that there is no real puzzle here: so, whatever his actual cue, the player knows that his job is to act 'asleep' until re-cued into action. Perhaps the actor will hear these post-part commands as simple confirmation of an acting choice already made. But there is a subtle difference between acting asleep on-stage whilst other action proceeds, and acting asleep on-stage whilst still being addressed—and more than that, whilst being lulled into sleep. It isn't that the physical acting need alter; it is that there is a phenomenological difference for the actor. An actor on-stage can never switch off—particularly when he is acting from parts and cannot be sure when his cue is coming. And here the text seems intentionally to script just such a liminal mental zone, between cued and not-cued, action and inaction, scripted and excluded.

There is a similar effect at Miranda's 'awakening'. Here is the Miranda-part:

_____ [slept] [well,] Awake.
The strangenes of your story, put
Heavinesse in me.

(TLN 438–4)

If we look at the same awakening in the full text, we will see that Miranda's cue to 'awake' is in fact spoken three times:

PROSPERO. **Awake**, deere hart **awake**, thou hast slept well,
**Awake**.
MIRANDA. The strangenes of your story, put
Heavinesse in me.
PROSPERO. Shake it off: Come on,
Wee'll visit *Caliban*, my slave ...

(TLN 438–43)

This is not a case where an interruption from Miranda seems particularly appropriate (though it would hardly be fatal for Prospero effectively to talk over her waking excuses and move seamlessly on to his next imprecation). Perhaps the Miranda-actor was given 'slept well, Awake' as his cue, so as to forestall interruption. Alternatively, instead of scripting cross-voices, the first 'Awake' might be a cue to mime waking up, the second a cue to arise, the third a cue to speak. Whatever the answer given on the part, the effect for the Miranda-actor is much the same. He will hear the repeated calls to 'Awake'; whether or not he speaks, he will begin acting 'waking up' the moment he hears himself addressed. Once more the actor is asked to inhabit a vaguely pre-linguistic zone, suggestive of dream, or spectral privacy, or indeed the 'dark-backward and Abisme of Time' (TLN 140) invoked by Prospero, of Miranda, a few minutes earlier. Above all, the echoing cue-word evokes gradations of consciousness. So the script bears directly upon the cued actor, but does not easily allow or invite speech. It becomes a means of embodying a world elsewhere, a psychic chamber beyond capture or apprehension.

If the Miranda-actor is in these cases left somewhat hanging, other things in his part-text are heavily over-determined: in particular, the striking opposition between the abhorred sight of the old (Caliban) and the wondrous sight of the new (Ferdinand). Here is the scene in full text:

MIRANDA. Abhorred Slave,
… who hadst
Deserv'd more then a prison.

CALIBAN. You taught me Language, and my profit on't
Is, I know how to curse …

PROSPERO. So slave, hence.

*Exit Cal.*

*Enter Ferdinand & Ariel, invisible playing & singing.*

ARIEL. Song
*Come unto these yellow sands,*
*and then take hands:*
*Curtsied when you have, and kist*
*the wilde waves whist:*
*Foote it featly heere, and there, and sweete Sprights beare*
*the burthen.*　　　　　　　　　　　　　*Burthen dispersedly.*
*Harke, harke, bowgh wawgh: the watch-Dogges barke,*
*bowgh-wawgh.*
*Hark, hark, I heare, the straine of strutting Chanticlere*
*cry cockadidle-dowe.*

FERDINAND. Where shold this Musick be? I'th aire, or th'earth?
It sounds no more: and sure it waytes upon
Some God'oth' Iland …

ARIEL. Song.
*Full fadom five thy Father lies,*
*Of his bones are Corrall made:*
*Those are pearles that were his eies,*
*Nothing of him that doth fade,*
*But doth suffer a Sea-change*
*Into something rich, & strange:*
*Sea-Nimphs hourly ring his knell.*
　　　　　　　　　　　　　*Burthen: ding dong.*
*Harke now I heare them, ding-dong bell.*

FERDINAND. The Ditty do's remember my drown'd father,
This is no mortall busines, nor no sound
That the earth owes: I heare it now above me.

PROSPERO. The fringed Curtaines of thine eye advance,
And say what thou see'st yond.

MIRANDA. What is't a Spirit?

Lord, how it lookes about: Beleeve me sir,
It carries a brave forme. But 'tis a spirit.

(TLN 494–553)

Miranda's part, however, would look like this:

_____ [Isle] [with] *Calibans.*
Abhorred Slave,
Which any print of goodnesse wilt not take,
Being capable of all ill: I pittied thee, ...
But thy vild race
(Tho thou didst learn) had that in't, which good natures
Could not abide to be with; therefore wast thou
Deservedly confin'd into this Rocke, who hadst
Deserv'd more then a prison.
_____ [thou] [see'st] yond.
What **is't a Spirit?**
Lord, how it lookes about: Beleeve me sir,
It carries a brave forme. But **'tis a spirit.**

(TLN 493–553)

Fifty lines intervene between Miranda's indignant speech to the 'Slave' and
her next cue—a period of time largely taken up with Ariel's mesmerizing
songs to Ferdinand. But nothing of these songs (presumably) appears on
Miranda's part. In full text Prospero says 'The fringed Curtaines of thine eye
advance, | And say what thou see'st yond' (TLN 551–2): Miranda is once
again being brought back into full consciousness, and has apparently been
spellbound, or in some way absent as Ferdinand enters. '*Enter Ferdinand
& Ariel, invisible playing & singing*' (TLN 519), says the stage-direction.
But how is Miranda to 'perform' *not* seeing the characters? Ariel's songs
proceed; in the interim the Miranda-actor might walk around, or stand
stock still, but either way he must listen 'inside' the music for his cue.
So, even though nothing of the song impinges upon the written part of
Miranda, her becoming is still partly beholden to the music—suspended
in it, suspended by it. Excluding the song from the part-text makes the
*experience* of it all the more hers. It has passed over her, and in that
sense become present to her: but neither the character nor the actor
can yet seize it. Shakespeare thus uses the exclusiveness of parts, and the
inescapability of being on-stage—the actor cannot but hear the song,
just as we cannot but see Miranda *not quite* being given the song as
her own—to instil and symbolize the imminence of love. The scene is

dramatizing 'fringes' of consciousness; sometimes the fringe opens on to others, sometimes not. Here, for Miranda and Ferdinand simultaneously, it does.

Falling in love—the *moment* of doing so—is the experience here orchestrated. As such, it is an epitome of what this long scene works repeatedly to reveal: the 'opened' mind, awakening into larger possibilities. The song for Ferdinand, as it floats over Miranda, intimates this imminence of love; and the Miranda-part's immediate premature cue—'is't a Spirit?' (TLN 553)—marking as it does her return to the action, embeds the necessity of such love 'in' Miranda. So, having identified that he is to speak the cueing phrase twice, the actor can treat the words that come in between the two cue-phrases as Miranda's own—not so much as asides as an inattentive or euphoric obliviousness to anyone else's definitions: 'Lord, how it lookes about', 'It carries a brave forme' (TLN 554, 555). Prospero might enter with his gentle correction, 'No wench' (TLN 556), but the cue-effect is working to reinforce the comic wonder of Miranda's category-eluding 'it's: no one but she can measure this wondrously alien vision; for as long as she is 'inside' her suspended cue-space, her mind is transported beyond anything but this single vision before her. The repeated cue is a sign, yet again, of gradations of mental presence: some of Miranda's mind is 'with' her interlocutor (Prospero, who humorously takes up her 'it', with '*it* eats and sleeps … '), but some of it is withheld. Miranda can be seen thinking along two channels, or leaping from one to another as she intuits hitherto impossible pathways of desire.

# Ariel

Here is Ariel's first entrance, in full text:

> PROSPERO.  **Come** away, Servant, **come**; I am ready now,
> Approach my *Ariel*. **Come**.
>
> *Enter Ariel.*
> ARIEL.    All haile, great Master, grave Sir, haile: I come
> To answer thy best pleasure; be't to fly,
> To swim, to dive into the fire: to ride
> On the curld clowds: to thy strong bidding, taske
> *Ariel*, and all his Qualitie.
>
> (TLN 298–305)

The script for Ariel's entrance pretty much repeats the technique used (in the immediately preceding three lines) for Miranda's passing into sleep. So, Ariel is potentially called for by Prospero a number of times: 'Come', 'away', 'Servant', 'come', 'I am ready now', 'Approach', 'my *Ariel*', 'Come'. Perhaps this is likely to come down to four or five commands in most performances—'Come away, Servant', 'come', 'I am ready now', 'Approach, my *Ariel*', 'Come'. But whatever the division into discrete units of speech, Ariel's entrance *per se* is clearly somehow at issue. Is he coming? Has he come? (If not, why not?) How has he come? Where is he? Is that he? And something of this—the dubiety, the tension, the thrill of unpredictable choice—must be experienced by the Ariel-actor. This, it would seem, is where the potentially premature cue contributes. If the Ariel-part has 'Come' as its first entrance-cue, then he will hear it three times. It is a warrant to enter early, perhaps before Prospero has seen him, perhaps in such an eccentric, teasing, or elusive way as to require repeated requests for him to 'Approach' more closely. At the same time, it opens up the possibility that Ariel's first line be distributed, mischievously or flirtily, throughout the interstices in Prospero's 'cue'. So, each word of Ariel's might follow or cue a sudden swoop into or out of sight:

PROSPERO.  Come away—
ARIEL.                    All haile—
PROSPERO.                          Servant—
ARIEL.                                    Great Master—
PROSPERO.                                          Come—
ARIEL.                                                    Grave Sir—
PROSPERO.  I am ready now—
ARIEL.                    Haile—
PROSPERO.                          Approach, my Ariel
ARIEL.                                                    I come—
PROSPERO.  Come—
ARIEL.      To answer thy best pleasure; be't to fly...

The question of Ariel's bodily presence is, of course, crucial; so too his prompt entry, a measure of his service and obedience, and so of his master's effective power. It is thus no small thing to render the original terms of Ariel's entrance mutable and teasing. For the effect of the repeated cues is to make Ariel's movement a simulacrum of his mind: one that is both traceable in the fluidity of his body and *not* reducible to, or discernible only in, this movement. That is, Ariel's circling and looping body intimates *mental* travel. This in turn suggests, if not quite a free mind, then a treasuring of thoughts that are not those of the master, that are not to be gainsaid by the master or indeed known to the master.

This is borne out by an early speech of Ariel's:

> ———————————————— [will] [discharge] thee.
> That's my noble Master:
> **What shall I doe?** say what? **what shall I doe?**

>                              (TLN 430–2)

Aware that his character is impatient for freedom, the actor might read the three brisk pleas for instruction as a simple sign of accelerating, tripping excitability. Alternatively, the three phrases allow for pauses in which Prospero withholds—teasingly, ponderingly, tortuously—the release into business for which his servant longs. But Ariel's speech also includes an 'early' cue: the question 'What shall I doe?' spoken fully at the beginning and again at the end of the line. The Ariel-actor will know that his interlocutor might well come in early; concomitantly, he will know that he can keep his second and third questions ('say what?', 'what shall I doe?) in reserve, to be doled out at opportune moments, in the hinges of whatever reply he receives from the 'Master'. The Ariel-actor's freedom begins to presage the Ariel-character's. Here is Prospero's reply:

> ——————————————— [shall] [I] doe?
> Goe make thy selfe like a Nymph o'th'Sea,
> Be subject to no sight but thine, and mine: invisible
> To every eye-ball else: goe take this shape
> And hither come in't: goe: hence
> With diligence.

>                              (TLN 432–7)

Prospero says 'goe' three times and 'hence' once: clearly open to the construction that he is struggling to command Ariel's attention. The exchange becomes rich in both comic and political potential. Instead of simply linking arms in co-operative endeavour, there are two different apprehensions of the future—one Prospero's, one Ariel's—that weave in and out of each other in a tantalizing dance. The early cue allows the actors to play at quite distinct velocities—mental *and* physical. For the combination of early cue and midline break offers prompts for tremendous physical freedom (a freedom which the specific engineering of the actor's body can immeasurably enhance). More than that, it proposes a highly suggestive separation of voice and body. Ariel's body can gather its own independent trajectory, its own whimsical eloquence:

> ARIEL.     What shall I doe? [*darting off*]
> PROSPERO.  Goe make thyself like a Nymph o'th'Sea,
>            Be subject to no sight but thine, and mine:
> ARIEL.     [*suddenly darting back*] Say what?
> PROSPERO.                    — invisible
>            To every eye-ball else. [*Ariel darts off*]
> [ARIEL.    [*darting back*]          What shall I doe?]
> PROSPERO.                    —Go, take this shape
>            And hither come in't: goe!      [*darting off*]
> [ARIEL.    [*returning*] What shall I doe?]
> PROSPERO.                    —Hence, with diligence!

There are many possible variations; the point is really the freedom for physical movement offered inside the speech. It is not so much that the speeches section the stage, as we have often witnessed; instead, they offer a sudden invitation to traverse, enter, and encompass that stage. As befits a mind in motion, Ariel's movements are as much in the angles of the air above the stage as upon its wooden boards. Set against the stillness of Prospero and his books, this mobility is powerfully expressive of a desire to possess place in an undetermined way. Single flashing clauses in Ariel's earlier account of his 'lightning' agency aboard the ship—'divide | And burne in many places' (TLN 310–11), 'flame distinctly, | Then meete and joyne' (TLN 312–13), 'momentarie | And sight out-running' (TLN 314–15)—exactly foreshadow the movements here engineered by cue and pause. The actor's body must now fulfil the promise of this earlier account of his off-stage action. Consequently, the performer should read these first speeches less as a recollection of recent improvisations than as instructions about *present* acting. Crucially, the script does not tie the actor into the relative barrenness, the physical stasis, of repartee. The effect recurs throughout Ariel's part: e.g. in IV. i when Ariel is called by Prospero's '**Come** with a thought; I thank thee *Ariel*: **come**' and leaves with '**I goe, I goe**' (TLN 1836, 1861). For as physical activity happens 'inside' the exchange, not so much in the words spoken as in the spaces between them, so the actor must decide precisely when and where he 'flies'. Like Miranda a moment earlier—but here *visibly*—Ariel is rushing into, rehearsing or anticipating, possibilities that are as yet inadmissible.

Anticipation is nine-tenths of the drama here. As we often find in *The Tempest*, meta-performative awareness segues into an articulated theme. So, the actor's thrill of mind, as he finds space and speed inside the constrictions of line and cue, is also where he taps into the romance genre and its transformations. The actor can indulge an unprecedented exuberance—but one still limited by the wires that represent both theatrical logistics and Prospero's continuing power. The pregnancy of these distinctively part-textual spaces is thus a consummate example of the responsibility given in this play to places and movement that are beyond simple semantics.

# Caliban (1)

The same techniques that we have witnessed with Miranda and Ariel now immediately engineer Caliban's first entrance. So, the Caliban-actor's cue to speak is '[Earth,] [thou:] speake' (TLN 450)—but the actor remains off-stage. His cue to enter does not come for a further seven lines. Again the entrance cue is very literal: '[Dam;] [come] forth' (TLN 458). This might seem straightforward enough—except that the two cues are surrounded by demands for him to enter or answer that are *not* his cue:

>                 … What hoa: slave: *Caliban*:
>                 Thou Earth, thou: speake. [SPEAKING CUE]
> CALIBAN *within*. There's wood enough within.
> PROSPERO.       Come forth I say, there's other busines for thee:
>                 Come thou Tortoys, when? [NOT A CUE]
>
>      *Enter Ariel like a water-Nymph*
>                 Fine apparision: my queint *Ariel*,
>                 Hearke in thine eare.
> ARIEL.           My Lord, it shall be done.     *Exit*.
> PROSPERO.       Thou poysonous slave, got by ye divell himselfe
>                 Upon thy wicked Dam; come forth. [ENTRANCE CUE]
>
>      *Enter Caliban*.
>
>                          (TLN 449–58)

Both cues are preceded by four directly addressed dictations to the character. The actor must hear them: but *he* is not quite being addressed. Again the cue-space is a contested one, here producing a moment in which agency is as equivocal and shadowy as presence. Is Caliban present or not? Is his actor present or not? For here the body of the actor, at once in and out of the scene, works as both metaphor and agent of the scene's profoundest concern: the uncertain interlinking of minds and bodies. Miranda's visible bodily suspension had evoked the movements of mind; Ariel's visible bodily arcs had simulated the same thing; here, the body of Caliban is lurking between shadow and light, occlusion and presence, presaging his similarly half-lit mind. In each case we see a mind moving outside the pre-emptive commands of Prospero, as of the linearly directing cue. However, with Caliban such resistance is more explicitly political. This is partly because the actor has no release into the liberty of flight or movement: he may well share in the frustrations and resentment of exclusion that his character feels. But the probability is that Shakespeare is once again scripting a surreptitious entrance—recollecting Ariel's a moment earlier, but also in radical contrast to it. Again this is allowed by a premature entrance cue ('Come forth'). It is spoken six lines 'early', and what happens in the interim is most telling: there is the brisk re-entrance of Ariel, then a *sotto voce* conversation between Prospero and his spirit, and then Ariel's exit. Clearly, the gap in time between the first and second 'Come forth' might be considerable, and certainly gives opportunity for Caliban to enter behind the backs of his enemy, but in full view of the audience. What might be the result? As we for the first time get an eyeful of the 'Tortoys', Caliban stares scornfully or disgustedly at the whisperers, or perhaps begins his lengthy and much-cogitated curse ('As wicked dewe, as ere my mother brush'd | With Ravens feather from unwholesome Fen | Drop on you both...' (TLN 459–61)).

This would be a classic example of the 'sectioned' stage. For just as we have now seen Caliban 'before' the master does, so we now hear him: the curse, or the first part of it at least, would then become an aside. Prospero's returning curse ('For this be sure, to night thou shalt have cramps...' (TLN 463)) is perfectly explicable as a response only to Caliban's final malediction, 'A Southwest blow on yee, | And blister you all ore' (TLN 461–2). Shakespeare might thus orchestrate the distinctive boundary-haunting centrality of Caliban—at once beyond the pale, yet intimately confidential. Once again, the opening struggle for full entrance and recognized presence, experienced in different but congruent ways by actor and by audience, sets the terms for the rest of the part.

# Ferdinand

The fourth in this uncanny tag-team sequence is Ferdinand, who enters immediately upon the first exit of Caliban. Again we need to see the full play-text if we are to reconstruct its performative invitations:

PROSPERO.  So slave, hence.                              *Exit Caliban.*

*Enter Ferdinand & Ariel, invisible playing and singing.*
ARIEL.          *Come unto these yellow sands,*
                        *and then take hands:*
               *Curtsied when you have, and kist*
                        *the wilde waves whist:*
               *Foote it featly heere, and there, and sweete Sprights beare*
                        *the burthen.*                 Burthen dispersedly.
               *Harke, harke, bowgh wawgh: the watch-Dogges barke,*
                        *bowgh-wawgh.*
               *Hark, hark, I heare, the straine of strutting Chanticlere*
                        *cry cockadidle-dowe.*

(TLN 518–29)

Ferdinand's precise entrance cue is unclear—it might be Prospero's final words to Caliban ('So slave, hence'), or Caliban's exit, or Ariel's music. But whatever the part-text dictates, the effect is familiar. The character enters centre-stage, not remotely ancillary or peripheral to the action, yet has nothing to say for quite some time; meanwhile his entrance is either cued or accompanied by disembodied noise (here Ariel's *'playing and singing'*), which will also be his eventual cue to speak. It thus reprises the 'immanent cue' effect of the play's opening scene. And again, as in the first scene, this enveloping cue is underlined, performatively nailed down, by more conventionally scripted repeated cues: in this case, the refrain of the song. These refrains were ritually repeated, and it is unlikely that the song simply ends with a single crisp *'cry cockadidle-dowe'*.[1] Furthermore, the burden is sung 'dispersedly': that is, not in harmonious unity. We should hear first a pack of dogs (*'bowgh-wawgh'*) and then a rabble of strutting cocks: this is less a sustaining chorus than a thoroughly disorientating 'alarum' of atavistic appetites and barely reined obedience, working inside and around any quelling courtly steps. These competing agencies, then, represent the conditions of Ferdinand's newly self-fashioning environment (courtly love, competitive agencies, male appetites, resistant obedience ... )

Shakespeare is careful not to disorientate his actor here. The part's first words tell him what is going on: 'Where shold this Musick be? I'th aire, or th'earth' (TLN 530). This information applies at once prospectively (it tells Ferdinand what to expect before he gets his cue to speak), in the present (the music is still playing as he begins speaking), and retrospectively (it applies on-stage to the immediate past). Shakespeare clearly wants his actors to feel their way into moments in which they are both played upon and, recognizing that they are in some sense instruments, self-playing. Active volition is partly suspended, partly distended; the performed result is likely to be some kind of slowing of motion.

The effect is repeated with Ariel's second song:

> *Full fadom five thy Father lies,*
> *Of his bones are Corrall made:*
> *Those are pearles that were his eies,*
> *Nothing of him that doth fade,*
> *But doth suffer a Sea-change*
> *Into something rich, & strange:*
> *Sea-Nimphs hourly ring his knell.*
> Burthen: ding dong.
> *Harke now I heare them, ding-dong bell.*
> (TLN 539–47)

The refrain ('ding dong' or 'ding-dong bell') again works as an echoing cue. The cue does not so much elicit a specific response as generate an enveloping aura. Again the song 'interrupts' Ferdinand's speaking, as though emerging out of it (' 'tis gone. | No, it begins againe' (TLN 537–8)). The character is present but acted upon; he is speaking but opened to other voices; he is transformed, rendered anew, in the action of listening. For the lines in the song enter and alter him, like pollen, or seed (or indeed the loathsome 'flesh-flie' invoked by Ferdinand at TLN 1309). The mix of song and response thus dramatizes the gestation of an archetypal romance character (capable in due course of fructifying, but only through exposure to an often hostile environment).

The intensity of interplay between character and environment should make it clear that discrete character is not here the be-all and end-all. With the same effects given to four characters in very quick succession, there can be no strict demarcation between one 'subjective field' and another. Thus, at the same time as Ariel's refrain surrounds and inter-lards Ferdinand's speech, the cues given on the Ariel-part—'it begins againe' and 'now above me'—indicate how the spirit's contribution to the scene is measured both in the playing of music and in the posi-tioning of *his* body. As before, Ariel's singing, swooping, and dancing are no less redolent of a mind-in-action than is Ferdinand's response to it. The 'ding dong' chorus possesses the same semi-corporeal, extem-porizing, floating freedom as does Ariel's body in receiving Prospero's commands. Meanwhile, through the echoing cue, the Ferdinand-part is at once spell-stopped inside and animated by the Ariel-part; equally, because Ariel is so at the service of Ferdinand, something inchoate, wistful, or simply ambitious in 'Ariel' is passed into Ferdinand. Similarly, the con-tent of Ariel's two songs (as much as they speak Prospero's plot) plants in Ferdinand the condition of his newly awakened sense of himself and his relation to the world. The space between repeated cues thus dou-bly epitomizes Ferdinand's situation: first, it is a concentrated version of his place on the larger stage (physically suspended, mentally expan-sive); second, it is a metaphor of a sexual longing that cannot yet be satisfied.

In all four parts that we have looked at, the individual actor remains paramount (though he is hardly likely to feel that he has orchestrating control of the play or the audience). In a sense the echoing cue-space—the space in between one repeating cue and another—is more than ever the actor's property, because he chooses how long or in what fashion to sustain the second cue or elude the other actor's sight. All four actors are put in the same condition, of being at once in the action, yet partly withheld from it. Each is cued to enter, but not yet to speak; or cued to 'act', but not to respond; each is, then, allowed a contingent presence, in which the actor can seem to be spying furtively upon matters that remain partly hidden. The result is a series of performances that are at once tersely determined and not *quite* or not finally scriptable. Whatever strategies the actor customarily employs to overcome a scenic hiatus—busy motion, statuesque invisibility, earnest nodding of the head—are all pretty redundant. Instead, it is the co-alescence of mind and movement—at times puzzled stasis, at others volatile animation—which both produces and symbolizes imaginative liberty. The writing demands that the actor be unusually aware of his movements *and* his thoughts. He absolutely feels the fact of choice, even if this choice is for the moment frustrated. He nurtures the possibility; it appears to be in his possession, and to derive some very basic kind of authenticity from the fact. The echoing cue-space thus gives a three-dimensional, almost reified presence to a turning mind, or to thinking at the edge of volition.

Cumulatively, *The Tempest* recommends performativity (not quite performance, because it includes the potential for such performance) as the source and symbol of subjectivity. However, as we are seeing, at its most characteristic this is anything but a histrionic form of play-acting. It is often closer to a fidget of the mind than to a grandstanding stealing of the stage. And this delicacy corresponds to the often furtive scripted locations for such mental/physical movement. In the decisive moments of self-discovery, the questions posed of the actor—where and when he enters, speaks, moves, hides—are repeatedly posed in the lapsed intervals or crannies of the part-script. Sometimes this means that the actor must simply wait—bewilderedly or not—and listen in more closely than ever to the world going on around him. At other times the actor must take a unilateral risk, and defer the claims of dialogue in favour of exploring a pocket of mind beyond the knowledge of any others.

This proposes a similarly tacit relationship between the actor and the audience. The sharing between the two is very different from the pantomimic jokes of, say, *Much Ado* or *Twelfth Night*, when one character is unaware of the creeping presence of another, and where furtive actor and colluding spectators share in a feeling of ironic superiority. Here there is no gloating identification with a character's 'secret' presence; the action obeys no well-known generic cliché whose pleasures we can blithely share. We instead witness the movement, but cannot quite touch or influence it; this is as true of Miranda's awakening as of Caliban's menacing first entrance. Moments such as these happen as though in a mime, and acquire that behind-glass, slow-motion quality which allows the action to be self-symbolizing. Because these nascent movements are founded *inside* the cueing space, as distinct from being singularly cued and immediately finished with, the minds engaged in the movements exist under semi-erasure, in a state of apprehension or intimation rather than achieved commission. This corresponds to subjective *and* political potential: the cue-space is like a kiln, in which the wet clay of the present can be felt working toward sustainable shape and form.

# Antonio and Sebastian

In I. ii repeated cues again and again produce a space of subjective 'becoming'. In II. i, by contrast, the villains' repeated cues *cramp* space. The effect is to mock the other characters' claims to unfinished potential. Consider the following:

ADRIAN.        Though this Island seeme to be desert.
SEBASTIAN. **Ha, ha, ha.**
ANTONIO.     So: you'r paid.
ADRIAN.        Uninhabitable, and almost inaccessible.
SEBASTIAN. **Yet**
ADRIAN.        **Yet**
ANTONIO.     He could not misse't.
ADRIAN.        It must needs be of subtle, tender, and delicate/temperance.

(TLN 710–18)

The crucial difference from the four characters introduced earlier is that Adrian, who wishes to harp upon rebirth or recovery (the clothes made new despite the shipwreck, the island in fact more temperate than a desert) is *not* given an early cue within which to dilate or dream. Instead, he is drowned out by the precipitous cues of others. First is Sebastian's hollow 'Ha, ha, ha'. As a repeating cue for his cynical confederate, Antonio, Sebastian's laughter can continue beyond Antonio's response, but in such a way that Adrian can do nothing except compete for airspace. Second is the double cue of 'Yet'. For Adrian, 'Yet' is a positive hinge-word, preparing for the close of his sentence in which he expresses faith in the island's delicacy and temperance. But Sebastian gets there first, *his* 'yet' working as a derisive and annihilating pre-echo of Adrian's. In turn, just as it is Adrian's undercutting cue, so it is simultaneously Antonio's cue; Antonio thus need not attend to Adrian's 'Yet' before saying 'He could not misse't'. The combination of pre-echo and early cue works to squash all buoyancy from Adrian's attempted cheer.

We find a similar effect twice more in the next few lines. First this:

GONZALO.   This *Tunis* Sir was *Carthage.*
ADRIAN.        *Carthage?*
GONZALO.   I assure you *Carthage.*
ANTONIO.     His word is more then the miraculous Harpe.
SEBASTIAN. He hath rais'd the wall, and houses too.

(TLN 757–60)

Antonio's cue, '*Carthage*', is spoken three times; the subsequent exchange between him and Sebastian might easily obliterate Gonzalo and Adrian's pedantic fussing over mytho-historical geography. And then this:

| SEBASTIAN. | Bate (I beseech you) **widow** *Dido*. |
| ANTONIO. | O **Widdow** *Dido*? I, **Widdow** *Dido*. |
| GONZALO. | Is not Sir my doublet as fresh as the first day I/wore it? I meane in a sort. |
| ANTONIO. | That sort was well fish'd for. |

(TLN 771–5; lineation ours)

Gonzalo's cue, 'Widdow *Dido*', is again spoken three times, shared between Sebastian and Antonio. The effect of the cue must be to crush Gonzalo's speech about whimsically fresh doublets inside their ricocheting mockery.

The cynics' denial of the dilated cue-space, and the creativity it allows, is a clear sign of their opposition to the island's dominant pulse. Here we can compare the opportunities experienced in I. ii's repeated cue-spaces, with the similar opportunity represented by the sleep into which all of Antonio and Sebastian's compatriots suddenly fall. This is now *their* moment: but it is crucially different from what we have seen hitherto. This difference is rooted in divergent approaches to the promise of repetition. To Antonio and Sebastian, repetition is as contemptibly routine as the ticks of a clock; for the 'younger' figures suspended between the repeating cues, repetition reflects glimpsed possibilities, ones that they hope may return. Compare the blithe historical confidence of 'What's past is Prologue; what to come | In yours, and my discharge' (TLN 947–8), with the recapitulative world of the island, and of the echoing cues that help bring its agents into being. The actors of Antonio and Sebastian will see from reading their parts exactly what is happening. Consequently, there is nothing surprising or serendipitous about the process of performance. The actors, like the villains they play, are simply given their cues for action: everything is explained to them, presented to them, by the speeches on their part-texts; cause and effect are scripted clearly and linearly. The actors of Miranda, Ariel, Ferdinand, and Caliban will all discover—or rediscover—their characters in the recesses of their part-scripts and the processes of performance. The actors of Antonio and Sebastian need not.

# Caliban (2)

The early scenes of the play thus establish a basic distinction between cue repetitions that hinder or constrict (collapsing down upon the would-be active mind and body) and cue repetitions that suspend or extend (awakening mind and body to opportunity). However, as we might expect from a play so powerfully engaged with historical possibility, the two options do not exist in isolation from each other. It is more accurate to say that they feed upon each other. This is exemplified in the second entrance of Caliban, which shows the two in symbiotic coalescence, or even collision.

This entrance is marked, '*Enter* Caliban, *with a burthen of Wood (a noyse of Thunder heard)*'; the part's speeches and cues follow thus:

> All the infections that the Sunne sucks up
> From Bogs, Fens, Flats, on *Prosper* fall, and make him
> By ynch-meale a disease: his Spirits heare me,
> And yet I needes must curse ... but
> For every trifle, are they set upon me,
> Sometime like Apes, that moe and chatter at me,
> And after bite me: then like Hedg-hogs, which
> Lye tumbling in my bare-foote way, and mount
> Their pricks at my foot-fall: sometime am I
> All wound with Adders, who with cloven tongues
> Doe hisse me into madnesse:
> Lo, now Lo,                                        *Enter*
> Here comes a Spirit of his, and to torment me     *Trinculo*
> For bringing wood in slowly: I'le fall flat,
> Perchance he will not minde me.
> ———————————————————— [here's] [my] comfort.
> Doe not torment me: oh.
> ———————————————————— [Breathes] [at'] nostrils.
> The Spirit torments me: oh.
> ———————————————————— [on] [Neates-]leather
> Doe not torment me 'prethee: I'le bring my/wood home faster.

(TLN 1040–1114; prose lineation ours)

This is a similar set-up to the play's opening scene: Caliban is cued to speak by thunder, and perhaps before that to enter; the threat or expectation of thunder persists throughout and beyond his seventeen-line soliloquy (witness Trinculo a moment later, 'another Storme brewing, I heare it sing ith' winde ... if it should thunder, as it did before, I know not where to hide my head' (TLN 1058–62)). In other words, Caliban's speech takes place inside an aural enclosure—not necessarily of continuing noise, but certainly of the memory and imminence of such noise. He is not, however, released into speech or action by the thunder, which is not his speaking cue. Instead, the noise hangs in the air as the force both provoking him into defiant outcries ('his Spirits heare me, | And yet I needes must curse' (TLN 1042–3)) and threatening the freedom of mind he ventures by so doing.

As in the play's first storm scene, the cue-effect here is as much a metaphor as a guide to the actor. So, the fear that the cue (thunder) may return is a symbol of the terrorizing surveillance which Caliban suffers. He imputes the thunder, one of any number of torments, to his master. The echoing cue thus partly expresses Caliban's raw memory (having experienced this before, he knows what to expect). But at the same time the enveloping cue is not simply owned by Prospero. It is the basic condition of Caliban's subjectivity, and as such the pressurized chamber within which his mind steams. If he dreams of release, then it is inside this cue-space—as an epitome of his condition on the island—that he will have to do it.

Once again, the situation of the character is shadowed by the situating of the actor. The player will see that he is given the rare privilege of a soliloquy (Prospero apart, only Ferdinand is similarly privileged). He will want to use that channel of intimacy to present his case directly to the audience. But the echoing cue, rumbling on throughout the soliloquy, frustrates this desire by forcing him to keep an eye over his own shoulder. It isn't that the actor is made to doubt whether or not he is in fact speaking a soliloquy (as happens with Macbeth, see pp. 477–88). There is no ambiguity as to who the actor addresses—himself—but there is uncertainty as to how porous or otherwise this self is in relation to the world crowding, or indeed pouring, in around him. The actor struggles for the clarity that comes with self-certain confidentiality. The questions that then hover at the actor's mental fringe become the questions that shape the character's emerging pathos. Can he ever be alone? What can it mean to be 'I'? Can he have any being independent of the 'bid[ding]', 'set[ting]', or 'tongues' of others? What freedom can he ever have from surveillance? Is there any liberty without an opposing violence? Is thought, however fiercely private, ever really free?

It is striking how intensively the Caliban-part requires of the *actor* a bunkered, deeply attentive concentration. In both of Caliban's appearances so far, the effect is the same. Whether he is being sought or ignored by the others on-stage, the Caliban-actor does not take his cue directly from anyone. The action goes on around him, and his character's basic mission is to avoid notice. He doesn't want to join in; he doesn't want to be asked in. Instead, the most intimate parts of his consciousness are focused and magnified in the desperate stillness of an essentially *appositional* body. Like Ariel's mercurial body, Caliban's resistant shell signifies a churning mind: and again, it is echoing cues that have vitally helped to create this.

To see how this works, we need to keep in mind two parts—Caliban's and Stephano's. Here again is the Caliban-part immediately after Trinculo's entrance:

> Lo, now Lo,                                              *Enter*
> Here comes a Spirit of his, and to torment me          *Trinculo*
> For bringing wood in slowly: I'le fall flat,
> Perchance he will not minde me.
> ———————————————————— [here's] [my] comfort.
> Doe not **torment me: oh.**
> ———————————————————— [Breathes] [at'] nostrils.
> The Spirit **torments me: oh.**
> ———————————————————— [on] [Neates-]leather.
> Doe not torment me 'prethee: I'le bring my wood home faster.
>
>                                   (TLN 1053–1114)

Four speeches in a row speak of present 'torment', two of them providing the actor with basically identical cues to give out. When conning the role, the actor is likely to think that everything describes a single 'feeling' or event, and that it all happens with urgent speed. But the reality is not so simple. First Trinculo has a long speech (twenty-four lines of dense prose, with numerous opportunities for improvised miming) in which he punctiliously studies the dead-still Caliban, trying to determine his genus, before eventually joining the strange 'islander' under his gaberdine to avoid the storm. Then there is the similarly lengthy intervention of the drunken Stephano:

> I shall no more to sea, to sea, here shall I dye ashore.
> This is a very scurvy tune to sing at a mans
> Funerall: well, **here's my comfort.**               *Drinkes.*
> *Sings. The Master, the Swabber, the Boate-swaine & I;*
> *The Gunner, and his Mate*
> *Lov'd Mall, Meg, and Marrian, and Margerie,*

*But none of us car'd for Kate.*
*For she had a tongue with a tang,*
*Would cry to a Sailor goe hang:*
*She lov'd not the savour off Tar nor of Pitch,*
*Yet a Tailor might scratch her where ere she did itch.*
*Then to Sea Boyes and let her goe hang.*
This is a scurvy tune too:
But **here's my comfort**. *Drinks*

(TLN 1082–95)

In the full play-script, neither Trinculo nor Caliban notice Stephano until the song is over and done with. This remains Trinculo's condition; his first words from under the gaberdine, 'I should know that voyce', mark the moment when he 'hears' Stephano; the only question is whether this could really be the voice of his friend, whom he assumes drowned. (The player of Trinculo has a number of repeated cues of his own to deal with in this scene, but they are of a predictable kind: his early cue of 'Trinculo' to Stephano when under the gaberdine helps orchestrate a little improvisatory freedom within slapstick (TLN 1144–5); then Stephano's repeated cue to Trinculo ('Sweare'), and Trinculo's twice-repeated cue of 'Monster', help establish his separateness from the other two as a mocking and cynical commentator.) But the part-text suggests that Caliban's experience is very different. So, Stephano enters singing, breaking off to speak the Caliban-actor's cue, 'here's my comfort'. He then has a drink—perhaps a lengthy swig—before proceeding to sing another sea-shanty. He now breaks off once more, and with surreal, slow-motion exactness repeats his earlier action: 'here's my comfort', followed by a long drink. In other words, the shanty is framed by a repeated cue-phrase. Stephano is in his own world: but where is Caliban?

To answer this, we need to 'place' his actor. So, he hears his cue, says or begins to say his line, but he finds that a sailor's shanty cuts across it. He doesn't after all have a quick scene, but a long and repetitive one, in which early cues redouble the fact that he cannot easily escape from this particular moment. The actor must now attend carefully to the song, assured that his cue will return. But the actor's relationship to the song has to be subtly different from his relationship to other dialogue. Normally he would have half an ear out for the cue-phrase and keep the rest of his mind for himself. In a situation like this one, it is different. He is 'in' his cue as he listens; he has been cued already, yet he is *still* being cued. He is thus experiencing, as he listens, a kind of bracket inside his cue. Instead of a clearly cued speech or action, one that gives to the actor (and often the character) an immediate motive for speaking, we see a *lapsed* motive, in which 'Caliban's' volition is briefly lent to this intervening singer.

Suspended thus between invitation and response, the Caliban-actor will surely listen with unusually intense interest. Perhaps he looks benignly upon the interruption (as a song of joy, impossible to him in his straitened position, but all the same affirming of his craft and ensemble); perhaps jealously (as a scene-stealing abrogation of his rights); perhaps he resents it because it lengthens his present discomfort, sweating and suffocating beneath a blanket with another actor sprawled on top of him. But whatever his specific orientation, part of his response must involve the most basic question: how does this song bear upon *my* part, *my* acting?

There is no simple answer to this; indeed, the moment seems scripted so as to hold opposite responses in tension. Let us take the possible responses one at a time.

First, it is clear that the repeating cue is not conferring the same kind of space as it does, for instance, with Ariel's songs to Ferdinand. In part, this is because it reinforces Caliban's already circumscribed playing space; just as Trinculo is lying on top of him, so the precipitous cue similarly besieges his mental space and invades his hopeful 'hibernation'. Secondly, and again conventionally, the cue trick helps establish zones on the stage. So it is clear that Caliban, who is all the time engaged with Trinculo, is nominally (verbally) cued by one figure (Stephano) whilst effectively (physically) 'cued' by another (Trinculo). To some degree the early cue releases the Caliban-actor to play the physical comedy; he has his cue in his safekeeping, and can robustly act his 'torment' throughout Stephano's song. Here is where the repeating cue on Caliban's part, 'torment[s] me: oh', comes into its own: the actor can dilate or repeat his final cue-word as he feels appropriate, whether giving out a long low moan or a quick yelp of apprehension. He might thus release differently tuned 'Oh's at intervals throughout Stephano's song, with clear comic potential ('For she had a tongue with a tang [Oh!] Would cry to a sailor go hang [Oh!]', and so on).

Thirdly—and quite opposed to facilitating slapstick—the coalescence of premature cue and song might offer a direct ingress into Caliban's otherwise unexpressed mind. Just as the song steals into the Caliban-part despite not being written into it, so it also steals into Caliban's consciousness despite there being no recorded response to it. Caliban can be engrossed both by the 'torment' of his resident spirit (Trinculo) *and* by Stephano's song. But again there are rival possible interpretations. So, Caliban may identify the song—as it mugs him, frightens him, paralyses him—as a further 'torment'. Accordingly, as much as his 'oh' has comic potential for an audience, it expresses for its speaker his simple and present pain—and perhaps the recognition of all-too-familiar provocations. After all, the sea-shanty's blithe celebration of collective merrymaking at a single victim's expense may well seem woundingly intimate; Caliban too has a 'tongue with a tang', and is scorned where others are adored. Understood in this way, Caliban's 'burden'—'oh … oh … oh'—works as piteous counterpoint rather than festive complement. For Caliban, the point is the mundane repetitiveness of his tortures. The elongated cue-space thus concertinas an entire recent history on the island into a single fearful act.

But the echoing cue-space is never simply about repeating the past; whatever animates this interim is always preparing for future repetitions. The same applies to the sea-shanty, with its perhaps enviably carefree cast of confederate sailors, loose women, and promiscuous tongues. Consequently, another way of Caliban possessing the song here comes to mind. Caliban has always in the past been the excluded and tormented one; now he can share in the dismissive and even atavistic satisfactions of inclusion. Caliban's own desiring (rather than fearful) mind can thus fugitively be *in* the song, finding in its boisterous spaces some hitherto barely imaginable freedom, jouissance, irreverence; perhaps a paean to the mental, physical, and erotic itinerance that he has for so long, and never more so than *now*, been cruelly forbidden. To be cued is to be controlled, and here is an opening in the envelope where he can slip out and breathe the air of 'freedom'. But still more enthralling is the simple, rambunctious, devil-may-care quality of the song's *sound*. As before with Ariel, the stolen cue-space allows the mind 'inside' it to rehearse a possibility or glimpse an idea that is yet not fully admitted to self-consciousness.[2]

Any conclusion about the significance of this particular sequence of repeated cues, then, must be ambiguous. We have seen how the particular promise of any repeating cue-space depends upon the time it gives the actor and character. In this instance, Caliban is appropriately suspended between constriction and expansion. On the one hand, this corresponds to the imminent disappointment of any union with the drunks; on the other hand, it corresponds to the political seriousness, the faithfulness to dream and resistance, of the mind that commits to such hope.

Caliban, unsurprisingly, is given the perfect gloss for the movement here dramatized:

> Be not affeard, the Isle is full of noyses,
> Sounds, and sweet aires, that give delight and hurt not:
> Sometimes a thousand twangling Instruments
> Will hum about mine eares; and sometime voices,
> That if I then had wak'd after long sleepe,
> Will make me sleepe againe, and then in dreaming,
> The clouds methought would open, and shew riches
> Ready to drop upon me, that when I wak'd
> I cri'de to dreame againe.
>
> (TLN 1492–1500)

'The clouds methought would open': this is precisely the effect of the cue-space's 'sliding door'. Has he heard the song or not? Is it a dream or not, a 'torment' or a 'sweet aire'? Or is it a falsely enthralling promise, only really offering a prolongation of Caliban's present subjection? It is the *furtiveness* of these extended spaces between repeating cues that allows all of this—a space that from any other perspective (or according to the full play-text) does not really exist. Only the actor can locate it, and then only in performance. Most importantly, the repeated cue creates a space that simultaneously opens and closes: that is at once open and closed; that seems to open only to close, or seems closed only to open, and so concentrates into itself the dynamism of history as it is subjectively experienced.

It is then appropriate that the scene should end with Caliban emphatically taking up for himself the ambivalent promise offered by giving out a repeated cue:

> *Caliban Sings drunkenly*
> **Farewell** Master; **farewell, farewell.**
> TRINCULO.   A howling **Monster**: a drunken **Monster**.
> CALIBAN.    *No more dams I'le make for fish,*
> *Nor fetch in firing, at requiring,*
> *Nor scrape trenchering, nor wash dish,*
> *Ban' ban' Cacalyban*
> *Has a new Master, get a new Man.*

> **Freedome**, high-day, **high-day freedome**, freedome **high-day,**
> **freedome**.

STEPHANO.     O brave monster; lead the way. *Exeunt.*

(TLN 1223–32)

The Caliban-actor is off on his own here. He will see that each of his speeches ends with triply repeated closing words: the actor is cueing his fellow players; but more profoundly, 'Caliban' is cueing himself. This of course is Caliban's most triumphant moment, and it is no coincidence that it is one in which the space between cues and action coincides: 'Caliban' alone creates the space, just as he alone acts inside it. Stephano has the nominal exit cue in this scene, but the repeated cues given to Caliban make it possible and perhaps desirable that he should 'lead the way' off-stage, with his repeating cue-word 'freedome' echoing off the rafters. If so, this is the only moment in the play when a single character *exits* inside his repeating cue-space: that is, the cue is not finished with, not decisively answered, and the cuer departs with it still in his keeping. Symbolically, this is highly suggestive. It means that the scene ends inside this space; it means that the bubble is in some basic sense not punctured. Even Ariel, for all the historical longing embodied in his songs and his movement, is never given this power to close a scene. This helps to explain the surprisingly uncontainable joy and passion of the moment: it is one of dream-come-true, as epitomized by the continuation of the repeating cue-space's power of wistful suspension beyond the span of the scene, and thus into a future 'off-stage'.

Of course, Caliban's plot is punished, and ends in ignominy. And, true to expectation, Shakespeare marks the plot's ultimate failure by a pointed reversal of the repeated cue technique. This happens when Stephano and Trinculo are waylaid by the clothes on the line:

STEPHANO.     … carry this.
TRINCULO.     **And this.**
STEPHANO.     I, **and this.**
              *A noyse of Hunters heard. Enter divers Spirits in shape/of Dogs and*
              *Hounds, hunting them about: Prospero/and Ariel setting them on.*
PROSPERO.     **Hey** *Mountaine* **hey.**
ARIEL.        *Silver:* there it goes, *Silver.*

(TLN 1926–33; prose lineation ours)

All four speakers are given premature cues—on top of the 'noyse of Hunters'. This is a classic example of using repeated cues to orchestrate a scene of crowded chaos. In thematic terms, the effect is clear: these are striking instances of repeated cues that shut down opportunity and seize up time and space (a sign of the way in which the drunken plot degenerates). We might see this as reminiscent of the vicious way in which Shylock's cue trick ricochets back upon him in *The Merchant of Venice* (see pp. 209–13). Nonetheless, it is suggestive that 'Caliban' is absent from this matrix of colliding cues. And indeed, Caliban's particular investment in the moment is uncertain. The repeated 'And this' | 'and this' together mark Stephano's and Trinculo's wish to load Caliban with garments—but whether he takes them is not clear. It is probable that Caliban is chased away with the others; but the part is written so that it is possible that he leaves before the dogs enter ('I will have none on't … '), or remains aloof, letting Stephano and Trinculo alone to be caught red-handed. Either way, this could hardly be more different from Caliban's 'freedom' song, which has an embodied spaciousness that this scene of punishment can do little to ridicule or annul. We are a long way here from the subtly working metaphysics of the central storm scene—and indeed of all of the intra-cue spaces earlier in the play. The integrity of such space remains powerfully inviolable, even if the final destination of Caliban's plot does not.

The repeated cue-space that we have seen time and again attending the 'young' characters' pivotal moments does not exist in isolation from the world of the island. It is perhaps Shakespeare's principal means of allowing his actors imaginatively to experience the geography of the island, and in particular the distinctively enclosed physical spaces out of which the island's desires, spirits, and energies must find release: the trees in which Ariel is imprisoned or in which Stephano finds his bottle, the clouds and thunder which batter one character after another, the cells of Prospero or Caliban. Most often we do not see these things—they are instead produced by the play's language, figurative or otherwise. They are thus at the edge between imagination and palpability, or moving between one and the other. And this is exactly the same condition in which the repeating cues again and again place the actors. For the elements in this play really do work like tendentious cues; here is Alonso:

> Me thought the billowes spoke, and told me of it,
> The windes did sing it to me: and the Thunder

(That deepe and dreadfull Organ-pipe) pronounc'd
The name of *Prosper*.

(TLN 1633–6)

Shakespeare works it so that all of the elder statesmen receive their lessons
'inside' exactly the kind of mental abeyance, cued by music, that we have
earlier witnessed being experienced by all of the younger characters. But
there is a crucial difference: the *actors* are not given any time inside this
space to make their own character-altering choices. Accordingly, the elder
statesmen are subject *to* rather than *of* the subduing spell-stopped space.
They are passive recipients, metaphorically offered one 'cue', and one only:
accept Prospero's right, and thus Prospero's forgiveness. They can tacitly
resist the cue, as Antonio does: but the echoing cue-space offers no other
positive options. As Prospero ties up the knots of his plot, Shakespeare
uses echoing cues a number of times, but always in a way that closes
down rather than opens up thought and action: e.g. Juno and Ceres'
song surrounding Ferdinand's praise of the masque; the sudden end to the
masque as 'Prospero *starts sodainly and speakes, after which to a strange hollow
and confused noyse, they heavily vanish*'; the 'living drollerie' of dancing and
salutations performed before Alonso and company, enveloped in 'solemne
and strange Musicke' (TLN 1535–67). But none of the characters is given
any personal 'space of becoming' within this spell-stopped moment; it is
not reinforced by local repeated cues that actually work upon the actors.
Such examples are quite unlike the final location in which we are asked to
imagine each of the young characters: the cell into which Caliban is sent to
'seek' grace; the discovery place in which Ferdinand and Miranda are found
playing chess; the elements into which Ariel is freed. All three recall and
recast—albeit in very different ways—the 'becoming space' continually
produced by repeated cues earlier in their parts.

# Conclusion

Because many characters experience similar processes, and because these
processes are in turn echoed or mirrored by the inanimate life of the
island, the ultimate subject of *The Tempest* is less any single individual
or even society than the energies that might go to make such a thing.
Sometimes in the play these energies are located in a tiny kernel, like the
seeds of the apple which Antonio (mockingly) imagines might 'bring forth

more Islands' (TLN 764–5); sometimes they are located in semi-embodied force-fields, like the sounds or weather which seem to sculpt so much of the island's activity. Whichever way we conceive of this potential—seed or force-field—the repeated cue-space embodies it. But before all else, the repeated cue-space is the *actor's* very own kernel (or perhaps kennel) of apprehended possibility. As such it both grounds and epitomizes *The Tempest*'s sustained exploration of incipience. For if this play, or its island, is Shakespeare's most audacious attempt at staging the theatre of the mind, then the actor held in an *extended* cue—stealing time where there seems to be none, stretching the 'horizontal' liberty of the scene so as to evoke the 'vertical' presence of consciousness—is its epitome.

In *The Tempest* Shakespeare takes the basic stakes in the cue—what happens if a cue is taken, what happens if it is not, what happens if it is taken twice—and creates an island in its image. The cue is always a hinge-point between one subject and another, and one subject's space-time and another. It is a point where minds *almost* meet, or where they overlap, commingle, and yet remain discrete and unknowable. It can be likened to a synapse—the junction between two neurons or nerve-cells. For the cue is likewise at once a terminal point, a beginning, and a supercharged gap between the two. But if the sensory or motor impulses of a part are relayed in its cues, there is never a simple forward movement, from one cell to another in an onrushing succession. This is the case with all cues, whatever their apparently orderly succession: but it is all the more emphatically the case with repeated cues. For with repeated cues we find that at crucial points the system is *not* relaying information as it supposedly should: the nerve impulses at issue start looping or ricocheting back upon their origin.

As a lived phenomenon, as experienced in practice or performance by the actor, the part becomes nervously alive with little hiccups, suspensions, and recursions. And as we have seen, it is in these 'interrupting' moments that the actor can most intensively feel what is at stake for his character. This is because the temporal disjunctions created by repeated cues both place action in abeyance (generating suspense or opportunity) and concentrate the mind (eliciting a recognition of choice). By refashioning experience as partially discontinuous, repeated cues help render the dramatic moment more authentically present.

Yet there remains a paradox. The most powerful moments of choice happen *as* suspension. Occasionally they are barely actable, though always powerfully felt. Furthermore, as we have seen, all of these effects are reproduced in a number of actors' parts, all contributing to a composite portrait of experience and possibility. As a result, the actors in *The Tempest* are perhaps forced to doubt as never before their power to possess the play or the audience. Perhaps this makes for a still more intense and protective identification with their parts; perhaps this just leaves them vaguely frustrated, or deferring unsurely to an increasingly remote author. But whatever the actor's specific response, it will be *because of* —rather than despite—the ongoing osmosis between actor and character demanded by the part-script.

# PART IV

## The Actor with his Part

I take this Offer then——pay the Bond thrice,
and let the Christian go.
———————————— take the Forfieture.
Give me my Principal, and let one go.
———————————— me that word.
Shall I not barely have my Principal?
———————————— at thy Peril, Jew.
Why, then the Devil give him good of it!
I'll stay no longer Question.
———————————— not for Anthonio.
Nay, take my life and all: pardon not that.
You take my house, when you do take the Prop
That doth Sustain my house: you take my life,
When you do take the means whereby I live.
———————————— dost thou say?
I am Content.
———————————— a deed of gift.
I pray you give me leave to go from hence;
I am not well; send the Deed after me,
And I will Sign it.

        Exit: P.S. at——— not the Front.

For Mr. Wm. Ward
Doncaster October ye 25th 1772
Lengths 10.

The part of Shylock from William Shakespear's *Merchant of Venice* (1772).

# 16
## History

### Interpreting Parts: Emotions

Here we will introduce some of the basic things that all actors would look out for in their written part-texts; we will go on to explore how Shakespeare adapts and transforms these widespread practices and expectations.

One of the first things that an actor would try to identify on a part is the 'passions' it contained. When Hamlet wants to find out how talented a player is (he desires 'a tast of [his] quality'), he suggests hearing 'a passionate speech' (TLN 1476–7). The player is then goaded into speaking the Hecuba set-piece from a failed play, a speech rich in the passionate intensity that Hamlet is unable to summon in himself. But later, Hamlet, keen to show how few similarities there are between his predicament and a show-piece speech, specifically expresses his distaste for actors who overact the passions and tear them 'to tatters' (TLN 1858). Examining Hamlet's outburst against overacting players, critics have suggested that Shakespeare himself is taking the opportunity inside his fiction to point a finger at some performer—perhaps Alleyn and his stalking Tamberlaine.[1] But in a nice irony, one of the earliest recorded references to Shakespeare's *Hamlet* occurs in a poem that also suggests something about the way in which Burbage performed the lead character: it talks of a man who strips to his shirt and then 'Much like mad-*Hamlet*; thus [at] Passion teares', implying that Burbage himself played precisely the kind of performance that his character decries.[2] We may see here another layer to the ironic reflexivity of *Hamlet*: Burbage/Hamlet is captive to the very mendacity and histrionics that his words tell him he (should) abjure. But such duplicitous aesthetic sensitivities are hardly unique to *Hamlet* (or Shakespeare, if

Hamlet is here the partial butt). The complaint that the passions were overacted was one frequently made: if an actor's part, wrote Robert Warner, 'prefigure passion, he raves, rages, and protests much by his painted Heavens'.[3]

A kinder description of Burbage's 'passionate' performance is given by Thomas Bancroft. It is seldom—if ever—quoted, yet it was written by someone who had seen the great man act. Bancroft praises particularly the way Burbage identifies and performs not just each mood but each mood change:

> *Burbage*...when his part
> He acted, sent each passion to his heart;
> Would languish in a scene of love; then look
> Pallid for fear; but when revenge he took,
> Recall his bloud; when enemies were nigh,
> Grow big with wrath, and make his buttons fly...[4]

A snappy and seemingly spontaneous change from one passion to another (called, from the Restoration period onwards, a 'transition') was one of the qualities for which an audience looked when judging a performance. Here Burbage is praised for having absolute control of his passions: he can blush and blench at will (a physical impossibility, we might think, but one often singled out as the hallmark of truly great acting). Similarly, Garrick, two centuries later, was praised for being able to sit in a chair and 'do' transitions from one passion to another: rage to grief, grief to anger, anger to sorrow. He was also said to be able to control the flow of blood to his face. Emotional intensity was prized only as much as speedy emotional changes.

Passions, in other words, were more than simply the units in which actors acted. They were entirely elemental to performances, so much so that the verb 'to passionate' became an alternative to the verb 'to act'. Asking 'whose person did you passionate?', Nicholson speculates which of the passions will be most occupying a particular actor as he cons his part:

> Belike your Swaines intend a Comedie, ...
> And love-sicke you these passions must descrie:
> Which to adorne with action and with grace,
> You daily thus make triall of your part,
> With sighes and teares that never pierce the hart.[5]

The noun 'passion', of course, had a broad theatrical meaning as well as a scientific one. Generally it described a specific emotion, as when sorrow is described as having 'no dissembled Action' in her depiction of 'The lively Passion of a pensive brest'.[6] But an attempt to identify and confine the passions to a certain number—five or seven—is not helpful as far as the early modern stage is concerned. Passions, in early modern scientific thought, were divided into two sets: concupiscible or irascible, one drawing the spirits, the other repelling them. However, within this basic demarcation, the way in which any single emotion was divided from any other was not entirely clear. So although treatises were written with the aim of explaining the inner causes and outward manifestations of the passions, they do not entirely agree with one another—despite their general recognition that the passions governed character and the way one ran one's life. The broad signification of passions on the stage, then, was like the treatises written about them: open to the actor to shape and the spectator to interpret. Often, for instance, the word 'passion' is used to describe the general rather than specific emotional qualities attending on a certain role, as when a boy player is criticized for putting on 'the attyre, the gesture, the passions of a woman'; or a young 'Popish rakehell' is able 'to act, & feigne the passions, and agonies of the devil'; or a 'King' is asked to 'Ascend Thy Throne, | And thence proceed, to act Thy Passion'.[7] Here the word 'passion' becomes almost a synonym for the embodying of emotion in acting, alluding in more or less generic terms to the intensity and verve with which a player performs his part. Indeed, a semantic opposition was drawn at the time between 'action' and 'passion': 'action' was physiologically the externalization (acting) of internal feeling (passion).

So although an actor considering how to perform his role would undoubtedly have worked to identify which passion was required at which moment, this is not to suggest that he would have conceived of either his part or of his life as consisting of one or two broad slabs of emotion. He would have seen his role as a collection of emotional units—coinciding with verbal units—and looked closely to decide which emotion he was 'in' at which moment, and when precisely it changed. The transitions remained the key. Thomas Riley, a university actor, is praised by Randolph in the same terms that Burbage was praised above: because he could not only nicely illustrate the passions, but also exchange with ease one powerful emotion for another:

> When thou art pleas'd to act an angry part,
> Thou fright'st the audience; and, with nimble art
> Turn'd Lover, thou dost that so lively too,
> Men think that Cupid taught thee how to wooe.[8]

Though the words 'humour' and 'passion' had different significations (humour being a subset of passion), both were looked for in a role. In science the four 'humours' were both passions and elements of nature: choler, relating to fire, being dry and hot and provoking anger; melancholy, relating to earth, being dry and cold and provoking grief; sanguinity, relating to air, being moist and hot and provoking love; phlegmaticism, relating to water, being wet and cold and provoking fear and astonishment.[9] The 'science' of humours is thus microcosmic, and so too was the theatrical mediation of it. So, even though the system of humours was said to be immanent in everything, in application it was unevenly discovered. Hence the way in which one found particularly 'humorous' moments or expressions, 'humorous' characters or dispositions, and, indeed, a 'humorous' genre all its own: 'men... on this Theatre, as Chance shall sway, | And on their humours work, their parts will play'.[10] Around the turn of the century, the 'comedy of humours' came to define an entire genre of writing which had as its source of interest the unique emotional physiology making specific characters behave in absurdly programmed, constitutionally unavoidable ways. The genre thus elevated—if that is the word—'temperamental' personality above plot or pathos.[11]

The humorous genre itself shows how prone playwrites and performers were to see writing as being essentially *about* emotion. Humorous comedies came in vogue after the performance of Chapman's *An Humorous Day's Mirth* (originally called *The Comedy of Humours*) in 1597 (Chamberlain records 'a new play of humors in very great request').[12] Any play thereafter that mentions humours is a homage to or a reaction against the humours genre: *Every Man in/out of his Humour, Every Woman in her Humour, An Humorous Day's Mirth*, etc. As Barnaby Rich put it in 1606, 'As for the humorous they have beene alredie brought to the stage, where they have plaide their partes, *Everie man in his humour*.'[13] For our purposes it is important simply to realize that while the 'humourous' aspect of the passions came to be the subject of certain kinds of comedy, 'passions' themselves were always one of the subjects of plays.

Somehow, then, actors' parts had to highlight not just emotions, but the particular *moments* when those emotions yielded to other emotions. The actor might occasionally have been 'told' to switch upon a particular cue, as when a stage-direction in Marston's *Insatiate Countess* tells the performer to 'fall in love' (or, perhaps, relates that he did so).[14] But equally often, such instructions had to be embodied in the shape, tone, and rhythm of discrete part-text's speeches.

## Playwrights and Emotions

'What is our life?' asks a common poem, often attributed to Raleigh. The answer is always 'A play of Passion'.[15] If actors were looking for passions and the transitions of the passions in their parts, playwrights were writing texts that contained those transitions. Both the nature of emotions and the relationship of emotions to people were at the core of what they wrote. One of the few accounts of poets gathering material for their writing shows them lurking in sundry places, observing not just people and types, but humours:

> For Humours to lie leidger they are seen
> Oft in a Tavern, and a bowling-green.
> They do observe each place, and company,
> As strictly as a Traveller or Spye.
> And deifying dung-hills seem t'adore
> The scum of people, Watch-man, Changling, Whore,
> To know the vice, and ignorance of all,
> With any Rags they'le drink a pot of Ale.[16]

They are looking, that is, for *observable* types, for striking emotional and temperamental affects communicable to the public eye. 'Transitions' are behind the jerkiness of early modern plays, the extraordinary rapidity with which one passion gives way to another, or, just as telling, the simulation or mockery of just such sudden switches: the abrupt insanity of Lear, jealousy of Leontes or Posthumus, love of Romeo or Malvolio. Unsurprisingly, Shakespeare was feted for his supreme ability to handle the passions ('Compar'd to [Shakespeare], for moving passion, | There's none know how to do't now [he is] gon') and the humours ('*Shakespeare* (most rich in humours) [could] entertain | The crouded theatres with his happy vein').[17] But other playwrights too were praised for the skill with

which they explored the passions: Beaumont and Fletcher 'coyn'd a golden
*Way*, | T'expresse, suspend, and passionate a *Play*'; Davenant 'forc't the
Audience leane | To th'passion of [his] Pen'; Ben Jonson, meanwhile,
'shew'd us how he could hit | Each humour now; and then be out
of it'.[18] It was even claimed, extravagantly enough, that a playwright's
ability to handle the passions well brought him near to God; he alone
could turn his own 'quicke passions, and witty humors … into matter and
forme as infinite, as Gods pleasure to diversifie mankinde'.[19] As such
quotations suggest, passions were not simply what playwrights depicted;
they were what motivated the writing in the first place. 'Passion' was
inceptive.

As writers wrote to the passions and the humours, and players performed to them, it is hardly surprising to learn that the audience watched
*for* them. At a time when mood was seen as being an external expression of bodily health and when 'character' was divided into four basic
mood types, humour was for everyone an available, pretty much intu-
itive unit or category of judgement. For instance, after a performance of
Shakespeare's *Othello*, one member of the audience writes in his commonplace book how impressed he was by the emotional villainy of Iago:
'Act: 3, ye scene betwixt Iago and Othello, and ye 1 sce: of ye 4 Act,
beetween ye same shew admirably ye villanous humour of Iago when hee
persuades Othello to his jealousy.'[20] Relishing the humour and passion
of the stage was, it was said, another way in which a member of the
audience could be corrupted. For watchers would often 'take on' the
passion of the performance, deriving their emotions from those simulated on-stage. Or the audience themselves might take 'instruction' from
an impassioned part. Viola's surrogate wooing scene in *Twelfth Night*
pokes gentle fun at those members of the audience who noted playhouse speeches, internalized them—and then used them in their flirtations:
like the lawyer's clark who 'dares attempt a mistresse … with Jests, or
speeches stolne from Playes', or Luscus, who speaks largely out of *Romeo
and Juliet*:

> If ere you heard him courting Lesbias eyes;
> Say (Curteous Sir) speakes he not movingly
> From out some new pathetique Tragedie?
> He writes, he railes, he jests, he courts, what not,
> And all from out his huge long scraped stock
> Of well penn'd playes.[21]

'Humours', writes Gayton of plays, 'are sodainly imitated' by the spectators: 'Many have by representation of strong passions been so transported, that they have gone weeping, some from Tragedies, some from Comedies; so merry, lightsome and free, that they have not been sober in a week after.'[22] This particular report might seem overstated, but there can be no doubt that playwrights wrote in the hope of effecting just such a 'passionate' conduit between a part and its viewer. Shakespeare in particular was famed for eliciting spellbinding transformations of the passions in his audience:

> So when thou find'st two contraries,
> Two different passions from thy rapt soule rise,
> Say, (who alone effect such wonders could)
> Rare *Shake-speare* to the life thou dost behold.[23]

The sense here is that the theatre was almost a 'learning school' for passions: that audiences went there to feel newly amazed, not only at an actor's or playwright's facility, but at their own capability to feel apparently impossible 'contraries' at one time, as though the theatre was introducing its 'rapt' spectators to new possibilities of feeling. At the very least, plays are praised for doing more here than stolid 'imitation'. They are arresting, audacious, transformatory. And at the heart of this is an openness to how we might *be* more than one thing at any one time. Passions were written into plays, identified by actors looking at parts, extracted by the audience: they were some of the major building-blocks that went to make up plays and defined what plays were. Consequently, it was one of the first jobs of the actor, upon receiving his part, to search out and animate his own 'cues' for passion; and it was one of the first heady tasks of the playwright to write them.

## Parts and Emphasis

Once an actor had identified his part's emotional transitions, he would have to address ways of manifesting the requisite feelings. Actors could not rely, as TV and cinema players can, upon subtle shifts in facial expression; they would often have been too far away for the audience (for whom corrective glasses for short sight had not yet been invented) to see what they were doing with their faces. So acting required full-bodied flamboyance. Accordingly, 'action' or 'gesture' (the motion of the body) and 'pronunciation' or 'emphasis' (the movement of the voice) were of supreme importance. These of course correspond to the two parts of rhetoric already referred to: *actio* and *pronuntio*. Students at both school and university were taught to portray with accuracy and finesse the relationship between the two. Good action and good pronunciation were life skills as well as acting ones. The crossover, however, was problematic. If a student, for instance, worked hard enough on his action and pronunciation to make them entirely 'perfect', he might become too good, too contrived—too much 'the actor':

> If a man have Emphasie and Elocution, ... whose vocal hands reign in mens affections, and inspire his auditory; in whom you may finde a continued strength without deficiency, without inequality: How comes he of? His classical friend will cry out he is a *Drammatist*, fitter to personate upon a Theatre a *Cassius* or a *Cataline*.[24]

Predictably, many texts about the theatre stress the necessity of a close relationship between action and words: plays are 'made more forcible by gesture and outward action'; 'the *Actor* ... puts life into ... mimicall Artillery by motion and voice'; good players 'are very wel deserving both for true action and faire deliverie of speech'; would-be good players 'must take heede of wrested and enforced action: for if there be not a facility in [their] deliverance, and as it were a naturall dexteritie, it must needes sound harsh to the auditour, and procure his distast and displeasure'.[25] No wonder, then, the urgency with which Hamlet tells the player to 'suit the Action to the Word, | the Word to the Action' (TLN 1865–6). But how were words selected to be highlighted by action?

First, how they were not. Pointing (punctuation) was not generally one of the ways in which words were pre-selected for the actor. How do we know? Because, though all remaining parts are lightly punctuated (as are all remaining manuscript plays), that punctuation varies markedly from script to script (in a far greater way than words do). Thomas Goffe's *The Courageous Turk*, a university and then a public theatre play of the 1620s to 1630, survives in manuscript, printed text, and actor's part, and in all three the punctuation of the same text differs. Would an actor, then, have relied on the punctuation in his part to tell him how to say what he had to say? Almost certainly not; he might have looked at it, but would not have used it as a basis for meaning. Poems of the time emphasize (invariably in typography and occasionally in theme) the fact that pauses are essentially the business of the reader rather than the writer. But if actors are selecting emphasis, they are of course automatically selecting punctuation also. Harington's poem 'To Sextus, an ill Reader', criticizes Sextus for ruining a good poem by his bad punctuation choices, and in doing so specifically shows pointing to be the responsibility of the speaker:

> That Epigram that last you did rehearse,
> Was sharpe, and in the making, neat and tearse,
> But thou doost read so harsh, point so perverse,
> It seemed now neither witty nor verse.
> For shame poynt better, and pronounce it cleerer,
> Or be no Reader, *Sextus*, be a Hearer.[26]

But wrong pointing could, of course, affect meaning. Gataker takes Psalm 13:1 and shows how various preachers have, through selecting bad punctuation, missed the sense—God's sense—in the lines. Note here both the suggestion that there is a 'right' place for pausing in the line, and that the unthoughtful preacher can miss it:

> 1. Some reade the words ... without stop or stay, as one continued sentence; *How long wilt thou forget me, O Lord, for ever?* ... 2. Others make a pause, but a pause misplaced; and they thus reade them; *How long, O Lord, wilt thou forget me? For ever?* ... 3. Others placing the pause aright, reade the words as *an Aposiopesis*, that is, a broken or imperfect sentence, not unfit to expresse passion ...[27]

Thus punctuation, if noticed at all when present, was seen to offer some breath-control suggestions, but was thought of as merely one in an array of facilitating rhetorical mechanisms; it was something that printers would freely add to texts themselves. For it was always 'Rhetorick', and its primary duty of persuasion, that was master: '[Rhetoric] not onely emboldens a scholler to speake, but instructs him to speake well, and with judgement, to observe his comma's, colons, & full poynts, his parentheses, his breathing spaces, and distinctions.'[28]

This means, of course, that private 'study' and 'instruction' had to determine which *were* the phrases and how to separate them fully from one another. Players were famous for having this skill, and for contrasting words and stops with magnificent grandeur: translating Lemnius, Thomas Newton advises young men to practise speaking aloud to music in order to attain the kind of 'bigge tuned sounds by stoppes and certayne Pauses, as our Comicall felowes now do, that measure Rhetorick by theyr ... Rhythmes'.[29] The result was that when actors were praised, it was for carefully selecting and isolating moments of punctuation and highlighting them with the use of appropriate action. So there was, for instance, the full stop, or 'period', that was recognized, chosen, and then further pointed by the act of weeping: 'every period had his sense made plaine, | With teares, which *Chorus*-like mine eyes did raine'.[30]

Punctuation is, of course, often latent in the sense of a piece. But as the actor started to work on the switches and changes of direction the author had inserted, pointing them, choosing some over others—this was where he started 'owning' the writing. Even those choices more or less demanded by the sense would, through being 'selected' by the actor, belong to him too. These days careful and 'accurate' punctuation makes choices for the reader, determining which words are important, which phrases are key: in the early modern period, making those choices and deciding how to manifest them was largely what private 'study' was.

Beyond that, though, 'Pronuntiation' needed to show 'sweetnes in distinction': the difference between one phrase and another or even one word and another. Burbage, again, was singled out for this skill. An epitaph on the actor speaks of how death first 'made seizure' on the actor's tongue in order not to be charmed away from his purposes by speech in which 'not a word did fall | without just weight to ballast it withall'.[31] Obviously, weighting the appropriate or 'just' words, selecting the emphasis, was another main task for an actor.

How would an actor discover which words to select? Iambic verse, of course, singles out words in a way that often requires no punctuation. This is no doubt one of the reasons why blank verse was so popular at the time: it made acting choices that much easier. And just as actors chose the words to stress according to the meter, so the audience would tap into not just those words but also the rhythm of the verse. Iambics were 'heard'; the thump or thrum of them was pronounced. Joseph Hall patronizingly describes 'gazing Scaffolders' as the people who are ravished by big-sounding sentences and 'pure *Iambick* verse'; he goes on to bemoan the popularity of tragic verse in general, and the facility with which it is poured out—'Unbid *Iambicks* flow from carelesse head'.[32] Pronunciation, then, was shaped by and to the rhythm of the verse. The point is in fact obvious: why write in verse at all, why change meter from prose to verse, if you do not wish to make the verse stand out? Modern acting, however, has softened the power of verse by naturalizing the way it is pronounced; often, when spoken, it sounds so

similar to prose that one cannot tell which is which or when one gives way
to the other.

But iambic verse, particularly very regular iambic verse, was clearly
identified with playwrights (often negatively): Digges thinks all successors
to Shakespeare will be worthless, and begs them not to take their second-
rate poetry to the Globe or Blackfriars, rather 'On Gods name may the
Bull or Cockpit have | Your lame blancke Verse, to keepe you from the
grave'.[33] He may be commenting on the fact that Shakespeare sophisticated
blank verse over time, rough-filing it to a state when it is often unclear
whether it *is* verse or some newfangled semi-metered prose. But he is also
commenting on the contemporary inevitability that playwrights composed
in verse, and that audiences had grown to expect and rely upon it. So
too had actors: but they must also have developed a powerfully efficient
sensitivity to shifting registers within verse (or between one manner of verse
and another), and to the gradations within a role between prose, couplet,
and blank verse. Parts were written in prose and verse (when they were)
for a reason, which is why a paean to Webster's *White Devil* particularly
praises the sparkling verse 'set' amidst the richly metallic prose:

> How pretty are thy lines, thy Verses stand
> Like unto pretious Jewels set in gold,
> And grace thy fluent Prose.[34]

Again, the magnification effected by the part-system ensured that such
stylistic shifts would be both plotted and seized upon. It is in such things
as much as anything that an actor is prompted into and guided through
a role; as with cues, such internal pointers are nodal points, where text
and action meet and the role branches into itself. How the actor might
have handled writing of Shakespeare's 'mature' complexity, how he knew
how to 'choose' his emphases, is another question that we will particularly
address.

The fact that actors were expected to select words for emphasis implies
something else about the theatre of the time. The theatre loved words.
What was repeatedly said by writers of the time was that the theatre
was a forum for coining words or for taking new words out for an
airing; both high rhetoric and bawdy jests were prone to relish novel
vocabulary, unwrapped as gifts for the audience to take home. Tarlton
the clown was famous for picking on new words and folding them into

his jokes: Harington lovingly recalls the time when Tarlton came by the Ramist's word 'prepuse' (foreskin) and admitted it 'into the Theater with great applause'; a catch-phrase of Tarlton's was 'without all the paraquestions'.[35] Shakespeare's clowns repeatedly play on this fascination with words: Costard in *Love's Labour's Lost* relishes the word (and idea of) 'remuneration'; Osric in *Hamlet* interposes 'palpable' into a sentence just as he offers superfluous flourishes with his hat. Such fascination with language, selecting the newer, grander, or more difficult word over the easier one is an illustration—almost a parody—of what almost all of these theatres were doing almost all of the time. Shakespeare and his contemporaries were lucky to live in a period when the English language was still in the process of becoming the main language of literature and governance as much as conversation, and when vocabulary was not yet 'set'. Shakespeare was far from alone among his theatrical contemporaries in making up words: the confidence and swagger of so much Elizabethan and Jacobean drama breathes such invention. Indeed, closing the theatres, feared Flecknoe, would retard the progress of language itself:

> The *Stage*... having much conferd and contributed to the inrichment of [language], it being the *Mint* that daily coyns new *words*, which are presently received and admitted as *currant*, ... the plucking downe of which will I feare, not only *retard* the perfectioning of our Language towards which it was advancing amain, but even quite hinder and *recoyle* it, and make it return to its former *Barbarisme*.[36]

One of the things that actors had to do in their parts, then, was pick out 'new' or unfamiliar words and *make* them work in context (and in Shakespeare, as we shall see, the context of grammatical innovation is by no means necessarily comic or meretricious). Reading from parts makes such concentration on *minutiae* all the more likely and, indeed, necessary: each actor was searching for his own piece of novelty or freshness. It is difficult to imagine a discursive economy more suited to Shakespeare's philological and dramatic audacity.

In part terms this means, of course, that one variety of 'selected' word for the actor to stress was the new or difficult word. And this was particularly the case when that word was a long one. The longer a word, the greater the actor's relish; playwrights would compete with one another to produce the most splendid polysyllabic tongue-twisters. So Greene follows up his famous attack on (what is probably) Marlowe's 'swelling bumbast of bragging blanke verse' by criticizing playwrights who turn 'to the spacious volubilitie of a drumming decasillabon'.[37] Any such grotesque ten-foot word ('decasillabon') is obviously an exaggeration, but a habitual complaint developed that playwrights regularly wrote words of six feet long, such as the 'sesquipedalia verba' that were, according to Milles, the common stock of actors.[38] Gayton went so far as to blame actors themselves for their 'wide' mouths, obliging playwrights to write words bulbous enough to fill them:

> I have heard, that the Poets of the Fortune and the Red Bull, had alwayes a mouth-measure for their Actors (who were terrible teare-throats) and made their lines proportionable to their compasse, which were *sesquipedales*, a foot and a halfe.[39]

Note here that it is the 'low' theatres, the Fortune and the Red Bull, that specialize particularly in verbosity. The less literate the audience, the more it was entranced by fat words; those very qualities that make modern spectators intimidated or confused by early modern plays were the qualities best loved and most demanded. Thus the contemporary prejudice that maintains that verbosity is necessarily 'difficult', or that grandiloquence—even mystifying splendour—would have been loathed by the 'groundlings', misunderstands what it was that people went to the theatre for. They wanted to be mesmerized and assaulted, teased and aggrieved, by language that drew attention to itself. Those wide-mouthed actors with their need for long words were a critical staple: 'your Poets take great paines to make your parts fit for your mouthes', says the cony-catching Ratsey to a group of strolling players, 'though you gape never so wide'; 'a wide-mouth'd *Poet*' writes Overbury [Webster?], 'speaks nothing but bladders and bumbaste'.[40]

A charge continually levelled at the theatre is that it is obsessed with 'bombast', preferring linguistic inflation to modest simplicity. 'Are not [plays'] Dialogues puft up with swelling wordes?' asks Crosse suspiciously; 'Let...Players, catch the eares of their Auditory and Spectators with faire bumbaste words, and set speeches', writes Cornwallis: 'It shalbe my course...to speake words that may be understood, and my power to meane wisely, rather then to speake eloquently.'[41] Words were there to be noticed, and it was the actor's job to find the noteworthy ones in his part. And word coining was associated not only with comic bathos, tragic bombast, or sheer thespian exhibitionism: Shakespeare imbued even the most taut tragic scenes with this kind of invention (as when he coined the word 'assassination' in *Macbeth*).

Perhaps this is why the very sound of the plays is so often mentioned, and mentioned as though it is in some way musical. Naturally this says a lot about the way an actor is rendering his text. There were fashions of writing and speaking that smacked of the playhouse, 'poeticall Play-house phrases, Clinches, and strong lines', ways so powerful that ministers of the church themselves might try to borrow them.[42] The experience of hearing well-written, clearly pronounced poetry on the stage is described as though a thing of sensuous and even demonic enthralment:

> Because the sweete numbers of *Poetrie* flowing in verse, do wonderfully tickle the hearers eares, the devill hath tyed this to most of our playes, that whatsoever he would have sticke fast to our soules, might slippe downe in suger by this intisement, for that which delighteth never troubleth our swallow.[43]

Anti-theatrical writings of the time feared that terrible subjects—'*Orestes* incest, *Cleopatres* crimes'—were being portrayed in '*eare-charming sense*', seducing the auditor beyond all due measure.[44] So, 'men come not to study at a Play-house, but love such expressions and passages, which with ease insinuate themselves into their capacities'.[45] The thrill of the word to playwright, actor, and audience is easy to forget: but in looking at parts, we need to get back to the primacy of scrupulously patterned words, of meanings weighted by rhythm as much as semantics, and of liquid variations in both prose and verse.

## Parts and Action

'One said a player had an idle imployment of it. O, you are mistaken, sayd another, for his whole life is nothing else but action.'[46] A player's 'work' *was* 'action' went the old joke—repeatedly.[47] But then 'action' was, held Demosthenes, the most important aspect of speaking, the chief part of an orator. Though action worked in tandem with pronunciation, setting up a counter-rhythm to the sound of the words, it also offered something more, something that a play when read could not give. What it could give at its best was variously described, but is often termed 'grace':

> A Play *read*, hath not half the pleasure of a Play *Acted*: for though it have the pleasure of *ingenious Speeches*; yet it wants the pleasure of *Gracefull action*: and

we may well acknowledg, that *Gracefulness* of *action*, is the greatest pleasure of a *Play*; seeing it is the greatest pleasure of (the Art of pleasure) *Rhetorick*.[48]

Like pronunciation, action was separately judged in its own right. Audiences were entranced by good action; actors could be applauded for their action even against the grain of the play. Action was something an actor could add, 'his' contribution to the words written by another. John Davies writes that if his friend Henry Butler were given a part to play on 'HONORS Stage', 'Thy *Wit* and *Courage* so that part would act | As ev'ry *Action* should be most exact. | *In few, thy many Parts well plaid by thee* | *Would gaine of most (at least) a* Plaudite'.[49] Because of this distinction between action and text, it was said that a good play could rescue an ill action ('New Playes and new Cloathes, many times help bad actions'), and that, similarly, bad actions could bring down a good text ('Had but thy severall plaies been managed | With skilfull actors, they had beene thy praise, | Where now they'r mention'd unto thy disgrace').[50] Yet action, too, had to be determined based on the words provided by the part—with, perhaps, some minimal stage-directions—and learned aside from the story to which it contributed.

What then constituted 'good' and 'bad' action, and how could an actor infuse appropriate 'action' into his severed script? The hand was extremely important.[51] That is clear when a new-made man is described as 'Out-acting famous *Roscius* with his hand' in order to 'Give passport to his phrase'; it brings us back to Hamlet's 'Sute the Action to the Word, the Word to the Action' (TLN 865–6) and 'Nor do not saw the Ayre too much your hand thus, but use all gently' (TLN 852–3) and to Titus's inability to do that because he has cut off a hand and, lacking it, is now unable to 'grace' his talk with proper gestures.[52] But regular significations for certain 'passions'—prescribed ways of doing anger, rage, grief, love—clearly extended beyond the hand to the face and body. When Othello gnaws his nether-lip (TLN 3290), when 'the *wanton* being wo-begon' is described as having 'deepe *sighes*' that 'pull in each panting *syde*', the entire body is manifesting the passions.[53] Perhaps the distinction is that the hand is 'gracing' particular words and phrases, while the body is more generally animating the emotional, passionate, or humorous content.

The audience's fascination with 'action' as movement is well demonstrated by the fact that English players built up an audience of foreign admirers who adored their performances despite being unable to understand English. On the Continent the acting of the English was acknowledged to exceed that of all others for reasons of gestural assurance and grace. When some 'cast dispised Stage players' went to Germany, the audience 'flocked wonderfully to see theire gesture and Action, rather then heare them, speaking English which they understoode not'; in Switzerland the response was yet more powerful: the people were enthralled and 'not understanding what they sayd, only for theire Action followed them with wonderfull Concourse, yea many young virgines fell in love with some of the players, and followed them from Citty to Citty, till the magistrates were forced to forbid them to play any more'.[54] A more measured response is provided by Horatio Busino, who went to the theatre in England on 8 December 1617, and was little moved by the experience, 'as I cannot understand a single word of English, though one may derive some little amusement from gazing on the sumptuous dresses of the actors and observing their gestures'.[55]

As the Swiss 'groupies' suggest, at least some of the players' 'action' was sexual; we might well envisage the actor combing his text for suggestive words to stress and manifest. It may well be that audience approval was most easily achieved through behaviour that enflamed desire; but we do not really know whether overtly sexual acting was exploited or despised by the more serious performers. Here, of course, is one of the difficulties of defining 'good' action: the same gestures can be variously described as wonderful or wanton, appropriate or scandalous. Predictably, almost all the evidence for sexually arousing acting is in the form of pejorative comment. Nevertheless, the repeated objections—that plays will turn the watchers into a tribe of adulterers, sodomites, masturbators—seems to witness to the same thing that made the virgins of Germany and Spain fall in love with the English players. 'These prophane and wanton stage playes or interludes', sighs Babington, 'what an occasion they are of adulterie and uncleanenesse, by gesture, by speech, by conveyances'; returning from the playhouse the audience is described as mentally 'infected' with the wicked passions they have just observed, 'so that … they play the Sodomits, or worse'; 'a lascivious … Play upon the *Stage,* … *not onely excites many adulterous filthy lusts, both in the Actors and Spectators; and drawes them on both to contemplative and actuall lewdnesse … but likewise instigates them to selfe-pollution, (a sinne for which Onan was destroyed)'.*[56] 'Bewitching vanities' is Lenton's description of the action of boys and their 'loose actions'; 'wantonizing Stage-gestures, can ingle and seduce men to heave up their heartes and affections', writes I.H.[57] Chettle even makes the dead Tarlton complain that these days players' 'gestures…are altogether wanton'.[58] It is difficult to determine precise social or semiotic practices from accounts composed from attitudes of such recoil and indignation. But as stylized as some parts of performance might have been, the sexual bits seem to have indeed been sexual: caressing, touching, kissing. This should be borne in mind when considering Othello and Desdemona, or Romeo and Juliet:

> [M]arke the madding and running to Theaters and Curtaines, daily and hourely, night and day, time and tyde, to see Playes and Enterludes. Where such wanton gestures, such dishonest speeches, such laughing and fleering, such lipping and kissing, such clipping and culling, such lustfull passions, such wincking and glancing of wonton eies and the like is used, as is wonderful and exceeding shamefull to behold.[59]

Inevitably, we cannot recover all such actions when looking at parts (though at times they are unequivocally called for). What we must be is meticulously alert to an individual part's prompts for action: in a part that, cues aside, excludes all others, there is nothing more fundamental for orientating the actor to a role's often quickly changing contexts. Such prompts are distributed throughout each part's speeches: however, as we will see in subsequent chapters, in anything but random fashion.

# 17

# Dramatic Prosody

## Introduction

The limitations of the part-script raise some very basic questions. How will the actor know what is going on around him? How will he know what he is responding to or working against? How will he know whom he is addressing at any one time? In other words, how can he escape a deadly situational vacuum? The semantic content of his speeches will obviously provide much essential contextual information; so too will his cues. But neither of these is sufficient for the actor confidently to place himself in an effectively unwritten world. Sometimes the part will have included stage-directions, or 'blocked' certain required movements. In the part of Orlando, for example, this happens during the 'mad' soliloquy, when the actor is required to perform various whimsical actions for which the speech alone does not prepare him. However, the very specific context of this speech—a big set-piece *tour de force* for the star actor Alleyn, alone up on the stage—makes such blocking more expected than it would be for regular dialogue. And certainly when transcribing all of the individual parts, the scribe could not possibly have added all of the 'to so and so' and 'aside' directions that pepper modern annotated texts: indeed, 'aside' did not come into common use as a stage-direction until considerably later. In the main, the actor had his cues and his speeches, and mapped his movements from them alone.

This meant that the playwright had to encode in the roll stylistic signs to direct and orientate his actors: among these are short lines, complete and incomplete pentameters, and shifts between prose, blank verse, and rhyme. All of these techniques help the actor to pace and measure the 'units' of his speech: they indicate a change in the tone or direction of acting; they single out transitions from one passion or humour to another, often within a single speech; and they direct stresses and enunciation, for instance by implicitly 'pointing' pauses. These are best thought of as aids or adjuncts to rhetoric, and as prompts to confident movement and embodiment. Above all, they make for a specifically *dramatic* prosody, in which shifts in the style or rhythm of the language indicate actable shifts in voice, gesture, or attitude. It is appropriate that the Latin term for the use of figures that shape syntax is *constructio*. As we shall see, in many ways each part's persona is built through them: prosody is less imitative than constitutive, allowing the actor to perceive, experience, and possess a 'reality' that is otherwise unknowable.

We are not of course claiming that such prosodic manipulations owe their existence to actors' parts. There is nothing more historical than poetic form, and a rich genealogy informs all these techniques. In pre-Shakespearean poetry, for instance, direct speech is always likely to involve interrupted rhythm. So a recurring device is the emotionally heightened 'list' of abrupt questions or expostulations, seen in works as formally different as Surrey's blank verse translation of Virgil, Marlowe's of Lucan, Spenser's rhyming *Shepheards Calendar*, and Sidney's sonnet sequence *Astrophil and Stella*. In all these works the line occasionally crams in multiple phrases, and 'regular' prosody defers to expressive immediacy. Nonetheless, what we *are* claiming is that working in parts—in particular, the combination of an elliptical script, private rehearsal, and ensemble performance—magnifies the importance and significance of such effects. It is the fact of missing explanations that forces imaginative engagement. What might in full text—because it doesn't beg questions, because the context is simply given—remain a measure mainly of how quickly or slowly to say the speech, becomes in part-text a cue for a tensely sensitive alertness to the options at hand.

It seems safe to assume that when Shakespeare considered prosodic questions, he always put practical results ahead of theoretical imperatives. It is difficult to believe, for instance, that Shakespeare could ever have worried himself, as did many prominent Elizabethan humanists, about trying to make his verse conform to a classical standard of prosodic 'quantity'—that is, dividing syllables according to their duration (long or short), rather than paying attention to their stresses (light or heavy).[1] The aural basis of performance, if nothing else, must have made Shakespeare's blank verse intuitively accentual. More than that, dramatic prosody requires a transformation of classical prosody's measuring of 'time' (*tempus*): for the dramatist and actor, what is important is the distribution of stresses, breath, and accompanying action in an embodied temporal space. Or again, the grammar books insist that the heart of good reading aloud is 'cleane sounding' and 'Dewe pausing', or in other words observing 'distinctions' between one unit of speech and another.[2] This is no less true for the actor. A pause means one thing in a silently internalized reading of a poem, and quite another in performance; time in a page-bound poem is abstract, hypothetical, or imaginatively reconstituted: in performance it is always spatial, always moving in three dimensions.

Shakespeare recognized this from the beginning. Certainly his narrative poems and sonnets are far more metrically predictable than any of his plays. The narrative poems, for instance, are as swift and immediate as any play could hope to be. But their pace is beholden throughout to a robustly consistent rhyming stanza (*ababcc* in *Venus*, *ababbcc* in *Lucrece*), in which the flow never wavers and in which every line finds point, finish, and momentum in its closing word. Just as these long poems (almost inevitably) eschew shifts between verse and prose, rhyme and unrhymed verse, and short and full lines, so do they essentially avoid 'space-making' midline pauses; even a two-part speech contained in a single line is usually turned into a flowing continuum by the simple device of a linking 'quoth she', or something similar ('She says "Tis so", they answer all "Tis so"' (*Venus and Adonis*, 851)). Shakespeare seems to have concluded early on that the potential in such effects lies dormant without physical bodies and physical space to enact them. It is *drama* that demands and refines Shakespeare's uses of shifts and pauses, drama that allows to such techniques the body and the room to rebound with consequence and reactivity.[3]

In exploring these techniques, we will generally try to avoid the technical language of metrical analysis (terms such as 'anapest', 'spondee', 'epic caesura'). This is not because such terms are misleading or imprecise. Nor is it because Shakespeare's actors were unlikely to use such terms (no doubt they used almost none of the terms we do). It is simply because this kind of masterful vocabulary can seem to encounter the verse effects as though in retrospect. It can remove us from the actor at the decisive moment of recognition, when he sees that 'something' of moment is happening in his text. We want to face the part-texts as though for the first time, as far as possible without presuppositions, and in layman's terms try to reconstruct, step by step, some of the things an actor might have noticed, and some of the expressive and performable consequences of such engagement.

First some brief words about a few things that are in the main *not* our primary subject, but that are indispensable tools for an actor. First and foremost is rhetoric. Classical rhetoric, as defined originally for public orators, had five parts: invention, arrangement, style, memory, delivery. Many rhetoricians in the early modern period tried to redefine rhetoric as an art primarily connected to writing rather than speaking, but drama powerfully retained—indeed replenished—the old classical values.[4] It is no coincidence that the five parts of rhetoric together encapsulate the basic progress 'through' an actor's part, first as constructed by the dramatist, then as appropriated by the actor. As plays were to be delivered rhetorically, so they were written for oral rhetorical delivery. Every actor was a trained rhetorician, irrespective of education, just as every part he received was an assemblage of tried and trusted rhetorical figures. He might look for two broad rhetorical forms: first, the many figures of speech that organized repetitions, symmetries, emphases, pauses, and antitheses; second, 'tropes' in which the words 'turn' from the customary to the novel (effects such as metaphor, metonym, simile, allegory, or the pun). It is easy enough to see how Shakespeare's actors grew to identify particular styles as specifically defining *their* type or character. They would be constantly looking out for repeated keywords or idiosyncratic phrases; for stately conceits or patches of lyricism; for ribald quibbles, latent puns, quizzical paradoxes; for quotations or misquotations, affectations, malapropisms, shifts in mode of address from 'thee' to 'you' and back—anything that might give edge, point, and shape to the role.

None of these effects *depends* upon working or thinking in terms of parts. But parts will always accentuate any rhetorical particulars (especially when configured in repeating or recurring formations), making them formidably expressive individuating tools. As we might expect with Shakespeare, rhetorical devices are far more than 'ornament' to an already existing part: a character is literally constituted by them, quite as much as by the part's metrical organization or the actor's speaking body. But because such linguistic features are generally humanistic rather than part-reliant, as well as easily studied in full text, they are not our primary subject. Nonetheless, rhetorical features visible in full text can have a very different effect (and can be read entirely differently) when seen on a part, and we will consider them when their presence seems to provide information specific to the actor, or when thinking in terms of parts adds something to their customary function.

Let us now sketch each of the main techniques of part-driven dramatic prosody: starting with prose/verse, and proceeding through couplets, broken lines, and short lines. First we will introduce each technique with a few typical examples; then we will look in more detail at how single parts can be mapped through various combinations of such instructions; and all the time we will be exploring a few interlinked questions. What kinds of expertise or expectations were being seeded in the actors? How did the writing satisfy or challenge them? What kinds of writerly innovations or expressive possibilities did these part-based techniques suggest to the playwright? And did the use or the usefulness of these techniques alter as Shakespeare's writing became technically more and more sophisticated?

## Verse/Prose

Of course, switches from prose to verse and back are occasionally found in other literary modes—witness the Book of Job, Sidney's *Arcadia*, *Jack and the Beanstalk*—but only in part-based drama are such shifts chiefly possessed by and definitive of a single, continuous, discrete character. This suggests a simple dramatic economy, an efficiency and transparency that any actor could quickly identify and use. So the switch from prose to verse or verse to prose as it occurs in an actor's part is like a visual stage-direction: it can be seen by the naked eye well before any attempt is made by the actor to learn the lines. The actor reading his part for the first time may well have noticed verse/prose switches before he took in anything else. Highly attuned to the allegorical 'meanings' of verse, prose, and the transition from one to the other, he would have had a repertoire of responses for sudden switches: tragic characters such as Othello, Lear, or Lady Macbeth tend to move into prose at moments of mental and social disintegration; comic characters such as Olivia or Beatrice move into verse when they fall in love. At its simplest, then, a verse/prose 'transition' might work as a quick crib to the mental development of the character in question.

Above and beyond its allegorical significance, prose allows the actor a differently tuned attentiveness to his own body. The actor will always feel that the prose arises in time with his own breathing and movement. This is not to say that prose dialogue necessarily resembles naturalistic conversation: simply that the words pan out more 'spaciously' in time. Generally lacking the elliptical syntax and concertinaed grammar of much of Shakespeare's verse, prose is much easier to absorb without strain. Similarly, freedom from the poetic line gives the actor more space for improvisation—not concerning the words spoken, but concerning their pace and rhythm. In particular, the prose-speaker can 'play' pauses with more freedom, dilating or suspending them for greater effect.[5] The audience is therefore usually 'with' the prose-speaker during any pause. As we shall see, in comic parts such as Portia, Beatrice, and Rosalind, the intimacy of prose channels the heroine's candour and confidence;[6] in tragic parts such as Lear, Othello, and Lady Macbeth, it embodies the character's base condition of rage, despair, and exposure. Either way, the mere *fact* of prose brings with it presumptions of confidentiality and a distinctively opened relationship to the audience. And in Shakespeare's hands this gift of confidence becomes immensely flexible.

In the part of Beatrice in *Much Ado About Nothing* everything is in prose, other than the single speech that marks her transition from disdain to love. Prose is, of course, aurally different—as well as visually different—from verse. Our quotation illustrates both; we do, however, use our own lineation rather than lineation that is shaped to the width of a Folio page (which we also illustrate through our use of slashes):

_____ [in] [the] message.
Yea just so much as you may take upon a knives/point, and choake a daw withall: you have no stomacke/signior, fare you well. *Exit.*
_____ [heare-say:] [now] begin,

*Enter Beatrice.*

_____ [some] [with] traps.
What fire is in mine eares? can this be true?
Stand I condemn'd for pride and scorne so much?
Contempt, farewell, and maiden pride, adew,
No glory lives behinde the backe of such.
And *Benedicke*, love on, I will requite thee,
Taming my wilde heart to thy loving hand:
If thou dost love, my kindenesse shall incite thee
To binde our loves up in a holy band.
For others say thou dost deserve, and I
Beleeve it better then reportingly.

(TLN 1075–1206)

In plot terms, Beatrice has exited throwing out scornful prose to Benedict, but has entered to overhear Hero, Margaret, and Ursula talk of

Benedict's love for her. But the actor playing Beatrice does not receive
this context on his part—although the cue (['some] [with] traps') may
well alert him to the fact that some trick is being played. Dividing his
part into transitions, the actor will be on the look-out for concomitant
changes in passion. Up until now, Beatrice has spoken a prose characterized by flinty dissidence and precision. Her verse, however, is not
a sophistication of that style of prose: it is something else entirely. So,
the first line betrays a struggle for prosodic definition: 'What fire is in
mine eares?' might be a prose question; the subsequent pause can stand
for Beatrice's (and perhaps the actor's) process of making a decision.
The immediately subsequent question—'can this be true'—resolves the
issue: the hope for clarity coincides with a perfect pentameter. From
this point on in the speech the pentameters flow with carefully conscious ease, while at the same time they fall into a regular rhyme scheme
(*ababcdcdee*, suggesting something like a foreshortened sonnet). The part
is *allowing* in rhymed verse just as the character is allowing in love; the
actor too must defer to the stylistic choice here committed to, pacing
the rhythms, observing the rhymes, and turning the 'holy band' of verse
into a powerfully observed, fulsomely performed ritual of passage.

Such switches from prose into verse invariably give the act of speaking
a new formality: the pace of delivery is prescribed and confined by the
strictures that the rhythm sets up. Often the shift in form accompanies a
symbiotic shift in content. There is a paired instance of this in the parts of
Jessica and her husband Lorenzo in *The Merchant of Venice*. The Jessica-part
has this:

Nay, you need not feare us *Lorenzo*, *Launcelet*/and I are out, he tells me flatly
there is no mercy for mee/in heaven, because I am a Jewes daughter: and hee
saies/you are no good member of the common wealth, for/in converting Jewes
to Christians, you raise the price of Porke.

——————————————————— [Lord] [*Bassiano's*] wife?
Past all expressing, it is very meete
The Lord *Bassanio* live an upright life
For having such a blessing in his Lady,
He findes the joyes of heaven heere on earth,
And if on earth he doe not meane it, [is
It] reason he should never come to heaven?
Why, if two gods should play some heavenly match,
And on the wager lay two earthly women,
And *Portia* one: there must be something else

Paund with the other, for the poore rude world
Hath not her fellow.

(TLN 1843–90; prose lineation ours)

And the Lorenzo-part this:

Yet more quarreling with occasion, wilt thou/shew the whole wealth of thy
wit in an instant; I pray/thee understand a plaine man in his plaine meaning:
goe/to thy fellowes, bid them cover the table, serve in the/meat, and we will
come in to dinner.
_____ [conceits] [shall] governe. *Exit Clowne.*
O deare discretion, how his words are suted,
The foole hath planted in his memory
An Armie of good words, and I doe know
A many fooles that stand in better place,
Garnisht like him, that for a tricksie word
Defie the matter: how cheer'st thou *Jessica,*
And now good sweet say thy opinion,
How dost thou like the Lord *Bassiano's* wife?

(TLN 1864–80; prose lineation ours)

Both of these parts are mainly in verse throughout: it is important to
recognize that the prose in this, their penultimate scene, is *not* inevitable
(Jessica speaks in verse to the clown's prose in her first scene). This
suggests that the fact of the prose—sustained long enough for Jessica
to have five prose speeches, Lorenzo six—might have been engineered
precisely so as to enable the subsequent switch back into verse shown
here. In both cases the prose, spoken in the presence of the clown, is
directly but humorously personalized, speaking respectively of Jessica's filial
and religious anxieties and Lorenzo's status-conscious impatience. The
verse of both, by contrast, distances the speaker from the subject (Portia
and Launcelot), whilst aspiring to formalize, almost canonize, sententious
generalizations about *other* people. There remain anxiously personal traces
in both speeches, but mainly sub-textually: the overwhelming effect of the
verse speeches is to suggest that the characters are worthy of a romantic
comedy, or more specifically of sharing in such a comedy's 'gentle'
denouements. In other words, the prose near each part's end is strategically
placed by Shakespeare: it is to be enjoyed by the actor, shared with the
audience—and then hastily left behind. The subsequent shift back into
verse thus helps bed down a feeling of new and earned possession: the
couple's satisfaction at having transcended origins, overcome obstacles, and

achieved completion. Equally, the studied formal obedience of the prosodic shift, with its hints of status anxiety, prepares for the couple's next and final appearance: their shared verse exchange, 'In such a night...', with its peculiar mix of shimmering moonlight and sworn deceit ('Stealing her love with many vowes of faith, | And nere a true one' (TLN 2428–9)). The actors may well experience in the reintroduced verse a relative straitening, a corseted kind of obedience. The anxiety to thus dress up in verse contributes to the tart aftertaste of this play's 'sweet winde' of an ending (TLN 2406).

Shakespeare plays differently with conventional expectations in the single shift from verse to prose in the part of Brutus in *Julius Caesar*. It is unusual for Shakespeare's dramatized public oratory to be in anything but blank verse. Yet in a play that is particularly dominated by blank verse, Brutus has a very public turn to prose. It occurs when he addresses the people of Rome, explaining Caesar's murder:

> Those that will heare me speake, let 'em stay heere;
> Those that will follow *Cassius*, go with him,
> And publike Reasons shall be rendred
> Of *Caesars* death.
> ————————————————— [is] [ascended:] Silence
> Be patient till the last.
> Romans, Country-men, and Lovers, heare mee for my/cause, and be silent, that you may heare. Beleeve me for/mine Honor, and have respect to mine Honor, that you/may beleeve. Censure me in your Wisedom, and awake/your Senses, that you may be the better Judge.

> (TLN 1534–47, prose lineation ours)

Brutus's verse is clear and commanding, admitting not the slightest hesitancy of address. However, set up by the portentous cue of 'Silence', the prose that follows is starkly different. The seemingly foreshortened pentameter line with which Brutus begins, 'Be patient till the last', is hardly propitious: for to whom is he speaking?[7] The actor may conclude that this is the nervous start of his public address; or that it is a brief aside, giving himself strength for the imminent ordeal; or, most likely, that Brutus is struggling to get the people's attention and to command the 'silence' that has nominally cued him. Whatever the answer, this is the context for his switch to prose. For the character it is a self-conscious choice for *performance*: Brutus here seeks to appropriate for his own purposes the mastery over a crowd presupposed by any prose-speaking actor.

However, everything that Brutus now says shows his struggle to find any such appropriately persuasive register. His stop–start rhythms are flanked by reiterated rebukes and pleas for respect: 'heare mee for my cause', 'be silent, that you may heare', 'Beleeve me for mine Honour, and have respect to mine Honour', 'Censure me in your Wisedom', 'awake your Senses'. But as much as he will see that his character's rhetorical hopes—for ease, flow, fulsomeness—are frustrated, the actor may still find for *himself* the channel of intimacy that the switch to prose will have led him to expect. If the character is still struggling for open access to his audience, the *actor* has it (the 'real' audience) in his palm. The switch to prose is thus as suggestive and exposing as ever: only what is exposed is just how vulnerable Brutus here is.

The role of Hamlet is unusual, in that it moves regularly between prose and verse, in pretty much equal measures, from the very start to very near the end. What he speaks depends fundamentally upon to whom he speaks. So, for most of the play Hamlet speaks in verse to himself and to his intimates (the Ghost, Horatio, and his mother), and in prose to everybody else (Claudius, Ophelia, Polonius, the players, Rosencrantz and Guildenstern, and Osric). The verse is usually intense and earnest, a speech of the heart that is often for and about himself; the prose is full of mercurial shifts between play-acting, aggression, instruction, and confession, being a more public discourse that is generally spoken for its effect upon others. The actor will notice a change, however, after the character's return from England. For the part has made a strategic shift into prose as its most quietly probing form of speaking; we see this throughout the conversation with Horatio and the grave-digger. By contrast, in the final act, Hamlet's verse becomes a mainly 'public' register. Consider the peculiarly burlesque verse of his outburst to Laertes in the grave and his subsequent 'apology'; the adventure story narration to Horatio of his actions on the boat; even his final speech, when he dies in the full glare of a chronicle-making audience—that is, moments when, if not play-acting, Hamlet is obtuse, abstracted, or removed from the access of others. Hamlet's prose becomes very different. In particular, it harnesses his 'late' movement between disgust, melancholy, and wise-eyed philosophic acceptance: in other words, the moments when he seems to 'come home' to himself—and to us—or at least to promise that he might.

Usually it will be the case that a particular dialogue is either in prose or in verse, but not always. Even in a fairly simple part like Jessica's in *Merchant* there is a scene—in fact, her first scene—in which her two verse speeches are separated by the Clown's prose. In this particular case the actor will experience no disjunction: Jessica has a short line, 'Farewell good *Lancelot*', which can be played as a 'prose' response to Lancelot's own lachrymose goodbye; only when he has left the stage does she begin her verse soliloquy ('Alacke, what heinous sinne is it in me ... ' (TLN 786–7)). But the juxtaposing of verse with prose is not always so straightforward.

For instance, in *Lear* (IV. vi) the mad King speaks *mainly* in prose, and the sane Gloucester *mainly* in verse: but neither is entirely prose or entirely verse, whilst neither is speaking in rhythmic concord with the other. These colliding or interpenetrating speech patterns are thus shaping a shared but emotionally profoundly discrepant moment. Here is part of that scene as it is presented in the Folio:

| | |
|---|---|
| GLOUCESTER. | O let me kisse that hand. |
| LEAR. | Let me wipe it first, |
| | It smelles of Mortality. |
| GLOUCESTER. | O ruin'd peece of Nature, this great world |
| | Shall so weare out to naught. |
| | Do'st thou know me? |
| LEAR. | I remember thine eyes well enough: dost thou/squiny at me? No, doe thy worst blinde Cupid, Ile not/love. Reade thou this challenge, marke but the penning/of it. |
| GLOUCESTER. | Were all thy Letters Sunnes, I could not see. |

(TLN 2574–84; prose lineation ours)

When analysing prose/verse patterns, it is usual to do so in context: one character's verse sets on or 'teaches' another. This is often true, and important. But there is another, different truth for the individual actor. As each part has its own unique pattern of prose and verse, when the actor learns the part away from the rest of the play, he will see and respond to 'his' context and 'his' transitions, not to any other. So the Gloucester-actor for the exchange above will probably identify his own speeches as in pentameter, albeit frequently foreshortened; he will almost certainly expect the cues he receives to be in the same basic metre—as they often seem to be:

_____ [money] [for] thee.
O let me kisse that hand.

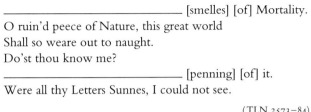

_____ [smelles] [of] Mortality.
O ruin'd peece of Nature, this great world
Shall so weare out to naught.
Do'st thou know me?
_____ [penning] [of] it.
Were all thy Letters Sunnes, I could not see.

(TLN 2573–84)

With their ambiguously addressed exclamations and pleading half-lines, the Gloucester-actor's speeches are already somewhat unstable. He might well have hoped for some rhythmic ballast from his partner in dialogue—a hope echoed in Gloucester's sudden switch out of elegiac verse-form into the heart-breaking directness of 'Do'st thou know me?' But the rhythmic pattern of Gloucester's speeches is in fact not remotely replicated in Lear's: the King speaks prose. So as much as the Gloucester-actor may try to 'hand on' or 'receive' a verbal pattern from his interlocutor, he will find that he is alone in his elegy, repeatedly unnerved and wrong-footed by the spasmodic 'anti-rhythms' of the King.

One final, more practical note on prose and verse. In Shakespeare's earlier plays, what is prose and what is verse is usually obvious. But as we see in this brief passage from _Lear_, this is not the case from mid-career on. The verbal or prosodic patterning in Shakespeare's later works is often experimental, hybridized, privileging dramatic considerations over clear stylistic taxonomies. Quartos and Folios confound the problem. In any play not printed in page order (seriatim), but in the order in which it will be bound (by formes), page layout may be shaped by printing-house contingencies. Passages of verse may be split to swell an underfilled page, for instance; alternatively, when a page is too full, they may be set as prose to save space. For our purposes, like editors (or perhaps early modern actors), we have had to make choices about whether lines are in verse or prose, and whether a split line is really a split pentameter—or one created by the printing-house. We will indicate when our choices are shaping the way we represent the text; some of our choices will of necessity be questionable as a result. But, like prompters or scribes in a busy early modern playhouse, we are trying to write parts—and to make 'part' sense—out of confusing and contradictory full texts. And, also like prompters, though we may make some mistakes, we will also highlight or draw attention to moments that have been missed when examining complete plays in full.

# Rhyme

The above example of the Beatrice-part's sole shift from prose to rhymed verse (*ababcdcdee*) illustrates how rhyme can help to signify actable transitions of emotion. This is particularly true of the far more common rhyming couplet—and not only because it is always a useful aid when memorizing lines. The most common location for a couplet is at the end of a speech, and in particular at the end of a soliloquy (such as Beatrice's). Examples are so numerous as to be unnecessary: such couplets always signify the snap of closure and a brisk passing of the baton to the next speaker. Of course the closing couplet in a soliloquy is still spoken *solus* to the audience. But it also very explicitly marks a movement from monologue back into dialogue—either because the scene is ending and the player needs to get off-stage, or because another player is entering. Either way, the soliloquy couplet is invariably accompanied by a movement of body and focus.

This very basic function of the couplet segues into its more sophisticated uses. First there is the couplet that ends an otherwise blank-verse piece of dialogue. These couplets will obviously help the actor to accentuate the fact that the speech is reaching a climax. In such cases the actor cued by the couplet will doubtless appreciate being alerted—by the distinctive rhythms and stresses of his interlocutor's couplet—to the fact that his cue to respond is coming. Equally, the rhythmic crescendo will reinforce the sense that the gauntlet has now been thrown: now it is for the addressee to rise to the moment's challenge (of honour, love, debate, or whatever). Usually such couplet-closed speeches are fairly lengthy, and take their place in a medley of similarly measured orations. It is a technique mainly limited to early Shakespeare. A classic instance is the first scene of *Richard II*. The part of Mowbray in this scene has seven speeches: the five most substantial are capped by couplets (one shared with the part of Richard); two of them also begin by completing a couplet started by Richard. Whatever the character is articulating with his rhyming words—in Mowbray's case variations upon honourable indignation or resolve—for the actor the rhymes are smoothly paved bridges to his addressor or from his addressee.[8]

We find a still more confident version of this expectant dependency when the dialogue shared between two or more actors is entirely in rhyme (exemplified by the lovers' parts in *A Midsummer Night's Dream*). Obviously the actor will see that his own speeches are in rhyme; any rhyming cues will tell him that his addressor's speeches are as well. The following exchange from *The Comedy of Errors* shows how seamlessly the part-texts even of multiple roles can accommodate the technique:

| | |
|---|---|
| ADRIANA. | Who is that at the doore yt keeps **all this noise?** |
| SYRACUSE DROMIO. | By my troth your towne is troubled with **unruly boies.** |
| EPHESUS ANTIPHOLUS. | Are you there Wife? You might have **come before.** |
| ADRIANA. | Your wife sir knave? Go get you **from the dore.** |
| EPHESUS DROMIO. | If you went in paine Master, this knave **wold goe sore.** |
| ANGELO. | Here is neither cheere sir, nor welcome, we would **faine have either.** |
| BALTHAZAR. | In debating which was best, wee shall **part with neither.** |
| EPHESUS DROMIO. | They stand at the doore, Master, bid them **welcome hither.** |
| EPHESUS ANTIPHOLUS. | There is something in the winde, that we **cannot get in.** |
| EPHESUS DROMIO. | You would say so Master, if your **garments were thin.** |

(TLN 708–24)

And so it goes for another fifteen rhymes. Or here is an example from the early scene of courtship in *Romeo and Juliet*; in full script the passage goes:

| | |
|---|---|
| JULIET. | Saints do not move, |
| | Though grant for prayers sake. |
| ROMEO. | Then move not while my prayers effect I take: |
| | Thus from my lips, by thine my sin is purg'd. |
| JULIET. | Then have my lips the sin that they have tooke. |
| ROMEO. | Sin from my lips? O trespasse sweetly urg'd: |
| | Give me my sin again. |
| JULIET. | You kisse by th'booke. |

(TLN 684–90)

Let us look at the actors' parts for this exchange. Romeo's part would have been something like this (with the rhyme words in bold):

————————————————— [for] [prayers] **sake.**
Then move not while my prayers effect I **take:**
Thus from my lips, by thine my sin is **purg'd.**
————————————————— [they] [have] **tooke.**
Sin from my lips? O trespasse sweetly **urg'd:**
Give me my sin again.

Juliet's would have looked like this (rhymes again in bold):

> Saints do not move,
> Though grant for prayers sake.
> _____ [sin] [is] purg'd.
> Then have my lips the sin that they have **tooke**.
> _____ [my] [sin] again
> You kisse by th'**booke**.

As the rhyme words indicate, the Romeo-actor will be certain that the scene is one of co-operative rhyming, because he has a cue ('prayer's sake') with which he immediately rhymes ('I take'). The Juliet-actor might *suspect* the same, seeing that he is given rhyming words ('tooke'/'booke') that get carried over Romeo's lines—but he has not been given nearly such clear information as the Romeo-actor. The part-script thus allows for a mingling of effects in performance. At least one of the actors will hope or anticipate that their characters are in sync: this hope will correspond to erotic excitement. The other might be more diffident: this corresponds to bubbling nervousness. When the parts do indeed fit serendipitously together in performance, as one part 'meets' another, the actors can share in the delight of satisfied expectations.

To the actor playing Romeo, this fragment is also full of prompts for action (which may have been flanked, in the actor's part, by stage-directions). Whether before, after, or during 'Thus from my lips', he must clearly kiss Juliet; in the pause after the line 'Give me my sin again', he must kiss her once more. Juliet's part, meanwhile, contains different information. Unless a stage-direction alerted the player to the kisses to come, 'Juliet' could suspect only *one* of the kisses (from her ensuing lines, 'You kisse by th'booke')—and would not know quite when it was going to come. As it happens, Romeo kisses Juliet while she is trying to complete their shared pentameter; perhaps the kisses are hurried, because the verse must go on; perhaps the rhymes are delayed, because the kisses must go on. Either way, the competing calls of compulsion and obedience—from the discrete part-scripts, from the shared rhymes and pentameters, and of course from the shared passion—make pretty much any decision a delightful one, in which fumbling cross-purposes are as appropriate as choreographed harmony.

These uses of the rhyming couplet all emphasize its coincidence with the speaking cue, and so its overt connection with other players. However, the couplet also has the capacity to be used for precisely the opposite effect—the movement *away* from others into privacy or inwardness. This potential is again inherent in the rhyming couplet's usual positioning at the end of a speech. For whilst a cue moves forward in time, from one player to the next, the second line in a couplet must also partly move backward in time, linking retrospectively with the previous line to form its own rival semantic/stylistic unit. This enables the couplet's powerful capability to be at once a cue—reaching to another—and a barrier, as the simultaneous loop back into one's own speech mentally screens off the 'rhymer' from the addressee.

The part of Hamlet—indeed, the character of Hamlet—exploits just this potential in his very first multi-line speech:

> Seemes Madam? Nay, it is: I know not Seemes:
> 'Tis not alone my Inky Cloake (good Mother)
> Nor Customary suites of solemne Blacke,
> … These indeed Seeme,
> For they are actions that a man might play:
> But I have that Within, which passeth show;
> These, but the Trappings, and the Suites of woe.
>                                              (TLN 257–67)

The entire speech is about the self-conscious performing of emotion: thus we are asked to assume that Hamlet brings to his speech the vocational awareness of an actor. No less than his actor, then, Hamlet *chooses* to speak the rhyme, out loud, to his mother. The technique's usual function on the stage is as a lubricant of conversation—a fact that Hamlet uses with taunting satirical intent. He is mocking any such glib social connectivity. In doing so, however, he also picks up on the couplet's debts to soliloquy, and thus its affinities with intense self-address. Consequently, in seeming to move 'out' to its addressee, the couplet simultaneously moves 'in' to Hamlet's inexpressible interior. This accords with what the actor (a mere four lines into the part) already knows: that this is a character who is *always* looking for occasions when publicly spoken words might peel off into asides, or into inhospitable implications whose import is partly for the nominal addressee and partly for himself ('A little more then kin, and lesse then kinde' (TLN 245); 'Not so my Lord, I am too much i'th' Sun' (TLN 246); 'I Madam, it is common' (TLN 254)). In a sense, then, we find in the tartly evasive couplet the part's very first soliloquy, albeit a frustrated and attenuated one.

Rhyming couplets can be especially suggestive for an actor when they are rare. An example of this is the part of Coriolanus, which features only two switches into rhyming couplets. Both are unprompted and unanswered couplets, occurring in between two intensely interlocutory passages. As such, they represent to the actor one thing above all: self-address. Thus it is no coincidence that these couplets come at perhaps the character's two moments of greatest emotional strain, corresponding to his rare moments of rhetorical equivocation. The first is when he is forced to humble his 'voice' to the citizens' voices. This immediately (and tellingly) succeeds the part's first use of prose. So he speaks in prose to the citizens, bids them farewell, and then, left for a moment alone, lurches almost viciously into rhyme:

> ———————————————————— [joy] [Sir] heartily.
> Most sweet Voyces:
> Better it is to dye, better to sterve,
> Then crave the higher, which first we do deserve.
> Why in this Woolvish tongue should I stand heere,
> To begge of Hob and Dicke, that does appeere
> Their needlesse Vouches: Custome calls me too't.
> What Custome wills in all things, should we doo't?
> The Dust on antique Time would lye unswept,
> And mountainous Error be too highly heapt,
> For Truth to o're-peere. Rather then foole it so,
> Let the high Office and the Honor go
> To one that would doe thus. I am halfe through,
> The one part suffered, the other will I doe.

> (TLN 1502–15)

The rhymes are anything but settled, peaceful, and closed; most of the rhymes do not finish the sentence, which instead rumbles on for a further dyspeptic half-line ('their needlesse Vouches', 'For Truth to o're-peere', 'To one that would doe thus'). This character is not one to be sated or appeased by harmonious verse-forms. He at once observes a rhyme and confutes its finality; any hints of triteness or accommodation in his speech are skewered by a profoundly obstinate contempt. But if this is what the verse-form suggests about the character, it is an attitude of which the actor is fully apprised and capable. The actor can three times recognize a kind of contingent sentence within the sentence: each time this 'secret sentence' embodies defiance and disdain, it girds him for unpleasant necessities, but never quite appeases his incorrigible edginess and scorn. Nevertheless, the actor still has to observe the rhymes, each of which achieves a perfectly satisfactory finality. The succeeding half-lines occupy their own pocket of auditory space-time, and can be played as poignantly or bitterly as the actor likes; the prosody is at once highly sophisticated, psychologically apt, and transparently actable.

The part's second use of couplets is when Coriolanus is struggling to respond to the supplications of his mother, wife, and son, as they kneel and plead before him. Here is the part in full from the moment he prepares to hear their request until his eventual capitulation:

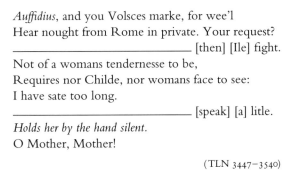

> *Auffidius*, and you Volsces marke, for wee'l
> Hear nought from Rome in private. Your request?
> —————————————————— [then] [Ile] fight.
> Not of a womans tendernesse to be,
> Requires nor Childe, nor womans face to see:
> I have sate too long.
> —————————————————— [speak] [a] litle.
> *Holds her by the hand silent.*
> O Mother, Mother!

(TLN 3447–3540)

For all of the intervening speeches' inordinate length—one speech of thirty lines, another of fifty, each of them packed with unanswered questions and untaken invitations to speak—it seems clear that Shakespeare writes the part to 'ensure' the actor, as best he can, against alienation or uncertainty. 'I have sate too long' is self-explanatory; so too the stage-direction (if transcribed on to the part); meanwhile the cue-phrase, if it is indeed 'speak a litle', reinforces the atmosphere—experienced by Coriolanus alone—of barely endurable discursive delicacy. In being forewarned of this silence, and subsequently in being able to control its duration after he has finally been cued, power returns to the Coriolanus-actor (an effect reinforced by the situational fulsomeness of his eventual words, 'O Mother, Mother! | What have you done?', which gives the actor the fullest possible possession of his character's sudden vulnerability).

It is the rhyming couplet that inaugurates this unwonted, thoroughly interiorized intimacy. Coriolanus doesn't want to be caught crying; but equally, he doesn't want anyone to hear him admitting that he might be thus caught: the couplets, that is, represent furtive self-address. In full text, the fact that his wife and son have just now added to his mother's pleas makes his imminent breakdown entirely explicable; all the more so when the theme of both is his son, 'this boy' who will 'keepe your name living to time' (TLN 3482). But the Coriolanus-actor does not have these words on his part; he receives only the seemingly adversarial defiance of 'then Ile fight' (TLN 3484). This is the context of the couplets, and the reason why his sentiment *had* to be couched in the prosodic form best suited to 'public' privacy: to ensure that the actor knows how intimate is this assault upon his character's very grounds of being.

## Short Speech Units (Short Lines, Midline Switches)

A crucial question when conning the part is how to 'point' each line or sentence. As we have shown, punctuation on parts is likely to have been sparse: the actor could not take his lead from it. Yet, wrongly pointed, an important speech would not make sense. The challenge is particularly acute when learning verse. The standard iambic pentameter was the actor's guiding measure. So the Lord Chamberlain's actors in the 1590s would have been taught to expect a basic congruence of thought to line; such metrical conventions make any 'deviations' stand out as clearly actable. Two more such deviations are the 'short' line of verse (a line that has less than five feet) and the 'broken' line of verse (a line that has one or more clear 'midline shifts' between one speech unit and another). Both are of paramount importance for the actor working from parts.

The usual explanation for the proliferation of short clauses or speech units in the drama is that they are realistic: short sentences are used in daily discourse; many questions, orders, and exclamations take only a few syllables to be said. However, although true as far as it goes, this explanation is inadequate. Verisimilitude is part of it, but no less important is basic dramaturgy. For the stopped, broken, or attenuated line in a verse passage is *never* defined only by its referential content. Such short speech units are always prompts for action. A rule of thumb can be identified whereby any 'missing' stress or syllable in the actor's iambic line implies a pause of roughly equal length. They invite the speaking actor to fill this space—a gap of one, two, three, four iambs—with some appropriate movement: perhaps of the whole body; perhaps merely a flicker of eye. Very often short lines also invite movement from other players. Actors today are perhaps unevenly aware of such 'pause prompts':[9] Shakespeare's actors could not afford to be. The early modern theatre's reliance upon actor's parts makes short and 'stopped' lines alive with implied—but indispensable—action.

## Short lines

Here is an example from the part of Desdemona's father, Brabantio, in *Othello*. It is the passage in which he responds to Desdemona's confession of love for Othello:

> God be with you: I have done.
> Please it your Grace, on to the State Affaires;
> I had rather to adopt a Child, then get it.
> Come hither Moore;
> I here do give thee that with all my heart,
> Which but thou hast already, with all my heart
> I would keepe from thee. For your sake (Jewell)
> I am glad at soule, I have no other Child;
> For thy escape would teach me Tirranie
> To hang clogges on them. I have done my Lord.
>
> (TLN 536–45)

The speech is packed with metrical and tonal variations, rhetorical stops and starts, and at least six or seven switches of address. But the very first thing the actor will see is almost certainly the stark two-iamb command in the speech's middle: 'Come hither Moore'. It is this graphic contrast with all that surrounds it—the sudden shrinking of the line—which tells the actor that physical consequences *must* follow. Brabantio is about to give away his daughter; for the character this means everything. The 'missing' half-line is thus the place to perform all that is at stake. First he will direct 'Othello' where to go, perhaps with a curt nod or finger. But the decisive movement, and the decisive acting, is all in Brabantio's emotions. Accordingly, the actor, reading ahead in the part so as to give content to this fearful gap, will fasten upon the pathetic repetition—'with all my heart'—that ends successive lines. The effect of the repetition is to split the erstwhile cliché in two, and thus to transform metaphor into literalism: he is performing a genuine act of heart loss, even mutilation. The ensuing marriage will indeed end him. Whatever particular mime he chooses, it should convey bitter and comprehensive desolation.

A similar effect is seen in this speech of Gloucester in *Lear*:

> _____ [Wherefore] [to] Dover?
> Because I would not see thy cruell Nailes
> Plucke out his poore old eyes: nor thy fierce Sister,
> In his Annointed flesh, sticke boarish phangs.
> The Sea, with such a storme as his bare head,
> In Hell-blacke-night indur'd, would have buoy'd up
> And quench'd the Stelled fires:
> Yet poore old heart, he holpe the Heavens to raine.

> (TLN 2127–34)

'And quench'd the Stelled fires' is a line of just three iambs, flanked by full pentameter lines above and below. The actor will clearly identify an invitation to pause, and probably to do so for roughly two iambs. But why? Is Gloucester supposed to 'do' something? Is another actor about to enter or intervene? The other actors, of course, can say nothing: the short line is cueing no one. If they cannot speak, what can they do? What *should* they do? The same questions, meanwhile, must be asked by the Gloucester-actor of his own performance. Here, obviously, is where he 'populates' the implied pause by resort to the surrounding context of the speech. As it happens, he has a number of choices: he might identify a cue to weep in the speech's invoking of 'poore old eyes', salt water ('The Sea'), and rain; alternatively, he may see the 'cruell Nailes' and 'boarish phangs' as cues to brandish his fists to the skies in impotent revenge. The options confronting the actor are neatly encapsulated in the short line itself: the teary 'quench'd' against the raging 'fires'. Of course, he might consolidate the implied directions and play both emotions simultaneously, taking into his own body the turbulence of a mutinous world.[10] Whatever the actor's decision, it will immediately provoke reaction from the watching Regan and Cornwall. Short lines such as these here regularly produce just such an effect: heightened expectation, worried attentiveness, momentary uncertainty, potentially experienced by *everyone*, on-stage and off-stage.

One final note about short lines, reprising a topic discussed in the Cues part of the book: as we have seen, many cue-lines are short lines. An actor working from parts will always identify a speech's closing line as a hinge between one mind or motion and another: a point of switching and transition, often of opposition and tension, usually of concentrated reaction. When this hinge-line is also a half-line—itself a sign that the lines act upon, reach for, or invite in other actors—the actors will be doubly alert to the imminence of such reactivity. The two instruments—cue and short line—here help to define each other's format and functions. So, the non-cueing short line will accrue some of its potential from the purpose of the cue: we can imagine the mid-speech short line as a 'false' or 'secreted' cue, prompting action but forbidding speech. Conversely, the clear dramatic potential of abbreviated lines almost certainly prompted their increasingly frequent use as cueing lines. For the conjunction of the short line with the cue intensifies the knowledge that someone—or something—is about to intrude.

## Midline switches

Another frequent and fundamental example of prosodic deviation is when syntactically there is a switch from one unit of speech to another in the middle of a line. Often a single speech or dialogue enacts one overall function (a debate, a proclamation, a soliloquy), whilst internally it is constituted of numerous smaller units or utterances. These small units may be made out of shifts of address from one party to another—including the shift between addressing others and an 'aside' to oneself—or, if the addressee remains the same, decisive shifts in tone. In such circumstances, the actor's pointing is all-important.

Here, for example, are two switches from the start of the Prince's part in *Romeo and Juliet*: one, where it might have been looked for, at the end of a line; one, slightly less expected, midline. The Prince enters to find apprentices and noblemen of the houses of Montague and Capulet alike with their weapons drawn:

> Rebellious Subjects, Enemies to peace,
> Prophaners of this Neighbor-stained Steele, [SHIFT]
> Will they not heare? [SHIFT] What hoe, you Men, you Beasts ...
> (TLN 83–5)

The actor learning this will see that the Prince's first impulse is to give a public speech: a formal, high-handed address to the fighters. But he only manages this for two lines. The third line, 'Will they not heare?' is addressed in exasperation to some other party: probably someone in his train, possibly himself, possibly the audience (an editor's added 'aside' would ruin this moment: 'aside'—to whom?). Clearly the actor will have to change tone when, having completed one line with 'Steele', he begins the next with 'Will'. As usual, the actor has choices: for a start, does he interpret the line as a question (as here in the Folio) or an exclamation? If it is a question, then who is it asked of? Perhaps, recognizing that no one is listening, his oratorical voice simply fades away into puzzled self-questioning; perhaps it becomes louder and angrier as he shouts the effectively rhetorical question over the oblivious combatants. The speaker's choices are made clear by the second half of the line: 'What hoe, you Men, you Beasts'. Here the direction of address—to the crowd—is unequivocal, as is its tone of escalating exasperation and rage, suggested by the fact that even this half-line contains three gradations, three distinct mini-speech units—what hoe!//you Men!//you Beasts!—in which the Prince tries to tame, name, and judge his 'Rebellious Subjects'. And whatever decision he makes will in turn produce effects in the other players on-stage—they must decide whether they are flagrantly ignoring authority, or recklessly ignorant of it.

In other words, the entire line—the opening half-line outcry, the subsequent half-line with its triple units of failed address, and the potential for 'action pauses' in between each one of these four distinct locutions—is a sequence of practical action cues for *all* of the players on-stage. Any unexpected or a-metrical shifts in a line always carry this kind of expressive potential. They are always moments, not so much for taking stock, as for instantaneously sizing things up: what is imminent, or appropriate, or unavoidable right *now*? As we can see in the Prince's speech, the shifts within the line are often competitive rather than shared; they open up various rival focuses and alternative orders, which may work against each other as well as against any residual 'order' enshrined in conventional metrical form. In this sense syntax *is* semantics: it signifies changes in meaning, mood, or movement.

This example, furthermore suggests, how we have to resist always as-sociating a line of iambic pentameter with evenly flowing, swiftly paced, carefully spoken delivery. Shakespeare's actors, working from parts, eager to 'magnify' flat-scripted lines into multi-dimensional action, were always on the look-out for the implicit space that an apparently fleeting ellipsis might present. Like the hiatus that follows an 'incomplete' pentameter, any such shift within a line can elicit intervening action, which may in turn delay the

line's completion. A striking instance of this actable dynamism, compacted
into a pentameter, is when *Lear*'s Gloucester loses his first eye: 'Give me
some helpe.——O cruell! O you Gods' (TLN 2142). The Folio punctuation we have here transcribed ('——') tries to emphasize an unusually
significant midline shift (in the Quarto this moment is marked—almost
more terribly—by the banal neutrality of a comma). However, there are
also other shifts in the single line. Two of them are signified by the manifest
grammar: one after 'helpe', another after 'cruell'. Gloucester's eye might
be removed in the pause after one of these words ('inside' the pentameter,
and thus swiftly), or at the end of the line; or, if the torture is particularly
cruel or ham-fisted, the violation might have been going on throughout
and beyond the line. It is of course possible that Cornwall's part specifically
cued the removal of Gloucester's eye at a certain word; or he might have
felt free to choose his moment within the line, toying with the actor playing
Gloucester. (Either way the eye must be 'out' by Regan's ensuing line:
'One side will mocke another: Th' other too' (TLN 2143).) If the verse
overrides the action, then that suggests something practical (the removal of
the eye must be relatively swift). Alternatively, the broken metrics of the
line may well encourage the actor to exploit more than two grammatically
inscribed breaks. He might see potentially *five* different units of speech
inside the single line:

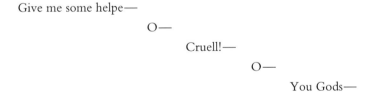

The actor will know the simple plenitude—of emotion, sound, time—that
a single 'O' can contain (as we saw with repeated cues). Here too this
brief plangent symbol may invite and allow considerable duration: and
certainly no one can interrupt Gloucester in his pentameter of anguish.
There is thus more than enough space here fully to allow the most vicious
on-stage act of Shakespeare's career—and yet for both actor and auditors
to retain an awareness, or a memory, of metrical observance. Any audience
can at once *see* the interruption and 'hear' the (eventually) completed line:
conventional prosody becomes a mocking allegory of false obedience, and
of governing orders sustained through scandalous violence.

As we see with both short lines and broken verse-lines, the rhythmic obligations of iambic pentameter give Shakespearean speech much of its existential edge: the feel of living people pressed by circumstances, seeking freedom or seizing space where neither is easily given. Equally, it keeps the actors on guard, alive to occasion and opportunity: not coming upon responses in easy complacency, or noting from a safe distance every moment of sudden transition or ratcheted-up intensity. Shakespeare wants his actors to grab their moments, almost to fight for them, with urgency and immediacy. In fracturing the form—sometimes loosening it, sometimes contracting it—these techniques allow dramatic verse to embody an experience that is always open to accident or surprise, always prone to be interrupted or challenged by the fact of other minds and bodies. Writing in parts thus helps to produce 'play' that, for the actors, resembles a taut game of sport, alive with sudden decision, with spotted opportunities and momentary wagers; for the characters, it produces experience continually defined by contingency, probation, and risk.

# 18

## Prosodic Switches:
## Pauses, Prompts, and
## Soliloquies

In this chapter we will continue to explore how Shakespeare uses prosodic shifts to help his actors calibrate their performances. But we will also move from this to suggest how this basic tool of working in parts—the short line or midline 'volta'—becomes a profound influence upon Shakespeare's writing: in particular, his development of ever more situationally layered, experientially pregnant verse, and the capability of this verse to suggest subjective and inter-subjective presence.

### Romeo and Juliet

There were of course fairly conventional, programmatic, typological uses to which Shakespeare put his prosodic shifts. Abrupt midline switches, for instance, are occasionally used as a particular 'type's' stylistic calling-card. Old Capulet in *Romeo and Juliet* is an example of such a type—the irascible and peremptory old man. Hence the little details that define his speeches: in particular, crabbed repetitions (' 'tis gone, 'tis gone, 'tis gone' (TLN 594); 'go too, go too' (TLN 659); 'more light, more light' (TLN 664); ' 'tis not so much, 'tis not so much' (TLN 606); 'How now? | How now?' (TLN 2190–1); 'take me with you, take me with you wife' (TLN 2181); 'I thanke you: and I thanke you not' (TLN 2192)) and blustering imperatives ('Give me my long Sword' (TLN 73); 'My Sword I say' (TLN 75); 'give roome' (TLN 596); 'Ile make you quiet' (TLN 665); 'hold your tongue' (TLN 2213)). Apart from one ingratiating speech of rhyming couplets (spoken in mollifying tones to his prospective son-in-law, Paris),

the Capulet-part is dominated by short phrases and abrupt switches. This
is typical:

> Well said my hearts, you are a Princox, goe,
> Be quiet, or more light, more light for shame,
> Ile make you quiet. What, chearely my hearts.
>
> (TLN 663–5)

Clearly a series of different people are here being addressed. Learning the
part in isolation, perhaps the actor will not know quite to whom he is
talking, or perhaps he is given a stage-direction supplying extra information.
Either way, the actor also has to make sense of the passage on-stage. So
in performance he may simply move his gaze around, addressing different
directions to different people; ideally, he will perform something like this,
his reasoning being supplied in italics:

> *Plural: to some guests?* Well said my hearts—*Singular: to Tybalt?*—you are a
> Princox, goe,
> Be quiet, or—*to a servant/some servants*—more light, more light for shame,
> *to Tybalt?*—Ile make you quiet. *To anyone*—What—*to some guests*—chearely
> my hearts.

The broken verse-line (broken here by discrete units of speech rather than
by punctuation) is a simple and efficient way of instructing actors about
the nature of the character. This is a part full of distinctive idiosyncrasies:
its verse is very close to prose, dotted with pauses, eschewing rhythmic
flow in favour of sudden stops, angry repetitions, and abrupt switches.
From the very start, its heavy caesuras—which the performer will pick
up on only when learning the part—provide space for a player to move
violently between obsessions ('How now? | How now? Chopt Logicke?
what is this?' (TLN 2190–1) or from one preoccupation and one addressee
to another ('Speake not, reply not, do not answere me. | My fingers
itch, wife…' (TLN 2205–6)). Capulet's highly individual metrics, his
midline irruptions and abruptions, often solicit no response whatsoever:
they reflect or create only Capulet's oblivious distemper.

Another conventional use of abrupt phrases or midline switches is to
indicate histrionic grief, distraction, or lamentation—seen at appropriate
points in the parts of both Romeo and, as we see here, Juliet:

> All this is comfort, [SWITCH] wherefore weepe I then? [SWITCH]
> Some words there was worser then *Tybalts* death

> That murdered me, [SWITCH] I would forget it feine, [SWITCH]
> But oh, it presses to my memory...
> *Romeo* is banished [SWITCH] to speake that word,
> Is Father, Mother, *Tybalt, Romeo, Juliet,*
> All slaine, all dead: [SWITCH] *Romeo* is banished...
>
> (TLN 1761–78)

Effectively, this kind of writing gives the actor a clearly performable transition into grief; both the prosody and the ensuing action follow established forms. Even in generic or short parts, we regularly find broken lines 'pointing' the violent caprice of passion. Metrical irregularity is an immediate allegory for distraction or volatility: theme and actability are equally served. So Lady Percy in *2 Henry IV* has a single scene only, consisting of two speeches, but peppered with over ten decisive midline breaks; here is a taste:

> He was the Marke, and Glasse, Coppy, and Booke,
> That fashion'd others. And him, O wondrous! him,
> O Miracle of Men! Him did you leave
> (Second to none) un-seconded by you.
>
> (TLN 989–92)

The breaks and stops suggest a programmatic, declamatory style of performing grief; this is in line with the more generic style of writing, fitted to broad types (here the lamenting spouse) rather than crafted for a more individuated part.

A variation upon this is Shakespeare's equally regular use of sinuous, irregular prosody for 'reporter' or 'narrator' parts. Shakespeare's plays contain many parts that have no real personality or distinctiveness, and that carry little narrative interest in or for themselves. Such parts are particularly crucial to the history plays, in which vast historical actions, large armies, swiftly switching fortunes, and the like have to be concentrated into stageable compass. The challenge for the playwright is to make such story-telling passages succinct, compelling, and swift. One of the main techniques that Shakespeare uses for this is to vary the point at which his sentences end, sometimes end-stopping them, sometimes dotting them with midline pauses. The midline caesura, as always, tends to be emphatic, to herald a shift in argument or location, or offer a quick qualification or modification of what comes before. For example, fractured metrics point the basically anonymous part of Lord Bardolph (not Bardolph of the fiery nose) in *2 Henry IV*, whose role, though little more than an evolving mouthpiece for the changing fortunes of the rebels, thereby brings in the listening spectators. Another example is Rumour in *2 Henry IV*, whose opening forty-line speech has eight midline stops—in meaning rather than/as well as punctuation—an extraordinary ratio for 1590s Shakespeare; a further example is the Chorus in *Henry V*. In each such part the stops are a sign for the actor to 'open out'—to prick up his ears, feel the physical presences, renew his alertness to context. However, this opening out is not to the character himself, nor to other characters: the technique's usual energies are instead opened out to the bated audience, here busily constructing in their minds what the stage will not in fact body forth.

The two types of speech that from early in Shakespeare's career are given a particularly liberal use of midline switches—passionate lamentation, and reportage—are both frequently performed solus on-stage. And examples such as Juliet's lament and Clarence's nightmare speech (*Richard III*, TLN 838–910)—both of them nominally dialogue, but effectively addressed to the speaker—will suggest one further mode that is consistently freer than other dialogue with midline switches, 'unmetrical' pauses, and unanswered interrogatories; one that often combines lamentation with reportage, and which is likewise invariably addressed solely to the audience: this of course is the soliloquy. The soliloquy is also where Shakespeare's experiments in representing inward doubt and division are starkest, and where future technical innovations in the writing of layered roles are most conspicuously presaged.

It is obvious enough why soliloquies might be so liberal with short speech units and brisk prosodic shifts. In the absence of other characters to respond to or react against, the discrete speech has to produce its own 'dialogue'. In a soliloquy, the midline switch will invoke for the actor the same expectations as it did when he was in company—change of address, switch of attention—but he will immediately adjust his delivery to the absence of interlocutors besides himself and the audience. For example, the Romeo-part ends with a long soliloquy (spoken over the 'dead' body of Juliet) that is full of short statements and midline sentence endings. The breaks in the line are all invitations to act histrionic passions in a particular way: by moving from one dead body to the next, from addressing one body to addressing the next, or from apostrophizing over a corpse to enunciating to the silent and spellbound off-stage audience:

Said he not so? Or did I dreame it so?
Or am I mad, hearing him talke of *Juliet*,
To thinke it was so? ...
How oft when men are at the point of death,
Have they beene merrie? Which their Keepers call
A lightning before death? Oh how may I
Call this a lightning? O my Love, my Wife ...
*Tybalt*, ly'st thou there in thy bloudy sheet? ...
Forgive me Cozen. Ah deare *Juliet*:
Why art thou yet so faire?

                                    (TLN 2932–55)

The frequent swift internal shifts within the line, moving between self-questioning and expostulation, clearly mark the speech as a soliloquy. However, the actor will also notice in the speech important continuities with rhetorical habits established earlier in the part—hyperbolical grand-standing, unanswerable questions, lexical circularity:

Is love a tender thing? It is too rough,
Too rude, too boisterous, and it prickes like thorne.
                                    (TLN 476–7)

Then plainly know my hearts deare Love is set,
On the faire daughter of rich *Capulet*:
As mine on hers, so hers is on mine;
And all combin'd, save what thou must combine
By holy marriage: when and where and how ...
                                    (TLN 1064–8)

Hence banished, is banish: from the world,
And worlds exile is death. Then banished,
Is death, mistearm'd, calling death banished ...
                                    (TLN 1822–4)

... and every Cat and Dog,
And little Mouse, every unworthy thing
Live here in Heaven and may looke on her,
But *Romeo* may not. More Validitie,
More honourable state, more Courtship lives
In carrion Flies, then *Romeo*: they may seaze
On the white wonder of deare *Juliets* hand ...
                                    (TLN 1833–9)

In learning the part of Romeo, the actor will identify fractured metrics as an instruction positively *not* to address others on-stage (an instruction that of course absolutely requires awareness of these others), and instead to apostrophize hyperbolically 'above' the other actors. Romeo often seems to be reaching out for an absent, transcendent addressee—Cupid, beauty, Rosaline, love, Juliet—and in this absence must be satisfied with himself. The part's final soliloquy is the ultimate example of this—the example which much of the preceding part has been waiting for, or been expecting. The soliloquy thus recapitulates, concentrates, and internalizes the prosodic habits that have characterized the part's most passionate speeches. Indeed, the prosody itself begins to reify the emotions it channels: that is, a love that transcends all order and annihilates all bodies is given its own concrete, appropriately riven body.

Romeo's is by no means the only part that does this: it becomes a signature of Shakespeare's early 'tragic' heroes, and a crucial example of how the very simple requirements of working in parts helps to produce increasingly sophisticated representations of personhood. Let us see how this works by tracing the midline shifts in the parts of Richard III and Richard II. In doing so, we will see just how formative the material necessities of working in parts were to Shakespeare's development as a writer.

## Gloucester/Richard III

In the part of Gloucester/Richard III, midline shifts carry an often frightening charge.[1] The actor is forced to forage hungrily in the spaces they create; the devilish Richard really does feed upon the carnage they invariably beckon. But, as we shall see, so too does Shakespeare. He knows the midline shift is a principal means of bringing a wider world into the actor's purview. However, this shift or lacuna is so volatile, so volatilizing, that it really does seem as though Shakespeare is gathering energy back from it, and realizing new expressive possibilities as he does so.

Richard's opening soliloquy ('Now is the Winter of our Discontent...' (TLN 3)) is an unmistakable gift to the actor.[2] Richard lets fly with sarcastic contempt for all who stand in his way; equally, he is witheringly disdainful of his own malformation. The actor will identify in the speech a consistent seam of pathological binaries: all at court are happy, fair, and proportioned; Richard is directly the opposite; the fact of such difference provides all the explanation the player needs. In acting the body—hunched, limping, and creeping in the margins—the actor will automatically enact mind, manner, and motive.

As a charismatic declaration of intent, the part's first speech bestows on the actor magnificent confidence in his character—he possesses both word and occasion. But how will the bare part tell the actor that this role is *more* than one of cascading (albeit witty) malevolence? As the part is such a patent show-stealer, the temptation must have been huge for Burbage to seize its thumping opening notes and magnify them throughout the rest of the play (perhaps on the recent model of Alleyn as Tamburlaine). At the very least, the actor will search his part-script for portals in which to recover the exhilarating mastery of this first speech. This belief in—even need for—self-centring demonic energy will give to any moment in which he actually does repossess it an electric supercharge. In turn, any disappointing of expectation, any shortfall in the actor/character's possession of the moment, becomes all the more experienced and meaningful.

One technique above all mediates and concentrates this particular drama: the unexpected half-line speech unit, and the shifts or pauses it commands. For it is the half-line or arrested line that most distinctively catalyses Richard's spell. Initially, the technique is used to show Richard dividing, imposing upon, and destroying others; at the end, it is used to show Richard dividing, imposing upon, and destroying *himself*.

Richard's opening soliloquy does not contain a single midline break. When Clarence enters, however, Richard says this:

> Brother, good day: What meanes this armed guard
> That waites upon your Grace?
>
> (TLN 45–6)

The midline shift from greeting to question is the simplest indication of Shakespeare's basic stagecraft. We see here a change in the mode of speech, an attendant change in tone (from false bonhomie to false solicitousness), and a direction to look at others on-stage (the guard that attends Clarence). The same thing happens a few lines later ('How say you sir? can you deny all this?' (TLN 100)). Again the hiatus marks both a transition in tone, here from bawdy ribbing to peremptory threat, and a sudden switch of attention (from Richard to his addressee, the guard Brakenbury). In each instance, the pause between both statements can be stretched as far as desired (and, perhaps, pentameter permits) by the actor playing Richard. The more the addressee, Brakenbury, acts (or indeed feels) discomforted, the more 'Richard' can relish his small torture. A pause is here less a moment of silence than a prompt for action—of the speaker, the addressee, or both.

Richard is soon alone on-stage once more, but his soliloquy again ends with an ominous mid-stopped line:

> Simple plaine *Clarence*, I do love thee so,
> That I will shortly send thy Soule to Heaven,
> If Heaven will take the present at our hands.
> But who comes heere? the new delivered *Hastings*?
>
> (TLN 125–8)

The break between 'hands' and 'But', together with the midline arrest, figure a change in tone and function (from smug revelling to curious attention) and a tacit instruction to look in a particular direction and at a specified player (the entering Lord Hastings). But the breaks also help the actor to manipulate *our* gaze, encouraging the audience to collude in his devilry. Part-based prosody is here scoring the very basics of performance.

Richard has another decisive midline switch during his exchange of brisk badinage with Lady Anne. It too marks a transition: from what Richard calls a 'keene encounter of our wittes' (TLN 301) to a placatory supplication. Here is the part:

> ——————————————— [place,] [but] hell.
> Yes one place else, if you will heare me name it.
> ——————————————— [Some] dungeon.
> Your Bed-chamber.
> ——————————————— [where] [thou] lyest.
> So will it Madam, till I lye with you.
> ——————————————— [I] [hope] so.
> I know so. [SWITCH] But gentle Lady *Anne*,
> To leave this keene encounter of our wittes,
> And fall something into a slower method…
>
> (TLN 292–302)

The three one-line speeches before the midline switch all follow the same pattern. Each cue is 'twisted'—'dungeon' becomes 'Bed-chamber', 'lyest' becomes 'lye with you', 'hope so' becomes 'know so'—as Richard moves with insolent imagination through the place, position, and commission of the sexual satisfaction he recommends. In this context, the sudden midline arrest following 'I know so' is coiled with tension. If the pause is played as Richard's to end or extend, then it might seem a further rhetorical ruse (even a kind of studied 'interruptus' to his seductive jabs): three aggressive moves are followed by an unexpected backing away; a rapacious but some-how irresistible menace echoes in the air. In full play terms, Anne might in the pause wish herself away, but be forced to remain merely petrified; or she might wish that Richard would continue with his assaults, because violence is easier to fend off than silence; similarly, the actor of Anne might begin to feel and act the puzzle of erotic capitulation. Alternatively, the line break might signal Anne's implacability, or her blank refusal of Richard's game. As she says nothing, so she offers him nothing—the pause in the line is the Richard-actor's cue to notice the fact and to try a new tack.

As this pivotal exchange proceeds, the line shifts themselves begin to gather an accumulating explosiveness, and to invite increasingly vigorous action—from both Richard and Anne. Here is Richard's speech (the stage-direction need not have been in the actor's part):

> _____ [Where] [is] he?
> Heere: *Spits at him*
> Why dost thou spit at me.

> (TLN 332–4)

Soon the technique of splitting lines heralds the scene's ultimate moment of transition: when Richard bares his breast to Anne's sword, asserts his crimes, and dares her to kill him:

> *He layes his brest open, she offers at it with his sword.*
> Nay do not pause: For I did kill King *Henrie*,
> But 'twas thy beauty that provoked me.
> Nay now dispatch: 'Twas I that stabb'd yong *Edward*,
> But 'twas thy Heavenly face that set me on.

> (TLN 371–5)

According to the next Folio stage-direction, Anne now '*fals her sword*', and she is his. Once more the midline shifts seemingly invite in other parts, other actions, other objects of focus. The first midline break—at the demand that Anne should 'not pause'—ironically ensures that she does just that. The second—after 'Nay now dispatch'—has the same effect. Thus the midline shift carries *more* compelling authority over the action than the words spoken; it pre-empts or even neuters semantics, pointing the irony in apparent imperatives ('now dispatch'), and effectively directing the players' motion. Richard becomes the arch-dramaturge, taunting his interlocutor with possibilities that she and her actor *know* they have no power to perform.

From this point on, Richard's passage into authority—and beyond—can virtually be plotted through the part's midline switches:

> A blessed labour my most Soveraigne Lord:
> Among this Princely heape, [switch] if any heere
> By false intelligence, or wrong surmize
> Hold me a Foe: [switch] If I unwillingly, or in my rage,
> Have ought committed that is hardly borne,
> To any in this presence, I desire
> To reconcile me to his Friendly peace:
>
> (TLN 1178–84)

Here the shifts, indicated chiefly by syntax ('if... If'), accentuate the menace underlying Richard's 'apology'. He appears to be addressing the King, but in fact is addressing the 'Princely heape' (itself redolent of piled-up corpses). The caesuras are an opportunity for the actor playing Richard to stop and look at his indirect addressees, to smile a false smile or to wipe away a smile, and either way to allow his words' double-speak to reverberate. The pauses indicate a shift in address (from King to princes) and a movement in focus (from Richard to his future opponents). Taking place in public, they are thus a means of *concretizing* power: of drawing the speech out of 'itself' and menacingly into its future effects.

Here is another example:

> Then be your eyes the witnesse of their evill.
> Looke how I am bewitch'd: [switch] behold, mine Arme
> Is like a blasted Sapling, wither'd up.
>
> (TLN 2038–40)

The switch tells everyone where they must look: at Richard's arm, which he claims to have been maimed by witchcraft, but which is all too clearly morphing into an evil wand of its own. In this way, the break again concentrates movement to and fro between agents. That Richard orders all to 'Looke' means that it is not only he (as the object of all gazes) that is a focus, but they (as the objects of his direction). Again the switch encapsulates the magnetism of power in action. These and similar peremptory switches ('If? ... Talk'st thou to me of Ifs ... Off with his head' (2045–8)) can be answered by nothing but dumbfounded tongues. The technique thus helps the staged action animate the fear and silence of surviving beneath tyranny.

Precisely because these shifts are so keyed to shifts in power, the actor must always be alert to any changes in the use of the technique. An important example occurs when Buckingham reports to the dismayed Richard what 'dumbe Statues, or breathing Stones' (TLN 2238) the people were when he tried to manufacture acclaim for the usurpation:

RICHARD.  How now, how now, what say the Citizens?
BUCKINGHAM. Now by the holy Mother of our Lord,
     The Citizens are mum, say not a word.

(TLN 2214–16)

Richard's response to this report is suggestive:

   What tongue-lesse Blockes were they,
   Would they not speake?
   Will not the Maior then, and his Brethren, come?
(TLN 2255–7)

The breaking of Richard's first pentameter into two lines can be explained by the Folio page on which the passage occurs—the compositor seems to have split the line to fill some space on a sparse page (in Q the words are on a single line). But there are certainly two distinct rhetorical questions here: one of contemptuous vehemence, one of real bewilderment and even fear. Crucially, this marks the first time in the part that Richard is given a midline switch over which he *lacks* complete control: the citizens he would put on the spot are inaccessible. The part makes clear that Richard's questions demand a response, but twice there is none: the 'tongue-lesse Blockes' are not there to feel his rage or reflect his potency, and the follow-up question—'Would they not speake?'—is *not* then answered by Buckingham. There is thus no stage action that can satisfy the metrical break or appease its troubled sentiment. What does the Richard-actor do to fill the gap? Some unpredictable movement between anger, puzzlement, panic? Certainly this moment signifies to the actor a new vulnerability in his hitherto ascendant character. The part-learning actor will from this point be finely attuned to any more unfilled gaps and unanswered questions; the part-playing actor, meanwhile, will be highly conscious of their potency.

When power is truly at work—minds at a cusp, fates undecided, fear and anxiety afoot—Shakespeare almost always marks this with midline switches. By contrast, Richard's most brazenly hypocritical speeches usually eschew them. The 'coronation' scene is a striking instance. In this scene Richard moves from pretending to refuse the crown to pretending unwilling acceptance of it (TLN 2324–2470). His long speeches of burlesque refusal and diffidence, set-pieces of studied, transparent performance, are notable for the absence of midline breaks:

> My Lord, there needes no such Apologie:
> I doe beseech your Grace to pardon me,
> Who earnest in the service of my God,
> Deferr'd the visitation of my friends.
> But leaving this, what is your Graces pleasure?
> _____ [this] [ungovern'd] Ile.
> I doe suspect I have done some offence,
> That seemes disgracious in the Cities eye,
> And that you come to reprehend my ignorance.
> _____ [amend] [your] fault.
> Else wherefore breathe I in a Christian Land.
> _____ [move] [your] Grace.
> I cannot tell, if to depart in silence,
> Or bitterly to speake in your reproofe,
> Best fitteth my Degree, or your Condition.
> If not to answer, you might haply thinke,
> Tongue-ty'd Ambition, not replying, yeelded
> To beare the Golden Yoake of Soveraigntie,
> Which fondly you would here impose on me.
> If to reprove you for this suit of yours,
> So season'd with your faithfull love to me,
> Then on the other side I check'd my friends.
> Therefore to speake, and to avoid the first,
> And then in speaking, not to incurre the last,
> Definitively thus I answer you …

(TLN 2324–74)

The lack of shifts in the line, or the openings or invitations they allow, accords with the already decided minds of those to whom Richard speaks. Of course the whole performance is a charade of participatory politics; this enacting of apparent power transition is a belated mockery of what has already happened.

This is the context for the peculiar part of the '*Citizens*' in this scene, assembled as they are on-stage to witness the effective coronation ('*Enter the Maior, and Citizens*' (TLN 2269); '[Richard] wonders to what end you have assembled | Such troopes of Citizens, to come to him' (TLN 2303–4)). Unusually, Shakespeare gives the people no tongue whatsoever; this despite allusions to just such voice (e.g. 'good my Lord, your Citizens entreat you', says the Mayor (TLN 2422)). Already they have been described as 'mum', as 'statues': now, *en masse*, they enact those qualities. This is easy for the supernumerary actors to do: they have no lines. But what is interesting is that their silence is also scripted into Richard's part: through the pointed *refusal* of midline breaks. As we have seen, the part's midline shifts have already produced some unwanted silences. Now, at this crucial moment of legitimation, it is Richard who—almost literally—will not allow anyone in. He will not risk an interruption, or dare the crowd of citizens *not* to answer his desires.

The metrical regularity here given to the actor therefore works as a pastiche of ideological regularity: perfect testimony to pseudo-humility, -piety, and -decorum. But it also shows Richard responding to the perilous nature of his achievement. He could be foiled by the slightest dissent: if one of these 'Stones' were to shift, an avalanche might follow. There is thus something almost wistfully holy about the speech blocs in which he takes refuge. They are a metrical version of the prayer—'meditating with two deepe Divines' (TLN 2291)—that Buckingham has just pretended to be Richard's habitual comfort. Richard uses the unbroken line, therefore, much as he uses religion: with a Machiavellian appreciation of its usefulness.

A sensitive actor, then, learning the progress of his part, will identify a micro-narrative in its employment of midline/short-line switches. Richard has used them to his advantage, then been used by them, then escaped from them into phoney metrical completeness. Whilst Richard measures his power over others, the player measures his metrics: mastery of one equates to mastery of the other. From now on, if Richard is to speak in abrupt speech units, he will want to do so with a massive presumption of violence behind them: interrupting, coercing, or invading the security of others. Conversely, if he suffers the broken metrics unwillingly, helplessly, or accidentally, then this will be a decisive allegory of Richard's gathering self-destruction.

If Richard's premonition of vulnerability leads him to take refuge in lyric regularity, then the return of the half-line shift must be suggestive. And this is exactly what happens as soon as Richard is crowned:

> Stand all apart. [SWITCH] Cousin of Buckingham.
> —————————————————— [My] [gracious] Soveraigne.
> Give me thy hand. [SWITCH]
> Thus high, by thy advice, and thy assistance,
> Is King *Richard* seated: [SWITCH]
> But shall we weare these Glories for a day?...

> > (TLN 2590–5)

The Quarto text transcribes more regular pentameters, which serves to make the midline shifts still more striking:

> Stand al apart. [SWITCH] Coosin of Buckingham,
> Give me thy hand: [SWITCH]
> *Here he ascendeth the throne.*
> Thus high by thy advice
> And thy assistance is king Richard seated: [SWITCH]
> But shal we wear the honours for a day?

> > (Q, H4b)

The heavily weighted breaks invite a particular kind of performance. The Richard-actor can take his time, commanding all eyes, making it clear that all other bodies must move in time to his. The half-lines are not questions, so they neither crave nor require verbal completion. Only King Richard can resume speaking after them, if and as he chooses. In this context, the statement 'Is King *Richard* seated' suggests an ominous moment of transition and possession. But studying his part, how precisely would the actor play the lines? Is Richard reporting a *fait accompli*? Or is this a nervous question, expressing the insecurity of Richard's power and the uncertainty of his claim to kingship? In the Folio lineation, given the free-standing resonance of a single line, the moment becomes still more taut with unresolved tensions.

For this particular moment is *almost* Richard's triumph. It is the first time he has used the royal name, 'King', for himself. He has, moreover, adopted the third person, as though at once smug and amazed, watching himself in objectified wonder. In a sense the long pause that follows in the folio ('Is King *Richard* seated——') contains all conceivable possibility: it might just have been feasible, had Richard so chosen, to rule from here with moderation and clemency. The line, in Folio and Quarto, receives no verbal response. No one moves or speaks; everyone awaits Richard's guidance. The midline lacuna is thus suspended tantalizingly between the achievement and the unmasking of absolute power. That all eyes and ears attend the King, we might think, testifies absolutely to his authority. However, the fact that this power is not in motion, that it is not taking effect upon others—attested by their silence and stillness—suggests that history for a moment is frozen, that judgements are in abeyance, and that everything is up for grabs. Audience attention perhaps shifts uneasily from the King to his subjects; or perhaps we cling to the King with bated expectation: but no direction is supplied from Richard. And because no one else's action is called for, or even possible, the motion—perhaps violence—that the midline switch invites must happen upon and *in* the King.

From this point on Richard (if not his actor) has lost full possession of the midline interstice—and with it the power to compel or dictate history. This is most clearly witnessed when Richard tries to persuade the kingmaker, Buckingham, that the 'Bastards' in the tower should be killed. Though Richard's first line in the scene—'Stand all apart. Cousin of Buckingham' (TLN 2590)—is a perfect illustration of how the part's midline breaks have customarily worked, the actor will identify a change from the moment his character begins talking in private with Buckingham:

Why *Buckingham*, I say I would be King.
_____ [thrice][-renowned] Lord.
Ha? [SWITCH] am I King? ]SWITCH] 'tis so : [SWITCH] but *Edward* lives.
_____ [True,] [Noble] Prince.
O bitter consequence! [SWITCH]
That *Edward* still should live true Noble Prince. [SWITCH]
Cousin, thou wast not wont to be so dull. [SWITCH]
Shall I be plaine? [SWITCH] I wish the Bastards dead,
And I would have it suddenly perform'd. [SWITCH]
What say'st thou now? [SWITCH] speake suddenly, be briefe.
_____ [doe] [your] pleasure.
Tut, tut, thou art all Ice, [SWITCH?] thy kindnesse freezes.

(TLN 2602–13)

Time after time the part has discrete speech units of less than a full line, which elicit no response ('Ha?', 'am I King?', 'O bitter consequence!', 'Shall I be plaine?', 'What say'st thou now?', 'speake suddenly'). Perhaps the scripting indicates Richard's desire for the kind of immediate response which his imperative commands have till now almost always provoked. Perhaps these mini-locutions are not so much seeking an answer as recommending an attitude in their addressee: hear my vexation, feel my menace, do my (implied) bidding. Either way, the simple absence of any response—the pauses in context forbid spoken and physical response from Richard's inter-locutor—means that the energy generated out of the shift is not taken up or away by any other agent; it is neither absorbed nor suffered by another. These midline switches are always provoking reactivity; if there is no one else to volatilize, the current has to return to the speaker. The midline lacuna, then, becomes haunted by Richard's isolation and vulnerability.

Learning his part from beginning to end, the actor would discover a brisk escalation in the frequency of these devices for Richard's final scenes. The Richard-part's dominant form soon becomes the half-line unit of speech (presented in Folio as shattered pentameters). Intermittently, the King's speeches as he heads toward his doom *cannot* be answered. Sometimes this is because he is asking rhetorical non-questions, impotent stabs into air that can produce nothing but blank permission from those whom he commands:

> Is the Chayre emptie? [SWITCH] is the Sword unsway'd? [SWITCH]
> Is the King dead? [SWITCH] the Empire unpossest? [SWITCH]
>
> (TLN 3267–8)

Indeed, it can seem as though the final decisive transition in the part—from command to impotence—is engineered precisely through prosodic breaks:

> *Catesby* come hither, [SWITCH] poste to Salisbury: [SWITCH]
> When thou com'st thither: [SWITCH] Dull unmindfull Villaine,
> Why stay'st thou here, and go'st not to the Duke?
>
> (TLN 3237–9)

Here Richard's bewildered irritation—'Dull unmindfull Villaine | Why stay'st thou here ... ?'—articulates the prosodic effect: the midline switch creates space and occasion for an explicit *failure* to move others.

The final scenes are organized around the swift cutting back and forth between Richard's camp and that of the invading Richmond (the future Henry VII). Whereas Richmond's speeches are commandingly self-possessed, intoned through swelling full-line sentiments, Richard's lines are cramped, his sentences short. He repeatedly surprises his interlocutors with abrupt questions; they try to answer, but the danger, quite clearly, is an unanswerable silence:

_____ [most] [gracious] Liege.
Norfolke, we must have knockes : [SWITCH?]
Ha, must we not? [SWITCH?]
_____ [my] [loving] Lord.
Up with my Tent, [SWITCH?] heere wil I lye to night,
But where to morrow? [SWITCH?] Well, all's one for that. [SWITCH?]
Who hath descried the number of the Traitors?

(TLN 3437–43)

What is't a Clocke?
_____ [nine] [a] clocke.
I will not sup to night, [SWITCH]
Give me some Inke and Paper: [SWITCH]
What, [SWITCH] is my Beaver easier then it was? [SWITCH]
And all my Armour laid into my Tent?
_____ [go] [my] Lord
Stir with the Larke to morrow, gentle Norfolk.
_____ [you] [my] Lord.
*Ratcliffe.*
_____ [My] Lord.
Send out a Pursuivant at Armes
To *Stanleys* Regiment: [SWITCH] bid him bring his power
Before Sun-rising…
Fill me a Bowle of Wine: [SWITCH] Give me a Watch, [SWITCH]
Saddle white Surrey for the Field to morrow: [SWITCH]
Look that my Staves be sound, [SWITCH] & not too heavy. *Ratcliff.*
_____ [My] Lord.
Saw'st the melancholly Lord Northumberland?
_____ [up] [the] Souldiers.
So, I am satisfied: [SWITCH] Give me a Bowle of Wine, [SWITCH]
I have not that Alacrity of Spirit,
Nor cheere of Minde that I was wont to have. [SWITCH]
Set it downe. [SWITCH] Is Inke and Paper ready?
_____ [is] [my] Lord.
Bid my Guard watch. [SWITCH] Leave me. [SWITCH]
*Ratcliffe*, about the mid of night come to my Tent
And helpe to arme me. [SWITCH] Leave me I say.

(TLN 3486–3519)

Richard is reduced to the barest forms of command. The frequent staccato
speech units—'Give me a Bowle of Wine', 'Set it downe', 'arme me'—are
empty of anything but an assurance of fugitive comfort (some wine, some

guards, the promise that he will not be left all alone). Obedience here can be no more than mechanical. This means that the focus of the midline shifts, as of the whole scene, is upon Richard's anxiety and isolation:

> ———————————————— [all] [his] pride.
> *Richard starts out of his dreame.*
> Give me another Horse, bind up my Wounds:
> Have mercy Iesu. Soft, I did but dreame.
> O coward Conscience! how dost thou afflict me?
> The Lights burne blew. It is not dead midnight.
> Cold fearefull drops stand on my trembling flesh.
> What? do I feare my Selfe? There's none else by,
> *Richard* loves *Richard*, that is, I am I.
> Is there a Murtherer heere? No; Yes, I am:
> Then flye; What from my Selfe? Great reason: why?
> Alacke, I love my Selfe. Wherefore? For any good
> That I my Selfe, have done unto my Selfe?
> O no. Alas, I rather hate my Selfe …
>
> (TLN 3638–51)

It is easy enough to identify the broken metrics as symptomatic of the King's internal fracture; that self-division or self-alienation is the overt theme of the speech makes such associations inevitable. But the prosody in no sense suddenly collapses into this broken internal dialogue. As we have seen, the movement has already been presaged by the gradual shrivelling of Richard's address to others. By this stage in the part, the midline pauses betoken no movement but that of Richard's mind: they evoke varieties of echo and recursion, embodying the mortal trap of 'Selfe'.

So, by tracing the midline shifts in the part of Richard III, we can see how an instrument designed to help the actor overcome the limitations of the actor's part is also the 'infrastructure' of a layered dramatic subjectivity. In particular, we can see how the half-line imperative spoken to others—used to elicit movement in these addressees—mutates into the half-line subjunctive spoken to oneself—used to indicate movement in the mind of the soliloquizer. This proposes two varieties of progression for the midline shift: from external to internal dialogue and division; and from actor's tool to expressive resource.

Shakespeare is on to something new. What is new is not the simple fact of a soliloquy peppered with short self-addressing statements (that is memorably achieved, for example, by Marlowe in Faustus's final speech).

It is the residual prosodic continuities between the early and later parts of
the same roll—the recognizable, meaningful signs that link what otherwise
might seem merely discontinuous. This writing is a consummate example
of the way in which Shakespeare's discursive patterns both draw upon and
feed into the processes and necessities of acting. More than that, it shows
his ability to ground his narratives (political, emotional, psychological)
in multiple 'languages' at one time; Shakespeare is allowing the midline
or short-line 'volta' to bear forward and backward meaning—indeed,
memory—like any other of his numerous semiotic resources.

# Richard II

Let us now look at the same techniques in the part of Richard II, written
perhaps two or three years after *Richard III*.

Initially, the part's midline shifts are alive with Richard's distinctive and
assured take upon kingship. Here are the first words in I. iv:

> We did observe. Cosine *Aumerle*,
> How far brought you high Herford on his way?
>
> (TLN 575–6)

What did Richard 'observe'? We do not know. All we know is that he
will say no more on the matter. Perhaps he is telling his addressee that he
already knows what he has just been told; perhaps he starts an observation
that he does not complete; perhaps he speaks haughtily, or collusively, or in
rebuke. The statement has no substance other than its situational context,
but it is a context that we are denied. All we are given is opacity of motive,
suggesting whimsicality. That the scene *begins* in this fashion—a half-line
statement followed by a break, both entirely in the King's control, both
unreachable to sense or intervention—becomes a striking illustration of
Richard's unplumbed power and arbitrary prerogative.

More flagrant examples soon follow. Here is Richard upon the death of
Gaunt:

> The ripest fruit first fals, and so doth he,
> His time is spent, our pilgrimage must be:
> So much for that. [SWITCH] Now for our Irish warres ...
>
> (TLN 800–2)

Richard offers a couplet containing three pseudo-saccharine clichés of mourning, followed by 'So much for that', as he devastatingly sweeps them aside. Thematically, the switch is the cue for the civil wars. But for the actor *and* the character, the midline switch here represents unmitigated opportunity and will. A similar explosive volte-face characterizes Richard's response to York's plea for moderation:

> ———————————————— [allegeance] [cannot] thinke.
> Thinke what you will: [SWITCH] we seise into our hands,
> His plate, his goods, his money, and his lands.
>
> (TLN 856–8)

Again the part displays the midline gear change (presaging tyranny, whimsicality, unreachability) and the exultantly gleeful rhyme. Signs such as these are very straightforward for the actor to 'read' and play. In these early scenes, Richard's caprice is (as it were) his own: he speaks it as he intends it. The actor can exult in the clarity of delivery, even as his character is sowing the seeds of self-destruction.

That is, the only real presence in these speeches is the King's—and indeed the actor's—controlling mind. However, if Shakespeare wants Richard's petulance to furnish 'tragedy', then this controlling mind has to be broken into, broken up—indeed, broken down. Such effects are achieved through fracturing the line so as to make space for split minds, alternative perspectives, or competing agents. As Shakespeare was quickly discovering, this is how verse can genuinely embody—rather than merely report or describe—the agitations of experience.

The first 'movement' of the part ends with Richard's exit in II. i ('Come on our Queene, to morrow must we part, | Be merry, for our time of stay is short' (TLN 870–1)), alluding to the short time that he and his wife have together before he leaves for Ireland. The actor will then see on his part a sudden transition from this imprecation to 'be merry':

> Come on our Queene, to morrow must we part,
> Be merry, for our time of stay is short.
> ———————————————— [and] [after] holliday. *Exeunt.*
> Barkloughly Castle call you this at hand?
> ———————————————— [the] [breaking] Seas?
> Needs must I like it well: I weepe for joy
> To stand upon my Kingdome once againe.
> Deere Earth, I doe salute thee with my hand,
> Though rebels wound thee with their Horses hoofes:

As a long parted Mother with her Child,
Playes fondly with her teares, and smiles in meeting;
So weeping, smiling, greet I thee my Earth,
And doe thee favor with my Royall hands.

(TLN 870–1371)

Whilst learning the part, the Richard-actor may not realize just how long the gap is between these two speeches, the first to 'our Queene', the second at 'Barkloughly Castle': it is about 500 lines, a gap in time in which his character's fortunes have been irrevocably transformed. There is no real narrative problem here for the actor: the part immediately recapitulates the essential information, briskly giving the circumstantial facts. Richard is near 'Barkloughly Castle'; he does not know the area; he feels alienated and unsure; he has to seek comfort and assurance from his attendants: and all this because 'rebels wound thee [the kingdom] with their Horses hoofes'. Nonetheless, the actor clearly cannot reproduce the same 'Richard' that we last saw—departing for Ireland full of shrill confidence, thin sarcasm, whimsical brutality. The switch into a newly pathetic register is the prompt for the actor to adopt a newly expressive manner—a new pose, voice, and style that will make or break the play.

Hence the part's immediate reversion to the midline switch ('Needs must I like it well: I weepe for joy'). Coming in the first line of a major set-piece speech, the break here is rendered full of portent. It brooks no interruption, seeming to prepare for some defining shift of mental gear. But we need to see just how *un*-inevitable the second half of the line is; how the first half is not the necessary predicate of the second. The prosody signals a definite decision: to switch from sulky resignation to the overt performing of his emotions. More specifically, the movement from 'Needs must' to 'I weepe for joy' sees the King adopt a mask of histrionic or hyperbolical emotion: the actor and character are strategically almost as one. By the third line of this speech, 'Deere Earth, I doe salute thee with my hand', the actor/character has decisively entered into a mode of self-presentation. He thus acts out a pantomime (some kind of prostration) to accompany his pathetic words. So the opening half of the 'broken' line, appropriately cued by 'breaking Seas', shows Richard emerging from his slough of weeping despair; and the second half shows him recovering a more dignified and sustainable frame for the tears that have already overcome him.

Throughout this pivotal scene (III. ii), the Richard-actor can trace his vacillations between kingliness and despair through the studied distribution of midline stops. This first pause is followed by about fifty lines of iambic pentameter, with barely a midline shift in sight: Richard is composing himself, cheering himself up, practising a rhetoric of assertion ('The breath of worldly men cannot depose | The Deputie elected by the Lord' (TLN 1411–12)). Of course this rhetoric is in many ways deluded; its careful observance of verbal decorum suggests that the King is seeking sentimental refuge in metrical forms that are already otiose or fractured. The latent strain and hysteria break out in the return of the midline switch:

> For everie man that *Bullingbrooke* hath prest,
> To lift shrewd Steele against our Golden Crowne,
> Heaven for his *Richard* hath in heavenly pay
> A glorious Angell: [SHIFT] then if Angels fight,
> Weake men must fall, for Heaven still guards the right.
>
> (TLN 1413–17)

Throughout the preceding speech Richard has related himself to the sun: as the 'Deputie elected by the Lord' (TLN 1412), he is the 'Eye of Heaven' (TLN 1393) who rises in 'the East' (TLN 1305), and 'darts his Lightning [Q: light] through ev'ry guilty hole' (TLN 1399); as such, he will outface and embarrass his dark and furtive opposition. However, nearing the midline shift, this extra-terrestrial imagery becomes profaned and trivialized. Richard's great chain of cosmic analogies ends up in a bathetic pun: the 'glorious Angell[s]' fighting in God's army are nothing more than common coins. Just as Bolingbroke 'presses' soldiers into action, so Richard will press more money from a quickly vaporizing royal mint. Richard's simulation of authority is likewise forced and unsustainable. The sudden midline arrest embodies the belated recognition of this. The actor has to stop for a moment; perhaps he sniggers, or giggles, as he shows the character trying to re-inflate the deflation. The pause is thus a moment for the player to *act* his self-derision, allowing the bastardized image of an 'Angell' to echo thinly through the air. And because it occurs inside an iambic pentameter, the midline break allows far more invasive, even subversive effects than would a simple end-line stop.

From this point in the scene, Richard basically gives up on authoritative blank verse. Extravagant conceits ('But now the blood of twentie thousand men | Did triumph in my face') and unruly rhymes abound; so too does the unanswered midline break, which has become a basic means of structuring subjective and political discomfort:

> I had forgot my selfe. Am I not King?
> Awake sluggard Majestie, thou sleepest:
> Is not the Kings Name fortie thousand Names?
> Arme, arme my Name: a punie subject strikes
> At thy great glory. Looke not to the ground,
> Ye Favorites of a King: are wee not high?
> High be our thoughts: I know my Unckle *Yorke*
> Hath Power enough to serve our turne.
> But who comes here?
>
> (TLN 1440–8)

That the speech here ends with a yearning half-line (one that the actor may hope or expect to be completed by his interlocutor—but is not) encapsulates the way in which the part is now measured by prosodic incompletion:

> Say, Is my Kingdome lost? why 'twas my Care:
> And what losse is it to be rid of Care?
> Strives *Bullingbrooke* to be as Great as wee?
> Greater he shall not be: If he serve God,
> Wee'l serve him too, and be his Fellow so.
> Revolt our Subjects? That we cannot mend...
>
> (TLN 1453–8)

Every second thought occupies a half-line. The actor may feel that each such half-line recalls its old function as a command, or as a demand for others' immediate response. But he will also 'play' the pauses, showing how they no longer prompt answering obedience or assuring movement—the only movement they proffer is back into Richard's impotence and abjection. As Scroope has it a moment later, 'I play the Torturer, by small and small | To lengthen out the worst, that must be spoken' (TLN 157–8).

As it proceeds toward Richard's end, the part regularly returns to this staccato manner of speaking:

> What must the King doe now? must he submit?
> The King shall doe it: Must he be depos'd?
> The King shall be contented: Must he loose
> The Name of King? o' Gods Name let it goe.
>
> (TLN 1731–4)

The half-lines continue to evoke Richard's inner pain. But here they also gesture toward a saving irony, as Richard attempts to protect himself through the distancing efficacy of style. In this there is even a suggestion of meta-dramatic playfulness, as he starts to relish the drama of the pauses. It is as though the pathetic capabilities of the half-line—so evident in Richard III's fall—have come to seem a staple of 'tragic' affect, irresistible to a player-king like Richard. Thus the prosody becomes as self-dramatizing as all of Richard's other rhetorical armoury: another 'shivered' glass in which he can enact and observe his disintegration.

This is one manifestation of the part's increasing prosodic sophistication. Another is the way in which arrested lines, or lines made up of distinct sentences or thoughts, become an organic part of longer set-piece speeches. In particular, the midline shift is assimilated into the part's gathering 'tragic' mode, as flowing blank verse is seamlessly intertwined with sudden suspensions:

> ——————————————— [are] [worthily] depos'd.
> Must I doe so? and must I ravell out
> My weav'd-up follyes? Gentle *Northumberland*,
> If thy Offences were upon Record,
> Would it not shame thee, in so faire a troupe,
> To read a Lecture of them?
>
> (TLN 2149–54; not in Q)

Here the first two midline breaks (after 'doe so?' and 'follyes?') are partly asking for a response: Richard wants to be spared humiliation, hoping for a remission of public accountability. As before, the half-line question is not answered; as before, this failure to prompt a response signifies lost power. But the questions are also in part simply 'rhetorical', expecting nothing in return but their own echo. This helps furnish the political weightiness of these midline breaks: they offer brief spaces in which the play's unresolved battles over legitimacy, equity, and efficiency can fester and circulate. But fundamental for the actor is the way in which midline silences are becoming specifically *Richard's* silences, a kind of self-communing. This is made very clear from the third midline switch, addressed directly to Northumberland: 'Would it not shame thee … To read a Lecture of them? [SWITCH].' Richard knows he will never have an answer; indeed, this pre-emptive knowledge directs the question. The midline switches have ceased to act upon anyone else, or to invite in anyone else's movement. Concomitantly—as we saw at a similar moment in the Richard III-part—any movement brought about by the switch has to be 'within' the speaker, as he quite consciously divides *himself* up into differently speaking parts.

We see this in the way in which key speeches of Richard's are now explicitly divided up into movements, each such movement positing or sculpting a slightly different self-image. So here only the opening riposte to Northumberland's cue is, in truth, addressed to anyone except Richard himself:

> ———————————————————— [My] Lord.
> No Lord of thine, thou haught-insulting man; [SWITCH]
> No, nor no mans Lord: [SWITCH] I have no Name, no Title; [SWITCH]
> No, not that Name was given me at the Font,
> But 'tis usurpt: [SWITCH] alack the heavie day
> That I have worne so many Winters out,
> And know not now, what Name to call my selfe. [SWITCH]
> O, that I were a Mockerie, King of Snow
> Standing before the Sunne of *Bullingbrooke*,
> To melt my selfe away in Water-drops.
>
> (TLN 2175–84)

Even when the line does complete the thought, the pause at its end takes a type of infection—a nervous exhaustion, an intimation of finality—from the midline caesuras that have begun to surround it:

> Give me that Glasse, and therein will I reade. [SWITCH]
> No deeper wrinckles yet? [SWITCH] hath Sorrow strucke
> So many Blowes upon this Face of mine,
> And made no deeper Wounds? [SWITCH] Oh flatt'ring Glasse,
> Like to my followers in prosperitie,
> Thou do'st beguile me. [SWITCH] Was this Face, the Face
> That every day, under his House-hold Roofe
> Did keepe ten thousand men? [SWITCH] Was this the Face,
> That like the Sunne, did make beholders winke?
> Is this the Face, which fac'd so many follyes,
> That was at last out-fac'd by *Bullingbrooke*?
>
> (TLN 2199–2209)

This solipsistic mode of address reaches its climax, appropriately enough, in Richard's one and only soliloquy. In this speech, Richard's 'still breeding Thoughts' turn the prison into the world and Richard into all its inhabitants:

> Thus play I in one Prison [Q: person], many people,
> And none contented. Sometimes am I King;

Then Treason makes me wish my selfe a Beggar,
And so I am. Then crushing penurie
Perswades me, I was better when a King:
Then am I king'd againe: and by and by,
Thinke that I am un-king'd by *Bullingbrooke*,
And straight am nothing.

(TLN 2697–2704)

Here the part of Richard II again recapitulates the technique seen in the part of Richard III: the passage away from power into its loss, and from community into isolation, is canonized in a set-piece soliloquy that very explicitly posits a split and multiplied self. The division of the speaker's self is *both* the constructive principle and the subject-matter of the two speeches. Richard III's soliloquy is made up of short phrases and brief sentences; Richard II's lines, by contrast, are frequently enjambed, but his long sentences often end midline—with the succeeding sentence proposing a real shift in direction, usually introducing another conceit, and another hypothetical projection of self. Consequently, even though the midline stops are not here following half-line speech units, the incipient energies compacted in the gap remain the same.

Clearly the fact of being in a soliloquy must change the way the technique can be acted. Whereas the midline shift in a dialogue produces a bracing challenge or invitation to the auditor on-stage, in soliloquy there is *no* acted-upon object. Consequently, there can be no shift of attention from speaker to addressee, and no invitation to stage action or bodily movement. The customary dynamism of the midline break (with its mixture of suspended momentum and sudden response) is in one sense simply frustrated. However, because it is externalized in nothing visible or audible, it produces a felt consciousness of a gap, or of silence ('no one is speaking…!'). The words spoken immediately before the switch may then echo in the emptiness; they can gather intensified portent, because unresolved by and unrecuperated into the line. The primary 'target' of the switch momentarily becomes the audience: we are given a newly intent engagement with the moment's tensions and opportunities. If anyone is there to respond, it is us. Instantaneously, however, our focus turns with renewed intensity back upon the speaker. A technique associated with the presence of others is being used in a context where there are no others; this intuition of something missing, consequently, accentuates the speaker's existential isolation.

In cases such as these, the dynamism of the midline shift is peculiarly concentrated. (It might have something of the force of unrequited desire, all the more violently experienced for not being returned.) The gap, however brief, becomes equivalent to—indeed, it creates—a space that belongs peculiarly to the speaker. Sometimes this space represents what is happening 'inside' the speaker, in which case the violence in the momentary pause reveals a new, intensely charged interiority. Alternatively, it represents a space 'around' the speaker, in which case the silence reveals a character's isolation: as the space in which he is enclosed gets larger, his own body becomes correspondingly dwarfed. In turn, these two subject-making spaces can be conceived of as folding into one another, constituting a genuinely new dramatic ontology: one defined by separation from others and by a magnification of one's own cognitive embodiment as the be-all and end-all.

The climactic soliloquies of the two Richards thus offer almost a commentary upon the mutation of the midline switch from an 'external' to an 'internal' mechanism. That both parts so explicitly show the broken line metamorphosing into the 'broken' soliloquy indicates that writing in parts—parts which absolutely *require* midline switches—may well have suggested to Shakespeare his innovations in characterization. If so, then this in turn implies a modification to the widely accepted genealogy of the soliloquy. It is clear that the soliloquy owes a lot to the 'psychomachia' or soul struggle, common in medieval writing, in which the battle against temptation is allegorized by a fight between embodiments of vice and virtue; in due course the sixteenth-century soliloquy reinternalizes these stark opposites into the self-questioning of a single speech and speaker. But thinking in terms of actors' parts suggests a sophistication of this genealogy, rooted in the way in which Shakespeare makes a single part's syntactic fluctuations or continuities embody that persona's story. The soliloquy's necessarily dialogical structure, instead of internalizing a simple binary (good versus evil), can now potentially be moving between all kinds of memories or possibilities. For it becomes haunted by the absent presence of whatever formerly animated the midline switches. As we shall see, the implications of this do not end with the soliloquy.

# 19

# Midline Shifts in 'Mature' Shakespeare: From Actorly Instruction to 'Virtual' Presence

It is well known that in the second half of Shakespeare's career his lines and sentences grew metrically much freer. By the late 1590s, the actors would have noticed a growing number of 'broken' lines that do not cap short statements, but that instead mark the completion of a sentence that has travelled over two, three, four, or more lines. Soon enough such overflowing sentences become the norm. By *Measure for Measure* (*c.*1602−4) it becomes almost unusual for any full pentameter line to complete a sentence. This is the case even in the most basic conversation; the technique is by no means limited to soliloquy or reverie. This might lead us to speculate that at some stage the midline switch lost its specificity for the *actor*, and ceased to be determined largely by the fact of working in parts: that it became merely a pause for breath, or a brief stop preparing for further reiteration. And certainly, this metrical sophistication proposes a different relationship between dramatic prosody and acting, and so the way a part 'scores' the actor's shifts and movements.

To identify precisely what is at stake here, we should briefly reiterate the actions or types for which the midline switch was normative in roughly the first half of Shakespeare's career. First, it indicates a range of acting options: a switch of address from one party to another; a physical opening out to other players, allowing the speaker to act upon them or for them to act upon the speaker; a shift in mental focus, or an alertness to the idea or necessity of such a shift, often but not necessarily visibly performed. Second, it is the hallmark of a few delimited types of role: the reporter or narrator, the lamenting or traumatized woman, the irascible or peremptory patriarch. Third, it characterized the self-dialogue of soliloquy. In the early part of Shakespeare's career, the instruction to the actor encoded in the midline switch is usually clear and single. It is possible, though fairly rare, for a single role to encompass all of these manners: but if it does, it will do so progressively, in understandable narrative order (as we saw in the parts of Richard III and Richard II). The prosody signifies to the actor that he should progress from one well-attested way of playing the midline switch to another equally established manner of playing it. If not quite programmatic, the acting is typological.

The big change that takes place in Shakespeare's writing is that midline switches cease necessarily to indicate one single, identifiable action. Often the syntactic gear change no longer discernibly affects other characters; nor does it redirect the speaker's relationship to other characters: instead, it often indicates a change in emotion, manner, or address that does not take over from a previous orientation, but rather coexists with it. In other words, the midline switch heralds *simultaneous* rather than consecutive mental or physical movements. For instance, a speech of lament or spleen, full of excitable short phrases, need not indicate that a character has mutated into a correspondingly lamenting or splenetic part: such passion might be no more than a momentary or occasional expression. The prosody, that is, begins to mark discontinuous facets of a nominally cohering persona.[1]

Perhaps the most significant sophistication is in matters of address. From the beginning of Shakespeare's career the midline switch has been available to direct the actor to move from addressing others to speaking 'asides':

> DUCHESS. God blesse thee, and put meeknes in thy breast,
> Love, Charity, Obedience, and true Dutie.
> RICHARD. Amen [SHIFT—ASIDE], and make me die a good old man,
> That is the butt-end of a Mothers blessing...
>
> (*Richard III*, TLN 1382–5)

An actor can clearly relish such opportunities to collude hammily with his audience. It is not long, however, before Shakespeare is regularly blurring the distinction between addressing others and addressing oneself. Often the midline switch occurs during a 'public' speech, with the technique indicating a brief moment in which the speaker 'checks in' with himself, listens to himself, as though for approbation or clarification. In other words, in the midst of conversation, there is self-policing, self-overhearing, self-consciousness.

A further sophistication is when the indicators of soliloquy become interspersed with those of dialogue. In fact, we see this happening from quite early in Shakespeare's writing career. Various moments in the role of Juliet illustrate this nicely. Here the actor, having begun the speech clearly addressing Romeo, will find his 'dialogue' complicated by a sequence of soliloquy-style short statements:

> [1] Faine would I dwell on forme, faine, faine, denie
> What I have spoke, [2] but farewell Complement,
> [3] Doest thou Love? [4] I know thou wilt say I,
> And I will take thy word, [5] yet if thou swear'st,
> Thou maiest prove false: [6] at Lovers perjuries
> They say *Jove* laught, [7] oh gentle *Romeo*,
> If thou dost Love, pronounce it faithfully.
>
> (TLN 886–92)

> [1] Faine would I dwell on forme, faine faine denie
> What I have spoke: [2] but farewell complements.
> [3] Doest thou love me? [4] Nay I know thou wilt say I,
> And I will take thy word: [5] but if thou swearst,
> Thou maiest prove false:
> [6] At Lovers perjuries they say Jove smiles.
> [7] Ah gentle *Romeo*, if thou love pronounce it faithfully.
>
> (Q1, D2a–b)

The Folio text has perfectly consistent lineation, but five successive lines are broken half-way through by a shift from one type of statement to another. The Quarto is somewhat more fluid: some of the breaks are at the ends of lines. What the actor's part was like, we cannot know; but we can see that the breaks are in the structure of the speech, as both Folio and Quarto compositors acknowledge. And, at each shift, the actor has to make a decision: does the movement from one variety of speech to another imply a new mode or new direction of address? Should she (add oblique) he speak to Romeo, or to herself? Clearly, any 'opening out' to Romeo is something of a dare; so she returns 'inward', half in hesitant self-checking, half to gird herself into renewed courage. It might go like this:

> [To herself] Faine would I dwell on forme, faine, faine, denie
> What I have spoke, (shift of voice) but farewell Complement,

(To Romeo) Doest thou Love? (to herself) I know thou wilt say I,
And I will take thy word, (to Romeo) yet if thou swear'st,
Thou maiest prove false: (to herself) at Lovers perjuries
They say Jove laught, (to Romeo) oh gentle *Romeo*,
If thou dost Love, pronounce it faithfully.

Of course, the various parts of the speech could be distributed in various ways. Juliet's use of 'thou', for instance, might indicate direct intimacy (spoken to the present Romeo) or wistful apostrophizing (spoken of an absent or future Romeo); similarly, Juliet keeps on referring back to an anterior wisdom, learned as though proverbially ('if thou swear'st | Thou maiest prove false', 'They say *Jove* laught'). The important point is that the midline gear change is, in each case, a direction to perform the character's debate with *herself*: the actor will recognize a 'soliloquial' structure inside putative dialogue. There is here in embryo much that Shakespeare went on to develop: in particular, the use of rhetorical machinery to direct shifts of attention and address between different characters and within a single speaker.

Instead of a simple demarcation between a public and a private being, or between rhetoric (for an audience) and confession (for oneself), such techniques help to furnish personae that are always in public even when most private, always partly private even when fully public. This gives us a much more delicate sense of gradations of *auditor*: the off-stage audience is always there, but sometimes more so than at other times. The same applies to the on-stage interlocutor who, even when directly addressed, might go in and out of the addressee's focus. And the same again applies to the speaker, who is always at some level his own addressee, just as the actor is always overhearing and assessing his own performance. Sometimes he 'hears' himself as he imagines his other addressees hear him, trying to anticipate responses and modulate his rhetoric and delivery accordingly; at other times his identification with 'their' attention diminishes, as he becomes more engaged with his own primary listening.

This technique becomes powerfully ubiquitous in the part of Hamlet. Consider this speech, immediately upon his first seeing the Ghost:

—————————————————————— [Lord], [it] comes.
Angels and Ministers of Grace defend us:
Be thou a Spirit of health, or Goblin damn'd,
Bring with thee ayres from Heaven, or blasts from Hell,

> Be thy events wicked, or charitable,
> Thou com'st in such a questionable shape
> That I will speake to thee. [SHIFT?] Ile call thee *Hamlet*,
> King, Father, Royall Dane: [SHIFT?] Oh, oh, answer me.
>
> (TLN 623–30)

The two midline shifts here would conventionally suggest to the actor that his address should move from one party to another, or that his manner of address, the basic intention directing his speech, should alter. But does it? It is possible that all three sentences framed by the two shifts are addressed directly to the Ghost, and in basically the same pleading register. Equally, it is possible that the opening five and a half lines are spoken to himself, and the shift after 'to thee' indicates that Hamlet has only then plucked up the courage to speak directly to the Ghost. Alternatively, 'Ile call thee Hamlet…' may remain a self-address, as he works out precisely how he is going to speak to the apparition: he is rehearsing options, before finally plunging in with 'Oh, oh, answer me,| Let me not burst in Ignorance; but tell| Why thy Canoniz'd bones…' (TLN 630–2). Or again, the sentence in between the two graphic midline shifts might be the sole example of self-address—he 'checks in' with himself before returning to the Ghost. (Indeed, each line from 'Be thou a Spirit of health' to 'or charitable' might contain two discrete questions, each separated by a quizzical pause.) The point to recognize is how the speech does *not* admit of a clear delineation between the actor addressing the Ghost and addressing himself. The midline switches—whether marked by punctuation or not—may easily have suggested a soliloquy style of acting; equally, they may have suggested a decisive switch (quite where is up to the actor) from fearful meditation to frantic address; or the actor may have recognized here an artful palimpsest, involving two styles of writing laid one over the other, so that he 'feels' soliloquy segue into dialogue, and dialogue into soliloquy, or feels the difficulty of deciding precisely when to switch, or indeed to switch back again: both experiences perfectly embodying his character's unprecedented dilemma, faced by a host who in the most basic sense truly is both an extension of himself and an unreachable other. It is not that the actor is left bereft or embarrassed here. He has real options, and they are immediately actable. He may well decide to leave a choice as it were undecided, and speak at once 'at' *and* 'over' the Ghost: again, this is all to the good. Indeed, precisely

because the Ghost is an 'externalized' version of Hamlet's present condition
(his temporal possibilities, metaphysical terror, spiritual angst, narrative
challenge, etc.), the actor can direct the movements implied by the
prosody to a clear target—even when hiding from or delaying addressing
this target.

The Hamlet-part often interweaves or confuses self-address and dialogue;
it is almost a predicate of the part, as suggested by its tart opening line
('A little more than kin'), or by the fact that it is impossible to determine
whether the 'To be or not to be' soliloquy is addressed to or heard
by anyone other than Hamlet. But this kind of layered midline switch,
interestingly, is used only when Hamlet is speaking to those characters
whose identity is intimately or even porously adjacent to his own: Horatio,
the Ghost, and his mother. He speaks almost exclusively in prose to
everyone else, which inevitably renders any sudden shifts or pauses more
shared with the audience and less tensely subjective. The effect is to establish
a uniquely teeming presence of *thought* 'in' the verse midline switch, or in
the invitations it presages.

This is exemplified in this speech, addressed nominally to Horatio, from
later in the Hamlet-part:

> ———————————————— [the] [businesse] there.
> [1] It will be short, [SWITCH]
> [2] The *interim's* mine, [SWITCH] [3] and a mans life's no more
> Then to say one: [SWITCH] [4] but I am very sorry good *Horatio*,
> That to *Laertes* I forgot my selfe; [SWITCH]
> [5] For by the image of my Cause, I see
> The Portraiture of his; [SWITCH] [6] Ile count his favours: [SWITCH]
> [7] But sure the bravery of his griefe did put me
> Into a Towring passion.
>
>                                    (TLN 3576–84)

There are numerous potential switches from one type of utterance to
another. However, there is no real *action* asked of any of them. Horatio
listens, but can do nothing; Hamlet speaks, his thoughts swirl, but his body
seems to all intents still. The movement is all in the mind, and repeatedly
pivots upon the midline or half-line switch. The actor will ask himself
which of these, if any, mark a shift from addressing Horatio to addressing
himself; he will see from the content that Hamlet is vacillating between
retrospective commentary ('to *Laertes* I forgot my selfe', 'the bravery of
his griefe did put me ... '), philosophical meditation ('The *interim's* mine',

'a mans life's no more ...', 'by the image of my Cause ...'), and present resolution ('Ile count his favours'). Only the first of these—and then only probably—makes more sense as dialogue. The other two modes are perhaps more compelling as 'internal' meditation. What seems clear is that at least half of the speech's gear changes can be read either way: moving from dialogue to monologue, or from monologue to dialogue, or continuing in one or the other; or, of course, performing both actions simultaneously, speaking to Horatio whilst more profoundly thinking out loud (Horatio, like the Ghost earlier, here serving as a double or sounding-board for the Prince's anxieties). The point of decision for the actor has to be the caesura, the pivot between one thought or one speech-action and the next. Above all, the midline shift becomes the location for *thinking*: for an effectively invisible process of coming to terms with the world, for slight shifts in attitude or orientation; for a self-conscious process of cognition; for a mind discovered, again and again, at the edge of volition; for an ongoing recognition of how every thinking moment presents choices, and elicits decisions, but how these decisions may issue forth only into renewed contingency; and above all, how neither consciousness nor communication is ever simply linear: both go backwards and forwards all the time, between one moment and another, and between one subject and another.

We can generalize from these instances about midline switches in 'mature' Shakespeare: even when no other actor or agent is at issue, the auditors (including the actor) can infer the presence 'in' the midline switch of rival lives or possibilities. In later Shakespeare, then, the stopped locution or syntactic ellipse continues to imply the imminence, expectation, or memory of another. But here is the radical change: this presence can now be phenomenological, rather than explicitly named or visibly embodied. An actor's daily practice and sensory antennae are thus transmuted into implicit or inferable experiential context. So, *every* speech with a midline switch, resonant as it must be with lurking silence, becomes in part a self-address. Conversely, there can be no such thing as a speech of absolute existential independence; we are always constructed and reconstructed interpersonally.

We can see this operating in powerfully affective apostrophizings such as the following. Each speech draws upon the metrical shifts conventional in 'narrator' roles; however, all of the midline caesuras are flooded with 'virtual' presences, with memories or associations that the specific situation evokes without quite naming. Here is a 'Gentleman' (or Horatio, probably mistakenly, in the Folio), speaking of the mad Ophelia in *Hamlet*:

> She speakes much of her Father; [SWITCH] saies she heares
> There's trickes i'th'world, and hems, and beats her heart,
> Spurnes enviously at Strawes, speakes things in doubt,
> That carry but halfe sense: [SWITCH] Her speech is nothing,
> Yet the unshaped use of it doth move
> The hearers to Collection; [SWITCH] they ayme at it,
> And botch the words up fit to their owne thoughts.
>
> (TLN 2749–55)

Here is Rosse speaking of Scotland under Macbeth's tyranny:

> Alas, poore Countrey,
> Almost affraid to know it selfe. [SWITCH] It cannot
> Be call'd our Mother, but our Grave; [SWITCH] where nothing,
> But who knowes nothing, is once seene to smile: [SWITCH]
> Where sighes, and groanes, and shrieks that rent the ayre
> Are made, not mark'd: [SWITCH] Where violent sorrow seemes
> A Moderne extasie [SWITCH] ...
>
> (*Macbeth*, TLN 2000–6)

Here is Miranda speaking of the opening tempest:

> The skye it seemes would powre down stinking pitch,
> But that the Sea, mounting to th'welkins cheeke,
> Dashes the fire out. [SWITCH] Oh! I have suffered
> With those that I saw suffer: [SWITCH] A brave vessell
> (Who had, no doubt, some noble creature in her)
> Dash'd all to peeces: [SWITCH] O, the cry did knocke ...
>
> (*Tempest*, TLN 84–9)

These midline spaces become populated by 'communal' experiences, associations, or expectations, intuitively supplied by the auditors to fill out the necessarily partly unarticulated mind of the speaker. But it is important to see how inferred presences such as these are not limited to narrative *tours de force* or emotionally loaded set-pieces. We can see the same basic associations at work in relatively banal conversation. Here is Polonius:

> I, Springes to catch Woodcocks. [SWITCH] I doe know,
> When the Bloud burnes, how Prodigall the Soule
> Lends the tongue vowes: [SWITCH] these blazes, daughter ...
>
> (*Hamlet*, TLN 581–3)

The speech's gear changes imply subtle shifts in Polonius's investment in his subject-matter—from proverbial advice to wistful memory—which at the same time invite us to 'fill in' the gaps with our own associations. Whether or not the syntactic shift prompts a tangible switch in focus or movement, it is always animated; it always suggests questions, or glints with past or possible life. Here is Lady Macduff:

> Wisedom? [SWITCH] to leave his wife, to leave his Babes,
> His Mansion, and his Titles, in a place
> From whence himselfe do's flye? [SWITCH] He loves us not,
> He wants the naturall touch. [SWITCH] For the poore Wren…
> (Macbeth, TLN 1719–22)

In 'mature' Shakespeare, then, the within-line shift is always populated by the busy minds or past experiences of others (including other versions of the speaker), and with a pre-apprehension of alternative judgements, differences, resistances, applause: that is, with all of the things that an *actor* seeks or expects, and which the part-generated midline shift has long accentuated. The result is profound. A dramatic verse built upon such effects, beholden to irregular prosody like a body to its joints, starts to animate its own 'sociality': we can sense a world listening in, whispering in the gaps. And in turn, this becomes a basic source of the permeating 'thickness' of Shakespearean dialogue—the way in which his syntax is flooding with consequence, agitating the blankness like wind over water, and suggesting as it does so *depth*. It helps explain that uncanny confidence that the speaking comes from living; that Shakespeare's given present always implies (seemingly) unarticulated hinterlands.

In the unreachable hiatuses of Shakespearean syntax sits some sort of basic recognition: we can never completely reach or know another; we can never completely be known or reached. In due course, as the technique takes over Shakespeare's verse, so these existential puzzles become perhaps Shakespeare's primary subject: the peril of love and the instability of any comforts; our mystery and our neediness, and the dependence of each upon the other; the fact that no one—wife, father, friend, servant, child, or oneself—can finally be possessed or transparent. As unlikely as it might sound, the midline break is an abiding home for all of this. It houses the permeating tremor, the catch in the voice, the barely enunciated breath; it allows the sharp intake or the swallowed word, the sudden aspiration or

abbreviating punctuation. The complete poetic line simulates a teleology
we can pretend to survive, or that otherwise protects and completes us; by
contrast, the decisive break in this line places us in a 'meantime' to which
we repeatedly return, definitively unfinished, reaching, and wanting. But
as much as this suggests a deep, profoundly human metaphysics in the
arrests and voltas of Shakespeare's speaking rhythms, it is also a simple
exdtrapolation of the most basic facts for the actor who grows up working
in parts, and of the apperceptive sensitivity that he necessarily develops. For
to the extent that other actors are absent from the part-text, they are implied
and therefore inferred in its ellipses; however exclusive or self-sufficient the
process of conning, rehearsing, or even performing the part might seem,
other actors are always at once echoing and imminent. In much the same
way, the lacunae of Shakespeare's syntax teems with ghostly others and
'virtual' lives, at once remembered and anticipated. It is of course we, the
hearers or readers, who have to intuit or animate these presences; to do
so Shakespeare relies upon *our* apperception, *our* imaginative populating
of absence. But the daily practice of his part-based actors got there first,
offering a powerful model for apprehending many lives in the gaps and
margins of one.

# 20

# Case Studies: Five Romantic Heroines and Three Lonely Men

In this final Part of the book we will look at a selection of parts that typify the contribution of prosodic switches to Shakespeare's increasingly sophisticated means of constructing character. We have seen how such effects are indispensable to the part-based actor, and how he always had to read very carefully through his part so as to pick up the vital points of climax and transition. Shakespeare expected much of his actors here; he required that they remain at once studious and alert—fully cognizant of customary practice, but always open to novelty. No doubt they in turn expected much of him: they can hardly not have been aware of Shakespeare's innovations in drawing character and situation; the company's principal actors must have received each new part eager to prove equal to whatever new combinations it held.

In the vast majority of cases, parts would have been learned in 'play order' from beginning to end (although, as *Hamlet* shows, an actor could be asked to con a particular addition or revision after he has learned the rest of the part, or even, we can presume, during his process of memorizing it). If we assume a part on a roll, then we can imagine a length of dialogue, fastened top and bottom about two sticks, which could be 'scrolled' with one hand; such parts would in the main have been studied linearly. Learning from a roll in this way, it may be difficult to compare passages that are any great space apart; flicking laboriously backwards and forwards would probably have been unusual. What would have been very clear with such a technology, however, is how one 'shape' of speaking precedes or proceeds upon another. By contrast, if the part were sewn into a 'magazine' or pamphlet form, or even handed out in single loose-leaf sheets, it would have been considerably easier to shuffle back and forth, comparing temporally distant scenes and passages (although as parts were sometimes distributed before plays were fully written, learning in 'play order' was still often a prerequisite). In practice, however, the type of subject or character being produced need not be foreclosed either way. There is no specific material shape that can preclude the actor's busy mental needlework, as he joins later bits with earlier ones and happens upon unanticipated patterns. Once the actor has read the part all the way through, he will inevitably supply a recursive perspective, bringing a fuller sense of the whole back to his understanding of each moment. And indeed, even actors with the most linear approach to a persona would intuitively be on the look-out for reprises and continuities that are seized upon precisely because they hark back to earlier things.

There is much at stake for the actor as he traces his part-script's shifts in shape, form, and rhythm. For in the absence of a framing narrator, explanatory glosses, or other characters, the speech bloc carries a massive weight of self- and situational definition for the actor. Perhaps before semantic referents, certainly before any play with or off others, prosody embodies emotion and directs performance: it lets the actor feel or intuit a characterized body to go along with the words. In this sense, dramatic prosody is 'performative' in a very foundational way. It allows the speech bloc to inhabit the actor as well as the actor to inhabit the speech bloc. We are perhaps accustomed to the idea that Shakespeare's polysemous words often exceed the full reach of the actor or possession of the character. But here we are suggesting something else: that the words exist in shapes or forms, visible as well as interpretable and speakable, that the actor might well recognize *before* he defines or deduces many other details; that he can take refuge in these shapes, or identify them as the place out of which any speech comes and into which the speaker returns. The recognition will be typological and generic, drawing upon allusions to or expectations of familiar precedents. But all the same, the recognition will 'feel' like intuition, enabling the actor to find confident embodiment, which will in turn create theatrical immediacy. The result is a character that seems ineffably to precede—and that will survive—the particular meaning of the words spoken. In other words, prosody furnishes the actor with his character's grounds of being—a temporary presupposing that this person/persona *is*. Dramatic prosody is here not so much about performing an act through speech, as proposing a consciousness before, beyond, and immanent in such an act. For the actor, prosody and ontology become one.

But if some such thing is the gift of dramatic prosody, then it is also the danger. For what if the actor's presuppositions are mistaken? Or what if the playwright decides to scramble the signs, and make the actor share in his character's struggle for self-possession? Shakespeare does not do this lightly; but when he does, it is always significant.

In this Part, then, we will look at the 'linear' unfolding of some of the part-based techniques we have already identified, and see how the character's story is progressively embodied in prosodic shifts and mutations. In particular, we will look at shifts into and out of rhyme, prose, and blank verse. These case studies are split into two sections. First, we will study a series of romantic heroine parts, quite possibly written for and played by the same actor: Portia, Rosalind, Olivia, Helena (*All's Well*), and Isabella. Second, we will study three more or less 'tragic' male parts, in which both the character and the actor experience a growing loneliness, even alienation: two whose stories we continue (having explored each part's indebtedness to repeated cues)—Mercutio and Shylock—and finally one major part, hardly touched on elsewhere, with which we end our book: Macbeth.

## Portia

When the actor scrolls through the part of Portia for the first time, he will see that the part begins with a lengthy prose scene, full of chatty and sassy humour; however, he will also see that the character never once speaks in prose again. This stark fact proposes an equally stark interpretive choice. Either the character changes radically and unalterably between her first and second scenes; or the 'Portia' of this first scene is filtered into what happens subsequently.

The early lines of Portia's part typify many of the opening scenes given to romantic heroines. The first line names the heroine's servant and confidante (the actor knows precisely to whom he is speaking), and sets an appropriately confidential tone: 'By my troth *Nerrissa*, my little body is a wearie of this great world' (TLN 196–7). The prose suggests a divided attitude: on the one hand it is intimate, socially assured, and sexually confident; on the other, it is itchy, edgy, and impatient. The opening lines present a deliberately ironic mock antithesis (little body–great world) : 'little' bespeaks concentrated self-reliance, 'great' sarcastic irreverence. Here is a rich girl who knows all too well how fat and inflated supposed 'great'-ness usually is. The actor will immediately recognize a scornful character, alert to contradictions, attracted by opposites—and in the very fluency of her pejoratives slightly bored:

> God made him, and therefore let him passe for a/man, but in truth I know it is a sinne to be a mocker, but he,/why he hath a horse better then the Neopolitans, a bet-/ter bad habite of frowning then the Count Palentine, he/is every man in no man, if a Trassell sing, he fals straight a capring, he will fence with his own shadow. (TLN 248–53; lineation ours)

In this chattering over-abundance the actor will identify a familiar comedic type (the high-born heroine whose irreverence, ascendance, and taste mark her out as a worthy erotic target): a character of wit and muscularity, for whom colloquial, confessionary prose is presently the frustrating 'home':

> I had rather to be marri-/ed to a deaths head with a bone in his mouth, then to ei-/ther or these ... (TLN 243–5)

> Very vildely in the morning when hee is sober,/and most vildely in the afternoone when he is drunke:/when he is best, he is a little worse then a man, and when/he is worst he is little better then a beast ... (TLN 276–9)

> I will doe any thing *Nerrissa*/ere I will be married to a spunge. (TLN 288–9)

> If I live to be as olde as *Sibilla*, I will dye as/chaste as *Diana* ... (TLN 296–7)

This is the actor's initiation into the part. If the candour and scorn disappear, so too, the actor may surmise, will the character's defining energy. From surveying the part, the actor will see that the rest of his speeches are to be in verse. One of his first jobs, then, will be to locate in this verse the 'Portia' he has already identified from the part's first prose scene. And the key to his continuities—and discontinuities—is the lines' prosodic shifts, and how these shifts carry a memory of the powerfully etched 'prose' Portia of the first scene.

The vital clue for the actor occurs at the very end of this opening scene. It is a speech of typically racy irreverence:

> If I could bid the fift welcome with so good/heart as I can bid the other foure farewell, I should be/glad of his approach: if he have the condition of a Saint,/and the complexion of a divell, I had rather hee should/shrive me then wive me. Come *Nerrissa*, sirra go before;/whiles wee shut the gate upon one wooer, another/knocks at the doore. (TLN 318–24)

Portia's exuberance finds simultaneous climax and release in two rhymes: 'rather hee should *shrive me* then *wive me*', and 'sirra go *before* … another knocks at *the doore*'. This is no longer straight prose, but nor is it quite metered verse. It is instead a bridge between the two: if this part has a 'prose mind' and a 'verse mind', then rhyming couplets partake of both. As we have seen, the *fact* of a rhyme always indicates some sort of switch, the nature of which depends upon the context. Usually it is one of two kinds: either towards union and companionship, or away from public discourse into private self-accounting. The two effects might seem opposite to one another, but they in fact own a profound affinity: the quick flick into rhyme presents a moment of mental clarification and emotional lucidity.

In this case, the prosodic transition goes in two stages. So, the 'shrive me'/'wive me' rhyme is of course not a metrically regular couplet; but the fact that the rhyme words are so close together ensures that the actor will relish their exuberant concatenation. Furthermore, the ribald juxtaposition is in the same contemptuous vein as the sentiments already spoken by Portia in unrhyming prose. This continuity of manner will suggest to the actor that the first rhyme is to be heard by—and shared with—Nerrissa. But it will also prepare him for the succeeding couplet. He will know that this second rhyme is not accidental (though still couched in a prose speech); but he may also know from numerous precedents that rhyming couplets like this one—unprompted and unanswered—are almost always a sign of private discourse. Consequently, as 'Portia' departs the scene on a couplet, she also leaves behind the overtly *performed* mode of witty prose. She swings (indeed, rather like the 'gate' she verbally plays with) into a brisk rhyme, which for all its authority brings in a newly equivocal note. So, as Portia moves into things unknown, dismissive nonchalance morphs into anxiety:

> Come *Nerrissa,* sirra go before;
> Whiles wee shut the gate upon one wooer, another knocks at the doore.
>
> (TLN 322–4)

The final line may well be spoken alone; certainly the sudden presence of rhyme can adumbrate a furtive private fear. The part of Portia as a whole has few verse couplets: but all are at story-and-character-defining moments; the actor will learn to shape his role around them.

From this point on, the role is entirely in verse. Partly this is because 'Portia' is always on display, and must tame her speech to conform to the formalities of public discourse. But the actor will search for continuities

despite this. Accordingly, he will immediately see how the first passage of
verse reprises the issues of the first prose scene—the frustration of being
without choice, the peril of being dependent upon another's will:

> _____ [my] [gentle] Queene.
> In tearmes of choise I am not solie led
> By nice direction of a maidens eies:
> Besides, the lottrie of my destenie
> Bars me the right of voluntarie choosing.
> But if my Father had not scanted me,
> And hedg'd me by his wit to yeelde my selfe
> His wife, who wins me by that meanes I told you,
> Your selfe (renowned Prince) than stood as faire
> As any commer I have look'd on yet
> For my affection.

> (TLN 529–39)

Reading in parts enables us to gather a much clearer sense of Portia's
grievances and edginess than does the full text, in which she seems more
or less politely to respond to the courtly Morocco. The part-script's recognition of who precisely is being addressed—'renowned Prince'—comes
belatedly; *seven* lines of complaint are spoken first. This has to make the
praise ('renowned Prince') feel like an afterthought, an obedience to the
rules of courtesy. In this it echoes the entire speech's straitened mimetic
obedience. And just as Portia has no real choice, but kicks impotently
against the fact, so too her metered speech is at once dictated by her dead
father and agitated by her own resistance. The actor will see this particularly
in the battle for control between the line and the sentence. The collision
of agitated pronoun and incarcerating verb encapsulates Portia's grievance:
she repeatedly places herself alongside contemptibly paralysing verbs ('Bars
*me*', 'scanted *me*', 'hedg'd *me*', 'yeelde *my selfe*'), just as she stresses the
sarcastic opposition between her father's 'wit' and 'my selfe'. Her very
being—witness the emphatic succession of 'I', 'a maiden', 'my', 'me',
'my', 'me', 'me', 'my selfe', 'me', 'I'—has been bartered by a dying man's
whimsy. Or consider the collocation, 'yeelde my selfe | His wife, who wins
me'. The enjambment invites the actor to 'flow' from one line to the next;
but the implicit ellipsis ('[*to be*] His wife'), followed by the immediate arrest
after 'wife', renders the speaking chillingly abrupt. 'His wife'—*stop*—comes
to seem an insult, a manifest impossibility, as the actor bites down upon the
very idea. The simple shape of the verse is here doing much of the actor's

work: and it is verse that posits the heroine as little less (or more) than a caged animal. Her wildness may be constrained by metrical form and good manners, remaining hidden from the other characters: but her private mind is thoroughly visible to the actor (and through him to the audience).

This edginess is going to find release in two places, both of which in some sense recover the liberties of Portia's opening scene: in rhyming couplets and in prose-like statements. One version of this latter is the short line of blank verse. In this second scene, the part has three short lines. Two of these are completed by Morocco to make a pentameter:

> For my affection.
> _____ Even for that I thanke you.
>
>                                 (TLN 539–40)
>
> Your hazard shall be made.
> _____ Good fortune then.
>
>                                 (TLN 564–5)

The other one completes a short line of Morocco's:

> And die with grieving.
> _____ You must take your chance.
>
>                                 (TLN 556–7)

Now, we do not know how much the Portia-actor knew, or whether or not he was conscious of the larger role his half-lines play in the scene's pentameters. What is clear is that the full play-text and the individual part-text are setting out potentially very different stories: the shared lines of the full text suggesting one prevailing mind-set (seeking or imposing union), the 'lonely' half-lines of the part-text suggesting a quite different mind-set (resisting union and deeply anxious about an unrevealed but imminent future). The discrepant fit between play and part is thus analogous to Portia's discomfort 'inside' conventional iambic pentameter: the actor's possession of and preference for his part-text can thus feed into *Portia's* possession of and preference for her own independent decision making.

Crucially, however, there is nothing assured or complacent about any such tenacious clinging to 'home truths'—on the part of Portia *or* her actor. For it is of the essence of these scenes that choice is threatened by coercion, and stubbornness niggled at by anxiety. Accordingly, Shakespeare is intentionally scripting a measure of actorly uncertainty. This is reinforced in Portia's next scene. Here the part-script repeats the short-line technique; but this time the lines are *not* going to be 'answered' by anyone. Here, then, is the part's entire third scene (in which, in the full play, Morocco chooses a casket):

> Goe, draw aside the curtaines, and discover
> The severall Caskets to this noble Prince:
> Now make your choyse.
> _____ [choose] [the] right?
> The one of them containes my picture Prince,
> If you choose that, then I am yours withal.
> _____ [as] [I] may.
> There take it Prince, and if my forme lye there
> Then I am yours.
> _____ [thus] [loosers] part. *Exit.*
> A gentle riddance: draw the curtaines, go:
> Let all of his complexion choose me so. *Exeunt.*

(TLN 973–1053)

The Portia-actor may not know that Morocco's speech leading up to the cue '[as] [I] may' proceeds for fifty lines—a long wait, suspenseful, nervous, and impatient, which may be felt by character and actor alike. Nor may he know that Portia's two short lines will here not be completed, instead echoing into a silence that is Portia's alone:

> Now make your choyse _____
> Then I am yours _____

Notwithstanding such potential insecurities, the part still gives a distinctive power to the actor when casting out short lines such as these: lines that because of the uncertainty of their acted moment (a perhaps literal and felt uncertainty for the actor, albeit very different from the uncertainty we impute to 'Portia'), and because of the fugitive independence of their prosody, can become all the more owned and individuating.

The part's very next line tells the actor how the casket choice went: the cue phrase is 'thus loosers part'. Portia remains unpossessed; in turn, the actor remains in possession of the part's defining wit and scorn. So, Morocco leaves, and the Portia-actor speaks his first full-verse rhyming couplet. Here it is that the character decisively returns to the caustic and quickly bigoted mind witnessed in the part's first scene:

> A gentle riddance: draw the curtaines, go:
> Let all of his complexion choose me so.
>
> (TLN 1052–3)

In a telling recursive move, the part first returns the actor to the word which started the scene ('Goe'), and then to the earlier prose couplet's concern with coming and going ('*go* before; whiles wee shut the gate upon one wooer, another knocks at the doore'). Once more the actor will identify a 'homing' device epitomized in the iterative rhythms and private pulse of Portia's couplets, just as he will in other strategically repeated words ('choose', 'me').

In story terms the next scene repeats what has just happened, though this time it is Aragon who chooses wrong; likewise, the Portia-part recapitulates the structure of the previous scene. But it also gives the actor hints of a further 'transition', again consistent with the sharp-minded individuation of the opening prose scene's sketch. This time the movement is from irritation, to exhaustion, to burgeoning parody:

> Behold, there stand the caskets noble Prince,
> If you choose that wherein I am contain'd,
> Straight shall our nuptiall rights be solemniz'd:
> But if thou faile, without more speech my Lord,
> You must be gone from hence immediately.
> _____ [and] [be] gone.
> To these injunctions every one doth sweare
> That comes to hazard for my worthlesse selfe.
> _____ [my] [fortunes] here.
> Too long a pause for that which you finde there.
> _____ [deserts] [no] better?
> To offend and judge are distinct offices,
> And of opposed natures.
> _____ [beare] [my] wroath.
> Thus hath the candle sing'd the moath:
> O these deliberate fooles when they doe choose,
> They have the wisdome by their wit to loose.
>
> (TLN 1117–94)

Read in part-terms, Portia's brusque impatience is tersely evident. As before with 'Goe', she starts with what she really wants of Aragon: 'You must be gone from hence immediately'. Her blank verse betrays not the slightest hesitation; the foreshortened line ('And of opposed natures') is peremptory rather than uncertain, emboldened by the noble prince's impotent cue-phrase ('deserts no better?'). Everything here is aimed at the bottom line—get it right or be gone. Yet whereas in the previous scene the long pause for the suitor's preamble was characterized by an uncertain tension, here the part mordantly footnotes the delay, pre-empting any tension it might have contained. So, Aragon's cue to Portia, after a speech of no fewer than thirty-four lines, is met with a derisively rhyming putdown:

> _____ [my] [fortunes] here.
> Too long a pause for that which you finde there.

For the actor playing Portia, rhymes such as these are the missing bridge between the candour of prose and the coercion of verse. 'Too long a pause ... ', she says, bored and contemptuous, and as though emboldened by the non-fatal outcome of the first trial. She can hardly wait to be released from the pseudo-deliberation. This release is then celebrated in another foreshortened line, and another 'stolen' couplet: 'Thus hath the candle sing'd the moath', rhyming with Aragon's 'wroath'. In play terms this line is a deliberate tetrameter that takes up and mocks Aragon's rhyming tetrameter ('Sweet adue, Ile keepe my oath, | Patiently to beare my wroath' (TLN 1190–1)). The Portia-actor will know from the cue that his response is a rhyme. But seeing the tetrameter in a passage mainly of pentameter, he may also choose to exploit the missing iamb, finding a brief gap in time and space to spot, relish, and then 'perform' his double-coupleted dismissal:

> ARAGON. ... Patiently to beare my wroath.
> PORTIA.  Thus hath the candle sing'd the moath:
>          O these deliberate fooles when they doe choose,
>          They have the wisdome by their wit to loose.
>
> (TLN 1191–4)

Recapitulating Portia's twin themes of 'choosing' and 'losing', the final lines function as powerfully self-centring asides. On neither occasion does the 'blinking idiot' Aragon remotely share in the rhyme. Each is for Portia alone: the first an aside in the midst of his endless contemplation over the caskets, the second offering snap-like closure, as she offloads her anxieties (choose/lose) on to this latest loser.

The first words of the next scene herald still another stylistic transition—now into flustered blank verse:

> I pray you tarrie, pause a day or two
> Before you hazard, for in choosing wrong
> I loose your companie; therefore forbeare a while,
> There's something tels me (but it is not love)
> I would not loose you …
>
>                              (TLN 1342–6)

Read in part-script, the effect is very clear. This longing for delay butts up immediately and comically against Portia's regular injunctions to 'go' and loathing of all 'pause' in the previous scenes. This new resistance to speed, the longing to remain in this moment of undisappointed possibility, duly informs the verse shape:

> … I could teach you
> How to choose right, but then I am foresworne,
> So will I never be, so may you misse me,
> But if you doe, youle make me wish a sinne,
> That I had beene forsworne: Beshrow your eyes,
> They have ore-lookt me and devided me,
> One halfe of me is yours, the other halfe yours,
> Mine owne I would say: but of [if] mine then yours,
> And so all yours; O these naughtie times
> Put bars betweene the owners and their rights.
> And so though yours, not yours (prove it so)
> Let Fortune goe to hell for it, not I.
> I speake too long, but 'tis to peize the time,
> To ich it, and to draw it out in length,
> To stay you from election.
>
>                              (TLN 1351–65)

Flushed with halting and prevarication, with midline arrests, nervous word-play, and extra syllables, the passage closes with a wry apology for its own manners ('I speake too long…') that is itself as drawn out as the foregoing speech. The actor will recognize a new mode of blank verse, embodying a nervously delighted, dilated stutter. Portia's verse up until this point has not displayed a single decisive midline switch (her parting dismissal of Morocco—'A gentle riddance: draw the curtains' (TLN 1052)—aside). Now barely a sentence goes by without one:

> Let musicke sound while he doth make his choise,
> Then if he loose he makes a Swan-like end,

Fading in musique. That the comparison
May stand more proper, my eye shall be the streame
And watrie death-bed for him: he may win,
And what is musique than? Than musique is
Even as the flourish, when true subjects bowe
To a new crowned Monarch...

(TLN 1386–93)

This is the verse of a mind energetically in motion, darting off at angles into glimpsed vistas of extinction or apotheosis. 'Pointing' this part as he learns it, the actor will be forced to pause repeatedly midline—at 'musique', 'him', 'than?' and 'Monarch' merely in the passage above. Each such momentary hiatus will seem to invite the voice of another, or await interruption, confirmation, or contradiction. Of course the speaker knows there will be no such interruptions—but he can play the possibility, all the while knowing that the absence of such intervention has its own resonance. Portia is grasping after the uncertain possibilities of others, waiting upon the not yet spoken choice of another—even as the only voice speaking is hers. The resultant pauses are thus Portia's alone, embodying moments of concentrated internal projection.

But the thing to notice, once more, is the movement between different prosodic registers. It is in these that the actor locates the part's deepest and most dependable psychological infrastructure; whatever the vicissitudes and interpolations of the full script, the actor will identify his own coherence and continuity. So, in the scene where Bassanio surveys the caskets, the Portia-actor will have learned these lines:

> I stand for sacrifice,
> The rest aloofe are the Dardanian wives:
> With bleared visages come forth to view
> The issue of th'exploit: Goe Hercules,
> Live thou, I live [.] with much more dismay
> I view the fight, then thou that mak'st the fray.
> ———————————————————— [be] [the] consequence
> How all the other passions fleet to ayre,
> As doubtfull thoughts, and rash imbrac'd despaire:
> And shuddring feare, and greene-eyed jealousie.
> O love be moderate, allay thy extasie,
> In measure raine thy joy, scant this excesse,

> I feele too much thy blessing, make it lesse,
> For feare I surfeit.

(TLN 1400–60)

The actor will see that Portia's speech of fractured blank verse ends with a rhyming couplet ('dismay'/'fray'); and that her next speech begins with a sestet of rhyming couplets, importantly *not* prompted by the inconclusive but premonitory cue-phrase ('be the consequence'). As it happens, Portia has to wait through a 'ding dong' song, and then another thirty-plus-line speech, before she is given the cue for the rhyming sestet. However, the actor learning the part may not know this. Instead, he is likely to presume a tight emotional link between the closing couplet of one speech and the opening couplets of the next. The fact that there is such an excruciating delay between them in performance means that he has to sustain his mood of anxious suspense for minutes on end. The player is likely to feel intensified identification with the couplets, to cherish them as his own. Because the chain of couplets on his part is interrupted for so long, he is asked to sustain his present agitation 'inside' them, at once 'in' the gap between his first and second couplets, and 'in' the couplets themselves, as though the authentic speech of Portia's heart. Simultaneously, the actor will locate a repeating pattern—this time a repeat that harks back to the close of Portia's opening scene, when rhyme first formed a bridge between prose and verse, private and public. Here the prosody mediates between broken blank verse and nervous couplets: the same mind inheres throughout. What the couplets do above all is keep the 'original' Portia (feisty, funny, nobody's fool) in view even as her social circumstances are more straitened and impotent than ever.

Once again we see the peculiar power of rhyme to create a moment that is shared with the audience, but with no on-stage character. The rhyming sestet subsists in the middle of another's blank verse. So, the sestet occurs at the moment in between Bassanio's making the choice of a casket and opening it. Of course, Bassanio cannot speak while Portia does: but in terms of the fiction, these are Portia's thoughts as Bassanio's hand reaches towards the box, as he gathers his courage, and raises the lid. The rhyme form purports to step out of an intensely suspenseful moment—rather like an animated thought bubble—at once seeking perspective upon what is at stake and searching for perspective beyond it. The suggestion is of Portia effortfully attempting to put her unruliness into a trance. But the violence of her sentiments—another transmutation of her earlier prose, loaded likewise with incorrigibly physical agitation—makes placation hopeless. The bare rhymes themselves convey this forcefully

————————————————— fleet to ayre,
————————————————— rash imbrac'd despaire:
————————————————— greene-eyed jealousie.
————————————————— allay thy extasie,
————————————————— scant this excesse,
————————————————— make it lesse.

(TLN 1454–9)

The rhymes are at once spellbinding and pendulum-like. This alone embodies Portia's paralysed inability to move beyond her present knowledge: her fate really is at a cusp. In other words, the rhyme form itself is an allegory of Portia's attempt at rational moderation, as she desperately tries to batten down what is within ('allay', 'scant', 'make it lesse'). For the Portia-actor, rhyme is much more than a merely formal framework. It is an *embodiment* of the passions at issue—almost a residual 'Portia-body', concordant with grace and refinement, but profoundly rocked from within.

Repeatedly, the part's brisk shifts from one mode of speech to another reveal indecorous prosody 'beneath' apparently more decorous prescripts. Any simulation of escape and closure in the rhyme form, therefore, intensifies the fact of felt emotion. This helps explain the way the rhymes conclude nothing, but instead give way to a terrified half-line: 'For feare I surfeit'. Once again, the part's determining directives to the actor—rhyme and broken line—work complementarily. The short line sums up the larger speech's anxiety (can I contain myself?), before exiting into a space of frightened apprehension. (Bassanio's incomplete half-line response, 'What finde I here?', cannot be wrestled to make a pentameter with Portia.) Nothing can be done but wait, as Portia hangs upon the next words of her beloved, desperate that the cue here given to Bassanio ('feare I surfeit') should not be unhappily prophetic.

The next time Portia speaks is when, in the story of the play, all of these anxieties have been resolved: Bassanio chooses the right casket, and the marriage is assured. The actor will be in no doubt what has happened—his next words are 'You see my Lord *Bassanio*'. But the simple shape of Portia's lines makes her new state equally clear. Overthrowing metrical irregularities and stylistic experimentation, her next speech instead offers

controlled conceits and swelling repetitions in a ritualized ceremony of
self-commitment:

> You see my Lord *Bassanio* where I stand,
> Such as I am; though for my selfe alone
> I would not be ambitious in my wish,
> To wish my selfe much better, yet for you,
> I would be trebled twenty times my selfe,
> A thousand times more faire, ten thousand times
> More rich, that onely to stand high in your account,
> I might in vertues, beauties, livings, friends,
> Exceed account: but the full summe of me
> Is sum of nothing: which to terme in grosse,
> Is an unlesson'd girle, unschool'd, unpractiz'd,
> Happy in this, she is not yet so old
> But she may learne: happier then this,
> Shee is not bred so dull but she can learne;
> Happiest of all, is that her gentle spirit
> Commits it selfe to yours to be directed,
> As from her Lord, her Governour, her King.
> My selfe, and what is mine, to you and yours
> Is now converted.
>
> (TLN 1496–1514)

Portia's passion play is in a basic sense over. Whereas with Morocco she
was jealously superintending of her personal pronouns (*I, me, my*), here she
happily gives them over: '*it* selfe to *yours*', '*her* Lord, *her* Governour, *her*
King', 'what is *mine*, to *you* and *yours*'. The character has to begin all over
again, in a newly humble, acquiescent register ('*she* is not yet so old | But
*she* may learne'). But interestingly—and as this new third-person idiom
might imply, pretending as it does to speak of some other 'she' whom
Portia watches, or may in the future observe—the *actor* never once has
to play this submissiveness. This is true even of this initiating speech of
wifely obedience: Portia declares her intention to renounce all possession
to her husband, but the act of so doing is itself sheer authority. This is her
choice, her act—and her gift to rescind if ever Bassanio should fail his part
in the bargain ('I give them with this ring, | Which when you part from,
loose, or give away, | Let it presage the ruine of your love, | And be my
vantage to exclaime on you' (TLN 1517–21)). The 'unlesson'd girle' she
invokes is simply not in the actor's part; like the 'nothing' she similarly
claims to have devolved into, it works more as a coy come-on to her man

(witness the slyly knowing ingenuousness of 'the full summe of me | Is sum of nothing: which to terme in grosse, | Is an unlesson'd girle') than as any genuine commitment to a new role.

For the Portia-actor this fact is crucial. He doesn't remotely need to 'put away' what he has by now internalized as the part's under-flowing mental *and* physical current—pro-activity, impatience, irreverence, virility. So, far from becoming the model good wife, 'Portia' is immediately redirected into energetic stage business: she hears of the misfortune of Bassanio's 'deere friend', gives her husband gold, and dresses up as a lawyer. All is dominance. Accordingly, what the actor will find is a role more emboldened than ever by raffish volition.

This transition is once again channelled through a simple change in the use of short lines and couplets. The part's very first words after its long speech of putative wifely submission are 'Is this true *Nerrissa*?' (TLN 1556). Once again Portia is the mistress, batting away interruptions ('So do I my Lord, they are intirely welcome' (TLN 1575)) and demanding answers:

> What summe owes he the Jew?
> ————————————————— [three] [thousand] ducats.
> What, no more?
> Pay him six thousand, and deface the bond;
> Double sixe thousand …
>
> (TLN 1654–8)

The short lines now speak only of Portia's power: her demand for information or her certainty of knowledge. This new manner is reinforced by the ensuing couplets:

> My maid *Nerrissa*, and my selfe meane time
> Will live as maids and widdowes; come away,
> For you shall hence upon your wedding day:
> Bid your friends welcome, show a merry cheere,
> Since you are deere bought, I will love you deere.
> But let me heare the letter of your friend.
>
> (TLN 1667–72)

The sense of the couplets is alive with ironies and double-speak, typified by the wry pun upon 'deere', as Portia girds herself for costly new challenges. But for the actor the crucial thing is not the referential content of the couplets but—as always—how they physically direct his acting. Being thus clearly addressed to intimates, these couplets resemble conventional parting rhymes—summative lines which allow one to exit a scene with a swing. But any such conclusive optimism is deceptive. The rhymes do not end the scene: they don't even end the speech. They enact instead a simulacrum of 'public' closure—and wifely obedience—before passing with resolute swiftness into what now takes over as the part's dominant manner: busy, purposeful, proto-masculine authority: 'But let me heare the letter of your friend' (TLN 1672). Strung between a request and an instruction, this prosy pentameter, sweeping away any predilection in the preceding couplets for harmonious joy or private doubt, marks the decisive transition into the Portia-part's third mode.

From this point on the role is timed by recurring prose-like lines—if seeking answers, then brisk stand-alone questions; if asserting authority, then abrupt openings to a longer speech. As always, the brusquely stopped line opens out to other actors: but now the fear or hope is limited to Portia's interlocutors. Portia is swift and commanding; so too is the actor: inwardness has given way to plot. (The part has only one more couplet, an epitome of the plot-driven departing rhyme 'therefore haste away, | For we must measure twentie miles to day' (TLN 1811–12).) This new boldness is typified by the fact that furtive locutions (couplets, pauses) are no longer needed to embody the character's restless energy. Instead, Portia puts on the disguise of the male lawyer, 'Balthazar'. The actor can stay 'in part', while the character can elude or defer the connubial leash by becoming precisely the play-actor.

Crucially for the actor, this new prosaic verse—made up of short commands acting upon others—is sustained whether he is playing a man or a woman. So, he speaks them as 'Portia':

> Come on *Nerrissa*. (TLN 1783)
> Fie, what a questions that? (TLN 1807)

As Balthazar:

> Which is the Merchant heere? and which is the Jew?          (TLN 2082)
> Is your name *Shylocke*?          (TLN 2084)
> Do you confesse the bond?          (TLN 2091)
> Then must the Jew be mercifull.          (TLN 2093)
> Is he not able to discharge the money?          (TLN 2119)
> Why this bond is forfeit          (TLN 2142)
> Why then thus it is          (TLN 2157)
> Therefore lay bare your bosom.          (TLN 2165)

Thy selfe shalt see the Act        (TLN 2231)
Why doth the Jew pause        (TLN 2252)
Take thy forfeiture        (TLN 2252)
Tarry Jew        (TLN 2064)
Art thou contented, Jew? What dost thou say?        (TLN 2311)
Clarke, draw a deed of gift.        (TLN 2313)

As Portia again:

Enquire the Jewes house out, give him this deed,
And let him signe it.

(TLN 2380–1)

As Balthazar once more:

That cannot be.        (TLN 2389)
I pray you shew my youth old *Shylockes* house.        (TLN 2392)

And as Portia to the close:

Away, make haste        (TLN 2400)
Are they return'd?        (TLN 2533)
Go in *Nerrissa*        (TLN 2537)
A quarrel hoe alreadie, what's the matter?        (TLN 2568)
You were too blame, I must be plaine with you        (TLN 2588)
What Ring gave you my Lord?        (TLN 2607)
Sir, grieve not you,        (TLN 2663)
Marke you but that?        (TLN 2669)
Then you shall be his suretie: give him this,
And bid him keepe it better then the other        (TLN 2680–1)
Speake not so grossely        (TLN 2693)
How now *Lorenzo*?        (TLN 2717)
It is almost morning        (TLN 2725)
Let us goe in.        (TLN 2727)

The part stays remarkably businesslike to the very end. The short lines give the actor space to 'allow' Portia's triumph, mainly by eliciting and observing the surprised gratitude of others. But in so far as any inwardness of *Portia* is concerned, the part remains as playfully self-deflecting and emotionally impregnable as it has been since Bassanio chose the correct casket. So, the final two short speech units appropriately occur in the part's very last speech:

*It is almost morning,*
And yet I am sure you are not satisfied

> Of these events at full. *Let us goe in*,
> And charge us there upon intergatories,
> And we will answer all things faithfully.
>
> (TLN 2725–9; our italics)

'It is almost morning' promises to release Portia's stooges from *her* version of the enthralling bond: but only 'almost'. 'Let us goe in' is similarly the Portia-character's command, and the Portia-actor's orchestration.

Neither political nor prosodic renunciation will happen in this part. The character may be about to take on the domesticity and obedience promised by her betrothal. But the actor never has to, instead remaining robustly faithful to the manners established in the part's very first prose scene—manners which the actor keeps steadily in view through all of the part's twists and turns. So, when 'Portia' returns in the final scene, there is a corresponding return to her familiar candour and iconoclasm: she exchanges impatient wit (in verse) with Nerrissa; when Bassanio does finally enter, she delays the revelation that she was Balthazar and that she has the ring until the very final moments, facilitating further boundary-bending ribaldry ('I will become as liberall as you, | Ile not deny him any thing I have, | No, not my body, nor my husbands bed: | Know him I shall, I am well sure of it' (TLN 2650–3)). We might explain away this episode as a series of temporary games, as a charade of independence and irreverence before the 'real life' of spousal obedience is assumed. But the actor does not need to project into futures beyond the part-script, or indeed even 'naturalize' the character he is to play. His job is to act the part: and this part is *always* at the edge of decorum, chipping away at obstructions, or seeking small easements wherein she (or he) might express impatience, mischief, or power. In the first half of this part, dramatic prosody is a vehicle and allegory of the self in process; in the second half, dramatic prosody is a vehicle and allegory of acting—indeed, of a particularly commanding style of play-acting that suggests an alternative (and perhaps prophetic) authority.


# Rosalind


If the same actor who played Portia did indeed also play Rosalind, then he would have noticed a number of similar prosodic devices in his part—though used to different ends. The most cursory survey of the part would tell the actor that this is a 'controlling' role. He would see that almost every speech is initiating and assertive rather than passive; he would see a tremendous extemporizing gusto, whether in prose or verse, and a fluid adaptability in which language is used to act *upon* others rather than to hide or explore oneself. At the same time, he would also see that Rosalind is a much longer role than that of Portia, and is far fuller of transitions from prose to verse and back. Throughout the play Rosalind is given scenes of confessional, garrulous prose (the kind of scene that Portia has only once), but she has, by contrast, far fewer moments of suspended, anxious, or 'silent' inwardness. Instead, the prose/verse shifts are dominated by Rosalind's multiple role-play, as she leads or guards against the affections of her country cousins. The actor confronted with the role must, then, analyse each prose/verse switch and decide how to play it—for when such a transition does convey psychic or emotional portent, then the actor can be sure that he is at one of the part's defining moments.

The first and third cues given to the actor establish the character's initial situation and disposition: '[Coz,] [be] merry' (TLN 172) and '[*Rose,*] [be] merry' (TLN 191–2). The hints are of melancholy, stubbornness, and perhaps capricious power: though fully aware that others rely upon her high spirits, she will choose when and when not to give of herself. Her subsequent movement into bantering prose ('What shall be our sport then?' (TLN 199)) and witty repartee ('Then shal we be newes cram'd' (TLN 261)) is thus clearly marked as both a concession to her friend and a compensation for her as yet unspoken sorrow. The actor is to show Rosalind doing her best in the circumstances, but also a pervading detachment from the merriment: something is to be kept in reserve.

All of this changes very suddenly, with the part's first excursion out of prose into verse. It occurs when Rosalind realizes that the young wrestler she has been admiring is the son of her exiled father's dear friend:

> _____ [come] [your] waies.
> Now Hercules, be thy speede yong man.
> _____ [by] [the] legge.
> Oh excellent yong man.
> _____ [heire] [to] *Fredricke.*
> My Father lov'd Sir Roland as his soule,
> And all the word was of my Fathers minde,
> Had I before knowne this yong man his sonne,

> I should have given him teares unto entreaties,
> Ere he should thus have ventur'd.

(TLN 371–402)

For the actor, the shift into verse is a clear sign of sudden emotional engagement. Its theme is love: Rosalind's father's love for his friend, Rosalind's love for her father, and, by extension, Rosalind's love for her father's friend's son. Whereas the prose speaks of wry deflection, the verse suddenly evokes the profoundest springs of selfhood: memory joins with possibility, father with son, a lost love with a future love. The part so far has been premissed upon half-buried grief; the verse is here the cable for its lifting. The brief trip into verse thus gives new layers to the part's emotional soil. The actor might identify almost a reversal of what happens in the Portia-part: in Portia's verse there remains a stubborn, necessary, but often furtive residue of her prose manners; in Rosalind, it is the 'verse themes' that carry through, mutated, into the prose:

> ————————————————————— [for] [your] Father?
> No, some of it is for my childes Father: Oh/how full of briers is this working
> day world.                                                     (TLN 469–71)

The prosodic to-and-fro does two things. It establishes that verse can symbolize a change in attitude; but that change once having taken place, it also establishes that it is not only in verse that this altered condition can find embodiment: a subsequent shift back to prose or verse need not imply a blank return to a former state of mind. Prosodic transitions can instead accrete, serving as markers of awakening or maturing emotional experience; they are invariably at once interruptive (because marking a sudden change) and continuous (because the change becomes part of the developing character). It thus tells as much about character as it does about plot; indeed, it is about character *as* plot.

But the actor of course has to know about 'external' transitions just as much as internal ones. When, for instance, Rosalind decides to dress as a man, the part then has to tell the actor about altered habits of mind, tongue, and body. Here is the Rosalind-part marking the entrance into the forest:

> O *Jupiter*, how merry are my spirits?
> ————————————————————— [were] [not] wearie.
> I could finde in my heart to disgrace my mans/apparell, and to cry like a
> woman: but I must comfort/the weaker vessell, as doublet and hose ought to
> show it/selfe coragious to petty-coate; therefore courage, good/*Aliena*.

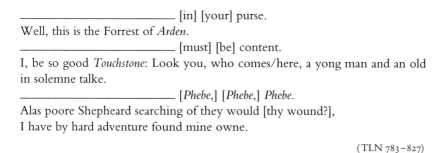

———————————————— [in] [your] purse.
Well, this is the Forrest of *Arden*.
———————————————— [must] [be] content.
I, be so good *Touchstone*: Look you, who comes/here, a yong man and an old
in solemne talke.
———————————————— [*Phebe*,] [*Phebe*,] *Phebe*.
Alas poore Shepheard searching of they would [thy wound?],
I have by hard adventure found mine owne.

(TLN 783–827)

The part-script establishes geography and situation with typical economy
('…my mans apparell', 'this is the Forrest of *Arden*' (TLN 787–8, 797)).
The actor of Rosalind could not be placed any more securely. Meanwhile,
the speeches are all exploring the implications and possibilities of the
character's new sex. So, whereas the role began with Rosalind's sorrow,
here Rosalind, as Ganymede, opens on her happiness: 'how merry are my
spirits'. The character is trying to refashion herself, perhaps not so much
into a man, as into a different emotional type. Obviously the male costume
gives both the actor and the character liberty not quite to inhabit either
the male or the female body (an ambiguity between player and part further
helped by the practice of casting boys or young men as women). This
liberty in turn licenses further shifting layers of self-identification in the
speeches: Ganymede could 'cry *like* a woman' (our italics); similarly, the
pronoun 'I' mutates between female self-reference ('*I* could finde in my
heart…') and male ('*I* must comfort the weaker vessell'). Just as the male
disguise permits a very overt probing of the character's individual identity,
asking 'Rosalind' to study herself with dispassionate objectivity, so too the
part-script asks the *actor* to pay close attention to his own moves: to stand
partially outside himself and observe the decorum of his motions. There is
thus an interesting congruity in the way the part sets up both its 'female'
and 'male' behaviour. It will be clear to the actor, whichever 'sex' he
is playing, that the swaggering public manner both deflects and displaces
unsettled inward feelings. The part (like the larger play) is all the time
testing the possibilities of playfully hypothesized selves or vocations. But
Rosalind's (or Shakespeare's) jazz-like improvisations are *always* variations
upon the strong central themes. The part never loses touch with the fact
of emotional layers, or that it is precisely these depths which are impelling
much of the role-play. And the actor would largely know this—know that
his acting remains accountable to genuine emotion and affect—through

its repeated stylistic *returns*. Neither verse nor prose is ever far away; the 'truth' of each inheres in the other: Rosalind remains Rosalind.

The actor will be reminded of this when, during his first scene as Ganymede, he is asked to switch back into plaintive blank verse:

> I, be so good *Touchstone*: Look you, who comes/here, a yong man and an old in solemne talke.
> ———————————————— [Phebe,] [Phebe,] Phebe.
> Alas poore Shepheard searching of they would [thy wound?],
> I have by hard adventure found mine owne.
>
> (TLN 802–27)

Clearly Rosalind's words mark a transition from external banter to a more internal earnestness. The switch appears unexpected, as though a sudden irruption of feeling into a hitherto breezy scene—but is it? For a start, the actor should pick up how the part is continuing to explore 'inward' feeling through 'external' displacements. 'Look you, who comes here', she/he says, 'a yong man and an old in solemne talke'. The actor is prepared to watch, and to find significance in whatever he is about to witness. But more than that, he needs to consider the import of the thrice-spoken cue-word, 'Phebe'. Of course it is possible that the part of Rosalind transcribed only a single 'Phebe' as the cue. But this seems unlikely. For the actor conning the part, the only clue to the nature of the 'adventure' is the cue itself, in which case the three words are inestimably more useful than one. He will guess easily enough that '*Phebe, Phebe, Phebe*' stands for a lovelorn lamentation. In full script this lamentation, spoken by Silvius, takes the form of three increasingly long speeches articulating the passion and pain of love, each climaxing with the refrain 'Thou hast not lov'd'. In full script, or of course performance, it is listening to this that has to stand for Rosalind's 'hard adventure'—nothing more. When the actor is learning the part, however, the same weight of vicarious experience must be inferred from the cue-words alone ('*Phebe, Phebe, Phebe*'). The Rosalind-actor will read the repeated cue in the light of his scripted response to it; he will anticipate being given the space (by the Silvius-actor) to locate and perform such a protracted experience. So, nominally cued to speak by the first '*Phebe*', Rosalind's 'searching' can now be going on inside the drip-fed misery or echoing wail of the cue-phrase. Rosalind's blank verse response thus retroactively transforms a brief speech-cum-song into hard-earned personal experience (something the play does throughout, as songs fill in for the absent experience of seasons and geography). The statement casts backwards to give length and depth to fleetingly staged time. At the same time, Rosalind's commentary is proleptic: by acknowledging the imperfectness of forgetfulness or repression, it works as a preparation for the *extension* of emotional accountability into the rest of the part. That is, Rosalind 'will' by 'hard adventure' search her 'wound' (or perhaps her 'would', if we accept the Folio reading, which thereby means 'what she would', or 'as she likes it').

Of course, placed in this picaresque comic landscape, the actor will know that much of the time this wound will be covered up: hence the basic Rosalind/Ganymede prose style, which is brisk, loquacious, assertive, decisive, and self-delighting. 'Ganymede's' repeated set-pieces are afire with comic antitheses, accumulating conceits, and mocking illustrations:

―――――――――――――――――――― [cure] [any] so?

Yes one, and in this manner. Hee was to ima-/gine me his Love, his Mistris: and I set him everie day/to woe me. At which time would I, being but a moonish/youth, greeve, be effeminate, changeable, longing, and/liking, proud, fantastical, apish, shallow, inconstant, ful/of teares, full of smiles; for everie passion something, and/for no passion truly anything, as boyes and women are/for the most part, cattle of this colour: would now like/him, now loath him: then entertaine him, then forswear/him: now weepe for him, then spit at him; that I drave/my Sutor from his mad humor of love, to a living humor/of madnes …

(TLN 1585–97)

With its buoyant humour and improvised stories, this is the prose of Rosalind the plot-maker. It is a discourse of unthreatened self-possession. A very different prose, however, marks the moment when she/he learns that her love for Orlando is requited:

―――――――――――――――――――― [(Coz)] [tis] he.

*Orlando?*

―――――――――――――――――――― *Orlando.*

Alas the day, what shall I do with my doublet &/hose? What did he when thou saw'st him? What sayde/he? How look'd he? Wherein went he? What makes hee/heere? Did he aske for me? Where remaines he? How/parted he with thee? And when shalt thou see him a-/gaine? Answer me in one word.

―――――――――――――――――――― [in] [a] Catechisme.

But doth he know that I am in this Forrest, and/in mans apparrell? Looks he as freshly, as he did the day/he Wrastled?

(TLN 1409–25)

Because the exchange is in prose, the actor can play all of the pauses between the sentences at any pace he wishes. The torrent of questions can come in one great rush, or they might come in separate spurts, in line with Rosalind's behest to Celia moments earlier, 'I pre'thee tell me, who is it quickely, and speake apace: I would thou couldst stammer, that thou might'st powre this conceal'd man out of thy mouth, as Wine comes out of a narrow-mouth'd bottle: either too much at once, or none at all' (TLN 1393–7). Here the unanswered—the unanswerable—question is a comic device, accentuating how Rosalind's bubbling nerves obliterate her addressee. But as such, it is also a genuine marker of emotional intensity. These brisk questions usually invite action from the addressee. And certainly the actor playing Celia has to decide how to perform while waiting for the cue of 'in one word'. However—ironically but tellingly—the cue comes at the end of a command, *not* a question. This reinforces something deliriously self-exclusive about the questions that precede it. There are ten of them in succession, and they are all in some fundamental sense addressed to Rosalind herself. In a curious way, therefore, the speech has few designs upon Celia at all, and asks for no responding action. The cue sentence—'Answer me in one word'—jokingly reinforces Celia's effective silencing.

The actor will notice how very unusual this kind of speaking is for Rosalind. Generally the character speaks *to* others, both expecting and dictating responses (even though her addressees are often oblivious to her plotting or pretence). In the pseudo-questions of this moment, therefore, we can identify a productive technique for portraying ecstatic communion with the self—an actable technique that helps furnish some of the more subjective nuances of the part. Rosalind's non-questions allow a pause in proceedings while the full significance of the news is absorbed. Ironically, the garrulous abandonment of rhetorical control produces something akin to the effect of silence. No one can reach 'Rosalind' within her questions; in this loquacious privacy, the speech is as close as the part comes to soliloquy. The distinctive elasticity of prose here helps to produce one of the part's pivotal moments: it signifies Rosalind's emotional homecoming and, allowed and emboldened by this, her leave-taking into the relaxed and superior confidence with which she orchestrates the remainder of the action.

# Olivia

Now let us imagine that the same boy performer were to be given the roll of Olivia to learn (admittedly, he might just as easily have been given Viola). Olivia, like Rosalind, moves regularly between prose and verse—but, as we shall see, for different reasons. In its very layout the part looks distinctive. It opens with a series of one-line prose exchanges, and regularly reverts to this: Olivia's basic mode throughout is the brisk command and curt question:

_____ [blesse] [thee] Lady.
Take the foole away.
_____ [away] [the] Ladie.
Go too, y'are a dry foole: Ile no more of you: besides you grow dishonest.
_____ [take] [her] away.
Sir, I bad them take away you.
_____ [you] [a] foole.
Can you do it?
_____ [Dexteriously,] [good] Madona.
Make your proofe.
_____ [virtue] [answer] mee.
Well sir, for want of other idlenesse, Ile bide your proofe.
_____ [why] [mournst] thou?
Good foole, for my brothers death.
_____ [in] [hell,] Madona.
I know his soule is in heaven, foole.
_____ [the] [Foole,] Gentlemen.
What thinke you of this foole _Malvolio_, doth he not mend?

(TLN 330–66)

The first switch away from prose into verse always indicates a change in emotional tenor; here the transition occurs (as we might expect) with the first approach of Viola/Cesario:

What kinde o'man is he?
_____ [Why] [of] mankinde.
What manner of man?
_____ [you,] [or] no.
Of what personage, and yeeres is he?
_____ [out] [of] him.
Let him approach: Call in my Gentlewoman.

> *Exit Malvolio*
> *Enter Maria*
> Give me my vaile: come throw it ore my face,
> Wee'l once more heare *Orsinos* Embassie.
>
> (TLN 444–60)

The actor will notice how the peremptory prose modulates, as though at once unwillingly *and* serendipitously, into a verse-line. So, the first two speech units here are roughly identical short questions; the next contains two questions, making a longer line that almost amounts to a pentameter ('Of what personage, and yeeres is he?'): the frustrated curiosity is drawing Olivia out of her armour of prose. The process continues in the next two lines, which both compact two discrete units of speech into full pentameters—'Let him approach' (TLN 456) and 'Call in my Gentlewoman' (TLN 456), then 'Give me my vaile' (TLN 459) and 'come throw it ore my face' (TLN 459). For the actor the effect is at once tense and portentous. In moving out of prose, the player must ratchet up expectation and concentration; at the same time the residual clinging to prose bespeaks a character who will resist the pre-empting or formulaic predilections of metre. As Olivia falls in love with 'Cesario', her tenacious identification with prose is whittled down—although not without a struggle.

When first meeting 'Cesario', Olivia reverts to the clipped, impatient, and haughty prose that has typified her previous disquisitions ('your will' (TLN 463); 'Whence came you sir?' (TLN 471); 'Are you a Comedian?' (TLN 476); 'Come to what is important in't' (TLN 486); 'Speake your office' (TLN 501); 'What are you? What would you?' (TLN 505–6); 'In his bosome? In what chapter of his bosome' (TLN 517); 'Have you no more to say?' (TLN 519–20)). However, as the questions proceed, they grow in ambiguity, and the actor is clearly instructed to play her emerging curiosity about the stranger. Once Olivia consents to 'draw the Curtain' (TLN 524) and show her face, actor and character have both come upon new possibilities for openness.

As he searches for signs of emotional transition, the actor must attend as much to the shape as the sense of his speeches. Viola/Cesario is the first to start speaking in verse. Crucially, however, this is the clichéd verse she has conned from her master's scripted part. Twice Viola's verse speeches end with a half-line—'And leave the world no copie' (TLN 534), 'The non-pareil of beautie' (TLN 545). The Olivia-actor may or may not be aware that he will be invited to complete the line and so suggest two minds in unison. The part certainly tells him to resist Viola's over-mediated, coercive stab at harmony. So, Olivia initially continues to speak in tough-minded prose; 'And leave the world no copie' is Viola's iambic cue line, to which Olivia returns:

> O sir, I will not be so hard-hearted: I will give/out divers scedules of my beautie. It shalbe Inventoried/and every particle and utensile labell'd to my will. As,/Item two lippes indifferent redde, Item two grey eyes,/with lids to them: Item, one necke, one chin, & so forth …

> (TLN 534–9)

When Olivia *does* respond with her own half-line, the effect remains ambiguous:

> _____ [The] [non-pareil] [of] beautie.
> How does he love me?

> (TLN 545–6)

The actor is unable to achieve any snappy co-operation: a pause between 'beautie' and 'How' is unavoidable, and the shared line is neither quite iambic (Olivia's 'How' receives a jarring stress) nor quite a pentameter. Eventually the Olivia-part does give way to verse. But it is very unlike the first such transition in the Rosalind-part. For it signals a movement *away* from, rather than towards, self-possession or -confession. Verse here is all about generic obedience, taking the form of Olivia's *imitation* of obedience to patriarchy. That this is a simulation is made apparent to the actor by the way the verse shape frustrates the part's usual pithy compression, and with it the character's stubbornly capricious comic will:

> Your Lord does know my mind, I cannot love him
> Yet I suppose him vertuous, know him noble …
> In voyces well divulg'd, free, learn'd, and valiant,
> And in dimension, and the shape of nature,
> A gracious person; But yet I cannot love him:
> He might have tooke his answer long ago.
> (TLN 549–55)

The switch to verse—as always—connotes a change in mental lighting or emotional heat: but of what precise kind only the context can tell. And again and again we see that this context is discernible more at the level of rhythm than semantics. The actor will know what the switch to verse in a love scene can—invariably does—portend. He will equally know that the newness, and therein the seriousness, of the verse-form (which according to the normal rules, should now hail the true love's virtues) is uncomfortably at odds with the trite clichés and paratactic formulae he is here asked to express (which of course hail Orsino's virtues rather than Cesario's). So, Olivia's list of worthy adjectives ('vertuous … noble … free, learn'd, and valiant') suggests a wearily rehearsed catalogue, while only the final line achieves the impulsion of a confident iambic pentameter. The feminine endings of the other lines here quoted reinforce an air of irresolution, or of a mind not fully committed to the speaking moment. The actor may well conclude that the scripting of his role is here playing with, or playing 'off', part-based conventions for scripting subjective change: that the prosodic transition is itself mere hollowed-out imitation.

For this is a language that by the late 1590s is as open to ironic or anti-typical appropriations as any other. Far from heralding emotional transformation, the verse speech takes its listless patterning from the immediately preceding prose speech. Here Olivia had very consciously, very formulaically iterated her physical merits ('Item two lippes indifferent redde, Item two grey eyes, with lids to them: Item, one necke, one chin, & so forth. Were you sent hither to praise me?' (TLN 538–40)). The main difference, as always so far in this part, is that the prose is more frank in its weariness with epideictic convention. When the actor comes to the similar rehearsal of Orsino's gifts ('In voyces well divulg'd, free, learn'd, and valiant' (TLN 553)), it cannot but be infected by Olivia's etiolated self-eulogy of a few moments earlier. What Olivia says about Orsino's attributes is unimpeachable; the fact that she so little cares or even believes in it, *her* substantive absence from the blazon of virtues, is almost entirely carried by the way her rhythms echo the exhaustion and ennui of her prose. And so it is that the only sentiment really invested in here takes its rhythmic cue unambiguously—rather than tacitly—from prose: Olivia's thrice-spoken confirmation that 'I cannot love him' (TLN 549, 554, 575), a sentiment that can hardly avoid sounding abruptly discordant.

The Olivia-part rarely puts up with such false observances for long; its repeated habit is to cut to the chase. The actor will know that Olivia's pre-eminent wish is to banish all thoughts of Orsino and to ingratiate herself into her new interlocutor's affections; to do so she needs to settle upon a mutually harmonious register. Again, the shape and swing of the lines alone tells the story:

> _____ [not] [understand] it.
> Why, what would you ?
> _____ [should] [pittie] me.
> You might do much:
> What is your Parentage?
> _____ [am] [a] Gentleman.
> Get you to your Lord: ...

(TLN 559–71)

The actor will see that Olivia repeatedly shortens her own line, and may assume—or know—that this is because she completes Cesario's. In full text, she twice completes Cesario's verse, but on the third occasion, Viola/Cesario, and then Olivia, appear to speak prose statements followed by long pauses (the two lines together do not comfortably make up a pentameter). Thus, throughout, the fit of one line into another lacks real grace or ease, while Olivia's content continues to suggest discrete prose statements rather than shared verse-lines. There is no comfortable prosodic folding of one person's speech into the other; correspondingly, the actor is told, there will be no harmonious merging of mind and emotion. Even when, later in the same scene, the part does achieve a clear and simple pentameter line, its rhythms continue to be choppy:

> I cannot love him: let him send no more,
> Unlesse (perchance) you come to me againe,
> To tell me how he takes it: Fare you well:
> I thanke you for your paines: spend this for mee.

(TLN 575–8)

The actor will fix upon the fact that all of the lines are in some fashion sliced through the middle—either by the juxtaposing of distinct statements or instructions, or by halting parenthesis '(perchance)'. By splitting the verse-line into commands and questions, none of which elicit an answer, the part maroons the actor within his own speech bloc, indeed within his own line. He must repeatedly kick-start the lines, as one by one they seem to expire half-way through (summarized by Viola in her subsequent soliloquy: 'me thought her eyes had lost her tongue, | For she did speake in starts distractedly' (TLN 675–8)).

The curious metrical mix of abruptness and hesitancy shows a character reaching for decisiveness, or for some releasing response. In the last two lines every word is a monosyllable, and none is particularly selected for emphasis; that the rhythms are more pyrrhic than spondaic is appropriate, in that Olivia's apparent directions are in truth more like hopeful pleas. The prosody instructs the actor to search 'visually' into the Viola-actor: for if the character is here hunting for reciprocity, then so too is the actor. But there will be no help here from his addressee, and the gaps are instead filled with Olivia's effortful yearning and fitful distraction. The shift in the line (recalling Rosalind on a similarly flustered occasion) becomes a moment to act this present impasse, and with it the effective *absence* of any emotional or experiential transition. Instead we see confusion, yearning, even a dismayed prescience of burnt bridges and shredded dignity ('spend this for mee' (TLN 578)).

Perhaps the decisive transition in the part of Olivia is marked by a switch from blank verse to rhyming couplets, which corresponds to a similar switch from anguished aside to direct address:

> O what a deal of scorne, lookes beautifull?
> In the contempt and anger of his lip,
> A murdrous guilt shewes not it selfe more soone,
> Then love that would seeme hid: Loves night, is noone.
> *Cesario*, by the Roses of the Spring,
> By maid-hood, honor, truth, and every thing,
> I love thee so ...
>
> (TLN 1360–6)

The first three and a half lines are clearly a blank-verse 'aside', ending with the half-line 'love that would seeme hid'. Olivia then wrenches herself out of this secret pain through the fearless, oddly self-stripping device of turning a private confession into a rhyming couplet that only she (as it were) can hear. This first couplet is thus a secret *rehearsal* for the 'confession' about to come. So, in the line immediately following this first couplet, the actor is directly instructed to address Cesario ('*Cesario*, by the Roses of the Spring' (TLN 1364)). It is as though Olivia must grit her teeth, and prepare through this device to go fully public with her (rhyming) declaration of love. There follow no fewer than five fully declared, fully public couplets. The strange and admirable recklessness in all of this is found in the way the part here stretches the normal range of the comic couplet. Usually a device either for internal meditation or for openly shared sentiments (whether of love or combat), here the first couplet pivots *between* the two. This unconventional use of rhyme—which takes its effect precisely by flouting a normative convention—is working as an allegory of this precipitate and surprising character's challenge to conventional female behaviour.

Couplets soon mark another important moment in the unfolding role of Olivia; again, she is responding to Viola/Cesario:

> ——————————————————— [will] [acquit] you.
> Well, come againe to morrow: far-thee-well,
> A Fiend like thee might beare my soule to hell.

(TLN 1733–5)

Olivia's first line here is characteristically broken. It contains three distinct speech units, each capable of marking both a considerable pause and a shift in orientation: 'Well -'/'- come againe to morrow -'/'far-thee-well'. Only the second of these is clearly addressed to Viola/Cesario. The first suggests a wry address—perhaps a sigh—to herself; 'come againe to morrow', meanwhile, may be the Viola-actor's cue to exit. If the player does walk off-stage with this remark, then Olivia's 'far-thee-well' is spoken to Viola's retreating back. The possibility that the midline break rather than 'far-thee-well' indicates Viola's exit is reinforced by the fact that 'far-thee-well' is the opening half of one of Olivia's closing couplets. A couplet is almost always spoken only *to* those who share in the sentiment: here such candour is likely to be for the speaker's ears alone. But the couplet is doing more: as it often does, it figures here a shift of address. The actor was speaking to the player of Cesario, but is now speaking to himself (and the audience). At the same time, the address is to the *absent* Cesario, as the double use of 'thee' suggests. Up until this point, when addressing Cesario directly, Olivia has used 'you': 'it hath no tongue, to vex you' (TLN 1726); 'beseech you come againe' (TLN 1727); 'I have given to you' (TLN 1732). Of course, there is a convention that 'thee' or 'thou' is used when the addressee is off-stage (confirming Cesario's exit). But this sudden switch to the familiar 'thee' also has the force of candid self-truth. Left alone, Olivia can at last speak of—speak *to*—her beloved as she would wish. Again we see how the part's prosodic shifts help orchestrate changes in address, which in turn allow for the unfolding of a mind at odds with its surroundings and in battle with itself.

Prosodic irregularities pepper Olivia's part right up until the betrothal with Sebastian (her first meeting with Sebastian is full of her habitual metrical violence). At this point the verse settles down, and in the final scenes the part returns to its earlier nature: 'Olivia' is free once more to command, which she does with either brisk prose questions (her conversational mode before the disruption of love) or solid blank verse (her achievement after the acceptance of love). We see here how the actor's part is scoring very simple but fundamental shifts in address, and in doing so orchestrating the basic stuff of the comedy: cross-purposes and humiliation; a hint of poignancy in the farce, an abiding centredness in the character: and all founded in uncertain rhythms, unanswered pauses, and by the unrelenting but somehow understanding gaze thus cast upon the halting speaker.

## Helena (*Alls' Well That Ends Well*)

Helena's part looks entirely different from Olivia's. It contains an unusual number of long speeches for a comic heroine. For the actor looking at the role, Helena might seem to be someone who misjudges her place (perhaps one who 'tragi-comically' thinks herself a heroine from a different kind of play). His impression will be confirmed as he starts to read and learn the role. For he will find that Helena, like many heroines before her, has couplets as her norm. When he acts the play, however, he will quickly realize that few other characters speak in rhyme at all. Unlike, say, *A Midsummer Night's Dream*, where rhyme signifies a concentration of emotion amongst a group of people, rhyme in the Helena-part is a mark of singularity.

As with all the heroine-parts, the first scene establishes the specific energies or potential that must be harnessed if the role is to gather comic-romantic authenticity. In Helena's case, the initiating speeches are a mix of stubborn but unforthcoming public paradox ('I doe affect a sorrow indeed, but I have it too' (TLN 56)) and, far more promisingly, unaffected private confession (her first soliloquy begins, 'O were that all, I thinke not on my father' (TLN 83)). This, then, is the challenge of the role: how to achieve self-truth, how to *be*, in a society that prevents precisely that? If not soliloquy—and soliloquy is plainly unsustainable as a medium of social success—then what? The answer, as the actor will soon realize, is rhyming couplets. For they are the single form that can carry both the soliloquy-like aside and a bonding invitation to others—and in carrying the two, potentially unite them.

The rhymes don't come immediately. Instead, after opening with a single brief line of characterizing paradox ('I doe affect a sorrow indeed, but I have it too' (TLN 56)), the part turns straight to a twenty-line verse soliloquy about Helena's love. The verse is sinuous and agile, the sentiments candidly informative. The mere fact of a soliloquy here establishes the character's basic place for actor and audience: Helena is at the centre of the play, but at the margins of the court. This defining spatial antipathy suggests just how difficult it is for Helena to speak frankly in public. The problem for an actor seeking confident access to both character and audience is made manifest in the part's next two stylistic transitions. First the role segues into prose ribaldry, in which it is less Helena than generalized womankind that is at issue ('Blesse our poore Virginity from underminers and blowers up', and so on (TLN 125–6)). This ribbing exchange, with a man she clearly disdains ('You go so much backward when you fight'), then yields to two speeches of wilfully enigmatic obtuseness:

> _____ [anything] [with] it?
> Not my virginity yet:
> There shall your Master have a thousand loves,
> A Mother, and a Mistresse, and a friend,
> A Phenix, Captaine, and an enemy …
> His humble ambition, proud humility:
> His jarring, concord: and his discord, dulcet:
> His faith, his sweet disaster: with a world
> Of pretty fond adoptious christendomes
> That blinking Cupid gossips …
>
> (TLN 168–79)

The speech starts with a pause after 'virginity yet': the theme of much of the role. It continues as a series of oxymorons, dwelling obsessively on Helena's contradictory feelings about her contradictory love. The effect is at once coy, monomaniacal, and strangely abandoned. This abrupt shift into obsession suggests to the actor that the character is here repeating a thought dwelt upon a million times. But the subject of this avalanche of paradox remains elusive. Learning this part in isolation, the actor may wonder what on earth she is on about. Is Helena imagining Bertram at court, meeting a succession of rivals for his possession? Or is she envisioning herself as Bertram's everything: his mother, mistress, and friend; his phoenix, captain, and enemy; his guide, goddess, and sovereign; his counsellor, traitoress, and dear? But if the actor is confused, or rendered semi-absent from the subject, then this probably serves the speech's tumid sense of self-alienation or -estrangement. So, just as the speech begins and proceeds upon what seem to be obsessive ellipses, it ends with a confusion of stopped lines and attenuated thoughts:

> ... Now shall he:
> I know not what he shall, God send him well,
> The Courts a learning place, and he is one.
>
> (TLN 179–81)

Two things at least will be clear to the actor: that the character is morbidly in love; and that the inequities in her station and situation confound the lucid articulation of inward truth. This in turn is the import of her very next speech, that the 'poorer born' can only speak truly when alone: 'we the poorer borne | Whose baser stares do shut us up in wishes ... shew what we alone must thinke, which never | Returnes us thankes' (TLN 186–90). Once more the speech's subject is elusive, its syntax at once dense, wandering, and elliptical. The actor will already be bursting to return to the lucid frankness with which the part began. This is where the rhymes come in.

For from this point on, the part's decisive moments will repeatedly be marked by rhyming couplets:

> Our remedies oft in our selves do lye,
> Which we ascribe to heaven: the fated skye
> Gives us free scope, onely doth backward pull
> Our slow designes, when we our selves are dull.
> What power is it, which mounts my love so hye,
> That makes me see, and cannot feede mine eye? ...
>
> (TLN 223–8)

(And so on for another eight lines.) The actor will see couplet pile upon couplet, never once being 'answered' by another character. There is nothing light or escapist about these rhymes. Instead, they embody a mind suspended above humdrum concourse, reflecting the intense concentration of focus and sense of forethought that separates Helena's mind from everybody else's.

We see this again in Helena's confession of love for the Countess's son. The emotional pressure of this speech is initially expressed through a tense mix of abbreviated lines and *physical* propitiation (Helena kneels):

> Then I confesse
> Here on my knee, before high heaven and you,
> That before you, and next unto high heaven, I love your Sonne:
>
> > (TLN 523–5)

This is how the Folio transcribes the moment: we might prefer to give 'I love your Sonne' its own line, but either way the effect is to send out Helena's confession into a perilous silence. The Countess does not respond; nor does she respond when Helena makes two, three, four more attempts (three marked by midline switches) to receive blessing or forgiveness for her presumptuous adoration:

> Be not offended, for it hurts not him
> That he is lov'd of me ...
>
> > (TLN 526–7)

> ... My deerest Madam,
> Let not your hate incounter with my love ...
>
> > (TLN 538–9)

> ... [B]ut if your selfe,
> Whose aged honor cites a virtuous youth
> Did ever, in so true a flame of liking,
> Wish chastly ...
>
> > (TLN 540–3)

This escalating desperation is the context for Helena's prosodic turn in the speech's final four lines:

> ... O then give pittie
> To her whose state is such, that cannot choose
> But lend and give where she is sure to loose;
> That seekes not to finde that, her search implies,
> But riddle like, lives sweetely where she dies.
>
> > (TLN 544–8)

Helena ends with two rhyming couplets, rehearsing her familiar preoccupations. By this stage in the part, the *fact* of rhyme has already garnered its own prestige for the actor, marking a pressure-point of physical longing and emotional intensity. The switch to rhyme—and particularly to *two* successive couplets, rather than the much more pat convention of closing a long speech with a single couplet—thus suggests a shift in address. Helena has throughout this nearly thirty-line speech been directly, pleadingly addressing the Countess; this has failed. The couplets do not mark an intensification of such address; it would hardly be possible to address anyone else with greater intensity than Helena already has. Instead, they mark a switch to partial—or even complete—self-address. That is, the actor can identify the couplets as a sign that Helena, recognizing the failure of her entreaties, takes refuge in the fierce and lonely ardour which, as her earlier couplets attested, has become her habit and her home: she 'riddle like, lives sweetely where she dies'. Perhaps the Countess hears the rhyme; perhaps Helena speaks the final three and a half lines as an aside, ending her direct entreaty to the Countess with 'O then give pittie | To her whose state is such, that cannot choose'. But either way, the rhyme tells the actor that the 'riddle' remains Helena's to cherish. Confession or not, it is not yet to be shared; the fiercest mode of address remains internalized.

Appropriately, therefore, in the full text the Countess does not respond in stylistic kind. Her blank verse is instead peremptory and ragged:

> Had you not lately an intent, speake truly,
> To goe to *Paris*?

(TLN 549–50)

This disjunctiveness will come as no surprise to the Helena-actor: the rhymes themselves prepare for it; indeed, they require it. Whereas a single closing rhyming couplet often suggests an openness to sharing, or an invitation for others to share or enter, these consecutive rhymes suggest something closer to 'self-rhyming' solipsism: the more isolated and exposed Helena's passion is, the more firmly etched and definitive is its expression.

There is another part-pivoting rhyme effect in Helena's next scene, when she tries to persuade the dying King to take her cure. Rhyme once again concentrates the part's distinctive manner: like Helena herself in this scene, it becomes an audacious agent of lulling permission and occult intensity.

——————————————————————— [busines] [follow] us?
I my good Lord,
*Gerard de Narbon* was my father,
In what he did professe, well found.
——————————————————————— [I] [knew] him.
The rather will I spare my praises towards him,
Knowing him is enough: on's bed of death,
Many receits he gave me, chieflie one,
Which as the dearest issue of his practice
And of his olde experience, th' onlie darling,
He bad me store up, as a triple eye,
Safer then mine owne two: more deare I have so,
And hearing your high Maiestie is toucht
With that malignant cause, wherein the honour
Of my deare fathers gift, stands cheefe in power,
I come to tender it, and my appliance,
With all bound humblenesse.
——————————————————————— [sence] [we] deeme.
My dutie then shall pay me for my paines:
I will no more enforce mine office on you,
Humbly intreating from your royall thoughts,
A modest one to beare me backe againe.
——————————————————————— [thou] [no] Art.

(TLN 706–42)

Helena begins speaking in blank verse of a nervous and irregular kind
(or perhaps even prose); next her script becomes orthodox and author-
itative. However, both methods prove impotent, as the actor learns by
the cue '[thou] [no] Art'. This heralds the decisive transition, into four
long speeches of rhyming couplets, through which Helena will try to
enchant the King into submission. Crucially, unlike in the previous scene,
Shakespeare does not make these couplets go 'unanswered'. This is because, true to decorum, it is the King who first speaks in rhyme to
Helena; indeed, the King has already ended two successive speeches
with couplets. This has a double effect. First, the Helena-actor, who
starts rhyming with a couplet of her own (rather than completing one
of the King's), may be unaware of the King's contribution. He may
identify his own sudden switch into couplets as another sign of portentous transition: something big is happening; she/he is trying to draw
someone inside the permissive audacity of *her* 'rhyme space'. In performance, however, the actor will recognize that this rhyme space is

already partly the King's—albeit presaged by the relatively conventional speech-closing single couplet. The moment is thus flush with both expectation and surprise: the move into rhyme is also a move into tantalizing connection.

Of course, this prosodic 'meeting' foretells the fact that the King will indeed try Helena's cure. And satisfaction draws closer with the part's next rhyming speech, which begins by rhyming *with* the cue—and thus the Helena-actor knowingly sharing a couplet with the King:

> _____ [for] [their] reward.
> Inspired Merit so by breath is bard,
> It is not so with him that all things knows
> As 'tis with us, that square our guesse by showes:
> But most it is presumption in us, when
> The helpe of heaven we count the act of men.
>
> (TLN 756–61)

By isolating and focusing the shared rhyme, the part-text makes Helena's mission crystal clear. She will both accede to others' speech patterns and try to bring others into hers; the shared rhyme is reaching toward mutuality, while all the time it is *itself* an active and actable agency, bending the King's will to her own.

However, as the scene goes on, the part-text makes it likewise clear that the King does not immediately succumb:

> _____ [thou] [my] cure?
> The Greatest grace lending grace,
> Ere twice the horses of the sunne shall bring
> Their fiery torcher his diurnall ring...
>
> (TLN 769–72)

By not giving Helena another couplet to complete, the part-text clearly raises questions for the actor to ponder. Does the part-script elide some decisive sea change? Is the King retracting? Has someone else intervened? Are the powers of hypnotic, occult verse simply inadequate? Any uncertainty the actor feels can only reinforce the scene's feel of risk taking and agitation: and as we so often find, it is performance rather than rehearsal that must resolve the doubts. So, the actor may not realize until performing the scene that 'Helena' is given another means of attempting connection. She will complete the King's arrested line, and at the same time she will turn the

King's (unrhyming) penultimate line into the first half of *her* rhyme. Here is the full play-text:

KING.    Art thou so confident? Within what space
        Hop'st thou my cure?
HELENA.  The greatest grace lending grace ...

(TLN 768–70)

There follows a confident succession of couplets, all from Helena ('shall bring'/'diurnall ring', 'occidental damp'/'sleepy lamp', 'pilot's glass'/'how they pass', 'shall flie'/'freely die'). In other words, this scene stages itself in one way, while being learned in another.

In modern performances Helena invariably continues to manipulate the King, fired by sublime and presumptuous confidence. But Shakespeare's first actor may well have endured a very different experience, founded in the discrepancy between part-script and play-script. He would know the words he is to speak, but he would not fully know what they mean—because their meaning is transformed once it becomes part of a rhyme. Literally unaware of what has been and what is to come, the actor may perform a Helena who is insecure, terrified, walking a tightrope: one slip, and it is all over. The discrepancy between part-script and play-script thus recommends an admixture of hesitant trembling and sudden, resolving surprise. To the extent that the rhymes are 'blind' improvisations or unexpected gifts that the actor extemporally embraces, the rhyme effect embodies the character's audacity. In its mix of neediness, coercion, impudence, improvisation—and eventual success—the technique epitomizes the entire role.

Hardly surprisingly, the technique is exactly repeated at the next moment of exchange; here again is the full play-text—in which Helena takes up the King's half-line, completes it, and by so doing rhymes with his preceding line:

KING.    Upon thy certainty and confidence,
        What dar'st thou venter?
HELENA.  Taxe of impudence,
        A strumpets boldnesse, a divulged shame
        Traduc'd by odious ballads: my maidens name ...

(TLN 779–83)

Perhaps the actor has now sussed out what his playwright is doing, and performs the manœuvre with renewed confidence; perhaps he again moves through lonely hesitancy into serendipitous resolution. What is certain is that the actor has to *catch up* with his own character's 'boldnesse'. In play-script, the 'certainty and confidence' spoken of by the King is all Helena's; in part-script, it is not the Helena-actor's at all. His cue is 'dar'st thou venter', and the question is powerfully meta-performative. The actor too must join 'impudence' with 'confidence'; he must first recognize the 'hidden cue' (the invitation to rhyme), and then seize it as his own. Helena's trembling passage into stage-centre power could hardly be better served than through such experiential shadowing of the character by the actor.

So it is that the King's next reply responds in rhyming kind:

> KING.       Sweet practiser, thy Physicke I will try,
>                 That ministers thine owne death if I die.
> HELENA.    If I breake time, or flinch in property
>                 Of what I spoke, unpittied let me die.

> (TLN 796–9)

Helena has won; the scene between her and the King now proceeds in rhyming mutuality until its close.[1] But if the part's orchestration of rhymes represents little less than a seduction (witness the reiterated pun upon 'die'), it is a seduction based on offering—and risking—all. Hence the clearly pointed repetition of 'I die'/'let me die': a 'shared' and 'perfect' rhyme that is at once bold, ominous, and an impudent invitation to imagine mutual orgasm.

When we read the role of Helena in part-text, it is this moment of union with the King that, more than any other, marks her triumphant coming-to-be. Of course, she has a still greater conquest in her sights. But the part-text tells quite another tale—one more in line with the play's notoriously problematic nature. So, the part sustains an assured self-control as Helena refuses the various lords offered her, her refusals couched in the familiar rhyming couplets. However, the moment that Helena claims Bertram is also the moment of her almost palpable fading away:

> I dare not say I take you, but I give
> Me and my service, ever whilst I live
> Into your guiding power: This is the man.
> (TLN 1000–2)

Helena's public commitment to Bertram is marked by the abrupt renunciation of rhyme in favour of a hesitantly broken line of blank verse—or, as the actor of Helena may see it, by sending out a statement ('This is the man') that *may* be answered by a rhyme. But it is not. Instead, this single line of blank verse initiates Helena's emergence from self-rhyming, and with it opens up her new vulnerability to another's responses. In fact, as the actor will learn in performance, 'Helena' says nothing more after this for fifty lines. The part eventually has 'That you are well restor'd my Lord, I'me glad; | Let the rest go' (TLN 1050–1)—and then again nothing until Helena is led off-stage after a further forty lines. In the interim the actor will be subject to the actions of others—the King tells Bertram to 'Take her by the hand' (TLN 1077); Bertram says, 'I take her hand' (TLN 1081)—but nothing of this is in the Helena-actor's part. As though a bitter parody of comic-romantic closure, the Helena-actor is led off in impotent, perhaps ignorant, silence.

This defeat in victory carries on, still more devastatingly, in Helena's next scene with Bertram. Again, the raw information of the part-text tells all. There are no more rhymes. Instead, having entered to the devastating cue, '[comes] [my] clog', Helena speaks to her new husband in hesitant, over-formal blank verse ('I have sir as I was commanded from you' (TLN 1326); 'But that I am your most obedient servant' (TLN 1346); 'I am not worthie of the wealth I owe' (TLN 1356)). This nice observance of metrical form informs the actor of yet another transition: it is an allegory of Helena's suddenly straitened and 'timorous' mind. Of course, there is more in this than simply a portrait of uxorial obedience. Helena desperately wants to be kissed, and she tries to win a kiss first by the subdued demeanour of her prosody, and then by a direct entreaty. Both fail: hence the further transition in verse-forms when she realizes that Bertram is set to give her absolutely nothing:

> Nor dare I say 'tis mine: and yet it is,
> But like a timorous theefe, most faine would steale
> What law does vouch mine owne.
> ———————————————— [What] [would] [you] have?
> Something, and scarce so much: nothing indeed,
> I would not tell you what I would my Lord: Faith yes,
> Strangers and foes do sunder, and not kisse.
> ———————————————— [hast] [to] horse.
> I shall not breake your bidding, good my Lord:
> Where are my other men? Monsieur, farwell. *Exit.*
>
> (TLN 1357–66)

Helena's hopeful, obedient verse-lines have simply broken down ('Something, and scarce so much: nothing indeed'). Part-fractured, part-flattened, the rhythms offer plaintive accompaniment to the character's similar razing. The hanging, lonely extra foot of 'Faith yes' embodies Helena's entrance into unprecedented desolation. It is all the more pathetic after the breathless aspirings and anxious inflations of the scene's earlier verse ('And ever shall | With true observance seeke to eeke out that | Wherein toward me my homely starres have faild | To equall my great fortune' (TLN 1348–51)). The break in her parting line shows her searching for some modicum of comfort or support: 'Where are my other men?' As so often, the midline break opens up to possible others; as so often, the silence, or the simple absence of others, returns the gaze to the lonely speaker. In this scene—pivotal for part and play alike—prosody is successively hope, heart-break, and abandonment.

Of course, neither part nor play ends here; indeed, in a sense the part has to start again from scratch (a similar pattern as witnessed in the parts of Portia, Rosalind, Olivia, and, as we shall see, Isabella). Accordingly, the actor has another long blank-verse soliloquy (ending in a couplet) in which Helena can secretly express her woes and plans. But in truth the part struggles to repossess the intensity of feeling so evident throughout the first half of the play (which contains well over half of the Helena-part). The speeches of plot making with the widow and daughter are in indistinctive and lacklustre blank verse. There are, however, three exceptions, when the part does attain to the nervous concentration of experience that so characterized the Helena of the first two acts. Unsurprisingly, all are in rhyming couplets. The actor will know just what this means: a recovery of inward intensity. So, here Helena moves from busy instructions to her 'underlings' to fiercely quizzical candour about male sexuality:

> But O strange men,
> That can such sweet use make of what they hate,
> When sawcie trusting of the cosin'd thoughts
> *Defiles the pitchy night, so lust doth play*
> *With what it loathes, for that which is away,*
> But more of this hereafter: you *Diana*...

(TLN 2463–8)

If the whole reflection is not definitively an 'aside', the couplet with which it ends certainly proposes a layered address, in which troubled or intrigued self-meditation usurps any sisterly sharing.

Moments later the part displays a similar shift from plotting with others to choric aside, alive with excited and anxious expectation:

> ... we must away,
> Our Wagon is prepar'd, and time revives us,
> All's well that ends well, still the fines the Crowne;
> What ere the course, the end is the renowne.
>
> (TLN 2477–80)

In turn, the part's next—and last—rhyming couplets invoke both of these two preceding ones: first, by remembering Bertram's 'wondrous' lust in the dark, and second, by claiming the 'ends well' to which she has long aspired:

> _____ [both,] [O] pardon.
> Oh my good Lord, when I was like this Maid,
> I found you wondrous kinde, there is your Ring,
> And looke you, heeres your letter: this it sayes,
> When from my finger you can get this Ring,
> And is by me with childe. & c. This is done,
> Will you be mine now you are doubly wonne?
>
> (TLN 3046–52)

Once again, the player will identify the fact of rhyme as an actorly prompt. Just as the couplets all pulse with the selfsame erotic intensity, so will the actor intuitively recover the embodied self in which all of his previous couplets found breath. And so it is that the actor comes to his part's very last rhyme:

> _____ [ever,] [ever] dearly.
> If it appeare not plaine, and prove untrue,
> Deadly divorce step betweene me and you.
>
> (TLN 3054–6)

The message in part-script seems dangerously but characteristically ambivalent: there is a hopeful cue, followed by a profoundly menacing couplet. However—again characteristically—the part-script as rehearsed and pondered is not *quite* the end. There remains, as always, performance. And here the Helena-actor may find one final surprise. So, the full play-script of this final conjugal exchange goes like this:

> HELENA.   ... This is done,
>           Will you be mine now you are doubly wonne?
> BERTRAM.  If she my Liege can make me know this clearly,
>           Ile love her dearely, ever, ever dearly.
> HELENA.   If it appeare not plaine, and prove untrue,
>           Deadly divorce step betweene me and you.
>
>                                          (TLN 3051–6)

Helena and Bertram remain separate, rather than one; complementary rather than conjoined: but the part gives the Helena-actor some warrant to seize Bertram's last rhyme with a gusto and confidence that its negative lexicon and threatening theme barely warrants.

To the end the Helena-part is characterized by searing desire and tremulous vulnerability. The two blank-verse soliloquies, starting up the part's two main movements, make it clear how busily and obsessively the character has lived in her pain. But one-note misery is no subject for a lead romantic part. The crucial speeches, when life is truly at a cusp, will not be in soliloquy. Love is inherently interpersonal; the part has to engage with others, and the character's pain has to be put to a proof. For the actor playing Helena, this proof is discovered in rhyme. We find rhyming couplets that are first given 'confidentially' to the part-conning actor, but which in performance are always liable to sudden mutation or mugging. They become vehicles for a subjectivity that is both fiercely internalized and perilously opened out. As such, they are the truest litmus of this troubled and troubling role.

## Isabella

We have seen with other heroines how changes in the basic shape of speech blocs or lines indicate responsiveness to context, and the ways in which context produces changes in the character. Uniquely for a role of its type, the Isabella-part does not shift back and forth between blank verse, rhyme, and prose. With Isabella, the part's prosodic forms remain broadly consistent: she speaks in a tightly reined blank verse, often rhythmically jagged and broken, and only very occasionally either heated or fluid (basically when roused to indignation). The sense the part gives is of a mind in control of the medium, retaining even in the midst of passion some power in reserve.

Isabella's scenes have a repeated rhythm. She enters determined to skate on the situation's surface, to remain personally untouched and unrevealed, but again and again she is forced into a violent commitment and baring of her self to the moment's challenge. In many scenes, therefore, we seem to witness Isabella warming up—or perhaps thawing—into a fuller revelation of what we infer is 'already' there: as though at the start of each scene she is some kind of statue or monument, waiting to be quickened into motion. This happens from the very beginning.

Isabella's first scene shows her commitment to the cloister immediately challenged by the claims of love. The scene presents a similar challenge to the character's forms of speech. The actor might expect the opening speeches of a novice to be in modest and decorous blank verse (the witty prose banter that opens most of Shakespeare's heroine roles would hardly be appropriate). But instead he will find a succession of shocked and internally broken lines:

> _____ [he's] [in] prison.
> Woe me; [SHIFT] for what?
> _____ [Tilth,] [and] husbandry.
> Some one with childe by him? [SHIFT] my cosen *Juliet*?
> _____ [your] [poore] brother.
> Doth he so, [SHIFT?]
> Seeke his life?
> _____ [warrant] [For's] execution.
> Alas: [SHIFT] what poore
> Abilitie's in me, to doe him good.
> _____ [powre] [you] have.
> My power? [SHIFT] alas, I doubt.

(TLN 375–432)

Each caesura forces a silence, however brief, depicting intense mental movement. The character's opening wish had been for close 'restraint'—but the breaks signal the extent to which she is denied this. Her seclusion is no sooner mentioned than it ceases to exist. This series of exchanges is markedly different from what happens in Isabella's next scene, which opens on a sentence that takes five lines to deliver:

> There is a vice that most I doe abhorre,
> And most desire should meet the blow of Justice;

> For which I would not plead, but that I must,
> For which I must not plead, but that I am
> At warre, twixt will, and will not.
>
> (TLN 773–7)

The airlessly unbroken lines suggest a stalling or retraction of full emotional commitment: this obedience to prosodic form is a mode of protection. Conversely, the very stiffness of the words she uses here establishes the importance of any return to broken lines (such a return will be a pointer to 'act' a changing or pressured mind). This technique swiftly becomes the chief way of pacing Isabella's cognitive and oratorical changes, as she moves through the gears, gathering the requisite heat and pace to force by turns Angelo, Claudio—and herself—to full emotional *and* physical account:

> _____ [by] [the] Actor.
> Oh just but severe Law:
> I had a brother then; heaven keepe your honour.
> _____ [Maiden,] [no] remedie.
> Yes: [SHIFT] I doe thinke that you might pardon him…
> _____ [are] [too] cold
> Too late? [SHIFT] why no: [SHIFT] I that doe speak a word
> May call it againe…
> _____ [waste] [your] words.
> Alas, alas: [SHIFT]
> Why all the soules that were, were forfeit once…
> _____ [die] [to] morrow.
> To morrow? [SHIFT] oh, that's sodaine, [SHIFT] ⎫ a single broken
> Spare him, [SHIFT?] spare him: [SHIFT]        ⎭ pentameter line?
> Hee's not prepar'd for death; even for our kitchins
> We kill the fowle of season…
>
> (TLN 787–839)

In each such instance, the break in the line—delineated by a self-sufficient speech unit ('why no', 'Alas', 'Spare him')—marks a moment of outward appeal and inward searching. Where to go from here? What tack to try next? How much of myself must I offer? In this crucial scene with Angelo, these uncertain lines give way to a newly liberated prosody of enjambed lines and stirring crescendos:

> Could great men thunder
> As *Jove* himselfe do's, *Jove* would never be quiet,
> For every pelting petty Officer

Would use his heaven for thunder;
Nothing but thunder: Mercifull heaven,
Thou rather with thy sharpe and sulpherous bolt
Splits the un-wedgable and gnarled Oke,
Then the soft Mertill: But man, proud man,
Drest in a little briefe authoritie,
Most ignorant of what he's most assur'd,
(His glassie Essence) like an angry Ape
Plaies such phantastique tricks before high heaven,
As makes the Angels weepe, who with our spleens,
Would all themselves laugh mortall.

(TLN 867–80)


Because Authoritie, though it erre like others,
Hath yet a kinde of medicine in it selfe
That skins the vice o'th top.

(TLN 892–4)

In the Isabella-part, however, this sort of rhetoric is an exception rather than the rule; the role customarily prefers a far less swelling manner. So, the start of her next two scenes sees an immediate return to hesitant half-lines and tersely abbreviated speeches. This is Isabella's 'habit', her chosen self-insuring refuge. In turn, each scene witnesses her unwilling passage back out of such self-enclosure. So, her return visit to Angelo begins like this:

I am come to know your pleasure
——————————————— [Brother] [cannot] live.
Even so: heaven keepe your Honor.

(TLN 1037–9)

Her second line offers a midline switch, but it is not one that posits any kind of appeal to Angelo. Equally, it doesn't indicate any inward probing. Instead, it speaks of a tightly coiled resistance to any unwinding of mind and soul. Isabella's opening exchange with Claudio in prison shows a similar recoil:

——————————————— [what's] [the] comfort?
Why, [SHIFT]
As all comforts are: most good, most good indeede.

(TLN 1262–4)

Her opening line (as printed in the Folio) is a single word only—
'Why'—almost certainly indicating an intense suspension of thought.
What is she going to say? How is she going to play it? But then returning to unambiguous iambics, she again determines upon evasion and
euphemism:

> Lord *Angelo* having affaires to heaven
> Intends you for his swift Ambassador,
> Where you shall be an everlasting Leiger.
> (TLN 1265–7)

Once again, the prosody appears to be the basic means of marking the
mutations in Isabella's sense of comfort and commitment. The prosody
often moves between different types of self-deferment, in which the shape
of the speaking doesn't quite carry a fully embodied mind. There is the
uncertain short phrase, when she wonders whether and how to commit to
the moment's demands; there is (as here) the pseudo-smooth, hermetically
sealed bloc of pentameters, often serving abstract analogies or casuistic hypotheses; there is the convoluted iambic pentameter, which suggests that all
possible interpretations or presumptions are being neurotically self-policed.
Uniquely among the heroines, there is no prosodic 'shape' that adequately
embodies what we infer as the true Isabella; if 'she' exists anywhere, it is
in the ellipses, whether before a scene or between two tightly clenched
clauses.

The Isabella-part's single shift from verse to prose in a sense proves
the point: for although such transitions may, as always, look like decisive
barometers of passion, they may not in practice prove to be so. The shift
to prose happens when Isabella meets the Duke—or when the 'hero'
meets the 'heroine'. However, far from ratcheting up the tension, or
focusing more intently upon the heroine's inwardness, this transition marks
an almost carelessly dismissive escape from interiority. Importantly, this
transition immediately follows what is in many ways the emotional pivot
of the play, when the disgusted Isabella dismisses her brother Claudio to
his death:

> Mercy to thee would prove it selfe a Bawd,
> 'Tis best that thou diest quickly.
> _____ [but] [one] word.
> What is your Will.
> _____ [your] [owne] benefit.

I have no superfluous leysure, my stay must be/stolen out of other affaires: but I will attend you a while.

(TLN 1372–81; prose lineation ours)

The Duke, disguised as the Friar, now begins his plot making, and Isabella's part follows suit. Its intensity quickly abates. In full-play terms Isabella becomes effectively the Friar's agent, unable to tell his truth from his lies, and correspondingly dislodged as the emotional and ethical pulse of the play. In part terms—unlike the similar moments in the parts of Portia, Rosalind, Olivia, and Helena—the shift to prose does not signal either the recovery of something lost or the development of something new. It simply posits a shutting down of untoward passion, and a return to self-effacing busyness ('I have no superfluous leysure …'). The switch, which the actor may have hoped was an opportunity to *show* Isabella changing and developing, simply displays in mid-scene what we have to infer happening 'before' Isabella's every appearance. She puts parts of herself away, in the name of modesty, virtue, fear, or Christ.

And all the time the actor, too, must feel subtly inhibited, frustrated by prosody which denies any fulsome propelling of mind or body toward its 'target'. In effect, Shakespeare's scripting of the part here is a strategic means of embodying repression and guardedness. The actor will know one thing for sure, almost as a matter of faith: if 'Isabella' sees something, she will be wary of it. But what if she/he does *not* see it? Might Shakespeare be setting up this particular character to be so passionately untouchable, so determined *not* to be coerced into making any untoward alteration, that the 'transition' required by tragic-comic lore will have to come upon her like an unseen mugging from behind?

The way this works will not be noticeable unless we read the character in both part-text and play-text. It revolves around two versions of a particular 'exclusion': that is, the way in which Isabella doesn't hear direct appeals to her sympathy or support, and the way in which *her* appeals for sympathy or support are left unheard. This happens because, in either case, the appeal is spoken, but it is not written down on the addressee's roll. More than once, this seems deliberate and even cruel: the appeal is the final word, and so the cue-word, to which the speaker specifically needs a response. But Shakespeare interlards another statement, sometimes of no real significance, sometimes gratuitously insulting, whose dramaturgical effect is to keep the addressed actor damnably ignorant of the appeal when learning his part.

This happens at the crucial moment when Isabella banishes her brother from her affections and attention:

> No word to save thee.
> _____ [heare] [me] *Isabell.*
> Oh fie, fie, fie:
> Thy sinn's not accidentall, but a Trade;
> Mercy to thee would prove it selfe a Bawd,
> 'Tis best that thou diest quickly.
> _____ [but] [one] word.
> What is your Will.
>
> (TLN 1369–76)

The part includes one flailing appeal from Claudio ('heare me *Isabell'*) which she contemptuously dismisses ('Oh, fie, fie, fie'). The Isabella-actor might expect that the next cue—'but one word'—is yet another attempt of Claudio's to get her to listen. But it is not. This cue instead comes from the disguised Duke, and marks the scene's swift movement away from the climactic sibling confrontation. Claudio has one more short speech ('Let me ask my sister pardon, I am so out of love with life, that I will sue to be rid of it' (TLN 1392–3)) before he exits; he doesn't return until the final moments, when he stands mutely on stage amid the Duke's orchestrations. We might think this dismissal puzzling enough for the Claudio-actor. But for the Isabella-actor it is still more so. For her brother—a primary focus of all her scenes so far—simply disappears. The part does not record his plaintive parting words; and indeed, Isabella does not once hear from or speak to him again in the play. But this is not all that the part-text elides. The Isabella-actor is also not given Claudio's second desperate response to her disgusted abandoning of him:

> Oh heare me *Isabella.*

For instead of cueing Isabella, these words cue the Duke—or, in other words, they cue the scene's sudden dropping of what has been hitherto its main focus.

ISABELLA.  Take my defiance,
         Die, perish: Might but my bending downe
         Repreeve thee from thy fate, it should proceede.
         Ile pray a thousand praiers for thy death,

No word to save thee.

CLAUDIO. Nay heare me *Isabell*.

ISABELLA. Oh fie, fie, fie:

Thy sinn's not accidentall, but a Trade;

Mercy to thee would prove it selfe a Bawd,

'Tis best that thou diest quickly.

CLAUDIO. Oh heare me *Isabella*.

DUKE.    Vouchsafe a word, yong sister, but one word.

(TLN 1364–75)

All kinds of stage action might animate this moment: Isabella's failure to respond might be in two torturous stages—'O heare me!', '*Isabella*!'—reinforcing the familial stakes and ethical finality of her silence; Claudio could scream the words while being held down by gaolers; or Isabella might already have walked away, and he sobs them hopelessly to himself. But what we need to recover is how cruel and abandoning the train of cues here is: Claudio is dismissed by Isabella, but has the dismissal as a cue ('' 'Tis best that thou diest quickly'); he appeals to Isabella who (according to the part-script) 'hears' nothing; instead, the Duke is nominally cued, but his address is all to Isabella. The moment is structurally and emotionally pivotal. The cues and parts are distributed in such a way as to maximize Claudio's abandonment. But more than that, they maximize Isabella's implacability—not to say her cruelty—in ensuring this abandonment, and in measuring out its aural and spatial loneliness.

This reading becomes all the more likely once we recognize that Claudio gives out effectively the same cue to two different characters: 'heare me *Isabell*' (cueing Isabella), and 'heare me *Isabella*' (cueing the Duke). The marginal difference (Isabell/Isabella) may have been there on the actor's parts, and may have been designed explicitly to prevent the Duke-actor from coming in too early. But it seems highly unlikely that the Duke-actor, 'conceal'd' on-stage throughout the long, gradually escalating exchange between the siblings, tensely waiting for *his* re-entrance, would be forestalled from entering by an ambiguously hanging vowel sound. Furthermore, he will notice that the Duke's first speech has three separate parts—'Vouchsafe a word'—'yong sister'—'but one words'—which might easily represent three attempts at getting the furious young woman's attention. If indeed he does come in early, the exchange might work something like this:

CLAUDIO. Nay heare me *Isabell*.
ISABELLA. [to Claudio] Oh fie, fie, fie—
DUKE.        [to Isabella] Vouchsafe a word—
ISABELLA.                    Thy sinn's not accidentall, but a Trade;
DUKE.                    —young sister—
ISABELLA. Mercy to thee would prove it selfe a Bawd.
DUKE.                                —but one word
ISABELLA. 'Tis best that thou diest quickly.
CLAUDIO. Oh heare me *Isabella*.
DUKE.        *Vouchsafe a word, yong sister, but one word.*
ISABELLA. What is your will?

Or like this:

ISABELLA. Mercy to thee would prove it selfe a Bawd,
              'Tis best that thou diest quickly.
CLAUDIO. Oh heare me *Isabella*.
DUKE.        —but one word.

There are numerous possible variations, but they all point to the same basic effects. Claudio is harangued and then utterly isolated; the Duke is struggling for access to Isabella; and Isabella is violently beyond the claims of anything or anyone but her own revulsion. So, whilst this moment effectively maroons Claudio in his desperation, it equally maroons Isabella in *herself*. Her ascendant responses to the Duke-Friar—'What is your Will', 'I have no superfluous leysure'—suggest a woman who has already, in the blink of an eye, secreted herself back in her refrigerator, where she might remain fresh, cold, and aloof from decay. And if so, it is the silent hiatus in the part—the elision of Claudio's would-be cue to her of 'heare me *Isabella*'—that marks this self-collection.

Effects such as this 'missing' cue must work in one of two ways. They may freeze the actor on-stage in a particular attitude; or they may force a seemingly spontaneous 'decision' in favour of the unrehearsed revision of priorities. In this instance, the first option seems the most likely; next time, however, it just might be different. Either way, such powerfully sudden and *compelled* choices can forge, out of the heat of crisis, the particular 'Isabella' being enacted. Perhaps this will be an Isabella defined by unwavering self-consistency, by obliviousness to others' voices, and by inertia or paralysis in the face of others' demands for sympathy, forgiveness, or compromise; or perhaps it will be one defined by the unexpected melting or fragmenting of precisely such implacability.

The next such orchestration occurs at the beginning of the play's long final scene, when Isabella greets the re-entering Duke, accuses Angelo of crimes, and calls for justice. The context of this moment is established by the Isabella-actor's two immediately preceding appearances. The first is a brief scene telling Isabella that her co-operation in the bed trick has been a waste of time, and that her brother is dead. After responding with grievous violence ('Oh, I wil to him, and plucke out his eies' (TLN)), Isabella reluctantly agrees to take direction from the Friar. In the next scene we learn that the 'Friar' has tutored Isabella about what and what not to say. But this is a 'part' with which Isabella is distinctly unimpressed:

> To speak so indirectly I am loath,
> I would say the truth, but to accuse him so
> That is your part...
>
> (TLN 2325-7)

Obedience to the Duke is clearly going to be a struggle. In her public appeal to the Duke for 'Justice', therefore, we might expect a tussle between two ways of acting: one showing the urge toward violent revenge, the other showing resentful agreement to another's script that promises a 'sweet end' via 'bitter' 'physicke'. Here is her actual plea:

> ——————————————————— [kneele] [before] him.
> Justice, O royall *Duke*, vaile your regard
> Upon a wrong'd (I would faine have said a Maid)
> Oh worthy Prince, dishonour not your eye
> By throwing it on any other obiect,
> Till you have heard me, in my true complaint,
> And given me Justice, Justice, Justice, Justice.
>
> (TLN 2369-75)

The belligerence and excessiveness of the culminating repetitions can be played as craft rather than as a genuine loss of composure. But an equally cogent interpretation is that Isabella starts off 'kneeling' as instructed, but that the pressure and scandal of the circumstances soon sends her role playing awry. For it is by no means clear what instruction the repeated cue of 'Justice' here encodes. As we have seen, these prematurely given cues often help orchestrate specific things: crowd scenes; mental isolation; emotional dislocation; pathetic climax. All are potentially appropriate—but it is the first that here opens up the possibility of the others. So it is clear that we are here in a crowd scene. The entrance direction includes '*Citizens at severall doores*'; Peter demands that she 'Speake loud'; Isabella pleads with the Duke not to look on any other 'object' but herself. This, then, is the context for the desperation of her cue-line. The Duke is ignoring her, lapping up the neediness of his citizens, enjoying the role of returning grace, and hammily pretending not to hear the kneeling maid before him. It might thus have been played like this:

| | |
|---|---|
| ISABELLA. | And given me Justice!— |
| DUKE. [to another] | Relate your wrongs— |
| ISABELLA. | Justice!— |
| DUKE. [to another] | —In what? |
| ISABELLA. | Justice!— |
| DUKE. [to another] | —by whom? |
| [to another] | be brief |
| ISABELLA. | Justice! |
| DUKE. [to Isabella] | —Here is Lord *Angelo* shall give you Justice. |
| | Reveal your self to him. |

The repeated 'Justice', echoing and unanswered, stands both for its present lack and for Isabella's present isolation. The more the plea is spoken, the more it is left hanging; it ceases to seem cosily insured by an agreed script. As the word echoes, it becomes increasingly plaintive. Equally, because the word is unanswered by anyone on-stage, it is directed out to the suddenly confidential audience. *We* will listen, in the knowledge that her plea is just and that repair is necessary.

This signals an important moment in the evolution of Isabella's part. Up to now Isabella has remained firmly beyond us, just as she has remained beyond the other characters. The part has one soliloquy, which works principally to reinforce Isabella's self-sufficiency ('Did I tell this, | Who would beleeve me?' (TLN 1185–6)) and her self-certainty ('Then *Isabell* live chaste, and brother die; | More then our brother, is our Chastitie' (TLN 1198–9)). Perhaps more striking and unusual, the part has no 'asides' whatsoever, whether to the audience or to another character; instead, Isabella's impermeable presence provokes asides from others, whether Lucio, the Provost, or, of course, Angelo. Her part is utterly full-frontal rather than angular, its direction of address always dead straight. This is what makes her particularly vulnerable to surprise from the side or behind; and equally what makes the *direct* address to the audience, as enabled by the repeated cues, so distinctively propitious for this character's fuller emergence. For notwithstanding the assaults and coercions of all the main male characters upon her, this is the first time that the audience has been empowered to take her side or (as it were) to give her strength. Until now the actor has never been encouraged to appeal to 'our' good natures, being always sufficiently buttressed by 'Isabella's' certainty. Here things are suddenly different. So, an appeal is made to the audience: however, it is not necessarily an appeal made with confidence, or from a position of absolute dramaturgical security. For the effect of giving out the repeated cues is to dislodge the Isabella-actor from a clear possession of centre-stage. If neither her addressee nor the on-stage audience attend her, then will the audience off-stage? If the Isabella-actor is in danger of feeling marginalized, then she/he might well suddenly feel in need of support. Perhaps here at last is Isabella's decisive emotional transition (into vulnerability, sympathy, fellow feeling): and it is facilitated by the actor's sudden neediness.

For despite the fact that the Isabella-actor speaks the repeated cue, it is the Duke-actor who is in control of the scene. This is so whether his cue from Isabella is a single 'Justice' or all four: in either case the Duke will be given the opportunity to come in early and repel Isabella's continuing appeals. More than this, it is the Duke who passes Isabella back to Angelo. He says it explicitly ('Here is Lord *Angelo* shall give you Justice' (TLN 2378)), but this insult is reinforced by others lurking in the part-text. For it might come as a nasty shock to find that the next cue given to Isabella on her part—the seemingly answering and estimable 'course of Justice'—is in fact spoken by *Angelo*. The Isabella-part is suddenly at the mercy of circumstances quite beyond the actor's control, measured by a new principle of mockery and entrapment. Furthermore, the next cue given out by Isabella (to the Angelo-actor) reprises the uncertainty of the 'Justice' cue: 'Heare me: oh heare me, heere' (TLN 2385), goes the cue-line. Perhaps the cue as received on the Angelo-part is 'heare me, heere'; perhaps it is simply 'heere'. Either way, there is a strong chance that the Angelo-actor will think himself cued as soon as he hears the words 'Heare me: oh heare'. If the cue is 'heere', then the decision is made: he will come in before Isabella's line is even half over.

The likelihood, consequently, is that the Isabella-actor is left to complete the line over the top or in between the pauses of Angelo's mendacious evasions:

> ISABELLA. Hear me!—
> ANGELO.  My Lord,
> ISABELLA. Oh!
> ANGELO.  —her wits I fear me are not firm
> ISABELLA. hear me!
> ANGELO.  She hath been a suitor to me
> ISABELLA. Hear!
> ANGELO.  —for her Brother
>          Cut off from course of Justice.
> ISABELLA. By course of Justice!

Both are seeking a clear channel of appeal to the Duke, but their criss-crossing, fractured lines show each of them sabotaging the other's ambition. At the same time, the Duke is primarily deferring to Angelo, persevering with his teasing game, pretending to ignore the madwoman. The audience is likely to 'correct' the Duke, and to absorb Isabella's pleas as its own: but it will do so partly because of the actor's sudden exclusion from rhetorical control.

Not only does the part-script surprise the actor of Isabella in her cuer's identity—it then makes a succession of the Isabella-part's new speeches an almost mocking ricochet of their (already unwelcome) cues:

> Heare me: oh heare me, heere.
> _____ [course] [of] Justice.
> By course of Justice.
> _____ [bitterly,] [and] strange.
> Most strange:

> (TLN 2385–91)

The space between cue and cued is contracted almost to nothingness; Isabella's response resembles a violent reflex, an almost physical yoking of self into dialogue, rather than any kind of measured decision making. The effect, then, is to rob 'Isabella' of her trademark moment of choice: the moment in between her cue and her speech, where she/he *accepts* the cue, takes what she/he wants from it, and determines upon a response. We might quickly compare the earlier scene between Isabella and Angelo, in which the cues were always a gift to the actor *and* the character:

—————————————————————— [him,] [I] say
Must he needs die?
—————————————————————— [Maiden,] [no] remedie.
Yes, I doe thinke that you might pardon him …
—————————————————————— [will] [not] doe't.
But can you if you would?
—————————————————————— [I] [cannot] doe.
But might you doe't & do the world no wrong …
—————————————————————— [are] [too] cold.
Too late? Why no: I that doe speak a word
May call it againe …
—————————————————————— [you] [be] gone.
I would to heaven I had your potencie …
—————————————————————— [waste] [your] words.
Alas, alas …
—————————————————————— [die] [to] morrow.
To morrow? oh, that's sodaine …
—————————————————————— [live] [to] end.
Yet shew some pittie.
—————————————————————— [morrow,] [be] content.
So you must be ye first that gives this sentence …
—————————————————————— [That's] [well] said.
Could great men thunder …

(TLN 794–867)

Cues like these had presupposed a certain power to allow or refuse. In the final scene, by contrast, both actor and character are made to feel their ignorance and impotence, and thus to become the coerced reactor to unexpected provocations. The one whom Isabella seeks to cue ignores her; the one whom she seeks to silence or obliterate keeps cueing her: Isabella's message has to override the on-stage non-hearers and reach the off-stage hearers (the audience). The effect is to propose a new Isabella, who lacks rhetorical control, who is for the first time fully extended, yet unable to reach her target, and who in casting after a decently returned cue is *revealed* to us: as a woman genuinely defined by a passion for 'Justice', or for a full and fair 'hear'-ing. It is by exploiting the ellipses in the part technology, then, that Shakespeare and his actor can finally begin to bring this estranged heroine 'home'.

However, there remain to the very end real problems with how to play the role. This is the part in full from Isabella's final re-entrance:

_____ [she'll] [be] asham'd.
*Enter Duke, Provost, Isabella.*
_____ [at] [your] service.
Oh give me pardon
That I, your vassaile, have imploid, and pain'd
Your unknowne Soveraigntie.
_____ [is] [your] Brother.
I doe my Lord.
_____ [for] [*Claudio*'s] death.
Most bounteous Sir.
Looke if it please you, on this man condemn'd,
As if my Brother liv'd: I partly thinke,
A due sinceritie governed his deedes,
Till he did looke on me: Since it is so,
Let him not die: my Brother had but Justice,
In that he did the thing for which he dide.
For *Angelo*, his Act did not ore-take his bad intent,
And must be buried but as an intent
That perish'd by the way: thoughts are no subjects
Intents, but meerely thoughts.

(TLN 2654–2846)

The part-script is brief and unremarkable. The cues tell the Isabella-actor that the Duke is present and that Claudio is dead. Her speeches seem to be marked by modesty, gratefulness, and forgiveness. In line with what we have seen of the earlier romantic heroines, it seems that Isabella's story is basically finished with. She now serves others, reconciled to everything past. Or so the actor conning and rehearsing the part may have assumed.

However, the part-script is (violently, comically?) oblivious to what is going on in the full script. If the actor were depending upon the part for his knowledge, he would be ignorant of at least three important things: first, that Claudio is alive; second, that Mariana pleads with her to kneel in supplication for Angelo's life; third, that the Duke (twice) proposes marriage to her. We might conclude from this that the actor could not in such circumstances have relied only or even principally upon the part for his knowledge of what happens, either to his own or to other characters. And of course it is possible that the big things—that Claudio is not really dead and that the Duke proposes marriage at the end—were relayed in the run-through or backstage (certainly they would be known by the second performance). But the example of Mariana's request for Isabella to kneel is still hard to explain. We might prefer to think that the margins of the written part would have contained such basic blocking/stage-directions as kneeling, whether from inception, or after consultation with other actors. However, the specific details of the Folio text may also point to a more loaded, purposively scripted principle of uncertainty and surprise.

The basic set-up of the part here is hardly designed to ensure confidence of movement or certainty of intervention; for, once again, we find unsettling discontinuities between the learned part and the performed play. First, the Isabella-actor must wait for no fewer than 120 lines between his cue for re-entrance and his cue to speak. Second, instructions which in the full text are spoken directly to Isabella do *not* appear on the part. Here it is in full text:

> MARIANA.  Oh my good Lord, sweet *Isabell*, take my part,
> Lend me your knees, and all my life to come,
> I'll lend you all my life to doe you service.
>
> DUKE.  Against all sence you doe importune her,
> Should she kneele downe, in mercie of this fact,
> Her Brothers ghost, his paved bed would breake,
> And take her hence in horror.
>
> MARIANA.  *Isabell*:
> Sweet *Isabel*, doe yet but kneele by me,
> Hold up your hands, say nothing: I'll speake all ...
> Oh *Isabel*: will you not lend a knee?
>
> (TLN 2821–34)

It is important to recognize what is at issue here. The final scene is packed with supplications and pardons; kneeling is everywhere. The decision whether or when to kneel matters: and it matters to no one as much as Isabella. This is clear from earlier in the scene when, recounting to the Duke her humiliating previous engagement with Angelo, she immediately recalls how 'I praid, and kneel'd' and 'How he refeld me' (TLN 2460–1). It is unlikely that the whole long scene was choreographed to the last detail, but in most cases the part-text makes it clear what is to be done. (This is the case before Isabella's 'Justice' speech, which is cued by Friar Peter's 'kneele before him'.) On this occasion, Mariana asks Isabella three times to kneel, while the Duke implicitly warns her not to kneel (or rebukes her for kneeling). The full text makes it clear that the stakes are high. But what of the Isabella part-text? It would have been very easy to make Mariana's

'Lend me your knees' or 'lend a knee' Isabella's cue. Here, by contrast, Mariana's first injunction is not a cue, while her second ('lend a knee') cues the Duke's 'He dies for *Claudio*'s death', which in turn cues Isabella's final speech. In other words, Shakespeare seems intent on making the request to kneel a surprise: at once to keep it from the 'addressee' as long as possible, and then to make it come from a part whose claims upon 'Isabella' lack prescriptive authority. The actor is left to make up his own mind when or how or whether to kneel—to locate his own space and moment for a vitally important action.

Furthermore, as we saw earlier with the prison scene, it is not only Isabella who is forced by the dislocated part-texts into puzzled and impotent isolation. The Mariana-actor would probably assume that his direct addresses to Isabella also cue the Isabella-actor: but neither in fact does. Any surprise or dismay felt by 'Mariana' would then amplify the two subsequent moments of silent and even embarrassing *impasse*: as Isabella fails to respond, and as both actors wait for a heavy second or two for whoever *is* cued to respond to do so. This would intensify the Mariana-actor's exasperation at his inability—or his character's—to seize the action. The sum effect has to be an escalation of indignation, bewilderment, and perhaps barely bridled violence.

The scripting—characteristically—both provokes and liberates the actors. Whatever the precise result, it is likely to be highly dramatic. Isabella might finally agree to kneel at 'Most bounteous sir'. She thus speaks her appeal to the Duke from her knees, managing to defer to the claims of both sisterhood and authority; this is the option preferred by most editions, and clearly the most decorous solution. Alternatively, Isabella might remain standing throughout, immovably resistant, so that even her eventual speech of pardon is spoken powerfully on her own terms. Or again, she may kneel at Mariana's initial request, before being dragged to her feet at the Duke's 'Against all sense you do importune her'; in this scenario, Isabella briefly becomes a rag doll, torn between irreconcilable injustices. This version might accord well with a more comic rendering of the final act, accentuating how it pushes the claims of restoration to the brink of absurdity. By the same token, exactly the same blocking—Isabella ordered down, then ordered up, her body never less her own than now—can serve a quasi-tragic reading in which Isabella is the coerced victim of a ruling order immovably 'measured' by occlusion and violence. But whatever decision is made—to kneel or not, to rise or not, to drag her to her feet or not—the fact is that it needs to made *again*, at least once and perhaps twice or more. She can be dragged to her feet by the Duke, yet still have to abide two more pleading '*Isabel*'s and two more requests to 'kneel' from the desperate Mariana.

This is a powerful example of how working in parts catapults the actor into a necessarily incomplete present; neither forethought nor hindsight can be of much help here. And it is not only the fact of being open to unforeseen surprises that allows this presentness: it is equally the facility of the technology to splice unsuspected expanses of time 'inside' apparently snappy or singular events. This is repeatedly achieved in Isabella's final scene. So, having waited for 120 lines between her first re-entrance and her first cue to speak, the effect is repeated, with a further fifty lines between her 'I doe my Lord' (TLN 2787) and what might have seemed to the actor the continuous (in theme and address), 'Most bounteous Sir ...' (TLN 2836); and then another tantalizing fifteen lines, including numerous direct pleas for her acquiescence, between first being asked to kneel and finally being allowed to speak. The elisions in the part require a *consciousness* of uncertainty, some weighing of options, and a—more or less—solving improvisation.

The challenge of the part, and the peculiar tensions that underpin it, is decisively located in the *process* of playing: in the unpredictable experience of learning, practising, and in due course enacting the part. This process, at its most intense and intimate, is founded upon terrible uncertainties and temptations. These are always to do with the Isabella-part's separateness from others (or not), and in turn the character's separateness (or not) from unsettling affiliations. The actor has to decide *what to do* when he 'accidentally' hears Claudio's plea for a saving ear, or Mariana's request to kneel—or of course her brother's return from the dead, or the Duke's proposal of marriage. Again and again, actions that bear intimately or fiercely upon Isabella are not prepared for in the actor's part. These unscripted impositions may well produce in the actor an objective knowledge of unpreparedness, estranged in his body, clinging to what he knows best, uncertainly casting about for solutions. It is not only that Isabella offers no response to either the survival of her brother or to the Duke's two attempts to propose marriage. More than that, her part-text gives her no clue that either of these things will even take place. Even when the actor 'knows' the raw facts from the run-through or performance, fulsome possession of any *fait accompli* may well be a struggle: partly because the events or decisions have not been learned and 'owned' through intense private rehearsal; more strikingly, because they cannot be acted without supererogatory 'direction' from other actors. These final two surprises do not suddenly kick in, as repeated cues often do, providing an immediate dramatic supercharge that makes gratifying emotional sense. They simply occur—or blankly remain—asking the actor for a response that is likely to feel troublingly after-the-event, at once belated and presumptuous.

These are real difficulties that the actor has to face, and which in the absence of choreographing, modern-style direction he can best resolve by working at the vertiginous lacuna between scripted part and acted play. The fact that the scripted words, and only the scripted words, must be spoken gives the spaces around or between them their experiential pressure and urgency. The result is compelling. For the 'inadequate' prescriptiveness of parts thus produces subjective freedom and singularity—making the actor/character possess unexpected spaces, or expand into unexpected periods of time, or respond to unexpected information or provocation. In this way, the ellipses in the part become at once an engine, a location, and an allegory of the character's emerging subjectivity.

And it is 'in' just such decision-making spaces that we both first discover and finally leave Isabella. It is a space in which she feels the puzzle, or insult, of how identified *she* may or must be with any 'outside' thing. For these are the part's defining problems: whose is her body, where is her mind, in which way are her senses 'prone'? Does she remain locked inside herself, committing only to what she already knows? In thus testing and occasionally traducing settled expectations, the challenges to the character and the player fold into one another. For in the anxious *impasses* we can identify between part-script and play-script, in the missing cue connections between Isabella's part and others, we can get close to the founding premiss of this fierce and alienated role. We find a consciousness by turns threatened and defined by isolation, and by the anti-comic *discomforts* of recognition—of others, and through this, of oneself. Both actor and character are repeatedly forced out of the complacent possession of either time or place: forced into openness to surprise and contingency, and so into the embodied recognition that no rehearsal can ever quite prepare for the moment when—and if—it comes.

# Mercutio

Mercutio is a good example of how changes between verse and prose often inaugurate shifts in manner that bespeak telling continuities as much as radical transitions. In particular, this part shows how Shakespeare could transfer the distinctive emotional or psychological weight found in the part's *verse* midline switches/short lines into its *prose* pauses—and then back again.

In his first scene there is barely a breath to let anyone else in, or indeed to allow the Mercutio-actor himself a moment's pause. Mercutio offers an onslaught of wit and conceitedness that is broken only by the exasperated 'Peace, peace, *Mercutio* peace' (TLN 545) of Romeo, which interrupts Mercutio in the full flow of his Queen Mab speech. Until this moment the actor of Mercutio simply seizes the public stage, with the adrenalin rush of his speeches precluding any pauses in which any other actors might perform *their* 'business'. The spellbound attention of his auditors—or Mercutio's violent assumption of it—is thus ensured by the rhythms of his part's scripting.

But this breathless, almost de-oxygenated delivery is never again allowed such scenic dominance. From Mercutio's next scene on, the actor will notice small chinks in the part's rhetorical armoury. So after trying and failing to conjure forth Romeo through another speech of extravagant fancy ('Appeare thou in the likenesse of a sigh' (TLN 758)), Mercutio has this:

> This cannot anger him, t'would anger him
> To raise a spirit in his Mistresse circle,
> Of some strange nature, letting it stand
> Till he had laid it, and conjured it downe,
> That were some spight.
> My invocation is faire and honest, & in his Mistris name,
> I conjure onely but to raise up him.
>
> (TLN 773–9)

If the actor's part looked as it does here in the Folio, then the short line ('That were some spight') is strikingly final; it marks the moment where verse stops and, seemingly, prose begins. In particular, the attenuated line gives pause enough to reflect back on the peculiarly needy and bitter tone of Mercutio's speech. Such foreshortened lines often open out to other actors. But here there is really no one else being acted upon, so no one else who can respond with action. His supposed addressee, Benvolio, can at the most shrug or nod or look bemused: the audience's attention remains firmly on Mercutio. For the actor playing Mercutio, this moment of pause might be affectively neutral: but it still embodies the fact that no one answers to Mercutio's 'invocation'. Mercutio speaks into absence, into the loneliness either of unrequited longing (for Romeo) or unsavoury sexual experience.

A variation of this technique—here with midline switches—recurs in Mercutio's next speech:

> *Romeo* goodnight, [SWITCH] Ile to my Truckle bed,
> This Field-bed is too cold for me to sleepe, [SWITCH]
> Come shall we go? [SWITCH]
>
> (TLN 789–91)

The actor clearly has three distinct speech units: his goodnight is to the absent Romeo; his 'Ile to my Truckle bed' is to Romeo or himself; his 'shall we go?' might be to Romeo, himself, or Benvolio. These shifts and silences within the verse-line nudge the Mercutio-part very close to pathos. He is desolate, and needy, at once anxious for company and hurrying into loneliness. The actor would then be keenly aware of how his very next appearance immediately recapitulates this wistful theme: 'Where the devle should this *Romeo* be? | came he not home to night?' (TLN 1106–7). From this point on, the part switches almost entirely to prose—in which it remains until just before Mercutio's death. But there is nothing escapist or diminishing about this movement into prose. Instead, Shakespeare is asking something of his actor that takes its method directly from the preceding verse. That is, the part of Mercutio has so far displayed two performative registers: grandstanding conceitedness and sudden halts into silence. The move to prose will unite the two.

It is now that Shakespeare sows Mercutio's dialogue with numerous echoing and premature cues. As we have seen (see pp. 186–91), he wants the actor to locate separateness and loneliness 'inside' his performance for the on-stage crowd: to present an actor exiled from community, intermittently left cueing no one but himself. The decision for prose reinforces this 'sad clown' manner. First, it reinforces the part's debts to familiar jesting roles. Second, prose helps to release the actor from playing needy self-consciousness or unrequited love. He can instead *perform*, with all the gusto that the situation warrants.

However, it is precisely performance as existential escape that is here in Shakespeare's sights. Consequently, by surprising the actor in his performance—suspending him alone with his short line or his unanswered cue, abandoning him momentarily to a world without an attentive audience—Shakespeare makes the *actor* apprehend the true terror of his persona. All of the Mercutio-part's repeated cues, broken lines, switches between verse and prose, are suspended between the comic and tragic potentiality of each such technique. In this they epitomize the character.[2] Appropriately, then, the part's final prosodic transitions are a way of achieving tragic pathos. So, in its last moments, with Mercutio preparing to fight as though entering a dance—little knowing that it will be the dance of death—his part returns to verse. The actor will thus see his first verse-line move from (other) 'mens' to 'I', from the external to the internal:

> Consort? what dost thou make us Minstrels? &/thou make Minstrels of us, looke to heare nothing but discords: heere's my fiddlesticke, heere's that shall make you daunce. Come consort.
> ————————————————————— [gaze] [on] us.
> Mens eyes were made to looke, and let them gaze.
> I will not budge for no mans pleasure I.
>
> (TLN 1477–86; prose lineation ours)

From now on his pauses and attenuations are given renewed experiential intensity by the framing pressure of the verse-line:

> ... I am hurt. [SWITCH]
> A plague a both the Houses, [SWITCH] I am sped: [SWITCH]
> Is he gone and hath nothing? [SWITCH]
> (TLN 1522–4)

The first line here completes a pentameter (although the actor may not know it); the second is a fragmented pentameter; the third is foreshortened: the triple irregularity is clearly begging the actor to *act*. So, each line, each part of each line, gestures out to other actors; the frequent potential pauses invite the players of Benvolio and Romeo to enact the desperate search for their friend's wound. Equally, the shifts all 'break back' into Mercutio, as he makes statements ('I am hurt') or asks questions ('Is he gone ...?') that definitively can get no answer:

> Helpe me into some house *Benvolio*,
> Or I shall faint: [SWITCH] a plague a both your houses.
> They have made wormesmeat of me, [SWITCH]
> I have it, and soundly [SWITCH] to your houses.
>
> (TLN 1539–42)

The short and broken lines here join with, and in a sense complete, the earlier ones. Both reach into a grief beyond reply: once the loneliness of unrequited love, now the loneliness of death. The prosody here is absolutely dramatic: each brief switch of speech or shortened line asks for a discrete and decisive action by the performer. But it is important to recognize that right to the end the part sustains its segueing between verse and prose. Mercutio's last but one speech returns to prose, and is the ultimate example of a comic display that tries in vain to counter pathos through performance:

> No: [SWITCH?] 'tis not so deepe as a well, nor so wide as a/Church doore, [SWITCH?] but 'tis inough, 'twill serve: [SWITCH?] aske for me to/morrow, and you shall find me a grave man. [SWITCH?] I am pepper'd/I warrant, for this world: [SWITCH?] a plague a both your houses./[SWITCH?] What, a Dog, a Rat, a Mouse, a Cat to scratch a man to/death: [SWITCH?] a Braggart, a Rogue, a Villaine, that fights by the/booke of Arithmeticke, [SWITCH?] why the dev'le came you be-/tweene us? [SWITCH?] I was hurt under your arme.
>
> (TLN 1530–7; prose lineation ours)

At the very least, prose and verse work here as each other's reflection, even each other's palimpsest: the same phrases, the same rhythms, the same invitations to suspend or contract the moment, each simultaneously though perhaps unequally visible. For the actor, the effect is to provide a tense alertness to opportunity: a reluctance to settle in any pre-ordained patterns; an openness to sudden or untoward pauses, and so to a semi-improvised dependence upon himself alone as the teller, or here the toll, of the passing moment.

# Shylock

It seems likely that the same actor played Shylock as played Capulet (discussed in Chapter 18). The similarities in the broad arc of each part are obvious: both are self-enclosed, jaundiced patriarchs, threatened by authority from one angle, by their daughters' independence from another—who suffer a devastating come-uppance for their rigidity. But hardly less stark are the prosodic resemblances between the two parts. 'Shylock' recapitulates many devices familiar from 'Capulet': the internal repetitions, the way the part continually refers back on itself, not allowing outside speakers in. But were the same actor to have received this role, he would also have noticed in it a considerable advance in sophistication—and difficulty.

The Shylock-part is always organized by the abrupt midline shifts familiar from the Capulet-part. Sometimes these shifts work fairly simply, indicating the change in direction from addressing others to addressing oneself. Here the shifts fit the context: Shylock is in his own house, harrying his daughter or his servant:

> I am bid forth to supper *Jessica*,
> There are my Keyes: [SWITCH *to self-address*] but wherefore should I go?
> I am not bid for love, they flatter me,
> But yet Ile goe in hate, to feede upon
> The prodigall Christian. [SWITCH *to addressing Jessica*] *Jessica* my girle,
> Looke to my house, [SWITCH *to self-address*] I am right loath to goe,
> There is some ill a bruing…
>
> (TLN 848–54)

> What are their maskes? [SHIFT *to Jessica*] heare you me *Jessica*,
> Lock up my doores, and when you heare the drum
> And the vile squealing of the wry-neckt Fife,
> Clamber not you up to the casements then,
> Nor thrust your head into the publique streete
> To gaze on Christian fooles with varnisht faces…
> Let not the sound of shallow fopperie enter
> My sober house. [SHIFT *to self-address*] By *Jacobs* staffe I sweare,
> I have no minde of feasting forth to night:
> But I will goe: [SHIFT *to Clown*] goe you before me sirra,
> Say I will come.
>
> (TLN 864–75)

However, the instructions to the actor in this part are not always so clear. For the actor will find from the start a very unusual—we might even say alien—use of prosody. The Jew in Venice inevitably suffers a kind of inward exile. But so too, perhaps, does the actor. For he is forced to come upon what may be familiar prosodic 'landmarks' in eccentric and uncertain ways.

So the player surveying the Shylock-part would immediately notice the early shifts from prose to verse. As we saw earlier when looking at the part's premature cues, the principal character of his prose is the pedantic variation upon a single repeated phrase, all spoken with arithmetical relish:

> There be land rats, and water rats, water theeves, and/land theeves, I meane Pyrats … I will buy with you, sell with you, talke with/you, walke with you, and so following: but I will/not eate with you, drinke with you, nor pray with you.
>
> (TLN 347–61)

The first shift into verse marks Shylock's sudden movement into self-address:

> How like a fawning publican he lookes.
> I hate him for he is a Christian:
> But more, for that in low simplicitie
> He lends out money gratis …
> (TLN 365–8)

As we might expect, this verse is as weighed and measured as the prose. But instead of the single phrase, the principal unit in which Shylock makes his meticulous considerations has now become the syllable—particularly the single syllable in a long word: Chris[t]-[t]i-[i]an; sim[p]-[p]lic-i[t]-[t]ie. These words end their lines, perfectly furnishing Shylock's exact and contemptuous human equations; still more, they exemplify his hyper-correct and perhaps disturbingly foreign enunciation. In such a carefully delineated metrical context, the actor will seize upon any variation:

> He hates our sacred Nation, and he railes
> Even there where Merchants most doe congregate
> On me, my bargaines, and my well-worne thrift,
> Which he cals interest: Cursed be my Trybe
> If I forgive him.
> (TLN 372–6)

Here, suddenly, the words have to be cramped, or indeed crushed, to make the pentameters work. 'Nation' must be two syllables, 'even' must be one, 'interest' perhaps two (although the temptation for the actor must be to linger on each syllable of this gorgeous word). The closing statement—'Cursed be my Trybe if I forgive him'—could of course be a free-standing pentameter. But the lineation in Quarto and Folio alike suggests two half-lines, potentially hedged by two pauses—after 'interest' and 'forgive him'. The effect is to isolate and amplify the closing statement. It becomes a summative and proleptic pledge: one spoken with violent certitude to everyone, anyone, no one.

Old Capulet's shifts—however capricious—are always answerable to the context. Shylock's movements, by contrast, are laced with menace. This is because they are measured by nothing but Shylock's *own* cogitations:

> I am debating of my present store,
> And by the neere gesse of my memorie
> I cannot instantly raise up the grosse
> Of full three thousand ducats: what of that?
> *Tuball* a wealthy Hebrew of my Tribe
> Will furnish me: but soft, how many months
> Doe you desire? Rest you faire good signior,
> Your worship was the last man in our mouthes.
>
> (TLN 378–85)

It is striking how difficult it is here to distinguish between one unit of speech and another. Dramatic speech always has a limited range of addressees: it might be direct address to all others on-stage; it might be address to one or more characters (to the exclusion of any others); it might be direct address to the audience, *sotto voce*, which no one but the audience 'overhears'; it might be *sotto voce* which one or more characters on-stage also overhear. However, Shylock's peculiarly taunting role threatens these familiar demarcations. And the part appears to be written so as to make the actor himself uncertain to whom he should direct his speeches. Just how declared, how candid, and how shamelessly should he 'play' this radically indecorous Jew? This is more than just a question about the character; it is a question for and about the actor. For how 'should' he approach these lines? What is *not* spoken out loud, in flagrant defiance of politeness or respect? Is anything kept within, as a secret or appetite too dark or shaming to be acknowledged?

So how will the actor play the above speech? He will know the convention that a midline transition from one unit of speech to another almost always indicates a shift in address: either from one character to another, or from public (to others on-stage) to private (to the audience off-stage). But is this the case here? The opening lines, 'I am debating ...' are scarcely a response to his cue from Bassanio, '[doe] [you] heare?' Is Bassanio then his addressee? Or is Shylock talking to himself? The first clear shift comes with the short phrase, 'what of that?', but from or to what exactly is unclear. He might continue to address himself; he might be thinking out loud; he might be directly addressing one or all of the Christians. Similarly, either Antonio or Bassanio might be the 'you' of the midline switch into 'but soft, how many months | Doe *you* desire?' The final shift then clearly has Shylock address Antonio ('Your worship'): 'Rest you faire good signior, | Your worship was the last man in our mouthes.' The joke in this last statement is not only the relish of anticipatory cannibalism. It is a comment upon this very speech—an artfully ordered appetizer in which Shylock (*almost* literally) 'mouths' his various addressees, one by one, as though tasting a little of each at a time.

Similar confusing prosodic shifts recur throughout Shylock's period of ascendance:

> O father *Abram*, what these Christians are,
> Whose owne hard dealings teaches them suspect
> The thoughts of others: Praie you tell me this,
> If he should breake his daie, what should I gaine
> By the exaction of the forfeiture?
>
> (TLN 489–93)

Again there is the change in focus of address, but once more the precise direction of this change is menacingly ambiguous. The actor may think that the line 'O father *Abram*, what these Christians are', indicates self-address (rather like Puck's 'what fooles these mortals be!' in *A Midsummer Night's Dream* (TLN 1439)). If that were the case, having vented his contempt, he then shifts back to addressing 'these Christians'. But the exclamation may actually represent more mock renunciation than genuine confession. So Shylock says of the Christians that their 'owne hard dealings teaches them suspect | The thoughts of others' (TLN 490–1): but Shylock, of course, is absolutely to be 'suspect'-ed; no one could drive a 'hard'-er bargain than him. Consequently, his putative addressee—'father *Abram*'—shades mendaciously and mockingly into Antonio. Shylock may thus be pretend-ing—grotesquely enough—to be in league with his fellow 'merchant' against the suspicious Bassanio. If so, Bassanio now stands for 'these Chris-tians'; Shylock now purports to address *Antonio* confidentially, as though he were a member of his own tribe. The midline shift—with 'Praie you tell me this'—thereby signals the switch in address from this burlesque Antonio to Bassanio. This in turn points the moment when he returns to a vicious attack on his old enemy: pretending that Antonio is not present, Shylock suddenly changes his mode of address to the third-person 'he': 'If *he* should breake *his* daie.'

It is from this context of shifting, problematic, ambiguous address that Shylock's most famous speech—'Hath not a *Jew* eyes?' (TLN 1270)—takes its bearings. Spoken nominally to Salarino, the speech is in prose. This immediately gives the actor huge liberty to shift the focus and pace of address, to seize pauses, to identify discrete units of speech, and thus to engage or confront more than one audience. Every link in this speech can be an invitation to switch from insult to confession, threat to apology, on-stage to off-stage audience. When the Shylock-actor speaks six times of the 'you' that repeatedly prick, tickle, poison, and wrong the Jew, he *may* speak directly to Salarino or directly to 'us'; he may shift from one to the other; he may implicate both throughout:

> _____ [that] [good] for?
> To baite fish withall, [SWITCH?] if it will feede nothing/else, it will feede my revenge; [SWITCH?] he hath disgrac'd me, and/hindred me halfe a million, laught at my losses, mockt at/my gaines, scorned my Nation, thwarted my bargaines,/cooled my friends, heated mine enemies, [SWITCH?] and what's the/reason? [SWITCH?] I am a *Jewe*: [SWITCH?] Hath not a *Jew* eyes? [SWITCH?] hath not a/*Jew* hands, organs, dementions, sences, affections, passi-/ons [SWITCH?], fed with the same foode, hurt with the same wea-/pons, subject to the same diseases, healed by the same/meanes, warmed and cooled by the same Winter and/Sommer as a Christian is: [SWITCH?] if you pricke us doe we not/bleede? [SWITCH?] if you tickle us, doe we not laugh? [SWITCH?] if you poison/us doe we not die? [SWITCH?] and if you wrong us shall we not re-/venge? [SWITCH?] if we are like you in the rest, we will resemble you/in that. [SWITCH?] If a *Jew* wrong a *Christian*, what is his humility,/[SWITCH?] revenge? [SWITCH?] If a *Christian* wrong a *Jew*, what should his suf-/ferance be by Christian example, [SWITCH?] why revenge? [SWITCH?] The vil-/lanie you teach me I will execute, [SWITCH?] and it shall goe hard/but I will better the instruction.

> (TLN 1265–83; lineation ours)

The difficult politics of the speech are all wrapped up in questions of address—questions as to who is being addressed and how—and therefore of inclusion and accusation. Prose always has this potential for overt shifts, particularly shifts *towards* addressing the audience, and in thus addressing the audience gaining some relief (from loneliness, responsibility, the seriousness of vice). There is no such relief in the Shylock-part: first, because if the audience is addressed, it is not his partner but his enemy; second, because if the speech contains both soliloquy and dialogue, or sustains both in the same moment, this is not for the first time. The actor has already experienced it in all of its tense irresolution in the earlier verse (see, for example, the ambiguous rhythms of TLN 448–53). It is perfectly possible that much of this great speech is addressed, as though in pain, to Shylock alone; or that much of it is jabbed jeeringly at his grossly trivial and bigoted interlocutor, Salarino; or again, that much of it is offered as combined mitigation and threat to the audience. One thing is clear: the actor is left with choices, no less difficult than potentially decisive.

The speech is so famous, and the part so ambivalent, that it can be difficult for us today to recover how confusing these choices might have seemed to the actor for whom the part was originally written. The point to recognize is that the choices are *not* pre-ordained or obvious. Rather, here, as with the earlier midline switches, the choices curiously grow from within the substance of the speech. The ethical provocation of the Shylock-part is well attested. But we can identify here where the *actor* might have located something of the same: in the part's inveterate double-speak; in the uncertain hinge-points between one unit of speech and another, and so between one addressee and another; and, not least, in the porous boundaries between 'verse' and 'prose', ostensibly distinctive registers which here keep chopping into or out of one another.

We have already witnessed how Shylock's distinctively jagged verse takes its shapes from the prose which begins the part: both are characterized by phrasal repetitions that seem at one and the same time to ignore, insult, and intentionally provoke their unaddressed overhearers. When his early verse seems to be tauntingly suspended between soliloquy and conversation—or when the actor is faced with difficult decisions concerning who to look at or who to 'cut'—any choices take their cue from the similar uneasiness of the prose. Likewise, in the 'Hath not a *Jew* eyes' (TLN 1270) speech, the heavy prose 'switches' come with the full knowledge of what preceded them. Rather than forgetting in the freedom of prose the fact of difficult choices, the recurrence forces the difficulty to the fore. They are contextualized, and partly predetermined, by the part's earlier midline verse shifts. The sudden leaps from one brief speech-act to another—whether in prose or in verse—therefore serve the Shylock-part's fastidious ability to expose anxious politics and slippery agency. Does he speak *to* him, or to them, or to me? Does he speak *of* him, or of them, or of me? In other words, these hinge-moments 'inside' speeches become powerful occasions—not only for 'Shylock', but for anyone, including the audience, who may be his momentary target—for *feeling* one's place, and for measuring one's relative belonging, complicity, or ethical responsibility. In this part there really is no such thing as free speech.

There is thus no refuge for Shylock—or his interlocutors—in either prose or verse. It is no accident that the part's numerous repeated cues—perhaps its chief technique for embodying Shylock's shamingly, shamefully interruptive relationship with others—are as likely to happen in prose as in verse.[3] Shylock is *always* out of kilter, as lone a wolf as Shakespeare ever depicted. And to become such a thing, the Shylock-actor has to be forever on edge—just as his character is forever on the edge. The part of Shylock is a powerful pioneer in the technique, reach, and attendant expectations of both acting and characterization.

# Macbeth

Let us begin this final section with a brief recapitulation. Shakespeare's actors would always have had to pay scrupulous attention to how their parts point transitions in emotion and address. This means searching out the usual range of instruments—cues, midline switches, short lines, rhyming couplets, movements between prose and verse—designed to help the actor overcome the exclusion of information about his fellow players that is a feature of part-scripts. As we have seen, such devices fill out missing context, providing dramaturgical instruction concerning the player's interrelationships with his fellows on-stage. They provide a way of mapping one's passage through a speech; they orientate the actor in what might otherwise be a radically unfamiliar environment. There is no doubt that Shakespeare's actors must often have 'seen' these signs before deciphering the argument of the more opaque or densely figurative speeches on their rolls. We can surmise, then, that Shakespeare's actors knew and depended on the specific range of options that were opened up by particular lexical signs. However, we have seen how Shakespeare's increasingly sophisticated metrics began to complicate once unequivocal acting signs: he starts introducing more than one 'instruction' at one time, or gives information with outcomes that are not visibly, physically actable but are found, instead, in the interpreting mind of the actor or auditor. This potential for interpretive overload is not necessarily a problem for the actor. The examples quoted earlier (pp. 383–6) from the part of Hamlet, for instance, all give the actor a mercurial power of choice that accords well with the prince's caprice, charisma, and facility to surprise. But there is clearly a danger—or a temptation—to puzzle the actors, or to play games with their expectations, or to make them doubt the adequacy of their responses. Of course, Shakespeare would hardly do this without a powerful expressive rationale, or unless a compelling imperative placed the actors' needs in the shade. In the part of Macbeth, we are going to suggest, this is precisely the case.

First, a necessary caveat: it is not easy to be confident about all the details in the Macbeth-part, simply because it is not easy to be confident about the *Macbeth* text. The provenance and authority of the only extant version of the play—in the Folio—has long been a matter of debate. There is a good chance that it is a more or less faithful record of a performance text, perhaps for Blackfriars (suggested by the probably interpolated scenes of singing and dancing), perhaps for court; equally, there is a strong possibility that the play has been cut down from Shakespeare's original2, and shortened and reordered, probably by Middleton. And many of the details of the Folio text—not least regarding lineation and versification—may reflect the work of the typesetters (compositors) rather than the script of the author or the working parts of the players. Textual critics agree that there were two compositors at work on Folio *Macbeth*—'A' until the end of iii. iii, 'B' from then until the conclusion—and that compositor A in particular was prone to arrange 'verse' in what seems, at face value, unlikely metrical units. Nonetheless, the single text we have can still tell us a lot about how (at least) one version of *Macbeth* was performed. For even if we agree that lineation is sometimes arbitrarily determined by a compositor, the organization of the Macbeth-part remains powerfully consistent and distinctive. Though not every detail can be depended upon, simple accumulation can stand for evidence of the kinds of acting signals that the player (probably Burbage) was looking for as he imagined and embodied the very first stage Macbeth.

As always, a basic question for the actor is how this part relates to other parts he has played. Macbeth is obviously a tragic hero, and Burbage would have been looking out for this part's particular angle on the conflicts within self and with others that so distinguished his earlier 'tragic' roles of Hamlet, Othello, and Lear (all identified as Burbage roles in the actor's epitaph poem). He would have searched out his script for moments of privacy, for points where suppression breaks out into violence, or for defining moments where thought provokes, inhibits, or replaces action.

At the opening of the Macbeth-part, the actor is immediately apprized of the most salient facts about his character. He will learn from his own lines the 'strange intelligence' that he is going to become Thane of Cawdor and King ('I know I am *Thane* of Glamis, | But how, of Cawdor?' (TLN 171–2)). His early cues, meanwhile, will tell him vital information concerning his mood and mode:

| | |
|---|---|
| _____ [Charme's] [wound] up' | (TLN 135) |
| _____ [you] [are] so' | (TLN 146) |
| _____ [Macbeth,] [all] haile | (TLN 169) |
| _____ [are] [they] vanish'd? | (TLN 181) |
| _____ [the] [Reason] Prisoner | (TLN 187) |
| _____ [shall] [be] king | (TLN 189) |
| _____ [Devill] [speake] true? | (TLN 213) |
| _____ [Have] [overthrowne] him | (TLN 224) |
| _____ [I] [pray] you' | (TLN 237) |

The cues paint a picture of uncanny influence, demonic temptation, and epistemological dizziness. They harp upon a single string: the supernatural or supra-rational force that will draw Macbeth into action. This *character* thus arrives in a world where reason, custom, and empiricism have all been superseded by some barely understood, self-estranging metaphysical determinism. But might something similar apply to the actor? For the peculiar bodilessness of the cues may already suggest to him the difficulty of finding any adequate on-stage 'counter' to his character, someone of roughly equal force to bounce off or interrogate.

Let's explore this question by concentrating upon two aspects of the Macbeth-part: first, the prosodic and locutionary distinction between soliloquy and dialogue; second, rhyming couplets.

## Macbeth's rhythms of address

Macbeth's six soliloquies all occur in the part's first half (before the appearance of Banquo's ghost, from which point onwards Macbeth is never alone, though always, as we shall see, at least partially addressing himself). Now the pace and syntax of Macbeth's soliloquies are more clearly 'pointed' for the actor than anything else in the part. So each soliloquy, long or short, is marked by a similar rhythm. The prosody is at first tentative and broken, with short phrases, abrupt questions, interrupted lines, clausal qualifications; it then gains a cascading momentum, marked by strongly flowing, often increasingly long sentences. The psychological effect is simple: confusion or prevarication resolving into coherence and decisiveness. A few examples will suffice:

> Present Feares
> Are lesse then horrible Imaginings:
> My Thought, whose Murther yet is but fantasticall,
> Shakes so my single state of Man,
> That Function is smother'd in surmise,
> And nothing is, but what is not.
>
>                          (TLN 248–53)

> Besides, this *Duncane*
> Hath borne his Faculties so meeke; hath bin
> So cleere in his great Office, that his Vertues
> Will pleade like Angels, Trumpet-tongu'd against
> The deepe damnation of his taking off:
> And Pitty, like a naked New-borne-Babe,
> Striding the blast, or Heavens Cherubin, hors'd
> Upon the sightlesse Curriors of the Ayre,
> Shall blow the horrid deed in every eye,
> That teares shall drowne the winde.
>
>                          (TLN 490–9)

> … no: this my Hand will rather
> The multitudinous Seas incarnardine,
> Making the Greene one, Red.
>
>                  (TLN 722–4)

> If't be so,
> For *Banquo*'s Issue have I fil'd my Minde,
> For them, the gracious *Duncan* have I murther'd,
> Put Rancours in the Vessell of my Peace
> Onely for them, and mine eternall Jewell
> Given to the common Enemie of Man,
> To make them Kings, the Seedes of *Banquo* Kings.
>
>                          (TLN 1654–60)

As always, a flowing soliloquy does not preclude midline switches ('Present Feares | Are lesse', '… no: this my Hand') or short lines ('And nothing is, but what is not', 'That teares shall drowne the winde', 'Making the Greene one, Red'). For the actor, as we have seen, such metrics are entirely conventional, and not the least confusing. The actor is simply speaking to himself, and not casting about for anyone else's response. Whatever the desolation of the character, the actor will be secure and confident. Any pauses he finds become pointers of self-collection; in marking a shift from one thought of self or projection of self to another, they are the 'centring' infrastructure of a mind in motion. Crucial in this instance, then, is a *distinction* between the actor's and the character's experience. The persona of Macbeth is premissed upon separateness from others, and increasingly from self; the main question is whether or not he can be at peace in this isolation—the answer, of course, is that he cannot. But the *actor* will feel that for a while he can, and that the place in which he finds this peace is in his soliloquies. (Or, more precisely, he will feel such confidence if he can be assured that he indeed *is* in soliloquy—a confidence which, as we shall see, is not always easily sustained.)

When Macbeth is speaking to or with others, it is quite another story:

```
_____ [who's] there?
A Friend. [SHORT: fourth iamb in incomplete line?]
_____ [in] [measurelesse] content.
Being unprepar'd, [SHORT and free-standing]
Our will became the servant to defect,
Which else should free have wrought. [SHORT—to be completed by Banquo]
_____ [shew'd] [some] truth.
                    I thinke not of them: [SHORT: completion of line]
Yet when we can entreat an houre to serve,
We would spend it in some words upon that Businesse,
If you would graunt the time. [SHORT—to be completed by Banquo]
_____ [your] [kind'st] leysure.
If you shall cleave to my consent, [SHORT]
When 'tis, it shall make Honor for you. [SHORT]
```

(TLN 584–604)

The actor reading these cues and lines will find various difficulties. For a start, the substance of the cues received is opaque, giving the actor no lead whatsoever concerning mood or context other than the oddly vacant compliance of his interlocutors. Equally, they are hard to receive without losing metrical regularity. Compiled in either halting blank verse or prose, the dialogue is almost impossible to speak lyrically or even confidently. Indeed, dialogue like this will disconcert both speaker and receiver. Am I taking or giving an iambic cue—or perhaps neither? Seven of Macbeth's ten lines are short, which itself embodies a hanging nervousness, reinforcing his mix of strangled courtesy and vaporized reference. An actor relying only on his part-text might be left grasping for something solid: uncertain what he is acting 'into' or moving against, and liable to suspect that any kind of stress in enunciation, indeed any actorly choice at all, is unearned or mistaken. Of course the character of Macbeth is here painfully ill at ease. But the actor is given no perspective upon this unease, and therefore precious little release from the exchange's claustrophobic, strangely bodiless politeness.

We see a different use of the same technology in Macbeth's next scene. Here the cues Macbeth receives are packed with content. Shorn of Macbeth's actual lines, they read:

———————————————————— [a] [sorry] sight.
———————————————————— [two] [lodg'd] together.
———————————————————— [not] [so] deepely.
———————————————————— [make] [us] mad.
———————————————————— [doe] [you] meane?
———————————————————— [Groomes] [with] blood.
———————————————————— [Seeme] [their] Guilt.
———————————————————— [in] [your] thoughts.

(TLN 675–736)

The actor knows he has 'done the deed' (TLN 665), and knows his interlocutor (Lady Macbeth) worries partly about his mind, and partly about the dead King's grooms. However, if we flesh out these cues with the actual words spoken *by* Macbeth, then something quite different emerges. As instructive as the cues are for the Macbeth-actor, they are repeatedly all but ignored by the Macbeth-character:

———————————————————— [a] [sorry] sight.
There's one did laugh in's sleepe...
———————————————————— [two] [lodg'd] together.
One cry'd God blesse us, and Amen the other.
———————————————————— [not] [so] deepely.
But wherefore could not I pronounce Amen?
———————————————————— [make] [us] mad.
Me thought I heard a voyce cry...

_____ [what] [doe] [you] meane?
Still it cry'd, Sleepe no more ...

(TLN 675–98)

Macbeth's single chilling remembrance—the grooms, the inability to say
'Amen'—is carried over from speech to speech, irrespective of any cues.
The character neither takes up nor pays heed to what is said to him. This
disparity between cue and speech encapsulates how Macbeth now operates
at an inescapable remove from others.

So, for the part-conning actor, one indicator that the character is not
really responding to his addressor is this growing discontinuity between cue
and speech. Another is any increasingly flowing or rhapsodic momentum,
implicitly denying appeal to other characters, or space in which they might
speak:

_____ [make] [us] mad.
Me thought I heard a voyce cry, Sleep no more:
*Macbeth* does murther Sleepe, the innocent Sleepe,
Sleepe that knits up the ravel'd Sleeve of Care,
The death of each dayes Life, sore Labors Bath,
Balme of hurt Mindes, great natures second Course,
Chiefe nourisher in Life's Feast.

(TLN 690–6)

Notwithstanding the interrogatory presence of his wife, Macbeth's speech
here replicates the lyrical momentum of his soliloquies. A similar gradual
crescendo distinguishes Macbeth's first public statement after the body of
Duncan has been discovered:

_____ [is] [not] so.
Had I but dy'd an houre before this chance,
I had liv'd a blessed time: for from this instant,
There's nothing serious in Mortalitie:
All is but Toyes: Renowne and Grace is dead,
The Wine of Life is drawne, and the meere Lees
Is left this Vault, to brag of.

(TLN 850–6)

Even though spoken in the presence of Macduff, Banquo, Lennox, Ross,
and Lady Macbeth, the enjambed accumulations of the last three lines
in particular suggest a perceptible movement into self-address. The gang

on-stage overhear everything, but the actor needs no one at all in his sight-lines.

Macbeth's next major speech presents a still further refining of the technique. For it offers the actor more than one interpretive option. The choice he makes depends upon which prosodic model he identifies as underpinning the speech: it might be the model of Macbeth's soliloquies; it might that of his far more tortured conversations:

> Who can be wise, amaz'd, temp'rate, & furious,
> Loyall, and Neutrall, in a moment? No man:
> Th'expedition of my violent Love
> Out-run the pawser, Reason. Here lay *Duncan*,
> His Silver skinne, lac'd with His Golden Blood,
> And his gash'd Stabs, look'd like a Breach in Nature,
> For Ruines wastfull entrance: there the Murtherers,
> Steep'd in the Colours of their Trade; their Daggers
> Unmannerly breech'd with gore: who could refraine,
> That had a heart to love; and in that heart,
> Courage, to make's love knowne?
>
> (TLN 873–83)

Is this pivotal speech to be played as monologue or dialogue? It can be interpreted as another 'virtual' soliloquy, a rhetorical conversation devoted to resolving its own puzzled question ('Who can be wise, amaz'd…in a moment?'). Accordingly, the speech again replicates the rhythmic sequence of his soliloquies: stop–start agitation succeeded by momentous resolution. Macbeth is speaking only nominally to others; he erases his audience as he appeases himself. But let us imagine the actor—fully aware that other actors are on-stage with him—deciding against modelling his approach to the speech upon the part's earlier soliloquies. He instead chooses to point the speech heavily, using the switches and changes in direction as clues for acting an increasingly desperate attempt at *dialogue*. He then produces something like this:

> Who can be wise, amaz'd, temp'rate, & furious,
> Loyall, and Neutrall, in a moment? [SWITCH] No man: [SWITCH]
> Th'expedition of my violent Love
> Out-run the pawser, Reason. [SWITCH] Here lay *Duncan*,
> His Silver skinne, lac'd with His Golden Blood,
> And his gash'd Stabs, look'd like a Breach in Nature,

For Ruines wastfull entrance: [SWITCH] there the Murtherers,
Steep'd in the Colours of their Trade; [SWITCH] their Daggers
Unmannerly breech'd with gore: [SWITCH] who could refraine,
That had a heart to love; [SWITCH] and in that heart,
Courage, to make's love knowne?

Parsing the speech in this fashion, the actor produces a frantically escalating attempt at justification. Macbeth is intensely aware of everyone who is listening: he is anxious for approbation, desperate not to hear the strain of his hyperbole echoing or, still worse, the silence that greets each attempt at explanation. The actor can decide whom to address, and can clearly switch between addressing all and sundry, to addressing a particular individual, or a specific cluster (Duncan's sons, for instance), to addressing himself. Each midline caesura, furthermore, is a pause in which Macbeth—if not the actor—hopes that someone else will speak: a word will do, any word of pity or sympathy or understanding. But nothing comes, so he must plough on, to the very end hoping for release. Rather than a proto-soliloquy, this becomes a failed attempt at conversation. The broken lineation thus resembles pretty much every dialogue that Macbeth endures: like them, it is full of fractured or arrested lines, reaching out for some answering completion that never comes.

It might just about be possible for the actor to reconcile in his delivery of the speech these two models—soliloquy and failed dialogue. The actor could begin by playing Macbeth's 'hope' for conversation; he could cast the first six speech units (and the hanging ellipses that follow) out in the direction of one or more of his fellow players; he could then pick up momentum from 'who could refraine', and turn away from his unresponding on-stage audience back to the only 'heart' that he now knows: his own. This is possible, but difficult. More to the point, perhaps, is simply how overloaded are Shakespeare's potential instructions to the actor (who, suggestively, gets no help whatsoever from the succeeding cues or speeches—the passage itself is brought to an end only by Lady Macbeth's notorious faint). For the part has taught the actor that line breaks and short lines mean one thing in monologue (where they are basically self-securing), another in dialogue (where they are self-isolating). This proposes two very different psychological narratives, and two quite distinct relations of the speaker to what he talks about: his crime. But in this instance, Shakespeare's peculiar intensity places the actor in a limbo-like mental space, demanding responses slightly outside customary precedents.

As a consequence, the actor is led to experience something like the authentic Macbeth miasma: he is haunted by others even when he is alone; he is alone even when he is with others; he is secure only in being unreachably cut off; he denies it all (because lying to others) even as he confesses it (because speaking to himself). What is at stake, therefore, is both a manner of acting (how declamatory, knowingly false, mock-theatrical, pleading, uncertain, etc.) and, embodied in this acting, a state of mind. Above all, the part is written—and must be acted—in a style that is very finely tuned to the ironies that can mediate speaking: how one may in different moments be differently revealed to or concealed from oneself.

This is (of course) a decisive moment for both the part and the play. Nothing can ever be the same. Not least, from this point on, Macbeth will speak of 'serious' things only to shadows or surrogates of himself. It is therefore appropriate that this moment should mark the point from which it becomes virtually impossible to determine what Macbeth's mode of address is, even though the largest questions of sin and sincerity must hang upon that decision. Time and again the actor is caught, unable to choose between addressing himself and addressing others. He has to seek ways of negotiating this impasse, one method one moment, another the next.

So Macbeth's next scene, his first as King, sees him resume his normal public manner—crabbed, glozing, nauseatingly insincere. But he is at the same time painfully labouring for release. This is why each midline suspension now carries a yearning proto-question:

> We heare our bloody Cozens are bestow'd
> In England, and in Ireland, not confessing
> Their cruell Parricide, filling their hearers
> With strange invention.
>
> (TLN 1016–19)

No longer daring to ask anything, the part resolves into diffident, querying statements. But any response, answer, or affirmation is icily withheld. So Macbeth carries on, forced to change the subject:

> But of that to morrow,
> When therewithall, we shall have cause of State,
> Craving us joyntly.
>
> (TLN 1019–21)

Again he gets nothing; again he switches tack:

> Hye you to Horse:
> Adieu, till you returne at Night.
> Goes *Fleance* with you?
>
> (TLN 1021–3)

The prosody, as usual, creates space, silence, and nervous expectation (on-stage and off-stage); everything here breathes the sickly want of reciprocity. This, then, is a consummate example of how Macbeth's dialogue becomes almost entirely superfluous. It apes political function and efficiency, but it is primarily a nervous iteration of unspeakable depths. Hence, having effectively bid Banquo 'adieu' two or three times already, he proceeds to do so two or three times more:

> _____ [does] [call] upon's.
> I wish your Horses swift, and sure of foot:
> And so I doe commend you to their backs.
> Farwell.                                    *Exit Banquo.*
>
> (TLN 1024–7)

The words are basically empty of content, representing no more than repeated attempts at saying goodbye. If the part-script includes Banquo's exit, as above, then the Macbeth-actor will know that Banquo does not respond to him. A dreadful mix of hollowness and echo is then epitomized in the 'missing' four feet of Macbeth's closing line. Whether the final 'Farwell' precedes or succeeds Banquo's actual departure from stage doesn't matter—fatally unanswered, marooned in his own lines' ellipses, Macbeth is talking to himself.

As Macbeth sedulously clears his passage into desolation, the part makes repeated use of short-line commands either to no one in particular or to no one with a name:

> Let every man be master of his time,
> Till seven at Night, to make societie
> The sweeter welcome:
> We will keepe our selfe till Supper time alone:
> While then, God be with you. *Exeunt Lords.*
> Sirrha, a word with you: Attend those men
> Our pleasure?
> _____ [the] [Pallace] Gate.
> Bring them before us.
>
> (TLN 1028–38)

There is a fundamental creative osmosis at work here between player and persona. Repeatedly there is no counterweight for the actor; no thrilling to and fro, no ensemble playing, no sustaining collegiality. Actors may love being the focus of attention, but the almost palpable refusal of adrenalin in these scenes, the casting of so many lines as *and* into unreturned taciturnity, the scratchy, nerve-end attrition of these exchanges—all of this means that the actor might well be left hanging, like his character, in edgy need of violence or other release. This, in more ways than one, is where the murderers come in (it helps explain the strangely compulsive and functionally redundant explosiveness of Macbeth's 'Catalogue' of mongrels, curs, demi-wolves, and the like).

Macbeth's first speech to the murderers epitomizes the bridled metrics and communicative isolation of all his preceding 'conversations'. The exchange is always re-lineated by editors, often from the Folio's jagged verse into prose. In truth, for the actor, such fidgeting is neither here nor there. He can do nothing but acknowledge each verbal change in direction, tacitly recognizing another sequence of unanswered prompts:

> Was it not yesterday, we spoke together?
> ————————————————— [please] [your] Highnesse.
> Well then, —— [?]
> Now have you consider'd of my speeches: —— [?]
> Know, that it was he, in the times past,
> Which held you so under fortune, —— [?]
> Which you thought had been our innocent selfe. —— [?]
> This I made good to you, —— [?] in our last conference, —— [?]
> Past in probation with you:
> How you were borne in hand, how crost: —— [?]
> The Instruments: —— [?] who wrought with them: —— [?]
> And all things else, that might
> To halfe a Soule, and to a Notion craz'd,
> Say, Thus did *Banquo*.

> (TLN 1067–80)

Contrary to what the actor might normally expect, the short lines here have no effect upon the addressees. But nor do they reach out to the audience (suggesting how detached *we* might presently feel from the anti-hero). The speech is itself a dark joke about the superfluousness of dialogue; Macbeth has already ('yesterday', he tells us) spoken of what he now takes so many laboured lines to repeat.

The scene of the feast brings this savage dialogical solipsism to a (literal) head:

*Enter First Murtherer*

See they encounter thee with their harts thanks
Both sides are even: [SWITCH: Macbeth sits] heere Ile sit I'th'mid'st,
Be large in mirth, anon wee'l drinke a Measure
The Table round. [SWITCH: sees/addresses Murderer] There's blood upon thy face.

(TLN 1266–9)

There are two or three points here (after 'even', 'mid'st', 'in mirth') where Macbeth might shift attention, uneasily or not, from one member of his table to another; typically, no addressee is specified in the part, or at least none before the murderer ('thy'). In this sense, the actor is decidedly *undirected* by the script—at least before turning to the murderer. The script encourages a certain abstraction, an absence of commitment to the ostensible occasion (a feast). When at last he gets the clear direction to speak to the murderer, the Macbeth-actor is given the release that, as we have seen, is so often denied him. The phenomenology of actor and character are here as one: the search for focus is like an arrow in flight, initially unsteady before suddenly claiming the target.

Here is another typical example:

_____ [*Fleans*] [is] scap'd.
Then comes my Fit againe: [SWITCH?]
I had else beene perfect; [SWITCH?]
Whole as the Marble, founded as the Rocke,
As broad, and generall, as the casing Ayre:
But now I am cabin'd, crib'd, confin'd, bound in
To sawcy doubts, and feares. [SWITCH?] But *Banquo's* safe?

(TLN 1278–84)

Macbeth is cued by the murderer, and ostensibly responds to him. But it is unclear what the two or perhaps three midline switches indicate. They will, as ever, suggest to the actor a shift of address: but of what kind? Either or both of the first two short lines may be 'asides' to himself; indeed, so may the entire first five and half lines, switching to a direct questioning of the murderer only with 'But *Banquo's* safe?' However, the preceding five lines may also be 'to' the murderer: enunciated out loud, in full hearing of his agent, albeit speaking of secrets that none of his guests must hear. Macbeth is on one level addressing himself throughout this speech. This is indeed no less true of the closing 'rhetorical' question—'But *Banquo's* safe?'—which seems to be directly addressed to another, but is more profoundly Macbeth's conscious repetition of a known fact. We might even doubt whether, on the actor's part, it did indeed close with a question-mark. For the apparent 'question' is more a compulsive murmur from a half-buried unconsciousness: a worried incantation, or a superstitious charm, not directed primarily *to* anyone. It is thus appropriate that Macbeth is speaking here to nameless agents whose main function is to mirror, echo, shadow, or fulfil the hero. In so far as he addresses others, he addresses himself. This is a consummate example of the midline shift that is a potential actorly instruction (open to be visibly acted upon or not) and also (because the physical response is an option rather than a direction) an implicit phenomenological 'movement'. Whoever is nominally being addressed, the midline shifts are the snakes and ladders inside Macbeth's consciousness.

## Macbeth's rhyming couplets

The distinctive challenges of the Macbeth-part are epitomized in its use of rhyming couplets. Couplets can usually be split into two basic forms: those that 'cap' a soliloquy and those in dialogue. The first generally offer the actor fairly straightforward information, being often summative statements that conclude largely meditative, internally directed monologue. They tend to signal a decisive movement 'out' to the audience, directing the actor to adopt a confidentially declaratory tone:

> The Prince of Cumberland: that is a step,
> On which I must fall downe, or else o're-leape,
> For in my way it lyes. Starres hide your fires,
> Let not Light see my black and deepe desires:
> The Eye winke at the Hand: yet let that bee,
> Which the Eye feares, when it is done to see.
>
> (TLN 336–41)

> Whiles I threat, he lives:
> Words to the heat of deedes too cold breath gives.
>
> (TLN 640–1)

> *Banquo*, thy Soules flight,
> If it finde Heaven, must finde it out to Night.
>
> (TLN 148–9)

Couplets such as these conform straightforwardly to the conventions: whether they take the form of a sequence of unanswered rhymes, or whether they are short 'teeing-up' lines supplying the first half of an unprompted, unshared couplet, they unequivocally direct the actor into 'inward' address. Unsurprisingly, the Macbeth-part regularly uses just such half-line/full-line couplets at moments of concentrated resolution. Now we might suppose that this private intensity is an obvious signature of the Macbeth-part: declared as such unproblematically from the start, and epitomized in its distinctively fierce and isolating rhymes. But it is not in fact so simple. For it is highly suggestive about Shakespeare's designs that the part's very first rhyme, whilst it certainly invokes customary expectations, at the same time seems to defer and complicate them.

So, this first couplet completes what is effectively Macbeth's first soliloquy:

> Come what come may,
> Time, and the Houre, runs through the roughest Day.
>
> (TLN 261–2)

As usual, the lone couplet presents a clear direction to the actor: it is spoken to himself alone, yet it indicates an imminent return to shared dialogue (clinched by the next cue that 'Macbeth' is given, '[upon] [your] leisure'). In all modern performances, the speeches that precede this couplet are treated as though they are a soliloquy beginning with 'Two Truths are told': a soliloquy broken into by other actors. But for the actor learning his part alone—learning it without presuppositions as to who or what Shakespeare's Macbeth 'is'—the nature of the speech might not have been quite so self-evident. Here is how the part would have framed this first couplet:

> My Thought...
> Shakes so my single state of Man,
> That Function is smother'd in surmise,
> And nothing is, but what is not.
> _____ [our] [Partner's] rapt.
> If Chance will have me King,
> Why Chance may Crowne me,

Without my stirre.
_____ [aid] [of] use.
Come what come may,
Time, and the Houre, runs through the roughest Day.
_____ [upon] [your] leysure.
Give me your favour:
My dull Braine was wrought with things forgotten.
Kinde Gentlemen...

(TLN 250–67)

It is clear from the surrounding information on the part that 'Macbeth' is not paying any attention to the others on the stage: he is told as much by the preceding cue, 'our Partner's rapt'. Moreover, Macbeth's return after the couplet to addressing others ('Give me your favour') will suggest to the actor that until then he continues to address himself alone despite the interjection of cues from others. But still, a small leap of faith is required before this broken passage can be *assumed* to be a soliloquy: more than that, with his own speeches 'interrupted' every few lines by others' cues, the actor cannot but retain a consciousness of others' voices. The actor sees this beforehand, wonders what these other speeches portend or contain, just as he is aware of these others in performance. Here is thus another indication of how Shakespeare scripts this part so as to embed in his actor a peculiarly *physical* temporizing: a forestalling of full physical abandoning to the moment and to the audience. In having to keep an ear out to others' interventions, the actor cannot assume an exclusively shared channel between actor and audience, or the confidence and relief that usually comes with soliloquy. Any such assurance has to be taken on trust. The character desperately wants to be scot-free and alone: but so too does the actor. The part is thus written so as surreptitiously to plant *in the actor* a desire for self-release, and for the exclusivity, clarity, and even violence of being securely alone (as Macbeth says later to the murderers, 'I require a clearenesse...To leave no Rubs nor Botches in the Worke' (TLN 1139–40)). There is no easy recourse to a pristine interiority: the actor's waiting corresponds to the character's tacit, buried, but explosive impatience. The role of Macbeth is all about pushing further and further into lonely spaces. But this will not happen without violence; moreover, it cannot happen without Macbeth's taking into himself *and* obliterating the rival selves that this first 'soliloquy' presents as edging in upon Macbeth's struggle for self-definition.

However, not every couplet in Macbeth's part speaks of Macbeth's hidden inwardness; and not every couplet excludes all addressees but himself. From early in the part the Macbeth-actor will notice a second variety of couplet—spoken during conversations with his wife:

> Away, and mock the time with fairest show,
> False Face must hide what the false Heart doth know.
>
> (TLN 556–7)

The opening word, 'Away', tells the actor that the couplet is addressed to another: Macbeth says directly to his wife the kind of thing that otherwise he would say only in private: in a soliloquy. In play terms, this is a sign of the demonic confederacy between the two, whose merged persona is here reinforced by Macbeth's singular 'Face' and 'Heart'. Later a similar direction is presented to the Macbeth-actor:

> Good things of Day begin to droope, and drowse,
> Whiles Nights black Agents to their Prey's doe rowse.
> Thou marvell'st at my words: but hold thee still,
> Things bad begun, make strong themselves by ill.
>
> (TLN 1211–14)

In this passage the third line ('Thou marvell'st...') makes clear that Macbeth's interlocutor, Lady Macbeth, must hear his first couplet; in turn, the succeeding couplet ('hold thee still'/'themselves by ill') is directly addressed to her.

The part thus appears to set up two distinct types of couplet: one for use when Macbeth is addressing himself (or the audience) alone, one for use when Macbeth is addressing Lady Macbeth. But this is a part that specializes in mingled and ambiguous signals, just as it repeatedly complicates apparent bifurcations (between agents, functions, judgements). So we might notice that every one of Macbeth's couplets, whether spoken to himself or his wife, is an incantation to crime or an abdication to evil. The same hypnotic rhythm is common to both, and represents pretty much the bass note of the Macbeth-part: a pervasive rumble 'beneath' all else, emerging into the spare finality of a rhyme each time that Macbeth renews his Faustian pledge. Consequently, even when Lady Macbeth is addressed, the actor is drawn back to 'playing' the rhyme as though it is unshared.

So, even though Macbeth's couplets are indeed sometimes addressed to Lady Macbeth, the actor is never speaking entirely *to* her. He is speaking around her, through her, over her, as he might a ghostly mirror, or ghostly emanation of self. The writing recommends a strange defocusing in the relationship of the Macbeth-actor to all others. It is as though he is asked to overlook his addressee's body in favour of a penumbra that surrounds, exceeds, and obscures it. He is speaking to his wife; he is speaking to nobody at all. The couplets embody Macbeth's enveloping pathology, as he at once engrosses and erases all others.

Apart from Macbeth's final words to Macduff, there is only one more occasion when rhyme in this part is clearly addressed to someone else. However, the shift into direct address during the rhyme also marks the character's immediate escape *from* rhyme:

> Sweet boadments, good:
> Rebellious dead, rise never till the Wood
> Of Byrnan rise, and our high plac'd *Macbeth*
> Shall live the Lease of Nature, pay his breath
> To time, and mortall Custome. Yet my Hart
> Throbs to know one thing: Tell me, if your Art
> Can tell so much: Shall *Banquo's* issue ever
> Reigne in this kingdome?
>
> (TLN 1640–7)

We might note here a new manner in the rhymes. The rhyme words do not complete the thought, but instead look to the succeeding half-line for grammatical definition. Obviously this makes the rhyme far less sure and portentous—apt enough, when Macbeth is flailing around for sure portents. The equivocating rhythm confers a half-erased rhyme that resists sure enunciation, one that is liable to be ignored or even missed by actor and audience alike. The couplets themselves appear to have become unmoored from their bearings: the rhymes drift, or seem to search for a fugitive finality. It is tempting to call them hypothetical—but in terms not so much of sense as of rhythm. This is because these lines are *both* in rhyme and in blank verse. The actor is asked to serve two prosodic measures simultaneously. This means that the observance of one such rhythm—for instance, stressing the rhyme word—can only be semi-committed, as though any decision for action thereby embodied is retractable. If conventional rhyming couplets clearly allegorize a decided state of mind (some sort of firming up of intention, whether in the form of inward meditation or outward invitation), here the accompanying state of mind is rendered provisional, as though Macbeth is auditioning for a future act, or imitating or recollecting a past state of certainty. But either way, the rhyme does not confirm sure-footed volition; it is not clicking in time to a surely apprehended fate.

And perhaps the actor is similarly caught here, marooned, like the rhyme word, half-way between premature closure and uncertain continuation. Usually, however dark or defeated the 'meaning' of a rhyming couplet, it represents a little island of the mind, an island *for the* mind. But what we here witness is a time-honoured acting sign—the unshared couplet—*not* being allowed its customary functions: this is neither a release into a secure 'private' home, nor a release into connection with others. Both such states offer (rather as conventional soliloquy does) the relief of clarity: the assurance of understood function, the shoring up of energies afforded by securely possessed space and time. There is no such relief given when the rhyming lines are also in blank verse. If Macbeth is trapped, the actor is likewise circling without a clear route of escape.

Macbeth has fifteen more rhyming couplets to speak, but they overwhelmingly take on a new form. First, they are neutral of address (until Macbeth's very last challenge, 'Lay on *Macduffe* | And damn'd be him, that first cries hold, enough' (TLN 2474–5)). Second, they offer a new take upon the rhyme form's customary harping upon existential end-games. Once Macbeth leaves the witches for the last time, his couplets always speak of fatalism, by turns stoic, reckless, and euphoric:

> No boasting like a Foole,
> This deed Ile do, before this purpose coole. (IV. i)
>
> (TLN 1706–7)

> The minde I sway by, and the heart I beare,
> Shall never sagge with doubt, nor shake with feare. (V. iii)
>
> (TLN 2223–4)

> I will not be affraid of Death and Bane,
> Till Birnane Forrest come to Dunsinane. (V. iii)
>
> (TLN 2283–4)

> But Swords I smile at, Weapons laugh to scorne,
> Brandish'd by man that's of a Woman borne. (V. vii)
>
> (TLN 2412–13)

For our purposes, what is important is the ambiguity of address—a purposeful lack of direction to the actor either about the action he is performing in saying the words, or about the effect these words have upon his listeners' actions. Consider the context of this couplet:

> ————————————————— [my] [good] Lord.
> Time, thou anticipat'st my dread exploits:
> The flighty purpose never is o're-tooke
> Unlesse the deed go with it. From this moment
> The very firstlings of my heart shall be
> The firstlings of my hand. And even now
> To Crown my thoughts with Acts: be it thoght & done:
> The Castle of *Macduff*, I will surprize,
> Seize upon Fife; give to th'edge o'th'Sword
> His Wife, his Babes, and all unfortunate Soules
> That trace him in his Line. *No boasting like a Foole,*
> *This deed Ile do, before this purpose coole,*
> But no more sights. Where are these Gentlemen?
> Come bring me where they are.
>
> (TLN 1696–1709, our italics)

The speech begins in clear response to the cue ('my good Lord'), but it is unclear from the first words until the end of the penultimate sentence to whom Macbeth is talking. Assuming the convention that midline switches indicate shifts in purpose or address brings us no closer to certainty. The couplet is no different from anything else in the speech. It may be spoken to Macbeth's men, or to Macbeth himself, or possibly to the audience (in such a way that it is unclear whether his men are meant to be overhearing or not). The line between Macbeth, his agents, and indeed his adversaries has all but vanished; so too has the line between monologue and dialogue.

And the first person to experience this difficulty of address has to be the actor. He repeatedly comes across the same difficulty in the part's final scenes. So the couplet 'heart I beare'/'shake with feare' (TLN 2223–4) is spoken with doctor and attendants on-stage, in a speech beginning 'Bring me no more Reports' and ending with Macbeth insulting his 'cream-fac'd Loone' of a servant. The couplet 'Death and Bane'/'Dunsinane' (TLN 2283–4) comes immediately after the direct address of the arrested line 'Bring it after me'. It seems clear from the doctor's reply to Macbeth's couplet ('Were I from Dunsinane away, and cleere...' (TLN 2285–6)) that the character as well as the actor 'hears' the couplet that cues him. The Macbeth-actor will not know this, pointing once more to a strikingly elusive performative effect—Macbeth is speaking 'to' no one, but in the full hearing of everyone.

Similar difficulties apply to the following three couplets:

> Arme, Arme, and out,
> If this which he avouches, do's appeare,
> There is nor flying hence, nor tarrying here.
> I 'ginne to be a-weary of the Sun,
> And wish th'estate o'th'world were now undon.
> Ring the Alarum Bell, blow Winde, come wracke,
> At least wee'l dye with Harnesse on our backe.

(TLN 2370–6)

There seem to be two orders to others here—'Arme, Arme, and out', and 'Ring the Alarum Bell'; meanwhile the middle couplet appears to be addressed to Macbeth himself as an aside. But any of these utterances could be taken otherwise. Shakespeare seems studiously intent upon making subject and agent slippery. All seven lines here could be spoken to others, or addressed to the self; they could be shouted to the audience, or beyond the battlements, to no one but the sun, the wind, and the oncoming wrack. This is partly because the subject changes in each speech unit: 'Arme' has a passive or absent subject; 'There is nor flying … nor tarrying' elides precisely who the verbs belong to; the middle couplet has the pronoun 'I'; the final couplet moves from unspecified agency ('Ring …'), to a semi-anthropomorphized nature ('blow … come'), to an irresolvably ambiguous 'we' and 'our', suspended between the royal and the collective plurals. This proposes something more nuanced than a simple division between public and private. The audience remains consistent throughout, but the relative appeal being made to that audience—or rather, *within* that audience—wanes and waxes along with the speech's unpredictable rhythms. We cannot speak with precision of any single audience, or auditor, or indeed addressee for the speech: once more, Macbeth is on one level addressing only himself throughout.

The frequent elusiveness of the part-script is peculiarly appropriate for this character. The actor is asked not so much to notice two options and decisively choose one, as to exist inside contradictions, or even irresolvable antinomies. Shakespeare's aim seems to be to cast, drag—almost drug—his principal actor into intermittent mental limbo precisely because it will help him to inhabit Macbeth's similar limbo. The actor is invited, or perhaps compelled, to allow all sides, and in so doing to commit finally to none; in this to turn paralysis into agency, or perhaps to identify agency as something closer to somnambulism than active volition: all of this virtually describes Macbeth.

At its most extreme—yet also at its most characteristic—the player is faced with writing like this:

> More shall they speake: for now I am bent to know
> By the worst meanes, the worst, for mine owne good,
> All causes shall give way. I am in blood
> Stept in so farre, that should I wade no more,
> Returning were as tedious as go ore:
> Strange things I have in head, that will to hand,
> Which must be acted, ere they may be scand.

> (TLN 1417–23)

Once again these couplets conflate two instructions for the actor in one: they are spoken 'to' or 'with' Lady Macbeth, but take the customary form of private address. But this is barely the beginning of their difficulty. For as we saw with the 'Yet my Hart | Throbs to know one thing: Tell me, if your Art' (TLN 1644–5) couplet, the speech intertwines blank verse and rhyme. So the clause, 'I am in blood' operates in two directions simultaneously—not so much grammatically (which often happens in Shakespeare) but in terms of the actable units of speech to which it belongs. It begins a discrete 'blank verse' sentence; it also completes a rhyme (with 'good') begun in the previous sentence; or, perhaps more to the point, it retrieves a rhyme out of a sentence that seemed to all intents buried. 'All causes shall give way'—which must be 'punctuated' by the actor with a full stop—stands as a decisive end to both the sentence and the thought. More than that, it invites a pensively lengthened midline pause before speaking 'I am in blood'. The sum effect is to make any putative rhyme with the earlier subordinate clause ('for mine owne good') seem strangely after the event—if not absent-minded, then perilously stretched.

This is typical of the oddly surreptitious violence—both creeping and brutal, rather like the assassination—with which Macbeth here forces through to his deathly rhyming couplets. Normally we expect a couplet to be prepared for by the metre: the closing word of the first rhyming line is usually stressed, anticipating a climactic rhyme. The rhythm of Macbeth's lines, by contrast, is beholden not to the line but to the sentence. When blank verse and rhyme are, as here, laid one over the other, we don't simply get unorthodox stops. We get two (or perhaps more) directions—to pause in speech, to reorientate focus, to shift in body, to open out or close off to others, to feel the presence or the absence of others—in brisk succession. But each is consequent upon quite different rhythmic and semantic movements, movements which it is difficult to allow the reality of, or to fully endorse, without blanking any possibility of a coexisting motive or momentum. This simultaneous inter-layering of rhyme and blank verse has to be disorientating to the actor. How does he make up his mind? Can he respond to both prosodic directions? What if he cannot *but* observe both, yet in doing so can do justice to neither? Any decision is likely to sound like a false obedience: perhaps half-baked, perhaps belated, perhaps, like the 'taste of fears', '*almost*' but not quite 'forgot'. Uncertain hermeneutics produces uncertain phenomenology. The question as to how the actor applies his technique thus inevitably becomes a question about the character's relation to his action. What does he decide? How decisive is any 'decision'? How ironized is Macbeth's resolve to 'know' of any single thing, or to 'act' in any particular fashion? How *little* might his mind get carried in his action—or in his acting?

If the actor is struggling for possession of such choices, the challenge does not end here. Consider the rest of the sentence begun by 'I am in blood'; again the rhyme depends more upon metrical misprision than easeful urbanity:

> ... I am in blood
> Stept in so farre, that should I wade no more,
> Returning were as tedious as go ore:

> (TLN 1419–21)

We might understand the contracted verb phrase, 'go ore', as befitting a Scottish accent.[4] A more likely explanation, perhaps, is simply that 'go ore' rather than 'go over' allows Macbeth to crush the words into a rhyming pentameter. The proper length of the line is already threatened by 'te-di-ous'; Macbeth's effort to crunch down the rhetorical gears into rhyme itself becomes an expression of violent retraction. The rhyme thus speaks for hasty cognitive shutdown—of doubt, retrospection, foresight—and allows Macbeth to bundle his thoughts into the order and refuge of an *action*. Furthermore, the rhyme here insinuates into the ear an alarming but characteristic aural joke: so, perhaps 'go ore' is not two syllables, but one; it is not two words, but one. This single sound ('go-ore') becomes a long, dilated, yawning word—it becomes 'gore': *I am in blood stepped in so far, that returning were as tedious as gore.* (We might compare the notorious sound-joke of 'Seyton'/'Satan', Macbeth's faithful servant.) There is no escape from circularity, and no escape from blood. The sentence begins with 'I am in blood', which closes a line; it ends with 'as go ore', which similarly ends a line. Just as 'blood will have blood', 'in blood' circles back into 'gore'. The ostensible end-line rhyme ('no more'/'go ore')—already rather furtive—is effectively trumped by the still more secret semantic 'rhyme' that begins and ends the sentence ('in blood'/'go ore'). This example shows a double subversion of rhyme's usual clarity: first, the metre fails to set it up clearly to be stressed and therefore noticed; second, the real rhyme is carried by a homophonic pun ('go ore'/'gore').

One thing is clear: however the rhyme here works, however many things it is doing, it is no longer the actor's reliable guide and instrument. And, more than this, the actor's uncertain relationship to his part works both to produce and to allegorize Macbeth's relationship to his own agency. For if the actor identifies a rhyme only belatedly, as though after the event; if it creeps up on him, and is gone before he knows it; if not even prosody, usually an actor's most dependable comfort, is in his sure possession, then the actor is likely to feel just as removed from his own body, as puzzled by barely apprehended machinations, as is his character.

Such prototypical 'mature' Shakespearean discourse has to threaten actorly tradition and frustrate actorly choice. Obviously the actor cannot simply declaim such things in the old high style; a part like Macbeth will defy, indeed embarrass, any 'robustious' display of this or that manner. But by the time of *Macbeth*, this had long been the case: from early on, Shakespeare's scripting elicits an intimately feeling style of acting, one that is exploratory, responsive, and anything but programmatic. But even for an actor applying the most sophisticated, questing, thoroughly trained critical sensibility, the part-text of Macbeth presents problems. It is difficult for any actor confidently to embody such writing, as though it really does find its origin and home 'in' him. But perhaps we have to go still further, and recognize that Shakespeare's accelerating liberties with compressed grammar, equivocal address, doubled-up prosodic palimpsests, latent word-play, ambiguous syntax (and so on) is not so much recommending a particular style of acting as pointedly defying any such recommendation. After all, what can the actor really do, faced with such linguistic density, other than try to speak the words clearly, observe the pauses (even when they seem obtuse or bewildering) and leave the rest to his auditors? Perhaps the performer must simply intone the given words, his body little more than a ventriloquist's dummy. By thus disarming the actor's power positively to seize language and occasion, or to give the moment any charismatic supercharge, perhaps Shakespeare ensures that the voice serves the words, is 'taken' by the verse (rather than vice versa).

Most of the instructions for actors that we have been identifying presume a linear approach to sense: 'changes of mind' or transitions in emotion happen in time; we can trace the pattern of cause and consequence; and when changes happen, they are decisive. But of course in reality this need not be the case. Mental states can be full of overlapping injunctions, rival priorities, a swarm of temporal confusions. This in turn suggests Shakespeare's larger ambition, pursued throughout his work but certainly reaching an acme of experimentation in *Macbeth*: he is developing a new means of embodying consciousness and experience. If Shakespeare was fully to embody 'real' minds in motion, then his writing in parts had to change. This is why we find the concentration of traditional directions for actors in single phrases; we get speech units that are performing, recalling, anticipating numerous actions at once. Of course, from the start of his career Shakespeare uses words to propose relations or judgements that are beyond the possession of any single individual (actor or character). But what we are drawing attention to in *Macbeth* is what might seem to be almost a sacrifice of this larger story: a superseding of prosody (rhyme, lineation, rhythm, etc.) that is primarily designed for actors.

In more functional writing for parts, the tried and trusted ways of pointing rhythm and rhyme were designed to bring clearly to the actor's mind the other players or the audience. The 'others' that dramatic prosody conventionally calls forth—that we should look at or look for, that should feel flattered, assaulted, cajoled, or otherwise implicated—have now become the speaker's virtual bodies, various memories, projections, or hypotheses of self. In the Macbeth-part they are designed to bring forth the character's mind—*his* otherness to any finished and unified sense of self; his interior conflicts, multiplicity, and mutability. Of course the experienced actor (like Burbage) may well trace or accompany the mutations in Macbeth's mind. But whether or not he does so is here not the point. Shakespeare is putting the character—or, more precisely, the character's embodied mind, his shifting relation to place, space, and time—before the actor.

It is a type of writing that fastidiously places the actor in uncertainties: where the very precision of the script demands holding in suspended tension apparently irreconcilable options, which admit of no resolution other than more or less blind improvisation. The actor becomes an emissary of mental activity that is most fundamentally embodied in the 'virtual' networks of words. This kind of linguistic economy can make fearsome demands on the actor, as we find repeatedly in the part of Macbeth: asking him to be in multiple mental places at one time, leaving it uncertain whom he addresses, loading his words with contrary impulses and warring emotions. Shakespeare is only rarely understood as a Beethoven-style genius, doing unexpected violence not only to generic form but to the capabilities of the voice or instrument. But perhaps, with Macbeth, this is precisely what he is doing: stretching the interpretive ingenuity and, more than that, the physical capability of his main actor as never before. Indeed, a suspicion begins to insinuate itself that the 'read' version of a part, or of its most pregnant moments, internalized alone, is not only logistically anterior to the staged version, but *ontologically* prior. Having spent much of his writing life orchestrating his parts' infrastructure so as to direct his actors into making the necessary choices, Shakespeare now wants to hold up choice itself as *always* a diminution, a kind of falsity to self: because no action can ever carry the mind.

Never again would Shakespeare put so much pressure upon the ability of individual parts to embody individual consciousness (that is, mental activity *per se*, whether self-conscious or sub-conscious, intentional or acciden-tal). The works immediately after *Macbeth* show a discernible releasing of this particular creative tension. The actors' parts have no less singularity or definition, but a manifest reduction in ambiguous or withheld actors' directions. They thus regain the instrumental clarity of many of Shake-speare's earlier parts. Whatever Shakespeare is up to in his later plays, he is not expecting his actors to share quite so mercilessly in his explo-rations. The tragedies that follow *Macbeth*—as technically and scenically audacious as they are in so many ways—do not in the main threaten the actor's security.

This is despite the fact that these plays are more metrically 'irregular' than ever, and have a greater proportion of short, shared, or 'squinting' lines. This is not to say that the part of Antony, for instance, returns to the old-fashioned (but comforting) demarcation between self-address and conversation, or between private and public discourse. Far from it: indeed, there is perhaps no other role that so blurs the distinction between the two. Partly this is because Antony is almost never alone on-stage—or if so, only for a few fleeting lines. Whatever he is talking about, both actor and character know that invariably someone is present to attend to it. But it is not like the Macbeth-role, in which it is frequently impossible to tell who is or is not being addressed, or whether it matters. Antony's gradations of address are often in a sense fickle and capricious, but (to risk an oxymoron) they are predictably so—or at least predictably so for the actor. Likewise, Martius/Coriolanus: whether speaking insultingly to the plebs or insinuatingly to the patricians, the part's speeches are almost always unequivocally 'directed'. The actor will easily glean from his part-script whom he is addressing, whom he is excluding, and any moments where he shifts from one to the other. Again, the prosody is of the utmost tautness and sophistication: but it is designed throughout to overcome the lacunae of the part-text. Whatever Shakespeare is doing here, bewildering his actor is not part of the contract.

The same applies to the (perhaps still more experimental) late 'romances'. In these plays character is not working quite as it has done; indeed, the relationship between a single body and an inferable mind frequently becomes as fluid and metamorphic as language itself.[5] Characterization becomes multiply centred, accreting from one scene to another, as various parts contribute to 'corporate' reformulations of subjecthood or subjectivity. All of this inevitably has consequences for the actor: but not, as we might perhaps expect, in the way of intensifying the assaults upon actorly sovereignty that we have seen throughout the Macbeth-part. Instead, Shakespeare seems to want his actors to feel that they know where they are and what they are doing. Often romance parts work more like a dance, something choreographed and externalized. The actors work to and along clearly described lines, giving a clarity which allows the attuned spectator to identify shared characteristics and thus accumulating constructions. In the late plays the individual actor is basically subdued to the company. In plays as serially itinerant in structure and location as *Pericles*, *Cymbeline*, and *The Winter's Tale*, in which supposedly central parts are suddenly stopped or silenced, or segue into an 'unknown' successor, the individual actors may know less than ever about how their parts fit in to the larger play. But they are not really pressed to find out; they are not made anxious by the ellipses, or not in any fashion that can then feed into the acting. Instead, the actor must simply perform his brief, more or less sure of the role's ambit (for *The Tempest's* sophisticated variations upon all of this, see pp. 275–303).

In many ways, therefore, the part of Macbeth marks the end of our particular story. It represents an overwrought climax to Shakespeare's long experimentation in making the actor's 'private' mind and experience—his confusions and ignorance, his dependence upon guesswork and inference, his vulnerability to surprise or suddenness—furnish the character's similar experiential peril. Nonetheless, Macbeth might seem a curiously antipathetic character with whom to close a book about actors' parts: not least because, for both the character and the player, 'acting' is experienced as the loss of clearly directing volition, thus threatening the radical annulling of vocation and even selfhood. But this very antipathy might also be seen to vindicate the actor and his part (or at least actors or agents less exhausted in their vocation than Macbeth). This is encapsulated in the closing rhyme of Macbeth's 'More shall they speake …' couplet sequence:

> Strange things I have in head, that will to hand,
> Which must be acted, ere they may be scand.
>
> (TLN 1422–3)

Here Macbeth imagines himself as an actor with his part. More than that, he is the playwright-actor, transcribing his 'will' on to the roll with barely a pause. Macbeth compares the speed with which things he thinks about must be acted on, with a part that must be written and performed before the verse can even be scanned. The densely punning 'will to hand' thus conflates the acts of writing, performing, and action: 'will' is author, promissory intention, and appetite; the 'hand' is that of writer with pen, actor with roll, and enactor with fist, sceptre, or knife. This overlapping of agents in the phrase is then repeated as the couplet unfolds: the phrases 'in head', 'to hand', 'be acted', 'be scand' can all apply equally to an author, an actor, or an individual subject. It might be all three, as Shakespeare was, and as Macbeth here imagines himself to be.

The crucial layering of meaning lies in the confused ordering of the statement, and in particular in its skewed time scheme. For the process Macbeth speaks of—from head, to hand, to acting, to scanned—is by any normal measure simply wrong. To scan the part after the acting is a belated mockery of efficient performance. (Of course, we might say that this is what Macbeth does throughout, as he desperately recalls, regrets, and purports to repair an irrevocably maladroit 'first night'—but if his lines do carry ironic self-reference, it is to a 'scansion' that he wants to ditch.) In so far as the lines refer to the processes of acting, they seem to present a flat denial of the actor's arts, and above all of the kinds of prevarication or uncertainty that bedevil the performing of this particular role. Alternatively, the couplet may affirm—how ironically or mercilessly it is difficult to measure—precisely the kind of acting required of this part: that is, conventional scanning is useless; just get out there and do it. Either way, it is as though Macbeth sees the doubts into which the part—for person and player both—is plunged, and he wants to be rid of them. He seeks an absolute 'now', a presence that wipes away all presentiment, apprehension, and indeed accountability. He would be done with the interventions of happenstance, the equivocations of doubt, or the terrible lacuna between possibility and commission. Still more, the 'will to hand'/'ere be scann'd' couplet neglects the very idea of rehearsal: of writing *for* actors who are then invited to go off alone, make the parts their own, and given them the life they need.

Of course, Macbeth's vow to act before scanning the script is far more than merely reckless or feckless. There *is* no performance without rehearsal: not least because, as we have found time and again, the supposed separation of 'rehearsal' from 'performance' is in truth factitious. Performance always carries a trace of rehearsal: partly because rehearsal cannot prepare finally for performance, partly because no performance is definitive or finished. There always remain decisions to be made, choices to be tested. Shakespeare's parts are written so that performance has to involve contingency, experimentation, and improvisation, a testing of possibility in the knowledge that if it doesn't work on this occasion there might—there should—always be another chance. But working from parts means that there is precious little chance to pre-emptively know what is coming; precious little of that practised, comprehensive foreknowledge that modern actors, rehearsing for week after week from a full text, hope or expect to secure. Shakespeare's actors had to play their parts *now*, perilously in the present. Often they are left waiting for something yet to come; often they are exposed to surprise, accident, and abruptness. Experience for these actors is repetitive *and* immediate: however haunted by memories or anticipations, however paralysed by fear or riddled with uncanny recapitulations, *this* particular thing has never happened before, just as *that* actor has never been exactly in this moment. We might know every last word, but still there is no securely predictive script.

We might protest here that the enacted moment may well *not* be unique: that it has often happened before, because the actor has already played the part. Now, if we were dealing in automata this may well be true; so too if the play could be animated effectively by actors reporting discoveries made (as it were) in the past. But we are not and cannot. The play is dead unless the actor is alive, and the actor is only alive if the part seems—to him and to the audience—to be happening for the very first time. If he once felt surprise and apprehension, it is precisely such feeling that he needs to recover, so that in acting the part he can always be a micro-moment 'before' any thought or movement, assuring the audience that his character, *now*, is the one who has the thought or makes the movement. This is what Shakespeare's writing in parts, again and again, appears to insist upon; it is essential if the high-wire act of daily public performance is to remain taut and transporting. The key to performing, in other words, is recovering that nerve-wracked gap between sketch and flesh, possibility and commission, expectation and commission; between the promise of a cue or the shape of a line and its final *irrecoverable* embodiment in speech. If he feels a paralysing clash of options, fears making the wrong decision, or feels tempted to make no decision at all; if he experiences in this moment the sudden apprehension of betraying the part or losing the audience—or, still worse, of professional embarrassment—then it is a trauma that he should be compelled to remember and repeat, to endure again in the interests of a popular entertainment that these first actors, in the process of making it work, can hardly not have experienced as intimately revealing.

The actor's part seems to make the individual subject the be-all and the end-all, or at least to make one's own mind and inferences the measure of all relevant things. This self-centring assurance of the part—as a discrete physical object, and as a specific actor's intellec-tual property—is the perfect technology for producing individuals with the power to watch themselves think and to be verified by doing so.

But the part's apparent completeness is also a form of splintered ex-clusion: each role is stripped of its protective bark and split from any cohering trunk. Likewise, the lacunae in actors' parts—sowing abrupt leaps in fortune divorced from clear motive—further questions how self-possessed any action can really be. The cued part thus focuses atten-tion upon the most basic questions of agency and responsibility. Who exactly is present in any action? Can any action, including any speech-action, carry all of a mind with it? Can any 'I' be independent of any other? Can any decision make sense, or even take effect, without the co-operation or coercion of another? But how to know these others when their sources, motives, or future direction are so constitutively opaque?

These questions can remind us just how intimate working in parts is to Shakespeare's recurring preoccupations: the inscrutability of oneself and others; minds and worlds that are beyond clear account, in which supposed reasons for action may be little more than rationalizations of blind opportunity or improvisation; the whimsicality of authority, or the stealing of authority by non-rational, atavistic, or serendipitous force; the basic tenuousness of almost any possession. Equally, the fact that part-based existing seems so threatened or determined by accident will prompt the actor to search for a more satisfying rationale—for what has been and what is to come—than an arbitrary pre-script or fortuitous opportunity.

In exploring something as lost and unfamiliar as actors' parts, we have nevertheless been led to perhaps surprisingly recognizable conclusions: that the actors were asked to act 'feelingly'; that the more open the actor, the surer his access to the writing and to his character; that Shake-speare's technical and expressive achievements were partly parasitic upon inherited agents and materials; that the reach of these materials expanded immeasurably in his hands. We have found a means of instruction and communication that is as inherently dramatic and collaborative a thing as we might possibly imagine. The part is written by the playwright, but it is written *for* the individual actor; unlike the full script, it is effectively meaningless, or a ghost of intended meaning, without the actor to give it body. But then, as much as it is the actor's—owned by him, loved and nurtured into being by him—it is still never fully *possessed* by the actor. He cannot understand it all; he cannot know all of the things it alludes to; still less can he know all the matters it elides. Given the procedures and necessities of Shakespeare's theatre—various plays on at one time, limited private rehearsal, old plays unpredictably renewed—it is obvious that no amount of tuition to an individual actor could ever have filled in all the gaps merely in *his* part; when we remember that a play might have thirty or more parts, we should realize just how many 'surprises' were likely to remain open. In the moment of its enacting, this kind of theatre has to remain potentially a thing of sudden, vertiginous, serendipitous discovery. Given no way to avoid this fact, Shakespeare very simply revels in it.

# Notes

## INTRODUCTION

1. Stephen Gosson, *The Ephemerides of Phialo* (1579), L5a.
2. For discussion of these clues and directions from an actor's point of view, see Patrick Tucker, *Secrets of Acting Shakespeare* (London and New York: Routledge, 2001).
3. See Tiffany Stern, *Rehearsal from Shakespeare to Sheridan* (Oxford: Clarendon Press, 2000), 107−9.
4. These additions may well be the ones for which Ben Jonson was paid; see Grace Ioppolo, *Revising Shakespeare* (Cambridge, Mass.: Harvard University Press, 1991), 56.
5. William Percy, *The Cuck-Queanes and Cuckolds Errants...*, ed. J. Haslewood (1824), 192−3.
6. Hence the unusual paucity of notes in the interpretive sections of our book.

## CHAPTER I. THE ACTOR'S PART

1. Edith Hall, *The Theatrical Cast of Athens* (Oxford: Oxford University Press, 2006), 43.
2. W. W. Greg's *Dramatic Documents from the Elizabethan Playhouses*, 2 vols. (Oxford: Clarendon Press, 1931), i. 173−5, considers 'Dux Moraud', Bodleian Library MS, Eng. Poet. F. 2 R.; the three 'Shrewsbury Fragments', 'third Shepherd' in *Officium Pastorum*, 'third Mary' in *Officium Resurrectionis*, 'Cleophas' in *Officium Peregrinorum*, and 'God' in a miracle play. Hansjürgen Linke describes German parts in 'Versuch über deutsche Handschriften mittelalterlicher Spiele', in Volker Honemann and Nigel F. Palmer (eds.), *Deutsche Handschriften 1100−1400: Oxforder Kolloquium 1985* (Tübingen: Max Niemeyer Verlag, 1988), 532. He writes of the rolls of Barabas, John, Merchant, Lucifer, and Synagogue from the *Alsfelder Passion Play* (1501−17), the Breslau roll of a Herald from a *Lent Night Play* (middle of the fourteenth century), the Gothaer roll of the Messenger (fifteenth century), the Himmelgarten roll of Mary from a Mary's Lamentation play (fifteenth century), a middle Dutch roll of the Praelocutor (end of the fifteenth century), the Rotherburg roll of Kaspar from a Resurrection play (beginning of the fifteenth century), the Steinach roll of Our Saviour (1520), the Vienna roll of Ruby (second half of the fifteenth

century), the Zwickau roll of Christ in an Easter play, and the Zwickau roll of Mary Salome in a Passion play (from *c.*1500). Draft rolls survive written by Raber: the Tirol rolls of Isaiah, Daniel, and Salome for a Mary's Lamentation play (all three of the sixteenth century). Our thanks to Max Liebermann for his help with translating this chapter. In Italy, three different parts for Judas and one for Pilate survive in a miscellany of 1531 belonging to the Gonfalone fraternity; one fourteenth-century part, 'Officium Quarti Militis', is in Sulmona; and there were rolls, now lost, including the 'Ludus Trium Regum' in Ivrea. For this information thanks to Professor Nerida Newbegin, University of Sydney (private correspondence).

3. Jean Fouquet, 'Sainte Apolline', in *Les Heures D'Ètienne Chevalier* (*c.*1420–81) in the Musée Condé, Chantilly; reproduced in *Les Heures* (Paris: Somogy, 2003), 85. See also two other medieval pictures of prompters (*régisseurs*) reproduced in A. M. Nagler, *Sources of Theatrical History* (New York: Theatre Annual, Inc., 1952), 50–1: Herald and Stage Director (with prompt-book), of Jakob Ruf's *Von des Herren Weingarten* (1539) and *The Stage Director of Valenciennes*, miniature by Hubert Cailleau (1547).

4. See Tiffany Stern, 'Behind the Arras: The Prompter's Place in the Shake-spearean Theatre', *Theatre Notebook*, 55 (2001), 110–18.

5. Bodleian Library MS, Ashmole 750, f. 168$^r$, repr. in Norman Davis, *Non-Cycle Plays and the Winchester Dialogues* (Oxford: Oxford University Press, 1979), 81–3, which corrects R. H. Robbins's misattribution in 'A Dramatic Fragment from a Caesar Augustus Play', *Anglia*, 72 (1954), 31–4.

6. Fully described in P. Aebischer, 'Fragments de Moralités, Farces, et Mystères retrouvés à Fribourg', *Romania*, 51 (1925), 511–27; *idem*, 'Quelques textes du XVIe siècle en patois fribourgeois', *Archivum Romanicum*, 4 (1920), 342–61; 7 (1923), 288–36; 15 (1931), 512–40; *idem*, 'Trois Farces Françaises Inédites Trouvées à Fribourg', *Revue du 16e siecle*, 11 (1924), 129–92; Graham A. Runnalls, 'The Medieval Actors' Roles Found in the Fribourg Archive', *Pluteus*, 4/5 (1986/7, pub. 1990), 5–67 (7–8).

7. Aebischer, 'Fragments de Moralités', 511.

8. Runnalls, 'Medieval Actors' Roles', 7–8.

9. Huntington Library MS, HM 4, f. 278.

10. Fully discussed in Runnalls, 'Medieval Actors' Roles', 32–3.

11. Discussed in ibid. 12.

12. Graham A. Runnalls, 'Towards a Typology of Medieval French Play Manu-scripts', in P. E. Bennett and G. A. Runnalls (eds.), *The Editor and the Text* (Edinburgh: Edinburgh University Press, 1990), 98.

13. Runnalls, 'Medieval Actors' Roles', 16.

14. 'Rôle of Tripet', Paris, Arch. nat., M 877B n° 24, ed. E. Elisabeth Lalou, 'Les Rolets de Théâtre: Étude Codicologique', in *Théâtre et Spectacles Hier et Aujourd'hui: Moyen Âge et Renaissance* (Paris: Editions du CTHS, 1991), 63–4; 'Rôle of the "Minister" in the *Mystère de saint André*', Gap, Arch. dép.

Hautes-Alpes, E 299 bis, ed. Lalou, 'Les Rolets', 64−7; 'Rôle of Saint Simon', Digne, Arch. dép. Alpes de Haute-Provence, C★852, ed. Lalou, 'Les Rolets', 67−8; 'Rôle of ("Péché") "Sin" in a morality play', Paris, Arch. nat., AB XIX Manche 1732, ed. Lalou, 'Les Rolets', 68−70; 'A Comic Rôle from Sion (Valais, Switzerland)', Sion, Archives cantonales du Valais, fond Flavien de Torrenté, A.T.F.1 MS 3, ed. P. Aebischer, 'Un fragment de rôle comique datant du début du XIV$^e$ siècle retrouvé dans un manuscrit déposé aux Archives cantonales du Valais à Sion', *Vallesia*, 22 (1967), 71−80; 'Rôle of Saint Barbara (Barbe)', Chambéry, Arch. dép. Savoie, no shelf-mark, ed. J. Chocheyras, in *Le Théâtre religieux en Savoie au XVIe siècle* (Geneva: Droz, 1971), 93−108; 'Farce of Thévot', Paris, Bib. nat., MS n. a. lat. 2374, ed. J. Maxwell, 'La Farce de Thévot le Maire, Perruche et Colin', *Humanisme et Renaissance*, 6 (1939), 539−46.

15. 'Rôle for Moréna in a Nativity play', ed. Lalou, 'Les Rolets', 70; 'Rôle of God' (fragment), ed. Lalou, 'Les Rolets', 71; 'Rôles for the Passion Play performed in Paris in 1539 by the Confrérie de la Passion', ed. Graham A. Runnalls, in 'Le Livre de Raison de Jacques Le Gros et le Mystère de la Passion joué à Paris en 1539', *Romania*, 118 (2000), 138−93. A fuller bibliography for surviving French roles is provided by Graham A. Runnalls in 'Actors' Roles from Medieval France', <http://www.byu.edu/~hurlbut/fmddp/roles/>.

16. Described by Graham A. Runnalls, 'An Actor's Role in a French Morality Play', *French Studies*, 42 (1988), 398−407.

17. Published as *Processus Satanae*, in *Malone Society Collections: II. 3*, ed. W. W. Greg (Oxford: Malone Society, 1931).

18. Linke, 'Versuch über deutsche', 532. The similarity to which he draws attention is that both parts are cued. He does not say whether the cue-speaker is named.

19. Dulwich College MS, I, Item 138. Reproduced as facsimile with transcript in Greg's *Dramatic Documents*, 2, and against the text of the 1594 Quarto of *Orlando Furioso* in W. W. Greg (ed.), *Two Elizabethan Stage Abridgements: 'The Battle of Alcazar' and 'Orlando Furioso'*, (Oxford: Malone Society, 1922).

20. Michael Warren, 'Greene's *Orlando*: W. W. Greg Furioso', in Laurie E. Maguire and Thomas L. Berger (eds.), *Textual Formations and Reformations* (Newark, NJ: University of Delaware Press, 1998), 67−91.

21. See Greg (ed.), *Two Elizabethan Stage Abridgements*, 128; Tiffany Stern, 'The Part for Greene's *Orlando Furioso*: A Source for the "Mock Trial" in Shakespeare's *Lear*?' *Notes and Queries*, 247 (2002), 229−31 (230).

22. Greg (ed.), *Two Elizabethan Stage Abridgements*, 156.

23. Harvard Theatre Library MS, Thr 10.1. 'Poore' is described and transcribed in N. W. Bawcutt (ed.), *Malone Society Collections: XV* (Oxford: Malone Society, 1993), 113−69, and discussed in David Carnegie, 'Actors' Parts and the "Play of Poore"', *Harvard Library Bulletin*, 30 (1982), 5−24. The other parts have not been written about.

24. See David Carnegie, 'The Identification of the Hand of Thomas Goffe, Academic Dramatist and Actor', *The Library*, 26 (1971), 161−5.

25. Carnegie, 'Actors' Parts', 12.
26. Bawcutt, 'Part of Poore', 149, 153. Carnegie, 'Actors' Parts', 10.
27. Thomas Goffe, *The Couragious Turke* (1632), D4a; bold face added.
28. Ibid. F2b–F3a.
29. Carnegie, 'Actors' Parts', 12–13.
30. W. J. Lawrence, 'Lengths', *The Stage* (11 Feb. 1932), 44.
31. *Ignoramus,* a Latin play by George Ruggle, was first performed in 1615 and published in 1630; this Restoration part is from the revised translation of that play by Ferdinando Parkhurst. The part is described in Edward F. J. Tucker, 'The Harvard Manuscript of Parkhurst's *Ignoramus*', *Harvard Library Bulletin*, 19 (1971), 5–24; its first act is transcribed in Edward A. Langhans, *Restoration Promptbooks* (Carbondale and Edwardsville: Southern Illinois University Press, 1981), 509–13.
32. Discussed in Edward A. Langhans, 'A Restoration Actor's Part', *Harvard Library Bulletin*, 23 (1975), 180–5 (183). His conclusion that this particular text 'did not see use in the theatre' is based on the fact that the part is 'clean' and not annotated by Medbourne; in fact, annotation is not necessarily a feature of parts.
33. Houghton Library MS, Eng 1258 (5), 7.
34. Langhans, 'A Restoration Actor's Part', Part of Trico, 181.
35. Part of Trico, 17.
36. Part of Falstaff, Folger Shakespeare Library MS, t.a.121.
37. Tate Wilkinson, *Memoirs of his Own Life,* 4 vols. (1790), ii. 65; David Garrick, *The Private Correspondence,* ed. James Boaden, 2 vols. (1831–2), i. 120 n.
38. Part of Shylock, Folger Shakespeare Library MS, y.d.42. See John Brownsmith, *The Theatrical Alphabet. Containing a Catalogue of Several Hundred Parts (both Mens and Womens) in Different Plays and Farces; with the Number of Lengths Noted that Each Part Contains* (1767).
39. For this and more on lengths, see Tiffany Stern, *Rehearsal from Shakespeare to Sheridan* (Oxford: Clarendon Press, 2000), 253–61.
40. Upwards of forty surviving part-books from the eighteenth century survive; they are listed in Edward A. Langhans, *Eighteenth-Century British and Irish Promptbooks: A Descriptive Bibliography* (Westport, Conn.: Greenwood Press, 1987).
41. From a book of MS parts belonging to Macklin: Harvard Theatre Library MS, TS 1197 54.5.
42. For Portsmouth, 15 Aug. 1734: Harvard Theatre Library MS, TS 1197 54.5. Business in this part is discussed in Bernard Barrow, 'Macklin's Costume and Property Notes for the Character of Lovegold', *Theatre Notebook*, 13 (1958/9), 66–7; three pages from the part are reproduced in that volume.
43. It is notable that the cuts to speeches in prompt-books—such as the Padua texts of 1625–35 and the Smock Alley ones from later in the century—tend to retain the cues. G. Blakemore Evans (ed.), *Shakespearean Prompt-Books of*

*the Seventeenth Century*, 8 vols. (Charlottesville: Bibliographical Society of the University of Virginia, 1960– ). For the revision of Shakespeare's *Hamlet* along 'part' lines, see Stern, *Rehearsal*, 107–10.

44. Folger Shakespeare Library MS, catalogued as 'manuscript callbook and related documents', w.b.469.

45. We consulted all thirty-four parts, but concentrated on the Shakespearean and early modern ones. They are: Part of Shylock (1784), MS t.a.30; Part of Lear (1788), MS t.a.17; Part of Benedict (1788), MS t.a.34; Part of Bajazet (1776?), MS t.a.22; Part of Jacques (1799), MS t.a.39; Part of Vincentio (1794?), MS t.a.35; Part of King John (1783), MS t.a.25; Part of King Henry V (1789?), MS t.a.38; Part of King Richard III (1783), MS t.a.13; Part of Macbeth (1785), MS t.a.11; Part of Paris (1796), MS t.a.29.

46. Folger Shakespeare Library MS of Garrick's part of King John (1745), w.a.172.

47. Folger Shakespeare Library MS of Kemble's part of Macbeth, dated 31 Mar. 1785, Theatre Royal, Drury Lane, MS t.a.11.

48. Folger Shakespeare Library MS, y.d.42.

49. William B. Wood, *Personal Recollections of the Stage* (Philadelphia: Henry Carey Baird, 1855), 442.

50. Philip Godfrey, *Back-Stage* (London: G. G. Harrap and Co., 1933), 37.

51. John Dolman, *The Art of Acting* (New York: Harper and Brothers, 1949), 78.

## CHAPTER 2. THE ACTORS

1. John Phillips, *Wit and Drollery* (1661), 93.

2. Robert Gomersall, *Poems* (1633), 69.

3. Nathaniel Richards, *Poems Sacred and Satyricale* (1641), 20; William Cartwright, 'Another on [Mr John Fletcher]', in *The Plays and Poems*, ed. G. Blakemore Evans (Madison: University of Wisconsin Press, 1951), 520.

4. Sir Richard Baker, *Theatrum Redivivum* (1662), 34.

5. Thomas Heywood, *An Apology for Actors* (1612), E3a.

6. T. Gainsford, *The Rich Cabinet* (1616), Q3a. See also Richard Brathwaite, *The English Gentlewoman* (1631), 95: 'in any Theatrall presentment…every one must bee suited to the person he presents'; Heywood, *Apology*, A4a: 'in this Theater, …every humor's fitted in his kinde'.

7. *Mercurius Melancholicus*, 58 (25 Sept.–2 Oct. 1648), 5–6.

8. John Boys, *Workes* (1622), 850. See also Epictetus, *Epictetus his Manuall*, trans. Jo Healey (1616), 28–9: 'Consider…thou hast that part to playe heere on this earthly stage, which thy maister hath vouchsafed to appoint thee: bee it a long part or a short, in a long playe or a short…It is thy duty to discharge thine appointed part with discretion, but what part thou shalt have allotted thee, is left unto the direction of another.' See also Sir Walter

Raleigh, *The History of the World* (1614), D1b: 'God, who is the Author of all our tragedies, hath written out for us, and appointed us all the parts we play.'

9. Thomas Heywood, *The Hierarchie of the Blessed Angells* (1635), 359.

10. Daniel Featley, *Clavis Mystica … Handled in Seventy Sermons* (1636), 381.

11. T. W. Baldwin in *The Organisation and Personnel of the Shakespearean Company* (Princeton: Princeton University Press, 1927) tried, prescriptively, to define an acting line for each player in Shakespeare's company; resultant criticism of his method has led to a neglect of the entire field. The theory has been recently revived, however. See Skiles Howard, 'A Reconsideration of Baldwin's Theory of Acting Lines', *Theatre Studies*, 26 (1985), 1−20, and David Grote, *The Best Actors in the World: Shakespeare and his Acting Company* (Westport, Conn., and London: Greenwood Press, 2002).

12. Thomas Overbury, *Sir Thomas Overburie, His Wife with New Elegies* (1616), M3a. See also D. Lupton, *London and the Countrey Carbonadoed* (1632), 81: 'A player often changes, now he acts a Monarch, to morrow a Beggar'; Robert Cawdry, *A Treasurie or Store-House of Similes* (1600), 380: 'As an Actor in a Comedie or Tragedy, which somtimes resembleth *Agamemnon*, somtimes *Achilles*, somtimes their enemie *Hector*, sometimes one mans person, sometimes an other: Even so an Hypocrite'; Francis Meres, *Palladis Tamia* (1598), 2S7a: 'As a stage player taketh upon him another mans person, sometimes being a servant, and sometime a Lorde'; Frances Quarles, *Argalus and Parthenia* (1629), 65: 'Who acts the King to day, by change of lot, | Perchance to morrow begs, and blushes not.' Mildmay Fane, Earl of Westmoreland, *Otia Sacra* (1648), 168: 'Thou act'st a King no more, no that's laid by, | Nor any's Parasite in flattery; | Thou hast put off the Clowns slops now, nor art | Wrapt with the fury of a Lovers Part … .'

13. See A. Gaw, 'John Sincklo as One of Shakespeare's Actors', *Anglia*, 49 (1926), 289−303; Mark Eccles, 'Elizabethan Actor IV', *Notes and Queries*, 238 (1993), pp. 165−76 (166). Fredson Bowers, 'The Copy for Shakespeare's Julius Caesar', *South Atlantic Bulletin*, 43 (1978), 29−31, suggests that the addition of the 'lean' Caius Ligarius after the play had been written out may reflect the doubling of this role and Cassius.

14. For more on this, see Shoichiro Kawai, 'Fat, Lean, Short, and Tall: Physical Characteristics of Dramatic Characters and Actors in the Age of Shakespeare' (unpublished Ph.D. thesis, University of Cambridge, 1999); Thomas Middleton, *The Wisdom of Solomon Paraphrased*, ch. 10, in *The Works*, ed. A. H. Bullen, 8 vols. (London: John C. Nimmo, 1886), viii. 215: 'Unhappy actor in death's tragedy … | A weeping part had earth in that same play, | For she did weep herself to death that day.'

15. Thomas Randolph, *The Jealous Lovers* (1632), 2¶1a.

16. Richard Flecknoe, *Love's Kingdom … with a Short Discourse of the English Stage* (1664), G7a−b.

17. Flecknoe never saw Burbage perform, and was happy to reuse this praise in a 'character' he wrote for a perfect, nameless actor. See Richard Flecknoe, *Aenigmatical Characters*, 2nd edn. (1665), 2. Here we are more interested in the praise than its designation.

18. Thomas Fuller, *History* (1662), 244. For chief actors consistently being cast as leading characters, see the evidence amassed from plots by T. J. King in *Casting Shakespeare's Plays* (Cambridge: Cambridge University Press, 1992), 17. Predictably, there is little extant information about which actor played which part—and none for Shakespeare's plays. But actually knowing the name of an actor who performed a role is not very telling when that actor no longer survives. What is more important is what range of roles a playwright conceived as being performable by the company he was with. Although we cannot 'cast' the plays we look at, we can investigate character-type, putting back what modern editorial policy removes when it exchanges 'type' for 'name' in speech-prefixes.

19. Thomas Dekker, *The Non Dramatic Works of Thomas Dekker*, ed. Alexander B. Grosart, 5 vols. (1884; New York: Russell and Russell, 1963), iii. 81.

20. Dekker, *The Wonderfull Yeare*, in *Non Dramatic Works*, i. 100. See also Samuel Torshell, *The Womans Glorie* (1645), 146: 'a sneaking *player* might as well be proud of the part he beares upon the *Stage*'.

21. Dekker, *Jests to Make You Merrie*, in *Non Dramatic Works*, ii. 282.

22. W. W. Greg, *Henslowe Papers*, 3 vols. (London: A. H. Bullen, 1907), iii. 125.

23. John Earle, *Micro-cosmographie … The fift edition much enlarged* (1629), H2b. See also Richard Brathwaite, *Times Curtaine Drawne* (1621), C3b: 'Some I know, that will not with their will | Put off their Suites, but love to weare them still; | That they (belike) of people might be knowne'; Cawdry, *Treasurie*, 600−1: 'as wee would laugh at a begger, who having borrowed princely apparell, to play the part of some King, upon a stage, wil needs afterward retaine and keep his apparell still, proudly and gloriously behaving himselfe in them, as if they were his owne'.

24. Steven Jerome, *Moses his Sight of Canaan* (1614), 2T3a−b: '[players] are all alike, Rogues by Statute, if they wander; or silken Beggers howsoever'; William Prynne, *Histrio-mastix* (1633), 325−6: 'Our *Players*, though they are *Rogues and Sturdy-beggers by Statute*, are yet so haughty in their mindes … that they disdaine the name of *Beggers*, though in truth they are no other, *then arrogant saucy Vagrants.*'

25. Robert Aylet, *The Brides Ornaments* (1625), 113.

26. John Davies, '*Against* Aesop *the Stage-player*', in *The Scourge of Folly* (1611), 85.

27. Stephen Gosson, *Plays Confuted* (1582), E6a.

28. Edmund Gayton, *Pleasant Notes upon Don Quixote* (1654), 144.

29. *Mercurius Pragmaticus*, 2 (21−8 Sept. 1647), 13.

30. Thomas Fuller, *The Holy State* (1642), 389.

31. *The Character or Ear-mark of Mr William Prynne* (1659), 4.

32. Gabriel Harvey, *Foure Letters and Certaine Sonnets Especially touching Robert Greene, and other parties, by him abused* (1592), 29.

33. Overbury, *Sir Thomas Overburie*, M3a; 'On Mr Richard Burbidg an excellent both player, and painter', in Commonplace Book (n.d.), Folger MS, v.a.97. The poem exists in various versions. Another punctuates this passage slightly differently, though the tenor remains the same: 'A Funerall Elegye on ye Death of the famous Actor Richard Burbedg who dyed on Saturday in Lent the 13 of March 1618', quoted in Edwin Nungezer, *A Dictionary of Actors* (New Haven: Yale University Press, 1929), 74, reads

> Hee's gone and with him what a world are dead.
> Which he reviv'd, to be revived soe,
> No more young Hamlett, ould Heironymoe,
> Kind Leer, the Greved Moore, and more beside,
> That lived in him; have now for ever dy'de.

34. Thomas Heywood's Prologue for Christopher Marlowe's *Famous Tragedy of the Rich Jew of Malta* (1633), A4b. See, too, the apologetic prologue to George Chapman's *Bussy D'Ambois* (1641), in *The Plays of George Chapman: The Tragedies*, ed. Allan Holaday *et al.* (Cambridge: D. S. Brewer, 1987), 31, written to explain how the play can still be performed though the actor Nathan Field 'is gone | Whose Action first did give it name'.

35. Meres, *Palladis Tamia*, 2Pb.

36. In the next century, similarly, Dennis was to declare that it was 'absolutely impossible … that any Actor can become an admirable Original, by playing a Part which was writ and design'd for another Man's particular Talent'; and Cibber was to rewrite his play *A Woman's Wit* (1697) so as to be able to offer it to the Lincoln's Inn company and the Theatre Royal company. See Tiffany Stern, *Rehearsal from Shakespeare to Sheridan* (Oxford: Clarendon Press, 2000), 150.

37. See Stern, *Rehearsal*, 150.

38. For the difference between the two varieties of text, see Andrew Gurr, 'Maximal and Minimal Texts: Shakespeare versus the Globe', *Shakespeare Survey*, 52 (1999), 68–87; Lukas Erne, *Shakespeare as Literary Dramatist* (Cambridge: Cambridge University Press, 2003).

39. John Marston, *Antonio and Mellida*, in Marston, *The Plays*, ed. H. Harvey Wood, 3 vols. (Edinburgh and London: Oliver and Boyd, 1934), i. 5.

40. Frances Quarles, *Argalus and Parthenia*, A3a.

41. See, e.g., Charlotte Charke, *A Narrative of the Life of Mrs. Charlotte Charke* (1755), 60: 'Mrs Heron having that Afternoon the Misfortune to bruise her Knee-pan, she was immoveable; and I was, at the second Musick, sent for to read the Part.' Nineteenth-century US actor William Davidge relates in *Footnote Flashes* (New York: The American News Company, 1866), 261: 'During one of Mr Barney Williams' successful engagements at the Broadway

Theatre, a piece called "Crossing the Atlantic" was produced... the second or third day after it was first acted, Mr Williams was taken ... seriously ill... about three quarters of an hour prior to the opening of the doors, I was solicited by the manager to read the part assigned to Mr Williams.' For more on understudies, see Stern, *Rehearsal*, 212.

42. Henslowe to Edward Alleyn, 14 Aug. 1593 in Greg, *Henslowe Papers*, iii. 38.

43. Richard Tarlton, *Tarltons Jeasts* (1613), C2b−3a. Similarly, M. Lluellin relates in his '*To the rich Memory of my Honoured Friend the Learned Author*' which prefixes William Cartwright's *Lady Errant* (1651), how a king doubles with a musician, 'And was though crown'd heard say, | Give us the Fiddle, we our self will Play'; see *Plays and Poems*, 4; and Jesus is compared to someone forced to play 'both a King and a Clowne in a Play' in John Gaule, *Practique Theories* (1629), 233.

44. Bodleian Library MS, Tenbury 1278, discussed in Robert Shay and Robert Thompson, *Purcell Manuscripts: The Principal Musical Sources* (Cambridge: Cambridge University Press, 2000), 257.

45. For some extended arguments about necessary and 'telling' doubles, see John C. Meagher, 'Economy and Recognition: Thirteen Shakespearean Puzzles', *Shakespeare Quarterly*, 35 (1984), 7−22, and Stephen Booth, 'Speculations on Doubling in Shakespeare's Plays', in Philip C. McGuire and David A. Samuelson (eds.), *Shakespeare: The Theatrical Dimension*, (New York: AMS Press, 1979), 103−31. See Ch. 6 for extended treatment of the part of Macduff.

46. Thomas Nabbes, *The Unfortunate Mother* (1640), A3a; John Cleveland, *The Character of a London Diurnall* (1647), 33; Anthony Munday et al., *Sir Thomas More* (3.2), ed. Vittorio Gabrielli and Georgio Melchiori (Manchester: Manchester University Press, 2000), 148−9. See also the depositions of witnesses respecting an affray at Norwich in 1583, when the Queen's Players were acting at the Red Lion Inn, reproduced in David Galloway (ed.), *REED: Norwich* (Toronto: University of Toronto Press, 1984), 75: 'after hym came one of the players in his players apperrell, with a players berd uppon his face'. For the beard as a prop of masculinity, see Will Fisher, 'The Renaissance Beard: Masculinity in Early Modern England', *Renaissance Quarterly*, 54 (2001), 155−87.

47. See King, *Casting Shakespeare's Plays*, for general records of doubling.

48. See ibid. 14−15, where King makes the same point from examining remaining playhouse 'plots'. He also, however, illustrates an occasion when a hired man, Parsons, playing very small parts in *The First Parte of Tamer Cam*, does have to make quicker changes; similarly very quick changes are required in George Peele's *Battle of Alcazar*.

49. Prynne, *Histrio-mastix*, 2L3b.

50. Robert Armin, *Foole upon Foole* (1600), D4a.

51. Josuah Sylvester, from *Du Bartas: His Divine Weekes and Workes Translated* (1621), 603. See also John Abbot, *Jesus Præfigured* (1623), 8: 'The swinish broode of this our present Age, | In their Sires vizardes plaie on the worlds

stage'; a Commonplace Book *c.*1612 in the Beinecke Library, Osborn b 144, 191: '& when thay have play'd their parts, & the time come that earth must to earth, then is their visards puld of ther faess & all the world may see them as naked at ther parting as they wear at their birth'; William Cowper, *A Holy Alphabet for Sion's Scholars full of Spiritual Instructions* (1613), A3b: 'For this world properly is compared to a Stage-play, wherin oftentimes Nobles are clad in beggars garments, and the beggar takes on the habite of a King; but when the guise is ended, and the maskes removed, then every one appeares to be that which he is'; John Collop, *Poesis Rediviva* (1655), 36: 'The world is but a Theater of ill; | Knaves, Fools, and madmen do the stage up fill; | Religion the vizard is which most put on | To act their parts; parts done, the vizards gone.'

52. John Lyly, *Rythmes against Martin Marre-Prelate* (1589), A2a. See also Robert Burton, *The Anatomy of Melancholy* (1621), 26: 'a new company of counterfeit visards, whiflers ... Maskers, Mummers'.

53. Thomas Fuller, *Mixt Contemplations on these Times* (1660), 9−10. See also *The Laughing Mercury*, no. 23 (8−16 Sept. 1652), 179: 'Actors, ... when their Vizards and brave Apparrel was taken off; they would appear to be at best but hyred to Act their Parts for a little silver.' For the absolute day-to-day theatrical normality of vizards as part of the theatrical experience, see Prynne, *Histrio-mastix*, 2R1b: 'theatricall Pageants, Apparitions, Attires, Visars, Garments, with such-like Stage-appurtenances'.

54. George Puttenham, *The Arte of English* (1589), 26.

55. Ben Jonson, *Christmas his Masque*, in *The Works*, ed. C. H. Herford and Percy Simpson, 11 vols. (Oxford: Clarendon Press, 1947), vii. 442. For the fact that vizards were usual for mummers or maskers, see Thomas Thomas, *Dictionarium linguae Latinae et Anglicanae* (1587), 2Xiia, where 'personatus' is described as one 'That hath a part in a play, a masker, or mummer, one disguised, that weareth a vizor, that taketh on him that he is not ... '.

56. Thomas Lodge, *Wits Miserie* (1596), 56: 'he ... looks as pale as the Visard of ye ghost which cried so miserally at ye Theator like an oisterwife, *Hamlet, revenge*'; Thomas Coryate, *Coryates Crudities* (1611), 273; Samuel Harsnett, *A Declaration of Egregious Popish Impostures* (1603), 91.

57. William Rowley, *A Search for Money* (1609), C2b.

58. R. Willis, *Mount Tabor* (1639), 111; Greg, *Henslowe Papers*, iii. 116−18.

59. William Percy, *Necromantes or The Two supposed Heds*, in *Plays*, Huntington Library MS, HM 4, 189b.

## CHAPTER 3. REHEARSING AND PERFORMING

1. *The Merrie Conceited Jests of George Peele* (1607), 22−3.

2. Thomas Dekker, *The Guls Horn-Booke*, in *The Non Dramatic Works*, ed. Alexander B. Grosart, 5 vols. (1884; New York: Russell and Russell, 1963), ii. 249. Sometimes such readings actually had a positive use. So Randolph's

brother-in-law writes of playwrights whose texts become 'of Age' when they have been blessed by 'the Councell of some friend'. See Richard Wets, 'To the pious Memory of my deare Brother in-law, M. Thomas Randolph', in Thomas Randolph, *Poems* (1652), B3b.

3. Robert Shaa to Henslowe, 8 Nov. 1599; Samuel Rowley to Henslowe, 4 Apr. 1601; in W. W. Greg, *Henslowe Papers*, 3 vols. (London: A. H. Bullen, 1907), iii. 49, 56.

4. Robert Daborne to Henslowe, 8 May 1613, ibid. iii. 69.

5. Daborne to Henslowe, 11 Mar. 1613/14, ibid. iii. 82.

6. Daborne to Henslowe, 16 May 1613, ibid. iii. 70.

7. Philip Henslowe, *Henslowe's Diary*, ed. R. A. Foakes, 2nd edn. (Cambridge: Cambridge University Press, 2002), 88.

8. Ibid. 201.

9. Marston, *Histrio-mastix*, in *The Plays*, 3 vols. (Edinburgh and London: Oliver and Boyd, 1934), iii. 259.

10. See Tiffany Stern, *Rehearsal from Shakespeare to Sheridan* (Oxford: Clarendon Press, 2000), 146−7, 207−11, 250−3.

11. For company rejections after readings, see ibid. 146−7.

12. Adrian Kiernander, ' "Betwixt" and "Between": Variant Readings in the Folio and First Quarto Versions of *Richard III* and W. W. Greg's Concept of Memorial Reconstruction', in Lloyd Davis (ed.), *Shakespeare Matters* (Newark, NJ: University of Delaware Press, 2003), 247.

13. William Prynne, *Histrio-mastix* (1633), 2R1a.

14. Richard Legge, *Richardus Tertius*, Bodleian Library MS, Lat. Misc. e. 16.

15. John Downes, *Roscius Anglicanus*, ed. J. Milhous and R. D. Hume (London: Society for Theatre Research, 1987), 2.

16. For the preference in early modern discourse for the word 'prompter' over 'book-holder', see Tiffany Stern, 'Behind the Arras:. The Prompter's Place in the Shakespearean Theatre', *Theatre* (*Notebook*), 55 (2001), 110. The term 'book-keeper', which, referred to the person who had official charge of the 'book'—indicated someone who was often, but not necessarily, the prompter.

17. N. W. Bawcutt, *The Control and Censorship of Caroline Drama* (Oxford: Clarendon Press, 1996), 183.

18. Daborne to Henslowe, 25 June 1613, in Greg, *Henslowe Papers*, iii. 73.

19. Giles E. Dawson (ed.), *Malone Society Collections: VII* (Oxford: Oxford University Press, 1965), 203.

20. Dekker, *Jests to Make you Merrie*, in *Non Dramatic Works*, ii. 345.

21. Stephen Gosson, *The Ephemerides of Phialo* (1579), K2a.

22. Sir George Mackenzie, *Aretina* (1660), 39.

23. Nicholas Breton, *Fantasticks Serving for a Perpetuall Prognostication* (1626), E4a.

24. John Fletcher, *Maid in the Mill*, in *The Dramatic Works in the Beaumont and Fletcher Canon*, ed. Fredson Bowers *et al.*, 10 vols. (Cambridge: Cambridge University Press, 1966−96), ix. 590.

25. *The Second Part of the Return from Parnassus*, in *The Three Parnassus Plays*, ed. J. B. Leishman (London: Ivor Nicholson and Watson Ltd., 1949), 218.

26. John Day, *Travails of Three English Brothers* (1607), B4a. See also Dekker, *The Seven Deadly Sinnes*, in *Non Dramatic Works*, ii. 73: 'Crueltie hath yet another part to play…severall companies in the Cittie have it in study, and they are never perfect in it.'

27. Thomas Middleton, *The Black Book* (1604), in *The Works*, ed. A. H. Bullen, 8 vols. (London: John C. Nimmo, 1886), viii. 25.

28. Marston, *Antonio and Mellida*, in *Plays*, i. 5.

29. Nathaniel Richards, *Poems Sacred and Satyricale* (1641), 21–2.

30. John Quarles, 'To my Muse', in *Gods Love and Mans Unworthiness* (1951), A3b. Instruction by playwrights was much more likely in a university environment. Writing of German university productions, Johannes Rhenanus maintains that it is there usual for the players to be 'daily instructed… even the most refined actors are obliged to let the poets instruct them'. See W. Creizenach, *Die Schauspiele der Englischen Komodianten* (1889), quoted and trans. in Stern, *Rehearsal*, 40.

31. Ben Jonson, *Cynthias Revels*, in *The Works*, ed. C. H. Herford and Percy Simpson, 11 vols. (Oxford: Clarendon Press, 1947), iv. 35.

32. Philip Massinger, *The Roman Actor* (1629), F3b; George Wilkins, *Miseries of Inforst Marriage* (1607), G2a.

33. Chapman, *The Gentleman Usher* (1606), in *The Plays of George Chapman: The Comedies*, ed. Allan Holaday *et al.* (Urbana: University of Illinois Press, 1970),144.

34. *Three Parnassus Plays*, 336–49.

35. See Stern, *Rehearsal*, 68.

36. 'Mr Ric. James gave all his books yt were printed to ye publiclibrary, with a coppie of verses of his owne making before them', in a Commonplace Book, Bodleian Library MS, Wood D 19 (2), 99; *The Actors Remonstrance, or Complaint* (1643), 4.

37. John Gee, *New Shreds of the Old Snare* (1624), 21.

38. Thomas Middleton, *Your Five Gallants* (1608), I1a.

39. Scott McMillin, 'The Sharer and his Boy: Rehearsing Shakespeare's Women', in Peter Holland and Stephen Orgel (eds.), *From Script to Stage in Early Modern England* (Basingstoke, London, and New York: Palgrave Macmillan, 2004), 231–45.

40. [Anthony Munday], *A Second and Third Blast of a Retrait from Playes* (1580), 110. See also William Crashaw, *The Sermon Preached at the Crosse, Feb. xiiii 1607* (1609), 170: 'he that teacheth children to play, is not an instructer, but a spoiler & destroyer of children'.

41. Heywood, *An Apology for Actors* (1612), C3b.

42. Thomas Tomkis, *Lingua* (1607), H3a.

43. *Three Parnassus Plays*, 341.

44. *Ratseis Ghost* (1605), B1a.

45. Downes, *Roscius*, 55, maintains of Betterton's Hamlet that 'Sir William [Davenant] (having seen Mr Taylor of the Blackfriars company act it, who being

instructed by the author, Mr Shakespeare) taught Mr Betterton in every particle of it'. Of Betterton's *Henry VIII* he says (p. 51) that Davenant taught it as he 'had it from Old Mr. Lowen, that had his instructions from Mr. Shakespear himself'. He can't be entirely right in his line of 'inheritance'—Shakespeare was dead by the time Taylor was of an age to play Hamlet—nevertheless Davenant may have seen and taught the performance as inherited from Burbage by Taylor.

46. Stern, *Rehearsal*, 253–66.
47. Edward Benlowes, *Theophila* (1652), C3a.
48. Greg, *Henslowe Papers*, iii. 123.
49. Richards, *Poems*, 20–1.
50. Stern, *Rehearsal*, 32.
51. Edmund Gayton, *Pleasant Notes upon Don Quixote* (1654), 94–5; Thomas Blount, *Glossographia* (1656), P7a.
52. Gee, *New Shreds*, 21.
53. Marston, *Antonio and Mellida*, in *Plays*, iii. 5; Chapman, *Gentleman Usher*, 146; Fletcher, *Maid in the Mill*, 601.
54. For this and other examples, see Stern, *Rehearsal*, 254.
55. From 'the Plot of *The Dead Man's Fortune*,' reproduced and transcribed in W. W. Greg, *Dramatic Documents from the Elizabethan Playhouses*, 2 vols. (Oxford: Clarendon Press, 1931), ii.
56. Jonson, *Every Man Out of his Humour*, in *Works*, iii. 467; Chapman, *Gentleman Usher*, 146.
57. William Percy, *Arabis Sitiens or A Dreame of a Drye Yeare*, in *Plays*, Huntington Library MS, HM 4.
58. Walter Raleigh, *The Poems: A Historical Edition*, ed. Michael Rudick (Tempe, Ariz.: Arizona Center for Medieval and Renaissance Studies, 1999), 184.
59. John Higgins, *The Nomenclature* (1585), 501; James Shirley, *Hide Parke* (1637), F2a.
60. Higgins, *Nomenclature*, 501; John Florio, *A World of Wordes* (1598), E2a.
61. For the prompters' strong association with playhouse curtains, see Stern, 'Behind the Arras'.
62. Nathaniel Woodes, *The Conflict of Conscience* (1581), A2b.
63. Jonson, *Staple of News*, in *Works*, vi. 280; Thomas Nashe, *The Works*, ed. R. B. McKerrow, 2nd edn., rev. F. P. Wilson, 5 vols. (Oxford: Oxford University Press, 1958), iii. 233.
64. Richard Brome, *The Antipodes*, in *The Dramatic Works,* ed. R. H. Shepherd, 3 vols. (1873), iii. 292.
65. Aaron Hill and William Popple, *The Prompter: A Theatrical Paper (1734–1736)*, ed. William W. Appleton and Kalman A. Burnim (New York: Benjamin Blom, 1966), 1.
66. Thomas Dekker, *The Blacke Rod, and the White Rod* (1630), 3.
67. Brome, *Antipodes*, 259.
68. John Stephens, *Essayes and Characters* (1615), 297.

69. Charles Gildon, *The Life of Mr. Thomas Betterton* (1710), 37.
70. Hill and Popple, *The Prompter*, 78; Roger Pickering, *Reflections upon Theatrical Expression in Tragedy* (1755), 52.
71. Stern, *Rehearsal*, 53.
72. John Taylor, *The Sculler*, in *All the Workes of John Taylor the Water-Poet* (1630), iii. 24; Thomas Fuller, *History* (1662), Hhh4a.
73. Marston, *Malecontent* (1604), in *Plays*, i. 141.
74. Jonson, *Cynthia's Revels*, 91.

## CHAPTER 4. HISTORY OF THE CUE

1. John Minsheu, *Minshaei emendatio ... sui Ductoris in linguas* (1625), 591.
2. Charles Butler, *English Grammar* (1633), C1b; Bodleian Library: Mal. 743.
3. Richard Brathwaite, *A Strange Metamorphosis of Man, Transformed into a Wildernesse* (1634), C11b.
4. Thomas Heywood, *The Royall King, and the Loyall Subject* (1637), C1a; Thomas Middleton and William Rowley, *A Faire Quarrell* (1617), B4b; Shakespeare, *Much Ado*, TLN 704.
5. John Clavell, *The Soddered Citizen* [*sic*], ed. John Henry Pyle Pafford and W. W. Greg (Oxford: Oxford University Press, 1936), 74.
6. Richard Brome, *Sparagus Garden* (1640), F2a; Thomas Dekker, *The Noble Spanish Soldier* (1634), in *The Dramatic Works of Thomas Dekker*, ed. Fredson Bowers, 4 vols. (Cambridge: Cambridge University Press, 1953–61), iv. 292.
7. William Shakespeare, *Shake-speare's Sonnets* (1609), C1b. [Archie Armstrong], *A Banquet of Jests* (1634), 213.
8. Lodowick Carlell, *Two New Playes. viz. The Fool would be a Favourit...* (1657), 74.
9. 'Mans lyfe likened to a Stage Play', in Thomas Howell, *H. his Devises* (1581), D3b.
10. Thomas Nashe, *The Works*, ed. R. B. McKerrow, 2nd edn., rev. F. P. Wilson, 5 vols. (Oxford: Oxford University Press, 1958), iii. 235.
11. Amongst other things, the reliance of actors on cues has ramifications for notions of 'memorially reconstructed' texts. Were the 'pirate' of a text an actor, then both his part *and* his cues should be accurate; he should be considerably less secure about lines belonging to fellow actors, particularly when his own character is not on-stage. In fact, this is never the case: the whole idea of 'pirate-actors', generally discredited anyway, needs to be fully rejected. Almost certainly textual thieves sat in the audience. See Tiffany Stern, 'Watching as Reading: The Audience and Written Text in the Early Modern Playhouse', in Laurie Maguire (ed.), *How to Do Things with Shakespeare* (Oxford: Blackwell, 2007).
12. James Boaden, *Memoirs of the Life of John Philip Kemble Esq*, 2 vols. in one (1825), i. 111.

13. Dekker, *The Guls Horn-Booke*, in *The Non Dramatic Works*, ed. Alexander B. Grosart, 5 vols. (1884; New York: Russell and Russell, 1963), ii. 250.

14. Thomas Adams, *Works*, 3 vols. (1861–2), i. 266. See also Thomas Fuller, *Church History* (1655), 236: 'My Cue of entrance is to come in, where the State-Writer doth go out.'

15. Thus important scholarship on the timing of entrances and exits is bound to be not entirely accurate, lacking the information about when such exits actually occurred. Mariko Ichikawa's *Shakespearean Entrances* (Basingstoke and New York: Palgrave, 2002), which designates two line-lengths for an entrance, is a useful starting-point—though one may then question why two line-lengths are not provided on a part preceding an entrance.

16. David Bradley, *From Text to Performance in the Elizabethan Theatre: Preparing the Play for the Stage* (Cambridge: Cambridge University Press, 1992), 89, makes a similar point: 'The Plot springs to life as a theatre document...as soon as it is put together with the actors' parts: those records together would be sufficient to direct an acted run-though.'

17. Samuel Harsnett, *A Declaration of Egregious Popish Impostures* (1603), *passim*.

18. Gabriel Harvey, *Works*, ed. Alexander Grosart, 3 vols. (1884), iii. 56. It was because of the cueing system that real animals were seldom put on-stage (which may answer the question of whether or not a real bear played the bear in *The Winter's Tale*): most animals could not take cues. Dogs may have been an exception, as *Two Gentleman of Verona* suggests.

19. Sir John Mennes, *Facetiae*, 2 vols. (1817), ii. 216.

20. Hansjürgen Linke, in 'Versuch über deutsche Handschriften mittelalterlicher Spiele', in Volker Honemann and Nigel F. Palmer (eds.) *Deutsche Handschriften 1100–1400: Oxforder Kolloquium 1985* (Tübingen: Max Niemeyer Verlag, 1988), 532. We are grateful to Anna Richards for translating this passage.

21. Gabriel Harvey's *Marginalia*, ed. G. C. Moore Smith (Stratford-upon-Avon: Shakespeare Head Press, 1913), 143.

22. John Lyly, *Pappe with an Hatchet* (1589), C3a.

23. James Shirley, *The Humorous Courtier*, ed. Marvin Morrillo (New York: Garland, 1979), 142.

24. George Wilkins, *The Painfull Aduentures of Pericles Prince of Tyre*, ed. Kenneth Muir (Liverpool: University Press of Liverpool, 1953), 97. For other references to cues of entrance see [Robert Daborne], *Ghost of Richard the Third* (1614), F2a: 'He lookes us oft; I came not on my Cue'; Jack Dawe, *Vox Graculi* (1623), 19: 'Next enters upon her Cu, that odiferous Lady Ver.'

## CHAPTER 6. CUES AND CHARACTERIZATION

1. Assuming each cue is not 'elongated' on Hamlet's part, the actor will learn to respond to his speeches sequentially—unlike a 'repeated cue', which we will discuss in the next section.

## CHAPTER 7. WAITING AND SUDDENNESS: THE PART IN TIME

1. The term 'target' is adapted from Declan Donnellan, *The Actor and the Target* (London: Theatre Communications Group, 2002).
2. That the same actor may 'already' have played the similarly, haplessly 'one note' Duncan reinforces both the likelihood of that player's presupposed performance style and the unactable ironies attendant upon it.
3. For more on this see Simon Palfrey, *Doing Shakespeare* (London: Arden Shakespeare, 2005), 213–20.
4. John Coleman, 'Facts and Fancies about *Macbeth*', *Gentleman's Magazine*, Mar. 1889, 222; quoted in *Shakespeare in Production: Macbeth*, ed. John Wilders (Cambridge: Cambridge University Press, 2004), 87.
5. For further extended examples, see in particular the analyses of the parts of Isabella and Macbeth, Ch. 20.
6. See Part IV for more on part-based prosody.
7. For more on repeated performances, see Ch. 3.
8. Samuel Johnson, *Johnson on Shakespeare*, ed. Arthur Sherbo, *The Works of Samuel Johnson*, 7 and 8 (New Haven: Yale University Press, 1986), 7: 404.
9. See George T. Wright, *Shakespeare's Metrical Art* (Berkeley: University of California Press, 1991), for a comprehensive study of such problems.
10. See Part IV, esp. Chs. 18 and 19.

## CHAPTER 9. FROM CROWDS TO CLOWNS

1. In Q1 Hamlet goes on to curse clowns still further, for having but one lame joke that they rehash interminably.
2. See Robert Weimann, *Author's Pen and Actor's Voice* (Cambridge: Cambridge University Press, 2000).
3. Repeated cues twice encourage the semi-improvised clowning of Dromio of Syracuse in *Comedy of Errors*, both times whilst being subject to his master's rote-repeating violence, e.g. at TLN 417–18, 430–42. One exception apart (TLN 340–50, again prompting 'disobedient' play from the servant/clown, here Dromio of Ephesus), the play elsewhere eschews repeated cues. Many of the scenes are written in shared couplets, and/or feature brisk witty repartee, both of which would be subverted by intentional repeated cues.

## CHAPTER 10. COMI-TRAGIC/TRAGI-COMIC PATHOS

1. Mercutio's repeated cue is in all three texts. Benvolio's repeated cue is not in the 'acting' text of Q1, and its main effect when present is simply to reinforce the separation that the first repeated cue allows Mercutio. Benvolio's repetition—'Here comes *Romeo*, Here comes *Romeo*'—is explicable in only two ways. Either he is excited, and says his words twice in happy succession;

or else he is conscious that Mercutio has ignored him, and he tries to get his attention. The second option is far more in keeping with the gradually escalating tension—even fear—surrounding Mercutio.

2. Q1 marks this moment with the repeated cue-phrase, 'a poxe on/of your houses' (F1a). These are Mercutio's last words, again cueing Romeo's soliloquy. The difference in Q1 is that the phrase first comes half-way through Mercutio's penultimate speech. In Q2/F this penultimate speech ends by cueing Romeo; in Q1 it ends by cueing the Boy: '_____ Wher's the Surgeon' *Boy.* 'Hee's come sir.' This means that the Romeo-actor is cued some eight or nine lines early which allows for a still more extravagantly sectioned stage than Q2/F seems to prescribe. In Q1 Mercutio's dying rage ('some peasantly rogue, some Sexton, some base slave shall write my Epitaph ... ') and Romeo's grief are both addressed primarily to the audience, each, again, in the interstices of the other.

### CHAPTER 11. THE BATTLE FOR THE CUE-SPACE:
#### *THE MERCHANT OF VENICE*

1. See analysis of the part of Portia in Ch. 20.

2. It is appropriate that the part of Falstaff, particularly in *2 Henry IV*, should use repeated cues in similar ways to the part of Mercutio. In comparison, the part of Shallow repeats phrases in almost every speech, often harping upon death and decay, but only on three innocuous comic occasions does the cue-phrase come early (TLN 1616 ('good Sir John'), 1643 ('well said'), 1753 ('come, come')). Shallow's specific mortality or inwardness is not the issue: the themes are either shared, or work contrapuntally upon Falstaff; isolating Shallow in his melancholy or morbidity would disperse rather than concentrate the scene's pathos.

### CHAPTER 12. TRAGEDY

1. This text is taken from *Shakespeare's Plays in Quarto: A Facsimile Edition of Copies Primarily from the Henry E. Huntington Library*, ed. Michael J. B. Allen and Kenneth Muir (Berkeley: University of California Press, 1981).

2. See e.g. Tobias Doring, 'Writing Performance: How to Elegize Elizabethan Actors', *Shakespeare Survey*, 58 (2005), 66–71.

3. The 1603 'Bad' Quarto recalls the repeated cue-effect even if it (presuming the text here bears marks of a memorial reconstruction) misremembers transcribes the actual words: 'God be with you Ladies, God be with you. *Exit Ofelia*' (G 46).

4. Simon Palfrey, *Doing Shakespeare* (London: Arden Shakespeare, 2005), 288–90. For discussion of the 'O' as a passionate apostrophe that goes at once

inward and outward (and much more), see J. H. Prynne, 'English Poetry and Emphatical Language', *Proceedings of the British Academy*, 74 (1988),
135–69.

## CHAPTER 13. THE CUE-SPACE IN *KING LEAR*

1. Cf. Mariko Ichikawa, *Shakespearean Entrances* (Basingstoke and New York:
   Palgrave, 2002).

## CHAPTER 15. REPEATED CUES AND THE CUE-SPACE IN *THE TEMPEST*

1. The burden could also refer to the bass part of a male voice, or a continuous
   undersong, such as the drone-like noise made by a bagpipe; see David Lindley
   (ed.), *The Tempest* (Cambridge: Cambridge University Press, 2002), 121, 247:
   either way we are on safe ground if we assume some kind of vibration
   or repetition echoing beyond the 'scripted' lyric. More generally on the
   practicalities of music in the play, see David Lindley, *Shakespeare and Music*
   (London: Arden, 2006), esp. 1–9, 218–33.

2. There is a fascinating precursor to Caliban's 'intra-cue' experience during
   Stephano's song in the experience of Bottom's 'dream' in *A Midsummer Night's
   Dream*—an experience likewise bracketed by repeated or privately cherished
   cues. So, during the play rehearsal, Bottom first misses his entrance cue ('never
   tyre'); he is called for by Peter Quince ('*Piramus* enter, your cue is past; it is
   never tyre'; this putative entrance cue is then spoken again by 'Thisby', 'O, as
   true as truest horse, that yet would never tyre' (TLN 909–17)). This makes
   'never tyre' a thrice-spoken cue: and now the cue for both Bottom the actor
   of Pyramus and the Bottom-actor. At some point after hearing 'never tyre'
   Bottom re-enters—it could be after the first, second, or third 'never tyre' (he is
   now barely recognizable as Bottom because of the ass's head; the comedy could
   be increased if Peter thinks 'Pyramus' hasn't come, but in fact he is standing
   there). At this point all of the other mechanicals run away, leaving Bottom to
   begin his 'translation' into Titania's lover and to experience barely imaginable
   delights. Eventually he awakes with 'When my cue comes, call me, and I will
   answer' (TLN 1728): his 'dream' of social and erotic conquest thus occurs in
   the 'bracket' between two cues, both of which are missed, repeated, or suspended; both of which work in the cued actor's mind quite distinctively from
   in anyone else's. Whether or not Shakespeare had this episode in mind when
   he came to write Caliban's travails in II. ii is impossible to know. Three things,
   however, are clear: Bottom's dream is explicitly framed by 'cue-slippage', and
   so by the metatheatrical openings that ensue; *Dream* is a clear precursor play
   to *The Tempest*, with its pastoral setting, fantastical cast, and intricate patterns
   of sleeping, dreaming, and waking; and Bottom's dream is clearly a palimpsest
   of Caliban's dreams (of rape, conquest, riches…), as his monstrosity is
   of Caliban's.

## CHAPTER 16. HISTORY

1. Cf. Robert Weimann, *Author's Pen and Actor's Voice* (Cambridge: Cambridge University Press, 2000).

2. Anthony Scolocker, *Daiphantus* (1604), E4b.

3. R. M. [Rob Warner?], *Micrologia Characters* (1629), B3a. See also W. S., *A Funerall Elegye* (1612), B3a: '[He could not] disgest as some loose Mimicks can, | An empty sound of over-weening passion.'

4. Thomas Bancroft, *Time's Out of Tune* (1658), 44.

5. Samuel Nicholson, *Acolastus* (1600), G3b.

6. Richard Brathwaite, *A Strappado for the Divell* (1615), L6b; Francis Quarles, 'The Argument' to sect. 9 in *Hadassa or the History of Queene Ester* (1621), G4a. See also Robert Tofte, *Alba* (1598), D6b:

> Thy Griefe (for me) a passion's in a play,
> Which men doth ravish with Melancholy:
> But acted once, and out of sight away,
> In minde, no longer there doth stay, but dy:
> Thou art the Actor playing such a part,
> My griefes neere deeply pearce into thy hart.

7. Stephen Gosson, *Plays Confuted* (1582), E5a; Samuel Harsnett, *A Declaration of Egregious Popish Impostures* (1603), 74; Robert Herrick, 'Good Friday: *Rex Tragicus*, or Christ going to his Cross', in *His Noble Numbers* (1647), 74.

8. Thomas Randolph, *The Jealous Lovers*, 2¶1b.

9. For the full scientific background to early modern ideas about the passions and humours, see Joseph R. Roach, *The Player's Passion: Studies in the Science of Acting* (Newark, NJ: University of Delaware Press, 1985), 23–57.

10. Bancroft, *Time's Out of Tune*, 138.

11. The best modern account of the genre of humour comedies and their relationship to Shakespeare is Martin Wiggins, *Shakespeare and the Drama of his Time* (Oxford: Oxford University Press, 2000), 64–78.

12. John Chamberlain, *Letters*, ed. Norman E. McClure, 2 vols. (Philadelphia: American Philosophical Society, 1939), i. 32.

13. Barnaby Rich, *Faultes Faults, and nothing else but Faultes* (1606), B4a.

14. John Marston, *Insatiate Countess*, in *The Plays*, ed. H. Harvey Wood, 3 vols. (Edinburgh and London: Oliver and Boyd, 1934), iii. 22.

15. Patrick Hannay, *A Happy Husband* (1619), L2b. Compare John Ford, *Fames Memoriall* (1606), in *The Nondramatic Works*, ed. L. E. Stock *et al.* (Binghamton, NY: Medeval and Renaissance Texts & Studies, 1991), 96: 'servile passion, theame for every stage'. Of course, life as a 'Passion Play' has another powerful resonance at the time, and one not at all irrelevant to the development of its drama: after all, Shakespeare's stage is a direct enough mutation from the Corpus Christi cycles, 'translating' Christ's passion into all kinds of context,

tragic, burlesque, scandalous. It is entirely likely that Shakespeare pressed upon this 'punning' conjunction of apparently disparate 'passions' in his work, in the role-play e.g. of Edgar in *Lear*, or Macbeth 'tied … to a stake' (TLN 2396) and hissed at by the audience.

16. Richard Wets, 'To the pious Memory of my deare Brother in-law, M. Thomas Randolph', in Thomas Randolph, *Poems* (1652), B3a.

17. Richard Flecknoe, *Epigrams* (1671), 51; Aston Cokain, *Small Poems of Divers Sorts* (1658), 108. See also George Daniel, *Trinarchodia* (1649), in *The Poems*, ed. Alexander Grosart, 4 vols. (private circulation, 1878), iv. 135: 'Falstaffe [was] an humor fram'd | To grace the Stage.'

18. Edward Benlowes, *Theophila* (1652), B6a; William Habington, 'To my friend, Will. Davenant', in Sir William Davenant, *Madagascar* (1638), A7b; 'S. W.', in Thomas Flatman, *Naps upon Parnassus* (1658), B5a.

19. John Stephens, *New Essays and Characters* (1631), 190.

20. Arthur C. Kirsch, 'Caroline Commentary on the Drama', *Modern Philology*, 66 (1969), 256–61, at p. 257.

21. John Marston, *Scourge of Villanie* (1598), H4a.

22. Edmund Gayton, *Pleasant Notes upon Don Quixote* (1654), 140.

23. 'Upon the Effigies of my worthy Friend, the Author Master William Shakespeare, and his Workes', in William Shakespeare, *Mr William Shakespeares Comedies, Histories and Tragedies* (1632), A5a.

24. Philip Kynder, *The Surfeit to ABC* (1656), 80–1.

25. Henry Crosse, *Vertues Common-wealth* (1602), P2b; John Gee, *New Shreds of the Old Snare* (1624), 17; *Ratseis Ghost* (1605), A3b; T. Gainsford, *The Rich Cabinet*, (1616), Q5b.

26. Sir John Harington, *The Most Elegant and Witty Epigrams* (1618), H5a.

27. Thomas Gataker, *Davids Remembrancer* (1623), 4.

28. Thomas Heywood, *An Apology for Actors* (1612), C3b.

29. Levinus Lemnius, *The Touchstone of Complexions*, trans. Thomas Newton (1576), G5a–b.

30. Nicholson, *Acolastus*, G4a.

31. Arthur Warren, *The Poore Mans Passions* (1605), G2b; 'On Mr Richard Burbidg', Folger Shakespeare Library MS, v.a.97.

32. Joseph Hall, *Virgidemiarum*, in *Poems*, ed. A. Davenport (Liverpool: Liverpool University Press, 1949), 14, 16.

33. Leonard Digges, 'Upon Master William Shakespeare, the Deceased Author, and his Poems', prefixed to William Shakespeare, *Poems* (1640), A3b.

34. Samuel Sheppard, *Epigrams* (1651), 133.

35. Sir John Harington, *A New Discourse of a Stale Subject, called the Metamorphosis of Ajax* (1596), C3b; idem, *Ulysses upon Ajax* (1596), D1a.

36. Richard Flecknoe, *Miscellania* (1653), 103–4. See also Francis Meres, *Palladis Tamia* (1598), 2N8a: 'the English tongue is mightily enriched, and gorgeouslie

invested in rare ornaments and resplendent abiliments by sir *Philip Sidney, Spencer, Daniel, Drayton, Warner, Shakespeare, Marlow* and *Chapman*'; James Howell, *Londinopolis* (1657), 399: 'And it was a true observation, that those comical, and tragical Histories, did much improve, and enrich the *English* Language'; *The Actors Remonstrance, or Complaint* (1643), 5: 'Comedies and Tragedies being the lively representations of mens actions, in which … the most exact and naturall eloquence of our English language [is] expressed and daily amplified.'

37. Preface to R. Greene's *Menaphon*, in Thomas Nashe, *The Works*, ed. R. B. McKerrow, 2nd edn., rev. F. P. Wilson, 5 vols. (Oxford: Oxford University Press, 1958), iii. 310–11.

38. Robert Milles, *Abrahams Sute for Sodome* (1612), D5b.

39. Gayton, *Pleasant Notes*, 24. In fact the Fortune players denied this allegation. When they moved temporarily to the Red Bull, a special prologue was written for them to explain in what ways they differed from the Red Bull's regular players. One was that they had 'ne'er | An Actour here [who] has mouth enough to teare | *Language* by th'eares' (see John Tatham, *The Fancies Theater* (1640), H3a).

40. *Ratseis Ghost*, A3b; Thomas Overbury, *Sir Thomas Overburie, His Wife with New Elegies* (1616), G6a. See also Thomas Heywood, *The Hierarchie of the Blessed Angells* (1635), 208: 'Whence growes this Innovation? How comes it, | Some dare to measure mouthes for every bit | The Muse shall tast?'; Hall, *Virgidemiarum*, 14: 'huf-cap termes … Such … as some brave-minded hungry youth, | Sees fitly frame to his wide-strained mouth.'

41. Crosse, *Vertues Common-wealth*, P2b; William Cornwallis, *Essayes* (1600), G5a.

42. William Prynne, *Histrio-mastix*, (1633), 6D1a.

43. Gosson, *Plays Confuted*, D8b.

44. M. Robert Anton, *The Philosophers Satyrs* (1616), 46.

45. Gayton, *Pleasant Notes*, 271.

46. Richard Chamberlain, *Conceits, Clinches, Flashes, and Whimzies* (1639), ed. James O. Halliwell (London: Thomas Richards, 1860), 10.

47. See also John Earle, *Micro-cosmographie … The fift edition much enlarged* (1629), H2a: 'He knowes the right use of the World, wherein hee comes to play a part and so away: His life is not idle, for it is all Action'; Jack Dawe, *Vox Graculi* (1623), 48: 'Players: … live not like lazy Drones, but are still in Action.'

48. Sir Richard Baker, *Theatrum Redivivum* (1662), 34–5. See also Warren, *Poore Mans Passions*, G2a: 'Oh with what action would I grace my part, | Had I a scene according to desart.'

49. John Davies, 'To my worthy friend Mr Henry Butler', in *The Scourge of Folly* (1611), 109. See also Anton, *Philosophers Satyrs*, 30: 'let your virtuous actions keepe such meane, | As Angels may applaud your lifes best Sceane'; Heywood, *Apology*, A4b: 'In which *Jehove* … by their evill actions doomes the rest, | To end disgrac't whilst others praise inherit.'

50. D. Lupton, *London and the Countrey Carbonadoed* (1632), 80; Richard Middleton, *Times Metamorphosis* (1608), printed in Richard Middleton of Yorke, *Epigrams and Satyres* (1608), 39.

51. This is not the place to reproduce again the hand gestures out of Bulwer's *Chirologia and Chironomia* (a book recording and suggesting hand gestures for deaf people), for that sets forth as rules what might be simply one man's take on gesture at the time: undoubtedly it is telling, but attempts to track down its suggestions inside early modern plays have not been entirely successful, and, anyway, Bulwer writes largely of hand gestures, not all gestures.

52. Richard Niccols, *The Furies* (1614), C7a–b.

53. John Davies, *Microcosmos* (1603), 82.

54. Charles Hughes (ed.), *Shakespeare's Europe: Unpublished Chapters of Fynes Moryson's Itinerary* (London: Sherrat and Hughes, 1903), 304, 373.

55. *The Journals of Two Travellers in Elizabethan and Early Stuart England: Thomas Platter and Horatio Busino* (London: Caliban Books, 1995), 121.

56. Gervase Babington, *The Workes* (1622), 60; John Green, *A Refutation of the Apology for Actors* (1615), 61; Prynne, *Histrio-mastix*, 2D4b.

57. Francis Lenton, *The Young Gallants Whirligigg* (1629), 8; I. H., *This Worlds Folly* (1615), B2a.

58. Henry Chettle, *Kind-Harts Dreame* (1593), E2b.

59. Green, *Refutation*, 61. This is an updated rephrasing of a similar outburst made by Philip Stubbes, in *Anatomie of Abuses* (1583), L7a.

## CHAPTER 17. DRAMATIC PROSODY

1. See Derek Attridge, *Well-Weighed Syllables: Elizabethan Verse in Classical Metres*, (Cambridge: Cambridge University Press, 1974).

2. See ibid. 34 *passim*; O. B. Hardison, jun., *Prosody and Purpose in the English Renaissance* (Baltimore: Johns Hopkins University Press, 1989), 5 *passim*.

3. See Hardison, *Prosody and Purpose*, 3, 21–2.

4. For the many ways in which humanist education nourished the popular drama, see Neil Rhodes, *Shakespeare and the Uses of English* (Oxford: Oxford University Press, 2004).

5. For more on the usefulness and distinctiveness of prose, see Simon Palfrey, *Doing Shakespeare* (London: Arden Shakespeare, 2005), ch. 6.

6. Although the part of Isabella in *Measure for Measure*, in this as in many such things, strikingly refuses or eludes such expectations. See Ch. 20.

7. See below for discussion of short lines.

8. See Palfrey, *Doing Shakespeare*, ch. 5.

9. Although see works by John Barton, Robert Cohen, Cicely Berry, Declan Donnellan, and Patrick Tucker in the Bibliography.

10. The Quarto perhaps makes the choice more straightforward: it retains the half-line pause, but in shifting it a line along directs the actor more towards 'rage':

The Sea with such a storme of his lov'd head
In hell blacke night indur'd, would have layd up
And quencht the steeled fires, yet poore old heart,
Hee holpt the heavens to rage.

(Q H1b)

## CHAPTER 18. PROSODIC SWITCHES:
### PAUSES, PROMPTS, AND SOLILOQUIES

1. We are quoting here from the Folio text for the sake of convenience. Where an important difference in meaning is suggested by the Quarto text, we will refer to it.
2. For extended analysis of the speech's rhetorical and semantic effects, see Simon Palfrey, *Doing Shakespeare* (London: Arden Shakespeare, 2005), 226–33.

## CHAPTER 19. MIDLINE SHIFTS IN 'MATURE' SHAKESPEARE:
### FROM ACTORLY INSTRUCTION TO 'VIRTUAL' PRESENCE

1. Of course, the midline switch does not achieve these effects in isolation, but rather in league with various other stylistic sophistications: word-play that is latent rather than displayed; grammatical units in which a single word or clause might qualify one phrase, modify another, and be a noun phrase in it own right; parts that are made up of two or more hitherto singular character types or humours: Hamlet as at once the prince, pastoral hero, revenger, lover, soldier, scholar, fool, clown, player, playwright, melancholic, malcontent, whore, lunatic, philosopher … See Simon Palfrey, *Doing Shakespeare* (London: Arden Shakespeare, 2005), *passim*.

## CHAPTER 20. CASE STUDIES: FIVE ROMANTIC HEROINES
### AND THREE LONELY MEN

1. There is one incongruous break from the shared rhymes: *King* 'Make thy demand.' *Helena* 'But will you make it even?' *King* 'I by my Scepter, and my hopes of *helpe*' (TLN 802–4). The text here is probably self-censored; the word being set up to complete the shared couplet is clearly 'Heaven', a term used elsewhere in the play with no problem.
2. For discussion of the terror and pathos in Mercutio's self-characterizing puns/conceits, see Simon Palfrey, *Doing Shakespeare* (London: Arden Shakespeare, 2005), 149–56.
3. See Ch. 11.

4. In his 1926 recording of the ballad about Ann Boleyn's ghost, 'With Her Head Tucked Underneath Her Arm', Stanley Holloway pronounces 'gore' to rhyme with 'hour' in a way that makes it homophonic with go o'er—in a tale that also has the ghost 'queering' Henry'sfeast rather as Banquo does Macbeth's. Downloadable at <www.archive.org/details/Stanley Holloway>. Thanks to Sylvia Adamson for alerting us to this.

5. See Simon Palfrey, *Late Shakespeare: A New World of Words* (Oxford: Clarendon Press, 1997; paperback, 2000).

# Bibliography

PRIMARY SOURCES

## Manuscript

Book of parts belonging to Macklin, Harvard Theatre Library MS, TS 1197 54.5.

Callbook and related documents for Garrick's *A Midsummer Night's Dream*, Folger Shakespeare Library MS, w.b.469.

Commonplace Book *c*.1612, Beinecke Library MS, Osborn b 144.

Commonplace Book, Bodleian Library MS, Wood D 19 (2).

Commonplace Book, Folger Shakespeare Library MS, v.a.9.

Commonplace Book, Folger Shakespeare Library MS, v.a.97.

Musical part for Richard Leveridge in Purcell's *Indian Queen*, Bodleian Library MS, Tenbury 1278.

Part of Bajazet (1776?), Folger Shakespeare Library MS, t.a.22.

Part of Benedict (1788), Folger Shakespeare Library MS, t.a.34.

Part of Falstaff, Folger Shakespeare Library MS, t.a.121.

Part of Jacques (1799), Folger Shakespeare Library MS, t.a.39.

Part of King Henry V (1789?), Folger Shakespeare Library MS, t.a.38.

Part of King John (1783), Folger Shakespeare Library MS, t.a.25.

Part of King John (1745), Folger Shakespeare Library MS, w.a.172.

Part of King Richard III (1783), Folger Shakespeare Library, MS, t.a.13.

Part of Lear (1788), Folger Shakespeare Library MS, t.a.17.

Part of Macbeth (1785?), Folger Shakespeare Library MS, t.a.11.

Part of Orlando, Dulwich College MS, I, Item 138.

Part of Paris, Folger Shakespeare Library MS, t.a.29.

Parts of 'Poore', Polypragmaticus, Amurath, Antoninus, Harvard Theatre Library MS, Thr 10.1.

Part for Secundus Miles, Bodleian Library MS, Ashmole 750, f. 168[r].

Part of Shylock, Folger Shakespeare Library MS, y.d.42.

Part of Shylock (1784), Folger Shakespeare Library MS, t.a.30.

Part of Trico, Houghton Library MS, Eng 1258.

Part of Vincentio (1794?), Folger Shakespeare Library MS, t.a.35.

Legge, Richard, *Richardus Tertius*, Bodleian Library MS, Lat. Misc. e. 16.

Percy, William, *Plays*, Huntington Library MS, HM 4.

**Print**

Abbot, John, *Jesus Præfigured* (1623).

*The Actors Remonstrance, or Complaint* (1643).

Aebischer, P. (ed.), 'Quelques Textes du XVIe siècle en Patois Fribourgeois', *Archivum Romanicum*, 4 (1920), 342–61, 7 (1923), 288–36, 15 (1931), 512–40.

Adams, Thomas, *Works*, 3 vols. (1861–2).

Anton, M. Robert, *The Philosophers Satyrs* (1616).

Armin, Robert, *Foole upon Foole* (1600).

[Armstrong, Archie], *A Banquet of Jests* (1634).

Aylet, Robert, *The Brides Ornaments* (1625).

Babington, Gervase, *The Workes* (1622).

Baker, Sir Richard, *Theatrum Redivivum* (1662).

Bancroft, Thomas, *Time's Out of Tune* (1658).

Bawcutt, N. W. (ed.), 'Part of Poore', *Malone Society Collections: XV* (Oxford: Malone Society, 1993).

Benlowes, Edward, *Theophila* (1652).

Blount, Thomas, *Glossographia* (1656).

Boaden, James, *Memoirs of the Life of John Philip Kemble Esq*, 2 vols. in one (1825).

Boys, John, *Workes* (1622).

Brathwaite, Richard, *The English Gentlewoman* (1631).

——*A Strange Metamorphosis of Man, Transformed into a Wildernesse* (1634).

——*A Strappado for the Divell* (1615).

——*Times Curtaine Drawne* (1621).

Breton, Nicholas, *Fantasticks, Serving for a Perpetuall Prognostication* (1626).

Brome, Richard, *The Dramatic Works*, ed. R. H. Shepherd, 3 vols. (1873).

——*Sparagus Garden* (1640).

Brownsmith, John, *The Theatrical Alphabet. Containing a Catalogue of Several Hundred Parts (both Mens and Womens) in Different Plays and Farces; with the Number of Lengths Noted that Each Part Contains* (1767).

Burton, Robert, *The Anatomy of Melancholy* (1621).

Butler, Charles, *English Grammar* (1633).

Carlell, Lodowick, *Two New Playes. viz. The Fool would be a Favourit... Osmond, the Great Twk* (1657).

Cartwright, William, *The Plays and Poems*, ed. G. Blakemore Evans (Madison: University of Wisconsin Press, 1951).

Cawdry, Robert, *A Treasurie or Store-House of Similes* (1600).

Chamberlain, John, *Letters*, ed. Norman E. McClure, 2 vols. (Philadelphia: American Philosophical Society, 1939).

Chamberlain, Richard, *Conceits, Clinches, Flashes, and Whimzies* (1639), ed. James O. Halliwell (London: Thomas Richards, 1860).

Chapman, George, *The Plays of George Chapman: The Comedies*, ed. Allan Holaday *et al.* (Urbana: University of Illinois Press, 1970).

——*The Plays of George Chapman: The Tragedies*, ed. Allan Holaday *et al.* (Cambridge: D. S. Brewer, 1987).

*The Character or Ear-mark of Mr William Prynne* (1659).

Charke, Charlotte, *A Narrative of the Life of Mrs. Charlotte Charke* (1755).

Chettle, Henry, *Kind-Harts Dreame* (1593).

Chocheyras, J. (ed.), 'Rôle of Saint Barbara (Barbe)', in *Le théâtre religieux en Savoie au XVIe siècle* (Geneva: Droz, 1971), 93–108.

Cibber, Colley, *A Woman's Wit* (1697).

Clavell, John, *The Soddered Citizen* [*sic*], ed. John Henry Pyle Pafford and W. W. Greg (Oxford: Oxford University Press, 1936).

Cleveland, John, *The Character of a London Diurnall* (1647).

Cokain, Aston, *Small Poems of Divers Sorts* (1658).

Collop, John, *Poesis Rediviva* (1655).

Cornwallis, William, *Essayes* (1600).

Coryate, Thomas, *Coryates Crudities* (1611).

Cowper, William, *A Holy Alphabet for Sion's Scholars full of Spiritual Instructions* (1613).

Crashaw, William, *The Sermon Preached at the Crosse, Feb. xiiii 1607* (1609).

Crosse, Henry, *Vertues Common-wealth* (1602).

[Daborne, Robert], *Ghost of Richard the Third* (1614).

Daniel, George, *Trinarchodia* (1649), in *The Poems*, ed. Alexander Grosart, 4 vols. (private circulation, 1878).

Davenant, Sir William, *Madagascar* (1638).

Davidge, William, *Footnote Flashes* (New York: The American News Company, 1866).

Davies, John, *The Holy Roode* (1609).

——*Microcosmos* (1603).

——*The Scourge of Folly* (1611).

Davis, Norman, *Non-Cycle Plays and the Winchester Dialogues* (Oxford: Oxford University Press, 1979).

Dawe, Jack, *Vox Graculi* (1623).

Dawson, Giles E. (ed.), *Malone Society Collections: VII* (Oxford: Oxford University Press, 1965).

Day, John, *Travails of Three English Brothers* (1607).

Dekker, Thomas, *The Blacke Rod, and the White Rod* (1630).

——*The Dramatic Works of Thomas Dekker*, ed. Fredson Bowers, 4 vols. (Cambridge: Cambridge University Press, 1953–61).

——*The Non Dramatic Works*, ed. Alexander B. Grosart, 5 vols. (1884; New York: Russell and Russell, 1963).

Downes, John, *Roscius Anglicanus*, ed. J. Milhous and R. D. Hume (London: Society for Theatre Research, 1987).

Earle, John, *Micro-cosmographie ... The fift edition much enlarged* (1629).

Epictetus, *Epictetus his Manuall*, trans. Jo Healey (1616).

Evans, G. Blakemore (ed.), *Shakespearean Prompt-Books of the Seventeenth Century*, 8 vols. (Charlottesville: Bibliographical Society of the University of Virginia, 1960– ).

Fane, Mildmay, Earl of Westmoreland, *Otia Sacra* (1648).

Featley, Daniel, *Clavis Mystica... Handled in Seventy Sermons* (1636).

Fitzgeffrey, Charles, *Sir Francis Drake* (1596), in *Poems* (1881).

Flatman, Thomas, *Naps upon Parnassus* (1658).

Flecknoe, Richard, *Aenigmatical Characters, second edition* (1665).

——*Epigrams* (1671).

——*Miscellania* (1653).

——*Love's Kingdom... with a Short Discourse of the English Stage* (1664).

Fletcher, John, *The Dramatic Works in the Beaumont and Fletcher Canon*, ed. Fredson Bowers *et al.*, 10 vols. (Cambridge: Cambridge University Press, 1966–96).

Florio, John, *A World of Wordes* (1598).

Ford, John, *Fames Memoriall* (1606), in *The Nondramatic Works*, ed. L. E. Stock *et al.* (Binghamton, NY: Medieval and Renaissance Texts & Studies, 1991).

Fouquet, Jean, 'Sainte Apolline', in *Les Heures D'Étienne Chevalier par Jean Fouquet: Les Quarante Enluminures Du Musée Condé* (Paris: Somogy, 2003).

Fuller, Thomas, *Church History* (1655).

——*History* (1662).

——*The Holy State* (1642).

——*Mixt Contemplations on these Times* (1660).

Gainsford, T., *The Rich Cabinet* (1616).

Galloway, David (ed.), *REED: Norwich* (Toronto: University of Toronto Press, 1984).

Garrick, David, *The Private Correspondence*, ed. James Boaden, 2 vols. (1831–2).

Gataker, Thomas, *Davids Remembrancer* (1623).

Gaule, John, *Practique Theories* (1629).

Gayton, Edmund, *Pleasant Notes upon Don Quixote* (1654).

Gee, John, *New Shreds of the Old Snare* (1624).

Gildon, Charles, *The Life of Mr. Thomas Betterton* (1710).

Goffe, Thomas, *The Couragious Turke* (1632).

Gomersall, Robert, *Poems* (1633).

Gosson, Stephen, *The Ephemerides of Phialo* (1579).

——*Plays Confuted* (1582).

Green, John, *A Refutation of the Apology for Actors* (1615).

Greg, W. W., *Henslowe Papers*, 3 vols. (London: A. H. Bullen, 1907).

Hall, Joseph, *Virgidemiarum* (1598), in *Poems*, ed. A. Davenport (Liverpool: Liverpool University Press, 1949).

Hannay, Patrick, *A Happy Husband* (1619).

Harington, Sir John, *The Most Elegant and Witty Epigrams* (1618).

——*A New Discourse of a Stale Subject, called the Metamorphosis of Ajax* (1596).

——*Ulysses upon Ajax* (1596).

Harsnett, Samuel, *A Declaration of Egregious Popish Impostures* (1603).

Harvey, Gabriel, *Foure Letters and Certaine Sonnets Especially touching Robert Greene, and other parties, by him abused* (1592).

Harvey, Gabriel, *Works*, ed. Alexander Grosart, 3 vols. (1884).

Gabriel Harvey *Marginalia*, ed. G. C. Moore Smith (Stratford-upon-Avon: Shakespeare Head Press, 1913).

Heath, Robert, *Clarastella* (1650).

Henslowe, Philip, *Henslowe's Diary*, ed. R. A. Foakes, 2nd edn. (Cambridge: Cambridge University Press, 2002).

Herrick, Robert, *His Noble Numbers* (1647).

Heywood, Thomas, *An Apology for Actors* (1612).

——*The Hierarchie of the Blessed Angells* (1635).

——*The Royall King, and the Loyall Subject* (1637).

Higgins, John, *The Nomenclature* (1585).

Hill, Aaron, and Popple, William, *The Prompter: A Theatrical Paper (1734–1736)*, ed. William W. Appleton and Kalman A. Burnim (New York: Benjamin Blom, 1966).

Howell, James, *Londinopolis* (1657).

Howell, Thomas, *H. his Devises* (1581).

I. H., *This Worlds Folly* (1615).

Jerome, Steven, *Moses his Sight of Canaan* (1614).

Johnson, Samuel, *Johnson on Shakespeare*, ed. Arthur Sherbo, *The Works of Samuel Johnson*, 7 and 8 (New Haven: Yale University Press, 1986).

Jonson, Ben, *The Works*, ed. C. H. Herford and Percy Simpson, 11 vols. (Oxford: Clarendon Press, 1947).

*The Journals of Two Travellers in Elizabethan and Early Stuart England: Thomas Platter and Horatio Busino* (London: Caliban Books, 1995).

Kynder, Philip, *The Surfeit to ABC* (1656).

*The Laughing Mercury*, no. 23 (8–16 Sept. 1652).

Lemnius, Levinus, *The Touchstone of Complexions*, trans. Thomas Newton (1576).

Lenton, Francis, *The Young Gallants Whirligigg* (1629).

Lodge, Thomas, *Wits Miserie* (1596).

Lupton, D., *London and the Countrey Carbonadoed* (1632).

Lyly, John, *Pappe with an Hatchet* (1589).

——*Rythmes against Martin Marre-Prelate* (1589).

Mackenzie, Sir George, *Aretina* (1660).

Marlowe, Christopher, *Famous Tragedy of the Rich Jew of Malta* (1633).

Marston, John, *The Malecontent* (1604).

——*The Plays*, ed. H. Harvey Wood, 3 vols. (Edinburgh and London: Oliver and Boyd, 1934).

——*Scourge of Villanie* (1598).

Massinger, Philip, *The Roman Actor* (1629).

Mennes, Sir John, *Facetiae*, 2 vols. (1817).

*Mercurius Melancholicus*, 58 (25 Sept.–2 Oct. 1648).

*Mercurius Pragmaticus*, 2 (21–8 Sept. 1647).

Meres, Francis, *Palladis Tamia* (1598).

*The Merrie Conceited Jests of George Peele* (1607).

Middleton, Richard, of Yorke, *Epigrams and Satyres* (1608).

Middleton, Thomas, *The Works*, ed. A. H. Bullen, 8 vols. (London: John C. Nimmo, 1886).

——*Your Five Gallants* (1608).

——and Rowley, William, *A Faire Quarrell* (1617).

Milles, Robert, *Abrahams Sute for Sodome* (1612).

Minsheu, John, *Minshaei emendatio ... sui Ductoris In Linguas* (1625).

Moryson, Fynes, *Shakespeare's Europe: Unpublished Chapters of Fynes Moryson's Itinerary*, ed. Charles Hughes (London: Sherratt and Hughes, 1903).

[Munday, Anthony], *A Second and Third Blast of a Retrait from Playes* (1580).

Munday, Anthony, *et al.*, *Sir Thomas More* (3.2), ed. Vittorio Gabrielli and Georgio Melchiori (Manchester: Manchester University Press, 2000).

Nabbes, Thomas, *The Unfortunate Mother* (1640).

Nashe, Thomas, *The Works*, ed. R. B. McKerrow, 2nd edn., rev. F. P. Wilson, 5 vols. (Oxford: Oxford University Press, 1958).

Niccols, Richard, *The Furies* (1614).

Nicholson, Samuel, *Acolastus* (1600).

Overbury, Thomas, *Sir Thomas Overburie, His Wife with New Elegies* (1616).

Peaps, William, *Love in it's [sic] Extasie* (1649).

Percy, William, *The Cuck-Queanes and Cuckolds Errants ...*, ed. J. Haslewood (1824).

Phillips, John, *Wit and Drollery* (1661).

Pickering, Roger, *Reflections upon Theatrical Expression in Tragedy* (1755).

*Processus Satanae*, in *Malone Society Collections: II. 3*, ed. W. W. Greg (Oxford: Malone Society, 1931).

Prynne, William, *Histrio-mastix* (1633).

Puttenham, George, *The Arte of English* (1589).

Quarles, Frances, *Argalus and Parthenia* (1629).

——*Hadassa or the History of Queene Ester* (1621).

Quarles, John, *Gods Love and Mans Unworthiness* (1651).

Raleigh, Sir Walter, *The History of the World* (1614).

——*The Poems: A Historical Edition*, ed. Michael Rudick (Tempe, Ariz.: Arizona Center for Medieval and Renaissance Studies, 1999).

Randolph, Thomas, *The Jealous Lovers* (1632).

——*Poems* (1652).

*Ratseis Ghost* (1605).

Rich, Barnaby, *Faultes Faults, and nothing else but Faultes* (1606).

Richards, Nathaniel, *Poems Sacred and Satyricale* (1641).

Rowley, William, *A Search for Money* (1609).

Ruggle, George, *Ignoramus Comoedia coram Regia Majestate Jacobi Regis Angliae* (1630).

Scolocker, Anthony, *Daiphantus* (1604).

Shakespeare, William, *Mr. William Shakespeares Comedies, Histories, and Tragedies* [*The Norton Facsimile*], ed. Charlton Hinman (New York: Norton, 1968).

Shakespeare, William, *Poems* (1640).

——*Shakespeare's Plays in Quarto: A Facsimile Edition of Copies Primarily from the Henry E. Huntington Library*, ed. Michael J. B. Allen and Kenneth Muir (Berkeley: University of California Press, 1981).

——*Shake-speares Sonnets* (1609).

——*The Tempest*, ed. David Lindley (Cambridge: Cambridge University Press, 2002).

Sheppard, Samuel, *Epigrams* (1651).

Shirley, James, *Hide Parke* (1637).

——*The Humorous Courtier*, ed. Marvin Morrillo (New York: Garland, 1979).

Stephens, John, *Essayes and Characters* (1615).

——*New Essays and Characters* (1631).

Stubbes, Philip, *Anatomie of Abuses* (1583).

Sylvester, Josuah, from *Du Bartas: His Divine Weekes and Workes Translated* (1621).

Tarlton, Richard, *Tarltons Jeasts* (1613).

Tatham, John, *The Fancies Theater* (1640).

Taylor, John, *All the Workes of John Taylor the Water-Poet* (1630).

Thomas, Thomas, *Dictionarium linguae Latinae et Anglicanae* (1587).

*The Three Parnassus Plays*, ed. J. B. Leishman (London: Ivor Nicholson and Watson Ltd., 1949).

Tofte, Robert, *Alba* (1598).

Tomkis, Thomas, *Lingua* (1607).

Torshell, Samuel, *The Womans Glorie* (1645).

W. S., *A Funerall Elegye* (1612).

R. M. [Warner?, Rob], *Micrologia Characters* (1629).

Warren, Arthur, *The Poore Mans Passions* (1605).

Wilkins, George, *Miseries of Inforst Marriage* (1607).

——*The Painfull Aduentures of Pericles Prince of Tyre*, ed. Kenneth Muir (Liverpool: University Press of Liverpool, 1953).

Wilkinson, Tate, *Memoirs of his Own Life*, 4 vols. (1790).

Willis, R., *Mount Tabor* (1639).

Wood, William B., *Personal Recollections of the Stage* (Philadelphia: Henry Carey Baird, 1855).

Woodes, Nathaniel, *The Conflict of Conscience* (1581).

### SECONDARY SOURCES

#### Parts

Aebischer, P., 'Un fragment de rôle comique datant du début du XIV$^e$ siècle retrouvé dans un manuscrit déposé aux Archives cantonales du Valais à Sion', *Vallesia*, 22 (1967), 71–80.

——'Fragments de Moralités, Farces, et Mystères retrouvés à Fribourg', *Romania*, 51 (1921), 511–27.

Aebischer, P., 'Trois Farces Françaises Inédites Trouvées à Fribourg', *Revue du 16e siecle*, 11 (1924), 129–92.

Barrow, Bernard, 'Macklin's Costume and Property Notes for the Character of Lovegold', *Theatre Notebook*, 13 (1958/9), 66–7.

Carnegie, David, 'Actors' Parts and the "Play of Poore"', *Harvard Library Bulletin*, 30 (1982), 5–24.

——'The Identification of the Hand of Thomas Goffe, Academic Dramatist and Actor', *The Library*, 26 (1971), 161–5.

Chocheyras, J., *Le Théâtre Religieux en Savoie au XVIe Siècle* (Geneva: Droz, 1971).

Golder, John, 'Rehearsals at the Comédie-Française in the Late Eighteenth Century', *British Journal for Eighteenth-Century Studies* (forthcoming).

Greg, W. W., *Dramatic Documents from the Elizabethan Playhouses*, 2 vols. (Oxford: Clarendon Press, 1931).

——(ed.), *Two Elizabethan Stage Abridgements: 'The Battle of Alcazar' and 'Orlando Furioso'* (Oxford: Malone Society, 1922).

Hall, Edith, *The Theatrical Cast of Athens* (Oxford: Oxford University Press, 2006).

Hawcroft, Michael, 'Comment jouait-on le rôle d'Hippolyte dans la Phèdre de Racine?: Témoignage d'un manuscrit inédit', *XVIIe Siècle*, 231 (2006), 243–76.

Kiernander, Adrian, '"Betwixt" and "Between": Variant Readings in the Folio and First Quarto Versions of *Richard III* and W. W. Greg's Concept of Memorial Reconstruction', in Lloyd Davis (ed.), *Shakespeare Matters* (Newark, NJ: University of Delaware Press, 2003).

Lalou, E. Elisabeth, 'Les Rolets de Théâtre: Étude Codicologique', in *Théâtre et Spectacles Hier et Aujourd'hui: Moyen Âge et Renaissance* (Paris: Editions du CTHS, 1991), 63–4.

Langhans, Edward A., 'A Restoration Actor's Part', *Harvard Library Bulletin*, 23 (1975), 180–5.

Lawrence, W. J. ['The Old Stager'], 'Lengths', *The Stage* (11 Feb. 1932), 44.

Linke, Hansjürgen, 'Versuch über deutsche Handschriften mittelalterlicher Spiele', in Volker Honemann and Nigel F. Palmer (eds.), *Deutsche Handschriften 1100–1400: Oxforder Kolloquium 1985* (Tübingen: Max Niemeyer Verlag, 1988).

Maxwell, J., 'La Farce de Thévot le Maire, Perruche et Colin', *Humanisme et Renaissance*, 6 (1939), 539–46.

McMillin, Scott, *The Elizabethan Theatre and the Book of Sir Thomas More* (Ithaca, NY: Cornell University Press, 1987).

——'The Sharer and his Boy: Rehearsing Shakespeare's Women', in Peter Holland and Stephen Orgel (eds.), *From Script to Stage in Early Modern England* (Basingstoke, London, and New York: Palgrave Macmillan, 2004).

Robbins, R. H., 'A Dramatic Fragment from a Caesar Augustus Play', *Anglia*, 72 (1954), 31–4.

Runnalls, Graham A., 'An Actor's Role in a French Morality Play', *French Studies*, 42 (1988), 398–407.

——'Le Livre de Raison de Jacques Le Gros et le Mystère de la Passion joué à Paris en 1539', *Romania*, 118 (2000), 138–93.

——'The Medieval Actors' Roles Found in the Fribourg Archive', *Pluteus*, 4/5 (1986/7, pub. 1990), 5–67.

——'Rôles for the Passion Play performed in Paris in 1539 by the Confrérie de la Passion', in 'Le Livre de Raison de Jacques Le Gros et le Mystère de la Passion joué à Paris en 1539', *Romania*, 118 (2000), 138–93.

——'Towards a Typology of Medieval French Play Manuscripts', in P. E. Bennett and G. A. Runnalls (eds.), *The Editor and the Text* (Edinburgh: Edinburgh University Press, 1990).

Shay, Robert, and Thompson, Robert, *Purcell Manuscripts: The Principal Musical Sources* (Cambridge: Cambridge University Press, 2000).

Stern, Tiffany, 'The Part for Greene's *Orlando Furioso*: A Source for the "Mock Trial" in Shakespeare's *Lear*?', *Notes and Queries*, 247 (2002), 229–31.

——*Rehearsal from Shakespeare to Sheridan* (Oxford: Clarendon Press, 2000).

——'Re-patching the Play', in Peter Holland and Stephen Orgel (eds.), *From Script to Stage in Early Modern England* (Basingstoke, London, and New York: Palgrave MacMillan, 2004).

Tribble, Evelyn B., 'Distributing Cognition in the Globe', *Shakespeare Quarterly*, 56 (2005), 135–55.

Tucker, Edward F. J., 'The Harvard Manuscript of Parkhurst's *Ignoramus*', *Harvard Library Bulletin*, 19 (1971), 5–24.

Tucker, Patrick, *Secrets of Acting Shakespeare* (London and New York: Routledge, 2001).

Warren, Michael, 'Greene's *Orlando*: W. W. Greg Furioso', in Laurie E. Maguire and Thomas L. Berger (eds.), *Textual Formations and Reformations* (Newark, NJ: University of Delaware Press, 1998).

Weingust, Don, *Acting from Shakespeare's First Folio: Theory, Text and Performance* (London and New York: Routledge, 2006).

Wilder, Lina Perkins, 'Toward a Shakespearean "Memory Theater": Romeo, the Apothecary, and the Performance of Memory', *Shakespeare Quarterly*, 56 (2005), 156–75.

## Actors and Staging

Baldwin, T. W., *The Organisation and Personnel of the Shakespearean Company* (Princeton: Princeton University Press, 1927).

Barton, John, *Playing Shakespeare: An Actor's Guide* (London: Methuen, 1984).

Bawcutt, N. W., *The Control and Censorship of Caroline Drama* (Oxford: Clarendon Press, 1996).

Beckerman, Bernard, *Shakespeare at the Globe, 1599–1609* (New York: Macmillan, 1962).

Bentley, G. E., *The Profession of Dramatist in Shakespeare's Time, 1590–1642* (Princeton: Princeton University Press, 1971).

——*The Profession of Player in Shakespeare's Time, 1590–1642* (Princeton: Princeton University Press, 1971).

Berry, Cicely, *The Actor and the Text* (London: Virgin Books, 2000).

Bevington, David, *Action is Eloquence: Shakespeare's Language of Gesture* (Cambridge, Mass.: Harvard University Press, 1984).

Booth, Stephen, 'Speculations on Doubling in Shakespeare's Plays', in Philip C. McGuire and David A. Samuelson (eds.), *Shakespeare: The Theatrical Dimension* (New York: AMS Press, 1979).

Bradbrook, M. C., *The Rise of the Common Player* (London: Chatto & Windus 1962).

Bradley, David, *From Text to Performance in the Elizabethan Theatre: Preparing the Play for the Stage* (Cambridge: Cambridge University Press, 1992).

Chambers, E. K., *The Elizabethan Stage*, 4 vols. (Oxford: Clarendon Press, 1923).

Cohen, Robert, *Acting in Shakespeare*, 2nd edn. (Hanover, NH: Smith and Kraus, 2005).

Dessen, Alan C., *Elizabethan Stage Conventions and Modern Interpretations* (Cambridge: Cambridge University Press, 1984).

——*Recovering Shakespeare's Theatrical Vocabulary* (Cambridge: Cambridge University Press, 1995).

Dolman, John, *The Art of Acting* (New York: Harper and Brothers, 1949).

Donnellan, Declan, *The Actor and the Target* (London: Theatre Communications Group, 2002).

Doring, Tobias, 'Writing Performance: How to Elegize Elizabethan Actors', *Shakespeare Survey*, 58 (2005), 66–71.

Eccles, Mark, 'Elizabethan Actor IV', *Notes and Queries*, 238 (1993), 165–76.

Fisher, Will, 'The Renaissance Beard: Masculinity in Early Modern England', *Renaissance Quarterly*, 54 (2001), 155–87.

Foakes, R. A., 'The Player's Passion: Some Notes of Elizabethan Psychology and Acting', *Essays and Studies*, NS 7 (1954), 62–77.

Gaw, A., 'John Sincklo as One of Shakespeare's Actors', *Anglia*, 49 (1926), 289–303.

Godfrey, Philip, *Back-Stage* (London: G. G. Harrap and Co., 1933).

Grote, David, *The Best Actors in the World: Shakespeare and his Acting Company* (Westport, Conn., and London: Greenwood Press, 2002).

Gurr, Andrew, *The Shakespearean Stage, 1574–1642*, 3rd edn. (Cambridge: Cambridge University Press, 1992).

——*The Shakespeare Company, 1594–1642* (Cambridge: Cambridge University Press, 2004).

Hattaway, Michael, *Elizabethan Popular Theatre* (London: Routledge & Kegan Paul, 1982).

Hodgdon, Barbara, and Worthen, W. B. (eds.), *A Companion to Shakespeare and Performance* (Oxford: Blackwell, 2005).

Holland, Peter, and Orgel, Stephen (eds.), *From Script to Stage in Early Modern England* (Basingstoke, London, and New York: Palgrave Macmillan, 2004).

Howard, Jean E., *Shakespeare's Art of Orchestration: Stage Technique and Audience Response* (Urbana: University of Illinois Press, 1984).

Howard, Skiles, 'A Reconsideration of Baldwin's Theory of Acting Lines', *Theatre Studies*, 26 (1985), 1–20.

Ichikawa, Mariko, *Shakespearean Entrances* (Basingstoke and New York: Palgrave, 2002).

Joseph, Bertram, *Elizabethan Acting* (London: Oxford University Press, 1951); rev. edn. (London: Oxford University Press, 1964).

Kawai, Shoichiro, 'Fat, Lean, Short, and Tall: Physical Characteristics of Dramatic Characters and Actors in the Age of Shakespeare' (unpublished Ph.D. thesis, University of Cambridge, 1999).

King, T. J., *Casting Shakespeare's Plays* (Cambridge: Cambridge University Press, 1992).

Kinney, Arthur F., *Shakespeare by Stages: An Historical Introduction* (Oxford: Blackwell, 2003).

Lindley, David, *Shakespeare and Music* (London: Arden, 2006).

Meagher, John C., 'Economy and Recognition: Thirteen Shakespearean Puzzles', *Shakespeare Quarterly*, 35 (1984), 7–22.

Menzer, Paul (ed.), *Inside Shakespeare: Essays on the Blackfriars Stage* (Selinsgrove, Pa.: Susquehanna University Press, 2006).

Nagler, A. M., *Sources of Theatrical History* (New York: Theatre Annual, Inc., 1952).

Nungezer, Edwin, *A Dictionary of Actors* (New Haven: Yale University Press, 1929).

Orgel, Stephen, *The Authentic Shakespeare, and Other Problems of the Early Modern Stage* (New York: Routledge, 2002).

Pasternak-Slater, Ann, *Shakespeare the Director* (Brighton: Harvester, 1982).

Roach, Joseph R., *The Player's Passion: Studies in the Science of Acting* (Newark, NJ: University of Delaware Press, 1985).

Stern, Tiffany, 'Behind the Arras: The Prompter's Place in the Shakespearean Theatre', *Theatre Notebook*, 55 (2001), 110–18.

——*Making Shakespeare* (London and New York: Routledge, 2004).

——'Watching as Reading: The Audience and Written Text in the Early Modern Playhouse', in Laurie Maguire (ed.), *How To Do Things with Shakespeare* (Oxford: Blackwell, 2007).

Thomson, Peter, *Shakespeare's Professional Career* (Cambridge: Cambridge University Press, 1992).

Wiggins, Martin, *Shakespeare and the Drama of his Time* (Oxford: Oxford University Press, 2000).

Worthen, W. B., *The Idea of the Actor* (Princeton: Princeton University Press, 1984).

——*Shakespeare and the Authority of Performance* (Cambridge: Cambridge University Press, 1997).

## Text

Blayney, Peter W. M., *The First Folio of Shakespeare* (Washington: Folger Shake-speare Library, 1991).

Bowers, Fredson, 'The Copy for Shakespeare's Julius Caesar', *South Atlantic Bulletin*, 43 (1978), 29–31.

Brooks, Douglas A., *From Playhouse to Printing House: Drama and Authorship in Early Modern England* (Cambridge: Cambridge University Press, 2000).

Clayton, Thomas (ed.), *The Hamlet First Published (Q1, 1603): Origins, Form, Intertextualities* (Newark, NJ: University of Delaware Press, 1992).

Cox, John D., and Kastan, David Scott (eds.), *A New History of Early English Drama* (New York: Columbia University Press, 1997).

Erne, Lukas, *Shakespeare as Literary Dramatist* (Cambridge: Cambridge University Press, 2003).

——and Kidnie, M. J. (eds.), *Textual Performances: The Modern Reproduction of Shakespeare's Drama* (Cambridge: Cambridge University Press, 2003).

Flatter, Richard, *Shakespeare's Producing Hand* (London: William Heinemann Ltd., 1948).

Gurr, Andrew, 'Maximal and Minimal Texts: Shakespeare versus the Globe', *Shakespeare Survey*, 52 (1999), 68–87.

Holland, Peter, and Orgel, Stephen, *From Performance to Print in Shakespeare's England* (Basingstoke: Palgrave, 2006).

Honigmann, E. A. J., *The Stability of Shakespeare's Texts* (Lincoln: University of Nebraska Press, 1965).

Ioppolo, Grace, *Dramatists and their Manuscripts in the Age of Shakespeare, Jonson, Middleton and Heywood: Authorship, Authority and the Playhouse* (London and New York: Routledge, 2006).

——*Revising Shakespeare* (Cambridge, Mass.: Harvard University Press, 1991).

Jones, John, *Shakespeare at Work* (Oxford: Clarendon Press, 1995).

Kastan, David Scott, *Shakespeare and the Book* (Cambridge: Cambridge University Press, 2001).

Kirsch, Arthur C., 'Caroline Commentary on the Drama', *Modern Philology*, 66 (1969), 256–61.

Langhans, Edward A., *Eighteenth-Century British and Irish Promptbooks: A Descriptive Bibliography* (Westport, Conn.: Greenwood Press, 1987).

——*Restoration Promptbooks* (Carbondale and Edwardsville: Southern Illinois University Press, 1981).

McLeod, Randall (ed.), *Crisis of Editing: Texts of the English Renaissance* (New York: AMS Press, Inc., 1993).

Orgel, Stephen, and Keilen, Sean (eds.), *Shakespeare and the Editorial Tradition* (New York and London: Garland Publishing, 1999).

Pollard, A. W., and Redgrave, G. R., *A Short-Title Catalogue of Books Printed in England, Scotland, & Ireland and of English Books Printed Abroad 1475–1640*, 2nd edn., revised and enlarged by W. A. Jackson, F. S. Ferguson, and Katharine F. Pantzer, 3 vols. (London: Bibliographical Society, 1986–91).

Taylor, Gary, and Warren, Michael (eds.), *The Division of the Kingdoms: Shakespeare's Two Versions of 'King Lear'* (Oxford: Clarendon Press, 1983).

Thompson, Ann, and McMullan, Gordon (eds.), *In Arden: Editing Shakespeare* (London: Thomson, 2003).

Wells, Stanley, and Taylor, Gary, with John Jowett and William Montgomery, *William Shakespeare: A Textual Companion* (Oxford: Oxford University Press, 1987).

Werstine, Paul, 'Editing after the End of Editing', *Shakespeare Studies*, 24 (1996), 47–54.

## Language, Prosody, and Rhetoric

Adamson, Sylvia, Hunter, Lynette, Magnusson, Lynne, Thompson, Ann, Wales, Katie (eds.), *Reading Shakespeare's Dramatic Language—Arden Shakespeare: A Guide* (London: Arden, 2000).

Attridge, Derek, *Well-Weighed Syllables: Elizabethan Verse in Classical Metres* (Cambridge: Cambridge University Press, 1974).

Davis, Philip, *Shakespeare Thinking* (London and New York: Continuum, 2007).

de Grazia, Margreta, 'Shakespeare and the Craft of Language', in Margreta de Grazia and Stanley Wells (eds.), *The Cambridge Companion to Shakespeare* (Cambridge: Cambridge University Press, 2001), 49–64.

Hardison, O. B. jun., *Prosody and Purpose in the English Renaissance* (Baltimore: Johns Hopkins University Press, 1989).

Hollander, John, *Vision and Resonance* (Oxford: Oxford University Press, 1975).

Hope, Jonathan, *Shakespeare's Grammar* (London: Arden, 2003).

Joseph, Sister Miriam, *Rhetoric in Shakespeare's Time* (New York: Harcourt, Brace and World, 1962).

Kastan, David Scott (ed.), *A Companion to Shakespeare*, Blackwell Companions to Literature and Culture (Oxford: Blackwell, 1999).

Kermode, Frank, *Shakespeare's Language* (London: Penguin, 2000).

Mack, Peter (ed.), *Renaissance Rhetoric* (London: St Martin's Press, 1984).

——(ed.), *Elizabethan Rhetoric: Theory and Practice* (Cambridge: Cambridge: Cambridge University Press, 2002).

McDonald, Russ, *Shakespeare and the Arts of Language* (Oxford: Oxford University Press, 2001).

——*Shakespeare's Late Style* (Cambridge: Cambridge University Press, 2006).

Murphy, James J., *Renaissance Eloquence: Studies in the Theory and Practice of Renaissance Rhetoric* (Berkeley and London: University of California Press, 1983).

Ong, Walter J., 'Tudor Writings on Rhetoric', *Studies in the Renaissance*, 15 (1968), 39–69.

Orgel, Stephen, *The Authentic Shakespeare, and Other Problems of the Early Modern Stage* (New York: Routledge, 2002).

Palfrey, Simon, *Doing Shakespeare* (London: Arden Shakespeare, 2005).

——*Late Shakespeare: A New World of Words* (Oxford: Clarendon Press, 1997).

Parker, Patricia, *Shakespeare from the Margins: Language, Culture, Context* (Chicago: University of Chicago Press, 1996).

Platt, Peter G., 'Shakespeare and Rhetorical Culture', in David Scott Kastan (ed.), *A Companion to Shakespeare* (1999), 277–96.

Poole, William, 'Unpointed Words: Shakespearean Syntax in Action', *Cambridge Quarterly*, 32 (2003), 27–48.

Prynne, J. H., 'English Poetry and Emphatical Language', *Proceedings of the British Academy*, 74 (1988), 135–69.

Rhodes, Neil, *Shakespeare and the Uses of English* (Oxford: Oxford University Press, 2004).

Smith, Bruce R., *The Acoustic World of Early Modern England* (Chicago and London: University of Chicago Press, 1999).

Thorne, Alison, *Vision and Rhetoric in Shakespeare: Looking Through Language* (New York: St Martin's Press, 2000).

Trousdale, Marion, *Shakespeare and the Rhetoricians* (Chapel Hill: University of North Carolina Press, 1982).

Vickers, Brian, *The Artistry of Shakespeare's Prose* (London: Methuen, 1968).

——*In Defence of Rhetoric* (Oxford: Oxford University Press, 1988).

——'Rhetoric and Poetics', in Charles B. Schmitt (ed.), *The Cambridge History of Renaissance Philosophy* (Cambridge: Cambridge University Press, 1988).

Weimann, Robert, *Author's Pen and Actor's Voice* (Cambridge: Cambridge University Press, 2000).

Wright, George T., *Shakespeare's Metrical Art* (Berkeley: University of California Press, 1991).

# Index of Shakespearean Parts by Character

For non-shakespearean parts see 'parts: non-shakespearean (by name) in main index'.

Adrian (*Tempest*) 294
Albany (*Lear*) 262–3
Alonso (*Tempest*) 280, 304, 305
Antonio (*Merchant*) 193, 197–9, 200–2,
    203, 205, 208, 211, 460–1
Antonio (*Tempest*) 276, 294–5, 305
Anthony (*Anthony and
    Cleopatra*) 266–70, 489
Ariel (*Tempest*) 279, 282, 284–8, 289,
    290–2, 295, 298, 300, 301, 304, 305
Ajax (*Troilus*) 225
Autolycus (*Winter's Tale*) 121

Banquo (*Macbeth*) 135, 469, 473
Bassanio (*Merchant*) 195–6, 197, 206–7,
    401, 402–4, 407, 408, 459–60
Beatrice (*Much Ado*) 332, 333–4, 340
Benedict (*Much Ado*) 333–4, 499
Benvolio (*Romeo and Juliet*) 186–7, 188,
    454, 510
Bertram (*All's Well*) 136–42, 424,
    430–1, 433–4
Bianca (*Othello*) 227–8, 229
Bottom (*Dream*) 157, 512
Brabantio (*Othello*) 347–8
Brutus (*Caesar*) 166–7, 170, 219, 336–7
Buckingham (*Richard III*) 363, 365, 367

Caliban (*Tempest*) 279, 281, 283, 288–9,
    290, 293, 295, 296–305
Canterbury (*Henry V*) 122
Capulet (*Romeo and Juliet*) 215–17,
    353–4, 456–7, 459
Cassio (*Othello*) 228, 229, 236

Celia (*As You Like It*) 135, 414
Charmian (*Anthony and
    Cleopatra*) 268–9
Chorus (*Henry V*) 356
Citizens (*Richard III*) 365
Cleopatra (*Anthony and
    Cleopatra*) 266–70
Cloten (*Cymbeline*) 271, 272
Clarence (*Richard III*) 356, 359
Claudius (*Hamlet*) 114, 220–3, 337
Cordelia (*Lear*) 108, 218, 258–61, 262
Coriolanus (*Coriolanus*) 98, 344–6, 489
Cornwall (*Lear*) 245–6, 351
Countess (*All's Well*) 426
Cressida (*Troilus*) 226

Diomedes (*Troilus*) 225
Doctor (*Macbeth*) 237–8, 482
Dogberry (*Much Ado*) 122
Dromio (*Comedy of Errors*) 510
Duchess (*Richard III*) 381
Duncan (*Macbeth*) 277, 510

Edgar (*Lear*) 96–7, 150–2, 240, 241,
    244, 247–55, 262, 264–5
Edmund (*Lear*) 96–7, 240–4, 246
Emilia (*Othello*) 233–5
Eros (*Anthony and Cleopatra*) 266,
    268–9, 270

Falstaff (*1 & 2 Henry IV*) 32, 124–5,
    498, 511, 514
Ferdinand (*Tempest*) 279, 282–3, 284,
    290–2, 295, 297, 300, 305

Feste (*Twelfth Night*) 179–80
Fool (*Lear*) 247–8, 249, 250, 253

Gentlemen (*Lear*) 256–7, 261
Gentlewoman (*Macbeth*) 238–9
Gertrude (*Hamlet*) 114, 221–2, 337, 385
Ghost (*Hamlet*) 115, 337, 383–5, 386
Gloucester (*Lear*) 108, 150–2, 240–7,
    248, 250–5, 263, 338–9, 348, 351
Gobbo (*Merchant*) 335, 338
Goneril (*Lear*) 108
Gratiano (*Merchant*) 209–10, 211, 212
Grumio (*Shrew*) 175–6, 177

Hamlet (*Hamlet*) 7, 96, 97, 114–15, 116,
    121, 171, 222–4, 263, 337, 343–4,
    383–6, 464, 499, 510
Hal (*1 Henry IV*) 100, 124
Hastings (*Richard III*) 360
Hector (*Troilus*) 225–6, 227
Helen (*Troilus*) 226
Helena (*All's Well*) 140, 141, 422–34,
    439
Henry V (*Henry V*) 499
Hero (*Much Ado*) 333
Horatio (*Hamlet*) 114, 223, 224, 337,
    385–6, 387
Hotspur (*1 Henry IV*) 99–101, 124

Iago (*Othello*) 229–30, 235
Imogen (*Cymbeline*) 271–4
Isabella (*Measure*) 434–52, 516

Jacques (*As You Like It*) 499
Jessica (*Merchant*) 193–4, 205, 334–6,
    337–8
Julia (*Two Gentlemen*) 174–5
Juliet (*Romeo and Juliet*) 148–50,
    158–62, 342

Kent (*Lear*) 253, 254, 260, 262, 264, 265
King (*All's Well*) 138, 141, 426–30
King John (*King John*) 35–6, 499

Lady Anne (*Richard III*) 360–1
Lady Capulet (*Romeo and Juliet*) 103–5,
    107, 113, 146, 148–9, 158–62, 187,
    189, 214–17, 228, 341–2, 354, 356,
    358, 382–3

Lady Macbeth (*Macbeth*) 218, 237–9,
    332, 333, 468, 469, 479–80, 484,
    499
Lady Percy (*2 Henry IV*) 355
Laertes (*Hamlet*) 116, 223, 337
Lear (*King Lear*) 108–10, 247, 248, 249,
    252, 253–4, 255–65, 332, 333,
    338–9, 464, 499
Lord Bardolph (*2 Henry IV*) 356
Lord Chief Justice (*2 Henry IV*) 122
Lorenzo (*Merchant*) 334–6
Lucius (*Cymbeline*) 272

Macbeth (*Macbeth*) 36, 97–8, 127, 133,
    134, 135, 144–5, 297, 464–94, 499
Macduff (*Macbeth*) 125–34, 469, 480
Malcolm (*Macbeth*) 127–8, 130–1, 133
Malvolio (*Twelfth Night*) 111–12, 113,
    114, 177–83, 184
Mardian (*Anthony and Cleopatra*) 270
Margaret (*Much Ado*) 333
Mark Antony (*Julius Caesar*) 167–71,
    219
Master (*Tempest*) 276, 277
Mercutio (*Romeo and Juliet*) 105–7, 113,
    186–91, 212–13, 224, 453–6,
    510–11
Miranda (*Tempest*) 279–84, 285, 288,
    289, 293, 295, 305, 307
Morocco (*Merchant*) 395, 396, 397, 400,
    404
Mowbray (*Richard II*) 340
Murderers (*Macbeth*) 475

Nerrissa (*Merchant*) 394, 408
Northumberland (*Richard II*) 377
Nurse (*Romeo and Juliet*) 103–5,
    158–62, 186, 187, 188, 189, 214

Olivia (*Twelfth Night*) 178, 180–1, 182,
    183, 332, 415–22, 432
Ophelia (*Hamlet*) 114, 116, 118, 218,
    219–21, 337, 387, 511
Orsino (*Twelfth Night*) 276
Othello (*Othello*) 107–8, 228–37, 332,
    333, 464

Pandarus (*Troilus*) 226
Paris (*Troilus*) 226

Parolles (*Alls Well*) 102–3
Peaseblossom (*Dream*) 34–5
Peter Quince (*Dream*) 157, 512
Petruchio (*Shrew*) 176–7
Pisanio (*Cymbeline*) 271–2
Polonius (*Hamlet*) 114, 115–18, 337,
    387–8
Portia (*Merchant*) 208, 210, 211–12, 333,
    335, 392–408, 409, 410, 432, 439,
    511
Posthumus (*Cymbeline*) 272, 273
Prince (*Romeo and Juliet*) 349–50
Prospero (*Tempest*) 276, 279–81, 282,
    283, 284, 285–8, 289, 290, 292,
    297, 304, 305
Proteus (*Two Gentlemen*) 101, 174–5

Regan (*Lear*) 108, 242, 243, 245–6, 351
Richard II (*Richard II*) 340, 358, 371–9,
    381
Richard III (*Richard III*) 122–3, 184–6,
    358–71, 378, 381, 499
Richmond (*Richard III*) 368
Romeo (*Romeo and Juliet*) 101–2,
    106–7, 112–13, 146–8, 149,
    186–8, 189, 190–1, 341–2, 354,
    356–8, 382–3, 453, 455
Rosalind (*Twelfth Night*) 333, 408–14,
    415, 417, 420, 432, 439

Rosse (*Macbeth*) 387
Rumour (*2 Henry IV*) 356

Salarino (*Merchant*) 194, 204
Sebastian (*Tempest*) 294–5
Shallow (*2 Henry IV*) 99, 511
Shylock (*Merchant*) 32, 37–8, 186,
    192–213, 245, 304, 456–63, 498,
    499
Silvia (*Two Gentlemen*) 173–4, 175
Silvius (*As You Like It*) 412
Solario (*Merchant*) 194, 200, 202–3,
    204
Speed (*Two Gentlemen*) 172–4
Stephano (*Tempest*) 298–301, 302–4

Thersites (*Troilus*) 226
Toby Belch (*Twelfth Night*) 177
Trinculo (*Tempest*) 296, 298–301,
    302–4
Troilus (*Troilus*) 225–6, 227
Tubal (*Merchant*) 204, 205–6

Valentine (*Two Gentlemen*) 173–4,
    175
Viola (*Twelfth Night*) 415, 416–17,
    419–21

Witches (*Macbeth*) 144–5, 276

# General Index

Plays are indexed under the names of their authors (when known). Shakespeare's characters are indexed separately under 'Index of Shakespearean Parts by Character'.

Abbot, John 503
act-breaks 54
action 1, 11, 65–9, 73–5, 96, 121–5, 134–6, 145–6, 169–70, ch. 15 *passim*, 312–13, 317–18, 320–1, 324–7, 342–3, 346–7, 349–51, 446, 449–52, 515
actors: and absence from stage 126–9, 132–3, 139; and audience 98, 105, 124, 131, 146, 173, 175, 178, 180, 192, 196, 197–8, 203, 208, 213, 226–7, 233, 246, 260, 289, 293, 297, 307, 356, 360, 378, 381, 383, 396, 444–5, 461–3, 478, 483; and decision making 124–5, 131, 135, 145–6, 149, 151, 160, ch. 8 *passim*, 184, 200, 203, 217, 232–3, 253, 254–5, 278–9, 292–3, 306–7, ch. 20 *passim*; and extemporisation 64, 124–5, 131, 160–2, 172–7, 185, 187–8, 189, 217, 227, 257, 442–3, 446–52; and ownership of part 92–3, 120–1, 125–34, 142, 181, 182–3, 232–3, 278–304, ch. 20 *passim*; and uncertainty 140–1, 148, 149, 252–5, 297, 397, 459, 462, 471, 480–8, 489, 490; core-group of 4–6, 11; their apperception 255, 293, 389
*Actors' Remonstrance* 506, 514
Admiral's Men 21, 76
Adams, Thomas 86, 509
Aebischer, Paul 17, 496, 497
Allen, Michael J. B. 511
Alleyn, Edward 20–2, 45, 49, 50–1, 58, 311, 328, 359, 503

Anton, M. Robert 515
*Antoninus Bassianus Caracalla* 24
Appleton, William W. 507
Armin, Robert 54, 503
Armstrong, Archie 508
Ashmole fragment 16, 18
Attridge, Derek 516
audience 45, 49, 52, 53, 54, 69, 74–7, 86, 89, 98, 111, 113, 124, 131, 144, 146, 146, 173, 175, 178, 180, 192, 196, 197–8, 203, 208, 213, 226–7, 233, 246, 260, 289, 293, 297, 307, 312, 316–17, 320–1, 325–6, 333, 337, 340, 351, 356, 360, 378, 381, 383, 396, 444–5, 461–3, 478, 483 508, 511, 513
Axen, Robert 54
Aylet, Robert 501

Babington, Gervase 326, 516
backstage plot 72, 73, 74, 86–7, 503, 507
Baker, Richard 42, 499, 515
Baldwin, T. W. 500
Bancroft, Thomas 312, 513
Barrow, Bernard 498
Barton, John 516
Bawcutt, N. W. 497, 498, 505
Beaumont, Francis 7; *Inner Temple Masque* 7 *see also* Fletcher
Benlowes, Edward 507, 514
Berger, Thomas L. 497
Berry, Cicily 516
Betterton, Thomas 69, 75, 506–7
Blackfriars Playhouse 321, 506
blocking 18, 22, 72–3

Blount, Thomas 71, 507
Boaden, James 32, 498, 508
Boleyn, Anne 517
book-holder, book-keeper *see*
    prompter
Booth, Stephen 503
Bowers, Fredson 500, 508
boy players 18, 42, 46, 62, 64, 66–8, 71,
    72, 73, 84–5, 313, 326
Boys, John 499
Bradley, David 509
Brathwaite, Richard 499, 501, 508, 513
Breton, Nicholas 63, 505
Brome, Richard *Antipodes* 74, 75, 507;
    *Sparagus Garden* 84, 508
Brownsmith, John 498
Bull Playhouse 51, 321
Bulwer, John 515
Burnim, Kalman A. 507
Burbage, Richard 20, 45, 48, 49, 67, 69,
    87–8, 137, 218, 311–12, 313, 320,
    359, 464, 487, 501, 502, 514
Burton, Robert 504; *Philosophaster* 24
Busino, Horatio 326, 516
Butler, Charles 83, 508
Butler, Henry 325, 515

Cailleau, Hubert 496
Capell, Edward 143
Carlell, Lodowick 71, 508
Carnegie, David 25, 28–9, 497, 498
Cartwright, William 42, 499; *Lady
    Errant* 503
Carlell, Lodowick *Fool Would be a
    Favourite* 85
casting 40–4, 60, 71, 501
Cawdry, Robert 500, 501
Chamberlain, John 314, 513
Chamberlain, Richard 515
Chapman, George 514; *An Humorous
    Day's Mirth* 314; *Bussy
    D'Ambois* 502; *Gentleman
    Usher* 66–7, 71, 72, 506, 507
*Character or Ear-mark of Mr William
    Prynne* 501
Charke, Charlotte 502
Chettle, Henry 326, 516
Christ Church, Oxford 24
Chocheyras, J. 497

Cibber, Colley 502; *A Woman's Wit* 49
Clark, Hugh 54
Clavell, John *So[l]dered Citizen* 84, 508
Cleveland, John 53, 503
clowns 43, 50, 51–6, 64, 89, 103, 106,
    122, 164, 171–7, 227, 299, 321,
    322, 335, 338, 510, 517
Cockpit Playhouse 29, 321
Cohen, Robert 516
coining words 321–4
Cokain, Aston 513
Coleman, John 510
Collop, John 504
commonplace books 316, 502, 504, 506,
    519
compositor 464
Confrérie de la Passion 19
con *see* study
Cornwallis, William 323, 515
Coryate, Thomas 504
couplets 340, 353, 372, 398, 402, 405,
    476–86; ambiguity of 480–8; and
    blank verse 480–1, 484; and
    change of passions 328, 340, 394,
    420, 426, 430, 432–3; and equivocal
    rhythms 480–2; and harmony 403;
    and monologue to dialogue 340,
    426–30, 479–80; and poetry 330;
    and self-address 343, 344–6, 394,
    398, 399, 402–3, 420–1, 423,
    424–34, 476, 477; as action
    prompts 342, 405, 433; as bridge
    between prose and verse 393–4,
    398–9, 402; as cue 341–3, 427–9,
    433–4; between private and
    public 421, 433, 479–83; in
    soliloquy 340, 423, 476, 477–8,
    479; possessed by actor 402–3; *see
    also* pentameter, rhyme
court performance 55
Cowper, William 504
Crashaw, William 506
Creizenach, W. 506
Crosse, Henry 323, 514, 515
cues: actor's expectation of ch. 7 *passim*,
    298–303, 397, 402, 414, 449; and
    apposition to play-text 91, 94,
    100–1, 103–10, 113–19, 125–34;
    and rhyme 342; and rhythmic
    shifts 142, 145–6, 149–50, 151,

cues: actor's expectation of ch. 7 (*cont.*)
182; and short lines 142–53,
347–9, 375 118–19, 120–1, 123,
134–5, 142, 149–50, 181–2,
451–2, 492 *see also* midline shifts,
short speech-units; annotating role
of 91–4, 253, 345, 360–1, 373,
397, 399, 402, 403, 409, 412, 427,
431, 467, 468–9, 478; appearance
of 91, 94; as mini-narratives 91,
254; attribution of 92–3; chains
of 91, 101–3, 129, 136, 141,
187–8, 209, 441, 465, 468;
enunciation of 145–6; of
entrance 97–101, 103, 110, 174–5,
186–7, 225, 255–7, 267–70,
272–3, 276–93, 296–305, 441 *see
also* entrances; of exit 31, 54, 72
86–8, 99, 174–5, 237–8, 242,
252–5, 256, 257–8, 269–71, 303,
421, 473, 509 *see also* exits; false or
secreted 182–3, 211–12, 213, 222,
243–4, 246, 250, 261, 263, 349,
439–43, 445–7, 448–52 *see also*
repeated cues; for action 123–5,
128–9, 130–1, 135, 449–52; first
and early (inaugurating) 97–110,
112, 279–93; length of 18, 21,
24–5, 29, 35, 38, 83, 89–90, 95, 99,
159, 195; 'owned' by more than
one speaker 93–4, 163, 231–7,
306; 'tail' of 21, 30, 83–4, 87–8,
91, 151, and *passim*; transitional
110–13, 136, 179, 242, 252, 296–8
*see also* cue-space, couplets:
co-operating with cues, repeated
cues
cue-space 100, 101, 146, 147–8, 152,
162, 169–71, ch. 11 *passim*, 206,
208, 211, 233, 236–7, ch. 13 *passim*,
ch. 15 *passim*, 446 *see also* cues
cued parts, cued scripts *see* parts
Curtain Playhouse 48, 327

Daborne, Robert 58, 60, 94, 505, 509
Daniel, George 513
Daniel, Samuel 514
Davenant, William 316, 506–7, 514
Davenport, A. 514

Davies, John 325, 501, 515, 516
Davidge, William 502
David, Lloyd 505
Davis, Norman 496
Dawe, Jack 509, 515
Dawes, Robert 70
Dawson, Giles E. 505
Day, John *Travails of Three English
Brothers* 64, 506
Dekker, Thomas 7, 46, 48, 57, 63, 86,
501, 504, 505, 506, 507, 509 *Noble
Spanish Soldier* 84, 508
Demosthenes 324
Dennis, John 49, 502
Digges, Leonard 321, 514
director 42, 496
distribution of parts *see* parts: distribution
of
Dolman, John 38, 499
Donnellan, Declan 510, 516
Doring, Tobias 511
doubling 50–6, 500, 503, 528
Downes, John 61, 505, 506–7
Dowton, William 32
Drayton, Michael 514
Duke's Company 29
Dulwich College 20, 497

Earle, John 501, 515
Eccles, Mark 500
Elizabeth I 84
emphasis *see* pronunciation
entrances 30–1, 33, 43, 72, 74, 76,
86–7, 89–90, 97–101, 103, 110,
125, 135, 174–5, 186–7, 225,
255–7, 267–70, 272–3, 276–93,
296–305, 441, 509, 511, 512, *see also*
exits; cues: of exit; cues: of entrance
Epictetes 42, 499
Erne, Lukas 502
Evans, G. Blakemore 498, 499
exits 31, 54, 72 86–8, 99, 509 *see also*
cues: of exit; cues: of entrance;
entrances
extemporisation *see* actors: and
extemporisation

Fane, Mildmay 500
*Farce of Théval* 19

Farquhar, George, *Beaux Stratagem* 33
Featley, Daniel 500
Field, Nathan 502
Fielding, Henry *The Miser* 33−4
Fisher, Will 503
Flatman, Thomas 514
Flecknoe, Richard 322, 500, 501, 513, 514
Fletcher, John 7, 42, 316; *Maid in the Mill* 63−4, 71, 505, 507 see also Beaumont
Florio, John 73, 507
Foakes, R. A. 505
fools *see* clowns
Ford, John 513
Fortune Playhouse 323, 515
Fouquet, Jean 16, 496
Fribourg archive 17−18
Fuller, Thomas 55, 501, 504, 508, 509

Gabrielli, Vittorio 503
Gainsford, T. 42, 499, 514
Galloway, David 503
Garrick, David 32, 34, 35, 36, 69, 312, 498, 499
Gataker, Thomas 319, 514
Gaule, John 503
Gayton, Edmund 71, 317, 323, 501, 507, 514, 515
Gaw, A. 500
Gee, John 71, 506, 507, 514
gesture *see* action
Gildon, Charles 508
Globe Playhouse 40−1, 90, 321
Godfrey, Philip 38, 499
Goffe, Thomas 61; *Courageous Turk* 24−7, 318, 498
Gomersall, Robert 499
Gosson, Stephen 1, 495, 501, 505, 513, 515
grammar books 329−30
Green, John 516
Greene, Robert 322−3, 514, 515; *Orlando Furioso* 16, 20−24, 28−30, 35, 86, 328, 497 see also parts: non-Shakespearean
Greg, W. W. 495, 497, 501, 503, 505, 507, 508
Greville, Curtis 54

Grosart, Alexander 509, 514
Grote, David 500
Gurr, Andrew 502

H., I 326, 516
Habington, William 514
half-lines *see* midline shifts, short speech-units
Hall, Edith 495
Hall, Joseph 320, 514, 515
Halliwell, James O. 515
Hannay, Patrick 513
Hardison, O. B. 516
Harington, Sir John 319, 322, 514
Harsnett, Samuel 87, 504, 509, 513
Harvey, Gabriel 88, 502, 509
Healey, Jo 499
Heavens 40, 312
Heminges, John 67
*Henry V* 51
Henslowe, Philip 46, 50−1, 56, 58, 70, 76, 503, 505
Herbert, Henry 61
Herford, C. H. 504, 506
Herrick, Robert 513
Heywood, Thomas 42, 49, 84, 499, 500, 502, 506, 514, 515; *Royall King* 508
Higgins, John 73, 507
Hill, Aaron 74, 507, 508
hirelings 50, 60, 503
Holaday, Allan 502, 506
Holcroft, Thomas 32
Holland, Peter 506
Holloway, Stanley 517
Honemann, Volker 495, 509
Howard, Skiles 500
Howell, James 514
Howell, Thomas 85, 508
Hughes, Charles 516
Hume, R. D. 505
humours 44, 122, 314−17, 325, 329, 499, 513, 514, 517

iambic verse *see* midline shifts, pentameter
Ichikawa, Mariko 509, 511
imitation *see* instruction
improvisation *see* actors: and extemporisation

individual rehearsal *see* instruction
inherited parts *see* parts: inherited
instruction 66–70, 72, 154, 319, 506–7
Ioppolo, Grace 495

James I 46
James, Richard 67, 506
Jerome, Steven 501
jigs 72
Job 332
Johnson, Samuel 71, 83, 142
Jonson, Ben 7, 49, 66, 77, 78, 95, 270,
        316, 495 *Bartholomew Fair* 270;
        *Christmas his Masque* 55, 504;
        *Cynthia's Revels* 66, 71, 77, 506,
        508; *Every Man Out* 72, 507;
        *Sejanus* 270; *Staple of News* 74, 507

Kawai, Shoichiro 500
Kemble, John Philip 25, 35, 36, 499
Kemp, William 43, 64, 67
Kiernander, Adrian 60, 505
King, Thomas 32
King, T. J. 501, 503
Kirsch, Arthur C. 514
Knight, Edward 61
Kyd, Thomas *Spanish Tragedy* 8–9, 71
Kynder, Philip 514

Lalou, E. Elisabeth 496, 497
Langhans, Edward A. 29, 498
*Laughing Mercury* 504
Lawrence, W. J. 29, 498
learning a part *see* study; parts: learned
        linearly
Legge, Richard *Richardus Tertius* 61, 505
Leishman, J. B. 506
Lemnius, Levinus 514
lengths 2, 32, 498 *see* parts
Lenton, Francis 326, 516
Leveridge, Richard 51–2
Lindley, David 512
Lincoln's Inn 49
Linke, Hansjürgen 88, 495, 497, 509
Lluellin, M. 503
Lodge, Thomas 504
Lord Chamberlain's Men 346
Lowen, John 507
*Lucerne Passion* 19

Lupton, D. 500, 515
Lyly, John 88, 504, 509

M., R. 512
Mackenzie, George 63, 505
Macklin, Charles 33–4, 50, 498
Macready, William Charles 135
Maguire, Laurie E. 497, 508
Malone, Edmond 83
Marlowe, Christopher 322–3, 329, 514;
        *Doctor Faustus* 370; *Jew of Malta* 49,
        56, 502; *Tamberlaine* 65, 311, 359
Marston, John 7, 514; *Antonio and
        Mellida* 50, 65, 71, 502, 506, 507;
        *Histriomastix* 59, 71, 505; *Insatiate
        Countess* 513; *Malcontent* 77, 508
Massinger, Philip 7; *Roman Actor* 54,
        66, 506
Master of the Revels 61, 94
Maxwell, J. 497
McClure, Norman E. 513
McGuire, Philip C. 503
McKerrow, R. B. 515
McMillin, Scott 67, 506
Meade, Jacob 70
Meagher, John C. 503
Medbourne, Matthew 29, 498
Melchiori, Georgio 503
Mennes, Sir John 87, 509
*Mercurius Melancholicus* 499
*Mercurius Pragmaticus* 501
Meres, Francis 500, 502, 514
*Merrie Conceited Jests of George Peele* 504
Middleton, Richard 515
Middleton, Thomas 7, 65, 464 500, 506;
        *Your Five Gallants* 67, 71, 506; and
        Rowley, *A Faire Quarrell* 84, 508;
        *Changeling* 47
midline shifts 123, 346–7, 349–52, 517;
        and actor's movement 346–7,
        361–2, 363, 456; and creation of
        time/space 350–1, 368, 379; and
        creation of 'virtual presence' 370,
        376–9, 386–9, 487–8; and
        immediacy of experience 352, 372;
        and inwardness 370, 376–9,
        381–2, 385–6, 400–1, 435–7, 454,
        467, 470–6, 487; and mental
        movement 346–7, 366–7, 378–9,
        385–6, 400–1, 435–7, 454, 467,

470–6, 487; and other players'
movements 346, 348, 350–1,
361–2, 366–7, 368, 375, 432, 436,
487–8; and pauses 130, 330, 346,
348, 351, 360, 361, 365, 374,
376–7, 384, 399, 401, 421, 425,
432, 435, 438, 454–6, 467, 471–2;
and self-address 349–50, 351, 354,
356, 367–8, 370, 375, 376, 381–2,
383–6, 470–6 see also soliloquy;
and switch of address 349–50, 351,
356–7, 358–89, 371–9, 380, 383,
384–6, 421, 457–63, 465–7,
470–6, 482; and switches in
power 358–9, 362–70, 371, 374,
376; and use in forming generic
'types' 353, 355–6, 380–1, 386; in
soliloquy 356–8, 370–1, 377–9,
381–2, 465, 466–7, 469–71; see also
short lines, short speech-units
Milhous, J. 505
Milles, Robert 323, 515
Minsheu, John 508
Moryson, Fynes 516
Muir, Kenneth 509, 511
Munday, Anthony 68, 506; Downfall of
Robert, Earl of Huntington 71; Sir
Thomas More 54, 503
Mystère de Saint André 19

Nabbes, Thomas Unfortunate Mother 53,
503; Hannibal and Scipio 54
Nagler, A. M. 496
Nashe, Thomas 507, 508, 515; Summer's
Last Will 74, 75
Newton, Thomas 319
Niccols, Richard 516
Nicholson, Samuel 312, 513, 514
Nungezer, Edwin 502

Officium Pastorum 495
Officium Peregrinorum 495
Officium Resurrectionis 495
Orgel, Stephen 506
Overbury, Thomas 48, 323, 500, 502,
515

Pafford, John Henry Pyle 508
Palfrey, Simon 510, 511, 516, 517

Palmer, John 86
Palmer, Nigel F. 509
Parkhurst, Ferdinando Ignoramus 29–31,
498
Parsons, Thomas 503
parts: actors' possession of 92–3, 120–1,
125–34, 142, 181, 182–3, 232–3,
278–304, ch. 20 passim; different
from full-text 97–110, ch. 7
passim, 396, 428–30, 439–52, 489;
distribution of 34, 51–2, 59–62,
391; inherited 69, 506–7; in
'books' 19, 20, 24–9, 31–8, 50, 52,
61, 390, 496, 498; in 'lengths' 2,
32, 498; in 'rolls' 17–20, 24, 31–2,
50, 52, 61–2, 88, 95, 390, 495–6; in
'sides' 2, 38; lacunae in 92, 113,
ch. 7 passim, 253, 373, 439–52, 493;
lay-out of 339; learned
linearly 390–1; revisions to 94;
writing of 20, 24–5, 29, 32, 60–1,
159, 339; and passim see also parts:
non-Shakespearean, 'Index of
Shakespearean Parts by
Character' 533
parts: non-Shakespearean (by name):
Amurath 24–7; Antoninus 24;
Antonio 47; Baltasar 18;
Bajazet 499; Barabas 495;
Christ 496; Cleophas 495; Comic
Role from Sion 19, 497;
Daniel 496 Dux Moraud 495;
God 19, 497; Hieronimo 48; High
Preist 19; Isaiah 496; Jesus 18;
John 495; Judas 496; Kaspar 495;
Lovegold 33–4; Lucifer 495;
Ludus Trium Regum 496;
Mary 495; Merchant 19, 495;
Messenger 495; Minister 19, 496;
Moréna 19, 497; Officium Quarti
Militis 496; Orlando 16, 20–24,
28–30, 35, 86, 328; Our
Saviour 495; Paris 499; Pilate 496;
Polypragmaticus 24–5;
Poore 24–5, 28, 497;
Praelocutor 495; Preist's role 18;
Ruby 495; Saint Simon 19, 497;
Saint Barbara 19, 497; Salome 496;
Scrub 33, 34; Secundus Miles 16;

parts: non-Shakespearean (by
name): (cont.)
19, 496; Vincentio 499 see also
'Index of Shakespearean Parts by
Character' 533
passions 59, 63, 76–7, 97, 111, 120–1,
126, 128, 129–32, 136, 137, 149,
179, 181, 209, 311–17, 325–27,
329, 334, 513 see also
transitions
pauses see midline shifts: and pauses;
prose: and pauses; prosody: and
pauses
Peele, George 57; Battle of Alcazar 503
pentameter 37–8, 138, 142–4, 145,
147–8, 149–52, 182, 256–7,
320–1, 346–8, 350, 351, 352, 358,
365, 370, 374, 388, 395–6, 400,
408, 412–13, 416–17, 431–2, 434,
436, 458; and rhythm 350–1, 395,
416, 420, 458, 465–7, 468, 469, 485
see also midline shifts, rhyme,
couplets, shared lines, short lines,
short speech-units
Percy, William 17, 56; Arabis Sitiens 73,
507; Cuck-Queanes and Cuckolds
Errants 8, 495; Faery Pastoral 8, 94;
Necromantes 504
performance 22, 23, 38, 49, 63, 65,
71–9, 85, 89, 90, 91–5, 103,
122–3, 126, 128,136, 140, 142,
145–6, 149, 153–4, 160, 163–4,
312, 316, 329–30, 342; and
suddenness 135, 137, 146, 152, 442,
446; and surprise in 100–1, 120,
122, 124, 135, 136–8, 141–2, 148,
149–50, 152–4, 203, 429, 449–52,
490–4; and waiting in ch. 7 passim,
397, 402, 414, 449; different from
rehearsal 92, 100–1, 103, 107–13,
119, 122–3, 136, 140, 153, 302,
396, 402, 428–9, 433, 491–4;
immediacy of 92–3, 153–4,
451–2, 491–4; foreign 325–6;
medieval 16, 18; modern 62;
second and repeated 75–9, 152–4,
160, 448, 492; university 24–5
Perkins, Richard 49
Peters, Hugh 47
Phillips, John 499

Pickering, Roger 508
platt see 'backstage plot'
Platter, Thomas 516
Plautus 49
play runs 70, 76
plot see 'backstage plot'
Pollard, Thomas 54
Popple, William 507, 508
Portland, Earl of 29
Prêtre Crucifié 18
Pritchard, Hannah 71
pronunciation 65, 68–9, 75, 317–21,
324–5, 331
prompt-book ('book') 34, 39, 61, 73,
78, 84, 85, 86, 93, 118, 498
prompter 16, 61–2, 73–4, 86, 108, 159,
339, 496, 505, 507
pronouns of address 383, 421
prose 122, 139, 143–4, 320–1, 324, 328,
330, 332–40, 344, 385, 410,
413–14, 516; and gradations of
address 413–14, 454, 456, 461–2;
and pauses 333, 414, 453–6,
461–3; and self-address 414, 458,
461; its relationship to
audience 332, 333, 335, 336,
385, 461–2 see also prose
to verse
prose to verse 332–9, 392–3, 409–11,
461–3; and actor's body 332, 411,
461; and allegory 332, 335; and
changes of passion 333–6, 344–5,
392–4, 409–12, 413–14, 416–18;
and narrative poetry 330;
as visual stage-direction 332 see also
prose
prosody: accentual 329; and
pauses 130–1, 181, 182, 183, 286,
329, 330, 333, 346, 348, 412–13;
and possession of character 391–2,
ch. 20 passim; and silence 123,
130–1, 145, 181, 211, 246, 259–60,
261, 345, 365, 367; continuities of
throughout part 357–8, 371, 376,
ch. 20 passim; psychological
infrastructure of 401see also midline
shifts, pentameter, prose, rhyme,
short speech-units
Proteus 45
Prynne, J. H. 511

Prynne, William 60, 501, 503, 504, 505, 515, 516
punctuation 22, 318–20, 346
puns 151–2, 168, 169, 171, 175, 187, 193, 249, 274, 331, 405, 486–7, 490
Purcell, Henry *Indian Queen* 51
Puttenham, George 55, 504

Quarles, Francis 50, 66, 500, 502, 513
Quarles, John 506
Queen's Players 21, 503
Quin, James 32

Raleigh, Walter 315, 499–500, 507
Randolph, Thomas 45, 313, 500, 505, 513
*Ratseis Ghost* 506, 514, 515
Ratsey, Gamaliel 69
reading 57–60, 62
Red Bull Playhouse 42, 323, 515
Red Lion Inn 503
rehearsal 25–6, 29, 34, 39, 42, 52, 62–8, 70–3, 78–9, 89, 100, 103, 122–3, 153, 157, 312, 451, 491;
ensemble 26, 34, 62, 67, 72, 74, 75, 78; full/group 62–3, 70–2, 100, 157 *see also* instruction, study
repeated cues 5, 26–8, 77–8, 115–16, 154, 157–307 *passim*, 331, 351, 509, 510, 511; actor's choice how to play 160–3, ch.'s. 9–15 *passim*; and clowns 171–7, 227, 299; and crowd scenes 165–71, 185–6, 219, 222, 224, 276, 278, 304, 443–4; and parody 266–7, 272–3, 274; and physical comedy 175–7, 299–301; and physical space 285–8, 300–5, ch. 15 *passim*; and post-tragic effects 266–75; and scenic jokes 174–5; and subjective 'becoming', ch. 15 *passim*; and tragic bathos 214–18; and tragic pathos 218–66; as metaphor 248, 275–9, 289, 297; as sound 249, 254, 276–8, 290, 296–7, 299–301; creating comedy 207–12; creating 'gradations of consciousness' 280–1, 284, 292–3, 299–305, 412; creating 'inwardness' ch.12 *passim*,
259–60, 281–94; creating split stage effect 174–5, 177, 180, 190–1, 198, 211, 218, 221, 228, 229–31, 237–9, 255, 262–5, 269–70, 273, 275, 277, 289, 443–5; ch. 12 *passim*, 259–60, 281–94; creating 'mental space' 281–90, 296–305, 412–13, ch.15 *passim*; defining genre through use of 207–8, 209–10, 212–13, 240, 275, 443–4; isolating a character through use of 163, 177–9, 185–6, 189, 190–1, 196, 213, 218, 219, 221, 224, 225, 227, 235, 237–9, 259–61, 262–5, 280–93, 443–4, 445, 463; making comic victims through use of 178–9, 185–6, 196, 205, 208, 211–12, 228, 241–2, 299; meta-theatrical 210–11, 248, 263, 288; recurring 113–18, 167–71, 182, 251–5; simultaneous not linear chs 9–15 *passim see also* cues: false or secreted
repeated performances *see* performances: second and repeated
*Return from Parnassus see Three Parnassus Plays*
Rhenanus, Johannes 506
rhetoric 68, 318–19, 321, 325, 329, 331
Rhodes, Neil 516
rhyme 18, 64, 151–2, 254, 328, 329–31, 332, 334, 340–6, 374, 394, 422, 517 *see also* couplets
rhyming couplets *see* couplets
Rich, Barnaby 314, 513
Richards, Nathaniel 41–2, 65, 66, 499, 506, 507
Riley, Thomas 45, 313
Roach, Joseph R. 513
Robbins, R. H. 496
Rogers, Thomas 73
roles *see* parts
rolls *see* parts
Rose Playhouse 20, 46
Rowley, Sam 47, 58, 505
Rowley, William 56, 504 *see also* Middleton
Ruf, Jakob 496
Ruggle, George *Ignoramus* 498

Runnalls, Graham 17, 496, 497
*Rythmes against Martin Marprelate* 55


S., W. 512
Samuelson, David A. 503
Scolocker, Anthony 512
*Second Part of the Return from Parnassus* see
    *Three Parnassus Plays*
second performances *see* performances:
    second and repeated
*Seven Deadly Sins* 48
Shaa, Robert 58, 505
Shakespeare, William: as actor 3–4;
    Works: *All's Well that Ends
    Well* 102–3, 136–42, 422–34;
    *Anthony and Cleopatra* 266–71, 489;
    *As You Like It* 53, 135; *The Comedy
    of Errors* 172, 341, 510;
    *Coriolanus* 98, 165, 278, 344–6,
    489; *Cymbeline* 43, 53, 271–4, 489;
    *Hamlet* 7, 8, 43–4, 53, 66, 68, 69,
    71, 96, 97, 114–18, 121, 218,
    311–12, 318, 322, 325, 337,343–4,
    387–8, 390, 499, 506, 510, 511,
    517; *1 Henry IV* 99–101, 122,
    124–5; *2 Henry IV* 99–101, 122,
    511; *Henry V* 43, 122, 153; *2 Henry
    VI* 166, 276; *3 Henry VI* 276;
    *Henry VIII* 69; *Julius
    Caesar* 166–71, 219, 336–7; *King
    John* 35–6; *King Lear* 7, 8, 43, 53,
    87, 96–7, 108–110, 150–52, 218,
    226, 240–65, 278, 332, 338–9, 348,
    351, 513; *Love's Labour's Lost* 43,
    85–6, 322; *Macbeth* 36, 43, 53,
    71–2, 97–8, 125–34, 135, 144–5,
    218, 237–8, 276–7, 278, 324, 332,
    387, 388, 464–94, 510, 513;
    *Measure for Measure* 380, 434–52;
    *The Merchant of Venice* 36–8, 186,
    192–213, 243, 304, 334–6, 337–8,
    392–408, 456–63; *A Midsummer
    Night's Dream* 2, 32, 34–5, 62, 64,
    71, 72, 89, 157, 212, 218, 341, 422,
    512; *Much Ado About Nothing* 84,
    122, 293, 333–4, 508; *Othello* 53,
    67, 74, 107–8, 218, 226, 227–37,
    273, 278, 316, 325, 327, 332,
    347–8; *Pericles* 90, 489; *The Rape of*

*Lucrece* 330; *Richard II* 340, 371–9;
    *Richard III* 48, 122–3, 184–6,
    358–71; *Romeo and Juliet* 43,
    101–2, 103–7, 112–13, 146–50,
    158–62, 186–91, 212, 214–18,
    316, 327, 341–2, 349–50, 353–8,
    382–3, 453–6, 510–11;
    *Sonnets* 508; *The Taming of the
    Shrew* 172, 175–7; *The
    Tempest*, 165–6, 275–307, 387;
    *Titus Andronicus* 325; *Troilus and
    Cressida* 224–7; *Twelfth Night* 2, 7,
    111–12, 113–14, 177–83, 276,
    293, 316, 415–22; *Two Gentlemen of
    Verona* 101, 172–5, 509; *Two Noble
    Kinsmen* 7; *Venus and Adonis* 330;
    *The Winter's Tale* 53, 94, 121, 489,
    509; *see also* 'Index of Shakespearean
    Parts by Character' 533
shared lines 28, 35–38, 138, 142–52,
    342 *see also* short lines, short
    speech-units
shareholder *see* sharer
sharers 41, 43, 44, 50, 58, 60
Shay, Robert 503
Sheppard, Samuel 514
Sherlock, William 54
Shirley, James *Hide Park* 73 *Humorous
    Courtier* 89, 509
short lines 142–52, 328–32, 336, 345,
    346–9, 352, 375, 403, 416–17, 419,
    424, 425, 431, 435, 437, 473;
    prose-like 405–8, 416, 419 *see also*
    short speech-units
short speech-units 346, 350, 351,
    359–61; acting upon others ch. 18
    *passim*, 405–8; and
    self-address 356–8, 396, 397, 403,
    453, 455–6, 467–71; and shifts of
    address 384, 405, 436; soliciting no
    response 367–8, 425, 435, 437,
    453, 459, 467–8 *see also* short lines
Shrewsbury fragments 495
sides *see* parts
Sidney, Philip 329, 332, 514
silence *see* prosody: and silence
Simpson, Percy 504, 506
Sincler, John 44
Smith, G. C. Moore 509
Smock Alley 498

soliloquy 148, 199–200, 236, 297,
    356–8, 359, 370–1, 385, 422–3,
    432, 444, 465, 469, 470, 477–8 *see
    also* midline shifts: and self-address;
    midline shifts: in soliloquy;
    couplets: in soliloquy
songs 26, 54, 72–3, 74, 280, 283–4,
    290–2, 299–301, 302, 305, 512
Spenser, Edmund 329, 514
stage-directions 16, 18, 22, 23, 25,
    26–8, 30–1, 73, 86, 124, 215, 270,
    315, 325, 328, 332, 342, 345, 354,
    361, 449
Steevens, George 143
Stephens, John 507, 514
Stern, Tiffany 495, 496, 497, 498, 499,
    502, 503, 505, 506, 507, 508
Stock, L. E. 513
strolling players 323
Stubbes, Philip 516
study 28, 32, 49, 61–75, 91–2, 120,
    319, 320, 346, 506
Surrey, Henry Howard Earl of 329
Sylvester, Josuah 503

Tarlton, Richard 48, 51–3, 77, 321–2,
    326–7, 503
Tatham, John 515
Taylor, John 76
Taylor, Joseph 506–7, 508
Terrence 49
textual variants 214–15, 217, 222–3,
    224, 229, 231, 233–4, 241, 245–6,
    247, 258, 259, 260–1, 263–4, 339,
    351, 363, 366, 382, 464
Theatre Playhouse 327
Theatre Royal 49
Thomas, Thomas 504
Thompson, Robert 503
*Three Parnassus Plays* 64, 506
tiring house 16, 54, 67, 71, 72, 73, 74, 86
Tofte, Robert 513
Tomkis, Thomas *Lingua* 68, 506

Torshell, Samuel 501
transitions 97, 106, 116, 130, 136,
    311–17, 329, 332–4, 338, 340, 349,
    352 *see also* midline shifts, passions,
    prose
Tucker, Edward F. J. 498
Tucker, Patrick 495, 516
'typecasting' and 'types' 41–5, 53, 54,
    62, 69, 99, 103, 121, 122, 126, 139,
    164, 166, 176, 353, 355–6, 380–1,
    386, 411

understudies 50–1
university parts 92, 143
*Ur-Hamlet* 55, 504

verse *see* midline shifts, pentameter,
    prose to verse, rhyme, couplets
vizards 54–6

Ward, William 32
Warner, Robert 312, 514
Warren, Arthur 514, 515
Warren, Michael 497
Webster, John 8, 48, 77, 323; *White
    Devil* 321
Weimann, Robert 510, 512
Wets, Richard 505, 513
Whitehall 29
Wiggins, Martin 513
Wilders, John 510
Wilkins, George *Miseries of an Inforst
    Marriage* 66, 506; *Pericles* 89–90,
    509
Wilkinson, Tate 32, 498
Williams, Barney 502–3
Willis, R. 56, 504
Wilson, F. P. 515
Wood, William B. 38, 499
Woodes, Nathaniel 507
Wright, George T. 510